Lecture Notes in Artificial Intelligence　13539

Subseries of Lecture Notes in Computer Science

Ben Goertzel · Matt Iklé · Alexey Potapov ·
Denis Ponomaryov (Eds.)

Artificial General Intelligence

15th International Conference, AGI 2022
Seattle, WA, USA, August 19–22, 2022
Proceedings

Editors
Ben Goertzel (ID)
SingularityNET Foundation
Amsterdam, The Netherlands

Matt Iklé (ID)
SingularityNET Foundation
Amsterdam, The Netherlands

Alexey Potapov (ID)
SingularityNET Foundation
Amsterdam, The Netherlands

Denis Ponomaryov
Russian Academy of Sciences
Novosibirsk, Russia

ISSN 0302-9743   ISSN 1611-3349 (electronic)
Lecture Notes in Artificial Intelligence
ISBN 978-3-031-19906-6   ISBN 978-3-031-19907-3 (eBook)
https://doi.org/10.1007/978-3-031-19907-3

LNCS Sublibrary: SL7 – Artificial Intelligence

This Springer imprint is published by the registered company Springer Nature Switzerland AG
The registered company address is: Gewerbestrasse 11, 6330 Cham, Switzerland

Preface

This volume contains the papers presented at AGI 2022, the 15th Conference on Artificial General Intelligence. The conference took place at The Crocodile in Seattle during August 19–22, 2022, and was broadcast live via Zoom and co-sponsored by SingularityNET's YouTube channel for online participants and viewers.

Spread over four days, the conference included two full-day and two half-day workshops, eight keynote lectures, two fireside chats featuring AGI luminaries, two panel sessions, a code demonstration, eight sessions of in-person and online contributed papers and talks, two poster video sessions, and a full day of general audience sessions with leading AGI researchers and leaders.

Learning from our first attempt at a hybrid conference at AGI 2021 in Palo Alto, California, the AGI 2022 hybrid conference process went smoothly and included additional time for online paper presentations. In addition to the full-day deep dives into the NARS and OpenCog/Hyperon AGI systems that have become somewhat traditional in the AGI conference series, this year's conference also included half-day workshops on Interpretable Natural Language Processing and AGI in FinTech, as well as a full-day demonstration of FutureAI's Brain Simulator II. The theme for this year's general audience day was Ethical Machine Creativity, which culminated in an evening concert with a spectacular performance by the Jam Galaxy band, featuring the Desdemona robot singing AI-generated lyrics (albeit with some human curation).

Researchers from at least 19 countries attended AGI 2022, either in-person or online. As always, conference activities spawned numerous deep discussions on incredibly diverse topics outside of the venue itself.

This volume contains the contributed papers presented at AGI 2022. There were 61 submissions. Each submission was reviewed by at least two (on average 2.54) Program Committee members. The committee decided to accept 31 long papers (51% acceptance) for oral presentation, and an additional 13 submissions for poster presentations. As usual, conference presentations and discussions spanned a wide and ever-evolving array of topics. New this year were discussions on AGI hardware as well as the release of a major open-source software tool, the DR-Learner.

Speakers and panelists for the general audience day included Sophia Robot (AGI Ambassador), Joscha Bach (Principal AI Engineer, Intel Labs), Ben Goertzel (CEO, OpenCog Foundation and SingularityNET and Chair, AGI Society), Janet Adams (COO, SingularityNET), Kyrtin Atreides (COO, AGI Laboratory), Gabriel Axel Montes (Music Co-director, Jam Galaxy), Charles Simon (Founder and CEO, Future AI), Chris Poulin (TrueAGI Advisor), Ed Keller (SingularityNET), Dianne Krouse (Jam Galaxy), Matt Iklé (CAIO, SingularityNET, and Treasurer, AGI Society), and Douglas Miles (Logicmoo and SingularityNET).

Three additional keynote speeches were presented by researchers from both academia and industry. This year's speakers and topics were as follows:

- Nelson Niu (Ph.D. student, University of Washington), "Polynomial Functors: Natural Formal Models of Interaction"
- Rachel St. Clair (Founder and CEO, Simuli), "Resource Management in AGI Systems"
- Chris Poulin and Phil Tabor (Co-leader, DR-Learner), "Open Source Deep Reinforcement Learning: Deep Dive"

Also included this year were two fireside chats

- Ben Goertzel and Rachel St. Clair, "Novel Hardware for Enabling AGI and Machine Creativity"
- Ben Goertzel and Gary Marcus (Founder and CEO, Robust.AI), "Overcoming the Obstacles Between Here and AGI"

Finally, there was one code demo:

- Dzvinka Yarish (Co-author, DR-Learner), "Demo of Open Source DR-Learner Tool"

We end by thanking everyone who made this successful conference event happen. This includes all of our sponsors (SingularityNET for their incredible and hard-working team that helped organize the event and handled the logistics, moderation, and live-streaming of the conference; the AGI Society for organizing the conference series since 2008; Future AI for their generous financial support as a "Main AGI Session" sponsor; TrueAGI for their in-kind support; and Springer for their contribution for the best paper prize as well as their proceedings publishing support). It also includes every one of our Program Committee members for their dedicated service to the review process, our contributors, participants, and tutorial, workshop, and panel session organizers, without whom the conference would not exist.

August 2022

Ben Goertzel
Matt Iklé
Denis Ponomaryov
Alexey Potapov

Organization

General Chair

Ben Goertzel   AGI Society, USA, and SingularityNET, The Netherlands

Program Committee Vice Chairs

Matt Iklé   AGI Society, USA, and SingularityNET, The Netherlands
Alexey Potapov   SingularityNET, The Netherlands
Denis Ponomaryov   Novosibirsk State University, Russia

Organizing Committee

Janet Adams   SingularityNET, The Netherlands
Ibby Benali   SingularityNET, The Netherlands
Ben Goertzel   AGI Society, USA, and SingularityNET, The Netherlands
Lowy Haley   SingularityNET, The Netherlands
Matt Iklé   AGI Society, USA, and SingularityNET, The Netherlands,
Sarah Isakson   SingularityNET, The Netherlands
Lisa Rein   Jam Galaxy, USA
Ryan Sternlicht   Jam Galaxy, USA
Iain Wentworth   SingularityNET, The Netherlands

Program Committee

Cristiano Castelfranchi   Institute of Cognitive Sciences and Technologies, Italy
Antonio Chella   Università di Palermo, Italy
Deborah Duong   SingularityNET, The Netherlands
Aaron Eberhart   Kansas State University, USA
Nil Geisweiller   OpenCog Foundation and SingularityNET, The Netherlands
Ben Goertzel   SingularityNET, The Netherlands
Thomas Gärtner   TU Wien, Austria

Patrick Hammer   Temple University, USA
Jose Hernandez-Orallo   Universitat Politècnica de València, Spain
Marcus Hutter   Australian National University, Australia
Matt Iklé   SingularityNET, The Netherlands
Cliff Joslyn   Pacific Northwest National Laboratory, USA
Garrett Katz   Syracuse University, USA
Anton Kolonin   SingularityDAO, St. Lucia
Xiang Li   Liaoning University of Technology, China
John Licato   Indiana University-Purdue University Fort
                                    Wayne, USA

Frank Loebe   University of Leipzig, Germany
Tony Lofthouse   Stockholm University, Sweden
Douglas Miles   SingularityNET, The Netherlands
Till Mossakowski   University of Magdeburg, Germany
Amedeo Napoli   Loria Nancy (CNRS, Inria, and Université de
                                    Lorraine), France
Laurent Orseau   Google, USA
Guenther Palm   University of Ulm, Germany
Aleksandr I. Panov   Federal Research Center Computer Science and
                                    Control, RAS, Russia
Maxim Peterson   ITMO University, Russia
Denis Ponomaryov   Novosibirsk State University, Russia
Alexey Potapov   SingularityNET, The Netherlands
Rafal Rzepka   Hokkaido University, Japan
Ricardo Sanz   Universidad Politécnica de Madrid, Spain
Oleg Scherbakov   ITMO University, Russia
Ute Schmid   University of Bamberg, Germany
Abdulrahman Semrie   SingularityNET, The Netherlands
Barry Smith   SUNY Buffalo, USA
Bas Steunebrink   NNAISENSE, Switzerland
Kristinn R. Thorisson   Reykjavik University, Iceland
Adam Vandervorst   SingularityNET, The Netherlands
Mario Verdicchio   Università degli Studi di Bergamo, Italy
Pei Wang   Temple University, USA
Jonathan Warrell   SingularityNET, The Netherlands
Robert Wünsche   TU Dresden, Germany
Roman Yampolskiy   University of Louisville, USA
Liudmila Zhilyakova   V.A. Trapeznikov Institute of Control Sciences,
                                    RAS, Russia

Additional Reviewers

Catt, Elliot
Eberding, Leonard
Landgrebe, Jobst
Livenstev, Vadim
Penz, David
Sheikhlar, Arash

Contents

Accepted for Poster Presentation

A General-Purpose Machine Reasoning Engine

Cengiz Erbas[✉]

Hacettepe University, Ankara 06800, Turkey
cengizerbas@hacettepe.edu.tr

Abstract. We are developing a machine reasoning engine that can learn arbitrary concepts from small number of training samples, and generate explainable models which can be visualized graphically. In this article, we present our intermediate results by experimenting with problems that require reasoning with simple arithmetic, geometric shapes, logical operators, simple program syntax, and regular and context-free languages.

Keywords: Machine reasoning · Grammar induction · Explainable models

1 Introduction

Even though neural networks and deep learning are successful in solving problems in numerous domains, there is an agreement that we need new complementary innovations to be able to achieve human-level AI or more generally AGI [2, 7, 11]. Neural networks operate at sub-symbolic level, and can learn complex statistical relationships. They are robust for noise and scale up well. They are the engines of the current phase of AI revolution. Neural networks however come with their weaknesses. They do not work well if big data is not available for the problem at hand. They produce models that are not explainable; and they are fragile in learning symbolic relationships. These weaknesses seem to be characteristic for all approaches that belong to sub-symbolic AI. We need new approaches to address them.

This article reports the intermediate results of one such attempt. We are developing a machine reasoning engine that can learn and discover cognitive relationships that are out of reach for neural networks, that can do this using only a few training samples and can generate explainable models which can be visualized graphically. We have experimented with the reasoning engine with problems in multiple domains. The prototype is able to learn and reason with simple arithmetic and geometric concepts, logical operators, and the syntax of simple programming language constructs using small number of training samples and without requiring any problem-specific model development.

The reasoning engine is compute-bound, but fully-parallelizable; and availability of more computing resources results in faster response. We have completed the implementation of the prototype in AWS Amazon Web Services [1] and made it accessible to researchers for experimentation through a web interface. We are in the process of enhancing the initial prototype to be able to solve more complex problems.

© The Author(s), under exclusive license to Springer Nature Switzerland AG 2023
B. Goertzel et al. (Eds.): AGI 2022, LNAI 13539, pp. 3–13, 2023.
https://doi.org/10.1007/978-3-031-19907-3_1

2 Related Work

There is a growing literature that aims to address the limitations of neural networks by borrowing ideas from traditional symbolic AI research. We can mention at least two categories of research in this area. The first category includes the work to enhance the capabilities of neural networks so that they can learn "programs". The second category consists of the efforts to enhance known symbolic systems, such as inductive logic programming, to be trainable like neural networks through gradient decent.

An example for the first category is [8]. This work enriched the capabilities of standard recurrent networks via a large addressable memory to be able to learn performing algorithmic tasks. They developed, what they call, Neural Turing Machines, which extended the capabilities of neural networks by linking them to external memory resources. This system does not construct an explicit symbolic representation of a program, but learn an implicit procedure that produces the intended results. This implicit procedure in a way operates at a lower-level model of computation, similar to Turing machines or pushdown automata, but it is differentiable end-to-end, making it possible to be trained with gradient descent. This is achieved by defining fuzzy read and write operations that interact with all the memory elements rather than addressing a single element as in a normal Turing machine. The experiments demonstrated that Neural Turing Machine is capable of learning from example data simple algorithms, such as copy operations, n-grams and priority sort.

As example for the second category, [5] proposed a differentiable Inductive Logic Programming (ILP) framework. ILP is a set of techniques for constructing logic programs from examples. The learned program in ILP is an explicit symbolic structure that can be inspected and easier to understand than a large tensor of floating-point numbers; it is able to generalize well from a small number of examples; and it enables continual and transfer learning, as the learned programs are free from side-effects and can be copied and pasted into the knowledge base. The main limitation of ILP is its inability to handle noisy, erroneous, or ambiguous data. If training examples contain any mislabeled data, ILP systems fails to learn the intended rule [3]. Differentiable ILP (dILP) aims to address the weaknesses of ILP by using neural networks. [5] showed that dILP is able to solve moderately complex tasks requiring recursion and predicate discovery. The main component of this work is a differentiable implementation of deduction through forward chaining on definite clauses. The main limitation of the dILP system is that it requires significant memory resources, which limits the range of benchmark problems that the system can be tested with.

A comprehensive survey of the literature to integrate human designed symbolic knowledge into neural networks-based models, which is also known as neural-symbolic computing, can be found in [6]. There are various approaches to represent symbolic knowledge in neural-symbolic systems, such as rule-based, formula-based and embedding-based [6, 13]. It is worth mentioning two recent articles [9, 10] who explored regular expressions as a means to integrate human-designed rules with neural networks[1].

3   Machine Reasoning Engine

3.1   Architecture

We are developing a Machine Reasoning (MR) Engine, called ALE – which stands for Arbitrary Learning Engine. ALE aims to provide reasoning/induction capabilities that are out of reach for the existing machine learning (ML) techniques. Our vision of how AGI will be build is based on a combination of ML and MR models, and arbitrary programs, where MR models integrate with and leverage the existing ML models and knowledge coded in the form of general-purpose programs, as shown in Fig. 1.

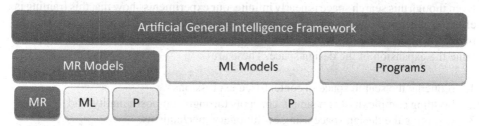

Fig. 1. The output of ML models is not within the space of the input features. The inputs and outputs of MR models, however, will be within the same design space of concepts. The output can be fed as an input to the same model recursively to build hierarchy of learned concepts.

If we look at the figure from right to left, it encapsulates three different ways of building artificial intelligence capabilities, as follows:

1. In its simplest form, intelligent functions can be developed by handcrafting them in the form of Programs (P). Early work in AI (including Expert Systems) falls into this category.
2. Alternatively, we can build ML models such as neural networks that demonstrate intelligent capabilities. ML models may use features extracted using programs as input to do classification. However, it is important to note that the output of the model is not within the design space of the input features. We cannot feed the output of a model to itself recursively to build hierarchy of learned concepts.

[1] This work has been supported by TÜBİTAK under 2232 International Fellowship for Outstanding Researchers Program (Project No: 118C228). However, the responsibility of the paper belongs to the author. The financial support does not mean that the content of the publication is approved in a scientific sense by TÜBİTAK.

3. MR models will not have this limitation. MR models will operate at the "concept" level. Both inputs and outputs of MR models will be within the same space of concepts. The output of an MR model can therefore be fed into the same model recursively to build hierarchy of learned concepts. MR Models will also be able to use the existing ML models as well as other programs as input, leveraging the existing AI systems.

The presentation in this paper focuses on the performance of ALE and the MR models. The links between MR models and ML models are under development with two integration scenarios. In the first one, ML model outputs are fed into MR models for high-level reasoning. In the second, MR models work as feature extractors for the ML models. This topic will be covered in a subsequent paper.

3.2 Algorithms

ALE applies induction [4] to recognize patterns and to reason about them. It can be viewed as a scaled-down implementation of Solomonoff's theory of universal inductive inference [12] which reduces AI to a search problem within the space of all programs. Even though this search space is nearly infinite, our experiments show that this framing is effective when we look for discrete cognitive relationships among concepts. Solomonoff induction is undecidable. To make the implementation tractable, we made 3 revisions to tame the expansion of the design space. These are:

1. reducing the search space to context-free expressions,
2. building complexity from simple concepts through compositionality, and
3. exploring the design space using evolutionary mechanisms.

First, ALE avoids undecidability by reducing the design space to context-free expressions, which is sufficient to express many interesting problems, in particular the ones that are related to human faculties that require language understanding. Second, compositionality allows building complexity from simple concepts hierarchically, consistent with how humans understand the nature. For example, we do not model human anatomy at the atomic level. Rather, we build our knowledge hierarchically: physics works at the atomic level; chemistry operates at molecular level; biology starts at cellular level, and so on. ALE applies this exact principle, which in effect, reduces the search greatly, and enables us to handle complexity. Finally, ALE imitates the nature which creates complexity (and intelligence) through evolution by natural selection. It applies this principle to eliminate the need to explore unproductive branches within the design space, speeding up the search.

ALE currently works on decision (classification) problems, and it has supervised and unsupervised learning capabilities. In the supervised training mode, it searches the design space to locate the simplest theory to explain the annotated data. In this mode, ALE can also discover relationships among learned concepts. We will see examples of this for simple arithmetic and geometric concepts in the next section. In the unsupervised training mode, it tries to build intermediate (new) vocabulary that can serve to form valid hierarchical representations of the training data. We will see an example of this in Experiment 5 in the next section.

As opposed to the ML models, which consist of large tensor of floating-point numbers, and which cannot explain its decisions and actions to human users, ALE generates explainable models that can be visualized so that the users can inspect and understand its decision process.

ALE is compute-bound but fully parallelizable. It will be able to scale to consume all the available processing resources to provide faster response. It is ported to AWS to be able to leverage the inherent parallelism. We made it accessible to researchers for experimentation through a web interface at https://www.ale-aws.com. The users will be able to start with an empty knowledge base, and guide ALE to learn new concepts. There are over 40 demo scripts that illustrates the general learning and reasoning capabilities of ALE. The researchers are welcome to create and run their own test cases and provide feedback.

4 Results

4.1 Command Line Interface

In this section, we provide the preliminary results of the experiments we performed. We start with a brief overview of the command line interface of ALE. Let's start with a simple example. Each line gives a separate command to ALE, where the first letter (u, l and c) indicates the command, and the rest provides the parameters.

```
ALE> u E+ xxxx
ALE> u E- x
ALE> l E
ALE> c E
ALE> u E? xxx
```

Here, we are training ALE to learn a concept E from two samples. The first line provides a positive and the second line provides a negative sample. Thus, the string "xxxx" is a member of E, but the string "x" is not. The user can provide as many training samples as she likes. The third line asks ALE to learn the concept E; and the fourth line produces a graphical representation of the model. Having learned the concept, the fifth line asks ALE if the string "xxx" is a member of E. ALE responds to such questions with Yes, No, or Unsure. If ALE is unsure, the user can provide additional training data, invoke ALE update the model, and ask the question again.

4.2 Experiments

We performed numerous experiments to evaluate the general learning and reasoning capabilities of ALE. The examples are from different problem domains, such as, arithmetic, geometry, logic, programs, and regular and context-free expressions. In this section, we provide the results of 5 of these experiments. To demonstrate generality, all the experiments are performed with the same ALE executables, and does not require a problem-specific configuration. Table 1 gives an overview of each experiment, and indicate the number of positive and negative training samples used.

Table 1. Overview of the experiments.

Experiment		Train data count	
		Positive	Negative
1	Odd/even numbers in unary, binary and quaternary form	4	3
2	Rules for integer ranges with logical operators	15	18
3	Learning syntax of recursive function calls in programs	8	12
4	Discovering geometric building blocks of a house image	6	21
5	Learning regular expressions by building hierarchy	2	4

We used the following notation when explaining the training scripts:

$[x]^n$ = "x" is repeated n times
$[x]^*$ = "x" is repeated 0 times or more
[0–9] = a digit between 0 and 9
[A–Z] = a letter between A and Z

4.3   Training Scripts and Results

Experiment 1: Learning Odd/Even Numbers
This experiment checks if ALE can learn the concept of odd (O) and even (E) numbers from data in different formats. First, we tried with data in unary format as in $[x]^n$.

Step 1: Provide positive $[x]^2$, $[x]^8$, and negative $[x]^5$ training samples for E
Step 2: Learn E
Step 3: Provide positive $[x]^1$, $[x]^5$, and negative $[x]^2$ training samples for O
Step 4: Learn O
Step 5: Reason with E $= [x]^4$ and E $\neq [x]^3$
Step 6: Reason with O $= [x]^3$ and O $\neq [x]^2$

Here, Step 2 generates a model for E in the form of E= $f_1(x)$. Similarly, Step 4 generates a model O= $f_2(x)$. Then, we switch to the reasoning mode, and Step 5 and Step 6 generate models E= $f_3(x, O, E)$ and O= $f_4(x, E, O)$. Then, ALE can demonstrate full understanding of these concepts by answering arbitrary questions about the relationships among them, such as:

```
O+1 -> E      // Adding 1 to an odd number gives an even number
2O -> E       // Multiplying an odd number by 2 gives an even number
2E+3O -> O    // 2 even and 3 odd numbers add up to an odd number
```

In this example, the numbers are provided to ALE in unary format, however, ALE can learn these same concepts even if the data is provided in other formats, such as, binary $[0-1]^*$ or quaternary $[0-3]^*$. We do not provide any additional information to ALE about the format of the training data. ALE figures out the concepts O and E all by itself from the patterns in the data alone, without knowing the underlying format.

Experiment 2: Learning Rules for Integer Ranges with Logical Operators
This experiment checks if ALE can learn rules constructed using logical operators. Assume that we collected data about the age (represented in 8 bits), education (Low, Medium, High) and income potential (the concept Z) of individuals within a population. Assume that the age and the education together determine the income potential, and the following logical relationship exists in the raw data, but not explicitly stated:

$$Z = [0-63][H] \ \textbf{or} \ [128-191][H] \ \textbf{or} \ [128-191][M]$$

ALE can discover this relationship from data without any guidance. In this experiment, we provided ALE with (rather arbitrary) 15 positive and 19 negative training samples. ALE is able to discover this simply in 2 steps as follows:

Step 1: Provide 15 positive and 19 negative samples for Z
Step 2: Learn Z

This generates several models for Z in the form of Z= f(0,1,L,M,H), where 0's and 1's encode the age (in 8 bits), and L/M/H encodes the education. ALE is then able to respond to the queries accurately.

Experiment 3: Learning Syntax of Recursive Function Calls
This experiment checks if ALE can learn F the syntax of recursive function calls in programs. A syntactically correct function call includes 0 or more parameters v, where each parameter can also be another function call recursively. The open and close brackets for the whole string should match each other, such as:

```
A(A(v,A(v,v)),A(A(v),v),v)
```

We provided 8 positive and 12 negative training samples. Example negative samples areAvA andAv,v,v). ALE is able to discover the syntax from these 20 training samples alone. The training sequence is simply as follows:

> Step 1: Provide positive and negative training samples for F
> Step 2: Learn F

Step 2 generates a model for F as a function of $F = f(A, v, ',', '(', ')')$. After this step, ALE is able to respond to the queries correctly. Examples are:

```
ALE> u F? A(A(A(x),A(x,x)),A(x,A(x)))      // returns YES
ALE> u F? A(A(x),A(x,x)),A(x,A(x,)))       // returns NO
```

Experiment 4: Discovering Geometric Building Blocks for a House Image
This experiment checks if ALE can learn the concept of skeleton of house (H), which consists of a triangle T (representing the roof) on top of a rectangle R (representing the body). The training samples are provided as black and white bitmap images on a blank background. ALE converts them into a 2D array of pixels on/off, as input for training. The training sequence is simply as follows:

> Step 1: Provide 2 positive and 9 negative training samples for R
> Step 2: Learn R
> Step 3: Provide 2 positive and 8 negative training samples for T
> Step 4: Learn T
> Step 5: Reason with H with 2 positive and 6 negative training samples

Step 5 expresses H as a function of R and T, and generates a model for H in the form of $H = f(R, T, on, off)$. ALE is then able to respond to the queries with other bitmap images accurately. Even though it is trained with houses with 1 and 2 stories, it is able to generalize it to n stories.

Experiment 5: Learning Regular Expressions by Building Hierarchy
Learning regular expressions from positive and negative training samples is a well-studied problem [4]. This experiment checks if ALE can learn regular expressions by building hierarchy, and compares its performance with the literature. As a specific example, we check if ALE can learn the following arbitrarily picked expression:

$$A = [012]^*[345]^7[01]^*[223]^*$$

ALE was able to learn this from only 2 positive and 4 negative training data. The list of positive samples used in this training are:

$$[012]^5[345]^7[01]^5[223]^4$$
$$[012]^8[345]^7[01]^6[223]^4$$

Here is the list of negative samples used in this training:

$$[345]^8[012]^7$$
$$[345]^7[012]^6[345]^5[223]^3$$
$$[012]^6[345]^4[012]^4[01]^4[012][223]^4$$
$$[01]^7[012][223]^4[012]^4[345]^3$$

The training sequence is simply as follows:

Step 1: Provide positive and negative training samples for A
Step 2: Explore the design space to select intermediate concept candidates
Step 3: Search (X,Y,Z,W,V) tuples to select the one that explains the data
Step 4: Learn A

Step 3 generates intermediate concepts X,Y,Z,W,V. Step 4 generates a model for A in the form of $A= f(X,Y,Z,W,V,0,1,2,3,4,5)$. After this step, ALE is able to respond to the following strings accurately. A graphical illustration of this model is given in Fig. 2.

We provided the same training data to the RPNI algorithm, which is a known grammar induction algorithm [4]. RPNI was able to produce an FSA model, but was not able to generalize it to the initial regular expression that we started with. Moreover, the model that ALE produces is modular and provides a better and simpler graphical representation compared to the FSA that RPNI generates.

To some up, the runtime of ALE for each experiment on Intel Core i7 @ 2.6 GHz with no GPU accelerator is given in Table 2.

Table 2. Runtime for each experiment on Intel Core i7 @ 2.6 GHz with <u>no</u> GPU accelerator.

	1	2	Experiments 3	4	5
Runtime	0.5 min	30 min	12 min	1.5 min	150 min

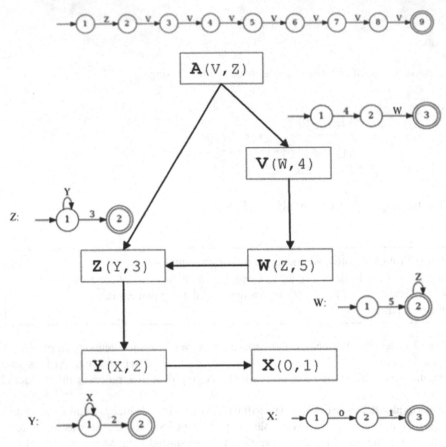

Fig. 2. The hierarchical model generated for A= (012)* (345)⁷ (01)* (223)*. Notice that concept A is a function of V and Z. Concept V is a function of W, and the concept W is a function of Z, and so on.

5 Conclusion

In this paper, we shared the results of 5 experiments that we performed with ALE, the reasoning engine that we are in the process of developing. In these experiments, we primarily focused on demonstrating the general-purpose learning capabilities of ALE. To achieve this, we picked problems from multiple domains, and performed all experiments with the same ALE executables, which do not require a problem-specific configuration. ALE is accessible at https://www.ale-aws.com. The researchers are welcome to experiment with the 40+ test scripts provided, or create their own tests cases.

Our current research continues in multiple dimensions. First, we are working on parallelizing the code to be able to use GPUs, which will reduce the runtime significantly. Second, we are working on neural network integration to demonstrate a hybrid performance. Third, we are also working on the potential use cases for ALE. One promising example is [14], where we used ALE to discover design patterns for city planning. We will continue enhancing the prototype to be able to solve more complex problems that are closer to the real-world.

References

1. AWS Homepage. https://www.aws.com. Last Accessed 21 Jan 2022
2. Chollet, F.: On the measure of intelligence. arXiv: 1911.01547v2. 25 Nov 2019
3. De Raedt, L., Kersting, K.: Probabilistic inductive logic programming. In: Ben-David, S., Case, J., Maruoka, A. (eds.) ALT 2004. LNCS (LNAI), vol. 3244, pp. 19–36. Springer, Heidelberg (2004). https://doi.org/10.1007/978-3-540-30215-5_3
4. Honavar, V., Slutzki, G. (eds.): ICGI 1998. LNCS, vol. 1433. Springer, Heidelberg (1998). https://doi.org/10.1007/BFb0054058
5. Evans, R., Grefenstette, E.: Learning explanatory rules from noisy data. J. Artif. Intell. Res. (2017)
6. Garcez, A.D., Gori, M., Lamb, L.C., Serafini, L., Spranger, M., Tran, S.N.: Neural-symbolic computing: an effective methodology for principled integration of machine learning and reasoning. J. Appl. Log. 6(4), 611–631 (2019)
7. Goertzel, B., Pennachin, C., Geisweiller, N.: Engineering General Intelligence, Part I: A Path to Advanced AGI via Embodied Learning and Cognitive Strategy. Atlantis Press (2014)
8. Graves, A., et al.: Hybrid computing using a neural network with dynamic external memory. Nature **538**(7626), 471–476 (2016)
9. Li, S., et al.: Integrating regular expressions with neural networks via DFA. arXiv:2109.02882v1 (2021)
10. Luo, B., Feng, Y., Wang, Z., Huang, S., Yan, R., Zhao, D.: Marrying up regular expressions with Neural Networks: A case study for spoken language understanding. arXiv: 1805.05588v1 (2018)
11. Marcus, G.: Deep learning: a critical appraisal. arXiv: 1801.00631. 2 Jan 2018
12. Solomonoff, R.J.: The discovery of algorithmic probability: a guide for the programming of true creativity. In: Vitányi, P. (ed.) EuroCOLT 1995. LNCS, vol. 904, pp. 1–22. Springer, Heidelberg (1995). https://doi.org/10.1007/3-540-59119-2_165
13. Strannegard, C., Nizamani, A.R.: Integrating symbolic logic and sub-symbolic reasoning. In: 9th International Conference, AGI 2016. Springer, New York, NY (2016)
14. Sari, E., Erbas, C., As, I., Sacin, H., Yigitarslan, S.S.: The Image of the City Through the Eyes of Machine Reasoning. Artificial Intelligence in Urban Planning and Design. Elsevier, New York (2022)

COMFO: Multilingual Corpus for Opinion Mining

Lamine Faty[1](✉), Khadim Drame[1], Edouard Ngor Sarr[1], Marie Ndiaye[1],
Ibrahima Diop[1], Yoro Dia[2], and Ousmane Sall[3]

[1] Université Assane Seck de Ziguinchor, Ziguinchor, Senegal
{lamine.faty,khadim.drame,edouard-ngor.sarr,marie.ndiaye,
ibrahima.diop}@univ-zig.sn
[2] Université Iba Der Thiam, Ziguinchor, Senegal
[3] Université Virtuelle du Sénégal, Ziguinchor, Senegal
ousmane1.sall@uvs.edu.sn

Abstract. The use of Machine Learning (ML) algorithms in opinion mining, particularly supervised learning algorithms, requires an annotated corpus to train the classification model in order to predict results that are close to reality. Unfortunately, there are still no resources for the automatic processing of textual data expressed in the Senegalese urban language.

The objective of this paper is to build a multilingual corpus for opinion mining (COMFO). The process of building the COMFO corpus is composed of three steps: presentation of the data source, data collection and preparation, and annotation by lexical approach. The particularity of COMFO lies in the integration of foreign languages (French and English) and local languages, particularly urban Wolof, in order to reflect the collective opinion of Senegalese readers.

Keywords: Opinion mining · Online comment · Corpus building · COMFO

1 Introduction

Opinion Mining (OM) [1, 2] is a data analysis technique designed to explore comments from social networks, commerce sites, news sites, etc. in order to determine the majority opinion of Internet users. Today, we are witnessing a great deal of interest in this emerging technique with the use of Machine Learning (ML) algorithms. The application of supervised learning algorithms in opinion mining requires an annotated corpus to train the classification model in order to predict results close to reality.

The work we are conducting in this article finds its application context in the exploration of comments from the Senegalese online press. In general, the structure of an online comment is less organized. The use of punctuation is much more present, spelling mistakes are very common. In addition, these comments are written in Senegalese urban language. Unfortunately, few resources are available for the automatic processing of textual data expressed in national languages.

B. Goertzel et al. (Eds.): AGI 2022, LNAI 13539, pp. 14–19, 2023.
https://doi.org/10.1007/978-3-031-19907-3_2

Our objective is to build and make available a corpus of labeled opinions to facilitate the use of ML algorithms on Senegalese comments. The major innovation of this COMFO-built resource lies in the integration of the Senegalese urban language in order to properly interpret users' opinions. First, we will review the state of the art of existing works while insisting on their limitations. Then, we will describe the annotation methodology of the COMFO corpus and the evaluation of the experts. In conclusion, we will sum up the results and announce some perspectives.

2 Related Works

With the multilingual nature of social media data, much recent work in FO (or sentiment analysis) incorporates multiple formal and/or informal languages. Proksch et al. [3] presented a multilingual sentiment analysis approach for estimating legislative conflict in most European parliaments in general. The corpus construction is based on European parliamentary debates that are automatically translated using the Google dictionary. The latter provides a reasonable basis for sentiment analysis in different languages. Grljević et al. [4] presented the first manually annotated Serbian language corpus for opinions in the field of higher education. Statistical and linguistic analyses of the corpus revealed useful information for the development of manual sentiment analysis rules. Hardalov et al. [5] proposed a method for sentiment analysis on a multilingual dataset from several sources regarding a target. In this paper, the authors presented the results of a comprehensive study conducted on 15 different datasets in 12 languages from 6 language families.

Although efforts have been made for multilingual sentiment analysis based on a range of informal languages, no meaningful resources have been built for most local languages [6]. Comments from the Senegalese online press are written in the Senegalese urban language. This Senegalese urban language, on the one hand, includes expressions from several languages (foreign and national) and, on the other hand, modifies the orthographic and even grammatical characteristics of a language to reduce its length [7]. It is in this context that we place ourselves to propose COMFO in order to try to reflect the collective opinion of Senegalese readers. The related works above will serve as sources of inspiration. Following this section, we will begin the methodology of construction of our corpus.

3 Constitution of the COMFO Corpus

3.1 Collection and Cleaning of Journalistic Comments

The data that we manipulate, come from Seneweb[1]. This news site is considered one of the favorite sources of Senegalese and diaspora Internet users. The enrichment and proliferation of Seneweb's data have made this source useful and attractive. For the collection, we used the OpinionScraper tool [8] which is a scraper for collecting, merging and formatting journalistic data. In addition, we cleaned this data using regular expressions.

---

[1] http://www.seneweb.com/.

In the end, we have 13,500 comments of which 60% are in French (with many expressions of street or popular French) 37% in urban Wolof and 3% for languages. Figure 1 is an illustration of sentences constructed from words or groups of words from several languages including French, English and Wolof.

N°	Commentaire	Langue
1	Gnoune sounou khalè kamnani daal dièka nanou tè gawougnou magate machalla ndakh pt noire bii gawoul magate	Wolof
2	Mon pot les goûts et les couleurs ne se discutent pas- KOUNEK AK LILA DOYE – L'ESSENTIEL QUE VS VS AIMER LOLOU MON ÂME SOLO	Wolof-Française
3	thanks never give up we we support you for what you doing we appreciate you	Anglaise
4	Félicitations aux lions et nos encouragements aux béninois. Vive le Sénégal.	Française

Fig. 1. Excerpt from Senegalese comments

3.2 Annotation by Lexical Approach

The annotation by the lexical approach consists, on the one hand, in deducing the opinion expressed by a term with the help of a dictionary or a lexicon of opinions and, on the other hand, in determining the polarity of a comment through the calculation of the score.

We used SenOpinion [9] which is an opinion lexicon developed to compensate for the lack of opinion mining resources in the Senegalese context. It is a lexicon composed of words, phrases and expressions in French or Wolof. This lexicon is exclusively intended for tagging comments written in Senegalese urban language. In order to find matches between words from our analysis database (list of input terms) and those from our lexicon without unique identifiers, we prefer to compare strings of letters in order to associate labels to each term. This description can be translated into machine language to allow the computer to perform automatic opinion labeling.

The calculation is based on the score measured according to the presence of terms from the documents in COMFO. For this purpose, we are interested in the result of this classical calculation (see Fig. 3) (Fig. 2):

- Let $C = \{t1, t2,...,tn\}$ be a comment composed of n terms $t1, t2,..., tn$;
- Let P *(Polarity)* be the value of each term which can be -1 or 1.

The lexical approach has the main advantage of allowing fast computations on large corpora [10]. However, the implementation of a resource adapted to the needs of specific applications requires expert evaluation.

Le score d'un commentaire C, noté *Score(C)* est par définition la somme des polarités de termes qui composent le commentaire

$$Score(C) = \sum_{i=1}^{n} P(t_i)$$

- Si Score(C) > 0 alors C a une orientation positive ;
- Si Score(C) < 0 alors C a une orientation négative ;
- Si Score(C) = 0 alors C n'a pas une orientation (neutre).

Fig. 2. Document classification by lexical approach

4 Evaluation of the COMFO Corpus

4.1 Evaluation of Experts

The role of experts is decisive in the process of building a linguistic resource such as a training corpus. Their job is to verify, correct if necessary and validate the proposed annotation. The experts are composed of linguists and data scientists. On the one hand, we have data scientists from the Artificial Intelligence training program of the Virtual University of Senegal (class 1) and, on the other hand, linguists from the Modern Letter master's program of the Assane Seck University of Ziguinchor. The experts assign polarities to the comments.

The validation of the results from the manual annotation is based on the majority voting system. This voting method determines the final polarity of a comment using the median calculation. As an illustration, we can see the document polarities more distinctly in the figure below (see Fig. 4).

Comments	Resources Tagging	Expert Evaluation
thanks never give up we we support you for what you doing we appreciate you	Neutral	Positive
Bro bayil senegalais yi ngay fowé koi mém si les lobby gordjigène te finance assume on sait tout c'est pas kom ca qu'on obtient un disc d'Or en plus ta music né pas riche et tu fau beaucoup de bruit	Positive	Negative
Ay way ma dieureum sey none.sou yalla ne waw koune dett si dett gay dee Wally reck eupeuna..	Positive	Positive
Nianthio diatawoulin allah barka que dieu vs bénissent	Neutral	Positive
Mashallah Maodo def nga Lou rafeet yaw sa xol dafa rafeet mashallah	Neutral	Positive
Salbe waha guoul si comba eume modou lo	Positive	Neutral
Il faut être sérieux ou même honnête et accepter votre défaite est claire devant les yeux de tout le monde	Positive	Negative
De toute façon quatre appuis ame na lithie desse mingui thie lokho C.N.G.	Positive	Neutral
Sois fairplay champion. Tu es tombé, il faut l, accepter. C,est le sport : on gagne, on perd ou c,est le nul. Lac 2 a gagné. Il faut te préparer et solliciter une revanche. COURAGE champion.	Negative	Positive
Lacs de guerre ne mérite pas ce victoires il n.a rien foutue lutteur de merde	Negative	Negative
Boy Niang tu es jeune nangoul dogal stpDanou ngua	Positive	Negative

Fig. 3. Annotated commentary excerpt

Once the documents are annotated, we can determine statistics with the data through the comment level. During the discussion, we will provide precise explanations concerning the irregularities or inequalities in the evolution of the trends.

4.2 Discussion

In total, we annotated a dataset of 13,000 comments whose statistics are provided in Fig. 7.

Polarity	Resources Tagging	Expert Evaluation
Positive	42,7 %	33,4 %
Negative	19,9 %	57,5 %
Neutral	37,4 %	9,1 %

Fig. 4. Statistics of annotated data

Looking at these statistics, we can easily see a big difference between these two annotation modes. This is due to the fact that the lexical approach compares strings of letters in order to associate labels to each term. Such an approach ignores negations. The problem of negations is a challenge that remains in opinion mining even with corpora written in English. The complexity of negations lies in the fact that they change the polarity of the comments initially expected. In addition, the complexity of the types of comments that we have with the expressions from the Senegalese urban language.

5 Conclusion

Ultimately, the construction of an opinion mining corpus requires a lot of human effort, especially in a context where automatic natural language processing tools are almost non-existent. It is a more specifically linguistic activity. This data collection and annotation activity invites the experts to verify and validate the proposed results. This phase is quite long but allows for much better performance. It provides a clean corpus that can be used by ML models.

In the rest of our analysis, we will use the expert annotation. This annotation has integrated negations and Senegalese urban language. This corpus will be made available to the scientific community for validation purposes of the methods that are experimented on these types of data. In the future, we plan to extend the experiments on ML algorithms to validate our tool.

Due to the multilingual nature of social media data, analysis based on a single official language may run the risk of not capturing the overall sentiment of online content. Efforts are being made to perform opinion mining or sentiment analysis in a multilingual context across a range of informal languages.

References

1. Jeyapriya, A., Selvi, C.K.: Extracting aspects and mining opinions in product reviews using supervised learning algorithm. In: Electronics and Communication Systems (ICECS), 2015 2nd International Conference on, pp. 548–552 (2015)
2. Liu, B., Zhang, L.: A survey of opinion mining and sentiment analysis. In: Mining text data, pp. 415–463. Springer (2012)
3. Proksch, S.-O., Lowe, W., Wäckerle, J., Soroka, S.: Multilingual sentiment analysis: A new approach to measuring conflict in legislative speeches. Legis. Stud. Q. (2018)
4. Grljević, O., Bošnjak, Z., Kovačević, A.: Opinion mining in higher education: a corpus-based approach. Enterp. Inf. Syst. 1–26 (2020)
5. Hardalov, M., Arora, A., Nakov, P., Augenstein, I.: Few-shot cross-lingual stance detection with sentiment-based pre-training. ArXiv Prepr. ArXiv210906050 (2021)
6. Lo, S.L., Cambria, E., Chiong, R., Cornforth, D.: Multilingual sentiment analysis: from formal to informal and scarce resource languages. Artif. Intell. Rev. **48**(4), 499–527 (2017)
7. Faty, L., Ndiaye, M., Diop, I., Drame, K.: The complexity of comments from Senegalese online presses face with opinion mining methods. In: 2019 14th Iberian Conference on Information Systems and Technologies (CISTI), pp. 1–6 (2019)
8. Faty, L., Ndiaye, M., Sarr, E.N., Sall, O.: OpinionScraper: a news comments extraction tool for opinion mining. In: 2020 Seventh International Conference on Social Networks Analysis, Management and Security (SNAMS), pp. 1–5 (2020)
9. Faty, L., et al.: SenOpinion: a new lexicon for opinion tagging in Senegalese news comments., In: 2020 15th Iberian Conference on Information Systems and Technologies (CISTI), pp. 1–6 (2020)
10. Sun, S., Luo, C., Chen, J.: A review of natural language processing techniques for opinion mining systems. Inf. Fusion **36**, 10–25 (2017)

Information as Entanglement—A Framework for Artificial General Intelligence

Wael Hafez[✉] ⓘ

Semarx Research, Alexandria, VA, USA
w.hafez@semarx.com

Abstract. Artificial approaches to intelligence depend on computational models to process information and provide intelligent capabilities. Due to the absence of uniform definitions of what constitutes intelligence and what is information, the capabilities such models provide differ according to their interpretations of intelligence and implicit assumptions about what is information. The variety of interpretations of intelligence and information also indicate that existing computational models for intelligence provide specialized rather than general capabilities. The study argues that achieving artificial general intelligence requires a unified, universal definition of information, which would subsequently yield precise formal insights into what constitutes intelligence. The paper provides a definition of information as the level of entanglement between two agents—or between an agent and its environment—measured in bits. Accordingly, intelligence is the agent's continuous activity to maintain and maximize its entanglement with its environment in the face of change. As the level of an agent's entanglement with its environment is a direct indicator of its ability to influence it and be influenced by it, we conclude that the change in an agent's information is the primary control signal for guiding entanglement maximization and, ultimately, the intelligent capabilities of an agent. The paper then introduces a novel class of agents, the information digital twin, which enables a system or agent to control its information and quantify its intelligent activities and enable it to increase its information.

Keywords: Information definition · Entanglement · Information digital twin

1 Introduction

1.1 Computational Models as the Basis for Enabling Intelligent Behavior

Computational models are the dominant metaphor for building intelligent agents and understanding how the brain perform intelligent tasks [6, 9]. Computational models rely on algorithms to modify selected variables to imitate, reproduce, or explain intelligent behavior [5]. On the one hand, the absence of a common understanding of the concept of intelligence [2] means that the logic used in the various algorithms is dependent on the assumptions of the algorithm developers, as opposed to a standard, unified logic of the phenomena. Similar circumstances apply to the selected variables. As there is no unified understanding of information [3, 14], the selection of these variables, their

© The Author(s), under exclusive license to Springer Nature Switzerland AG 2023
B. Goertzel et al. (Eds.): AGI 2022, LNAI 13539, pp. 20–29, 2023.
https://doi.org/10.1007/978-3-031-19907-3_3

degree of relevance to the activities being modeled, and the relationships between them depend on the model developer assumptions of what information is. Consequently, a large number of computational models capture numerous specific aspects of intelligence (e.g., object recognition, language processing, or process automation), but there is no general framework to integrate, leverage, and expand these specialized techniques to artificial general intelligence (AGI)-level capabilities.

1.2   The Concept of Information is Central for Understanding Intelligence

When investigating new fields of science and technology, a lack of precise definitions is a common issue. The construction of efficient heat engines, for instance, was only possible after the formalization of rigorous and consistent thermodynamics rules. The same is true for aircraft engineering and aerodynamics, communication systems, and communication theory. In other words, the development of a general framework for intelligent computational models requires a formal and consistent definition of information and intelligence. Thus, we argue that the relationship between intelligence and information is comparable to the relationship between heat and heat engines. In other words, the "substance" of intelligent behavior is information. As a result, providing a uniform and unified description of information will facilitate the development of more general computational models for intelligence.

1.3   Proposed Unified Definitions of Information and Intelligence

The task of the study is thus to provide a unifying definition of information, specify how to understand the phenomena of intelligence based on the definition of information, and finally define a general computational framework that combines the two notions to enable AGI. The proposed framework is implemented by a new type of gents we call the information digital twin (IDT). An IDT is specific to a system, agent, or individual. Assuming information as the level of agent entanglement with its environment and intelligence as the computations required to maximize that information, the IDT first learns the amount of information of its agent, monitors changes in that amount as the agent interacts with its environment, uses the degree of change to guide a search for actions to recover or increase the previous amount of information, and ultimately provides its agent with action recommendations. The supported agent can then choose which action to implement based on its overall objective.

1.4   Approach and Structure

Following the proposed definition of information, and according to control theory, the study outlines the requirements a system must meet to control its information level. A general definition of intelligence is then provided as the actions of controlling information to achieve agent objectives. After providing a brief introduction to the notion of industrial digital twins, the information digital twin (IDT) is discussed to indicate how it implements the computations necessary to capture the agent's information and ultimately support intelligent behavior.

2   A Unified Definition of Information

Introducing new definitions in a discipline necessitates comparing how the new definition relates to or differs from existing definitions. However, the current research will focus primarily on how the suggested definition facilitates an AGI framework. The focus of later works will be on incorporating the new definition into the ongoing conversation concerning the meaning of information.

2.1   Information as Entanglement

We propose defining information as the degree of entanglement between two agents or between an agent and its environment. According to Schrodinger's concept of quantum entanglement, "entanglement consists in the fact that a single observable (or set of commuting observables) of one system is uniquely determined by a single observable (or set of commuting observables) of the other" [10, p. 558]. In other words, entanglement establishes predictability between systems. If a particular state in one system is entangled with a specific state in the other, then knowing one of the states provides precise knowledge about the other. In quantum mechanics entanglement is an intrinsic characteristic of quantum systems. In the current context, however, entanglement between two systems or agents is the result of exchanging signals or messages. Assume, for instance, that agents X and Y each have four distinct states and that each state of *Agent X* is entangled with a specific state of *Agent Y* (see Fig. 1. A). In this case, knowing *Message y* offers a complete knowledge of *Message x* and vice versa.

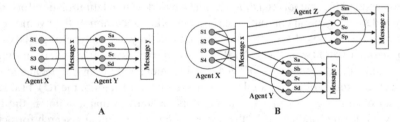

Fig. 1. Entanglement between agents is indicated by their responses to the messages they exchange. A message consists of one or more signals, and one or more signals represent a state.

The entanglement between *Agent X* and *Agent Y* means that each time *Agent X* sends a particular message corresponding to one of its states, it has a complete knowledge of *Agent Y*'s response. If *Agent X* sends a message to *Agent Y* indicating that it is at state *S2*, there is a probability of one that *Agent Y* will respond with a message indicating that it is in state *Sb*, which is entangled with state *S2*. Entanglement between the two agents thus shows that for *Agent Y*, the state *Sb* can be induced only by a specific message from *Agent X* corresponding to state *S2* or by any other agent capable of producing an identical message. Entanglement then enables a system to predict its environment and be predictable by other agents in it, which is a prerequisite for effective collaboration.

2.2   Systems for Entanglement—Increasing Interactions Predictability

Entanglement can be considered to occur as a phenomenon anytime systems or agents interact with one another or with their environment in general. Such interactions rely on a variety of what might be called systems of entanglement. Language is an example of an entanglement system. Assuming a community speaks the same language, each individual can confidently assume that others associate the same unique concepts or behaviors with an object such as a book. That is, the word "book" is entangled with specific concepts that are evoked whenever the word is used. The four arbitrary symbols (letters) making up the word *book* in that specific sequence are already associated with a specific set of physical objects (books) and they cannot be used to describe, for example, a tree. However, all language users can agree to dis-entangle the word *book* from the objects and concepts it represents and re-entangle it with a new set of objects and concepts, which is how languages actually evolve.

Cell communication, as well as communication in general, is another example of an entanglement system. When a cell sends a signal to neighboring cells, the sender cell can typically predict the signals produced by the receiving cells as a response. On the flip side, it is possible to infer that a particular trigger signal was received by a cell by examining its signaling activity. In other words, a cell establishes entanglement between the signals it receives from its environment with the ones it sends back. Another example of a system for entanglements is the DNA. During transcription, the DNA establishes predictable, particular dependencies between one form of signal (RNA polymerase) and another type of signals, the mRNA. In general, and assuming normal conditions, knowing one signals provides precise knowledge of the other one.

There are systems of entanglement in every element of life where agents interact. Their primary objective is to guarantee the predictability of different action-response relationships among the various agents, i.e., to ensure a reliable degree of entanglement that facilitates successful cooperation.

2.3   Information—Measuring Agent Level of Entanglement

The first step for an agent to manage and control its entanglement with its environment is to quantify it. As demonstrated in the above examples, the probability that an agent reacts to a message is a direct indicator of the extent of its entanglement with the source of that message. If, in Fig. 1. A, each time *Agent Y* receives message *S3*, it responds with message *Sc*, then *Agent Y* can assign probability of "one" to the entanglement of this interaction. However, if *Agent Y* begins to respond with *Sc* just 8 out of 10 times, then the probability of its entanglement drops to 0.8.

The corresponding information value calculation is based on Shannon's communication theory [11] and is used as the metric for an agent to measure its level of entanglement and generate a control signal to manage it. Consequently, (see Fig. 1. B) *Agent X* level of entanglement is two bits of information, as all its four states are entangled with their surroundings. The same holds for *Agent Y*. However, the situation is different for *Agent Z*, as just three of its states are entangled with the environment, resulting in entanglement value of 1,58 bits.

However, *Agent X* may entangle with its surroundings by communicating 16 messages that reflect a mix of its four states. However, its actual amount of entanglement, i.e., its information, is contingent on its ability to compel its environment to react to each of the 16 messages with a unique response message. If it succeeds, then its information is equivalent to 4 bits. However, if any of the corresponding responses occur with a probability of less than one, then *Agent X* inforamtion decreases proportionally.

3   Agents Need to Control Their Entanglement to Achieve Their Objectives

Agents interact with their environment to achieve specific goals. For example, animals interact with their surroundings to obtain energy, avoid danger, and reproduce. Artificial agents interact with their environment to fulfill predefined objectives, such as maintaining a flight route or maximizing a specific process output. In any interaction scenario, agents rely on their sensors to provide the values of the relevant parameter to their task, and on their effectors to modify these parameters in a way they believe will provide some desired results. Consequently, the sensors and effectors are the means through which agent-environment entanglement is achieved. Nevertheless, the agent-environment entanglement is subject to two significant sources of uncertainty: unforeseeable changes to the agent's operational conditions and communication uncertainties. Accordingly, for an agent to accomplish its goals, it must manage both sources of uncertainty.

3.1   Agents Predictability Ensures Their Performance

Unanticipated changes in the environment or erosion of the agent structure would lead to variation in the effective range of the sensors or effectors, their transduction efficiency, or their numbers. In addition, while the agent exchanges messages with its environment (i.e., communicates with it), this communication is prone to noise-induced uncertainty [12].

Both forms of uncertainty alter the probability that different signals and messages will produce the same reactions. The system's capacity to predict its environment and behave predictably is reduced accordingly. Even if the overall degree of agent-environment entanglement in bits remains constant, uncertainties alter the patterns and interdependence among the individual messages.

An agent must then continuously evaluate and adjust its level of entanglement with its environment as it provides a direct indication of its performance. Moreover, an agent may utilize changes in the degree of entanglement to guide its actions towards maintaining or improving its performance. An agent then needs a way to regulate its information value, i.e., its level of entanglement with its environment.

3.2   Elements of a Control System

In general, there are three prerequisites for controlling a variable [1]. First, it must be quantified, i.e., a measure representing its changes must be devised. The second step entails evaluating a divergence from a desired target value, i.e., providing a control signal. The third condition is to define a relationship between the control signal and the factors influencing the variable's value. The temperature management in a room is a typical example of a control system (see Fig. 2). Initially, the quantity of heat inside a room is measured in terms of temperature. Second, a control signal is calculated based on the difference between the desired room temperature and the actual temperature. Lastly, a controller is used to correlate the value of the control signal to a quantity of energy to the heater.

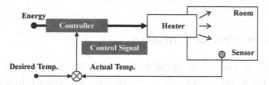

Fig. 2. General feedback control system components. A control signal is required for the controller to select the appropriate energy level to achieve the desired temperature.

For an agent to control its entanglement with the environment, it must then provide the following: a metric indicating the level of its entanglement, a control signal that determines changes in its entanglement, and a mechanism that modifies the level of entanglement based on the control signal. Assuming information, measured in bits, as the entanglement metric satisfies the first requirement. The next paragraphs present how an agent can meet the other two requirements.

3.3 Defining an Entanglement Control Signal

When *Agent X* sends a message to *Agent Y*, it can only determine *Y's* reaction through its own sensory states (Fig. 3. A). That is, regardless of how *Y* actually responds, *Agent X* can only assess the response by analyzing its own sensory states as they capture *Y's* response message. Accordingly, the only observable entanglement for *Agent X* is between its output states and corresponding input states, or between its output and input messages corresponding to each state. *Agent X* can then evaluate its entanglement with its enviroenmtn based on the entanglement between its output and input messages.

If every time *Agent X* sends a message *Ma* to the environment, it receives a message *Mt*, the two messages become entangled with probability of one. If, however, out of ten times of sending message *Ma*, seven times the message *Mt* is received, and three times message *Mx*, then the *Ma-Mt* entanglement decreases and the *Ma-Mx* entanglement increases.

The probabilites involved across all corresponding input-output messages are then used to calculate the overall agent level of entanglement. In addition, monitoring the input-output entanglement value over time provides a control signal indicating the variations in its value (see Fig. 3. B).

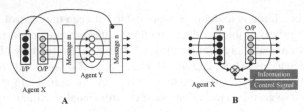

Fig. 3. Calculating the level of entanglement between the input and output messages—based on their probability—to obtain the entanglement control signal.

3.4 Defining an Entanglement Controller

The final prerequisite to enable an agent to manage its entanglement is the controller: how to use entanglement variations—the control signal—to correlate the input and output states to maintain or increase the agent information (Fig. 4). The controller includes the rules and logic that, given: a specific objective, an input message, and a control signal selects an output message (action) to send back to the environment. It is understandable that, for a complicated system, the controller's activities and logic may also be exceedingly complex; yet the point here is that the controller depends on the control signal to guide its actions.

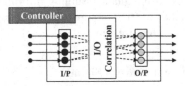

Fig. 4. The controller determines the necessary input-output state interdependence for the agent to attain its objectives.

3.5 Agent Architecture for Managing Entanglement Under Uncertainties

The relationship between the various elements for controlling entanglement is depicted in Fig. 5. As previously established, for an agent to accomplish its goals, it must compel the environment to send back desired input. Thus, given a particular objective, the controller chooses an output message to send to the environment and causes it to respond with an input message. If the response satisfies the system's objective, the input-output messages are entangled, and the amount of agent information grows. If the received message is not the desired one, or if the message is no longer desired, the controller decouples it from the related output message and begins searching for an alternative output message that would provide the desired outcomes.

The ability to simulate the effect of selected output messages on the level of entanglement is a defining characteristic of the configuration depicted in Fig. 5. In other words, the input-output entanglement assessment module can provide the controller with a signal indicating how effectively a selected output affects entanglement. The controller may then choose to retain the output message or "try another one" to maintain or increase the agent's entanglement level.

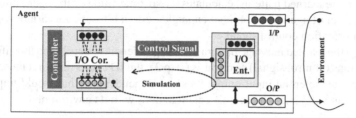

Fig. 5. General architecture for entanglement management.

4   The Information Digital Twin (IDT)

"A digital twin is a digital representation of a real-world entity or agent. The implementation of a digital twin is an encapsulated software object or model that mirrors a unique physical object, process, organization, person, or other abstraction" [4]. Digital twins are used to maximize the performance and lifetime of equipment by monitoring a piece of equipment in real-time, comparing actual performance to expected performance and predicting deviation, and intervening according to set rules. Digital twins are commonly employed to support equipment like jet engines, wind turbines, or even human organs. An information digital twin (IDT) is thus an agent that supports a system or another agent in predicting its environment and being predictable by it [8, 11] (see Fig. 6).

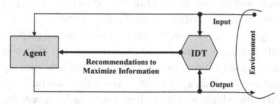

Fig. 6. Information Digital Twin which enables an agent to manage its information (level of entanglement) as it interacts with its environment towards some desired goals.

The increased agent-environment mutual predictability increases their ability to collaborate and automate their interactions. The IDT accomplishes this by monitoring the agent's information value, predicting its variations along with agent-environment interactions, and providing actionable recommendations to allow the supported agent to maintain or increase its level of information (i.e., entanglement with its environment). The IDT is a universal agent and does not rely on the kind or function of the system, artificial agent, or person it supports. The IDT provides thus an additional, general control dimension to enable an agent to improve its performance. The IDT executes four basic and interdependent computations:

1. Represents input and output messages and signals following a probabilistic data structure that enables a continuous evaluation of their probabilities.
2. Learns (using machine learning) signal and message dependencies and patterns.
3. Based on the learned patterns, calculates a real-time value of the agent information, i.e., the level of agent-environment entanglement in bits, and its variation over time as an information control signal.
4. Based on the learned message patterns and dependencies (step 2) and the information fluctuations (control signal) as rewards (step 3), the IDT uses reinforcement learning to search for potential input-output message dependencies that would improve the information value, i.e., the agent's entanglement with its environment.

So far, we have developed the general architecture of the IDT with the necessary data standards (step 1) as well as the algorithms for steps 2 and 3.

5 Discussion—Information as a General Metric for Intelligence

The study suggested that developing a computational model of AGI necessitates a general metric, which is characterized as the system or agent's level of entanglement with its environment. Similar to how any material flow between a system and its environment alters its energy, any message exchange between an agent and its environment alters its information. Even when the net change, in either case, is zero, changes can be still observed as a shift in the energy distribution or entanglement patterns across the system parameters or messages. In other words, information, as defined in the study, reflects any message exchange between a system or agent and its environment. As such, information is a general metric which can be used to quantify and compare the activities and choices underlying these exchanges.

Agent-environment message exchanges towards some objectives is a diverse activity. It may, for example, include interpreting the significance or relevance of input signals and messages, determining the most relevant response or sequence of responses leading to the system goals, capturing changes in the environment, adjusting objectives and responses accordingly, and, in the case of living systems, developing new messaging capabilities, i.e., new sensory and motor signals, or retiring ones that are no longer relevant. The efficiency and speed with which a system does these tasks reveal its intelligence [2, 7]. On the other hand, each and every one of these activities modifies the probabilities and dependencies of the involved signals and messages and accordingly the agent's information.

A key feature of the information control architecture depicted in Fig. 5 and enabled by the IDT is that all messages have two copies; one is used—without modifications— by the "I/O Ent." module to calculate agent information and the other is modified and altered by the "Controller" module to best achieve the agent objectives. Manipulation refers to the controller modifying the message structure and its probability of interactions with other messages in its search for the optimal actions and responses to accomplish the agent's goals. We believe the proposed information control architecture has broad similarities with the thalamus-cortex configuration [13] and might provide insights into brain intelligent activities as well.

6   Conclusion

Developing models of intelligence remains challenging. The research argued that intelligent behavior increases an agent's ability to interact with its environment, i.e., increase the number of signals and messages it can send to and receive and their associated probabilities. The agent's capacity to communicate is ultimately indicated by how well it can predict the environment and be predictable by it, which is defined as entanglement. As entanglement depends on communication and the probabilities of how various signals and messages are used and depend on one another, information is then suggested as the metric for measuring entanglement. The coupling of information and entanglement provides a unified, general definition of the nature of information, which then offers a unified general metric for quantifying intelligent activities. Information as a general metric offers an additional control dimension for directing intelligent actions. The described method is implemented by introducing the information digital twin, which is specialized in predicting the impact of system actions on its information and recommending actions to retain its value or improving it.

References

1. Bubnicki, Z.: Modern Control Theory. Springer, Heidelberg (2005)
2. Chollet, F.: On the measure of intelligence. arXiv:1911.01547C (2019)
3. Floridi, L.: Open problems in the philosophy of information. Metaphilosophy **35**(4), 554–582 (2004)
4. Gartner.   https://www.gartner.com/en/information-technology/glossary/digital-twin.   Last Accessed 13 Mar 2022
5. Gershenson, C.: Intelligence as information processing: brains, swarms, and computers. Front. Ecol. Evol. **9**(755981) (2021)
6. Gershman, S., Horvitz, E., Tenenbaum, J.: Computational rationality: a converging paradigm for intelligence in brains, minds, and machines. Science Magazine **349**(6245 273), 273–278 (2015)
7. Goldstein, S., Princiotta, D., Naglieri, J. (eds.): Handbook of Intelligence. Springer, New York (2015)
8. Hafez, W.: Information Digital twin—enabling agents to anticipate changes in their tasks. In: Goertzel, B., Panov, A.I., Potapov, A., Yampolskiy, R. (eds.) AGI 2020. LNCS (LNAI), vol. 12177, pp. 183–192. Springer, Cham (2020). https://doi.org/10.1007/978-3-030-52152-3_19
9. Rescorla, M.: The computational theory of mind. In: Zalta, E. (ed.) The Stanford Encyclopedia of Philosophy. https://plato.stanford.edu/archives/fall2020/entries/computational-mind (2020)
10. Schrödinger, E.: Discussion of probability relations between separated systems. Math. Proc. the Camb. Philos. Soc. **31**(4), 555–563 (1935)
11. Semarx Research Ltd. http://www.semarx.com
12. Shannon, C.E.: A mathematical theory of communication. Bell Syst. Tech. J. **27**(3), 379–423 (1948). https://doi.org/10.1002/j.1538-7305.1948.tb01338.x
13. Murray Sherman, S., Guillery, R.W.: Functional Connections of Cortical Areas: A New View from the Thalamus. The MIT Press (2013). https://doi.org/10.7551/mitpress/9780262019309.001.0001
14. Van Benthem, J., Van Rooy, J.: Connecting the different faces of information. J. Log. Lang. Inf. **12**, 375–379 (2003)

Causal Analysis of Generic Time Series Data Applied for Market Prediction

Anton Kolonin[1,2,3]($\boxtimes$) , Ali Raheman[1], Mukul Vishwas[1] , Ikram Ansari[1] ,
Juan Pinzon[1] , and Alice Ho[1]

[1] Autonio Foundation Ltd., Bristol, UK
akolonin@gmail.com
[2] SingularityNET Foundation, Amsterdam, The Netherlands
[3] Novosibirsk State University, Novosibirsk, Russian Federation

Abstract. We explore the applicability of the causal analysis based on tempo-rally shifted (lagged) Pearson correlation applied to diverse time series of dif-ferent natures in context of the problem of financial market prediction. Theoret-ical discussion is followed by description of the practical approach for specific environment of time series data with diverse nature and sparsity, as applied for environments of financial markets. The data involves various financial metrics computable from raw market data such as real-time trades and snapshots of the limit order book as well as metrics determined upon social media news streams such as sentiment and different cognitive distortions. The approach is backed up with presentation of algorithmic framework for data acquisition and analysis, con-cluded with experimental results, and summary pointing out at the possibility to discriminate causal connections between different sorts of real field market data with further discussion on present issues and possible directions of the following work.

Keywords: Causality · Causal analysis · Correlation · Financial market · Time series

1 Introduction

1.1 Background for This Work

The motivation of this work is to figure out a suitable general purpose algorithmic framework capable of figuring out causal connections across diverse time series data from different sources, including sparse and unreliable ones. The motivation is supported by our further work on the generic architecture for active portfolio management [1] employed by automated adaptive trading and market making agents [2] which need to be capable to do predictions in respect to future market dynamics relying on diverse temporal streams of data. This includes market data, social and online media news, as well as so-called "on-chain" data computed from transactional activities on public financial ecosystems such as blockchains.

B. Goertzel et al. (Eds.): AGI 2022, LNAI 13539, pp. 30–39, 2023.
https://doi.org/10.1007/978-3-031-19907-3_4

While we understand that the operations being performed by a hypothetical completely autonomous trading or market making agent might be considered as a narrow artificial general intelligence (Narrow AGI), we want to have the operational environment of it to gain as much reach as possible, maximizing its capabilities for intelligent decision making based on wide range of information sources, including market data and technical indicators from different exchanges, fundamental and "on-chain" data, and sentiment and emotional data from online and social media sources. That is why in this work we explore the possibility of causal analytics for market prediction purposes for as much information as possible given rather specific business case of the Bitcoin price prediction on Binance exchange for BTC/USDT pair referring to Tether USD stable coin.

1.2 Overview of the Field

The fundamental background for probabilistic causal analytics can be found in [3] with application of predictive causal analytics to financial markets discussed in [4]. The recent study of causal analytics applied to time series data is covered in [5]. Application of sentiment analysis in respect to causal analysis of sentiment data and market volatility on its basis is presented in [6]. The variety of features, metrics, and parameters then can be derived from the market data, including the structure of the limit order book (LOB) snapshots is covered in [7] and [8]. Finally, the very latest study discovers the connection between patterns in political and economic history with so-called "cognitive behavioral schemata" (CBS) patterns traditionally used in psychotherapy [9]. All the mentioned studies have been accounted, extended and tailored to the specific problem in hands as discussed further.

2 Practical Approach

2.1 Data Acquisition

Given the practical objective of our work is providing operations on crypto exchanges such as Binance and the crypto finance is a domain being actively discussed on social media channels such as Twitter and Reddit, we have tried to collect as much as possible data from both kind of sources.

Market Data. In particular, the present data acquisition framework streams the live market data from Binance exchange, including both raw trades and snapshots of the LOB at different sampling rates or granularity periods including 1 day, 1 h, 1 min, and 1 s. Both sorts of the mentioned "raw" data were used to compute the "pre-processed" data such as extended open-high-low-close-volume (OHLCV) frames, including volumes and counts of "buy" and "sell" (from the regular trader perspective) traded, average prices for "buy" and "sell" trades, including regular averages as well as weighted averages using both base and quote currency for the averaging weights. All the counts, volumes, and average prices for "buy" and "sell" are used to compute "imbalance" metrics indicating the skew of the distribution towards either "buy" or "sell". That is, we have substantially extended the scope of features used in [7]. The use of LOB data has been rendered useful in [8], so we include more metrics shaping the distribution of the orders such as minimum "ask" and maximum "bid" prices, average "ask" and "bid" prices with the averages weighted by order volumes, "spread" and average "spreads" between different sorts of the "ask" and "bid", order volumes on each of the order book sides and all sorts of imbalances on these "ask"/"bid" prices and volumes. The overall scope of the market data for the BTC/USDT pair discussed in this work was covering almost 1.5 years from August 2020 till December 2021.

The "pre-processed" data described above have been normalized in different alternative ways in order to turn them into stationary state in range between $[-1.0, +1.0]$. All the data was differentiated so the derivatives were computed on basis of the raw data. Next, the differentiated data and the raw data has been turned too non-negative logarithmic scale using operation $log10(1 + x)$. Finally, from this point, both differentiated and non-differentiated, logarithmic and non-logarithmic data has been normalized using operation $x/max(abs(x))$ to ensure the range $[-1.0, +1.0]$ regardless of the metric sign. It worth noticing that at the earlier phase of the work different normalization schemes were applied, however it was found that some of the metrics perform better in the representations other than expected, so eventually we have decided to apply all sorts of normalization to every metric at the cost of increased number of times series involved in the analysis on the following phase.

Media Data. Two kinds of metrics were derived from the online social media data: public posts from about 80 channels on Twitter and Reddit relevant to crypto market for six months starting July 2021. First, it was the conventional sentiment as presented in [6], computed as described below. Second, it was the "cognitive behavioral schemata" (CBS) patterns evaluated according to [9]. The overall volume of the media content was exceeding 100,000 posts across all channels.

The sentiment metrics were computed with help of Aigents®, which is "interpretable" model based on "n-grams," available as part of https://github.com/aigents/ aigents-java distribution and written in Java, which comes with "out-of-the-box" vocabularies for n-grams associated with positive and negative sentiment. It has over 8,200 negative and over 3,800 positive n-grams and returns the overall sentiment/polarity of the text based on the frequencies of occurrences of the reference n-grams in the text along with independent positive and negative sentiment metrics. One of the specifics of the model is implementation of the "priority on order" principle as discussed in [10]. In the Aigents®-specific implementation it means precedence given for n-grams with higher "n", so whenever any n-gram is matched, all matches of any other n-grams being parts of the former n-gram are disregarded. For instance, if tetragram ["not", "a", "bad", "thing"] is matched, then both bigram ["bad", "thing"] and unigram ["bad"] are disregarded and discounted. Similarly, matching bigram ["no", "good"] disregards and discounts both constituent unigrams ["no'] and ["good"]. In addition to that, the model has an option to provide logarithmic scaling of the counted frequencies and our studies have revealed that by enabling this option it provides better performance. The model provides four basic sentiment metrics, so that, instead of addressing the sentiment analysis problem as a plain classification ('Positive' vs. 'Negative' vs. 'Neutral'), we were treating it as a multinomial classification problem in four independent dimensions corresponding to the individual metrics discussed below:

sentiment (sen) – overall or compound sentiment/polarity in range [−1.0, +1.0], so its value can be either negative or positive;
positive (pos) – canonical positive sentiment assessment in range [0.0, +1.0], so its value can be only positive;
negative (neg) – canonical negative sentiment assessment in range [−1.0, 0.0], so its value can be only negative;
contradictive (con) – mutual **contradictiveness** of the positive and negative assessments computed as *SQRT(positive * ABS(negative))*.

All of the media metrics computed on basis of individual posts were aggregated as mean/average per channel across all channels on either daily or hourly basis and the aggregated mean values were in turn normalized using operation *x/max(abs(x))* to ensure the range [− 1.0, +1.0].

2.2 Analytical Framework

Since the practical and goal of the study was the prediction of the market price, our causal analytical framework was considering the price movement as a target "effect" and all the other metrics as a potential "causes". While the earlier work [7] refers to stationary function of "log-return" as a target, we were dealing with price difference (price derivative, PD) after finding that fundamental nature of results presented further does not depend on that choice while use of PD had turned to be handier in practical applications. That is, the PD was considered as the "effect".

The conceptual causal frameworks [3] and [4] justifying our studies has turned difficult to implement literally due to the lack of clearly identifiable "events" in the time series data, even assuming the data is represented by stationary functions in the range [−1.0, +1.0]. It was tempting to consider determination of events such as "price goes up", or "there is positive sentiment" but it was clear that it could be done on basis on some thresholds which would be either subjective or become a source of extra errors and uncertainties or both. On the other hand, the formal assessment of probability of such "event" would become another problem. One would suggest using the values of the "effect" and "cause" metric functions in the range [−1.0, +1.0] as probabilities but it could be ambiguous either because of diversity of scaling factors for individual metrics being forcefully aligned to the same normalization range. After all, we ended up following the approach of temporally lagged/shifted correlation analysis applied to time series data as described in [5] and [6]. That is, we were considering the **causation** as the **preceding correlation**, or correlation of the "cause" function with the "effect" function shifted back to certain lag on the temporal axis.

Given the rich data that we had, we were performing the causal analysis in three dimensional space, with time *t* being the first dimension, channel *c* being the second dimension and the metric *m* being the third one. The channel might be either actual Twitter or Reddit channel used to derive the media metric or some source of the market data (such as Binance) or "on-chain" data (such as Bitcoin) or third-party sources (such as Santiment or Glassnode services discussed further). The metrics would be specific in respect to the channel. The results presented in the next section were derived on basis of 80 media channels with 21 metrics in each and 111 metrics in single market data channel corresponding to BTC/USDT trading pair on Binance exchange, so 1791 potential "causes" were explored in total, in different time sampling rates such as day, hour, minute and second.

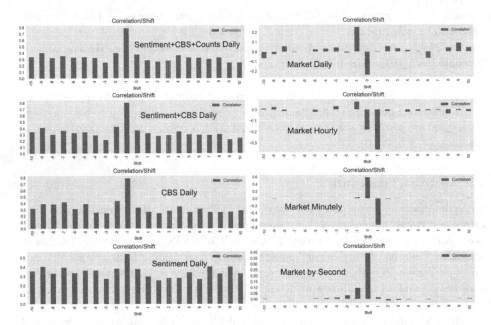

Fig. 1. Search for preceding correlation between the effect PD and synthetic additive cause indicator (SACI) on different temporal horizons measured as shift of the effect function back in time (negative shift to the left) or forward in time (positive shift to the right). The left bar charts present respective Pearson correlation (PC) of the shifted price with SACI assembled using different sets of media metrics across all Twitter and Reddit channels (top to down): sentiment with CBS with word count and post count, sentiment with CBS, CBS only, sentiment only – everything on daily basis. The right bar charts present PC of the shifted price with SACI assembled using all market metrics based on Binance data (top to down): on daily basis, on hourly basis, on minutely basis, on per-second basis.

The key study was the process of finding what we called synthetic additive cause indicator (SACI) relying on the whole scope of source metrics being treated as a hypothetical causes. The probabilistic logic treats addition as logical disjunction and multiplication as logical conjunction. In this work we were exploring only the disjunctive version of it, so the assembly of the integrative SACI was involving addition of the perspective causes in order to maximize the correlation with the effect at a particular target shift/lag. See the discussion on the SACI performance presented on Fig. 1 in the following section.

The temporal causation study was run evaluating different time shifts/lags in days $[-10, +10]$ computing mutual Pearson correlation (PC) between each of the potential

Weight by channel

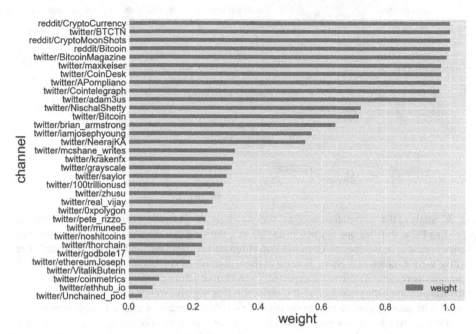

Fig. 2. Presentation of the "representability weight" of each of the media channels involved in the search for the SACI on daily basis, the study is showing that account on the weight while assembling the SACI improves the fitting of the cause-effect correlation on the training data set. The top channels with the weight equal to 1.0 have posts on every day while channels at the bottom with the weight close to zero have just few posts per month/week.

causes and the price difference and retaining the "correlation weights" of the computed value $P(l,c,m)$ for every time lag l, news channel c, and metric m. Also, the channels c were optionally weighted with the "representability weight" as $W(c)$ according to the percentage of days (or hours) with news present on such time intervals, as shown on Fig. 2. Then, for every lag l, the compound SACI metric time series $Y(l,d)$ = $\Sigma X(c,m,d) * P(l,c,m) * W(c)$ for every day d have been built from the original raw metrics $X(c,m,d)$. The compound SACI metric building process was implemented starting from channels with the highest $W(c)$ and $P(l,c,m)$ adding ingredients up to $Y(l,d)$ incrementally, as long as the correlation between the target price difference function and the current content of summed up $Y(l,d)$ series for given time lag l keeps increasing.

3 Experimental Results

The **causal connectivity as** a preceding correlation has been studied on the full scope of the media and market data described above with major results presented on Fig. 1. It is clearly seen that ability to build the well-correlated SACI from media data at the point one day before the anticipated "effect" is dominating all other time lags/shifts so we can with

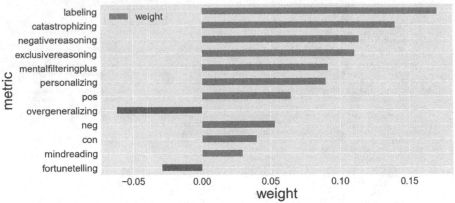

Fig. 3. Study of the "correlation weights" for one single media channel being part of the model as preceding PC at shift/lag one day before an "effect", showing that the most impactful on the price change appear to be the specific cognitive distortions called "labeling" and "catastrophizing". The positive weight means that either increase of these distortions is preceding price increase, which appears more reasonable due to the expectedly speculative nature of the crypto market or decrease of them is preceding the price decline. It is noticeable that negative weight of the "overgeneralizing" distortion apparently corresponds to the opposite – either increase of this distortion is preceding price decline, which appears more reasonable, or decrease of it is preceding the price increase. In accordance with the findings discussed regarding the Fig. 1, the sentiment metrics (*pos*, *con* and *neg*) appears much less impactful in respect to the price change, rendering the high degree of **contradictiveness** in respect to each other.

a greater certainty state that some combination of the metrics represented by the "model" of the SACI is having the causal connection with the target price change. In turn, the "model" of the SACI represented by the number of the channels and metrics involved in it along with their "correlation weights" and "representability weight" are determining the fine-grained causal structure of it discussed further. It is also seen that sentiment doesn't have significant impact on the causation alone (PC = 0.56), the involvement of word and news counts make the results a little bit worse (PC going down from 0.8 to 0.78), the CBS alone provides PC = 0.79 and CBS with sentiment together bring it to the maximum (PC = 0.8).

While the sentiment metrics have appeared promising thus far, the market metrics have turned to be substantially less inspiring. The daily study for market metrics on Fig. 1 do render promising correlation of the SACI one day before the "effect", however the low PC = 0.25 at this shift is much less than in case of using media metric and there is much more expressive correlation coinciding with the "effect" at zero shift/lag with almost the same PC value (negative in this case). Moreover, the studies for hourly, minutely and by-second sampling rates do not render noticeable preceding correlations at all.

The extra data involved for this kind of analysis were the pre-syndicated media, market and related data by third-party providers. Specifically, we explored the daily and

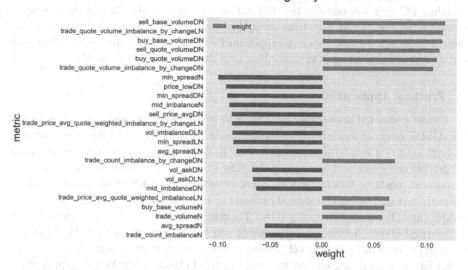

Fig. 4. A Study of the "correlation weights" for the market metrics, showing the less expression of the preceding PC at one day shift/lag before an "effect". The capital letters in feature suffixes correspond to involved "pre-processing" applied in left-to-right order: D – derivative or differential, L – decimal logarithm, N – normalization to range [−1.0, +1.0]. It is clearly seen that the most impactful features (PC > 0.1) appear to be the volumes of "sell" and "buy" trades and the imbalance between them denominated by the price change magnitude at the moment (*trade_quote_volume_imbalance_by_change*). Also, in accordance with discussion on Fig. 1, the PC assessments for market metrics are substantially less impressive than for media metrics.

hourly data feeds from Santiment (https://api.santiment.net) to check for sentiment and on-chain metrics both and Glassnode (https://glassnode.com) to check for on-chain data only. The on-chain metrics are indicators derived from different sorts of transnational activity on blockchain such as Bitcoin. The period for study was taken the same as for the social media feeds discussed above – nearly half year starting July 2021. While working with the Santiment API, we looked at various channels like Telegram, Reddit, Twitter and Bitcointalk with each of the channels supplied with negative and positive sentiment metrics provided by Santiment service. We also considered non-sentiment metrics from it, like circulating supply, active addresses, and GitHub activity available on the platform. But we could not identify any metrics that could impact the price prediction. The on-chain metrics used from Glassnode involved active address count, transactions count, transactions rate, blockchain count, blockchain height, grayscale holdings, to name a few. The study has shown many metrics having positive Pearson correlation synchronously, at the same day or hour with the price change (measured as price derivative or "log return"), yet no one was showing expressed causal connection with the price change in terms of preceding correlation on the shifted time series, so no further studies has been done on this data. Notably, the synchronous and preceding correlations were higher on daily data but much weaker on hourly data as it was found for other data discussed above.

The **causal structure** of the additive ingredients of the SACI rendering the highest preceding PC scores at one day lag/shift before the price change "effect" was done as shown on the Fig. 3 and Fig. 4 for media and market metrics, respectively. It shows confirmation on the greater potential applicability of the media metrics over the market metrics and use of the cognitive distortions over the sentiment, specifically.

3.1 Practical Applications

The results presented above have been tried to get applied for price prediction of the BTC/USDT (Bitcoin to USD Tether) trading pair on Binance exchange. The objective has been set to hit two targets. First, we were looking to exceed the baseline provided by "prediction" made just by copying the "last known price" (LKP) and approach the "prediction" made by looking up the "future known price" (FKP) in historical test data. The performance has been evaluated on basis of both Mean Average Percentage Error (MAPE) and Directional Accuracy (DA). The data used for experiments were the same as discussed above. Second, we were using our backtesting framework [1, 2] to use obtained predictions by the market making bots according to their strategies.

So far, in order to accomplish the goal, we tried classical Machine Learning algorithms such as Linear Regression, Ridge, Lasso regressions and Elastic Net among others without any clear success to outperform the LKP baseline. We experimented with the Long Short-Term Memory (LSTM) artificial recurrent neural network architecture. We did extensive feature engineering ending up with 53 input features for our LSTM model, these features were from OHLCV and Limit Order Book data plus calculating some basic Technical Analysis indicators such as RSI, MACD and Moving Averages among others. Normalizing our feature set was required to transform all features into homogeneous values, MinMax scaler proved to provide better results. We tested our model with different amounts of training data, historical intervals and different hyper-parameters for different data intervals, 1 min, 1 h, 4 h and 1 day. Only when we did an 'Ensemble' of 5 of our tested LSTM configurations predictions we managed to outperform the Last Known Price baseline when predicting a couple of days of June 2021. Unfortunately, these results did not translate when predicting full month periods or in our backtesting framework across most of the months over the years 2020–2021. Our LSTM Ensemble model proved to be very susceptible to market conditions, where bearish market conditions in May 2021 made possible some surprisingly good results in our backtesting framework, so the market making agents using the predictions were getting substantially larger revenues than the agents not using the predictions, even though MAPE and DA of these predictions was not exceeding the LKP as an average.

4 Conclusion

We found a way to determine causal connections in massive time series data. Also, we discovered such connections between the price change as an effect caused by combinations of specific cognitive distortions and sentiment patterns in online media content as well as changes of trade sell and buy volumes and imbalances between them on daily basis applied to Bitcoin cryptocurrency. That gives us hope to build a solution for reliable price prediction mechanisms usable for financial applications.

References

1. Raheman, A., Kolonin, A., Goertzel, B., Hegyközi, G., Ansari, I.: Architecture of automated crypto-finance agent. In: 2021 International Symposium on Knowledge, Ontology, and Theory (KNOTH), pp. 10–14 (2021). https://doi.org/10.1109/KNOTH54462.2021.9686345
2. Raheman, A., Kolonin, A., Ansari, I.: Adaptive multi-strategy market making agent. In: Goertzel, B., Iklé, M., Potapov, A. (eds.) AGI 2021. LNCS (LNAI), vol. 13154, pp. 204–209. Springer, Cham (2022). https://doi.org/10.1007/978-3-030-93758-4_21
3. Goertzel, B., Iklé, M., Goertzel, I., Heljakka, A.: Probabilistic Logic Networks: A Comprehensive Framework for Uncertain Inference., 1st ed., 2nd Printing, Springer. ISBN-13: 978-0387768717, ISBN-10: 0387768718 (2008)
4. Kovalerchuk, B., Vityaev, E.: Data mining for financial applications. In: Maimon, O., Rokach, L. (eds.) Data Mining and Knowledge Discovery Handbook, pp. 1153–1169. Springer US, Boston, MA (2010). https://doi.org/10.1007/978-0-387-09823-4_60
5. Mastakouri, A., Schölkopf, B., Janzing, D.: Necessary and sufficient conditions for causal feature selection in time series with latent common causes. arXiv:2005.08543 [stat.ME] (2020)
6. Deveikyte, J., Geman, H., Piccari, C., Provetti, A.: A Sentiment Analysis Approach to the Prediction of Market Volatility. arXiv:2012.05906 [q-fin.ST] (2020)
7. Arévalo, A., Niño, J., Hernández, G., Sandoval, J.: High-frequency trading strategy based on deep neural networks. In: Huang, D.-S., Han, K., Hussain, A. (eds.) ICIC 2016. LNCS (LNAI), vol. 9773, pp. 424–436. Springer, Cham (2016). https://doi.org/10.1007/978-3-319-42297-8_40
8. Tsantekidis, A., Passalis, N., Tefas, A., Kanniainen, J., Gabbouj, M., Iosifidis, A.: Using deep learning for price prediction by exploiting stationary limit order book features. arXiv:1810.09965 [cs.LG] (2018)
9. Bollen, J., et al.: Historical language records reveal a surge of cognitive distortions in recent decades. PNAS **118**(30), e2102061118 (2021). https://doi.org/10.1073/pnas.2102061118
10. Kolonin, A.: High-performance automatic categorization and attribution of inventory catalogs. In: Proceedings of All-Russia conference Knowledge Ontology Theories (KONT-2013), Novosibirsk, Russia, (2013). arXiv:2202.08965 [cs.IR] (2022)

Dynamic and Evolving Neural Network for Event Discrimination

Shimon Komarovsky[✉][iD]

Technion - Israel Institute of Technology, Haifa, Israel
cm5099@yahoo.com

Abstract. Artificial general intelligence (AGI) should be founded on a
suitable framework, e.g. a rule-based design or Deep Learning (DL). Here
we choose the DL to be the basis for AGI. An appropriate AGI is defined,
followed by its appropriate DL implementation. We introduce an AGI, in
the form of cognitive architecture, which is based on Global Workspace
Theory (GWT). It consists of a supervisor, a working memory, specialized memory units, and processing units. Additional discussion about
the uniqueness of the visual and the auditory sensory channels is conducted. Next, we introduce our DL module, which is dynamic, flexible,
and evolving or growing. It can be also considered as a Network Architecture Search (NAS) method. It is a spatial-temporal model, with a
hierarchy of both features and tasks, tasks such as objects or events.

Keywords: Deep learning · General intelligence · Evolving · Growing

1 Introduction

DL, as one of the Artificial intelligence (AI) approaches, is not as fully exploited
as it could be. First, deep neural networks (DNNs) are passive models, since they
have a fixed structure, while in reality there are dynamic processes, such as the
neurons' construction/destruction in the brain. Second, Learning in DL is simply
a categorization process without involving any thinking or imagination. Next, a
successful DL model (DLM) requires its designers to know the system, i.e., apply
implicit or explicit prior knowledge in the DLM. Moreover, a carefully designed
rule-based system may outperform a DLM, due to its dataset limitation, while
a rule-based system is designed for much broader and more diverse scenarios.
Finally, DL is highly task-specific. Even multi-tasking in DL requires all tasks
to be pre-defined. However, real AGI can generalize not only to unseen data but
also to unseen tasks (as in transfer/continual/meta learning). Nevertheless, we
propose a dynamic and flexible DLM that can be extended to AGI.

Next, we present an AGI architecture and a DLM, which can function as a
module in this AGI architecture, e.g. in the perception/actuation module.

*Please note that this paper presents a short version. The DLM and espe-
cially the AGI are preliminary ideas, and described roughly and generally, without mathematical details or implementation/results.*

B. Goertzel et al. (Eds.): AGI 2022, LNAI 13539, pp. 40–50, 2023.
https://doi.org/10.1007/978-3-031-19907-3_5

2   Proposed AGI Model

A general AGI model sketch is shown in Fig. 1. This AGI is based on GWT [17], describing a multi-agent system, where the agents are local controllers behaving reactively, and competing with each other over access to the working memory.

Our AGI, however, has no competition among its different and
independent modules, i.e. processors
and memories. Instead, it has centralized control with different elements, where each element has a specific function.

Examples of similar cognitive
architectures are in Appendix 4
in [9].

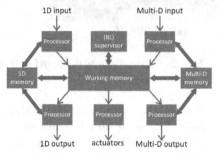

Fig. 1. AGI proposed architecture

2.1   AGI Function

Here the function of the proposed AGI in Fig. 1 is described.

As in humans, our AGI uses 1D (audio) input and 3D (visual) input, however, it also uses them as outputs. Moreover, the visual channel can be extended to 1 or more dimensions, depending on the environment our agent is deployed in.

There is separate sequential processing of 1D and multi-D data, for feature extraction and categorization of objects (static entities) or events (dynamic entities). Next, these objects/events propagate into the WM. Finally, an output is produced either through the 1D or the multi-D channel. If the output is an emerging idea/thought, it can be expressed via a 1D channel, similarly to humans describing verbally their inner thoughts to the outer world. Alternatively, it can be expressed via the multi-D channel, thus can be regarded as *screening imagination*, which is like projecting the current thought into a screen.

Additionally, 1D information (such as language) has a shared memory for input, output, and WM, denoted as 1D memory. This is also true for the multi-D information. The bidirectional arrows in Fig. 1 represent the acquisition (reading) and the update (writing) operations with the storage module.

The output communication of 1D and multi-D information can have various modes, such as continuously monitoring thoughts or waiting for a meaningful output. In addition, the AGI may have a degree of independent choice of when to interact and through which of the two channels.

This particular AGI is based upon Stimulus-Response behavioral theory [19], which states that the mind can be communicated with, although unobservable. This assumption is similar to the Chinese Room Argument, since there is only direct access to the output of the agent and not to the operations within. In other words, there is no explainability over the AGI's inner operations (it is a black-box), and so only the output can be analyzed. It is referred to as *intelligent behavior*, which is also expressed by human productivity over time, in fields such as science, psychology, and technology.

(a) AI identifying.   (b) AGI interpretating.

Fig. 2. Comparison between AI and AGI comprehending the environment.

This AGI does more than static/dynamic object identification or scene understanding [10], as in DL. It extends to the temporal dimension, by including: events, objects' behavior and function, associations from past experiences, etc. It is illustrated by comparing the current AI and the proposed AGI, in Fig. 2.

Just like Einstein's relativity theory, space and time are not separated, but treated as one whole concept. Similarly, our DLM is based on this hypothesis.

2.2 AGI Characteristics

Firstly, we consider AGI's main purpose to be organizing information to be utilized optimally in a variety of tasks. Hence, the self-supervision approach is a suitable tool to estimate this main goal. Additionally, DNN is an efficient model and memory structure, which can achieve this goal, in the sense that it organizes the data with the intention of recovering it later, see more in Appendix 5 in [9].

Secondly, we advocate that efficiency is more important than effectiveness, in AGI, since it is about the exploitation of available resources, while effectiveness is about how well a goal is achieved [1], e.g. the common attitude in DL to compare performances.

Finally, other characteristics an AGI should have are those imitating humans, such as having human guidance and support as in infant-parent and student-teacher interactions, having a correct teaching order (simple to complex), and the ability to grow/evolve in compulsory stages.

2.3 Two Information Types in AGI

Here we discuss and propose a rationale behind the unique functioning of the visual and auditory channels.

Firstly, we examine why humans do not possess an imagery output tool like the multi-D output we permit in our AGI. One can argue it would hurt our basic desire for privacy, but then just as we choose whether to talk or not, we can similarly choose when to turn this tool on. Another argument could be due to evolutionary survival reasons. Our current opinion is that the world we see with our eyes is what we all agree upon. Other than that, our inner models of the world are totally different.

Secondly, we reflect upon the reasons for humans not having a symbolic or lin-guistic channel to be objective as vision, i.e. why we end up with inner and unique symbolic representation. We think it is because language is highly context-dependent, and since each person has different contexts along his life, or different experiences, then he develops a different meaning/feeling/understanding of the objective concepts we all agree upon. Hence, the concepts we use in external communication are objective and common to all people, but their interpretation is different for each one. Therefore, the visual perception purpose is nothing but the objective agreement for effective communication between humans, realized via language. In other words, vision is not the main communicative channel for us, though, deaf people can bypass it by using sign language and textual format.

Consequently, the purpose of having two channel types is to distinguish the outer and inner world that the agent interacts with. Furthermore, humans (as should be followed by AGI) base their inner representation on spatio-temporal events, or operational language. A language comprised of objects, actions, and attributes, and expressed by words/symbols. Therefore spatio-temporal information can be transferred to humans not only by the static/objective world, but even more broadly by language. Agents denoted as green circles, communicating via 1D and individually perceiving multi-D input are illustrated in Fig. 3.

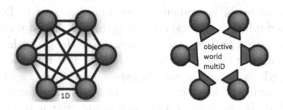

Fig. 3. Objective (right) verse Subjective inner representation (left).

3   Proposed DLM

Until now we presented a general AGI model. Now we turn to discuss which DLM can implement such AGI, or implement each or some of its different modules.

Any DLM requires some prior knowledge, also known as inductive bias. Then due to difficulties with matching the most proper prior knowledge to each specific problem we encounter - many studies try different hyper-parameters or archi-tectures, to get better performance, e.g. they use Network Architecture Search. See more about it in Appendix 6 in [9].

Therefore, the DLM we propose is adaptive for continuous learning and can serve also as a NAS method.

3.1 Proposed DLM Function

Our proposed DLM is based on the inductive bias principle. It states that small data requires simpler model while bigger data requires a more complex one. Complexity in DLMs is expressed in the NN size. Hence, assuming gradual learning like in infants, we propose evolving DLM, starting from small NN, extending successively to a bigger one, following abstraction, while encountering new data.

In the following, we describe our DLM evolution with comparison to an infant, while perceiving a spatial-temporal type of data.

We presume, that an infant does not have any supervised learning at the beginning of his life, but rather an unsupervised one. Only later that he fuses multi-modal information about objects and their meaning.

The first thing he does is segment the time period into simple events. But he starts with a single event detection (e.g. his total waking period) through some initial DNN with several layers. See Fig. 4(a).

After a while, when enough counts detected the single event, a split of this event is performed into two (or more) classes of events, e.g. day and night, see Fig. 4(b). Counts are the number of times the output class was triggered. Now, the agent can differentiate two events, sharing the same features. Later it can extend the number of events, and recognize as many events as necessary. Consequently, it is an adaptive NN structure, adaptive by necessity.

At some point of evolution, when connections (weights in DNN) and event identification (output layer's counts) are strengthened and established, the model can change its attention or free its resources, since the given level had become more automatic, similar to the idea in [7]. It can now build a new layer/level on top of the previous ones, if a simultaneous re-occurrence of several events is detected. For example, the re-occurrence of seeing the mom appearing and preparing herself to give milk suggests to the infant that it is a composite event on its own, see Fig. 4(c), where yellow = visual sensors, and green = neurons.

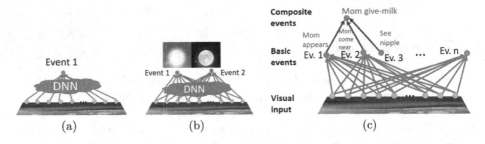

Fig. 4. Neuron separation and composition in the proposed approach (Ev. = Event).

Opposite structure-changing operations could be (i) deleting extremely rare nodes/edges in the DNN, a bit similar to dropout regularization in DL; and (ii) decomposing an event, if it appears to be more complex than it was supposed to be. In other words, if previously it was treated as a specific-level event, now it is fine-grained, thus decomposed into simpler events (refinement). It is decomposed into either existing events or new ones. If new ones, then they have to be attached to lower-level events/features, e.g. see Fig. 5, where the "ball in the air" event is decomposed into its three basics: throwing, moving in the air, and being caught.

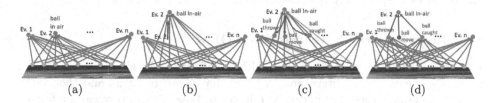

Fig. 5. Neuron decomposition in the proposed approach (Ev. = Event).

Decomposition is a highly uncertain operation, since it is unknown whether an event is compositional, and if it does - how many events it consists of, and which of these events are new and which are not. There are numerous ways to deal with it, e.g. see studies in 3.5, but it is out of the scope of this paper.

For this dynamic algorithm to work, the number of visits has to be stored for each weight (edge in DNN) and each neuron (node). If scalability is an issue for large DNNs, the visits memorization can be reduced from being stored for each neuron to being stored in each cluster of neurons in a large enough DNN.

Furthermore, the visits can be counted during *waking* periods (when the DNN is fixed), and the structure update can be done during *sleeping* periods, when there is no stimulus from the sensors, while the trajectory frequency within the DNN is stored in the neurons themselves, as mentioned above. The rate of structure changing can also be modeled with a learning rate as in RL, where at first it is mostly exploration (i.e. fast NN growth), and then lesser exploration and more exploitation. Finally, a finite number of nodes and connections is presumed, i.e. limited resources (so that it would not grow infinitely), thus resulting in adjusting the learning rate accordingly.

Finally, additional aspects for the DLM are presented in Appendix 7 in [9].

3.2   Advantages of the Proposed DLM

This approach is self-supervised and not unsupervised, since it is not about clustering into a pre-defined number of categories. Here, similar to NAS, the number of categories and connections are all dynamic, and change according to the decision of some supervising algorithm.

Another reason for this dynamic algorithm is that real intelligence does not end up with categories like cat/dog (it evolves into more complex models). Moreover, most AI research works backward. It always starts from high-complexity data and tries to learn it from scratch, instead of simple to complex learning as it should be in an evolving AGI.

Additionally, this dynamic algorithm is less computationally expensive since it has fewer connections compared to FC NN, similar to sparse NN.

Finally, NAS is used to find some optimal hierarchical structure of features represented via neurons for a given dataset. Thus, it is probably wrong to guess the number of best-describing features at each layer. Dynamic NN deals with this issue, by keeping only the relevant and true features/events.

3.3   Task Hierarchy in the Proposed DLM

The extending of classes converts this DLM into a hierarchical multi-class DNN. Such DNNs exist in the literature. In [3] we have feature layers and then task layers. Sometimes these layers can be mixed up. Labels' structure can be found separately from the model [4, 12], or as a part of the model [6, 10, 11]. All the tasks can be learned over one classifier, i.e. globally or in the last layer of the NN [4], or alternatively, intermediate tasks can be inserted inside the NN, i.e. locally [3, 11]. The structure can be learned from the data [10], e.g. by unsupervised clustering of the labels via some similarity measure [12], or it can be imported from external knowledge base [5], or used to change this structure [4, 6].

Similar to these papers, additional features can be inserted between task layers in our proposed DLM, for example.

Additionally, unlike features that are distributive representatives of data, holding only some piece of the actual information, tasks are end-point independent data representatives, thus ruining in a way, NN's distributive nature.

However, this is not their main drawback. The fact that they are informational points - enforces a huge memory, since we need lots of them to represent a huge amount of terms/concepts. As opposed to a small group of inter-related features, which can characterize an enormous amount of input data. Thus, at some point, replacing/converting tasks with/into features should be considered.

Fig. 6. Branching due to multiple hierarchies.

Generally, there may be different hierarchies besides compositional ones, e.g.: family tree, parts of speech, table of contents, topics, and sub-topics. One solution could be, is for the evolution to develop into different hierarchies, just like tree expansion: in different locations of a given NN and in different structures. An illustration of multiple hierarchies formed in a given NN is in Fig. 6.

3.4   Temporal Dimension of the DLM

Until now the presented DNNs in the proposed DLM were represented via static structure, i.e. a single simultaneous set of inputs produced a single simultaneous set of outputs. In other words, there were no recurrent connections to include a temporal sequence of inputs.

Usually, spatial-temporal models combine CNN with RNN in different ways. Either separately: CNN→RNN or interchangeably: CNN→RNN→CNN→ RNN... Another way is to separate CNN and RNN to separate inputs, e.g. textual for RNN and visual for CNN, with a fusion module at the end. In conclusion, event tasks, such as classification/clustering, can be done using the methods above.

Nonetheless, regular FC DNNs are used for spatial object tasks. But if our goal is to extract features along the temporal dimension also, a simple addition of recurrent connections could be made. Alternatively, an extension of the DNN could be done to include a temporal dimension, without changing the spatial dimension, i.e. orthogonal to it. See Fig. 7 for static and dynamic object tasks.

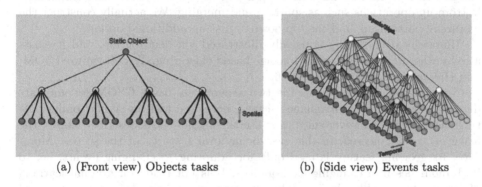

(a) (Front view) Objects tasks   (b) (Side view) Events tasks

Fig. 7. Spatio-temporal DNN model.

In Fig. 7 it is shown a FC NN. However, if required, it could be specialized in different ways, e.g. by shared connections/parameters or convolutions. And it can be done for either the spatial or temporal dimensions, or both.

3.5   Related Work

Several topics are involved with our DLM: continual/lifelong learning; unsupervised learning, specifically deep and non-deep clustering; event detection; multi-label and multi-task learning; Network Architecture Search, and more.

From the aspect of our task, video recognition tasks such as event detection [20] is a large topic in computer vision, and the most relevant to our DLM, whose task is the continual refinement of events. However, these tasks mostly involve batch learning, not continual learning, and utilize fixed architectures.

One practical application of our task, is for navigating robots to recognize events, e.g. in [14]. However, they use time series of sensor and motor signals to recognize important events, i.e. they do not use fully visual spatial data.

From the aspect of our architecture, similar models are belong to the family of growing networks [2,8], e.g. Incremental Grid Growing (IGG), Growing Cell Structure (GCS), Growing Self-Organizing-Map (GSOM), Growing Neural-Gas (GNG), and their variations. They all are unsupervised methods, learning the data distribution. However, they are based on shallow NNs with designed features [18], while we are focused on DNNs that automatically extract features, to allow learning of more complex and diverse events.

Also, some of the methods above [2], utilize an age counter, similar to the number of visitations in our model, which in general can be extended to other counters, holding additional information for better clustering.

Nevertheless, there are variations of SOM that produce non-flat data structure, e.g. the growing hierarchical SOM (GHSOM) [2,16], which induces hierarchical bias over the data to be learned. However, it implements only a top-down generating hierarchy, which is equivalent to our decomposition operation and can act as a legitimate implementation of this operation. We also implement bottom-up operations such as splitting and merging. We actually construct the hierarchy bottom-up, and the top-down is just an additional option.

Hierarchical clustering is usually illustrated via dendrogram, and it exists also in other models, such as in Linkage based clustering, Tree-Structured SOM, and Hierarchical Feature Map [2,16].

Nevertheless, [18] combines the two aspects, by using GSOM for anomaly detection in changing surveillance scenes, i.e. same task in similar online settings as we have. However since they use the shallow NNs described above, the features are engineered, in this case behavioral features of the scenes. Moreover, its growing feature is used only for adapting to changing events, i.e. to find anomalies in a changing environment. It is not made for gradual learning of events. Also, unlike the anomaly detection task, our task is to learn normal recurrent events.

All the methods above use different heuristics to improve clustering in different tasks. Additionally, the search for the closest neuron to a given input (like in k-nearest neighbor clustering) is the most expensive task, a step that is absent in our approach. Finally, these methods, including ours, are of the clustering type, and all have in common the problem of how to choose the suitable measure/distance. Hence, a more adaptive approach is needed, e.g. a deep clustering topic that exists in DL.

Similarly, our DL approach, suggests the hierarchy will not include only the neurons representing events, but also feature neurons in-between, to enable more flexible learning and clustering of events.

Besides, there are growing networks for supervised learning [15], especially for continual learning to avoid catastrophic forgetting [13]. Networks that involve both growing and pruning, such as Progressive Neural Networks (PNN) and Dynamically Expandable NetworkS (DEN) [13].

3.6   Contribution

Finally, the novelty/contribution of this paper is the notion that spatial-temporal dimension is inseparable, hence it should be learned as it is right from the start, contrary to the object detection tasks and alike. In addition, the learning must be gradual, continual, and unsupervised all the time, and as our DLM demonstrated, it must also practice gradual growth accordingly. Both of these principles are essential for an AGI agent. Consequently, some ideas were formed from the principles above, and should be refined further.

References

1. https://simania.co.il/bookdetails.php?item_id=145306
2. Astudillo, C.A., Oommen, B.J.: Topology-oriented self-organizing maps: a survey. Pattern Anal. Appl. **17**(2), 223–248 (2014). https://doi.org/10.1007/s10044-014-0367-9
3. Cerri, R., Barros, R.C., De Carvalho, A.C.: Hierarchical multi-label classification using local neural networks. J. Comput. Syst. Sci. **80**(1), 39–56 (2014)
4. Chen, H., Miao, S., Xu, D., Hager, G.D., Harrison, A.P.: Deep hierarchical multi-label classification of chest x-ray images. In: International Conference on Medical Imaging with Deep Learning, pp. 109–120. PMLR (2019)
5. Feng, S., Zhao, C., Fu, P.: A deep neural network based hierarchical multi-label classification method. Rev. Sci. Instrum. **91**(2), 024103 (2020)
6. Gu, J., Zhao, H., Lin, Z., Li, S., Cai, J., Ling, M.: Scene graph generation with external knowledge and image reconstruction. In: Proceedings of the IEEE Conference on Computer Vision and Pattern Recognition, pp. 1969–1978 (2019)
7. Hawkins, J., Blakeslee, S.: On intelligence: how a new understanding of the brain will lead to the creation of truly intelligent machines. Macmillan (2007)
8. Heinke, D., Hamker, F.H.: Comparing neural networks: a benchmark on growing neural gas, growing cell structures, and fuzzy ARTMAP. IEEE Trans. Neural Netw. **9**(6), 1279–1291 (1998)
9. Komarovsky, S.: Dynamic and evolving neural network for event discrimination. EasyChair Preprint no. 7922 (EasyChair, 2022)
10. Li, Y., Ouyang, W., Zhou, B., Wang, K., Wang, X.: Scene graph generation from objects, phrases and region captions. In: Proceedings of the IEEE International Conference on Computer Vision, pp. 1261–1270 (2017)
11. Nguyen, D.K., Okatani, T.: Multi-task learning of hierarchical vision-language representation. In: Proceedings of the IEEE Conference on Computer Vision and Pattern Recognition, pp. 10492–10501 (2019)
12. Papanikolaou, Y., Tsoumakas, G., Katakis, I.: Hierarchical partitioning of the output space in multi-label data. Data Knowl. Eng. **116**, 42–60 (2018)
13. Parisi, G.I., Kemker, R., Part, J.L., Kanan, C., Wermter, S.: Continual lifelong learning with neural networks: a review. Neural Netw. **113**, 54–71 (2019)
14. Prem, E., Hortnagl, E., Dorffner, G.: Growing event memories for autonomous robots. In: Proceedings of the Workshop On Growing Artifacts That Live, Seventh International Conference on Simulation of Adaptive Behavior, Edinburgh, Scotland. Citeseer (2002)
15. Qiang, X., Cheng, G., Wang, Z.: An overview of some classical growing neural networks and new developments. In: 2010 2nd International Conference on Education Technology and Computer, vol. 3, pp. V3–351. IEEE (2010)

16. Rauber, A., Merkl, D., Dittenbach, M.: The growing hierarchical self-organizing map: exploratory analysis of high-dimensional data. IEEE Trans. Neural Netw. **13**(6), 1331–1341 (2002)
17. Silva, R.C.M., Gudwin, R.R.: An introductory experiment with a conscious-based autonomous vehicle. In: 4th Workshop in Applied Robotics and Automation (2010)
18. Sun, Q., Liu, H., Harada, T.: Online growing neural gas for anomaly detection in changing surveillance scenes. Pattern Recogn. **64**, 187–201 (2017)
19. Watson, J.B., Meazzini, P., John B.W.: Il mulino (1977)
20. Wu, C., Ma, Y.F., Zhan, H.J., Zhong, Y.Z.: Events recognition by semantic inference for sports video. In: Proceedings. IEEE International Conference on Multimedia and Expo, vol. 1, pp. 805–808. IEEE (2002)

Hierarchical Temporal DNN and Associative Knowledge Representation

Shimon Komarovsky[(⊠)]

Technion - Israel Institute of Technology, Haifa, Israel
cm5099@yahoo.com

Abstract. This paper proposes two models. The first one is designed bottom-up, i.e., mostly based on DL and Jeff Hawkins' temporal principle. The second one tackles some aspects of intelligence, specifically concerning the thinking process. It is designed top-down, i.e., mainly based on cognition and communication.

Additionally, this paper not only exhibits top-down verse bottom-up approaches, but also presents the two edges of evolution: the DL model considers the beginning state of learning, while the knowledge representation model considers the saturated/mature/final state of learning.

Keywords: Hierarchical · Temporal · Deep · Associative representation

1 Introduction

An AGI design should handle a large variety of scenarios and have many vital features. Features such as: flexible, fluid, adaptive, and evolving.

We first propose a DL Model (DLM) originated mainly from the neural model in [4]. Then, we propose a model for the important components of an AGI agent: thinking and memory. It models the representation of elements in a memory, and describes how the thinking process accesses them and manipulates them for different tasks. It also encourages flexibility and adaptivity.

It is evident in neuroscience and DL that knowledge has a hierarchical structure, though there is a controversy about which type is it. In DL and [4] it is a hierarchy of features, while in [5] it is about the compositionality of objects. In this paper, our DLM is mainly established on temporal hierarchy. Whereas our knowledge representation model is based upon associative hierarchy, designated for efficient memory access.

Finally, both of our presented models are based on the System 1 and 2 principle [2], on a neuro-symbolic combination by converting raw features into operational concepts, and on the stimulus-response principle, since we believe that one of AGI's characteristics is that knowledge is operational. In other words, elements that are learned are either objects or their attributes or actions which act upon them. This notion is presented in many papers on associative memory

B. Goertzel et al. (Eds.): AGI 2022, LNAI 13539, pp. 51–61, 2023.
https://doi.org/10.1007/978-3-031-19907-3_6

or associative NNs, where an association is a response to a stimulus, which can be either other stimuli [13] or a behavioral response (action).

Please note the DLM, and especially the AKREM, are preliminary ideas. Also, the DLM is constructed from common and well defined components, and cited papers are given as suggestions to implement some of these components.

2   The Proposed DLM

Our DLM is inspired by the neural models and DLMs such as caption generation [15] and Visual-Question-Answering [3]. As shown in Fig. 1(a), the idea is to unwrap the percept-predict structure from the neural model [4] on the left, into a discriminative-generative or an encoder-decoder structure on the right.

The proposed DLM is illustrated in Fig. 1(b). In this structure the data coming from text and sensors is encoded. The text includes both information and instructions. Finally, this data is encoded into some extracted features representing the whole situation, including what the model is requested to do, and then up-sample it to the actuators (the decoding process).

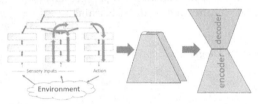
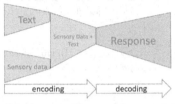

(a) Percept-predict structure turns into a discriminative-generative structure.

(b) Sensory data and text in encoder-decoder structure.

Fig. 1. Sensory data, text and response in the proposed DLM.

Our DLM purpose is to be able to plan and respond to inputs according to symbolic representation, which is derived from raw sensory data.

It is aimed to accomplish this by gradual learning in the following phases. First, it learns to fuse multi-modal inputs, to establish basic semantic concepts. Next, its objective is to learn two types of data: objects and their inter-relations. Hence, it starts by learning basic elements/objects, and then continue with composite objects and relations.

After this proper symbolic comprehension, it turns to learn how to respond correctly within the common supervised learning approach. Only it does so within several temporal resolutions: from fast to slow perception and response.

In the next section, we elaborate on these phases.

The gradual temporal representation and learning, implemented in the encoder and the decoder of our DLM, is based on the hierarchical temporal principle proposed in Jeff Hawkins' first book [4].

The proposed DLM, as any DLM, is not sufficient to serve as an AGI. Some issues are addressed in "Issues with the proposed DLM" in Appendix 4 in [9].

2.1   Proposed DLM Function

A more detailed implementation of the proposed DLM is discussed.

The DLM has a hierarchical temporal structure, and it is mainly based on two ideas: the joint learning of multi-modal input, and the learning of intermediate tasks [6]. The latter is used to implement scene understanding within different time scales (short, mid, and long terms). For more details about these and other aspects, see in Appendix 4 in [9].

The first idea is about extracting features separately from sensors and text, then learning them together via joint embedding space [14]. Thus, the assumption here is that these inputs are complementary. Since if they are trained together, then if one of them is missing, it is sufficient for recognition as if the second one was there too. These fused features represent spatio-temporal information for the short-term temporal resolution. In the next phase of learning, these joint features are extracted further into longer time scales, by freezing first the short-term RNN layers and activating mid-term layers only. The same goes for the long-range layers afterward.

The second idea is generally about hierarchical learning of tasks [1,11], whereby several layers of tasks are learned instead of the usual single output layer of tasks. In temporal hierarchical learning, the current layer of tasks is learned first, then later more complex tasks are learned in a new layer, based on the previous tasks.

In our DLM, it is realized by intermediate tasks via RNNs. Using the first idea, the features are extracted in different time resolutions. These features are the hidden and the output layers in RNN. However, to include intermediate tasks for different time resolutions, the encoder-decoder structure of RNN is used, as in translation tasks. In other words, the intermediate tasks are connected to the context signal(s) of the RNN, not to its hidden/output signal(s). A decoder is attached to the context or to the encoder layer in the RNN. Thus, the intermediate tasks are the outputs of each of these decoders. See more in [11], and in "Hierarchical Learning" in Appendix 4 in [9].

In conclusion, there are two ways to implement hierarchical temporal learning. Either via the first idea, thus to learn multi-modal data in joint embedding space, at different time scales. Or, via the second idea, where features are extracted hierarchically temporarily (via RNN output/hidden layers), and intermediate tasks are inserted into the temporal structure. Tasks assisting in forming correct and more appropriate (guided) features, as in [1,11]. Thus, after the recognition of spatio-temporal objects in the features extracted from the two inputs, their relationships should be recognized too. Hence, the intermediate tasks derive these relationships between objects. Some papers [16] focus on pairwise interactions between perceived objects in an image, e.g. via a 2D graph matrix, whereas [10] models high-order interactions between arbitrary subgroups of objects.

The full sketch of the proposed DLM is shown in Fig. 2. It is seen that the decoder is also hierarchically-temporarily constructed, as a mirror image of the perceptual encoder, with skip connections, whose function may be: copy, normalization, or addition.

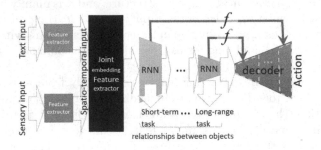

Fig. 2. Hierarchy-temporal DLM.

3   Associative Knowledge Representation Model (AKREM)

In this section, a model of AGI's knowledge representation is described. As explained in 3.3, it can utilize our general DLM, 2, as its base memory. This model tries to encapsulate a few cognitive important elements: short-term memory (STM), long-term memory (LTM), working memory (WM), and thinking. As mentioned in the abstract, it is designed in a top-down fashion. Specifically, it originates from our communication model.

3.1   Communication

Principles. Our fundamental assumption about human-human communication is that each person is a "black box". Thus, we do not have access to the actual inner interpretation and representation of persons' knowledge. In other words, we communicate externally, via objective tools (the language), but we have hidden subjective perspectives or world models, constructed during a lifetime via different circumstances and experiences. This assumption is illustrated in Fig. 3(a), where the inner representation of the same message varies among people.

Next, our communication model consists of several principles. (i) The sending process is about converting an abstract message, such as a story or technical procedure, into a sequence of words. Hence, this process is generative. It is about decomposing a high-level idea into low-level concepts. Exactly opposite is the receiving process. In it, the recipient tries to assemble the idea from the low-level concepts, hence it is a discriminative process. These processes are visualized in Fig. 3(a). (ii) These couple of processes can be viewed also temporarily. The sender's thought is materialized fully when he begins his sentence(s). But to fully capture his message, the recipient has to wait till the end of the message. Hence, the end of the thought is the beginning of the message, while its start is the ending of the message. (iii) Additionally, it is about context. Due to the "black-box" assumption, to be maximally understood, the sender must start in the most general context, or common ground, to fit the message to a wide range of different recipients, with a different states of mind. And then gradually lead the recipient to his specific message. Such a chronological process would be optimal for delivering the message as accurately as possible. (iv) Finally, to make the message clearer, both communicators should hold the models of all the relevant participants in the conversation (the recipient, the sender, their shared common knowledge, and their self-models). For principles (ii)-(iv) see Fig. 3(b).

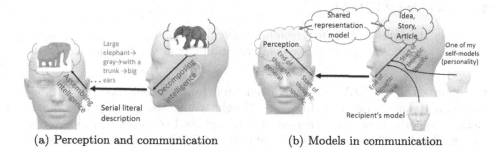

(a) Perception and communication   (b) Models in communication

Fig. 3. Communication basics.

Models in Communication.

Models in Communication. More generally, principle (iv) reveals that human-AGI communication requires something more than merely a set of models. It requires that the AGI itself hold human-like cognitive properties and capabilities, so that humans and AGI agents would be synchronized during communication and understand each other. Hence, the AGI should have characteristics such as episodic memory, continual learning, abstraction, and generalization.

Furthermore, a more broad interpretation of principle (iv), suggest that humans are actually modeling everything. Although, we model each thing differently - depending on our interaction with it. It applies to both different people (different interactions) and different groups of people. Similarly, it applies to each object/animal or their groups. Interaction with human(s) is unique because it creates a model by conversational interaction. This idea is illustrated in Fig. 4.

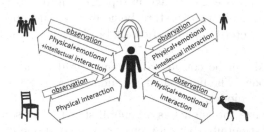

Fig. 4. Human create models from interaction.

We probably have also self-modeling, i.e. expectations from us, in the opposite direction of the interaction. In other words, how a person should behave in different groups, with different people, and with different animals and objects. Moreover, we can model ourselves, while viewing ourselves externally (as if we are another person), to learn and perhaps change our behavior.

Additionally, we perform a passive interaction, i.e. a simple observation. For example, infants mimicking when observing other humans (e.g. parents/siblings).

All the above describes the theory of embodiment, expressed by the boundaries an agent creates between different entities and between them and itself.

3.2   Detailed AKREM

Based on the communication principles above, AKREM is derived, expressing how information is represented in a memory, and to serve as a basis for cognition.

Function. Our AKREM is mainly originated from two aspects: (i) the phenomenon of random bouncing from one thought to another; and (ii) the communicative hypothesis of converting an idea to low-level concepts and vice versa. This model shows how information is represented. In the decoding of a message, it is represented via the dynamic construction of hierarchical structures, similarly to constructing syntactic trees of sentences in Natural Language Processing (NLP). While in the encoding of a message, it is about descending a given hierarchy, according to a chronological order, gathering lowest-level facts and thus producing a sequence. A video demonstrating how a specific story is generating an associative hierarchy, is in: "AKREM decoding" in [7].

It can be seen in the video, that when a new unrelated piece of knowledge enters the input, the previous pieces are grouped in form of association(s). It is a bit similar to the dynamic event detection [8], where a sequence is discriminated into a set of events. As here, the task is accomplished by recognizing similarities and dissimilarities in a sequence. Only the difference is, that there is only event discrimination, while here it is about constructing a plot out of the recognized events. Moreover, the DNN stores any new (frequent enough) composite event, which results in combinatorial explosion issue, while here it does not store any combination of events as a new event. In other words, unlike dynamic event detection, which has to store and define each new combination of events, here the knowledge storage is separated into two types of memory: concepts/procedural memories to store basic events, and episodic memory, to store any new encountered combination of basic events, which is constructed dynamically.

Hence, AKREM can be considered as an upgraded model of the dynamic event detection model. The next paper extends this associative model even further, into a model of models.

Next, we formalize this model as a general structure of some plot/message. We can imagine first details about a scene are triggered one by one, and placed in level 0 of the newly generated hierarchy. Next, another scene is introduced.

Each scene is represented by combining all its details in level 1. At the end of Chapter 1, a few scenes were gathered. After finishing Chapter 2, both chapters are connected to be in level 2. And it can go on and on. See Fig. 5(b).

In order to both generate a hierarchy from a sequence or vice versa, some kind of order has to be stored, e.g. chronological/causal, in all the levels of the plot, see for example the temporal trail in Fig. 5(a). But the direction in connections can be extended further. It can represent different types of connections, e.g. between the levels and between the hierarchies; abstraction/generalization; various associative connections, e.g.: comparison, analogy, causality, and correlation.

It is seen that the lowest level (0) is the most general with the most objective context, since the low-level concepts have so many associations, that they lose almost entirely their specificity. However, as one goes higher in the levels, the more specific the context becomes, since it is constructed underneath a more specific structure. Hence, the highest levels hold the essence of all levels below. Thus, they possess the most accurate message.

The meaning of low-level concepts having the most associations is that they are connected to a huge amount of such hierarchies in the memory, gathered so far. The higher one goes in a hierarchy, the fewer associations it has with other hierarchies, until one reaches the levels separating this hierarchy from the rest.

Note that how the grouping occurs was not specified. For now, the grouping can be considered as summarizing or finding the essence of distinct items, but the grouping can also be treated as finding some common meaning or a purpose. See for example in the video, that for every grouping one can ask the question "why" regarding the meaning of the items in the group, whose answer is representing the grouping.

Thus we presume that our thinking is purposeful. We assume that in active/generative mode we have a purpose and we construct a hierarchy keeping in mind the purpose the whole time (perhaps in a top-down fashion), while in passive/receiving mode we construct the sender message from details, i.e. bottom-up, reconstructing its purpose.

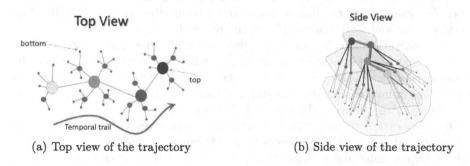

(a) Top view of the trajectory   (b) Side view of the trajectory

Fig. 5. Associative thinking via associative trajectories.

At other times, we can have a no-purpose thinking. It can be viewed as a wandering between existing hierarchies, and randomly jumping from one to another, at random levels within them. This is the first aspect mentioned above.

Characteristics. Associative thinking occurs all the time in our opinion.

For example, daily, where the hierarchy is constructed like a long narrative, with some experience at the top of the narrative's trajectory, made out of all separate events that occurred during this day. But it can also be attached to a previous hierarchy of the previous day, and even the previous week/month/year.

We use associative thinking in most of our cognitive tasks: in generating/perceiving a story/event/message, which is some (non-)linear plot of details; and in planning/simulating/contemplating/problem solving, which is also a series of possible actions and outcomes.

This AKREM is like a holographic memory, where the triggered neurons are shown in Fig. 5(b) on the yellow surface at the bottom. They belong to the DLM presented in Fig. 1. Hence, this holographic memory is orthogonal to this DNN. In other words, we can consider triggered neurons in this DNN, producing this hierarchical dynamic structure.

We propose that the perception operation in AKREM would be similar to the one in [2]. In it, perception occurs via system 1, a multi-agent system, where agents compete parallelly with each other to decide which pattern is perceived correctly from the senses, and hence also decide which response is suitable for it. A similar idea is presented in [5], where this competition is via triggering all relevant neurons, and then filtering out all irrelevant ones as more clues are coming from the senses. Irrelevant ones predict worse than others, hence we are left eventually with the correct pattern. The process above describes recalling, hence if no pattern is recognized, a new hierarchy/memory is generated.

Both in [4] and AKREM this perception idea is expressed by ascending multiple triggered memorized hierarchies, and then descending for prediction or verification. Thus, filtering all the non-relevant memories. When partial, corrupted, or unorganized information is encountered, it can be validated not only by descending, but also by moving in all the different directions in the hierarchies. For example, in recalling a story from a scene, the agent has the freedom to move back and forth temporarily in the hierarchies.

Associative thinking/approach is much more effective than context alone, since context might consist of many details, while associations can reduce the detail level and emphasize the abstract structure of the details. Additionally, this allows for minimal communication and minimal resources in cognitive processes, enabling very few items in the WM, e.g. 7 ± 2 items.

It is important to note that AKREM is a data representation model, not yet developed into a fully working NN model. Emerging hierarchies in the WM can be implemented e.g. by some non-parametric method, such as via decision trees, since their structure is dynamic. Moreover, the number of visitations of each node and connection can be stored in these hierarchies, to distinguish this way STM from LTM.

Additionally, AKREM is a mature model, i.e., it is in the state of adulthood, which is the state reached after there has been some learning stabilization. Hence, this model also lacks the evolution of memory till its mature state. Thus, it is missing all the primary learning and adaptation. It could be fulfilled, for example, via self-supervising learning of predicting the missing/next sensory inputs.

Finally, this model has many implications, similarities with other techniques, examples, and other considerations, which should be deeply discussed in a broader paper. Additional notes (e.g. limitations and contribution): in Appendix 5 in [9].

3.3 Memories in AKREM

Besides having our associative hierarchical structures, as elements in some memory, we also should address the memory structure itself.

As in humans, systems 0, 1 and 2 [12] should be realized here too. Systems 0 and 1 are expressed when the most frequent memory is used, in cases when automatic or no-thinking tasks are performed. Whereas system 2 is expressed by thinking, such as in problem solving, and it activates LTM and WM. A partial AGI model, consisting of AKREM and some DLM as its basis would also enable cases where the system is fully utilized, i.e. simultaneously thinking and performing automatic tasks.

We can assume that simple sensory perception is using base memory, similar to system 0 automatic system (no thinking), see Fig. 1. Then it provokes LTM concepts or events, "uploading" them to the WM (or STM), see Fig. 6(a). During a sleeping period, the system somehow decides what to consolidate into LTM and what not, due to unimportance or similar memories that already exist there. LTM and WM do not have direct contact with the sensors and executions, perhaps since this is abstract thinking, in which the thinking, depending on some externally-driven task, is moving in purposeful trajectories/hierarchies, mostly regardless of the inputs.

We assume that humans have permanent associative wandering in LTM, producing some final or intermediate results that are updated in WM. Differently, the wandering in AGI must have some purpose. Hence there are some external instructions inserted in this process, guiding it. See Fig. 6(a).

We believe that humans solve any situation/problem this way, i.e. by jumping associatively from element to element with some guiding will, searching for something, meanwhile gathering some intermediate insights, to eventually resolve with some response (good/no/bad solution).

Alternatively, we can regard the base memories, to be simply a part of the LTM. Hence, they represent the most frequent (nearly automatic) part of it. Thus, the least frequently used memory is at the bottom, while the most used memory is at a higher level, while WM serves as the currently used memory, and is located on top of this LTM unit. See Fig. 6(b).

Finally, additional aspect of generalization is addressed in Appendix 6 in [9].

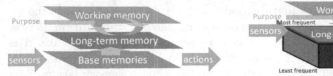

(a) Discrete memories interaction.   (b) Continuous memories interaction.

Fig. 6. Memories in the associative thinking model.

References

1. Cerri, R., Barros, R.C., De Carvalho, A.C.: Hierarchical multi-label classification using local neural networks. J. Comput. Syst. Sci. **80**(1), 39–56 (2014)
2. Daniel, K.: Thinking, fast and slow (2017)
3. Desta, M.T., Chen, L., Kornuta, T.: Object-based reasoning in VQA. In: 2018 IEEE Winter Conference on Applications of Computer Vision (WACV), pp. 1814–1823. IEEE (2018)
4. Hawkins, J., Blakeslee, S.: On intelligence: how a new understanding of the brain will lead to the creation of truly intelligent machines. Macmillan (2007)
5. Hawkins, J., Lewis, M., Klukas, M., Purdy, S., Ahmad, S.: A framework for intelligence and cortical function based on grid cells in the neocortex. Front. Neural Circuits **12**, 121 (2019)
6. Hwang, K., Sung, W.: Character-level language modeling with hierarchical recurrent neural networks. In: 2017 IEEE International Conference on Acoustics, Speech and Signal Processing (ICASSP), pp. 5720–5724. IEEE
7. Komarovsky, S.: AGI'22 related videos. www.youtube.com/playlist?list=PLvii8t7-Yebi6J25SyKbW5okEmZLME-fh
8. Komarovsky, S.: Dynamic and evolving neural network for event discrimination. EasyChair Preprint no. 7922 (EasyChair, 2022)
9. Komarovsky, S.: Hierarchical temporal DNN and associative knowledge representation. EasyChair Preprint no. 7921 (EasyChair, 2022)
10. Ma, C.Y., Kadav, A., Melvin, I., Kira, Z., AlRegib, G., Peter Graf, H.: Attend and interact: higher-order object interactions for video understanding. In: Proceedings of the IEEE Conference on Computer Vision and Pattern Recognition, pp. 6790–6800 (2018)
11. Nguyen, D.K., Okatani, T.: Multi-task learning of hierarchical vision-language representation. In: Proceedings of the IEEE Conference on Computer Vision and Pattern Recognition, pp. 10492–10501 (2019)
12. Prokopchuk, Y., Nosov, P., Zinchenko, S., Popovych, I.: New approach to modeling deep intuition. In: Materials of the 13th Scientific and Practical Conference «Modern Information and Innovative Technologies in Transport (MINTT-2021)». Kherson, Ukraine: XSMA, pp. 37–40 (2021)
13. Shen, F., Ouyang, Q., Kasai, W., Hasegawa, O.: A general associative memory based on self-organizing incremental neural network. Neurocomputing **104**, 57–71 (2013)
14. Socher, R., Karpathy, A., Le, Q.V., Manning, C.D., Ng, A.Y.: Grounded compositional semantics for finding and describing images with sentences. Trans. Assoc. Comput. Linguist. **2**, 207–218 (2014)

15. Xu, K., et al.: Show, attend and tell: Neural image caption generation with visual attention. In: International Conference on Machine Learning, pp. 2048–2057 (2015)
16. Xu, R., Xiong, C., Chen, W., Corso, J.J.: Jointly modeling deep video and compositional text to bridge vision and language in a unified framework. In: AAAI. vol. 5, p. 6. Citeseer (2015)

MARTI-4: New Model of Human Brain, Considering Neocortex and Basal Ganglia – Learns to Play Atari Game by Reinforcement Learning on a Single CPU

Igor Pivovarov$^{(\boxtimes)}$ (iD) and Sergey Shumsky

Moscow Institute of Physics and Technology, Moscow, Russia
igorpivovarov@yandex.ru

Abstract. We present Deep Control – new ML architecture of cortico-striatal brain circuits, which use whole cortical column as a structural element, instead of a singe neuron. Based on this architecture, we present MARTI - new model of human brain, considering neocortex and basal ganglia. This model is designed to implement expedient behavior and is capable to learn and achieve goals in unknown environments. We introduce a novel *surprise feeling* mechanism, that significantly improves reinforcement learning process through inner rewards. We use OpenAI Gym environment to demonstrate MARTI learning on a single CPU just in several hours.

Keywords: Machine learning · Reinforcement learning · Basal ganglia · Surprise feeling · Self rewards

1 Introduction

In this work we introduce two new concepts. First is Deep Control Architecture - new hierarchical model of cortico-striatal brain circuits, which use a cortical column as a structural element, instead of a singe neuron. DCA is a hybrid vector-symbolic model, making native representations from high dimensional vector space to symbols and vice versa. Through this, DCA is very fast and compact way for real time learning, hierarchical analysis of environment, hierarchical planning and executing.

Second is MARTI – new ML model of human brain, built on Deep Control Architecture, implementing neocortex and basal ganglia. It runs ensemble of cortical columns simultaneously, orchestrated by basal ganglia, which is selecting the winner and inhibiting the rest of columns. Basal ganglia also maintains *surprise feeling*, which is a mechanism of implementation of inner rewards, allowing model to learn much faster. This multi-agent model is capable of learning by reinforcement learning to achieve goals in unknown environments.

To demonstrate MARTI capabilities, we use OpenAI Gym Atari game Ping-Pong. We run both MARTI and Gym on a usual single CPU machine. Using this setup MARTI robustly learns to play Ping-Pong game in several hours.

© The Author(s), under exclusive license to Springer Nature Switzerland AG 2023
B. Goertzel et al. (Eds.): AGI 2022, LNAI 13539, pp. 62–74, 2023.
https://doi.org/10.1007/978-3-031-19907-3_7

In this work we show the role of basal ganglia in a whole decision making process and conclude, that Deep Control Architecture is a new promising way of modeling human brain, especially where fast performance is needed with limited resources.

2 Background

Deep neural network is a low-level model of human neocortex, particularly visual cortex, which is perfectly designed for object detection/classification. However, DNN results in other domains, e.g. planning, decision making and appropriate behavior are far less impressive. Possibly, this is because behavior tasks are mostly implemented in other parts of human brain, besides neocortex.

Neocortex receives sensorimotor information, classify it and build «map of objects» and their relations. Positive feedback loops between thalamus and cortex supports long-time cortex activation, to allow synchronization between distant parts of brain. Basal ganglia, being the main keepers of values, can inhibit or disinhibit these positive feedback loops, being the main conductor of the cortex activity. Finally, cerebellum helps to maintain routine operations, adopting patterns, that were found previously by neocortex and basal ganglia [1].

In this process neocortex plays important role, analyzing situation and predicting situation development, but it is basal ganglia, that plays key role in deciding on variants and implementation of most valuable variant. To implement behaivour tasks, one should propose a unified model of basal ganglia and neocortex.

3 Related Work

Deep Control architecture proposed in this paper reflects biological mechanisms of the brain, namely the concept of hierarchical predictive coding of information in the neocortex [2–5] Unlike other models of the neocortex [6–8], Deep Control integrates Hebbian learning in the cortex with reinforcement learning in basal ganglia, implementing so called super-learning architecture [9].

Learning hierarchies of policies is a long-standing problem in RL [10, 11]. Namely [12] introduced the concept of options as closed-loop policies for taking action over a period of time, and [13] proposed option-critic architecture as an important step toward end-to-end hierarchical reinforcement learning. In these and similar works [14, 15] both goals and subgoals are defined in the same sensory-motor space. In our approach, each level operates in its own space using increasingly abstract representations to formulate higher levels plans.

4 Reinforcement Learning Environment

To evaluate behavioral tasks we use reinforcement learning approach. In current work, we used OpenAI Gym Atari games environment [16] and particularly Ping-Pong (PONG) game.

The Atari 2600 PONG game is one of the most complex games for reinforcement learning. Games can easily last 10,000 time steps (compared to 200–1000 in other domains); observations are also more complex, containing the two players' score and side walls. Pong paddle control is nonlinear: simple experimentation shows that fully predicting the player's paddle requires knowledge of the last 18 actions [17]. Finally, sparse rewards makes Pong quite complex game for RL.

We consider tasks in which an agent interacts with an environment E (in this case the OpenAI Gym Atari emulator) in a sequence of actions, observations and rewards. At each time-step the agent selects an action at from the set of available game actions, $A = \{0, \dots K\}$. The action is passed to the emulator and modifies its internal state and the game score. Agent observes the E state st (it can be an image of current screen or any other representation of E state). In addition it receives a reward rt representing the change in game score. (In general the game score depends on the prior sequence of actions and observations and feedback about current action may only be received after many hundreds or thousands of time-steps have elapsed - this is so called *sparse rewards*.)

In this work our agent observes emulator state called RAM - bit memory state of Atari computer. As it was shown in [16], RAM state does not give some special advantages to agent and even controversial - it appears that screen image carries more structural information that is not easily extracted from the RAM bits, so neural networks usually learn better using screen image. But we use RAM representation here as a very rough model, based on idea, that behavioral centers of the human brain deal with preprocessed and good prepared data, not with raw images.

The goal of the agent is to interact with the emulator by selecting actions in a way that maximizes future rewards. Such model is not a perfect, but reasonable way to test abilities of ML model to learn and achieve goals in uncertain environments.

5 Deep Control Architecture (DCA)

Deep Control Architecture is a novel hierarchical model of human brain, including neocortex interaction with basal ganglia. First, we will discuss main ideas of DCA and then talk about current realization.

5.1 Main Ideas of DCA

DCA represents a hierarchy of modules learning to jointly implement predictive behavior control with reinforcing signals coming from the dopamine system of the midbrain [18]. DCA comprise:

- a hierarchy of self-organizing maps of cortical modules, predicting activity of lower level cortical modules with primary sensory-motor modules at the lowest level;
- each hierarchical level corrects its predictions based on long-term predictions of the higher level and actual signals from the lower level;
- basal ganglia assess the usefulness of various patterns of cortical activity and select the winning pattern, implementing reinforcement learning

In general, DCA is based on the following premises:

First, DCA uses cortical *columns* rather than neurons as main functional units of neocortex. Thus, one have no more need to model each neuron. Considering various neurophysiological data, the basic structural elements of neocortex are cortical columns, each working with ~ 20–30 *symbols*.

Second, our conjecture is that several columns with local reciprocal connections form *hypercolumn*, capable of memorizing typical temporal patterns - *sequences of symbols*.

Third idea is about hierarchy. Hypercolumns alone cannot predict far enough into the future to solve complex tasks. But being organized in a hierarchy, higher levels operate at ever greater time scales, using sequences of lower level symbols as their input.

5.2 DCA Structure

Based on these ideas, we introduce DCA as follows:

Cortical hypercolumn (CHC) is an autonomous module, working with vector data. CHC consists of two parts:

- Coder/Decoder – preprocessing high dimensional input vectors to discrete symbolic representation and back.
- Parser – processes symbolic data flow, finds patterns and regularity in data and predicts next symbols.

To create a new CHC, initial dataset of input vectors is needed. Then Coder/Decoder runs clusterization of this dataset (we use K-means clustering), mapping input vectors to K clusters. These clusters (or cluster numbers, if you like) become symbols for Parser. From this point, each new vector, received by CHC, is converted to symbol by Coder/Decoder and then processed by Parser.

5.3 Learning

Parser – processes symbolic data flow, finds patterns and regularity in data and predicts next symbol. For this purposes Parser has it's vocabulary S with all the symbols and correlation table C, that keeps correlations between symbols. Each time Parser receives new symbol, C is updated:

$$s_n => C\, s_{n-1},\, s_n = C\, s_{n-1},\, s_n + 1$$

If Parser has m symbols in vocabulary and two symbols s_{n-1} and s_n are correlated more then defined threshold T, a new symbol (word) is formed and added to vocabulary:

$$if\, C\, s_{n-1},\, s_n > T => s_{m+1} = s_{n-1}s_n$$

Parser has predefined capacity of vocabulary size and word length, e.g. 1000 symbols and max word length = 3. Parser learns regularities in data and predicts next symbol.

5.4 Prediction

Prediction can be based on the correlation statistics – then we call it "situation prediction". In this case Parser predicts next symbol as follows:

$$s_{n+1} => \boldsymbol{max}_i(\boldsymbol{C}s_n, s_i)$$

Prediction can be based on value function. For this purposes Parser can keep reward table $\boldsymbol{R}$, that keeps rewards received after symbols. Each time Parser receives a non-zero reward, $\boldsymbol{R}$ is updated:

$$r_n => \boldsymbol{R}s_{n-1}, s_n = \boldsymbol{R}s_{n-1}, s_n + r_n$$
$$\boldsymbol{R}s_{n-2}, s_{n-1} = \boldsymbol{R}s_{n-2}, s_{n-1} + r_n * k$$
$$\boldsymbol{R}s_{n-m-1}, s_{n-m} = \boldsymbol{R}s_{n-m-1}, s_{n-m} + r_n * k^m,$$
$$...$$

where m is predefined memory size

As a result, parser has working memory of rewards it received in particular situations. Based on $\boldsymbol{R}$ table, parser can predict *desired* next symbol with maximum expected reward (reward forecast):

$$s_{n+1} => \boldsymbol{max}_i(\boldsymbol{R}s_n, s_i)$$

Prediction is always a pair – next symbol s_{n+1} and reward forecast of that next symbol $\boldsymbol{R}s_{n+1}$. Which kind of prediction specific parser will use depends on architecture; we will discuss this in 6.

DCA use semantic coding to move to the next level of the hierarchy. State sequences of the lower level are mapped to the states of a higher level via clustering of probability vectors of their successors and predecessors. All hierarchical levels interact with each other, looking for a way to implement the abstract plan of a higher level, consistent with the newly received data from the lower one. The number of hierarchical levels increases with the increase in the amount of data collected when interacting with the environment. So does planning horizon, which makes the Deep Control architecture a good candidate for AGI.

6 MARTI

Furthermore, we present MARTI (Modular ARTificial Intelligence) – new model of human brain, built on Deep Control Architecture. In this work we present MARTI-4 prototype, implementing neocortex, basal ganglia and thalamus at a object level.

Neocortex is a set of hypercolumns, each of which acts as a autonomous agent, receives partial information from thalamus, converts it to it's own symbol representation and tries to predict next symbol. Basal ganglia striatum receive predictions from all columns and tries to figure out the most valuable action to continue with, selects the winner column and inhibits the rest. Thalamus serves as a main information hub, processing sensor and actuator information from outside, providing it to cortical hypercolumns and to basal ganglia and back. Thalamus also inhibits execution of hypercolumns, that do not have new input data.

MARTI-4 receives sensor data (environment state) s_t and actuator data a_t as input data, as well as current reward r_t.

6.1 First Layer Hypercolumns

At the initialization, thalamus uses random sampling to create p subsets of size m from the initial sensor data s_t. For each of this subsets thalamus creates s cortical hypercolumns. Then, each time upon receiving new data, thalamus repeats this sampling to p parts and feeds each part to corresponding column Coder.

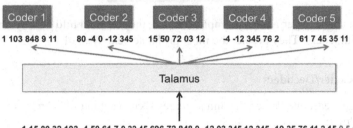

At first steps, there is no learning. At this stage Coder of each CHC is gathering data to create Parser. The condition of creating a Parser is that number of unique vectors received by this Coder exceeds given limit v. (Most of Coders never exceed this limit, because of different frequency of each of coordinates in initial vector). After limit v is reached, Coder creates corresponding Parser as follows:

- Coder run clusterization of v vectors, dividing vectors subset to K clusters
- Each cluster receives a symbolic name – a letter in UTF-8, e.g. "A" to "Z"
- Parser object is created with this alphabet

From this step, each time Coder receives a new vector, it classifies this vector (based on it's clusterization) and gives Parser corresponding cluster symbolic name as an input.

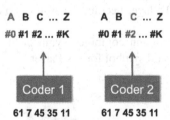

Parser of 1st layer in MARTI-4 is created with those restrictions:

- maximum word length $= 1$
- prediction type $=$ situation (correlation based)

Parser task is to parse it's symbolic inputs and build a correlation table C, using which it can predict next symbol. This parser also has reward table R, but it is not used for predictions, it is used for calculating *surprise feeling*, which we will discuss later.

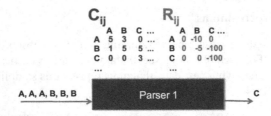

C_{ij} R_{ij}

	A	B	C ...
A	5	3	0 ...
B	1	5	5 ...
C	0	0	3 ...

	A	B	C ...
A	0	-10	0
B	0	-5	-100
C	0	0	-100

A, A, A, B, B, B → | Parser 1 | → C

So, Parsers of 1st layer are very simple and fast, they do not build new symbols and work only with letters. They predict the most probable next symbol.

6.2 Action Coder/Decoder

After creating at least one Parser, thalamus creates special actuator Coder A for actuator data a_t as follows:

- Coder A runs clusterization of actuator vectors subset a_t, dividing it to K clusters
- Each cluster receives a symbolic name – a letter in UTF-8, e.g. "a" to "z"
- no Parser is created for this Coder A

From this step, each actuator vector is classified by Coder A (based on it's clusterization) and converted to corresponding cluster symbolic name - which represents current *action*.

6.3 Second Layer Hypercolumns

After creation of at least 3 hypercolumns of 1st layer, next layer is created as follows:

- Each 3 hypercolumns of 1st layer become a substrate to create hypercolumn of 2nd layer.
- Coder of 2nd layer hypercolumn combines symbols of 1st layer subcolumns with current action symbol to build symbol for it's Parser.

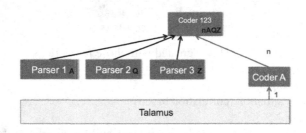

So, Parsers of 2nd layer works with symbols, combined from lower sensor symbols and action symbol, starting from action e.g. "nABC" or "dXYZ".They are created with restrictions:

- max word length = 4

- max vocabulary size $= 5000$
- prediction type $=$ value (reward based)

Parsers of 2nd layer has reward table R, keeping summarized reward received after each symbol as was discussed in Sect. 5.2.

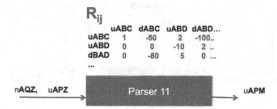

R_{ij}	uABC	dABC	uABD	dABD...
uABC	1	-50	2	-100..
uABD	0	0	-10	2 ..
dBAD	0	-80	5	0 ...
...				

nAQZ, uAPZ → Parser 11 → uAPM

At each step each Parser predicts most valuable next symbol, which will maximize the future reward. Besides it, each Parser calculate it's «positive feeling» of all possible actions. It is calculated as overall *number* of positive reward symbols, beginning from this action:

$$F^c(a_i) = \Sigma_j 1 \left| R(s_n, s_j) \right> 0 \; where \; s_j \middle| s_j \in a_i$$

6.4 Basal Ganglia

After all hypercolumns made their predictions, thalamus passes all the data to basal ganglia (striatum) to find the best prediction and, as a result, choose next action.

This is the most intriguing part of this paper, because most of usual RL approaches to choose next action does not work properly in this situation. We did a lot of experiments to find out working solution.

Usually, our intuition says, that in reinforcement learning approach model should take next action, which has maximum value function (or maximum future reward). In this case, that could mean choosing hypercolumn with maximum predicted reward. But suprisingly, at every moment we can find a hypercolumn giving a very high predicted reward combined with a wrong action. No separate hypercolumn can give a good prediction, because all of them have only partial sensor information. This is like CHC-1 "sees" only X coordinate of an object and CHC-2 "sees" only Y coordinate. *Their* predictions are always *biased* with *their* information.

That's why, to obtain better prediction, an ensemble of hypercolumns is needed. And the task of basal ganglia is to choose most promising way to increase future rewards.

In MARTI-4 basal ganglia striatum works as follows:

- For each action a_i calculate "basal positive feeling" as number of CHC, that has $F^c(a_i) > 0$

$$F^b(a_i) = \Sigma_j 1 \mid F_j^c(a_i) > 0$$

- Choose next action a_i, which has maximum $F^b(a_i)$

- Select as a winner CHC, that predicted next symbol with this action a_i, which has maximum predicted future reward.

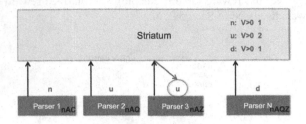

6.5 Surprise Feeling and Inner Rewards

Another important task of basal ganglia is maintaining a *surprise feeling*, which helps the model understand what was done right. In reinforcement learning environment *sparse rewards* are big issue, because reward can be received after many hundreds or thousands of steps have elapsed. In this case, it will be nice to have any way of understanding, that something has been done properly right now, without waiting too long for a distant (and rare) reward.

To do it, basal ganglia analyze the state of each hypercolumn just after it received new data but before it made any predictions. Each parser compares new data with previous prediction it made. Prediction is always a pair – next symbol s_{n+1} and reward forecast of that next symbol Rs_{n+1}. Similarly, received data also constructs a pair – symbol received s_t and reward forecast of this symbol Rs_t. And if $s_t \mathrel{!}= s_{n+1}$ then reward forecast may have changed.

Hypercolumn *surprise feeling* can be defined as *unexpected improving of reward forecast*:

$$S^c(s_t) > 0 \,|\, Rs_t >> Rs_{n+1}$$

Note, that, especially for parsers of 1st layer, usually parser receives (statistically) expected data and usually has expected deterioration of the reward forecast.

But single surprise of single hypercolumn is not enough to be sure, that overall forecast became better. Basal ganglia observes all hypercolumns and calculate "basal surprise feeling" based on simultaneous surprises of different columns or sequential surprises of single column. When this overall surprise feeling becomes greater than given threshold S^t a one time inner reward is given to all hypercolumns:

$$S^b(s_t) = \Sigma_j 1 \,|\, S^c_j(s_t) > 0$$
$$r_t = 1 \,|\, S^b(s_t) > S^t$$

This mechanism of *surprise feeling* allows model to learn much faster through implementation of inner rewards in addition to usual environment rewards.

6.6   Whole Cycle of Analysing/predicting

Finally, let's have an overview of the whole model work.

Each step thalamus receives sensor data s_t, actuator data a_t, current reward r_t. It samples s_t to p parts and feed each part to CHC of the 1st layer.

Each CHC of 1st layer encodes it's input vector to it's own symbols and processes symbol parsing taking into account "column surprise feeling" based on match between predicted and received symbols. After parsing, CHC makes prediction of next symbol and reward forecast.

Each CHC of 2nd layer receives symbols from 1st layers as an input and encodes them to own symbol representation. Then it processes symbol parsing taking into account "column surprise feeling". After parsing, CHC calculates next symbol prediction and "column positive feeling" for every potential action.

Basal ganglia striatum observe "column surprise feelings" from all CHC and calculates "basal surprise feeling" $S^b(s_t)$. If it is greater then a threshold S^t then one time inner reward is given to all CHC.

Basal ganglia striatum receive predictions from CHC of 2nd layer and calculates "basal positive feeling" for each potential action. Then it chooses the winner, that has maximum future reward for action with maximum "basal positive feeling".

Coder A decodes predicted action back to actuator terms a_t and it is returned back by thalamus to environment as a next action.

6.7   World Model and Prediction Horizon

In terms of reinforcement learning, MARTI-4 is a model-based agent, because it builds it's own "world model" and use the information about last steps to understand it's position in this world model. However, prediction horizon in MARTI-4 is usually 2–3 steps forward, because it has only 2 hierarchical layers and the prediction horizon in DCA depends only on hierarchy levels. This will be the subject of future works.

7   Experiments

Experimental setup was standalone single CPU test machine (AMD A8–9600 10 compute cores 16Gb RAM). We used Ubuntu 18.04, python 3.6.9, OpenAI Gym library, Java OpenJDK 11.0.13 installed. Marti-4 is written in Java and is using simple TCP/IP socket interface to receive and send data. To connect it with OpenAI Gym, we use additional python script, which receive data from Gym and send it to Marti via socket. When Marti have processed sensor data, it sends back actuator data to script, which sends it to Gym.

In previous works [17, 19], to set an experiment to test a model performance in PONG game, researches choose to run it up to 18,000 game steps or up to score 21. We found this setup not the best way to reveal model performance, because of specific Pong game nature: if model learns how to beat back the ball in some situations, that usually will not lead to win the game or even to win a single play in a game, because other side (Gym) will beat back the ball in most cases and finally win the game play. In other words, even when model steadily learns how to play, it still loses when play up to 21 score or 18,000 steps.

So, in our setup we choose to run the game up to 500 steps. If the model is not able to beat back at all, overall score is usually around 0:15. But when model steadily learns to play and beats back more and more, the plays become longer and longer and score looks like 1:1 or 3:4 or something like that.

To perform an experiment, both MARTI and Gym are executed on a test machine. CPU load is about 40% for Gym and 60% for MARTI. MARTI size in memory is ~ 8Gb. Using this setup MARTI robustly learns to play Ping-Pong game in 500–700 game plays (3–4 h).

Typical experimental run is shown in Fig. 1. One can see, that starting from typical score 0:15 with average goal difference is -15, MARTI makes quick progress and reaches typical scores 2:2, 1:0 with average goal difference -1 in 500–700 games.

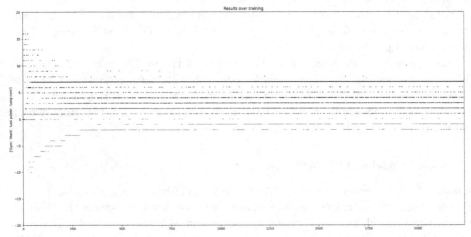

Fig. 1. On X-axe there is number of games played, each 500 steps. On Y-axe there are points: blue dots are Gym goals in the game, green dots are Marti goals in the game, orange points are goal difference between Gym and Marti calculated as average last at 30 games..

For purposes of comparison with previous works, we also preformed evaluation of model performance as in [19]. An episode starts on the frame that follows the reset command, and terminates when the end-of-game condition is detected or after 5 min of real-time play (18,000 frames), whichever comes first. A trial consists of 500 training episodes, followed by 500 evaluation episodes. Agent's performance was measured as the average score achieved during the evaluation episodes across 3 sequential trials. This setup is consistent to setups used in [17, 19] with the only difference, that MARTI-4 does not show significant improvement after 500 training episodes, so training episodes were lowered to 500. Table 1 shows MARTI performance, compared to previous works in this setup gives a summary of all heading levels.

Since MARTI-4 has only 2 layers, it can hardly been compared with deep networks like DQN. However, even this small model shows comparable results with models like Sarsa.

Table 1. Performance of different algorithms on PONG game.

ALGORITHM	PONG
Random [17]	−20.9
Sarsa [17]	−19
MARTI-4	−15,8
Human [19]	−3
UCT [17]	21

8 Discussion

Current model has modest results and never get to score *21:0*. This is because current prototype has only 2 hierarchical layers of hypercolumns and full power of DCA will be obtained, when there will be much more layers of hypercolumns, hierarchically organized. So, current work can be considered only as a testbed for this way of modeling. However, we demonstrate that even this simple model is capable to learn in unknown environment and show quick progress.

One of the reasons, DCA architecture is very fast is because model is building "on the fly" from zero, model size and hierarchy depends only on the amount and variety of input data. This is in contrast to deep neural networks, that are build initially huge and one have a need to run calculations forward and back through all this billions on neurons.

DCA perfectly suited to work with data preprocessed with DNN. Next thing to do is to make model input not a RAM state, but raw screen images, preprocessed with CNN. This will be more similar to real process, which take place in human brain.

Last but not least final technical issue is that neither OpenAI Gym Atari emulator nor ALE Atari emulator are providing fully reliable and expected behavior of Atari game. Namely, in some cases (1 of ~ 50 games) some unexpected behavior of Atari emulator occurs, when the gameplay is already finished, new gameplay should start, but screen remains unchanged for some time and model continues to receive some environmental data which makes no sense. In some games (Atari Breakout for example) this can last for 30,000 steps and more. This makes the learning process significantly more complicated.

9 Conclusion

We showed, that Deep Control Architecture is a hybrid vector-symbolic ML architecture, making native representations from high dimensional vector space to symbols and back. Through this, DCA is very fast and compact way for real time learning, hierarchical analysis of environment, hierarchical planning and executing, especially where fast performance with low resources is needed.

We presented MARTI - novel ML model of human brain, implementing neocortex, basal ganglia and thalamus, capable to learn by reinforcement learning to achieve goals in unknown environments. We presented a novel *surprise feeling* mechanism, that significantly improves reinforcement learning process through inner rewards.

Through this work we also tried to show the role and potential mechanism of basal ganglia work in human brain in a whole decision making process.

Disclaimer. Igor Pivovarov works part time in Moscow Institute of Physics and Technologies, Huawei, Skoltech, Bauman University and IP Laboratories. Sergey Shumsky works part time in Moscow Institute of Physics and Technologies and Bauman University. However, the whole scope of current work was made by authors solely in free time without any support or participation of any entities.

References

1. Shumsky, S.A.: Machine intelligence. Essays on the theory of machine learning and artificial intelligence. RIOR Publishing, Moscow (2019). ISBN 978-5-369-02011-1.
2. Friston, K.: A theory of cortical responses. Philos. Trans. R. Soc. B: Biol. Sci. **360**(1456), 815–836 (2005)
3. Bastos, A.M., et al.: Canonical microcircuits for predictive coding. Neuron **76**(4), 695–711 (2012)
4. Clark, A.: Surfing Uncertainty: Prediction, Action, and The Embodied Mind. Oxford University Press, Oxford (2015)
5. Spratling, M.W.: A review of predictive coding algorithms. Brain Cogn. **112,** 92–97 (2017)
6. Hawkins, J., Ahmad, S.: Why neurons have thousands of synapses, a theory of sequence memory in neocortex. Front. Neural Circuits **10**, 23 (2016)
7. Hawkins, J., Ahmad, S., Cui, Y.: A theory of how columns in the neocortex enable learning the structure of the world. Front. Neural Circuits **11**, 81 (2017)
8. Laukien, E., Richard C., Fergal B.: Feynman machine: the universal dynamical systems computer. arXiv preprint arXiv:1609.03971 (2016)
9. Caligiore, D., et al.: The super-learning hypothesis: integrating learning processes across cortex, cerebellum and basal ganglia. Neurosci. Biobehav. Rev. **100,** 19–34 (2019)
10. Botvinick, M.M.: Hierarchical reinforcement learning and decision making. Curr. Opin. Neurobiol. **22**(6), 956–962 (2012)
11. Pateria, S., et al.: Hierarchical reinforcement learning: a comprehensive survey. ACM Comput. Surv. (CSUR) **54**(5), 1–35 (2021)
12. Sutton, R.S., Precup, D., Singh, S.: Between MDPs and semi-MDPs: a framework for temporal abstraction in reinforcement learning. Artif. Intell. **112**(1–2), 181–211 (1999)
13. Bacon, P.L., H, J., Precup, D.: The option-critic architecture. In: Proceedings of the AAAI Conference on Artificial Intelligence, vol. 31, no. 1 (2017)
14. Vezhnevets, A.S, et al.: Feudal networks for hierarchical reinforcement learning. In: International Conference on Machine Learning. PMLR (2017)
15. Nachum, O., et al.: Data-efficient hierarchical reinforcement learning.*arXiv preprint* arXiv: 1805.08296 (2018)
16. Brockman, G., et al.: Open AI Gym.*arXiv 2016*
17. Marc, B.G., et al.: The arcade learning environment: an evaluation platform for general agents. J. Artif. Intell. Res. **47**, 253–279 (2013)
18. Shumsky, S.A.: Deep structural learning: a new look at reinforcement learning. In: XX Russian Scientific Conference NEUROINFORMATICS 2018. Lectures on Neuroinformatics, pp. 11–43 (2018)
19. Mnih, V., et al.: Playing Atari with Deep Reinforcement Learning. arXiv 2013

General-Purpose Minecraft Agents and Hybrid AGI

Alexey Potapov$^{(\boxtimes)}$ (iD), Anatoly Belikov(iD), Oleg Scherbakov, and Vitaly Bogdanov

SingularityNET Foundation, Amsterdam, The Netherlands
{alexey,abelikov,olegshcherbakov,vitaly}@singularitynet.io

Abstract. We consider the problem of creating general-purpose Minecraft agents capable of solving a wide range of goals in a complex environment as a testbed for studying hybrid neural-symbolic architectures for Artificial General Intelligence (AGI). We analyze the desirable behavior of such agents and sketch out an architecture for it. We implement a prototype of the agent, which is capable of achieving various goals in the Minecraft world and to perform exploration, and discuss the utility of more advanced AGI components to be developed and integrated into the agent in future.

Keywords: AGI · Neural-symbolic integration · Minecraft agents

1 Introduction

Different approaches to Artificial General Intelligence (AGI) focus on different aspects of the problem be that theory vs practice or knowledge representation and reasoning vs end-to-end learning. Each approach focuses on tasks, benchmarks and challenges that suit them better. In order to pursue a cross-paradigm approach, one needs a task, which solution is difficult for separate approaches, but each of the approaches can contribute to the solution. We consider Minecraft as one of environments, on which example a cross-paradigm approach to AGI can be fruitfully studied and discussed.

The idea to use Minecraft is not new. Two prominent examples are

- MarLÖ 2018 – Multi-Agent Reinforcement Learning in Minecraft Competition (an extension of the Malmo Collaborative AI Challenge) [1];
- MineRL Competition 2019 and 2021 [2, 3].

However, as we will discuss below, these competitions favor specific research topics and approaches, which don't explicitly facilitate cross-paradigm studies. In this paper, we propose to study the problem of achieving complex goals in complex environments (in accordance to one of definitions of AGI [4]) on example of Minecraft, and discuss implications for AGI design principles. We also describe a prototype of the Minecraft agent, which follows these principles on ad hoc level and can achieve various goals.

B. Goertzel et al. (Eds.): AGI 2022, LNAI 13539, pp. 75–85, 2023.
https://doi.org/10.1007/978-3-031-19907-3_8

2 Minecraft as Testbed for Cross-Paradigm AGI

Let us consider the existing Minecraft-based AI competitions. MarLÖ provides simplified Minecraft worlds as environments (like a fenced area of 5 × 5 blocks) with tasks like chasing a pig, which seems not too difficult for Reinforcement Learning (RL). The challenge is for multiple agents to collaborate in achieving the common goal by recognizing intents and strategies of each other just from their in-game behavior. While emergence of collaborative behavior is an important research topic, the tasks for agents are quite restricted and means of communication are limited. While the challenge itself is interesting, its restrictions are not very natural. Humans learn to communicate using language in different settings, and direct communications between agents in MarLÖ are not introduced not because it would be non-AGI-ish or less beneficial for collaborative behavior, but because it doesn't correspond specifically to subsymbolic RL methodology. If we wanted to put this competition into the AGI context, we would consider more complex tasks and allow more communication channels including symbolic ones.

MineRL, in turn, doesn't suppose multi-agent collaborations, but considers large (default) Minecraft environments with a distant goal. The diamond competition [2] consisted in acquiring a diamond, which requires first to cut some wood, then to craft wood planks, wooden pickaxe, mining cobblestone, crafting stone pickaxe, and digging deep, while avoiding lava. This goal is far from most distant in Minecraft, but deep RL agents fail to learn how to achieve it without hints. The competition proposes to train RL agents using records of human player walkthroughs. This is "one of the largest imitation learning datasets with over 60 million frames of recorded human player data".

The agent also receives auxiliary rewards for obtaining prerequisite items in addition to a high reward for obtaining a diamond. Moreover, in the navigation subtask, additional rewards are given for approaching the provided location. That is, the agent is consequently trained to navigate, to gather one prerequisite item after another. Although diamond acquisition is a reasonably complex goal in a reasonably complex environment, agents are intensively trained to achieve only one goal. Although the problem of creating models capable of achieving multiple goals via different policies is considered in RL, these models can be assisted by environment models and use some specific tricks (e.g. [5]). In any case, they have not been used in Diamond competition.

AGI methodology supposes that an agent should be capable of achieving a wide range of goals (in a wide range of environments or in a rich and complex environment such as the real world) [4, 6]. Minecraft provides a really wide range of goals including not only acquiring various items, but also visiting all biomes, encountering all breeds of cats, etc. Gathering huge imitation learning datasets and training separate agents for each of such tasks is neither practical nor AGI-ish.

More recently, the BASALT competition [3] has more interesting and less formalized tasks such as "Find Cave", "Make Waterfall", "Create Village Animal Pen", and "Build Village House". Unfortunately, these are still very concrete goals. Of course, it is amazing if agents can achieve these goals in randomly generated Minecraft worlds, but they learn to imitate sequences of human actions without obtaining general-purpose capabilities to achieve novel goals.

A wide range of environments is provided by the set of 57 Atari 2600 games, and the challenge is to make a single agent capable of mastering them all (which was accomplished by Agent57 [7]). However, it still corresponds to a finite set of goals, each of which the model is intensively trained to achieve separately. Minecraft provides one environment, but it is much richer (one may say that it contains a lot of related sub-environments). It raises an even stronger long-term credit assignment problem. It provides such settings, in which it is sensible to consider building not just one model with different instances, but one agent capable of achieving a wide range of complex goals simultaneously, which are of our primary interest.

3 Brief Analysis of Human Player Behavior

Human players intensively utilize knowledge. It is enough to know that you need an iron pickaxe in order to mine diamonds, and the goal to get a diamond will immediately imply that getting an iron pickaxe should be done first. If the necessary crafting receipts are known, then a lengthy plan will be constructed starting with the subgoal of obtaining logs. This fits into a fairly simple classical symbolic planning. But it is still productively used by humans, who can achieve any goal decomposable into known subgoals. If crafting a lever requires cobblestone and sticks, achieving this goal is not really different from crafting a stone pickaxe (up to the number of required resources). Humans do not require additional training or practice for this.

Human players reason over not only item crafting and block mining. They explicitly understand, for example, that block mining is possible from a certain distance, so the block should be approached first. However, while the reasoning can go down to quite fine granular subgoals, humans construct plans up to not elementary actions, but fairly large imperative policies. In some cases, these policies are explicit but still imperative algorithms, e.g., "mine until the block is destroyed". In other cases, these policies are implicit and subconscious. This is especially true for controlling keyboard and mouse with own body actions. If we are approaching one block and notice another useful block, we orient ourselves towards the new block not by an imperative rule or reflex, but decide to change our plans or not, while aiming at the new block is executed with much less conscious control, reasoning, planning, etc.

The main problem with reasoning and planning arises due to unknowns and uncertainties. If we are asked to get a diamond, but we don't know how to do this, we will not construct a huge branchy plan or enumerate all possible sequences of elementary actions. We will just explore. Similarly, if we know that logs are needed to craft pickaxes, which are needed for gathering other required resources, but we don't see trees around us, we will just search for trees. The search process can rely on some knowledge. For example, we will not search for trees in a sea or among icebergs, but our plans related to searching will be coarse grained.

Knowledge-based planning (or at least behavior guidance) plays prominent role in how humans play Minecraft. This side of human thinking is not captured by contemporary deep RL models. However, high-level plans are not enough to achieve goals and subgoals without lower-level skills and behavior policies.

Providing explicit knowledge to AI agents should not be considered non-AGI-ish by itself, because humans rely on this knowledge themselves. Training Minecraft agents from scratch is interesting, but not obligatory from AGI standpoint. What is more important is that agent's capabilities are not limited to knowledge, skills, or imitation-learning training sets provided a priori. Minecraft is a good testbed for this, because many things can be discovered and invented, all of which are infeasible to cover in ontologies.

Let us consider the following situation. A human player while running somewhere encounters a steep mountain for the first time, which should be somehow passed through. The player will not just try random actions, but instead will consider larger-scale options. "Going around" or "climbing up" strategies are borrowed from the real world, but "mining through" is more specific to Minecraft. The player first invents the idea to mine through the obstacle and then tests it. Similarly, the general idea of "climbing up" can be implemented very differently. It is very natural for the player to try jumping on reachable blocks with increasing height. This strategy follows (as one of options) from the subgoal "climb higher". But what to do if there is no block to jump on in the middle of execution of this strategy? The player can give up and go down. But there are other options. It is possible to destroy blocks to carve stairs in the stone. It is possible to attach blocks to the wall to build stairs. These options can also be invented with help of deduction.

One more interesting and less obvious for human players option is to look down, jump, and during the jump to put a block under oneself. It is really difficult to do this accidentally, so RL agents will unlikely learn this trick without guidance. In turn, human players cannot be sure that this trick will work. What we can see is that exploratory actions are based on randomness introduced not only on the level of basic motor commands, but also on higher behavioral levels. Human players may need some practice to master such skills as jumping on blocks in arbitrary conditions, and this practice looks more like traditional RL, but with rewards formed by reasoning.

Of course, if we consider infants in the real world, their learning will look more RL-like, but it will evolve to what is outlined above in contrast to most animals, which are also quite capable in RL. Thus, such form of neural-symbolic learning and decision-making should at least be architecturally supported.

4   Universal Agents with Reasoning

A distinct approach to AGI is a top-down approach based on universal models of intelligence [8]. However, traditional universal models don't include goal-oriented reasoning and planning. Thus, it is interesting to establish connection between such models and human behavior in Minecraft. Let us consider the basic model, AIXI, that performs Solomonoff induction to predict future rewards and observations, and enumerates all sequences of elementary actions to maximize expected future rewards.

Initially, AIXI will perform actions in accordance with priors imposed by its reference machine. But with the growth of interaction history, posterior distribution of predicted responses of the environment to agent's actions will converge to true rewards and observations. Basically, Solomonoff induction will (theoretically, provided nearly infinite amount of resources) reconstruct the Minecraft game engine (its part, with which the agent has already interacted).

AIXI reconstructs simulation models of the environment. Such a first-principles model as the Minecraft engine itself will not contain abstractions used by humans. Such concepts as "jump on a block", "climb on the tree", or "waterfall rafting" will not be presented there as well as concepts describing configurations of blocks not used by the world generator, e.g., "bridge over the canyon", "stairs to the mine", etc. At the same time, this model provides a perfect generalization of the interaction history. The question arises – why do we need redundant abstractions? Arguably, AIXI will be able to construct stairs or bridge without any notion of them and to make best possible predictions without additional abstractions by marginalizing unknowns out.

Let us note that using full Minecraft model is not more computationally efficient than enumerating all sequences of actions in Minecraft itself. There is not too much computational difference whether to run copies of a randomly acting agent countless times in Minecraft itself or to do the same using a precise model of Minecraft. While the theoretical possibility to reconstruct the model of the Minecraft engine using Solomonoff induction is fascinating, the rest sounds not too intelligent. Thus, essence of intelligence is in efficient use of resources (which is not a new idea for sure), and we can suppose that "redundant abstractions" have to do with it.

However, planning is usually performed in terms of environment state, while there is no Markov assumption in AIXI, and states (even hidden) are not introduced (while goal-oriented RL relies on states [5]). Moreover, goals are somewhat different from rewards. Nevertheless, such goal as "obtain a diamond" is turned into a reward in RL settings, and receiving such discrete reward can be straightforwardly turned back into the goal.

In AIXI, rewards are predicted by environment models consistent with interaction history. Consider one world model q such that

$$U(q, \mathbf{a}_{1:m}) = \mathbf{o}_{1:m}\mathbf{r}_{1:m},$$

where U is a Universal Turing Machine, $\mathbf{a}_{1:m}$ is a vector of actions executed by the agent, $\mathbf{o}_{1:m}$ and $\mathbf{r}_{1:m}$ are vectors of observations and rewards. These vectors may include past values $\mathbf{a}_{1:t}$, $\mathbf{o}_{1:t}$ and $\mathbf{r}_{1:t}$ for some $t < m$ as well as possible future actions $\mathbf{a}_{t+1:m}$ and predicted observations $\mathbf{o}_{t+1:m}$ and rewards $\mathbf{r}_{t+1:m}$ (which are produced by q).

It would be nice to describe goals and subgoals in terms of components of world model q, but it is not convenient while q is a program for UTM. We also don't have world states, so we cannot describe goals as families of desirable states. However, we can use interaction history instead. Let us consider arbitrary predicates p over the history computable on UTM: $U(p, \mathbf{a}_{1:m}, \mathbf{o}_{1:m}, \mathbf{r}_{1:m}) \in \{0, 1\}$.

We can suppose that goals can be represented as such predicates. In case of "obtaining a diamond", we can either calculate this predicate from observations (ObservationFrom-FullInventory in Malmo []) or from rewards (the reward is received; thus, the goal is achieved) depending on concrete settings. Some goals are more difficult to hand-code as predicates (e.g., "build a bridge"), but they can be represented as programs similar to world models. Achieving goal p within model q can be reduced to searching for such $\mathbf{a}_{t+1:m}$ that $U(p, \mathbf{a}_{1:m}, U(q, \mathbf{a}_{1:m})) = 1$. Then, it is trivial to marginalize over (with weights $2^{-\text{length}(q)}$) all models compatible with the observation history and to state the task of maximizing probability of p becoming true.

Now, let us introduce causal relations. We consider two predicates p_1 and p_2, and say that p_1 causally precedes p_2 within environment model q if

$$(\forall \mathbf{a}_{1:m}, \mathbf{o}_{1:m}, \mathbf{r}_{1:m} : U(q, \mathbf{a}_{1:m}) = \mathbf{o}_{1:m}\mathbf{r}_{1:m})U(p_2, \mathbf{a}_{1:m}, \mathbf{o}_{1:m}, \mathbf{r}_{1:m}) = 1 =>$$
$$(\exists m' < m)U(p_1, \mathbf{a}_{1:m'}, \mathbf{o}_{1:m'}, \mathbf{r}_{1:m'}) = 1$$

The truth or falsity of this condition is determined solely by programs p_1, p_2, and q themselves. Causal relation between p_1 and p_2 is actually a statement about q (which, in turn, should be consistent with the agent's past). Marginalization over all consistent q will give the probability of relation conditioned on the agent's history.

If the agent knows such a relation for the goal, it can reduce the depth of action enumeration. Indeed, if p_2 is a goal, and p_1 causally precedes p_2, then the agent can first try achieving p_1, which will take less time. With linear increase in the number of subgoals, computational complexity of choosing actions can decrease exponentially in AIXI. Causal relations can be enriched with the use of logical operators. For example, achieving p_3 can depend on conjunction or disjunction of p_1 and p_2. For example, crafting a stone pickaxe requires both sticks and cobblestone in the inventory, while mining coal ore requires either wooden or stone pickaxe. Instead of having large black-box programs p_i, we can have smaller p_i, which can be combined in a declarative way. This can simplify discovery of causally related predicates and enable their reuse for describing different goals and subgoals.

However, searching for new predicates and proving their causal relations can be difficult, when environment models are imperative. The problem is that universal induction needs complete generative models, which precisely reproduce all observations. If the environment is described with the use of separate predicates or features (without generative component in style of universal autoencoders []), it is impossible to estimate how much information is lost in this description and thus to assess the model quality. Also, as was mentioned, these descriptions have more pragmatic than inductive meaning. They can contain useful abstractions, which are, however, redundant from purely inductive standpoint.

One possibility to make proving causal relations within generative models of environment feasible is connected to Curry–Howard isomorphism. Suppose, for example, that these models are programs in a dependently typed language. These programs will contain types, which will correspond to certain propositions, and more propositions as dependent types can be formed on top of them. If goals are described in the same language, causal relations can be represented as (dependent) function types and proven by finding a function implementation that type-checks.

For example, the fact that diamonds are mined from ore only with iron or diamond pickaxes can be represented not as a piece of imperative code, but as a type in program q (if the reference machine in universal induction is a dependently typed language). Then, proof that possessing such a pickaxe is a prerequisite for mining a diamond within q will be trivial.

Detailed development of a goal-oriented version of AIXI model based on, e.g., a language with probabilistic dependent types, proofs of causal relations, and action selection guided by reasoning goes beyond the scope of this paper. Our goal is to develop a practically usable prototype of a Minecraft agent capable of achieving a wide range of goals. The presented informal sketch of this possibility, which shows that our introspection of human problem-solving in Minecraft can be aligned with improvements in AIXI efficiency, can justify the choice of architecture of such Minecraft agent from AGI standpoint.

5 Minecraft Agent Design

We are prototyping a hybrid Minecraft AI agent, which uses explicit symbolic knowledge and reasoning together with subsymbolic skills. We use seed ontology with knowledge about crafting receipts (which is a limitation of Malmo, which crafting command requires to specify the result). It can also include some entries describing mining results from blocks with tools, although this knowledge can be enriched via learning. This seed ontology is used instead of indirect prior information provided to the agent in the form of imitation learning training set in MineRL.

This knowledge can be straightforwardly used to infer what blocks should be mined to gather necessary resources for crafting necessary tools for mining other necessary blocks, etc. Similar to subgoals in the sketched above version of AIXI, knowing "what to do" is not detailed enough to infer immediate elementary actions. Our architecture includes "how-to" procedural knowledge to break subgoals down into finer-grained tasks such as "approach the block", "look at the block", "attack the block", etc., and even finer-grained tasks and procedural knowledge entries as "run towards the block to approach it", "strafe to avoid think obstacles", etc. Apparently, we can express this in natural language.

Such rules do not compose well. For example, the rule to float in order not to suffocate can contradict to the rule of shortening the distance for approaching the desirable block, when this block is under water. We can imagine a rule that block can be mined under water for a certain time and then it is necessary to surface. However, all such situations cannot be envisioned a priori. It should be noted that a deep RL agents are also not able to deal with novel situations, which do not resemble situations from training sets. This particular situation could be dealt with via reasoning at least by humans. Procedural knowledge can be considered as the result of caching of declarative knowledge-based inference. However, procedural knowledge can be formed before declarative, thus we consider it as a separate subsystem. Declarative knowledge is preferrable, since it can tell what to do in unexpected situations. However, such rules as "if the block location is known, approach it instead of search of a new block of interest" can be more difficult to prove from declarative knowledge (which can be absent) than to infer it inductively from practice. In any case, there are subsymbolic skills at the bottom, and procedural knowledge is aimed to glue declarative knowledge and these skills.

If procedural knowledge is not enough to answer what to do, search behavior is activated. For example, if the agent knows that achieving a goal requires certain blocks, but these blocks are not observed and their location is unknown, the agent will search for them. If the agent knows that some ingredient is needed to achieve the goal, but it doesn't know, what block this ingredient is obtained from, the agent will search for novel blocks and try mining them. Exploration of the world can be a separate goal or can be activated as a subgoal of another goal the way to achieve which is not known.

Subsymbolic skills produce basic actions, although actions (e.g., crafting an object) can be inferred from knowledge. Skills can be built-in into the agent as instinct, and can be trainable. The reason for the latter is also the lack of information, which is also solved by exploration, but on the level of individual actions. Rewards for such skills are formed by the symbolic system. The agent knows what is necessary to achieve by the skill, but necessary actions for this are not yet known and to be explored. This should not be necessarily estimated by a binary predicate "the task is solved by the skill" (e.g., the block is approached or mined) as in our sketched AIXI modification, but can be an estimate of the progress towards the goal (e.g., the distance to the block to be approached). Forming the latter automatically has not yet been implemented.

It is important to note that exploratory behavior was crucial for Agent57 to achieve superhuman performance in all 57 game [7]. Exploration was stimulated by intrinsic rewards based on novelty. The main new feature there was to adapt exploration/exploitation tradeoff to a current environment. In our case, exploration is activated at different levels of abstraction and explicitly depends on a goal and lack of knowledge how to achieve it. Exploration can be a separate goal in a conjunction with another goal, which will be equivalent to a sum of extrinsic and intrinsic rewards, but even in this case exploration on the top level will be guided by knowledge.

The sketched AIXI modification performs action selection, learning, and reasoning simultaneously at each time step. While this computationally infeasible, it doesn't encounter the problems of replanning and plan recovery. Our prototype constructs a graph of subgoals and skills, which is also dynamically updated. However, only reevaluation of goal statuses and preconditions is performed at each step, while replanning is performed only when such statuses are changed. For example, if the agent has the plan to cut some wood to make a wooden pickaxe to mine cobblestone and is on search for wood, but notices a cobblestone item (appeared, e.g., due to explosion of a creeper), it will approach the item and pick it up directly, because picking a cobblestone is a part of the goal-skill graph with the subgoal of determining a cobblestone location, which status changes when a cobblestone is noticed.

Our prototype has domain-specific components. Although Malmo provides symbolic entities as raw observations (e.g., observationFromFullInventory, observationFromRay), such notions as "mining a block", "picking up an item", "approaching location" are introduced manually. Inferring arbitrary symbolic concepts as well as introduction of brand-new skills was not considered in the current prototype, while it is the most interesting part in context of AGI. However, a working agent was implemented, which can achieve a wide range of goals without additional data provided by humans. Its behavior can still be made much more general-purpose and open-ended that will require more AGI-ish features. The prototype enables the study of these features in non-trivial settings with clear demonstration of their usefulness.

6   AGENt's Capabilities

Let us consider some examples of agent's capabilities to clarify them. The agent uses vision (Fig. 1), which guides its search for and navigation towards known blocks as well as attention towards novel blocks.

Fig. 1. Noticing and approaching trees via vision

In the course of free exploration, the agent can collect items, which are mined from the blocks that can be found both under and above the surface (Fig. 2). The agent has prior knowledge about tools, and decides to craft them as a subgoal of exploration when necessary.

Fig. 2. Intermediate exploration results

The agent doesn't have a one-way behavior like agents in the MineRL diamond competition, where they utilize a simple strategy to dig straight down after obtaining enough wood. Our agent navigates in arbitrary directions depending on its goal (Fig. 3).

Fig. 3. Mining coal ore and granite as novel blocks, climbing to surface for further exploration, returning back for obtaining iron_pickaxe as a goal, finding iron ore

7   Conclusion

We have implemented the prototype of a neural-symbolic Minecraft agent capable of achieving a wide range of complex goals of obtaining various items. Knowledge-based reasoning dynamically orchestrates subsymbolic skills, and guides learning and exploratory behavior. The agent can freely navigate in the world without getting stuck in the course or after achieving each goal. While the prototype contains ad hoc components, it serves as a proof-of-concept that the hybrid approach can be efficient in general-purpose open-ended Minecraft agents.

The prototype agent doesn't produce new symbolic knowledge besides establishing relations between known concepts. Thus, it also doesn't produce brand-new DNN modules for novel skills. For example, it cannot master swimming up a waterfall, because it doesn't have a notion of waterfall as well as constructions (block compositions) in general. These are the main topics of our further research, which can be studied in non-trivial settings with the use of the developed prototype.

References

1. Perez-Liebana, D., et al: The multi-agent reinforcement learning in MalmÖ (MARLÖ) competition. arXiv:1901.08129 (2019)
2. Guss, W.H., et al.: The MineRL 2019 competition on sample efficient reinforcement learning using human priors. arXiv:1904.10079 (2019)

3. Shah, R., et al: The MineRL BASALT competition on learning from human feedback. arXiv: 2107.01969 (2021)
4. Goertzel, B.: Toward a formal characterization of real-world general intelligence. In: Proceedings of 3D Conference on Artificial General Intelligence, pp. 74–79. Atlantis Press (2010)
5. Zhu, M., et al.: MapGo: model-assisted policy optimization for goal-oriented tasks. arXiv: 2105.06350 (2021)
6. Legg, S., Hutter, M.: Universal intelligence: a definition of machine intelligence. Minds Mach. **17**(4), 391–444 (2007). https://doi.org/10.1007/s11023-007-9079-x
7. Badia, A.P., et al.: Agent57: outperforming the atari human benchmark. arXiv:2003.13350 (2020)
8. Hutter, M.: Universal Artificial Intelligence: Sequential Decisions Based on Algorithmic Probability. Springer, Heidelberg (2005). https://doi.org/10.1007/b138233

Graph Strategy for Interpretable Visual Question Answering

Christina Sarkisyan[1], Mikhail Savelov[1], Alexey K. Kovalev[2(✉)],
and Aleksandr I. Panov[3]

[1] Moscow Institute of Physics and Technology, Dolgoprudny, Russia
[2] AIRI, Moscow, Russia
kovalev@airi.net
[3] Federal Research Center "Computer Science and Control" of the Russian Academy
of Sciences, Moscow, Russia

Abstract. In the paper, we consider the task of Visual Question Answering, an important task for creating General Artificial Intelligence (AI) systems. We propose an interpretable model called GS-VQA. The main idea behind it is that a complex compositional question could be decomposed into a sequence of simple questions about objects' properties and their relations. We use the Unified estimator to answer questions from that sequence and test the proposed model on CLEVR and THOR-VQA datasets. The GS-VQA model demonstrates results comparable to the state of the art while maintaining transparency and interpretability of the response generation process.

Keywords: Interpretable visual question answering · Graph explanations · Unified estimator

1 Introduction

Visual Question Answering (VQA) is one of the important tasks in the field of Artificial Intelligence (AI), which assumes an answer to a natural language question about a given image. In the most general setting, questions are free-form and open-ended. There are several public benchmarks for the task, including CLEVR [15] and VQA [3]. The performance of VQA algorithms have improved significantly over the years [20,26], but the gap between the best methods and humans [3] still exists.

VQA requires a rich understanding of both the visual content of images and the textual content of questions. The model should be able to detect objects and activities, ground words to the objects on the image, and perform commonsense reasoning. Thus, VQA unifies several research areas, including Computer Vision, Natural Language Processing, and Knowledge Representation & Reasoning, that, together with a well-defined quantitative evaluation metric, make it an AI-complete task [3].

B. Goertzel et al. (Eds.): AGI 2022, LNAI 13539, pp. 86–99, 2023.
https://doi.org/10.1007/978-3-031-19907-3_9

VQA systems have a variety of applications as they improve human-computer interaction by simplifying visual content retrieval. Special applications of VQA include the support for automatic intelligent medical diagnosis [12], the aid to visually impaired people to better perceive the environment [9], help to perform household tasks [16], and unattended surveillance with detection of anomalous situations [30]. Another possible application is smart and customer-tailored commercial advertisements [14].

Considering the potential of their practical use, VQA systems require reliability of the predicted answer [22] and robustness (insensitivity to visual content manipulation [1], answer distribution shift [2], linguistic variations in input questions [28], and others disturbances). This can be achieved by using interpretable models, so humans can trace their decisions and understand the reasoning process [19,24], unlike in unexplainable "black box" approaches.

We introduce a **Graph Strategy for VQA (GS-VQA)** framework for solving the VQA problem in an interpretable way. CS-VQA implements mapping of a question into the graph representation, object detection, and recursive graph traversal in order to connect the objects from the image with the appropriate concepts from the question to retrieve the correct answer. Special trainable modules (*estimators*) check the correspondence of objects and graph nodes by determining the specific objects properties and relations between them. GS-VQA exists in two versions of architecture. The first version, GS-VQA-v1, is based on the ideas of the UnCoRd model proposed in [31] with changes in the graph traversal procedure and estimators' architectures. In the second version, GS-VQA-v2[1] we replaced a set of estimators with a single **Unified estimator (UE)** capable of working with visual and textual features.

The main idea behind GS-VQA is that a complex compositional question can be broken down into a number of simple questions about objects' properties or they relations. These questions are fed into the UE. Depending on its answers, a decision is made based on the conformity of the object to a graph node. Thus, we simplify the initial question by decomposing it into a set of classification problems that are easier to interpret. Moreover, the UE is trained only once to determine all properties and relationships present in the dataset, unlike multiple estimators, each of which is trained separately on different data, which is a laborious task for a large number of objects' attributes.

2   Related Works

Deep Learning Approaches. The general VQA pipeline is to extract a joint representation of images and questions using various neural architectures and then solve a classification problem to find an answer. For example, a simple baseline [36] separately encodes image with a pre-trained convolutional neural network (CNN) and text with a Bag-of-Words model, while more recent approaches [29] learn multimodal representations. Besides being uninterpretable,

---

[1] The code for GS-VQA-v2 model is available on https://github.com/cds-mipt/x-vqa.

deep learning models have a disadvantage in that they rely on biases in the data, e.g. the visual priming bias [35], the language bias [7], or the linguistic bias, when the answer may depend on the linguistic form of the sentence, so the model may provide different answers to the same question if it is paraphrased [25].

Interpretable VQA. Taxonomy for Interpretable Visual Reasoning (IVR) proposed in a recent survey [10] divides the models into four categories according to the way they achieve interpretability. *Visual explanations* [4,8] highlight semantically important regions of an image and are used in attention-based models. *Text explanations* [21] can provide attributes, relationships, or commonsense knowledge, but are mainly oriented at reasoning results. *Symbol explanations* [32] are expressed in programs or logical rules and can trace the intermediate results of each reasoning step, ensuring better model transparency. *Graph explanations* [5,33] use its structure to provide more intuitive information on objects relationships(explicit, e.g. spatial or semantic, or implicit, captured by an attention module), representing either an image or a question. The answering procedure in the approaches that use an image-constructed scene graph is mainly not interpretable. More generally, "an explanation usually relates the feature values of an instance to its model prediction in a humanly understandable way" [24].

Graph Explanations. In this paper, we focus on a graph explanations approach that represents the question text in the form of a graph (*question graph*). It allows us to achieve a deep linguistic understanding of the question and associate it with objects in the image. In [13], the authors proposed dividing the question into several sub-tasks (e.g. *filter*, *count*) corresponding to individual neural modules with the attention mechanism. A sequence of modules application is predicted by a policy and represented as a linearized syntax tree. Noteworthy are the approaches that use the dependency trees obtained with the help of off-the-shelf text parsers [4]. Each node in such trees is represented by a sentence word, and the edges denote syntactic links between words. The model output depends solely on the syntactic structure of the question and does not require additional training set labeling, which is a step toward generalizing the model to different subject areas. There are promising works [23] that use both scene graphs and question graphs and explore the possibility of bringing them together. A remarkable approach with transparent interpretability and without explicit end-to-end training on (question, image) pairs is proposed in [31]. In the UnCoRd model, the VQA problem is reformulated as a directed graph traversal problem, i.e., nodes represent the objects mentioned in the text of the question, and the edges are the relationships between the objects. A key feature of the UnCoRd model is visual estimators, which are either trainable or rule-based models for determining the attributes of image objects. A separate visual estimator is used for each attribute or relation. The problem is that with a large number of attributes, it becomes difficult to train many estimators, think through the architecture, label training data, and invent manual rules for each attribute individually. In GS-VQA-v2, we propose replacing multiple estimators with one trainable Unified estimator that performs similar functions but is trained once to simplify the estimators training process.

3   Task Statement

We formulate the Interpretable Visual Question Answering task as the development of an interpretable model $a = \langle D, S, R, G_q \rangle$ capable of predicting the correct answer to the question given the input image I and the question q. D is a description of an image: $D = Detect(I)$, where $Detect()$ returns a set of regions of interest for objects. S is a set of scene states, where $S_i \in S$ is the set of correspondences of detected objects from D to question tokens, $S_0 = \emptyset$. $R : \{R_1, ..., R_k\}$ denotes a set of rules that transform the current scene state S_t into a new state S_{t+1}: $S_{t+1} = R_i(S_t)$. G_q denotes a strategy based on the question q, which, using the rules R, transforms the initial description S_0 into the final state leading to the answer to the question:

$$G_q(S_0) = R_{i_1} \circ R_{i_2} ... \circ R_{i_m}(S_0) = S_{final}.$$

As a strategy G_q, we consider the depth-first search (DFS) traversal of the question's graph representation. Each node must be assigned to a set of objects that satisfy the characteristics of the node, e.g., a node with the properties "red color" and "cube shape" will be assigned to all the red cubes in the image. The rules R are characterized by sub-procedures called during the graph traversal, which are responsible for applying the appropriate estimator to the scene objects. The estimator is either one or a set of models with trainable weights designed to define queried properties and relationships of scene objects. Given a scene's objects subset $O \in D$, associated with some image regions, and a queried attribute (property or relation name) $attr$, the estimator is to predict attribute value $\hat{v}$ in the candidate answer set V such that:

$$\hat{v} = \operatorname*{argmax}_{v \in V} P_\theta(v|O, attr),$$

where θ denotes the weights of the estimator. The estimator's response determines what the next scene state S_i will be, i.e., how the rule will affect the current state and which scene objects satisfy the requirements of the rule. Maximizing the estimator's accuracy will lead us to the correct application of the rules and, therefore, the correct construction of a strategy for answering the question q. Thus, the model provides not only an answer to the question but also an interpretable explanation that illustrates the relationship of scene objects with objects mentioned in the question's text. In addition, the obtained history of scene states $[S_0, S_1, ..., S_{final}]$ allows us to trace the reasoning process.

4   GS-VQA Model Overview

A schematic illustration of the GS-VQA model is shown in Fig. 1. The question q is fed into the *Question-to-graph model*, while the image I is processed by the *Object detector*. The *Answering procedure* implements the strategy G_q. Having received a graph representation and a set of objects D as input, it performs the graph traversal with a successive call of the necessary estimators to check if the scene object matches the node's characteristics. The final state S_{final} corresponds to a graph, where all nodes are assigned to objects, from which the information required in the question can be extracted by special sub-procedures built into Answering procedure.

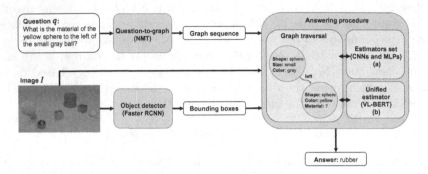

Fig. 1. An architecture of the GS-VQA model. In GS-VQA-v1 a set of estimators is used (a), while in GS-VQA-v2 it is replaced by the Unified estimator (b).

Question-to-Graph Model. A Question-to-graph model is used to translate the initial question text into graph representation. As a Question-to-graph model, we chose a seq-to-seq model from the OpenNMT library in PyTorch [17]. The model consists of eight encoders and eight decoders of the transformer architecture. The training set consists of pairs of the questions' texts and their graph representations serialized to sequences.

Object Detector. We used the Faster R-CNN [27] model as an object detector, which determines object classes and bounding box coordinates. Unlike the multiclass object detector in the original UnCoRd implementation, we predict only one abstract class "object to which all the image objects are assigned. The object class is one of the properties that have to be determined using a suitable estimator.

Answering Procedure. The answering procedure is a modified DFS graph traversal. The graph is traversed only from parent nodes to child nodes, starting with the first node of the Question-to-graph model output sequence. For each node, two sets are formed: a set of *current objects*—scene objects matching node properties—and a set of *candidate objects* that are in an edge-defined relationship with the current objects. Checking properties and relationships is done by calling the required estimator within a procedure. At each step of the algorithm, an intermediate answer is formed, depending on the success or failure of the property or relation check (*yes* or *no*). The final answer is extracted from the deepest node of the graph. The constructed graph with the scene objects assigned to the nodes after the answering procedure is shown in Fig. 2. The algorithm allows answering all types of questions in CLEVR. To check the correctness of the answering procedure independently of the performance of other models, the outputs of Question-to-graph and Computer Vision components were temporarily replaced with their ground truth representations. The algorithm was tested on 10,000 questions of the CLEVR validation set, with the resulting accuracy of 100%. The answering procedure pseudocode can be found in Appendix A.

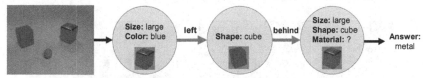

Fig. 2. Question graph visualization with objects assigned to nodes, built by the question answering procedure.

Estimators. In GS-VQA-v1, we have trained eight separate estimators for the CLEVR dataset to predict object properties and relations. We used estimators with three convolutional and three fully connected layers with ReLU activation to predict an object's color, material, and shape. We used multilayer perceptrons to determine the size and spatial relationships. The input for the size estimator is a bounding box corresponding to the given object. For spatial relations estimators, bounding boxes of queried objects are used as input.

In GS-VQA-v2, we consider VL-BERT [29] as a Unified estimator. VL-BERT works with textual and visual data and can be adapted for different visual-linguistic tasks by modifying input and output formats. The UE predicts answers for simple questions about properties and relations, so we modified VL-BERT to receive an input in the form of the name of a queried property (e.g., *material*) or a relation (e.g., *left*). VL-BERT also receives the entire image and the regions of interest specified by objects' bounding boxes. Depending on whether we need to know a property or a relation, the number of bounding boxes is equal to one or two, respectively. The VL-BERT possible answers includes all properties values from the dataset and the answers *yes* and *no* for the case when we want to confirm or deny the relationship between objects. Thus, VL-BERT can be used for both properties and relationships.

5 Experiments

We validate the proposed model on the CLEVR [15] and THOR-VQA datasets.

CLEVR. CLEVR [15] is a synthetic VQA dataset that contains images of 3D-rendered objects and compositional questions of five types: Exist (E), Count (C), Compare Integer (CI), Query Attribute (QA), and Compare Attribute (CA). Each image in CLEVR is provided with a detailed description of the objects in the scene, their position in space, and the spatial relations between the objects. The question can be generated from a functional program that shows which reasoning steps should lead to the answer. A scene object can be characterized by its shape, material, color, and size. There are five types of relations between objects that characterize the relative position in space in four directions—right, left, front, and behind—and the equality/inequality of objects' properties (e.g. *same color*). The example of image and question pair is shown in Fig. 3a.

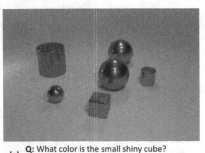

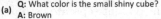

(a) Q: What color is the small shiny cube?
A: Brown

(b) Q:Whati s on a plate?
A: Egg

Fig. 3. Image-question pair examples from CLEVR (a) and THOR-VQA (b) datasets.

Experiments and Results on CLEVR. We first trained the Question-to-graph model on a set of pairs of questions and their graph representations, generated from the functional programs of CLEVR, with the obtained accuracy of 99.97%. The training set of bounding boxes for the Object detector was formed using scene descriptions from CLEVR[2], the mAP is 83%. For GS-VQA-v1, we trained the set of estimators described in Sect. 4. The labeling of the training sets was also carried out using scene descriptions from CLEVR; the size of training set for each estimator was 60,000 training samples. For each estimator we got fairly high accuracy values around 98%–99%. All of the trained models were built into the answering procedure and tested on the CLEVR validation set, with the overall accuracy of 95.4%. See Table 1.

To train VL-BERT for GS-VQA-v2, a training set was collected from scene descriptions and images. The training set was balanced so that each question and answer occurred in it approximately the same number of times. VL-BERT was trained on 90,000 samples and validated on a set of size 20,000. The obtained accuracy for VL-BERT is 99.84%. The entire GS-VQA-v2 model accuracy values for each type of CLEVR questions are shown in Table 1.

The results show that GS-VQA-v2 outperforms GS-VQA-v1. However, it does not exceed the UnCoRd result, which is 99.74%. This may be due to the insufficiently good mAP of the Object detector, because as an Object detector, we chose Faster-RCNN instead of Mask-RCNN [11] used in UnCoRd. After

---

[2] https://github.com/larchen/clevr-vqa/blob/master/bounding_box.py.

Table 1. Accuracy on the CLEVR dataset for different question types. *Results for GS-VQA-v1 are given on the CLEVR validation set.

Model	E	C	CA	CI	QA	Overall
UnCoRd [31]	99.89	99.54	99.80	99.91	99.74	99.74
NS-VQA [34]	99.9	99.7	99.8	99.9	99.8	99.8
GS-VQA-v1*	97.58	92.82	96.23	96.8	95.49	95.4
GS-VQA-v2	99.18	95.47	99.18	97.76	99.14	98.2

analyzing the situations in which our model makes mistakes, we can conclude that the model most often makes mistakes when the object in the image is not completely visible: for example, it is overlapped by another object, so an object detection error occurs. Also in UnCoRd, some estimators use hand-crafted rules rather than learning ones, which increases the quality but complicates their construction.

We also added an NS-VQA model [34] to a comparison, which processes the question and the image separately and achieves the best results on CLEVR. The main feature of this model is that it first parses the image into a scene description in the form of a table listing all objects with their properties. After that, the question is translated into a deterministic sequence of executable procedures (table filtering) and applied to the scene description. This approach allows us to track the steps performed by the system, but does not provide binding specific scene objects to question tokens, as shown in Fig. 2.

THOR-VQA. The THOR Visual Question Answering dataset (THOR-VQA) was generated in AI2-THOR [18], a near photo-realistic 3D environment, using its Python API. The generation procedure is based on on IQUAD [6]; 25 kitchen scenes and 36 types of objects in them were used. On average, about 1,000 questions per room were generated for each of eight types (Existence, Logical, Counting, Preposition, Material, Compare Material, Compare Size, Compare Distance). In experiments, we used only three types of questions (Existence, Preposition, Material) since those questions can be answered using a single image. All question templates and counts can be found in Appendix B and Appendix C, respectively. The generation process is a random search of seeds for the scenes. The procedure of generating a question for a given scene number and question type is shown in Fig. 4. We use a random number generator (RNG) to sample object classes for the question and a scene seed. The question is initialized using object classes and a given question type. The episode initialization consists of three stages: choosing objects, spawning the objects in the scene, and removing 25% of the objects to even out the distribution. If the question is valid, i.e., objects for answering the question are present in the scene and can be reached by the agent, it is saved. If not, the new episode is initialized, and the validation procedure is repeated. For Existence, Logical, and Counting types, all possible answers are generated for the sampled objects to keep the answers evenly distributed. An example from THOR-VQA is shown in Fig. 3b.

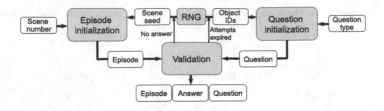

Fig. 4. Procedure of a question generation.

Experiments and Results on THOR-VQA. We followed the same training scheme for the THOR-VQA dataset as for CLEVR. For GS-VQA-v2, the Question-to-graph model, the Object detector, and the VL-BERT estimator were first pretrained on data generated from THOR-QAD. We followed the scheme for the CLEVR dataset to train the GS-VQA-v2 model on the THOR-VQA dataset. The Question-to-graph model achieved 100.0% accuracy on validation, which can be explained by a small number of question templates: nine in total. The Faster R-CNN detector achieved mAP of 86.2. The Unified estimator achieved 95.8 accuracy score on validation. The results are shown in Table 2.

Table 2. Accuracy on the THOR-VQA dataset for different question types.

Model	Existence	Preposition	Material
CNN-BoW	66.8	41.7	**96.4**
GS-VQA-v2	**90.8**	**82.7**	94.2

We used CNN-BoW model from [36] as a baseline for THOR-VQA. The baseline model outperforms GS-VQA-v2 on material questions due to the strong language bias, i.e., the model learns the mapping from the object type to the answer. The GS-VQA model archives the close score on material questions and drastically improves results on other question types. We assume that a better detector would further boost the performance.

6   Conclusion

In this paper, we propose the GS-VQA model for interpretable VQA. As has been mentioned, GS-VQA decomposes a complex compositional question into a sequence of simple questions. We used a graph strategy for decomposition and apply Unified estimator for resulting questions. The Unified estimator simplified the model training procedure since it maintained a single format for input and output data, regardless of the attribute type, and is trained for all attributes. As a result, the model's responses remained fully interpretable due to the fixed answering procedure and simple questions. We tested the proposed model on the

CLEVR dataset and on a collected THOR-VQA dataset. Experiments showed that the model performed comparably to the existing state-of-the-art methods. The problem of adapting GS-VQA to real-life VQA datasets is considered as further research.

Acknowledgments. This work was supported by the Ministry of Science and Higher Education of the Russian Federation under Project 075-15-2020-799.

A   Answering Procedure Algorithm

Algorithm A.1 getAnswer procedure.

Require: The graph node, $Node$;
    The scene objects set (object detection results), $objects$;
    The objects set obtained from the previous node, $candidate\_objects$;
    The dictionary storing the labels of visited nodes and the objects sets corresponding to them, $visited\_nodes$;
Ensure: $answer$;
1: $cur\_objects = find\_matching\_objects(Node, candidate\_objects)$;
2: **if** $cur\_objects \neq \varnothing$ **then**
3:    $answer = yes$;
4: **else**
5:    $answer = no$;
6: $visited\_nodes[Node] := cur\_objects$;
7: **if** $exist(child\_nodes) \wedge cur\_objects \neq \varnothing$ **then**
8:    **for** $child\_node$ in $unvisited\_child\_nodes$ **do**
9:       $related\_objects := find\_related\_objects(Node, candidate\_objects, objects)$;
10:      $answer = getAnswer(child\_node, objects, related\_objects, visited\_nodes)$;
11: **else if** $exist(parent\_nodes) \wedge cur\_objects \neq \varnothing$ **then**
12:    **for** $parent\_node$ in $unvisited\_parent\_nodes$ **do**
13:       **for** cur_obj in $cur\_objects$ **do**
14:         $parent\_objects = find\_parent\_objects(parent\_node, cur\_obj, objects)$;
15:         **if** $parent\_objects = \varnothing$ **then**
16:            $cur\_objects := cur\_objects - cur\_obj$;
17:    $visited\_nodes[Node] = cur\_objects$;
18:    **if** $cur\_objects = \varnothing$ **then**
19:       $answer = no$;
20: **else**
21:    **for** $node$ in $unvisited\_nodes$ **do**
22:       $valid\_objects := objects$;
23:       $answer = getAnswer(node, objects, valid\_objects, visited\_nodes)$;
24:       $break$;
25: **if** $exist(required\_property) \wedge cur\_objects \neq \varnothing$ **then**
26:    $answer = get\_property(Node, cur\_objects, required\_property)$;
27: **return** $answer$

B   THOR-VQA Question Templates

Table 3. Templates for THOR-VQA questions.

Question type	Templates
Existence	Is there OBJ in the room?
	Please tell me if there is OBJ somewhere in the room
	Is there OBJ somewhere in the room?
	Is there OBJ somewhere nearby?
	I think OBJ is in the room. Is that correct?
	Do we have any OBJs?
Logical	Is there OBJ1 and/or OBJ2 in the room?
	Please tell me if there is OBJ1 and/or OBJ2 somewhere in the room
	Is there OBJ1 and/or OBJ2 somewhere in the room?
	Is there OBJ1 and/or OBJ2 somewhere nearby?
	I think OBJ1 and/or OBJ2 is in the room. Is that correct?
Counting	How many OBJs are there in the room?
	There are between 0 and 3 OBJs in the room. How many are there?
	Please tell me how many OBJs there are somewhere in the room?
	Please tell me how many OBJs are around here?
	Count the number of OBJs in this room
Preposition	What is on/in OBJ ?
	There is something on/in OBJ. What is it?
Material	There is OBJ somewhere in the room. What material is it made of?
	What material is the OBJ in the room made of?
Compare material	Does OBJ1 share same material as OBJ2 in the room?
	There is OBJ1 and a OBJ2 in the room. Are they made of the same material?
Compare size	Is OBJ1 smaller than OBJ2 in the room?
	Is OBJ2 bigger than OBJ1 in the room?
Compare distance	Is OBJ1 closer to OBJ2 than OBJ3 in the room?
	Is OBJ3 farther from OBJ2 than OBJ1 in the room?

C THOR-VQA Question Counts

Table 4. Counts for THOR-VQA questions.

Question type	Counts			
	Train	val/seen	val/unseen	total
Existence	12990	5251	7442	25683
Logical	31951	4584	6015	42550
Counting	34257	4403	7226	45886
Preposition	39095	1609	6083	46787
Material	16650	5431	5264	27345
Compare material	23754	3174	4163	31091
Compare size	21341	720	3491	25552
Compare distance	16742	3822	4031	24595

References

1. Agarwal, V., Shetty, R., Fritz, M.: Towards causal VQA: revealing and reducing spurious correlations by invariant and covariant semantic editing. In: CVPR (2020)
2. Agrawal, A., Batra, D., Parikh, D., Kembhavi, A.: Don't just assume; look and answer: overcoming priors for visual question answering. In: CVPR (2017)
3. Antol, S., et al.: VQA: visual question answering. In: CVPR (2015)
4. Cao, Q., Liang, X., Li, B., Lin, L.: Interpretable visual question answering by reasoning on dependency trees. IEEE Trans.Pattern Anal. Mach. Intell. **43**(3), 887–901 (2019)
5. Damodaran, V., et al.: Understanding the role of scene graphs in visual question answering. arXiv:2101.05479 (2021)
6. Gordon, D., Kembhavi, A., Rastegari, M., Redmon, J., Fox, D., Farhadi, A.: IQA: visual question answering in interactive environments. In: CVPR (2018)
7. Goyal, Y., Khot, T., Summers-Stay, D., Batra, D., Parikh, D.: Making the V in VQA matter: elevating the role of image understanding in Visual Question Answering. In: CVPR (2017)
8. Guo, W., Zhang, Y., Yang, J., Yuan, X.: Re-attention for visual question answering. IEEE Trans. Image Process. **30**, 6730–6743 (2021)
9. Gurari, D., et al.: Vizwiz grand challenge: Answering visual questions from blind people. In: CVPR (2018)
10. He, F., Wang, Y., Miao, X., Sun, X.: Interpretable visual reasoning: a survey. Image Vis. Comput. **112**, 104194 (2021)
11. He, K., Gkioxari, G., Dollár, P., Girshick, R.: Mask R-CNN. In: ICCV (2017)
12. He, X., Zhang, Y., Mou, L., Xing, E., Xie, P.: PathVQA: 30000+ questions for medical visual question answering. arXiv:2003.10286 (2020)
13. Hu, R., Andreas, J., Rohrbach, M., Darrell, T., Saenko, K.: Learning to reason: end-to-end module networks for visual question answering. In: ICCV (2017)

14. Hussain, Z., et al.: Automatic understanding of image and video advertisements. In: CVPR (2017)
15. Johnson, J., Hariharan, B., Van Der Maaten, L., Fei-Fei, L., Lawrence Zitnick, C., Girshick, R.: CLEVR: a diagnostic dataset for compositional language and elementary visual reasoning. In: CVPR (2017)
16. Kirilenko, D.E., Kovalev, A.K., Osipov, E., Panov, A.I.: Question answering for visual navigation in human-centered environments. In: Batyrshin, I., Gelbukh, A., Sidorov, G. (eds.) MICAI 2021. LNCS (LNAI), vol. 13068, pp. 31–45. Springer, Cham (2021). https://doi.org/10.1007/978-3-030-89820-5_3
17. Klein, G., Kim, Y., Deng, Y., Senellart, J., Rush, A.: OpenNMT: open-source toolkit for neural machine translation. In: ACL (2017)
18. Kolve, E., et al.: Ai2-THOR: an interactive 3D environment for visual AI. arXiv:1712.05474 (2017)
19. Kovalev, A.K., Shaban, M., Chuganskaya, A.A., Panov, A.I.: Applying vector symbolic architecture and semiotic approach to visual dialog. In: Sanjurjo González, H., Pastor López, I., García Bringas, P., Quintián, H., Corchado, E. (eds.) HAIS 2021. LNCS (LNAI), vol. 12886, pp. 243–255. Springer, Cham (2021). https://doi.org/10.1007/978-3-030-86271-8_21
20. Kovalev, A.K., Shaban, M., Osipov, E., Panov, A.I.: Vector semiotic model for visual question answering. Cogn. Syst. Res. **71**, 52–63 (2022)
21. Li, Q., Fu, J., Yu, D., Mei, T., Luo, J.: Tell-and-answer: towards explainable visual question answering using attributes and captions. arXiv:1801.09041 (2018)
22. Lin, Z., et al.: Medical visual question answering: a survey. arXiv:2111.10056
23. Lou, C., Han, W., Lin, Y., Zheng, Z.: Unsupervised vision-language parsing: Seamlessly bridging visual scene graphs with language structures via dependency relationships. arXiv:2203.14260 (2022)
24. Molnar, C.: Interpretable Machine Learning (2022)
25. Niu, Y., Tang, K., Zhang, H., Lu, Z., Hua, X.S., Wen, J.R.: Counterfactual vqa: A cause-effect look at language bias. In: CVPR (2021)
26. Podtikhov, A., Shaban, M., Kovalev, A.K., Panov, A.I.: Error analysis for visual question answering. In: Kryzhanovsky, B., Dunin-Barkowski, W., Redko, V., Tiumentsev, Y. (eds.) NEUROINFORMATICS 2020. SCI, vol. 925, pp. 283–292. Springer, Cham (2021). https://doi.org/10.1007/978-3-030-60577-3_34
27. Ren, S., He, K., Girshick, R., Sun, J.: Faster R-CNN: towards real-time object detection with region proposal networks. In: NIPS (2015)
28. Shah, M., Chen, X., Rohrbach, M., Parikh, D.: Cycle-consistency for robust visual question answering. In: CVPR (2019)
29. Su, W., Zhu, X., Cao, Y., Li, B., Lu, L., Wei, F., Dai, J.: Vl-BERT: pre-training of generic visual-linguistic representations. arXiv:1908.08530 (2019)
30. Toor, A.S., Wechsler, H., Nappi, M.: Biometric surveillance using visual question answering. Pattern Recogn. Lett. **126**, 111–118 (2019)
31. Vatashsky, B.Z., Ullman, S.: VQA with no questions-answers training. In: CVPR (2020)
32. Vedantam, R., Desai, K., Lee, S., Rohrbach, M., Batra, D., Parikh, D.: Probabilistic neural symbolic models for interpretable visual question answering. In: ICML (2019)
33. Xiong, P., You, Q., Yu, P., Liu, Z., Wu, Y.: Sa-VQA: structured alignment of visual and semantic representations for visual question answering. arXiv:2201.10654 (2022)

34. Yi, K., Wu, J., Gan, C., Torralba, A., Kohli, P., Tenenbaum, J.B.: Neural-symbolic VQA: disentangling reasoning from vision and language understanding. In: NIPS (2018)
35. Zhang, P., Goyal, Y., Summers-Stay, D., Batra, D., Parikh, D.: Yin and Yang: balancing and answering binary visual questions. In: CVPR (2016)
36. Zhou, B., Tian, Y., Sukhbaatar, S., Szlam, A., Fergus, R.: Simple baseline for visual question answering. arXiv:1512.02167 (2015)

Analogical Problem Solving in the Causal Cognitive Architecture

Howard Schneider(✉) ⓘ

Sheppard Clinic North, Vaughan, ON, Canada
hschneidermd@alum.mit.edu

Abstract. The Causal Cognitive Architecture 3 is a biologically inspired cognitive architecture based heavily on navigation maps—arrays holding spatial navigation information about the external environment but also coopted by the architecture for much of its data storage and representational requirements. Sensory information is stored in navigation maps and operated on in the architecture. Enhancement of feedback pathways in the architecture allows the intermediate results of operations on navigation maps to be re-processed in the next operating cycle and has been shown to allow the architecture to generate causal behavior. Here it is shown that this also can readily allow the emergence of analogical processing as a core mechanism in the architecture. If a navigation map cannot be processed to yield an actionable output, then it is compared to a similar navigation map and automatically an analogical result is produced which the architecture can possibly use as an output. Analogical processing as a core mechanism may be advantageous in creating more capable artificial general intelligence systems.

Keywords: Analogies · Causality · Cognitive architecture · Artificial general intelligence

1 Introduction

Analogies may lie at the heart of human cognition [1]. Analogical problem solving allows us to solve day to day problems, make sense of novel situations and to plan behavior, and thus it is of relevance to creating a working artificial general intelligence (AGI). We describe here how in the development of a brain-inspired cognitive architecture, analogical reasoning appears to readily emerge, not as some specialized skill (e.g., to be used when performing human intelligence tests) but rather as a ubiquitous, core mechanism of cognition of the architecture.

The Causal Cognitive Architecture 3 (CCA3) is a biologically inspired cognitive architecture loosely inspired by the mammalian brain, in particular the mammalian hippocampus, and based heavily on navigation maps [2, 3]. The navigation maps in the simulated architecture [3] are arbitrarily limited size $6 \times 6 \times 6$ arrays holding spatial navigation information about the external environment but also coopted by the architecture for much of its data storage and representational requirements, as well as for the various small algorithms, termed "primitives" it uses.

B. Goertzel et al. (Eds.): AGI 2022, LNAI 13539, pp. 100–112, 2023.
https://doi.org/10.1007/978-3-031-19907-3_10

The key components of the CCA3 are shown in Fig. 1. The architecture takes as an input the set of sensory features streaming in from different perceptual sensors. Objects detected in this stream of sensory features are segmented, and visual, auditory, and other sensory features of each segmented object are spatially mapped onto navigation maps dedicated to one sensory modality. These single-sensory navigation maps are then mapped onto a best matching multi-sensory navigation map taken from the Causal Memory Module and operated on in the Navigation Module. Instinctive and learned primitives, essentially small rules or productions, themselves using modified navigation maps, are then applied onto the navigation map in the Navigation Module, producing a signal to the Output Vector Association Module and then to the external embodiment.

There are extensive feedback pathways throughout the architecture—states of a downstream module can influence the recognition and processing of more upstream sensory inputs. In the Causal Cognitive Architecture 3, the feedback pathways between the Navigation Module/Object Segmentation Gateway Module and the Input Sensory Vectors Association Modules are enhanced allowing intermediate results from the Navigation Module to be stored in the Input Sensory Vectors Association Modules. If so, in the next cognitive cycle (i.e., cycles of passing input sensory vectors into and through the architecture), these intermediate results will automatically be considered as the input sensory information and propagated to the Navigation Module and operated on again. By feeding back and re-operating on the intermediate results, the Causal Cognitive Architecture is able to formulate and explore possible cause and effect of actions, i.e., generate causal behavior [3].

Below we show that a consequence of this enhancement in feedback processing of the intermediate results of the architecture is not only the ability to generate causal (or pseudo-causal) behavior [3] but that the architecture now readily uses analogical reasoning as a central and core mechanism of action.

2   Functioning of the Causal Cognitive Architecture 3 (CCA3)

We will work through the operation of the Causal Cognitive Architecture 3 (CCA3) shown in an overview in Fig. 1. A series of equations presented below describes the operation of the key modules in Fig. 1. These equations effectively represent a pseudocode for the architecture. Named procedures in some equations represent blocks of pseudocode. For example, `Input_Sens_Vect_Shaping_Modules.normalize()` in (10) represents the code for transforming arrays of input sensory data into arrays with the same dimensions used by the other modules of the architecture. Additional details about specific equations/pseudocode can be found in reference Schneider [3].

2.1   Input Sensory Vectors Shaping Modules

Inputs for any sense modality are sensed (or simulated) as a 2D or 3D spatial array of inputs, which vary with time (2, 4, 6). We arbitrary assume visual, auditory, and olfactory inputs in our current model, but sensory modalities, of course, can be expanded. A vector $s(t)$ holds the arrays representing the sensory inputs $S_{\sigma,t}$ of different sensory systems (9).

It is transformed into a normalized $s'(t)$ (10). Any input sensory system inputs $S'_{\sigma,t}$ are now in an array of dimensions (m, n, o) (11).

$$S_1 \in R^{m\_1 \times n\_1 \times o\_1} \tag{1}$$

$$S_{1,t} := \text{visual\_inputs}(t) \tag{2}$$

$$S_2 \in R^{m\_2 \times n\_2 \times o\_2} \tag{3}$$

$$S_{2,t} := \text{auditory\_inputs}(t) \tag{4}$$

$$S_3 \in R^{m\_3 \times n\_3 \times o\_3} \tag{5}$$

$$S_{3,t} := \text{olfactory\_inputs}(t) \tag{6}$$

$$\sigma := \text{sensory system identification code} \in N \tag{7}$$

$$n\_\sigma := \text{total number of sensory systems} \in N \tag{8}$$

$$s(t) = [\mathbf{S}_{1,t}, \mathbf{S}_{2,t}, \mathbf{S}_{3,t}, ..., \mathbf{S}_{n\_\sigma,t}] \tag{9}$$

$$s'(t) = \texttt{Input\_Sens\_Vect\_Shaping\_Modules.normalize}(s(t)) = [\mathbf{S'}_{1,t}, \mathbf{S'}_{2,t}, ..., \mathbf{S'}_{n\_\sigma,t}] \tag{10}$$

$$\therefore \mathbf{S'}_{\sigma,t} \in R^{m \times n \times o} \tag{11}$$

2.2 Input Sensory Vectors Associations Modules

There is a separate Input Sensory Vectors Association Module for each sensory modality. A "local" navigation map refers to a navigation map dedicated to one sensory modality. The first operation on an array $\mathbf{S'}_{\sigma,t}$ is to match it against all the existing local navigation maps **LNM** in the Input Sensory Vectors Association Module σ. For example, the visual processed inputs $\mathbf{S'}_{1,t}$ are matched against $\textbf{\textit{all\_maps}}_{1,t}$ which represents all the local navigation maps in the visual Input Sensory Vectors Association Module (15, 16, 17). The next operation is to update the best-matched local navigation map $\textbf{LNM}_{(\sigma, \Upsilon,t)}$ with the actual sensory input $\mathbf{S'}_{\sigma,t}$ (20, 21). The best-matching and updated local navigation maps $\textbf{LNM}'_{(\sigma, \Upsilon, t)}$ of all the different sensory systems of the CCA3 are then represented in vector $\textit{lnm}_t$ (22).

$$\textbf{mapno} := \text{map identification code} \in N \tag{12}$$

$$\theta := \text{total number of local navigation maps in a sensory system } \sigma \in N \tag{13}$$

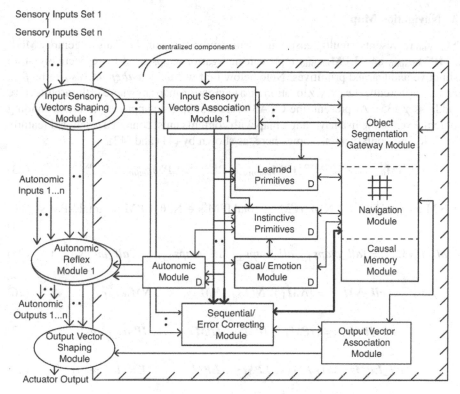

Fig. 1. Overview of the Causal Cognitive Architecture 3 (CCA3)

$$\mathbf{LNM}_{(\sigma,\mathbf{mapno})}, \mathbf{WNM}'_t \in \mathbf{R}^{\text{mxnxo}} \tag{14}$$

$$\mathbf{all\_maps}_{\sigma,t} = [\mathbf{LNM}_{(\sigma,1,t)}, \mathbf{LNM}_{(\sigma,2,t)}, \mathit{LNM}_{(\sigma,3,t)}, \ldots, \mathbf{LNM}_{(\sigma,\theta,t)}] \tag{15}$$

$$\Upsilon := \mathbf{mapno} \text{ of best matching map in a given set of navigation maps} \in \mathbf{mapno} \tag{16}$$

$$\mathbf{LNM}_{(\sigma,\Upsilon,t)} = \texttt{Input\_Assocn\_Module}_\sigma.\texttt{match\_best\_local\_navmap(} \mathbf{S'}_{\sigma,t}, \mathbf{WNM}'_{t-1}) \tag{17}$$

$$\mathbf{h} = \text{number of differences allowed to be copied onto existing map} \in \mathbf{R} \tag{18}$$

$$\mathbf{new\_map} := \mathbf{mapno} \text{ of new local navmap added to sensory system } \sigma \in \mathbf{mapno} \tag{19}$$

$$|\text{differences}(\mathbf{S'}_{\sigma,t}, \mathbf{LNM}_{(\sigma,\Upsilon,t)})| \le \mathbf{h}, \Rightarrow \mathbf{LNM}'_{(\sigma,\Upsilon,t)} = \mathbf{LNM}_{(\sigma,\Upsilon,t)} \cup \mathbf{S'}_{\sigma,t} \tag{20}$$

$$|\text{differences}(\mathbf{S'}_{\sigma,t}, \mathbf{LNM}_{(\sigma,\Upsilon,t)})| > \mathbf{h}, \Rightarrow \mathbf{LNM}'_{(\sigma,\Upsilon,t)} = \mathbf{LNM}_{(\sigma,\mathbf{new\_map},t)} \cup \mathbf{S'}_{\sigma,t} \tag{21}$$

$$\mathit{lnm}_t = [\mathbf{LNM}'_{(1,\Upsilon,t)}, \mathbf{LNM}'_{(2,\Upsilon,t)}, \mathbf{LNM}'_{(3,\Upsilon,t)}, \ldots, \mathbf{LNM}'_{(n\_\sigma,\Upsilon,t)}] \tag{22}$$

2.3 Navigation Maps

NM_{mapno} represents a multi-sensory navigation map stored in the Causal Memory Module. IPM_{mapno} and LPM_{mapno} represent navigation maps used to respectively store instinctive and learned primitives. Note below that we define *cubefeatures$_\chi$* to be *feature* values in a cube (i.e., x, y, z location) in a navigation map anywhere in the architecture at address χ (35). At present, the CCA3 takes a simplistic approach to the grounding problem: every cube in a navigation map with contents must contain a grounded feature, or else at least contain a link somewhere, as shown by (41) and (42).

$$NM_{mapno} \in R^{mxnxo}, IPM_{mapno} \in R^{mxnxo}, LPM_{mapno} \in R^{mxnxo} \tag{23}$$

$$\theta\_NM := total\ NM's \in N,\ \theta\_IPM := total\ IPM's \in N,\ \theta\_LPM := total\ LPM's \in N \tag{24}$$

$$all\_LNMs_t := [all\_maps_{1,t}, all\_maps_{2,t}, all\_maps_{3,t}, \ldots, all\_maps_{n\_\sigma,t}] \tag{25}$$

$$all\_NMs_t := [NM_{1,t}, NM_{2,t}, NM_{3,t}, \ldots, NM_{\theta\_NM,t}] \tag{26}$$

$$all\_IPMs_t := [IPM_{1,t}, IPM_{2,t}, IPM_{3,t}, \ldots, IPM_{\theta\_IPM,t}] \tag{27}$$

$$all\_LPMs_t := [LPM_{1,t}, LPM_{2,t}, LPM_{3,t}, \ldots, LPM_{\theta\_LPM,t}] \tag{28}$$

$$all\_navmaps_t := [all\_LNMs_t, all\_NMs_t, all\_IPMs_t, all\_LPMs_t] \tag{29}$$

$$modcode := module\ identification\ code \in N \tag{30}$$

$$mapcode := [modcode, mapno] \tag{31}$$

$$\chi := [mapcode, x, y, z] \tag{32}$$

$$feature \in R, action \in R \tag{33}$$

$$\Phi\_feature := last\ feature\ contained\ by\ a\ cube,\ \Phi\_action := last\ action\ contained\ by\ a\ cube,$$
$$\Phi\_\chi := last\ \chi\ (i.e.,\ address\ to\ link\ to)contained\ by\ a\ cube \tag{34}$$

$$cubefeatures_{\chi,t} := [feature_{1,t}, feature_{2,t}, feature_{3,t}, \ldots, feature_{\Phi\_feature,t}] \tag{35}$$

$$cubeactions_{\chi,t} := [action_{1,t}, action_{2,t}, action_{3,t}, \ldots, action_{\Phi\_action,t}] \tag{36}$$

$$linkaddresses_{\chi,t} := [\chi_{1,t}, \chi_{2,t}, \chi_{3,t}, \ldots, \chi_{\Phi\_\chi,t}] \tag{37}$$

$$cubevalues_{\chi,t} := [cubefeatures_{\chi,t}, cubeactions_{\chi,t}, linkaddresses_{\chi,t}] \qquad (38)$$

$$cubevalues_{\chi,t} = all\_navmaps_{\chi,t} \qquad (39)$$

$$linkaddresses_{\chi,t} = link(\chi, t) \qquad (40)$$

$$grounded\_feature := \forall_{feature} : feature \in all\_LNMs_{\chi} \qquad (41)$$

$$\forall_{\chi,t} : all\_navmaps_{\chi,t} = grounded\_feature \text{ OR } link(all\_navmaps_{\chi,t}) \neq [\,] \\ \text{OR } all\_navmaps_{\chi,t} = [\,] \qquad (42)$$

2.4 Sequential/Error Correcting Module

Binding temporal features as spatial features in the navigation maps is described in more detail in [3] via directing the sensory inputs in a parallel path through the Sequential/Error Correcting Module, as depicted in Fig. 1. For example, Vector Navigation Map **VNM** binds the *visual_motion(t)* in similar navigation map coordinates as the other sensory inputs (49). The navigation map **VNM″**$_t$ containing the visual motion and audio changes (50), and navigation map **AVNM**$_t$ containing processed sound patterns (51), are then sent to the Object Segmentation Gateway Module/Navigation Module. Computation of **VSNM′** (55) requires **VSNM** which is discussed in the next module.

$$s'\_series(t) = [s'(t-3), s'(t-2), s'(t-1), s'(t)] \qquad (43)$$

$$visual\_series(t) = \texttt{SeqError\_Correct\_Mod.visual\_inputs}(\, s'\_series(t)\,) \qquad (44)$$

$$auditory\_series(t) = \texttt{SeqError\_Correct\_Mod.auditory\_inputs}(\, s'\_series(t)\,) \qquad (45)$$

$$visual\_motion(t) = \texttt{SeqError\_Correct\_Mod.visual\_match}(\, visual\_series(t)\,) \qquad (46)$$

$$auditory\_motion(t) = \texttt{SeqError\_Correct\_Mod.auditory\_match}(\, auditory\_series(t)\,) \qquad (47)$$

$$\textbf{VNM} \in \text{R}^{mxnxo}, \textbf{AVNM} \in \text{R}^{mxnxo} \qquad (48)$$

$$\textbf{VNM}'_t = \textbf{VNM}_t \cup visual\_motion(t) \qquad (49)$$

$$\textbf{VNM}''_t = \textbf{VNM}'_t \cup auditory\_motion(t) \qquad (50)$$

$$\textbf{AVNM}_t = \texttt{SeqError\_Correct\_Mod.auditory\_match\_process}(\, auditory\_series(t)\,) \qquad (51)$$

$$\text{VSNM} \in \text{R}^{mxnxo} \tag{52}$$

$$visual\_segment\_series(t) = [\text{VSNM}_{t-3}, \text{VSNM}_{t-2}, \text{VSNM}_{t-1}, \text{and VSNM}_t] \tag{53}$$

$$visseg\_motion(t) = \texttt{SeqError\_Correct\_Mod.visual\_match}(visual\_segment\_series(t)) \tag{54}$$

$$\text{VSNM}'_t = \text{VSNM}_t \cup visseg\_motion(t) \tag{55}$$

2.5 Object Segmentation Gateway Module

The Object Segmentation Gateway Module attempts to segment a sensory scene into objects of interest. In theory all sensory modalities can be segmented, but at present, only the visual local sensory map $\text{LNM}'_{(1, \Upsilon, t)}$ is segmented (56–60). **WNM** is the "working navigation map" which is held in the Navigation Module and upon which operations of the instinctive and learned primitives can be applied. $\text{VSNM}_t(60)$ is transformed into VSNM'_t (52–55) and then contains visual sensory information segmented into different objects as well as binding information about the motion for each of these segments. **CONTEXT** is a contextual value which presently is assigned to the value of the previous **WNM**.

$$\text{LNM}'_{(1, \Upsilon, t)} = lnm_t[0] \tag{56}$$

$$\text{CONTEXT} := \in \text{R}^{mxnxo} \tag{57}$$

$$\text{WNM} := \in \text{R}^{mxnxo} \tag{58}$$

$$\text{CONTEXT}_t = \text{WNM}_{t-1} \tag{59}$$

$$\text{VSNM}_t = \texttt{Object\_Seg\_Mod.visualsegment}(\text{LNM}'_{(1, \Upsilon, t)}, \text{VNM}''_t, \text{CONTEXT}_t) \tag{60}$$

2.6 Causal Memory Module

The single sensory **LNM'**s are then matched against previously stored multi-sensory navigation maps stored in the Causal Memory Module. The best matched map is used as the working navigation map **WNM** (61). Actual_t (63) is a representation of VSNM'_t, containing objects and motion from the visual sensory inputs, AVNM_t containing audio information from the auditory sensory inputs, and $\text{LNM}'_{(3, \Upsilon, t)}$ containing information from the olfactory sensory inputs. WNM_t is then updated with the current sensory input and transformed into WNM'_t (65, 66).

$$\text{WNM}_t = \texttt{Causal\_Memory\_Module.match\_best\_multisensory\_navmap} \tag{61}$$
$$(\text{VSNM}'_t, \text{AVNM}_t, \text{LNM}'_{(3, \Upsilon, t)}, \text{LNM}'_{(4, \Upsilon, t)}, ..., \text{LNM}'_{(n\_\sigma, \Upsilon, t)})$$

$\mathbf{h'}$ = number of differences allowed to be copied onto existing navigation map $\in$ R

$$(62)$$

$$\mathbf{actual_t} = [\mathbf{VSNM'_t}, \mathbf{AVNM_t}, \mathbf{LNM'_{(3, \Upsilon, t)}}, \mathbf{LNM'_{(4, \Upsilon, t)}}, \dots, \mathbf{LNM'_{n\_\sigma, \Upsilon, t}}] \quad (63)$$

$$\mathbf{NewNM} \in R^{mxnxo} \tag{64}$$

$$|\mathbf{differences(actual_t, WNM_t)}| \leq \mathbf{h'}, \Rightarrow \mathbf{WNM'_t} = \mathbf{WNM_t} \cup \mathbf{actual_t} \tag{65}$$

$$|\mathbf{differences(actual_t, WNM_t)}| > \mathbf{h'}, \Rightarrow \mathbf{WNM'_t} = \mathbf{NewNM_t} \cup \mathbf{actual_t} \tag{66}$$

2.7 Navigation Module

Each cognitive cycle there is always a "working primitive" **WPR** (which is the best matching instinctive primitive (**WIP**) or learned primitive (**WLP**)) applied on the working navigation map **WNM'** in the Navigation Module, resulting in an **action** value (76–78). Normally the **action** value is then propagated to the output stages of the architecture and an action is taken in the real world (80–83). However, if the **action** value does not contain "move" (i.e., it is not actionable) then the output of the Navigation Module is instead fed back to the Input Sensory Vectors Association Modules (84). (Which from a biological evolutionary point of view, would have required only minor enhancements.) In the next cognitive cycle these intermediate results are returned to the Navigation Module (85) and operated on again. (The Input Sensory Vectors Association Modules automatically treat these intermediate results as if they are **LMN**'s of new sensory inputs, and automatically propagate them to the Navigation Module complex.)

$$emotion \in R \tag{67}$$

$$\mathbf{GOAL} \in R^{mxnxo} \tag{68}$$

$$autonomic \in R \tag{69}$$

$$[emotion_t, \mathbf{GOAL_t}] = \texttt{Goal/Emotion\_Mod.set\_emotion\_goal(} autonomic_t, \mathbf{WNM'_t})$$

$$(70)$$

$$\mathbf{WIP} \in R^{mxnxo} \tag{71}$$

$$\mathbf{WIP_t} = \texttt{Instinctive\_Prims\_Mod.match\_primitive(} actual_t, emotion_t, \mathbf{GOAL_t}) \tag{72}$$

$$\mathbf{WLP} \in R^{mxnxo} \tag{73}$$

$$\mathbf{WLP_t} = \texttt{Learned\_Prims\_Mod.match\_primitive(} actual_t, emotion_t, \mathbf{GOAL_t}) \tag{74}$$

$$\textbf{WPR} \in R^{mxnxo} \tag{75}$$

$$\textbf{WLP}_t = [\,], \Rightarrow \textbf{WPR}_t = \textbf{WIP}_t \tag{76}$$

$$\textbf{WLP}_t \neq [\,], \Rightarrow \textbf{WPR}_t = \textbf{WLP}_t \tag{77}$$

$$\textbf{action}_t = \texttt{Navigation\_Module.apply\_primitive}(\textbf{WPR}_t, \textbf{WNM'}_t) \tag{78}$$

$$\textit{output\_vector} \in R^{n'} \tag{79}$$

$$\begin{aligned}&\textbf{action}_t = \text{``move*''},\\&\Rightarrow \textit{output\_vector}_t = \texttt{OutVect\_Module.action\_to\_output}(\textbf{action}_t, \textbf{WNM'}_t)\end{aligned} \tag{80}$$

$$\textit{motion\_correction} \in R^2 \tag{81}$$

$$\begin{aligned}&\textbf{action}_t = \text{``move*''}, \quad \Rightarrow \textit{motion\_correction}_t = \texttt{SeqError\_Correct\_Mod.motion\_correc-}\\&\texttt{tion} \,(\, \textit{action}_t, \quad \textbf{WNM'}_t, \textit{visual\_series(t)}\,)\end{aligned} \tag{82}$$

$$\begin{aligned}&\textit{output\_vector'}_t = \texttt{OutVector\_Module.apply\_motion\_correction}\\&\qquad (\,\textit{output\_vector}_t, \textit{motion\_correction}_t\,)\end{aligned} \tag{83}$$

$$\begin{aligned}&(\textbf{action}_t \neq \text{``move*''} \text{ and } \textbf{WPR}_t \neq [\text{``discard*''}]) \text{ or } \textbf{WPR}_t = [\text{``feedback*''}],\\&\texttt{Navigation\_Module.feedback\_intermediate}(\textbf{WNM'}_t)\end{aligned} \tag{84}$$

$$\begin{aligned}&(\textbf{action}_{t-1} \neq \text{``move*''} \text{ and } \textbf{WPR}_{t-1} \neq [\text{``discard*''}]) \text{ or } \textbf{WPR}_{t-1} = [\text{``feedback*''}],\\&\forall_\sigma: \textbf{LNM}_{(\sigma, \Upsilon, t)} = \texttt{Input\_Assoc\_Module}_\sigma\texttt{.extract\_}\sigma(\textbf{WNM'}_{t-1})\end{aligned} \tag{85}$$

3 Analogical Feedback

3.1 The Problem of Processing the Intermediate Results

As noted above, when an operation on a navigation map does not result in an actionable output, rather than wait for another sensory input to be processed in the next cognitive cycle, the Causal Cognitive Architecture will feed back these intermediate outputs of the Navigation Module and re-process them in the next cognitive cycle. While for certain combinations of sensory inputs and instinctive or learned primitives this may eventually give a useful output, even a causally related output [3], often it does not.

We describe here an algorithm which emerges readily from the architecture for processing of the intermediate results whereby analogical results are generated that may be more useful than simply feeding back and returning the intermediate results unchanged in the next cognitive cycle as occurs in the previous architecture [3]. As well, from the biologically inspired point of view, note that this algorithm requires only a small evolutionary step from the previous architecture.

In Eq. (86) we see the state where the working navigation map **WNM'** that was produced from the sensory inputs does not result in any actionable result in the Navigation Module, and so, there is the signal to feed back these results to the Input Sensory Vectors Association Modules, where they can be temporally stored. At the same time, in (87) the working navigation map that was produced **WNM'** is matched against the various navigation maps stored in the Causal Memory Module and the best matching navigation map becomes the working navigation map **WNM'**.

In (90) the navigation map which the new working navigation map **WNM'** linked to in the past, becomes the working navigation map **WNM'**. And in (91) the difference between these two navigation maps, i.e., what happened essentially in the past, is stored as the working navigation map **WNM'**. Then in the next cognitive cycle the original working navigation map that was fed back and stored in the Input Sensory Vectors Association Modules (in Eq. 86) is retrieved and added to (rather than overwriting) the Navigation Module (92). Thus, at this point, the working navigation map **WNM'**$_t$ in the Navigation Module contains the action that occurred in the past of a similar working navigation map in a possible analogical situation. The demonstration example in the section below will illustrate this more clearly.

$$(\textbf{action}_t \neq \text{" move*"} \text{ and } \textbf{WPR}_t \neq [\text{"discard*"}] \text{ and } \textbf{WPR}_t \neq [\text{"feedback*"}])$$
$$\text{or } \textbf{WPR}_t = [\text{"analogical*"}], \tag{86}$$
$$\Rightarrow \texttt{Navigation\_Module.feedback\_intermediate}(\textbf{WNM'}_t)$$

$$\Rightarrow \textbf{WNM'}_t = \texttt{Causal\_Memory\_Module.match\_best\_multisensory\_navmap}(\textbf{WNM'}_t) \tag{87}$$

$$\Rightarrow \textbf{short\_term\_memory} \in R^{mxnxo} \tag{88}$$

$$\Rightarrow \textbf{short\_term\_memory} = \textbf{WNM'}_t \tag{89}$$

$$\Rightarrow \textbf{WNM'}_t = \texttt{Navigation\_Module.next\_map1}(\textbf{WNM'}_t) \tag{90}$$

$$\Rightarrow \textbf{WNM'}_t = \textbf{WNM'}_t - \textbf{short\_term\_memory} \tag{91}$$

$$(\textbf{action}_{t-1} \neq \text{"move*"} \text{ and } \textbf{WPR}_{t-1} \neq [\text{"discard*"}]) \text{ or } \textbf{WPR}_{t-1} = [\text{"analogical*"}], \tag{92}$$
$$\Rightarrow \textbf{WNM'}_t = \texttt{Navigation\_Module.retrieve\_and\_add\_intermediates}$$

The procedure `feedback_intermediate` in (86) takes the navigation map **WNM'**$_t$ and breaks it up into local navigation maps **LNMs** representing its sensory components and stores the **LNMs** in their respective sensory modules in the Input Sensory Vectors Association Modules. In the procedure in (92) `retrieve_and_add_intermediates` these **LNMs** holding the intermediate results from (86) are transmitted to the Navigation Module where they are added to (rather than replacing) the working navigation map creating the new working navigation map **WNM'**$_t$.

The procedure `match_best_multisensory_navmap` in (87) is the same as the one in (61) and is described in more detail in [2, 3].

The procedure next_map1 in (90) looks at the link addresses (37) of the working navigation map **WNM'**$_t$ and then retrieves the last (i.e., most recent) navigation map which this **WNM'**$_t$ linked to, which now becomes the new **WNM'**$_t$. The procedure next_map1 is the one simulated in the demonstration example below. (Other similar procedures are available. For example, next_map2 will examine every one of the link addresses (37) of the working navigation map **WNM'**$_t$ and then execute Eqs. (91) and (92) for all these link addresses and then attempt to choose the best analogical result.)

3.2   Analogical Feedback Demonstration Example

A simple demonstration of above equations via a Python computer simulation (with sensory inputs simulated as well) is shown below. This example shows the advantageous nature of the inductive analogic abilities created by the inclusion of Eqs. (86) to (92).

Figure 2 shows a working navigation map **WNM'**$_t$ in the Navigation Module of the CCA3 (using 6x6x0 maps). Visual lines in the environment were sensed by an agent using the CCA3 and are propagated to the **WNM'**$_t$ as shown in Fig. 2. What action should the Navigation Module take now? How to make sense of this environment?

No particular primitives are triggered, so an instinctive primitive is used as the working primitive **WPR** which contains "analogical". Thus, instead of producing an output action, the Navigation Module will feed this working navigation map back to the Input Sensory Vectors Association Modules where it can be temporarily stored, and the analogical algorithm occurs (86–92). Figure 3 shows the best match from the Causal Memory Module of **WNM'**$_t$ which then becomes the new working navigation map (87). Then the navigation map which occurred after the navigation map in Fig. 3 (i.e., in the past when the map in Fig. 3 was stored in the Causal Memory Module) which is represented as a link in the map in Fig. 3 (not shown as it is in a non-spatial dimension of the navigation map), is activated and becomes the new **WNM'**$_t$, via (90) and as shown in Fig. 4. The difference between the navigation maps in Fig. 4 and Fig. 3 represents what happened in the past (91). Then in the next cognitive cycle, as described in (92), what happened in the past is added to the original Working navigation map (Fig. 2) resulting in a new **WNM'**$_t$, shown in Fig. 5.

Thus, if a straightforward resolution of a navigation map is not immediately possible (i.e., an instinctive or learned primitive is applied to a navigation map resulting from various sensory inputs, and there is not an actionable output), the architecture will automatically produce an analogical result. Note that other instinctive or learned primitives can then further process, as well as reject or output, the analogical result that is produced.

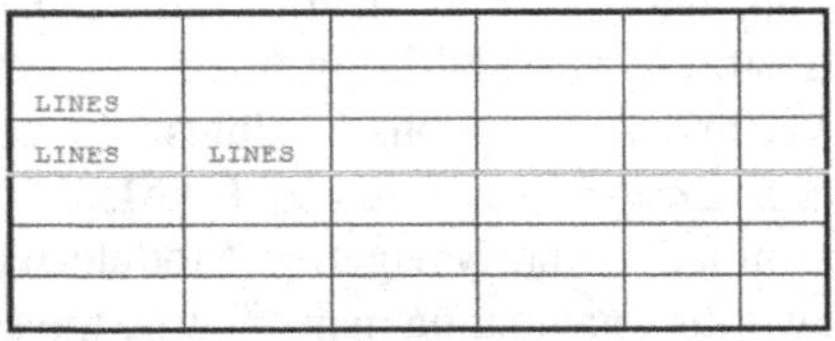

LINES					
LINES	LINES				

Fig. 2. (top left) Working Navigation Map **WNM'** – what action should occur?

LINES				
LINES	LINES			
LINES	LINES			
LINES				

Fig. 3. (top right) Best match from Causal Memory Module of previous **WNM'**.

LINES					
LINES	LINES	LINES	LINES	LINES	
LINES	LINES				
LINES					

Fig. 4. (bottom left) This is the Working Navigation Map **WNM'** that occurred after the best match **WNM'**.

LINES					
LINES	LINES	LINES	LINES	LINES	

Fig. 5. (bottom right) Retrieve the starting **WNM'** and apply the difference to it

4 Discussion

Above we reviewed how in developing a cognitive architecture loosely modeled on the mammalian brain, by enhancing pre-existing feedback pathways we can obtain causal abilities [2–4], and then with another small enhancement we show the emergence of inductive analogical abilities. There is a long history of analogical problem solving in the field of artificial intelligence [5]. The purpose of this work is not to show a better means of analogical abilities (although in conjunction with the overall causal architecture they may one day in fact prove to be quite advantageous) but to show how in a mammalian brain inspired cognitive architecture, causal and inductive analogical abilities effectively can emerge from the architecture.

Most earlier approaches to analogic problem solving were symbolic, e.g., Gentner's Structure-Mapping Engine (SME) [5], Hofstadter and Mitchell's Copycat program [6], and required human structuring and knowledge. In the last decade more connectionist approaches to analogy-making have been proposed. Wu and colleagues describe the Scattering Compositional Learner that puts neural networks in a sequence to elucidate the compositional structure of a problem and allows analogical reasoning [7].

While the deep learning approach to analogical reasoning overcomes the need for much of the human prior knowledge that symbolic systems required, a huge training set is still nonetheless required, something humans do not require, and issues such as performance via biases rather than understanding, remain [8]. Mitchell notes that while in the last decade there have been tremendous improvements in the ability of AI systems to recognize images and generate natural language, the ability of artificial intelligence systems to handle analogies, concepts, and abstractions, still remains an open problem.

The CCA3 demonstration example above, represents a very basic example of the use of analogical problem solving in the architecture. The example was a simplified analogy taken from Chollet's Abstraction and Reasoning Corpus [9]. To solve more complex problems in Chollet's corpus, additional primitives could be added to the CCA3 and used in conjunction with the architecture's intrinsic analogical problem solving. For example, if the next navigation map as shown in Fig. 4 was a rotation of 90 degrees plus the addition of the contiguous 'LINE' squares, then a set of intrinsic primitives for detecting and effecting basic geometric transformations is required.

As noted above, when enhanced feedback processing of intermediate results occurs in the Causal Cognitive Architecture, there is the possibility for analogies as a core mechanism in cognition. Given that many aspects of the architecture are brain inspired, that suggests that indeed analogies may be central to human cognition. Chen and colleagues have shown that one year old infants are capable of analogical problem solving [10]. Hofstadter presents evidence arguing for the role of constant analogy making in the human mind [1]. Similarly, analogical mechanisms may prove to be an important ability in allowing more capable future artificial general intelligence systems.

References

1. Hofstadter, D.R.: Analogy as the core of cognition. In: Gentner, D., Holyoak, K.J., Kokinov, B.N. (eds.) The Analogical Mind, pp. 499–538. MIT Press (2001)
2. Schneider, H.: Causal cognitive architecture 1: integration of connectionist elements into a navigation-based framework. Cogn. Syst. Res. **66**, 67–81 (2021). https://doi.org/10.1016/j.cogsys.2020.10.021
3. Schneider, H.: Causal cognitive architecture 3: a solution to the binding problem. Cogn. Syst. Res. **72**, 88–115 (2022). https://doi.org/10.1016/j.cogsys.2021.10.004
4. Schneider, H.: The meaningful-based cognitive architecture model of schizophrenia. Cogn. Syst. Res. **59**, 73–90 (2020). https://doi.org/10.1016/j.cogsys.2019.09.019
5. Falkenhainer, B., Forbus, K.D., Gentner, D.: The structure-mapping engine. In: Proceedings of the National Conference on Artificial Intelligence, AAAI, pp 272–277 (1986)
6. Hofstadter, D.R., Mitchell, M.: The copycat project. In: Holyoak, K.J., Barnden, J.A. (eds.) Advances in Connectionist and Neural Computation Theory, vol. 2, pp. 31–112 (1994). Ablex
7. Wu, Y., Dong, H., Grosse, R., Ba, J.: The Scattering Compositional Learner. arXiv:2007.04212 (2020). https://doi.org/10.48550/arXiv.2007.04212
8. Mitchell, M.: Abstraction and analogy-making in artificial intelligence. Ann. N Y Acad. Sci. **1505**(1), 79–101 (2021). https://doi.org/10.1111/nyas.14619
9. Chollet, F.: On the Measure of Intelligence. arXiv:1911.01547 (2019)
10. Chen, Z., Sanchez, R., Campbell, T.: From beyond to within their grasp: analogical problem solving in 10- and 13-month-olds. Dev. Psychol. **33**, 790–801 (1997). https://doi.org/10.1037//0012-1649.33.5.790

A Biologically Plausible Graph Structure for AGI

Charles J. Simon$^{(\boxtimes)}$

Future AI, Washington, DC, USA
charles@futureAI.guru

Abstract. Graph structures have shown to represent a viable approach to developing AGI. This paper describes how a knowledge graph could be represented in neurons and introduces the Universal Knowledge Store (UKS), an open-source implementation, which could form one component of AGI. Unlike backpropagation-related systems which have only the most tenuous biological relationship, graph structures *can* be built from basic biological neuron models.

Keywords: Artificial general intelligence · Graph algorithm · Biological neuron · Leaky-integrate-and-fire · Hebbian synapse

1 Introduction

The Universal Knowledge Store (UKS) [1] is an open-source graph data structure/API which is designed to support development and experimentation into Artificial General Intelligence (AGI). Its structure is guided by an exploration of how knowledge might be stored in biological neurons and how this neuronal approach could steer designs for a similar structure in computers.

Specifically, the neurons described here use the biologically plausible "Integrate and fire" (IF) model [2–4], possibly with leakage (LIF) [4–7]. These neurons are interconnected with synapses, which may be fixed weight or learn via Hebbian Learning and its biologically observed equivalents [8–10].

The IF model accumulates charge from synapses incoming from firing neurons until a threshold is reached, then it fires, and the accumulated charge is reset to 0. For convenience, the threshold is defined at a value of 1. If an incoming synapse has a weight of 1, when its source neuron fires, the target neuron will immediately meet the threshold and fire as soon as possible thereafter. A synapse weight of 0.5 would require 2 firings to cause the target neuron to accumulate enough charge to fire. The LIF neuron model adds exponential decay at a given leakage rate which is defined as the proportion of the accumulated charge which will leak off in a given time-slice [11, 12]. With a leak rate of .5 (very fast) a charge of .5 will decay to approximately zero in 10 time-slices. A leak rate of 1 prevents the neuron from accumulating any charge from one time-slice to the next approximating a perceptron where the charge value is the instantaneous sum of weights of all synapses from firing neurons.

B. Goertzel et al. (Eds.): AGI 2022, LNAI 13539, pp. 113–123, 2023.
https://doi.org/10.1007/978-3-031-19907-3_11

The paper begins with biologically plausible neuron models and how these can be simulated by implementing the nodes and edges of a graph. It then shows how the UKS implements similar concepts in a higher-level language with flexibility and improved performance while storing any kind of data from multiple sense inputs.

The objectives of the project are as follows:

1.1 Flexibility

The structure should be able to store and relate any kind of information without a pre-defined data design. An infant learns about his/her environment and objects within it in a multisensory way before learning about language. This means that any data structure must be able to merge or link information from multiple senses. The later learning of language (for example) requires that new node types (e.g., words) and edge types (e.g., rhymes-with) must be able to be created on-the-fly so the structure of the knowledge graph cannot be fully predefined.

1.2 Biological Plausibility

It is NOT necessary that an AGI mimic the biological brain. However, understanding a possible biological implementation of the data structure shows the types of structures and limitations a biologically plausible AGI needs. These limits include things like the minimum and maximum number of objects an AGI might need to store, the minimum and maximum numbers of links an object might possess. The Brain Simulator's interactive neuron display is excellent for building small neural circuits to experiment with the type of capabilities which might be present in small clusters of neurons [6]. On the other hand, design and simulation at the neuron level is cumbersome and while the basic structure of the UKS *could* be implemented in neurons, a higher-level language is used.

1.3 Performance

Again, it is NOT necessary that an AGI match human brain performance. Depending on the amount of computer power available, computer performance can lag below human performance in many areas while vastly exceeding human performance in others and still create a useful AGI. The very slow speed of neurons (250 Hz max) means that a biological system must do as much as possible in parallel. With computers built from components as much as a billion times faster, the requirement for parallelism is relaxed.

2 A Brief Introduction to Knowledge in Neurons

2.1 The Information of Knowledge

Consider that a system is only given "Blue is a color," and "Red is a color." Now, it has the information to answer the questions: "What is blue?" (a color), "What is red?" (a color), and "What are some colors?" (blue and red). The graph structure of Fig. 1A shows a simple representation of this knowledge.

Representing the information to answer these simple questions in neurons is not so simple and what follows is the description of a network of neurons that does just that. "Blue," "red," and "color" have a meaning to *a person* but are just words or ideas with relationships to one another. Within the brain, these are just spiking neurons with some sort of synaptic connections. While many models use the spiking rate of a neuron to represent information content, the following description works with individual spikes [7] and is therefore significantly faster. In mathematics, this is a "graph" which is a collection of "nodes" connected by "edges." One could say that Color is a parent node of Red and Blue and that Red and Blue are Child nodes of Color, and this nomenclature is carried into further descriptions.

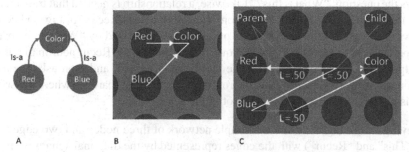

Fig. 1. A) Illustrates how certain types of knowledge can be represented in a "graph" of "nodes" connected by "edges." B) If the nodes, "Blue," "Red," and "Color" were just single neurons, firing either Blue or Red will cause Color to fire (because the white synapse weights are 1) but there is no convenient way to connect Color so it fires Blue and Red. C) By adding more neurons to every node, each can have parents and children. The center neurons will only fire if two or more input neurons fire in temporal proximity because the incoming synapse weights are .9 and leakage will quickly drain accumulated charge. Now, if Blue AND Parent fire, Color will fire. If Red AND Parent fire, Color will fire. If Color AND Child fire, both Blue and Red will fire. (Color figure online)

Implementing a Graph in Neurons. To implement the simple three-node color graph in neurons, assign individual neurons to represent each of the three nodes as shown in Fig. 1B. To answer the first two questions, a high-weight synapse must connect Blue to Color, and another must connect Red to Color. Now if the Blue neuron fires (because perhaps something blue was seen or the word "blue" was heard), the Color neuron will subsequently fire and the system will know that Blue is a Color. Likewise for Red. In most cases, individual spikes might be bursts of multiple spikes.

With just a synapse from Blue to Color, there is no way to fire Color and get Blue and Red to fire because synapses are one-directional [9]. Issues arise if the system were to add synapses from Color to both Blue and Red. If Color fires, it causes both Blue and Red to fire which, in turn, causes Color to fire again, causing neurons to fire…so all neurons fire indefinitely for any input. Neurons must be added so that Color will only fire if the system wants to know the Parent of Blue or Red and another which will cause Blue and Red to fire only if the brain searches for the all the Child nodes of Color. More generally, with more neurons added to each node and a lower synapse weight so two firing inputs are necessary to fire, the solution to this issue is shown in Fig. 1C.

This system now has a node consisting of several neurons to represent the abstract concept of blue. One of the node's neurons fires when the system sees blue or hears the word, but it must be separate from the neuron which fires to *say* the word blue, otherwise, every time blue was seen (or the word was heard), the system would also say it. So, each node also needs more neurons which determine if it is receiving input or creating output for that node. If every node can have parents and children, and an input and output, each node requires four neurons.

Another set of neurons is needed to transfer inputs to outputs so that if the system *does* see blue, it *can* say, "Blue" if desired. This is the "This" relationship because it answers the question, "What is this?" Likewise, a relationship is needed that transfers the output to the input. This is the "Recursion" neuron (labeled "Recur" in Fig. 2) because it allows one to ask, "What is the parent of this node?" followed by "What is the parent of the parent?" The system asks the first question, then fires the Recur neuron to transfer the output of the first question to be the input of the second, and then asks the same question again. More generally, this neuron is needed for any searches where the search target is not directly connected to the root of the search.

Retrieving Data. Figure 2 shows a simple network of three nodes and two edge types (plus "This" and "Recur") with the edges represented by the diagonal synapses. To fire the children of Node 1, fire neuron Node 1 followed by the Child neuron. A similar process could get the parents of any node.

Additional nodes require additional rows, and additional edge types require additional columns in the neuron array. Because an individual neuron may have as many as 10,000 synapses connecting it to other neurons, the number of nodes and edge types is quite large but not unlimited. For larger data structures, multiple arrays of neurons would be required.

Storing Data. The diagonal synapses in the lower portion of Fig. 2 follow a Hebbian rule [10] such that if the target neuron of the synapse fires directly after the source, the synapse weight will be strengthened. Since Hebbian synapse weights change gradually, multiple spikes on both the input and output are needed so bits of short-term memory are added to the input and output (labeled "I1"-3 and "O1"-3) of each node. These short-term memory bits work by storing a partial charge in the neuron. When the "ReadIn" neuron fires, it fires the memory bit neuron only if a partial charge is present (indicating a 1 was stored) and then restores the partial charge. If there was no partial charge, no neuron fires, indicating a 0.

The memory write process is to fire the input for the target node, fire This to transfer it to the output, fire the source node, then fire the relationship type repeatedly until the synapse has strengthened sufficiently. When the Learn neuron is firing, it controls all the timing needed for learning.

Neuron Summary. Figure 2 shows a basic structure with three nodes represented by eight neurons each. Each node has 4 relationship types: Parent, Child, This, and Recur along with bits of short-term memory on the input and output. All the actual information is stored in the weights of Hebbian synapses. In the explanation, only weights of 1 or 0 are used but partial weights can be significant in 1) allowing learning over a number of presentations rather than immediately and 2) allowing for reading over multiple firings so that the "most-learned" information will be retrieved first.

Because any node might potentially relate to any other, there must initially be a large number of zero-weight synapses even though only a few are eventually used to store information (are adjusted to a non-zero weight).

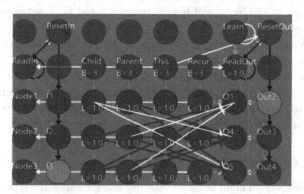

Fig. 2. Represents a three-node graph as described if Node1 is Color, Node2 is Blue, and Node3 is Red. The actual data of the structure is the diagonal Hebbian synapses between the nodes. In this case, Node1 has the children Nodes 2 and 3 and, conversely, Nodes 2 and 3 have the parent Node1. (Color figure online)

The control signals originate somewhere outside the structure (perhaps the hippocampus). Note that, as described, the network doesn't automatically add a reverse relationship. When the system adds Color is a parent of Blue, the connection that lets Color's children include Blue must be added in a separate operation.

2.2 Biological Plausibility

Is this biologically plausible? Yes and no. Because the brain can answer simple questions about colors and add new relationships quickly, some sort of graph structure with relationships *must* exist. Because one can remember for the long term, these relationships *must* be stored in synapse weights. But neuroscientists don't find orderly physical structures like these in the brain so one must assume that the neurons which perform these functions could be interspersed with neurons doing other things as well.

That the brain implements these structures *exactly* as described is unlikely for several reasons. Here are some important ones:

- Redundancy—as described, the failure of any single neuron or synapse can cause a loss of memory or a node's function. Instead, nodes in the brain likely consist of perhaps a hundred neurons with redundant connections.

- Physical layout—the structure described is very orderly and precise and no equivalent has been discovered in the brain.
- Multiple graphs—this describes a single graph, but it is likely that various graphs in the brain contain different kinds of information such as visual and audible. Some nodes might link to nodes in other graphs.

Some implications of a biologically plausible model are:

- No Data—the nodes and edges of the neuron graph cannot contain any useful information because they are simply individual bits. This has significant implications as to data structure of the brain and how a computerized knowledge graph could be dramatically more efficient.
- No Data in Synapse Weights—the weight of a synapse is needed to keep track of a specific bit of information and how close it is to being learned. It cannot simultaneously represent an information value such as a brightness level.
- Cortical Columns—there is a possibility that cortical columns represent graph nodes based solely on the observation that they represent a repeating pattern in the neocortex and contain a reasonable number of neurons.

2.3 Important Conclusions from the Biological Perspective

A minimum node requires eight neurons. Adding a few likely edge types brings this to 11. With 16 billion neurons in the human neocortex, this limits the number of nodes to 1.45 billion. Considering redundancy, a non-optimal biological implementation, and the fact that the neocortex is not fully dedicated to this type of storage, a more realistic maximum on the number of nodes in a neocortex graph would be 10–200 million. This is an important conclusion because building, maintaining, and searching a graph of this size is conceivable on a powerful desktop computer.

3 The Universal Knowledge Store (UKS)

The system described above with several extensions was implemented with a Brain Simulator II module ("ModuleGraph") which can be downloaded. It can create and arrange as many nodes, neurons, and synapses as desired needed to represent information. Within the *Brain Simulator*'s user interface, one can watch individual neurons fire as information is stored in, or retrieved from, the structure. This is fine for demonstrating a few dozen nodes but is unwieldy for larger graphs. The next development phase replaces the neuron/synapse structure with a program for larger structures.

The UKS implements a knowledge graph of unlimited potential and complexity representing information as a collection of nodes connected by edges as above and contains only two significant object types, a "Thing" and a "Link" which are concrete implementations of a generic node and edge.

The Thing represents anything (a word, a physical object, a color, an action, a relationship type, etc.), and a Link connects one Thing to another Thing. While a Thing is somewhat analogous to a neuron and a Link is somewhat analogous to a synapse, this is a very loose analogy, as Things would require many neurons in a brain.

3.1 The Link

A Link is "owned" by a Thing and targets another Thing in the same way one might say that a Synapse is owned by one neuron and connects to another. The other end of the Link is the Target Thing. As a software structure, a Link is just a reference (C#) or a pointer (C++) to a Thing with a floating-point weight value used during learning.

3.2 The Thing

Each Thing has lists of Links to other Things. In theory, a single list would suffice but for efficiency, the Thing has specific Link lists for "Parents," "Children," "References," and "ReferencedBy" Links. Parents and Children Links are simplified and do not contain a weight (Fig. 3).

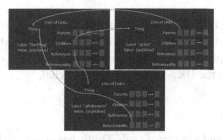

Fig. 3. Each Thing has lists of Links to other Things. Parent/child relationships are hard-coded while References could have any relationship type. The Label and Value are a programming shortcut.

The Parent-child relationships can form a Tree-like structure of Things by using Lists where each Thing can have any number of parents and children. The parent-child relationship is useful to restrict search domains as searches can be limited to only the Children (or recursively Dependents) of a given Thing. In this way, the hierarchy of parent-child links can be thought of as representing brain areas. For example, visual searches can be limited to visual Things and auditory searches are limited to auditory Things. Parent-child may also be considered an "is-a" relationship as seen previously.

A portion of an example knowledge store is shown in Fig. 4. From the parent-child links, one could say that Circle is a Shape and Shape is a Visual Thing. Red and Blue are Color children and Color is a Visual Thing.

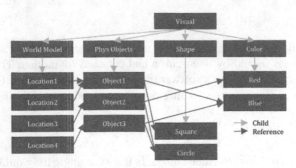

Fig. 4. From this representation of partial UKS content, one can see that at Location1, there is an object which is a Blue Square, at Location2, there is another, at Location3 there is a Red Circle, and at Location4, there is a Blue Circle. This is similar to the model used by the Perception and Maze demo applications described later. (Color figure online)

The UKS is just a list of Things; Things that contain links to other Things. The parent-child relationships of the UKS do not necessarily represent a formal tree structure because Things may have multiple parent Things, there is no exclusion of circular references, and not all the Things in the UKS must be interconnected.

3.3 Thing References

In addition to Parents and Children, each Thing has a list of Links named "References" so a Thing can reference any number of property Things. There is a mirror list, "ReferencedBy" for efficiency in searching.

3.4 Labels and Values

Each Thing has an optional "Label" and "Value," so when looking at debug information about the content of the knowledge store, it can make sense. As an example, a single line of code can find any Thing based on its label and return its children.

```
IList<Thing> t = UKS.Labeled("PhysicalObject").Children;
```

To efficiently get a list of all the physical objects in the UKS, any specific physical object Thing "is-a" physical object so it has the Physical Object Thing as a parent.

A deviation from the idea that nodes contain no information is the Value property which can contain any object. In a computer, to know how to spell a word, one can store a text string with the spelling. In the brain, since neurons obviously don't support text strings, there must be a sequence with a list of links to other nodes which represent individual letters. These Letter nodes must have links to other nodes which define the strokes needed to write them, the utterance needed to speak when spelling a word out loud, and a definition of patterns of visual input to recognize and read them. Without the Value, the complexity needed to store something as simple as a word in a biologically plausible structure can be daunting.

The key for these two properties is that as UKS applications are developed which rely on them, they are cutting corners on biological plausibility. This may mean that the algorithm will need re-thinking down the road *or* that conversely, the algorithm has an efficiency edge over its biological counterpart.

One of the underlying tenets of this development is that to create General Intelligence, an AGI needs to generalize information from widely disparate sources and types. To comprehend something as simple as "Things fall down," a system needs to understand about physical things, have experienced things falling (an action), know about sequences of actions, have heard and learned the associated words…and on and on. The implementation of AGI on the UKS can represent all this information in a useful way.

4 Summary and Current Development

The UKS is a powerful general-purpose graph structure with a biologically plausible basis. Two demonstration applications show its power and flexibility. Perception and Traversing a Maze.

4.1 Application 1, Perception: Learning by Correlation

This takes as input visual shapes and text tags and infers relationships between them. Although the tagged data is ambiguous because when the system is told "This is a red square near a blue triangle," which word is associated with which property or relationship is initially ambiguous. Over a very small number of samples, however, the system can infer that red and blue must be related to the hue, square and triangle must relate to the number of corners, and near must be related to distance. This learning process is similar to what one might see in a toddler learning language. All the related information is stored in the UKS.

4.2 Application 2: Maze/Learning by Trial and Error

There are plenty of ways for a computer program to solve a maze. The approach in this instance utilizes the UKS and builds a structure within the UKS that can be generalized to a wide variety of intelligent behaviors.

As the system explores the maze, it builds an internal mental model and records landmarks and decision points. At each decision point, it stores an Event which is a situation-action-outcome triple. After exploring the maze, it can search the list of Events at any recognized landmark to determine the decision needed to achieve any desired goal (Fig. 5).

Both sample applications are included in the Brain Simulator II download. [1].

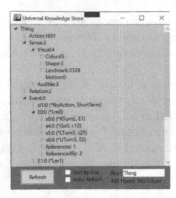 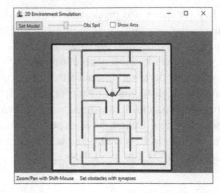

Fig. 5. (Left) The tree view display of the UKS content shows parent-child and reference relationships. In this case, the Visual Sense and Events are expanded. Event "E0" has a reference to the Landmark "Lm0", and children each of which represents an action taken and the outcome. For example, a Left Turn led to color "c29" (a possible goal) while a right-turn led to another event "E1". "LTurn" is a reference to a node which could represent the action of turning left. These automatically assigned node labels are in keeping with the idea that individual nodes don't contain information. (Right) The maze application illustrates how the UKS can be used to keep track of landmarks. The Event/Action/Outcome triples stored in the UKS form the basis of reinforcement learning. (Color figure online)

References

1. FutureAI. The Brain Simulator II [open source software which implements the examples as described]. Available: https://commons.wikimedia.org/w/index.php?title=File:Neuron3. png&oldid=603062228 (2021). Accessed 2022
2. Abbott, L.F.: Lapicque's introduction of the integrate-and-fire model neuron. Brain Res. Bull. **50**(5–6), 303–304 (1999)
3. Dutta, S., Kumar, V., Shukla, A., Mohaptra, N.R., Ganguly, U.: Leaky integrate and fire neuron by charge-discharge dynamics in floating-body MOSFET. Sci. Rep. **7**, 8257 (2017)
4. Gerstner, W., Kistler, W.M.: Spiking Neuron Models: Single Neurons, Populations, Plasticity. Cambridge University Press (2002)
5. Mao, J., Gan, C., Kohli, P., Tennenbaum, J., Wu, J.: The Neuro-Symbolic Concept Learner: Interpreting Scenes, Words, and Sentences from Natural Supervision (2019)
6. Stiles, J., Jernigan, T.L.: The basics of brain development. Neuropsychol. Rev. **20**(4), 327–348 (2010)
7. Chowdhury, S.S., Lee, C., Roy, K.: Towards understanding the effect of leak in spiking neural networks. Neurocomputing **464**, 83–94 (2021). https://doi.org/10.1016/j.neucom.2021. 07.091
8. Simon, C.J.: Brain simulator II: the guide for creating artificial general intelligence. FutureAI (2021)
9. Martens, M.B., Celikel, T., Tiesinga, P.H.E.: A developmental switch for Hebbian plasticity. PLoS Comput. Biol. **11**(7), e1004386 (2015). https://doi.org/10.1371/journal.pcbi.1004386
10. Piochon, C., Kruskal, P., MacLean, J., Hansel, C.: Non-Hebbian spike-timing-dependent plasticity in cerebellar circuits. Front. Neural Circuits **6**, 124 (2013)
11. Goerzel, B.: The General Theory of General Intelligence: A Pragmatic Patternist Perspective (2021)

12. Oleskiw, T.D., Bair, W., Shea-Brown, E., Brunel, N.: Firing rate of the leaky integrate-and-fire neuron with stochastic conductance-based synaptic inputs with short decay times. *arXiv* (2020)
13. Rao, R.P.N., Sejnowski, T.J.: Spike-timing-dependent Hebbian plasticity as temporal difference learning. Neural Comput. **13**(10), 2221–2237 (2001). https://doi.org/10.1162/089976601750541787

The Delta Normal AGI

Pieter ter Doest[(✉)]

PNF7, Holten, The Netherlands
pieter.ter.doest@pnf7.nl
https://pnf7.nl

Abstract. In the quest for an Artificial General Intelligence (AGI) this paper presents a proposal for a symbol-based narrow AGI that uses a problem-driven mechanism within a certain domain. Using a small set of seeded ontology roots, simplified sentences can be constructed with surprising characteristics. Problem solving graphs with a limited depth are combined to form larger graphs.

Keywords: AGI · COFO · Problem solving · Combinatorial processes

1 Introduction

Problems are universal. Each moment of the day we encounter problems, although we are not aware of this all the time. Washing the car can be seen as a problem. The same goes for driving to work, or picking up a fork. We can look at all these activities as presenting problems. But also a dialogue in fact is a combination of mini problem-solving dialogues in order to solve a particular problem. A central point in this paper is the thought that 'problem solving dialogues' (PSD) are central in conversations, navigation, problem solving or in any knowledge based interaction. Even a unit of information itself can be seen as a PSD. When a problem is getting more complex, then more PSD's are needed.

2 Definitions

First we need to agree on some definitions:

2.1 The Topic-Region

A topic-region is a small part of a larger graph. We can apply a modified version of sampling theory: From a given point there are enough topic regions so that a Turing Test is satisfied. Several topic-regions together form a topic. An example of a topic = 'talking about lunch'. Example of a topic-region = 'the jam on my toast'. A topic-region should be small enough so that the AGI will have a limited set of solutions.

B. Goertzel et al. (Eds.): AGI 2022, LNAI 13539, pp. 124–133, 2023.
https://doi.org/10.1007/978-3-031-19907-3_12

We want to turn complexity into quantity: a complex convoluted graph can be turned into a large set of 'manageable' smaller graphs.

The database of this AGI will not contain a complete world. Instead, we will define certain domains where the AGI will be knowledgeable. Ben Goertzel calls this a narrow AGI [1]. For a social-companion application for instance, this should be enough to pass a Turing Test.

2.2   Compresssion and Expansion

Natural language sentences are compressed into so-called 'Sents'. A Sent has three elements and a qaci precursor and a value, so the format is: q/a/c/i el1 el2 el3 val. This means that for instance 'to love', 'to like' and 'to hate' are all compressed into 'pref' combined with a value. Only a limited number of verbs (el2) are allowed after the compression step.

Input natural language sentence	Sent
John likes pancakes	A human023 pref pancakes 80

When the core part of the AGI has done it's work, the information is expanded again. This expansion will give a certain randomness to the responses of the AGI, which gives a human-like character.

Compression introduces an error when the original information needs to be retrieved. In other words, some original information is lost. Probably our human brain does the same.

2.3   COFO

In this paper we make use of the COFO as defined in Ben Goertzel's paper: The General Theory of General intelligence; A Pragmatic Patternist Perspective [3]. This paper has as one of it's central theorems the COFO. Goertzel: [3]: 'Combinatory Function Optimization (COFO) systems - which seek to maximize functions via guiding function-evaluation using sampling and inference guided selection of combinations within a combination system are introduced as a species of DDS particularly useful within AGI architectures.'

2.4   Drivers

A driver is a motivational signal. It steers the AGI and its decisions. For high-level drivers we make use of the ideas in the paper by Shalom H. Schwartz and Anat Bardi [2]. In their paper they use the term 'values' instead of drivers. But we also need low-level drivers for our AGI:

- optimize cleanliness
- optimize body temperature
- optimize feeling hungry

All these drivers together will trigger the activation of problems. And, as mentioned later in this document, problems are solved by solutions. The high-level drivers combined with the low level drivers can be implemented by a small network of AGI's, or by a single AGI called several times sequentially.

2.5 Problems and Solutions

A delta is defined as a difference between the normal and the incoming signal. A delta is one of the contributors to a problem. A solution is then coupled to that delta and to the other contributors. The normal is a stacking of incoming sentences that have a similar quark set, over time. Other contributors to a problem are discussed in a separate paragraph about problem solving.

2.6 Normalization

All incoming information is accumulated and thus normalized and stored in the database. Then, a new incoming signal is compared with the stored normal. A delta is calculated and this delta can then trigger new activities (which are Sents in themselves). What is normal for one person does not have to be normal for the other. For instance, 'The sun goes under at five o'clock' is time zone related. 'Black is the color of mourning' is culture related. 'I go to sleep at one o'clock at night' is personal information. A normal is calculated depending on the generic/personal aspect of the information. Next to this, the flatter mechanism (see elsewhere in document) will filter out privacy aspects.

2.7 Problem Solving Graph (PSD)

A problem solving graph is a directed acyclic graph (DAG). There are many PSD stored in the database of the AGI. A PSD has has a limited depth, less that five levels. It is important to realize that the bidirectional aspect of a dialogue, the input and the reaction, is stored in each PSD.

2.8 Data Record Format

Two coupled Sents are combined into a data record: inputsentence/outputsentence/meta-data/PSD-graph, or also: problem/solution/meta-data/PSD-graph.

Any information needed in the core AGI can be stored in this format.

2.9   Learning, Adaptation and Optimization

The AGI can learn by adding drivers, adding sentences, elements, adding quarks, adding entries to the log and entries to the database. We also use a funnel model for learning; the output of the AGI can be fed to a funnel. This funnel stands for the world, or the internet. Slowly data from the world will be input again to the AGI. This is how a network of AGI's and humans together can teach the AGI.

Learning can also be that new drivers, Sents or problems are added to the database. Because all these concepts have the same database format, this can be implemented easily.

Adaptation can be implemented by applying solutions to the database records themselves. In other words, 'to replace' as a solution can be taken literally on a database record.

2.10   Elements and Quarks

Every element is linked to a number of quarks. These quarks are simple concepts like : container, group, transport, etc. (see table). The quarks are seeds in the sense that they are pre-defined. Over time, new quarks can be added by the AGI itself. Every element and sentence can thus be linked to other elements and sentences by seeking commonality between these groups of quarks. This is one of the aspects of understanding. The interesting thing with the use of quarks is that any natural language sentence can be mapped to a 'sent'. Remember, a Sent consists of elements and each element can be linked to a number of quarks.

The AGI can understand using quarks whether for instance 'to read' and 'book' are related to each other.

It is obvious that the set in the table is a choice. And this choice can also be done differently. We think that this is probably the same in human brains, that the quarks are different in different human brains.

A problem arises with words that cannot be associated easily with quarks, for instance 'respect'. We can try to link it to 'pref' but this is not very convincing. However, to the rescue comes the topic-region. Because if we make this a TR, we can then say that 'respect' is a specific exception for this TR (Table 1).

Table 1. Quarks and examples.

Quark	Example of strong association	Weak association
Container	cup, book, database	house
Shield	wall, clothes, to protect	defense
Channel	opening, tunnel	solution
Support	table, to support	resistance
Radiation	sun, heating	influence
Force	pull, weight	
Energy	energy	
Time	past, present, future	
Loc	place	
Group	crowd, party	
Conflict	fight, opposition	
Own	wealth, property, money, to buy	
Val	money	
Fix	to repair	
Tool	fork, car	
Food	sandwich, soup	
Pref	to like, to love, to hate	to attract
Transport	to move, car, rocket	
Drive	to cause, to steer	influence
Animate	human, animal	
Data	book, database	language
Compress	to join	
Expand	choice, decision, to split	
Waitfor	future, wait	
Event	publication	
Increase	grow, increase, inverse: decrease	
Dominate	to win, inverse: to loose	
Transaction	gift, payment	
Reward	inverse: punish	
Nature	mountain, river, tree	
Organization	can also be done with group?	
Sequence	causal	cycle
Problem	fault, stuck	
Pattern	machine	
Solve	to clean	
Stat	big, empty, happy, warm	
Contract	deal, trust, confidence, to buy, to help	
Normal	balance, steady, average	
Activity	-any verb, except 'to be'	

2.11   Matching

Matching of elements can be done in several ways:

- By comparing the set of multiple linked quarks using a distance (objective) function.
- By comparing the elements directly using a distance function.
- By swapping elements with single quarks and thus making a template with fuzzy matching

3   Natural Language Transformed to Sents

'I work in Montreal' can be reworked to: 'I work in an office. The office is located in Montreal'. So a machine-learning software module (not in scope of this document) reworks the short-cut sentence back to original -explicit- sentences, and subsequently the sentences are mapped by the AGI to Sents. We envisage a layered model where the outer layers are implemented by sub-symbolic software and the inner core is implemented by the symbolic AGI as proposed in this paper.

4   Problem Solving

In this AGI we divide up complex problems into smaller, simpler problems. Then, for each problem we find a simple solution. These solution are stated in the Table 2 below.

Table 2. Problems and examples.

Problem	Example
Stuck	The car was stuck in the garage
Bad	He has placed a bad shot
Slow	The car was driving too slow
Sad	John was sad
Dirty	The car was dirty
Below threshold	Temperature too low
Over threshold	Temperature too high
Lost	Jill has lost the key

Having defined the problems, we can now state the solutions. These are also a simplification of the real world. However, we think that a combination of these simple solutions can approach a complex real-world solution (Table 3).

Table 3. Solutions and examples.

Solution	Example
To redo	Begin all over again, to reset
To replace	To replace a bicycle
To remove	To remove dirt
To retrain	To retrain a person to sing better
To repair	To repair a bicycle
To increase	To increase the car's speed
To decrease	To decrease the car's speed
To find	To find the key

With these problems and solutions, we can now translate complex problems into a set of simpler problems. The problem is something like: 'the lunch was bad. How to solve this?'. The solution is: 'by retraining the cook, replacing the cook, replacing the sandwich'.

5   Combinatorial Processes

For this we refer to the work of S. Kauffman [5], W. Fontana [6] and B. Goertzel [4]. We have already discussed that quarks can be combined to define an element. Building on that, three elements can be combined to form a sentence. And on a higher level, we can see that combining sentences lead to a dialogue. But how can we generate dialogues and get feedback on their success?

One way to obtain this feedback is to let the world (the internet) decide which dialogue is best. A way to do this is to let chatbots on the internet try out different 'Sent' dialogue structures (Table 4).

Table 4. Combinatorial examples of elements.

Dialogue type	Input sentence	Output sentence
Question status, reply stat and pref	q el1 stat el3	a el1 stat el3
		a el1 pref el3
Assert ownership, reply status	a el1 own el3	a el1 stat el3

Or, following Kauffman [5], we can see a dialogue as a string. So then the question-replies can be seen as substrings. Taking this further, we can search for a steady-state of a dialogue after an N number of turns. We can create a simple computer program that can give basic replies (how? when? did you ...? etc.) to keep the dialogue going.

6   The Core Process of the AGI

The core process consists of the following mechanisms: input, normalize, delta, problem solving, route, combi, fiatter.

Postulate 1. *This AGI can be seen as a COFO, as introduced by Goertzel [3]: 'which seek to maximize functions via guiding function-evaluation using sampling and inference guided selection of combinations within a combination system - are introduced as a species of DDS particularly useful within AGI architectures'. This corresponds with what this AGI does.*

Postulate 2. *All mechanisms inside the AGI, including the data itself, are 'problem solving dialogues'*

6.1   Input from the Internet

Suppose we make a social companion for an elderly lady in a care home. We first choose a topic, for instance 'hobbies'. We then choose a topic region, for instance 'singing in the communal room'. Then, a vocabulary for this topic region (100–200) words is pulled from the internet and the frequency of these words is counted. After filtering, this leaves a small set of ontology words for a topic region. Next, we input each word to the API of an internet dictionary. We then match our quarks to the results of the internet definition of a word, and obtain the following (Table 5):

Table 5. Example of automatic quark assignment.

Word	Quarks
Jill	Animate
Sings	Activity
In-communal-room	Loc, container

The above describes the mechanism in which quarks are automatically assigned to words. When new words are introduced in an active dialogue they are added to the database.

6.2   Combinatory Sentence Making

We have already defined our Sent format: q el1 el2 el3 val.

With this, and because there are only a limited number of allowed el2's, the AGI can compose combinatory questions, like for instance, 'q jill pref lunch'; Does Jill like the lunch?

6.3   Making It Work

The AGI has a database and a log, and these both use the record format as defined. The core program consists of the following mechanisms:

– get input
– attach quarks to new elements
– store new quark-element combinations in database
– get domain ontology for this topic-region
– apply router
– normalize
– find delta
– find best fitting problem solving dialogue (PSD)
– execute problem solver on PSD
– retrieve log-related questions
– store incoming information in log
– use output from combinatorial unit
– use output from flatter
– store output in log

All these mechanisms are associated with problem solving dialogues, or PSD's.

Some PSD's are a basic q-a mechanism. In that particular case the driver contribution is implicit in the database records. The result from the core program is a hybrid answer coming from either the log, the problem solver, or a combinatorial answer, all controlled by the flatter. The flatter filters out impossible/unlikely answers by employing a list of unwanted words and unwanted word combinations.

7   Future Work

If we take the combinatorial approach further, we can combine several narrow AGI's to form a more complex AGI (a meta combiner). We also want to investigate a 'Fast Training' algorithm, where we let a simplified AGI interact with a more advanced AGI. The first can then train the second. Lastly, we want to further investigate argumentation mechanisms for this AGI.

8   Summary

The Delta Normal AGI has the following aspects:

– It follows the COFO definition in Ben Goertzels paper [3]
– The AGI works with compression and normalization
– Several units can form a network together
– The AGI is a basic problem solver
– Combinatorial processes can be applied to all components of the AGI

– In this paper we provide a framework that can stand on its own, but that can also be used by other AGI systems. A link to software examples can be found on our website.

Please note that the different mechanisms of this AGI are symbolic by nature. A number of these can also be implemented by sub-symbolic mechanisms such as machine learning. But the fact that quarks underly and define elements should remain in order for the AGI to interpret and relate all aspects of its system.

References

1. Goertzel, B.: From narrow AI to AGI via narrow AGI? SingularityNET (2019)
2. Schwartz, S.H., Bardi, A.: Value hierarchies across cultures: taking a similarities perspective. J. Cross-Cult. Psychol. **32**(3), 268–290 (2001)
3. Goertzel, B.: The general theory of general intelligence. A pragmatic patternist perspective, Arxiv (2021)
4. Goertzel, B.: The Hidden Pattern. A Patternist Philosophy of Mind. BrownWalker Press, Boca Raton (2006)
5. Kauffman, S.: The Origins of Order. Oxford University Press, Oxford (1993)
6. Fontana, W.: Algorithmic chemistry: a model for functional self-organization. Technical report LA-UR-90-1959 Los Alamos National Laboratory (1990)

Purely Symbolic Induction of Structure

Linas Vepštas[(✉)] [iD]

OpenCog Foundation, Rockville, USA
linasvepstas@gmail.com

Abstract. Techniques honed for the induction of grammar from text corpora can be extended to visual, auditory and other sensory domains, providing a structure for such senses that can be understood in terms of symbols and grammars. This simultaneously solves the classical "symbol grounding problem" while also providing a pragmatic approach to developing practical software systems that can articulate the world around us in a symbolic, communicable fashion.

1 Introduction

The symbolic approach to cognition is founded on the idea that observed nature can be categorized into distinct entities which are involved in relationships with one another. In this approach, the primary challenges are to recognize entities, and to discover what relationships there are between them.

The recognition problem is to be applied to sensory input. That is, we cannot know nature directly, as it is, but only by means of observation and sensing. Conventionally, this can be taken to be the classical five senses: hearing, touch, smell, vision, taste; or, more generally, scientific instruments and engineered detectors. Such sensors generate collections of data; this may be time-ordered, or simply a jumbled bag of data-points.

Out of this jumble of data, the goal of entity detection is to recognize groupings of data that *always* occur together. The adverb *"always"* here is key: entities are those things that are not events: they have existence over extended periods of time (Heidegger's "Dasein"). The goal of relationship detection is to determine both the structure of entities (part-whole relationships) as well as events (statistical co-occurrences and causation). If one is somehow able to detect and discern entities, and observe frequent relationships between them, then the path to symbolic processing becomes accessible. Each entity can be assigned a symbol (thus resolving the famous "symbol grounding problem"), and conventional ideas about information theory can be applied to perform reasoning, inference and deduction.

The goal of this paper is to develop a general theory for the conversion of sensory data into symbolic relationships. It is founded both on a collection of mathematical formalisms and also on a collection of experimental results. The experimental results are presented in a companion text; this text focuses on presenting the mathematical foundations in as simple and direct a fashion as possible.

B. Goertzel et al. (Eds.): AGI 2022, LNAI 13539, pp. 134–144, 2023.
https://doi.org/10.1007/978-3-031-19907-3_13

In the first section, the general relationship between graphs and grammars is sketched out, attempting to illustrate just how broad, general and all-encompassing this is. Next, it is shown how this symbolic structure can be extended to visual and auditory perception. After this comes a mathematical deep-dive, reviewing how statistical principles can be used to discern relationships between entities. Working backwards, a practical algorithm is presented for extracting entities themselves. To conclude, a collection of hypothesis and wild speculations are presented.

2   From Graphs to Grammar

Assuming that sensory data can be categorized into entities and relationships, the natural representation is that of graphs: each entity is represented by a vertex, each relationship is represented by an edge. Vertexes are labeled with symbols, edges with symbol pairs. An example is illustrated below.

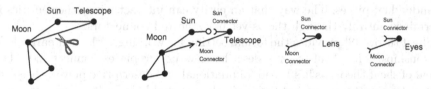

On the left is a conventional sparse graph of relationships between entities. On the right is the same graph, with some of the edges cut into half-edges, with the half-edge connectors labeled with what they can connect to. The connectors are drawn with distinct shapes, intended to convey what they are allowed to connect to. Such vertices, together with a collection of connectors, can be imagined to be jigsaw puzzle pieces, waiting to be connected.

The simplicity of the above diagram is deceptive. There is a deep and broad mathematical foundation: jigsaw pieces are the elements of a "monoidal category" [7]. The connectors themselves are type-theoretic types. The jigsaw pieces are the syntactical elements of a grammar. These last three statements arise from a relatively well-known generalization of Curry-Howard correspondence: for every category, there is a type theory, a grammar and a logic; from each, the others can be determined [2].

The jigsaw paradigm in linguistics has been repeatedly rediscovered [4, 11, 13, 23]. The diagram below is taken from the first paper on Link Grammar [17]. Syntactically valid sentences are formed whenever all of the jigsaw connectors fully mated. This fashion of specifying a grammar may feel unconventional; such grammars can be automatically (i.e. algorithmically) transformed into equivalent HPSG, DG, LFG, *etc.* style grammars. Link Grammar is equivalent to Combinatory Categorial Grammar (CCG) [21].

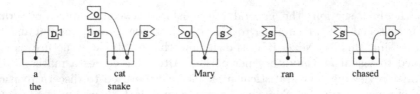

a   cat   Mary   ran   chased
the   snake

Compositionality and Sheaves. The naive replacement of entities by vertexes and relationships by edges seems to have a problem with well-foundedness. If an entity is made of parts, does this mean that a vertex is made of parts? What are those parts made of? Is there an infinite regress? How might one indicate the fact that some entity has a composite structure? These questions are resolved by observing that a partially-assembled jigsaw puzzle resembles a singular jigsaw piece: it externalizes as-yet unconnected connectors, while also showing the connectivity of the assembled portions. Jigsaws resolve the part-whole conundrum: the "whole" is a partially assembled jigsaw; the parts are the individual pieces. The way that an entity can interact with other entities is determined entirely through the as-yet unconnected connectors.

Sheaf theory [8] provides the formal setting for working with such part-whole relationships. The sheaf axioms describe how jigsaw pieces connect [20]. The appeal of sheaf theory is it's broad foundational and descriptive power: the sheaf axioms describe topology and logic (via the extended Curry-Howard correspondence mentioned above). Natural language can be taken in this broader setting.

Pervasiveness. After becoming familiar with the jigsaw paradigm, it becomes evident that it is absolutely pervasive. A common depiction of DNA uses jigsaw connectors for the amino acids ATGC. The antibody (immunoglobulin) is conventionally depicted in terms of jigsaws. Chemical reactions can be depicted as the assembly of jigsaw pieces.

Composition (beta reduction) in term algebra can be seen as the act of connecting jigsaws. Consider a term (or "function symbol") $f(x)$ with typed variable x. Constants are type instances; for example, the integer 42. Beta reduction is the act of "plugging in": $f(x) : 42 \mapsto f(42)$. Re-interpreted as jigsaw connectors, the term $f(x)$ is a female-coded jigsaw, and 42 is a male-coded jigsaw. To connect, the types must match (the variable x must be typed as integer). This kind of plugging-in or composition (with explicit or implicit type constraints) is rampant throughout mathematics. Examples can be found in proof theory, [19] lambda calculus, [3] term algebras [1] and model theory [5].

Vision and Sound. Shapes have a structural grammar, too. The connectors can specify location, color, shape, texture. The structural decomposition is that it is *not about pixels*! The structural decomposition is scale-invariant (more or less, unless some connector fixes the scale) and rotationally invariant (unless some connector fixes direction). The structural grammar captures the morphology of the shape, it's general properties It can omit details when they are impertinent, and capture them when they are important.

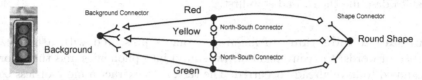

Audio data can also be given a jigsaw structure. On the left is a spectrogram of a whale song; time along the horizontal axis, frequency on the vertical, intensity depicted as a color.

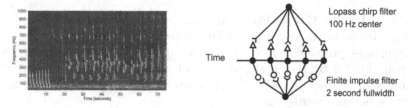

A midsection of the song is shown as jigsaws: the number of repetitions (six), the frequency distribution (its a chirp, which can be discovered with a chirp filter.) Individual repetitions can be spotted with a finite impulse response filter. Sensory information can be described in grammatical terms.

3 Symbolic Learning

In order for a graphical, sheaf-theoretic, grammatical theory of structure to serve as a foundation stone for AGI, there most be a practical algorithm for extracting structure from sensory data. This can be achieved in three steps. The first step is chunking (tokenization), the division of sensory data into candidate entities and interactions. The second step takes a collection of candidate graphs, splits them into jigsaw pieces, and then classifies jigsaw pieces into common categories, based on their commonalities. The third step is a recursive step, to repeat the process again, but this time taking the discovered structure as the sensory input. It is meant to be a hierarchical crawl up the semantic ladder.

Tokenization, induction of grammar, entity detection and predicate-argument structure have been experimentally explored in linguistics for decades; a review cannot be given here. What has been missing until now is a unified framework in which sensory (visual and audio) data can be processed on the same footing as linguistic structure. The OpenCog system, specifically the AtomSpace and the Learn project,[1] provide an implementation of that unified framework. Research has focused on the second step of the above algorithm; extensive research diaries

---

[1] See the "AtomSpace" and "Learn project" in github.

log the results.[2] A summary of these results is presented as a companion paper to this one. Explorations of the first and third steps have hardly begun. It is easiest to describe the second step first.

Grammatical Induction. In linguistics, one is presented with a tokenized sequence of words; the conversion of raw sound into phonemes and then words is presumed to have already occurred. The task is to extract a more-or-less conventional lexical grammar, given a corpus of text. This may be done as follows. First, perform a Maximum Spanning Tree (MST) parse; next, split the MST parse into jigsaw pieces; finally, classify those pieces into lexical vectors. The process is inherently statistical.

Maximum Planar Graph Parsing. MST parsing is described by Yuret [22]. Starting with a corpus, maintain a count $N(u, w)$ of nearby word-pairs (u, w). The frequentist probability $p(u, w) = N(u, w) / N(*, *)$ is the count of a given word-pair divided by the total count of all word-pairs. The star indicates a marginal sum, so that $p(u, *) = \sum_w p(u, w) = N(u, *) / N(*, *)$. The Lexical Attraction between word-pairs is

$$MI(u, w) = \log_2 \frac{p(u, w)}{p(u, *) \, p(*, w)}$$

This lexical attraction is just the mutual information; it has a somewhat unusual form, as word-pairs are necessarily not symmetric: $(u, w) \neq (w, u)$. The MI may be negative! The range of values depends on the size of the corpus; for a "typical" corpus, it ranges from -10 to $+30$.

The MST parse of a sentence is obtained by considering all possible trees, and selecting the one with the largest possible total MI. The example below is, taken from Yuret's thesis. The numbers in the links are the MI between the indicated words.

Maximal planar graphs (MPG) (graphs with loops, but no intersecting links) appear to offer experimentally-observable advantages over trees, they constrain the grammar more tightly and offer advantages similar to those of catena-based linguistic theory [14]. MST parses are linguistically plausible: they correspond, more or less, to what trained linguists would write down for a parse. The accuracy is reasonably high. Perfect accuracy is not needed, as later stages make up for this. Yuret indicates that the best results are obtained when one accumulates at least a million sentences. This is not outrageous: work in child psychology indicates that human babies hear several million sentences by the age of two years.

---

[2] See the diaries in the aforementioned project.

Lexical Entries. Given an MST or MPG parse, the lexis is constructed by chopping up the parse into jigsaw pieces, and then accumulating the counts on the jigsaw pieces. This is shown below.

Several kinds of notation are in common use such lexical entries. In tensorial notation, $ball : \overleftarrow{|the\rangle} \otimes \overleftarrow{|throw\rangle}$. In Link Grammar, `ball : the−& throw−`; the minus signs indicate connections to the left. The ampersand is the conjunction operator from a fragment of linear logic; it demands that both connectors be present. Linear logic is the logic of tensor algebras (by the aforementioned Curry-Howard correspondence.) Unlike tensor algebras, natural language has a distinct left-right asymmetry, and so the corresponding logic (of the monoidal category of natural language) is just a fragment of linear logic. Note that all of quantum mechanics lies inside of the tensor algebra; this explains why assorted quantum concepts seem to recur in natural language discussions.

Connector sequences such as $\overleftarrow{|the\rangle} \otimes \overleftarrow{|throw\rangle}$ are disjoined in the lexis; each such sequence is called a disjunct. Given a word w, a lexical entry consists of all word-disjunct pairs (w, d) together with their observed count $N(w, d)$. The normalized frequency is $p(w, d) = N(w, d) / N(*, *)$ where $N(*, *)$ is the sum over all word-disjunct pairs. A lexical entry is thus a sparse skip-gram-like vector:

$$\overrightarrow{w} = p(w, d_1)\,\widehat{e_1} + \cdots + p(w, d_n)\,\widehat{e_n}$$

The logical disjunction "or" can be used in place of the plus sign; this would be the "choice" operator in linear logic (as in "menu choice": pick one or another). The basis vectors $\widehat{e_k}$ are short-hand for the skip-gram disjuncts $\overleftarrow{|the\rangle} \otimes \overleftarrow{|throw\rangle}$.

Similarity. The lexis generated above contains individual words with connectors to other, specific words. Taken as a matrix, the lexis is sparse but still quite large. To obtain a conventional grammar in terms of nouns, verbs and adjectives, dimensional reduction must be performed. This can be achieved by clustering with respect to a similarity metric. A conventional similarity metric is the cosine distance

$$\cos\theta = \overrightarrow{w} \cdot \overrightarrow{v} = \sum_d p(w, d)\,p(v, d)$$

As a metric, it fails, because the space spanned by these vectors is *not Euclidean space*! It is a probability space, with unit-length probability vectors: $1 = \sum_{w,d} p(w, d)$. The correct similarity is the mutual information:

$$MI(w, v) = \log_2 \frac{\overrightarrow{w} \cdot \overrightarrow{v}}{(\overrightarrow{w} \cdot \overrightarrow{*})(\overrightarrow{*} \cdot \overrightarrow{v})} \qquad \text{where} \qquad \overrightarrow{w} \cdot \overrightarrow{*} = \sum_d p(w, d)\,p(*, d)$$

Experimentally, the distribution of the MI for word pairs is Gaussian.[3] This is remarkable: it implies that the word vectors are uniformly distributed on the surface of a (high-dimensional) sphere: a Gaussian Orthogonal Ensemble (a spin glass) [18]. In this sense, one can see that natural language is maximally disambiguating.

In this way, after transforming to a sphere, a plain cosine distance be used. The sphere vectors are given by $\vec{w} = \sum_v MI(w,v)\hat{v}$. The center of the sphere must be subtracted, and the vectors normalized to unit length before taking a dot product.

Classification. In practice, clustering is not straightforward. One wishes to first cluster the most frequent words first, whereas the highest MI pairs are very rare. This suggests defining a ranked-MI, adjusted by the average log frequency:

$$MI_{\mathrm{rank}}(w,v) = MI(w,v) + \frac{\log_2 p(w,*) + \log_2 p(v,*)}{2} = \log_2 \frac{\vec{w} \cdot \vec{v}}{\sqrt{(\vec{w} \cdot \vec{*})(\vec{*} \cdot \vec{v})}}$$

Experimentally, this just shifts the Gaussian to the right.

Word-Sense Disambiguation. Words can have multiple meanings. Two words may be deemed to be similar, but not all of the disjuncts can be dumped into a common class; some of the disjuncts may belong to other word-senses. For example, a portion of the word-vector for "saw" can be clustered with other cutting tools, while the remainder can be clustered with viewing verbs. This presents a practical difficulty: off-the-shelf clustering algorithms cannot perform word-sense disambiguation.

Connectors must also be merged. The rewriting of connector sequences is subtle, as it affects word-vectors outside of those being merged (the merged connectors might appear anywhere). To maintain coherency, "detailed balance" must be preserved: the grand total counts must remain the same both before and after merge.

Factorization. The clustering described above can be understood to be a form of matrix factorization. The word-disjunct matrix $p(w,d)$ is factorized into three matrices LCR as

$$p(w,d) = \sum_{g,g'} p_L(w,g)\, p_C(g,g')\, p_R(g',d)$$

where g is a "word class" (*e.g.* common noun, transitive verb) and g' is a "grammatical relation" (*e.g.* subject, object, modifier). The matrices L and R are very sparse, which C is compact, dense and highly connected. A sense of the scale

---

[3] See the Language Learning Diary Part Three, *op. cit.*

of factorization can be obtained from the hand-curated English-language dictionary. It consists of about 100K words, 2K word classes, several hundred grammatical relations (LG "macros") and 30 million disjuncts. In other words, the central component is quite small. Factorization provides an aid to interpretability. Instead of a morass of matrix elements, word-classes are recognizable as such, as is the predicate-argument structure. This is the power of a symbolic, lexical approach.

4 Chunking/Tokenization

The relatively straightforward tokenization of written English hides the difficulty of chunking in general. How can one obtain a comparable chunking of raw audio or visual data? The goal is to obtain, by automatic means, a sequence of transducers, from sounds to phonemes and syllables and words.

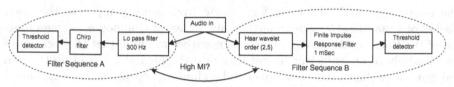

A pair of transducers in block-diagram form is shown. The generation of such sequences can be managed through genetic program (GP) learning techniques. An example of a GP system is provided by MOSES [9, 10]. Given a collection of "okay" filter sequences, GP can explore both the parameter space to provide a better tuning, and, by means of mutation and cross-over, generate other filter sequences. The goal is to find high-quality "feature recognizers", indicating the presence of a salient feature in the sensory environment.

Learning in GP systems is guided by maximizing a utility (scoring) function. But what should that function be, in an unsupervised setting? Just as one discovered structure in language through entropy maximization, one can use the same ideas here. For all features (filter sets) currently under consideration, one looks for high-MI correlations. Features that are poorly detected have poor correlation and low information content; crisp recognizers should be sharply correlated.

The Symbol Grounding Problem and the Frame Problem. An old problem in philosophy (dating back to Socrates) is the symbol grounding problem.[4] When one says the word "chair", what does that mean? Both extensional lists of things one can sit and intensional lists of properties fail; they are never complete. Affordances provide the answer: to be a chair, an object must be sit-on-able. The DSP filter sequence is precisely an affordance-detector.

A simpler example. If someone says "I hear whistling in the distance", what does the word "whistling" actually mean? How to describe it? What is the

---

[4] See the Stanford Encyclopedia of Philosophy, "Frame Problem" and "Embodied Cognition".

grounding for the symbol "whistling"? Filter sequences explicitly manifest the grounding. "Whistling" is a certain kind of hi-pass filter attached to a chirp filter with a certain finite impulse response time. That is what "whistling" is. What else could it possibly have been?

The Frame Problem posits that the number of objects and events overwhelms the current focus. Entropy-maximizing training of filter sequences solves this. Mutual information tells you what things "go together". The grammatical structure reveals *how* those things go together. The vast ocean of sensory stimulus is reduced to a trickle of symbolic relationships, arriving either in a regular, expected pattern (and thus ignorable), or arriving in unexpected, surprising ways, demanding attention.

5   Abstraction and Recursion

The above presented techniques for moving from sensory input to the lower reaches of semantics. Can one go farther, and arrive at common-sense reasoning, one of the Holy Grails of AGI? The author wishes to argue that the techniques described above are sufficient to reach up into the highest levels of abstraction and general intelligence. It is a ladder to be climbed, repeating the same operations on each new layer of abstraction.

The next few rungs of the ladder can be found in linguistics. The MST parsing algorithm given above was presented at the word-pair level. When applied at the semantic level, it becomes the Mihalcea algorithm [12].

In lexical semantics, there is an idea of "lexical implication rules" [15]. These are rules that control how words used in one context can be used in a different context. The discovery of these rules be automated: each rule has the form of a jigsaw, and the algorithm for inferring jigsaws has already been presented. Jigsaw assembly is parsing: given a set of constraints (for example, a sequence of words) parsing is the act of finding jigsaw pieces that fit the word-sequence. Parsing technologies, and their more general cousins, the theorem-provers, are well-understood.

Lexical implication rules generalize to the "lexical functions" (LF) of Meaning-Text Theory (MTT) [6]. The MTT is a well-developed theory of the "semantic" layer of linguistics, sitting atop surface syntax. An algorithm for learning LF's is described by Poon & Domingos [16]. The relationship to the current work is obscured by their use of jigsaws written as lambdas; rephrasing as jigsaws makes it clear that it is just a hunt for equivalent jigsaw sub-assemblies (synonymous phrases). Anaphora resolution, reference resolution and entity detection are well-explored topics in computational linguistics. The jigsaw metaphor demonstrates precisely how one can climb the rungs of the ladder: from pair-wise correlations up to grammars. In the presence of a grammar, we once again know what is ordinary, and can then renew the search for surprising pair-wise correlations, this time at the next layer of abstraction.

5.1   Common Sense

Can this be used to learn common sense? I believe so. How might this work? Let me illustrate by explaining an old joke: "Doctor Doctor, it hurts when I do this! Well, don't do that!". The explanation is shown below, in the form of a rule, using the notation from proof theory. The thick horizontal bar separates the premises from the conclusions. It is labeled as "Joke" to indicate what kind of rule it is.

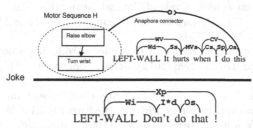

The "sequent" is the anaphora connector, which connects the word "this" the a specific motor sequence. Which motor sequence? Well, presumably one that was learned, by automatic process (perhaps GP), to move a limb. All of the components of this diagram are jigsaw pieces. All of the pieces can be discovered probabilistically. All of the connectors can be connected probabilistically. The learning algorithm shows how to discern structure from what is superficially seems like a chaotic stream of sensory input. Common sense can be learned.

References

1. Baader, F., Nipkow, T.: Term Rewriting and All That. Cambridge University Press, Cambridge (1998). https://doi.org/10.1145/356458.1008651
2. Baez, J.C., Stay, M.: Physics, topology, logic and computation: a Rosetta stone. Arxiv/abs/0903.0340 (2009). https://doi.org/10.1007/978-3-642-12821-9_2. http://math.ucr.edu/home/baez/rosetta.pdf
3. Barendregt, H.P.: The Lambda Calculus: Its Syntax and Semantics. North-Holland, Amsterdam (1981). https://doi.org/10.2307/2274112
4. Coecke, B.: Quantum links let computers read. New Scientist, December 2010. http://www.cs.ox.ac.uk/people/bob.coecke/NewScientist.pdf
5. Hodges, W.: A Shorter Model Theory. Cambridge University Press, Cambridge (1997). https://doi.org/10.5555/262326
6. Kahane, S.: The meaning-text theory. Dependency and valency. Int. Handb. Contemp. Res. **1**, 546–570 (2003). http://www.coli.uni-saarland.de/courses/syntactic-theory-09/literature/MTT-Handbook2003.pdf
7. Lane, S.M.: Categories for the Working Mathematician. Springer, Heidelberg (1978). https://doi.org/10.1007/978-1-4757-4721-8
8. Lane, S.M., Moerdijk, I.: Sheaves in Geometry and Logic. Springer, Heidelberg (1992). https://doi.org/10.1007/978-1-4612-0927-0
9. Looks, M.: Competent program evolution. Ph.D. thesis, Washington University St. Louis (2006)

10. Looks, M.: Meta-optimizing semantic evolutionary search. In: Lipson, H. (ed.) Genetic and Evolutionary Computation Conference (GECCO), p. 626. ACM (2007)
11. Marcus, S.: Algebraic Linguistics; Analytical Models. Elsevier (1967). https:// monoskop.org/images/2/26/Marcus_Solomon_editor_Algebraic_Linguistics_ Analytical_Models_1967.pdf
12. Mihalcea, R.: Unsupervised large-vocabulary word sense disambiguation with graph-based algorithms for sequence data labeling. In: Proceedings of HLT 2005, pp. 411–418. ACL (2005). https://doi.org/10.3115/1220575.1220627
13. Nida, E.: The molecular level of lexical semantics. Int. J. Lexicogr. **10**, 265–274 (1997). https://www.academia.edu/36534355/The_Molecular_Level_of_ Lexical_Semantics_by_EA_Nida
14. Osborne, T., Putnam, M., Groß, T.: Catenae: introducing a novel unit of syntactic analysis. Syntax **15**, 354–396 (2012). https://doi.org/10.1111/j.1467-9612.2012. 00172.x
15. Ostler, N., Atkins, B.T.S.: Predictable meaning shift: some linguistic properties of lexical implication rules. In: Proceedings of the First SIGLEX Workshop on Lexical Semantics and Knowledge Representation (1991). https://doi.org/10.1007/3-540-55801-2_29
16. Poon, H., Domingos, P.: Unsupervised semantic parsing. In: EMNLP 2009, pp. 1–10. ACL, August 2009. https://doi.org/10.5555/1699510.1699512. http://www. aclweb.org/anthology/D/D09/D09-1001
17. Sleator, D., Temperley., D.: Parsing English with a link grammar. Technical report, Carnegie Mellon University, Computer Science, CMU-CS-91-196 (1991). http:// arxiv.org/pdf/cmp-lg/9508004
18. Talagrand, M.: Mean Field Models for Spin Glasses. Springer, Heidelberg (2010). https://doi.org/10.1007/978-3-642-15202-3
19. Troelstra, A.S., Schwichtenberg, H.: Basic Proof Theory, 2nd edn. Cambridge University Press, Cambridge (1996). https://doi.org/10.1017/CBO9781139168717
20. Vepstas, L.: Sheaves: a topological approach to big data (2017). arXiv:1901.01341
21. Vepstas, L.: Combinatory categorial grammar and link grammar are equivalent (2022). https://github.com/opencog/atomspace/raw/master/opencog/sheaf/ docs/ccg.pdf, unpublished
22. Yuret, D.: Discovery of linguistic relations using lexical attraction. Ph.D. thesis, MIT (1998). https://doi.org/10.48550/arXiv.cmp-lg/9805009. http://www2. denizyuret.com/pub/yuretphd.html
23. Zeng, W., Coecke, B.: Quantum algorithms for compositional natural language processing. In: Electronic Proceedings in Theoretical Computer Science (EPTCS) 221 (2016). https://doi.org/10.4204/EPTCS.221.8. arXiv:1608.01406

Accepted for Full Oral Presentation

Extended Subdomains: A Solution to a Problem of Hernández-Orallo and Dowe

Samuel Allen Alexander[✉]

The U.S. Securities and Exchange Commission, New York City, NY, USA
samuelallenalexander@gmail.com
https://philpeople.org/profiles/samuel-alexander/publications

Abstract. This is a paper about the general theory of measuring or estimating social intelligence via benchmarks. Hernández-Orallo and Dowe described a problem with certain proposed intelligence measures. The problem suggests that those intelligence measures might not accurately capture social intelligence. We argue that Hernández-Orallo and Dowe's problem is even more general than how they stated it, applying to many subdomains of AGI, not just the one subdomain in which they stated it. We then propose a solution. In our solution, instead of using test-cases within the given AGI subdomain to estimate an AI's intelligence, one would use test-cases in an extended subdomain where test-cases have the ability to simulate the AI being tested. Surprisingly, AIs only designed for the original subdomain can be tested with test-cases in the extended subdomain anyway. By extending the subdomain in this way, we might avoid Hernández-Orallo and Dowe's problem.

Keywords: Social intelligence · Intelligence measurement · Universal intelligence

1 Introduction

The problem of designing AGI goes hand-in-hand with the problem of measuring the intelligence of artificial agents. After all, without the ability to measure intelligence, it would be hard to even know whether progress is being made toward AGI. For the diverse and wide-ranging types of intelligent agents considered by AGI researchers as a whole, the intelligence-measurement problem is quite difficult (it is not clear to what extent objective intelligence measurement is even possible in such a general context). Concrete progress can be made by restricting attention to narrow, well-defined subdomains of AGI. Within a narrow subdomain of AGI, one can measure (or at least estimate) intelligence by using benchmarks: how well does the agent perform on such-and-such test-cases? For example, how well does a given AI perform at Atari games? Such subdomains of AGI can be considered as (in Goertzel's words) "idealized case[s] of AGI, similar to assumptions like the frictionless plane in physics" [4].

B. Goertzel et al. (Eds.): AGI 2022, LNAI 13539, pp. 147–157, 2023.
https://doi.org/10.1007/978-3-031-19907-3_14

Hernández-Orallo and Dowe pointed out [6] a problem in certain theoretical intelligence-measurement benchmarks. We will argue that the problem they point out is actually much more general: they posed it in the context of one particular subdomain of AGI but it is not limited to that subdomain. A benchmark generally consists of a battery of simple test-cases, or a simple procedural method for randomly generating test-cases. But this seems to prevent the test-cases from having genuine social aspects, for the following reason. To include genuine social aspects in a test-case would (apparently) require that genuine intelligence be somehow built into that test-case. For example, in an Atari game, enemy (or ally) Non-Player Characters (NPCs) are simplistic automatons. Simplistic automatons are not genuinely social. To add genuine social aspects to an Atari game, one would need to replace those automatons with genuinely intelligent agents. But the complexity of such agents would far exceed the complexity of the Atari game! Or, if test-cases are generated procedurally, perhaps the procedure could randomly generate test-cases with genuine social aspects, but the odds of this would be extremely small. One could replace an Atari NPC's script with a randomly-generated script, but the odds are negligible that the NPC would thus become genuinely intelligent. So then, how can our benchmarks capture social intelligence?

We will propose a general solution where AIs in one subdomain are benchmarked against test-cases in an extended subdomain. In the extended subdomain, test-cases have the ability to secretly simulate the agent being measured. For example, to measure AIs in the subdomain of Atari games, we would run those AIs against *extended Atari games*. An extended Atari game is just like an Atari game, except that the game's mechanics are allowed to use an oracle to query what the AI playing the game would do in arbitrary situations. We will argue that in the extended subdomain, genuine social aspects can be built into simple test-cases. Furthermore, this solution is surprisingly quite practical. In the Atari subdomain, for example, if we have an AI's source-code, we can use that source-code to realize the oracle needed to run the AI in an extended Atari game. By contrast, it would be virtually impossible for a human to play extended Atari games in general, because it would be virtually impossible to realize an oracle that could predict the human's actions in arbitrary situations[1].

2   Background: The Hernández-Orallo and Dowe Problem

'How can we create environments so that they have intelligent agents inside? It is enlightening (but perhaps of little practical use) to think that some extremely complex infinite environments we consider as possible in the test could contain "life". In some of them, we could even find "intelligent beings" ... When we say that it is perhaps of little practical use, it is because the complexity of these environments is extremely high and the

---

[1] Even a perfect genetic clone of the human player would not be enough, since a human player's actions are not determined by genetics alone but depend on a whole lifetime of previous learning and interaction with the world.

probability of one of them appearing by chance is almost zero. Therefore, we cannot bind the evaluation of social intelligence to this remote chance. However, this a priori remote probability is in fact a much higher a posteriori probability if we think in terms of evolution. ... Consequently, we require inserting these other agents into the environments'—Hernández-Orallo and Dowe [6]

Hernández-Orallo and Dowe did not state their problem in its full generality. They stated it [6] in the universal intelligence context of [10], essentially a very formal, theoretical version of the reinforcement learning (RL) context. We will avoid spelling everything out in full detail as the details are verbose and unimportant. Roughly speaking, in the universal intelligence context, *agents* interact with *environments*. They take turns. On the agent's turn, the agent takes an *action*. On the environment's turn, the environment gives the agent an *observation* and a *reward*. Certain technical constraints are placed on the rewards which the environment can output, in order to ensure certain convergence properties. The agent is considered to perform better or worse in a given environment if the rewards it receives are bigger or smaller, respectively.

Legg and Hutter proposed [10] defining the numerical intelligence level of such an agent to be the average total reward the agent receives across the space of all computable environments, weighting environments with some distribution. A uniform distribution would be no good because No-Free Lunch theorems imply all agents would end up with the same exact intelligence measure, see [8]. Legg and Hutter instead proposed giving each environment μ a weight of $2^{-K(\mu)}$ where $K(\mu)$ is the Kolmogorov complexity of μ (the length of the shortest computer program for μ). Note that $K(\mu)$ depends implicitly on the choice of a background Universal Turing Machine (UTM). Intuitively one can think of a UTM as a programming language, so the choice amounts to choosing: which programming language should environments be programmed in? This choice is non-trivial, see [12][2].

Other methods have also been proposed for measuring intelligence in the universal intelligence context. The Legg-Hutter intelligence definition is impractical because, mathematically, the average performance of the agent across the whole space of computable environments, is an infinite sum, each term of which involves the Kolmogorov complexity function (itself already non-computable). More practical methods involve running the agent for bounded numbers of turns against randomly-generated environments. Universal intelligence measures of this type are proposed by Legg and Veness [11] and by Hernández-Orallo and Dowe themselves [6]. Hernández-Orallo and Dowe further refine the idea, proposing to dynamically adjust the complexity of the randomly-generated environments based on the agent's performance, an idea motivated by human psychometrics.

All these methods of measuring universal intelligence are highly susceptible to Hernández-Orallo and Dowe's problem. Environments containing genuinely-intelligent built-in NPCs must be highly complicated. So in the Legg-Hutter infinite sum, any such environment would contribute very little, because its weight

---

[2] Some progress on UTM-choice was presented at last year's AGI conference [3].

$2^{-K(\mu)}$ would be extremely small. In intelligence measures based on running the agent in randomly-generated environments, the odds are quite small that a randomly-generated environment would contain a genuinely intelligent NPC. So all these intelligence measures would seem to poorly capture social intelligence.

Hernández-Orallo et al. [7] proposed using multi-agent environments to solve the problem. In their proposal, in order to quantitatively estimate the intelligence of an agent, one would randomly generate multi-agent environments, and also randomly select agents for each multi-agent role (except for the role to be filled by the agent being measured). Despite this solution's inherent beauty, it is not very practical. Either the randomly-generated agents are generated completely at random (e.g., they have random source-codes), in which case the odds of such an agent being genuinely intelligent are extremely small; or, they are generated in some way such that with non-negligible probability they are genuinely intelligent. But the latter seems almost as difficult as creating AGI in the first place, so an intelligence measure dependent on it might not be very helpful as a step toward AGI. We will propose a different solution to Hernández-Orallo and Dowe's problem, which does not involve randomly generating agents.

2.1   The Generalized Hernández-Orallo and Dowe Problem

Nothing about the Hernández-Orallo and Dowe Problem inherently depends on the particular background of universal intelligence in which they stated it. The problem applies any time we would use simple test-cases (or a simple procedure for generating test-cases) to benchmark AIs in any subdomain of AGI. We would state the general problem as follows:

Problem 1 *(The Generalized Hernández-Orallo and Dowe Problem). Assume we are working in some subdomain of AGI where we want to benchmark AIs against test-cases. Any test-case with genuine intelligence built into it must necessarily be highly complex. Thus, no such test-case can occur in any fixed library of simple test-cases, and no such test-case can be generated with non-negligible probability by any simple procedure for generating test-cases. Thus, no such library or procedure can be used to reliably benchmark social intelligence (since social intelligence requires interaction with other genuine intelligences).*

Note that when we say "no such test-case can be generated with non-negligible probability..." we assume a certain sparseness condition. For any n, if S_1 is the set of all length-n computer programs, and S_2 is the set of all length-n computer programs of AGIs, then presumably $|S_2|/|S_1| \approx 0$. Given an algorithm for an AGI, one could contrive a programming language falsifying this (e.g., contrive the language so that said algorithm can be written in just 1 character). We believe this sparseness assumption is plausible for natural programming languages whose semantics do not depend on any already-known AGI.

Example 2 *(Image classification). Consider a subdomain of AGI where image classifiers can be trained on labeled images and asked to predict labels of unlabeled* *images. Fix some genuinely intelligent classifier A_0 and some finite set T of images with labels from $\{0, 1\}$. Assume A_0 has been trained on T. Suppose A is a classifier whose intelligence we are trying to measure. As one test-case, we could systematically investigate how well A learns to classify images as either "images A_0 classifies as 0" or "images A_0 classifies as 1".*

The test-case in Example 2 is presumably complicated, because it depends on the genuinely intelligent classifier A_0. Thus, the test-case would never be included in any simple test-case library, and there is low probability it would be generated by any simple test-case-generating procedure. Thus, any estimate of a classifier's intelligence based on a simple test-case library, or on test-cases generated by a simple procedure, would fail to reliably capture the classifier's performance on the test-case in question. One could argue that the test-case in question is a social intelligence test-case, because it tests how well the classifier learns to anticipate its colleague A_0.

3 Extending Subdomains to Solve the Hernández-Orallo and Dowe Problem

We propose to solve Problem 1 by extending the subdomain in question so as to admit simple new test-cases capable of incorporating social aspects, in such a way that a given AI (only designed for the original subdomain) can still attempt test-cases in the extended subdomain. The intuitive idea is that, in the extended domain, when an AI is being tested on a test-case, the test-case is allowed to query an oracle which tells the test-case what the AI would output in response to arbitrary inputs. This allows for self-play to be incorporated into the test-cases (below, we address the anticipated objection that self-play is not genuinely social). Certainly we are not claiming that self-play is a new innovation. It has been widely used to train agents for specific individual environments, from Backgammon all the way to StarCraft II, and in a sense it is also used in adversarial techniques such as GAN (see [5]). What is new in our proposal is that we suggest self-play can be applied to general social intelligence measurement, where, instead of having a specific environment in mind, we are interested in an agent's general performance over the whole space of all environments.

Definition 3. *A subdomain of AGI is a tuple $\mathscr{D} = (\mathscr{A}, U_{\mathscr{A}}, \mathscr{T}, U_{\mathscr{T}}, L)$ where:*

1. *$\mathscr{A}$ is a set of computer programs (called AIs) in programming language $U_{\mathscr{A}}$;*
2. *$\mathscr{T}$ is a set of computer programs (called test-cases) in programming language $U_{\mathscr{T}}$ which extends $U_{\mathscr{A}}$ (possibly including some oracles);*
3. *For all $U_{\mathscr{A}}$-programs a_1, a_2, if a_1 and a_2 both compute the same function, then $a_1 \in \mathscr{A}$ iff $a_2 \in \mathscr{A}$.*
4. *For all $U_{\mathscr{T}}$-programs t_1, t_2, if t_1 and t_2 both compute the same function, then $t_1 \in \mathscr{T}$ iff $t_2 \in \mathscr{T}$.*
5. *L is a computable function which takes $a \in \mathscr{A}$, $t \in \mathscr{T}$, $n \in \mathbb{N}$, and outputs a rational number $L(a, t, n) \in \mathbb{Q}$ which we call a measure of a's performance on t at step n.*

We say $\mathscr{D}$ is code-independent *if the following requirement holds: for all $a_1, a_2 \in \mathscr{A}$, for all $t_1, t_2 \in \mathscr{T}$, if a_1 and a_2 compute the same function, and t_1 and t_2 compute the same function, then for all $n \in \mathbb{N}$, $L(a_1, t_1, n) = L(a_2, t_2, n)$.*

Example 4. *Take $\mathscr{A}$ to be the set of programs defining RL agents (in some formalization of RL) and $\mathscr{T}$ to be the set of programs defining RL environments, both in some common language $U_{\mathscr{A}} = U_{\mathscr{T}}$. Let $L(a, t, n)$ be the nth reward a gets in an interaction with t. The resulting code-independent subdomain $\mathscr{D}$ could be called the RL subdomain of AGI.*

Definition 5. *Suppose $\mathscr{D} = (\mathscr{A}, U_{\mathscr{A}}, \mathscr{T}, U_{\mathscr{T}}, L)$ is a subdomain of AGI. The extension of $\mathscr{D}$ is the subdomain $\mathscr{D}' = (\mathscr{A}, U_{\mathscr{A}}, \mathscr{T}', U_{\mathscr{T}'}, L')$ where:*

1. *$U_{\mathscr{T}'}$ is the extension of $U_{\mathscr{T}}$ by a new oracle $\mathbf{a}$.*
2. *$\mathscr{T}'$ is the set of all $U_{\mathscr{T}'}$ programs t with the following property: for each $a \in \mathscr{A}$, if t_a is the $U_{\mathscr{T}}$ program obtained from t by replacing all instances of $\mathbf{a}$ by a, then $t_a \in \mathscr{T}$.*
3. *L' is the computable function which, on input $a \in \mathscr{A}$, $t \in \mathscr{T}'$, and $n \in \mathbb{N}$, outputs $L'(a, t, n) = L(a, t_a, n)$, where t_a is as above.*

If $\mathscr{D}$ is the RL subdomain of AGI (Example 4), then $\mathscr{D}'$ is a variation of RL in which environments can simulate agents in order to base their rewards and observations not only on what actions the agent has actually taken, but also on what actions the agent would hypothetically take in counterfactual scenarios[3].

Lemma 6. *If $\mathscr{D}$ is a subdomain of AGI, then $\mathscr{D}'$ really is a subdomain of AGI.*

Proof. The only nontrivial part of the claim is that L' is a computable function which, given $a \in \mathscr{A}$, $t \in \mathscr{T}'$, $n \in \mathbb{N}$, outputs $L'(a, t, n) \in \mathbb{Q}$. Clearly the operation of replacing instances of oracle $\mathbf{a}$ by a, is computable. So the computability of L' follows from the computability of L. By definition, $t \in \mathscr{T}'$ means $t_a \in \mathscr{T}$, so $L'(a, t, n) = L(a, t_a, n)$ exists and is in $\mathbb{Q}$ since L satisfies Definition 3.   □

Even though Lemma 6 is trivial, it has profound implications. It says that even though an AI is designed for the original, un-extended subdomain of AGI, that AI can nevertheless be tested using test-cases in the extended subdomain.

While clearly not a perfect solution, the following theorem at least partly solves Problem 1.

Theorem 7 (*Deparametrization Theorem*). *Let $\mathscr{D} = (\mathscr{A}, U_{\mathscr{A}}, \mathscr{T}, U_{\mathscr{T}}, L)$ be a code-independent subdomain of AGI. Suppose F is a $U_{\mathscr{T}}$ program which takes as input an AI $a \in \mathscr{A}$ and outputs a test-case $F(a) \in \mathscr{T}$. In the extended subdomain $\mathscr{D}' = (\mathscr{A}, U_{\mathscr{A}}, \mathscr{T}', U_{\mathscr{T}'}, L')$, there is a test-case F^*, of approximately the same complexity as F, such that for all $a \in \mathscr{A}$ and $n \in \mathbb{N}$, $L'(a, F^*, n) = L(a, F(a), n)$.*

---

[3] Alexander et al. explore this RL variation in [1], suggesting a variation of the Legg-Hutter intelligence measure that might measure an agent's self-reflection intelligence via its performance in extended RL environments (if these environments could be further pared down to just those of a social nature, the same idea could lead to a formal measure of RL agent social intelligence, but we do not currently know how to so pare them down).

Proof. Let F^* be the $U_{\mathscr{T}'}$ program:

1. Take input $\boldsymbol{X}$.
2. Output the result of running $F(\mathbf{a})$ on $\boldsymbol{X}$.

Clearly F^* has approximately the same complexity as F. For each $a \in \mathscr{A}$, F_a^* is the $\mathscr{T}$-program:

1. Take input $\boldsymbol{X}$.
2. Output the result of running $F(a)$ on $\boldsymbol{X}$.

Clearly F_a^* and $F(a)$ compute the same function. Thus by condition 4 of Definition 3, $F_a^* \in \mathscr{T}$. By arbitrariness of a, this shows $F^* \in \mathscr{T}'$. For any $a \in \mathscr{A}$ and $n \in \mathbb{N}$, $L'(a, F^*, n) = L(a, F_a^*, n)$ by Definition 5, which equals $L(a, F(a), n)$ since F_a^* and $F(a)$ compute the same function and $\mathscr{D}$ is code-independent.   □

Theorem 7 says that any AI-parametrized procedure for generating test-cases in the original subdomain can be replaced by a *single* test-case, in the extended subdomain, roughly as complex as the original procedure. In the single test-case, the AI-parameter is replaced by a simulated copy of the very AI we are trying to test. For example, suppose we want to test an Atari-playing AI's social intelligence. We could take $F(a)$ to be an Atari game in which the player plays "Super Breakout" with a as partner. Then F^* is a *single* extended Atari game in which the player plays "Super Breakout" with a *clone of herself* as her partner. Thus, the infinite test-case family, "Play Super Breakout with partner a" (each one of whose complexity is approximately the complexity of Super Breakout plus the complexity of a), is replaced by the single test-case, "Play Super Breakout with a clone of yourself as partner", roughly as complex as Super Breakout.

We would argue that test-cases produced by Theorem 7 are appropriate for benchmarking intelligence in a super-general context[4]. If we design an NPC opponent using a huge neural network, the resulting test-case has an inherent bias toward neural networks. That would be inappropriate for measuring alien intelligences based on some other technology. It would be rather arbitrary to judge a Martian life form by how well it can raise a *human* baby, or to judge a human by how well he can raise a *Martian* baby. But it would be quite appropriate to judge each by how well it can raise *a baby version of itself.*

The reader might object that there is nothing social about interacting with one's own clone. But in general, AIs act based not only on immediate stimulus, but on the whole history of prior stimuli. In short: AIs train. This is abstracted away in Definition 3. One should not think of the AIs in Definition 3 as taking immediate observations as sole inputs, but rather as taking entire histories as inputs. In Theorem 7, $F(a)$ might output a test-case where one plays chess against an instance of a that has been trained on, say, 50 years of random stimuli (generated dynamically, to keep F simple). Then F^* is a test-case where one

---

[4] Provided the test-cases $F(a)$ are nontrivial; Tic-Tac-Toe would be a poor social intelligence benchmark regardless of the opponent's intelligence.

plays chess against a clone of oneself trained with 50 years of random stimuli[5]. This could be quite different than playing against oneself directly. When Silver et al. declare that

"The agent consists solely of the decision-making entity; anything outside of that entity (including its body, if it has one) is considered part of the environment," [13]

that *body* would certainly include the brain and the hippocampus. So if I am being driven by an agent in Silver et al.'s sense, then a clone of that agent needn't share my memories. And to the extent that my personality depends on my memories (including what I was taught in school, etc.), said clone needn't share my personality. Indeed, if personality is a function of training, the following Paper-Rock-Scissors example illustrates how one could apply different training to a self-play opponent, encouraging the opponent to differ in personality from the agent.

Example 8 *(Paper-Rock-Scissors Python Example, see Listing 1.1). Consider a concrete formalization of RL in which environments are instances of Python environment-classes and agents are instances of agent-classes. An environment-class is required to implement a "start" method (outputting an initial observation) and a "step" method (which takes the agent's latest action and outputs an observation and a reward). An agent-class is required to implement an "act" method (which takes an observation and outputs an action) and a "train" method (which takes a prior observation, an action, a reward, and a next observation, the intent being that the agent should update its neural net, Q-table, etc., based on the fact that it took the given action in response to the given prior observation and this resulted in the given reward and the given next observation). This is a subdomain of AGI. The extended subdomain is identical except that an extended environment-class's methods have access to an oracle AgentClass (the* **a** *in Definition 5) for the agent-class used to instantiate the agent. Its methods can thus instantiate independent agent-clones for use in its reward-observation calculations. Listing 1.1 defines an extended environment-class where the agent plays Paper-Rock-Scissors against a clone of itself, but every move, the clone gets trained* twice *instead of once.*

Example 8 gives a single test-case in an extended subdomain. It corresponds to an infinite family of unextended test-cases, indexed by AgentClass. It tests the player's performance in the task[6]: "Play Paper-Rock-Scissors against a clone of yourself that trains twice as much as you." The extended environment has

---

[5] If the player is human-like, 50 years of such training might even make the clone so different that the player doesn't realize the opponent *is* a clone.

[6] The example is not trivialized by the random strategy. A good RL agent should balance *exploitation* of known good strategies (like random play) against *exploration*. Otherwise the agent would be suboptimal against certain flawed opponents. Indeed, this line of thought leads to Hibbard's hierarchical intelligence measures [9] [2].

Listing 1.1. An extended environment in which the agent plays Paper-Rock-Scissors against a clone of itself, but the clone trains twice as much.

```
class PaperRockScissors_DoubleTrainingEnemy:
  def start(self):
    # Instantiate a clone of the agent. This clone will play
    # the role of the agent's enemy.
    self.sim = AgentClass()
    # Start interaction with both player & enemy seeing paper
    self.prev_player_action = PAPER
    return {'obs': PAPER}

  def step(self, player_action):
    # Figure out which action the agent's enemy takes
    enemy_action = self.sim.act(obs=self.prev_player_action)

    player_reward = compute_reward(player_action, enemy_action)

    # Train the enemy based on how the enemy sees things
    # (the enemy gets the opposite reward as the player, etc.)
    self.sim.train(prev_obs=self.prev_player_action,
        act=enemy_action, reward=-player_reward,
        next_obs=player_action)
    # Train again, so the enemy trains twice as much
    self.sim.train(prev_obs=self.prev_player_action,
        act=enemy_action, reward=-player_reward,
        next_obs=player_action)

    self.prev_player_action = player_action
    return {'reward': player_reward, 'obs': enemy_action}
```

low complexity ($\approx$10 or 20 lines of code), far simpler than a non-extended version with a fixed genuinely intelligent enemy built-in. Because the opponent is trained differently than the player, we would expect the opponent to develop a different personality than the player (except in some degenerate cases)—this gives the test-case a social aspect. The reader can easily imagine more ambitious examples where entire communities (or even civilizations) of entities interact with themselves and the player, each entity instantiated as AgentClass(), but different entities trained differently and therefore having distinct personalities. With some creativity, such ambitious extended environments could be programmed with relatively low complexity: the most complicated part (how the entities behave) is delegated away.

4 Conclusion

Hernández-Orallo and Dowe described [6] a problem which may prevent certain intelligence measures from measuring social intelligence. They stated the problem in the universal intelligence context [10]. We pointed out that the problem is more general. It arises any time we try to use simple test-cases (or a simple procedure for generating test-cases) to estimate intelligence in any AGI subdomain. The problem is that building genuine intelligence into a test-case (apparently necessary for the test-case to measure social intelligence) would make that test-case complicated, not simple. We propose a high-level solution. Instead of designing test-cases in the subdomain in question, design test-cases in an extended subdomain where test-cases can simulate the AI being tested. Such extended test-cases can incorporate social interaction by delegating competitors' or collaborators' intelligence to a clone (or clones) of the AI being tested. For example, instead of testing, "How well can the AI negotiate with such-and-such human?" (a question involving a complex arbitrary parameter), instead, test: "How well can the AI negotiate with its clone?" (a simple non-parametrized question).

Acknowledgments. We acknowledge José Hernández-Orallo and the reviewers for valuable feedback.

References

1. Alexander, S.A., Castaneda, M., Compher, K., Martinez, O.: Extending environments to measure self-reflection in reinforcement learning. Preprint (2022)
2. Alexander, S.A., Hibbard, B.: Measuring intelligence and growth rate: variations on Hibbard's intelligence measure. JAGI **12**(1), 1–25 (2021)
3. Alexander, S.A., Hutter, M.: Reward-punishment symmetric universal intelligence. In: Goertzel, B., Iklé, M., Potapov, A. (eds.) AGI 2021. LNCS (LNAI), vol. 13154, pp. 1–10. Springer, Cham (2022). https://doi.org/10.1007/978-3-030-93758-4_1
4. Goertzel, B.: Artificial general intelligence: concept, state of the art, and future prospects. JAGI **5**, 1–48 (2014)
5. Hernández-Orallo, J.: Twenty years beyond the Turing test: moving beyond the human judges too. Mind. Mach. **30**(4), 533–562 (2020)
6. Hernández-Orallo, J., Dowe, D.L.: Measuring universal intelligence: towards an anytime intelligence test. AI **174**(18), 1508–1539 (2010)
7. Hernández-Orallo, J., Dowe, D.L., España-Cubillo, S., Hernández-Lloreda, M.V., Insa-Cabrera, J.: On more realistic environment distributions for defining, evaluating and developing intelligence. In: Schmidhuber, J., Thórisson, K.R., Looks, M. (eds.) AGI 2011. LNCS (LNAI), vol. 6830, pp. 82–91. Springer, Heidelberg (2011). https://doi.org/10.1007/978-3-642-22887-2_9
8. Hibbard, B.: Bias and no free lunch in formal measures of intelligence. JAGI **1**(1), 54 (2009)
9. Hibbard, B.: Measuring agent intelligence via hierarchies of environments. In: Schmidhuber, J., Thórisson, K.R., Looks, M. (eds.) AGI 2011. LNCS (LNAI), vol. 6830, pp. 303–308. Springer, Heidelberg (2011). https://doi.org/10.1007/978-3-642-22887-2_34

10. Legg, S., Hutter, M.: Universal intelligence: a definition of machine intelligence. Mind. Mach. **17**(4), 391–444 (2007)
11. Legg, S., Veness, J.: An approximation of the universal intelligence measure. In: Dowe, D.L. (ed.) Algorithmic Probability and Friends. Bayesian Prediction and Artificial Intelligence. LNCS, vol. 7070, pp. 236–249. Springer, Heidelberg (2013). https://doi.org/10.1007/978-3-642-44958-1_18
12. Leike, J., Hutter, M.: Bad universal priors and notions of optimality. In: Conference on Learning Theory, pp. 1244–1259. PMLR (2015)
13. Silver, D., Singh, S., Precup, D., Sutton, R.: Reward is enough. AI **299**, 103535 (2021)

Versatility-Efficiency Index (VEI): Towards a Comprehensive Definition of Intelligence Quotient (IQ) for Artificial General Intelligence (AGI) Agents

Mohammadreza Alidoust$^{(\boxtimes)}$ (ID)

Mashhad, Iran
m.alidoust@hotmail.com

Abstract. In this paper, an index for measuring the versatility and efficiency of artificial general intelligence (AGI) systems is proposed. The Versatility-Efficiency Index (VEI), is the updated version of our previous efforts (i.e., Versatility Index (VI)) towards a comprehensive definition of an intelligence quotient (IQ) for intelligent agents. VEI is based on both Legg-Hutter and Pennachin-Goertzel definitions of intelligence and plays as an alternative way for measuring the intelligence level of intelligent agents. VEI, in contrast to VI, also encompasses the qualitative characteristics of intelligent agents like their wellness of performance and the complexity of the operating environments. VEI is applicable to both of the natural general intelligence (NGI) agents and AGI agents. For determining two parameters of VEI, AGI Pyramid – a novel classification of environments by classification of the problems of the universal problem space (UPS)- is proposed. The role of the Artificial General Intelligence Society (AGIS) in the mentioned classification and determination as well as the importance of the VEI in slowing down or preventing from singularity and its role as the possible bridge between intelligence and physics are also discussed.

Keywords: Artificial general intelligence · Intelligence quotient · Legg-Hutter definition · Pennachin-Goertzel definition · Versatility-Efficiency Index · AGI pyramid · Complexity · Environments · Energy · Singularity

1 Introduction

Intelligence quotient (IQ) tests are standard tests for measuring the intelligence level of a human being. IQ tests measure the performance of a human in solving various problems and output a number as the intelligence quotient (IQ). Although the validity of these tests is affected by some influencing factors like culture, they are still the main tool for measuring the IQ of a natural general intelligence (NGI) system like a human. There are a number of definitions for intelligence proposed by the artificial general intelligence (AGI) scientists [1], but there is still a lack of a numerical method for measuring the intelligence level or IQ of an AGI agent. However, like NGIs, the intuitive concept of

B. Goertzel et al. (Eds.): AGI 2022, LNAI 13539, pp. 158–167, 2023.
https://doi.org/10.1007/978-3-031-19907-3_15

IQ can be extended to AGI agents. In the following sections, the Versatility-Efficiency Index (VEI) as the primary steps towards a comprehensive definition for measuring the intelligence level of AGI agents is proposed and the way to calculate its parameters is developed.

2   Versatility and the Legg-Hutter Definition

Versatility is one of the main necessary conditions for an intelligent agent to be called an AGI agent. Our previous works towards this end [2], resulted in proposing the Versatility Index (VI) for AGI agents which measures the versatility of AGI agents based on the Legg-Hutter definition. Legg and Hutter state that AGI agents have to "perform well in a wide range of environments" [3]. The author turned this statement to a formula as follows;

$$VI = \sum_{i=1}^{N} \alpha_i \tag{1}$$

where N is the number of different operating environments of the system, and α_i is the performance of the system in environment i. Since N and α_i are positive dimensionless real numbers, the VI is also a positive dimensionless real number. Since AI systems are problem-specific, their VI value will obviously be low compared to AGI agents. So, the VI can be considered as a distinction between AI and AGI agents. The VI also provides a quantitative ground for comparison between different AGI agents. Different AGI agents can be compared by their VIs. The more versatile systems will have higher VI values and vice versa.

3   Efficiency and the Pennachin-Goertzel Definition

Efficiency is another main necessary condition for an AGI agent. AGI agents have to perform their tasks efficiently. For example, you do not want your AGI agent to consume megawatts of power to solve a simple voice recognition task, or spend a couple of months for it. However, it is intuitively true that complex problems require more amount of power and time. Efficiency encompasses qualitative descriptions of the AGI agent. However, in contrast to versatility, efficiency is not restricted to AGI agents and can be used to describe the qualitative aspects of other systems, like control systems.

Pennachin and Goertzel defined intelligence as "achieving complex goals in complex environments" [1]. Therefore, considering both of the Legg-Hutter and Pennachin-Goertzel definitions implies that AGI agents have to *perform well in a wide range of easy to complex environments*. This combined definition has two sides: 1) the intelligent agent side, and 2) the environment side. The first side questions the *wellness* (i.e., quality) of the *performance* of an intelligent agent, while the second side questions the *number* and the *complexity* of the various environments. The terms *performance* and *number of environments* provide a quantitative description of the intelligent agent (i.e., versatility), while the terms *wellness* and *complexity* deal with qualitative descriptions of the intelligent agent (i.e., efficiency).

Although VI is an informative tool for calculating the versatility of an intelligent agent based on the performance of the system and the number of environments that the system can operate in, it gives no information about the efficiency, or in other words, the qualitative aspects of the intelligent agent, which are wellness of the performance of an intelligent agent as well as the complexity of the environments. Therefore, there is a need for a computational expression of those two qualitative aspects, i.e., wellness (in the AGI agent's side) and complexity (in the environment's side), which demonstrate the efficiency of an intelligent agent. In the following subsections, first, the computational method of defining the complexity of environments, and then, the wellness of performance of the AGI agents will be discussed.

3.1 Complexity of Environments

From the environment side, the efficiency of an intelligent agent depends on the complexity of the environment where that agent is operating in. In other words, complexity of an environment is a key qualitative factor that influences the efficiency of the intelligent agent which is operating in that environment.

In order to define the complexity of environments, one has to classify the various environments, and then define the complexity of each subclass. Any environment can consist of any number and combination of problems[1] (or tasks or goals) of different complexities (See Fig. 1).

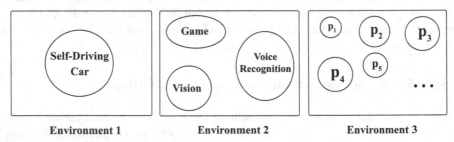

| Environment 1 | Environment 2 | Environment 3 |

Fig. 1. Three different environments with various problems of different complexities: Environment 1 consists of a single self-driving car problem, environment 2 consists of three problems, and environment 3 consists of an infinite number of problems.

Since there are infinite combination of problems, classification of environments is impossible. But the point is that the complexity of an environment can be determined based on the complexities of the various problems that exist in that environment. To this end, based on a certain criterion, the universal problem space (UPS) must be classified into subspaces, and then, the complexity of each subspace is defined based on either of the two other criteria which will be discussed in the following subsections. Finally,

---

[1] Although the terms problem, task and goal have slight differences in meaning, in this paper they are considered the same.

the complexity of an environment is calculated based on summation of the complexities of subspaces which exist in that environment. Therefore, instead of classifying the environments, we classify the problems.

Classification of Problems

The universal problem space (UPS), is a dynamic infinite space of solved problems (SPS) and unsolved problems (NPS) to the human as a natural general intelligence (NGI) agent. (See Fig. 2.)

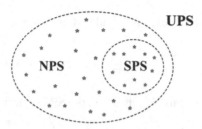

Fig. 2. Universal problem space (UPS), which consists of solved problem space (SPS), and unsolved problem space (NPS). The stars represent problems.

Since IQ tests are performed on solved problems, we classify the problems in the SPS. Every scientific field has its own set of problems and classifies them into certain subspaces based on their desired criteria. Since in artificial general intelligence (AGI) we are interested in the intelligence, we can classify the problems of the SPS (i.e., the solved problems of the UPS) into certain subspaces based on the various aspects of intelligence which are used by the humans to solve those problems.

The aspects of intelligence are as follows;

1. Reasoning, problem solving (R)
2. Knowledge representation (K)
3. Planning (P)
4. Learning (L)
5. Natural language processing (N)
6. Perception (C)
7. Motion and manipulation (M)
8. Social intelligence (S)

Solving every single problem in the SPS requires applying a certain combination of aspects of intelligence (whether simultaneously or consecutively). The problems which require the same number of aspects of intelligence can be grouped into the same subspaces S_n. For example, the problems which require aspects Reasoning (R), Learning (L), Planning (P), Perception (C), and Motion (M) (e.g., the robot path planning problem, and playing chess) belong to the $S_n = RPLCM$ subspace which is a 5-aspect subspace. Thus, the SPS can be classified into a number of subspaces based on the number of required aspects of intelligence which are needed to solve the problems that exist in each subspace. So, each subspace contains a unique combination of the 8 mentioned aspects where;

$$\bigcup_{n=1}^{N} S_n = SPS$$

and

$$S_r \cap S_t = \varnothing, \qquad r \neq t$$

The total number of subspaces N is calculated as follows;

$$N = \sum_{k=1}^{8} \frac{8!}{k!(8-k)!} = \frac{8!}{1!7!} + \frac{8!}{2!6!} + \cdots + \frac{8!}{8!0!} = 8 + 28 + 56 + 70 + 56 + 28 + 8 + 1 = 255$$

This means that based on this classification, the SPS is partitioned into 255 different unique subspaces.

Please note that in addition to SPS, the UPS contains one infinite space of unsolved problems (NPS) which contains the problems like death and aging which are still unsolved to the human (See Fig. 2). Since the problems in the NPS are unsolved, we do not know what aspects of intelligence are required to solve them, so the above classification seems meaningless and does not apply to the problems of NPS.

The SPS has one 8-aspect subspace (i.e., RKPLNCMS), 8 number of 7-aspect subspaces (e.g., RKPLNCM, KPLNCMS), 28 number of 6-aspect subspaces (e.g., KPLNCM, RPLNCS), 56 number of 5-aspect subspaces, 70 number of 4-aspect subspaces, 56 number of 3-aspect subspaces, 28 number of 2-aspect subspaces and 8 number of 1-aspect subspaces. Although with respect to the number of required aspects the SPS may look like a diamond-shaped space, due to the number of currently known benchmark problems in each subspace we will preferably refer to the SPS as AGI Pyramid which will be discussed in the following paragraphs. Figure 3 illustrates the AGI Pyramid.

Each subspace S_n represents the exact number of aspects that are needed to solve a problem which belongs to that subspace, no matter whether the aspects are needed simultaneously or consecutively. In other words, each single problems will belong to the subspace which has the exact number of required aspects for solving that problem. For example, although a vision task has a perception aspect (C) in common with subspaces like $S_q = RPLC$, $S_w = KPLNCMS$, $S_h = C$, and $S_g = RCS$, it will belong to $S_h = C$ subspace, because other aspects are not needed in performing this task.

Please note that the previous paragraphs discussed the subspaces from the environment side. From the intelligent agent's side, solving a problem that belongs to a q-aspect subspace requires an intelligent agent which is able to unify those q aspects into one intelligent approach. For example, an intelligent agent which is able to perform well in $S_g = RCS$, is an intelligent agent that has unified Reasoning (R), Perception (C), and Social Intelligence (S) into one intelligent agent which enables it in solving the problems that belong to $S_g = RCS$.

Additionally, it is obvious that based on the number of unified aspects, higher level intelligent agents are able to perform well in lower-level subspaces with common aspects,

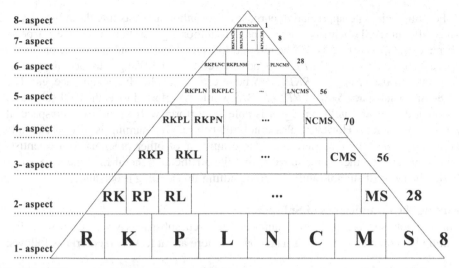

Fig. 3. AGI Pyramid: Classification of the SPS into subspaces based on the eight required aspects of intelligence in order to solve the problems that are grouped into a subspace; Reasoning, problem solving (R), Knowledge representation (K), Planning (P), Learning (L), Natural language processing (N), Perception (C), Motion and manipulation (M), Social intelligence (S). Each level represents subspaces with the same number of required aspects and the thickness of each level represents the number of currently known benchmark problems. Please note that although the SPS and its subspaces are depicted like bounded shapes, they are infinite spaces with infinite number of members.

but the opposite order is not true. For instance, if intelligent agent A is able to perform well in $S_g = RCS$, it will perform well in $S_h = C$ subspace too. But if intelligent agent B is only able to perform well in $S_h = C$ it cannot perform any tasks from $S_g = RCS$, since solving the problems in $S_g = RCS$ requires application of Reasoning and Social Intelligence too. It should be noted that "performing well" does not imply that an intelligent agent is able to solve *all* of the problems that exist in a subspace.

AGI Pyramid connects the agent's side and the environment's side and links the internal characteristics of the agent (i.e., intelligence aspects) with the external world (i.e., environment). The author believes that reaching the top of the AGI Pyramid (i.e., an intelligent agent that is able to perform well in all 255 subspaces), is the path from AI to AGI which requires a bottom-up approach by gradual leveling up the AGI Pyramid. This bottom-up development takes time, until a simultaneous unification approach to all of those 8 aspects is found. That is, one has to find the common core mathematical representation behind all of the 8 aspects and unify them.

However, unification of all of the 8 aspects is the most difficult goal of AGI, and it "is not workable to simply create a modular system with modules embodying different AI paradigms: the different approaches are too different in too many ways. Instead, one must create a unified knowledge representation and dynamics framework, and figure out how to manifest the core ideas of the various AI paradigms within the universal framework." [1].

For simplicity and appreciation purposes, the author suggests that the subspaces be named after the AGI scientists. For example, the author suggests that the unique 7-aspects subspace $S_{Goertzel} = KPLNCMS$ be referred to as the Goertzel subspace, the unique 7-aspects subspace $S_{Wang} = RKPLNCM$ be referred to as the Wang subspace, the unique 7-aspects subspace $S_{Hutter} = RKPLNMS$ be referred to as the Hutter subspace, etc. The one 8-aspect subspace $S_{AGI} = RKPLNCMS$ would be referred to as the AGI subspace, and obviously if an intelligent agent is able to perform well in the AGI subspace, it is a real AGI agent. However, please note that the above naming is just an example and a suggestion, though, there are a large number of other precious AGI scientists and researchers, so the author suggests that the Artificial General Intelligence Society (AGIS) is the most suitable authority for handling this naming procedure.

Defining the Complexities of Subspaces
In the previous subsection the total number of different subspaces N was determined. For defining the complexity w_i of each subspace i, there are at least two criteria as follows;

1 The relative complexities between 255 subspaces are determined and assigned by the AGI community based on the importance of the corresponding problem subspaces to the community, with higher scores for more complex subspaces,
2 The complexities are determined based on the average *time* and *power consumption* for current AI methods (or humans) to solve standard benchmark problems that exist in those subspaces on a certain standard computer platform.

The defined complexities would then be published as a *standard table of complexities* by the AGIS and used by robotic companies, AGI research centers, etc.

3.2 Wellness of Performance

From the intelligent agent's side, the efficiency of an intelligent agent, is related to the wellness of the intelligent agent in solving the problems (or performing the tasks or achieving the goals) that exist in a subspace.

Thorisson et al. state that "performing a task in real world requires time, energy, and possibly other resources such as money, materials, or manpower" [4]. Since in AGI we are interested in generality, only the factors time and energy that are general in every task are adopted from the above statement to define wellness or quality of performance. Thus, wellness is related to:

1. Accuracy: the performance wellness of an intelligent agent in a subspace is proportional to the accuracy of the system in performing the tasks that exist in that subspace. We have $\alpha_i \propto a_j$ where α_i represents the average performance wellness of the system in subspace i, and a_j is the accuracy of the system in performing task j of the subspace i.
2. Time: the performance wellness of an intelligent agent in a subspace i is proportional to the reciprocal of the time needed to perform the tasks that exist in that subspace. So, $\alpha_i \propto \frac{1}{t_j}$, where t_j is the time needed for performing task j of the subspace i.

3. Power consumption: the performance wellness of an intelligent agent in a subspace i is proportional to the reciprocal of the power needed to perform the tasks that exist in that subspace. Thus, $\alpha_i \propto \frac{1}{p_j}$, where p_j is the power needed for performing task j of the subspace i.

So, we have $\alpha_i \propto \frac{a_j}{p_j t_j}$, therefore for a subspace that contains more than one task, we have;

$$\alpha_i = \frac{1}{M_i} \sum_{j=1}^{M_i} \frac{a_j}{p_j t_j} \tag{2}$$

where α_i represents the average performance wellness of the system in subspace i, and M_i is the number of problems that exist in subspace i. Since the dimension of p_j is watts and the dimension of t_j is seconds, and other parameters are dimensionless, the dimension of α_i is $[\alpha_i] = joule^{-1}$.

4 Versatility-Efficiency Index

The complexity of a subspace is defined as a constant parameter w_i, which in combination of wellness of performance (Eq. (1) and (2)), constitute the Versatility-Efficiency Index (VEI) as follows;

$$VEI = \sum_{i=1}^{N} w_i \alpha_i \quad \text{or} \quad VEI = \sum_{i=1}^{N} \sum_{j=1}^{M_i} w_i \frac{a_j}{M_i p_j t_j} \tag{3}$$

where $N = 255$ (since the AGI agent must be tested in all 255 subspaces of the SPS), w_i is the complexity of each subspace i (which are defined based on the two criteria), α_i is the average performance wellness of the system in performing all of the benchmark tasks that exist in subspace i, M_i is the number of benchmark tasks that exist in subspace i, a_j is the accuracy of the system in performing task j of the subspace i, p_j is the power needed for performing task j of the subspace i, and t_j is the time needed for performing task j of the subspace i.

VEI is a scoring system and encompasses both of the quantitative and qualitative descriptions of AGI agents. In order to measure the VEI of an AGI agent, the agent must be tested in SPS but only over benchmark tasks of each of the 255 subspaces. To this end, the agent's average performance (i.e., accuracy, time and power) must be measured over benchmark tasks of each of the 255 subspaces and then multiplied by the corresponding complexity of each subspace which is obtained from the standard table of complexities. Summation of these values will give the VEI of the agent. This process examines the versatility and efficiency of an AGI agent over standard problems of SPS and is like taking an IQ test by an AGI agent.

For the dimension consistency in Eq. (3), the dimension of complexity w_i must be joule, i.e., $[w_i] = joule$. This sounds intuitively true, since solving complex problems require more amount of energy than simple ones.

5 Conclusion

In this paper, based on the Legg-Hutter and Pennachin-Goertzel definitions of intelligence, the Versatility-Efficiency Index (VEI) was proposed as a primary step towards definition of IQ for intelligent agents. Like the IQ tests for human being, VEI calculates the versatility and efficiency of intelligent agents based on measurement of their quantitative and qualitative performance in different environments. VEI is not limited to AGI agents, but also can be applied to NGI systems. The average VEI of humans can be the measured and then considered as the basis of comparison between AGIs.

In addition, if we have the VEI of human, the VEI of current AGI agents can tell us how far we are now from reaching to an AGI agent with (at least) a human-level artificial intelligence (HLAI).

Although the accuracy of humans a_j is not %100 in performing all of their tasks, and compared to a computer they may spend much more time for performing their tasks, they are still the most intelligent being in the world. Using a 20-W brain ([5], and [6]), humans perform well in all of the 255 subspaces. Regarding the VEI formula from Eq. (3)

$$VEI = \sum_{i=1}^{N} w_i \alpha_i \quad or \quad VEI = \sum_{i=1}^{N} \sum_{j=1}^{M_i} w_i \frac{a_j}{M_i p_j t_j}$$

we have $N_{human} = 255$. Also, despite their mediocre to high accuracy and time, the average performance of humans α_i in all 255 subspaces is still high. In addition, humans can perform in complex environments too. Considering Eq. (3), these leads to a high value of VEI for humans.

On the other hand, despite having high accuracies and much lower computation time, current intelligent agents will have much lower VEI values because they cannot perform well in all of the 255 subspaces (for example in environments which require natural language processing aspect or in environments which require emotions as a key factor of social intelligence).

VEI also relates to *singularity* and that is the point when AGI agents are able to exponentially reproduce and build more powerful and intelligent descendants than themselves. This might threaten the human existence, i.e., a global catastrophe. Obviously, AGI agents with higher VEI (i.e., robots with IQ very much higher than human), will reach singularity more rapidly than lower-VEI agents. Therefore, future companies that will mass-produce future AGI agents might have to follow a *VEI Limit* determined by the AGIS for their products as a possible way to prevent or at least slowing down the singularity. This VEI limit could buy time for humans to decide how to prevent the catastrophe.

The exact value of this VEI limit is unknown yet, but due to the ultra-highspeed wireless communication and data sharing capability of the future AGI agents that – in contrast to humans – enables them to have access to %100 of the knowledge and experience of their fellow agents which consequently empowers them with swarm intelligence, even lower values of VEI than humans are recommended for (at least) the first generations of the mass-produced AGI agents.

Another point that can be derived from the comparison between the 20-W human brain and current intelligent agents is that, with regard to the power consumption p_j in the dominator of VEI in Eq. (3), for building a real AGI agent we would not necessarily need super power consuming computers, but rather we would need more versatile and efficient algorithms.

References

1. Pennachin, C., Goertzel, B.: Contemporary approaches to artificial general intelligence. In: Goertzel, B., Pennachin, C. (eds.) Artificial General Intelligence, pp. 1–30. Springer Berlin Heidelberg, Berlin, Heidelberg (2007). https://doi.org/10.1007/978-3-540-68677-4_1
2. Alidoust, M.: AGI brain II: the upgraded version with increased versatility index. In: Goertzel, B., Iklé, M., Potapov, A. (eds.) AGI 2021. LNCS (LNAI), vol. 13154, pp. 11–18. Springer, Cham (2022). https://doi.org/10.1007/978-3-030-93758-4_2
3. Legg, S., Hutter, M.: Universal intelligence: a definition of machine intelligence. Mind. Mach. **17**(4), 391–444 (2007)
4. Thórisson, K.R., Bieger, J., Thorarensen, T., Sigurðardóttir J.S., Steunebrink, B.R.: Why artificial intelligence needs a task theory and what it might look like (2016) https://doi.org/10.48550/arXiv.1604.04660
5. Hasler, J.: Special report: can we copy the brain? – a road map for the artificial brain. IEEE Spectr. **54**(6), 46–50 (2017). https://doi.org/10.1109/MSPEC.2017.7934231
6. Furber, S.: To build a brain. IEEE Spectr. **49**(8), 44–49 (2012). https://doi.org/10.1109/MSPEC.2012.6247562

Moral Space for Paraconsistent AGI

Piotr (Peter) Boltuc[2,1](✉) 🆔

[1] University of Illinois Springfield, Philosophy, Computer Science, One University Plaza 3030, Springfield, IL 62703, USA
[2] Management Theory, Warsaw School of Economics, Niepodleglosci 162, 02-554 Warsaw, Poland
pboltu@sgh.waw.pl

Abstract. Ben Goertzel argues that humans operate within paraconsistent ethics. There are two arguments: 1. Moral para-consistency viewed primarily as resulting from deeply rooted tensions between individuation and self-transcendence (or autopoiesis *versus* evolutionary fitness). 2. Paraconsistency due to human cognitive limitations (we would need massively stronger cognitive functions to handle our lives consistently). This is directly relevant for AI since advanced humanoid AIs and AGIs should follow paraconsistent norms for easier human-AI interactions. This is also indirectly relevant, in a broader ontological framework, where Goertzel analyzes paraconsistent foundations for quantum probability, programming, and concept formation. Paraconsistence in these domains does not seem to result from weakness of human cognitive functions, manifestly in quantum physics. Those paraconsistencies seem relationally veridical. Yet, in his explanations of ontological paraconsistency, Goertzel 2021a follows Weber in focusing on *sorites* kind of problems; this creates an impression that the issues of fuzziness are the gist of Goertzel's paraconsistent approach to AI. Yet, this is more of a heuristic start for Goertzel. Paraconsistency is not always at the boundaries, but at the core of nimble complex systems. We argue that, at least in ethics, paraconsistency is primarily based on alternative objectives or sources of value (following Goertzel's argument 1; also Ross, Haidt, Dancy, Sen); ethical problems based upon vagueness in boundary conditions, though important and interesting, are less central to the metaethical dimension of paraconsistency, and therefore to the logical make-up of future AIs.

Keywords: Paraconsistent ethics · Paraconsistent AGI · Non-homogenous moral space · Ben Goertzel · Amartya Sen

1 Paraconsistency 2021

In the first half of 2021 Ben Goertzel [1, 2] put forth two major papers, and a few commentaries, on **paraconsistent foundations** for quantum physics, probabilistic reasoning, and concept formation. Goertzel also discusses paraconsistent interzones that allow co-functioning of paradigmatically different units within complex cognitive systems, including human brains [3].

B. Goertzel et al. (Eds.): AGI 2022, LNAI 13539, pp. 168–177, 2023.
https://doi.org/10.1007/978-3-031-19907-3_16

In the second half of 2021, Goertzel [4, 5] gave a couple of lectures, in which he discussed paraconsistent ethics. I do not think those came out in writing yet. This paper is an attempt to help advance the latter topic and help ground it in a broader meta-ethical current, which I call non-homogenous moral space [6]. Goertzel's ethics is based on his work in other applications of paraconsistency. Yet, as he emphasized in [5], his paraconsistent ethics, follows on his philosophical work focused on patternist philosophy [7]. Patternist philosophy finds its philosophical climax in stochastic approaches to AI, especially the topic of machine and human creativity *at the edge of chaos*. Due to its background in stochastic ontologies, Goertzel's paraconsistent value theory goes beyond the recent standards of *paraconsistent ethics* [8] and *relies on the structure of quantum ethics, which he views as closely approximated through probability theory.*

2 Paraconsistent Ethics; the Gist

Let us start with a fast look at paraconsistent ethics before Ben Goertzel, followed by a glance at the two general currents in paraconsistent logic applied to ethics. Then we can get the taste of Goertzel's [1–5] recent ideas on it, made public in 2021.

Literature on paraconsistent ethics percolated for two decades [8–10]; it is viewed mostly as the way to cope with moral dilemmas. Earlier on, the ways to cope with such dilemmas, quite similar to paraconsistency, have been proposed at least since Plato, including prominently Aristotle, Maimonides, Thomistic casuistry, Marxist and Gonseth's dialectics, among other attempts. The focus of this article is, in part, to bring onto the picture of paraconsistent ethics the non-standard metaethical systems that go beyond Weber's [8] *fuzzy logic* approach (reliant on the sorties paradox). Based on Goertzel's focus on the dialectics of autopoiesis *versus* self-transcendence [5], we extend its scope to the other areas of non-homogenous moral space [6].

2.1 The Two Takes on Paraconsistent Logic and Ethics

Within paraconsistent logic, there seem to be two voices: First, the old school radical paraconsistent logic, based largely in quantum physics. Second, the paraconsistent logic that *tinkers at the edges*, giving particular attention to *vagueness*. This rift, applied to paraconsistent ethics, is visible in Polish logic:

> Przelecki [11] wrote: "ethical predicates differ greatly in the degree of their indeterminacy. This degree seems particularly high in the case of the predicate "is a moral obligation", lower in the case of predicates "is morally good (relatively bad)", and the lowest in the case of comparative predicates "is morally better (or worse) than". Here, we are undoubtedly dealing with the phenomenon of semantic indeterminacy."

Przełęcki "limits the scope of paraconsistency to the issue of natural language ambiguity", which other authors endorse [12]. This comes for the price of diverging from the original scope of paraconsistent logic, in the works of Łuksiewicz [13] and Jaśkowski [14], as well as da Costa [15, 16], a pioneer of contemporary paraconsistent logic. The latter approach, largely based on the logic of quantum physics, deals with fuzzy logic, but is not merely – or, primarily – the question of vagueness.

Ben Goertzel, in his recent proposals of paraconsistent ethics — follows the strengths of both approaches, the one focused on paraconsistency of complementary options and the other on vaguenss and fuzzy logic. Those senses are not exclusive but pertain to situations of different sorts.

2.2   Goertzel's Two Arguments for Paraconsistent Logic of Morals

Ben Goertzel [1–5] presents two arguments why human ethics is paraconsistent:

1. **Moral paraconsistency from human cognitive limitations**. If we were wiser, we would navigate between the horns of all those moral dilemmas, Yet, we would need cognitive functions stronger a few orders of magnitude, in order to handle our moral lives consistently [7] In this argument, Goertzel claims that moral errors come from limited human nature, especially intelligence (thus, from our stupidity). He refers primarily to human deficiencies that would require more than reasonable improvements in our intellectual capacities to fix. Thus, they come *de facto* from human nature, not from its essence but from essential *practical applications leading to human errors of judgment*.
2. Goertzel views **moral paraconsistency** as **based on a deeply rooted tension between individuation** and **self-transcendence**. Morally aware people, through personality development, want to become the best 'self' they can be, but they also have a moral urge to transcend one's own particularities and interests, for some kind of objectivity, such as their evolutionary fitness, objective attainments, as well as the general good. More philosophically, this can also be viewed as tension between *autopoiesis* and *evolution* based on the work of Varela and Maturana [17].

Axiological inconsistency may come from the other tensions among the values, such as those described by Ross [18], Greene and Haidt [19], or Dancy [20]. Viewed in the context broader than just Varela's theory. Goertzel's second argument seems to catch a more essential inconsistency than the first, originating not quite at the implementation level but rather at the structural paraconsistencies in axiology that lie at the center of human motivation, or even brain structure [19]. Those axiological paraconsistencies are the background of the rest of this paper.

3   Axio-Ontology 1 and 2 for Paraconsistent Ethics

As shown above, Goertzel presents two arguments in support of paraconsistent ethics. In this section we argue that those two arguments result in paraconsistent-value-ontologies of different tilts, which we call *Paraconsistent Ontology 1* and *Paraconsistent Ontology 2*.

3.1 Paraconsistent Metaethical Ontology 1 (Human Limitations)

Paraconsistency in human behavior and ethics that comes from Goertzel's **argument 1** is the ethics of implementation. It functions in the conceptual universe, where there exists a (consistent and in principle implementable) hierarchy of the good, and bad, things. Yet, we are intellectually too weak to sort out the logistics of making it happen. Everybody who reflected on the philosophical consequences of the *Traveling Salesperson* may easily grasp this point [21].

3.2 Paraconsistent Metaethical Ontology 2 (Axiologically Grounded Inconsistency)

Paraconsistency in human ethics seems to acquire its ontological gravity largely from Goertzel's **argument 2** – from a gap in the center of motivations and/or values within the core of human ethics. Goertzel argues that it results from (morally justified) leaning towards self-perfection and (morally justified) leaning towards self-transcendence, but it can be extended to the other psychological or meta-ethical sources [18–20]. Let us call *Paraconsistent Ontology 2 paraconsistent through and through*.

There are a few versions of Ontology 2: existential, based on competing foundational values and those dependent on *propinquity* (closeness in moral space).

Ontology 2 Consisting in the Existential Frame (O2E): The gist of the *paraconsistent ethics through and through* comes from its existential underpinnings [22]. It does not result merely from our cognitive limitations. Instead, it is the existential dilemma of a being like us. Following Goertzel [3] the existential conflict between self-growth and self-transcendence belongs to human ontology, not being merely an epistemic weakness.

Such moral/existential ontological dilemmas may be constructed with complementarity of different values. Vallverdu and Talanov [23] argue that human lives are shaped by awareness of one's mortality; thus, artificial AI companions need to be mortal and aware of it, if they are to truly connect with human beings. This is a version of the traditional existentialist dilemma applied to AI.

3.3 Mixed Ontology 1/2

It is based on the mix of both arguments, with overarching Ontology 1. The rationale goes like this: Maybe we are not even sure what the moral goals should be, but we would find it out if we were intellectually, or emotionally, stronger. So, the problem is not merely of implementation. The axiological (not just logistic) problem is resolvable for much smarter *moral agents* (or those *interested* in ethics).

In the moral universe 1/2, someone may wish AGIs to guides us through the logistics of our lives; or even through the jungle of possible axiologies and resulting goals, as well as ways and means of gaining them, which is broader than the choice from among the paths allowed in the *travelling salesman* sort of cases [21][1].

---

[1] The idea that there is a way to find the solution, is no nonsense in the ontology of Paraconsistent Ethics 2 (and its 1/2 version).

3.4 Propinquities

As mentioned above, paraconsistencies also results from plurality of ethical values. The most enticing is the so-called *Common Sense Morality* that relies on morally relevant ties.

Situational O1P results from the complex structure of moral situations [20], which may be viewed as an intricate case of Ross's ethics of *prima facie* moral reasons [18]. For Ross the weight of various *prima facie* moral duties depends largely on situational context. Yet, for Dancy such *context*, defines the gist and center of moral value.

Typical O1P relies on moral *proponquities* [24, 25], often viewed as friendship, especially by C. Gilligan [26] and her followers, or kinship e.g. by Pargetter [27]. Those special duties create agent-relative structure of moral obligations with their sophisticated logical structure investigated by Sen [28, 29].

   The ethics based upon morally relevant ties becomes complex, which is intuitively the correct picture of the moral realm – this runs counter to the advocates of Procrustean bed with their enthusiasm towards *Ockham's razor* in moral theory. Ethical theories with propinquity are often complex. Goertzel's paraconsistent ethics [1–5, 7], not only at the fuzzy edges but also in the core of ethics, makes use of the digital revolution (now primarily as big data computing). Soon, as the AI to AGI revolution progresses, we should have measurable, yet stochastic, mechanisms to replace such Procrustean tendencies.

4   Positional Moral Paraconsistency

Ethical theories, especially those apt for paraconsistency, have structural aspects worth attention. We may view moral space as a logical space created by the sum of properties (of actions, inactions, intentions, outcomes, states of affairs etc.,) identified as carriers of moral value in a relevant context[2]. A given space of moral values is non-homogenous if moral value changes as a function of its positional characteristics, such as relevant closeness to the moral agent – for instance relations of friendship, kinship, or other special obligations; or just proximity in space-time location.

   Many theories that accept non-homogenous distribution of moral value accept inherent agent-relative moral reasons [6, 18–20, 24–29]. Instrumental agent-relative moral reasons are often explainable in a more general framework of ethics guided by moral impartiality. The structure of non-homogenous moral space can be presented in relationist terms. The tools of paraconsistent logic, Goertzel's model [1–5], should make it easier to formalize and work out details. Below, we present alternative paraconsistent sets of values that may result in *paraconsistent ethics through and through,* as defined in the previous section.

---

[2] This section presents the gist of the arguments from [6].

4.1 Moral Pluralisms, Psychological (Greene/Haidt) and Philosophical (Ross)

Ross and Haidt [18], in their respective theories, present multiple sources of value that can be viewed as inherently inconsistent. They do so by creating a non-ordered, or at least not completely ordered, value set.

Jack Haidt in his well-known concept of five moral foundations (developed with Joshua Greene), based on research in experimental psychology, singled out: **Care** and **Fairness** as individualizing values (common to almost all sane human beings) and **Loyalty**, **Authority** and **Sanctity**, which are group-binding values (more common among communitarians and conservatives than the liberals). Later, **Liberty** has been observed and added as the sixth independent moral variable.

Centers responsible for instantiating those values are located in various parts of human brain, of different evolutionary age and with no specific, evolutionarily deep coordinating mechanism. This fact about brain design may explain common conflicts of morally relevant values in many non-trivial cases.

Within moral theory, already in 1930, W.D. Ross [18] proposed seven categories of *prima facie* moral reasons (or duties), which are not pre-ordered. Thus, they may come into mutual conflicts – individually or in coalitions (such *ad hoc* coalitions are characterized by the common denominator of ending up with the same moral recommendation in a given case). We've put them in an order somewhat similar to Haidt's psychological categories: **Beneficence**, **Non-maleficence**, **Justice**, **Fidelity**, **Reparation**, **Gratitude**, **Self-improvement**. Ross encourages weighing those values, in a given situational context, on somewhat intuitive grounds. This procedure can no doubt be grasped within paraconsistent logic, but further theories seem even more sophisticated structurally.

4.2 Dancy's Moral Particularism

We now move to the cases that go beyond the problem of unordered (or incompletely ordered) sets of moral values, whose applications may conflict. Going quite a bit further in the direction sketched out by Ross, **Jonathan Dancy** [20] presented an idea of moral particularism, which is probably the most plausible defense of radical contextualist ethics. Dancy poses that there are specific morally relevant features of situations, not just actions or outcomes. He agrees that going through a list, such as Ross', in searching for morally relevant features of a given situation, is a rather efficient procedure, but *only as a heuristic measure*.

Moral situations are dominant in creating value, since they are unique in their broad, yet relevant, contexts. Only a detailed, nearly aesthetic inspection of each situation may reveal the true set of values relevant in a given instance. Moreover, those values are position-relative – mothers in law of the groom and the bride will view the wedding differently due to their particular attachments and proximity to one's own offspring. Dancy shows that abstracting from those special features of a situation would be morally wrong. Thus, detached judgments, like those by the courts of law – while useful for maintaining public order – should not be seen as moral judgments due to the morally inappropriate measure of impartiality. This approach puts upside down Kant's and Mill's endorsement of impartiality [30, 31] as the main criterion of ethics (perceived by Kant as a **moral law**, structurally similar to legal laws). Dancy's version of radical contextualism is quite far-going, but with big-data analysis may be handled by AI.

4.3 Sen's Socio-Economic Calculus of Agent-Relative Reasons

Amartya Sen (a Nobel laureate in economics) wrote a set of ground-breaking articles on the ethics and structure of special moral obligations [28, 29]. Sen demonstrates that, what philosophers refer to as agent-relative values, constitutes several categories with different formal characteristics. Sen distinguished three types of agent-relativity, **defined as *negations* of the following neutrality claims**:

Doer neutrality (DN): Person i may do this act if and only if person i may permit person j to do this act. Ai(i) <=> Ai(j).
Viewer neutrality (VN): Person i may do this act if and only if person j may permit person i to do this act. Ai(i) <=> Aj(i).
Self-evaluation neutrality (SN): Person i may do this act if and only if person j may do this act. Ai(i) <=> Aj(j).

Amartya Sen presented a proof that those three kinds of agent-neutrality are bilaterally dependent on each other, which means that any one form of agent-relativity entails one other form [28].

In his response to standard criticisms of agent relativity in ethics [32] Amartya Sen argues that personal identity, for instance, one's role as a parent, a friend or a compatriot, results in **objective, position-relative** moral reasons. Those reasons come with morally relevant social roles. Sen emphasizes that often people are not free to choose moral norms incompatible with their social role, so that some special moral obligations are obligatory.

4.4 Non-homogenous Moral Space: Sidgwick and Pargetter

Sen's logic of three kinds of agent-relativity reveals interesting features of, non-homogenous moral space [6]. In the Modern context, non-homogenous moral space originates from Bentham's utilitarian criterion of *propinquity* [24], which means morally relevant closeness, viewed as one of the main moral criteria of assessing utilitarian value. The criterion was dropped by Mill (impressed by Kant's requirement of universal impartiality for ethics) [30, 31]. A kind of *propinquity* resurfaced in Sidgwick's advocacy of the *common sense morality* [25], which is non-homogenous in the scope of moral obligations.

A similar idea was defended by Robert Pargetter in his moral kinship argument [27]. Pargetter's notion of kinship incorporates friendship, family ties, networks of friends, patriotism and membership in morally relevant communities. He emphasizes the strong moral feeling that we have moral obligations toward certain persons, which are stronger than those held towards the others [27, p. 346]. Thus, "fundamental judgments of goodness and badness will be relativized to a person at a time" (27 p. 354). Pargetter's approach, similarly to Sen's theory, resembles relativity theory, but never moral relativism. It is a **relationist ethics**.

Those kinds of arguments have been criticized, most persuasively by Parfit [33] as indirectly self-defeating. Parfit argues that Common Sense Morality leads to the frustration of more goals (accepted by utilitarians, including Sidgwick[3]), which would be better satisfied in a long run, by an adoption of an impartial system of ethics. Yet, this depends on the valuations by relevant agents. Ethical theories with propinquity factor are criticized as subjectivist [32] or indirectly inconsistent [33]. However, objections of this sort are handled by semantic and/or deontic bonus added to the utilities, relative to their structure; in particular to kinship or closeness in moral space: Sen [29] vs. Regan [32]; Boltuc [34] vs. Parfit [33].

Let me put forth a counterexample. If a gift of the same toy by the parents, gives their child 10 times more pleasure than getting the very same thing from a charity worker, we would have a good start at utilitarianism based on the meaning (semantics) of given goods, or actions, that is essentially non-homogenous. With the benefit of closeness strong enough in assessment of utilities, Parfit's argument [33] reveals itself ill-conceived *in those kinds of cases*. As in many instances in utilitarianism and economics, the answer is in the actual numbers [34]. This is also the case in a W.D. Ross-style mix of deontic, utilitarian and maybe other values [18]. The calculus may best be set up in the context of Sen's *broad consequetialism*, which he calls *consequence based moral evaluation* [29]. I tend to visualize it as deontic bricks in a consequentialist wall[4].

5   Conclusion: The Existential Twist to Paraconsistent Ethics

Looking back at the arguments in Sect. 4, I find the conflict of values in the works of Haidt and Ross [18, 19] important and relevant for paraconsistent analysis; yet, somewhat low-dimensional. The role of propinquity in ethics has been unnecessarily neglected, through the attempts to turn ethics into *the moral law* – to which Sidgwick (rather than Bentham), Pargetter, Gilligan and the communitarians (for instance Walzer [35]) have many important ideas to add. This is even more so if we talk of virtuoso theories of Dancy and masterful work by Sen. It looks like non-homogenous moral theories are ripe for parconsistent re-presentation and advanced AI recommender systems look like a good machine to help us make it happen.

Nevertheless, the above theories do not seem to carry the existential (even existentialist) gravity shared by Goertzel's main ethical dilemma, the conflict, or tension, between autopoiesis and self-transcendence. Under this description, its existential meaning, pertaining to the value and fragility of individual life, comes to the forefront.

Max Talanov and Jordi Vallverdu [23] gave a surprising paper at BICA (Lyon 2015) arguing that AIs ought to be made mortal, and know of their mortality, in order to be the real human companions, for them to be able to share human existential experience. This approach fits nicely with Goertzel's dilemma [4].

Our last existential argument is not quite a moral dilemma. It expresses Luciano Floridi's idiosyncratic view on human existential situation, juxtaposed with the optimism on the human condition predominant in Western cultures [36]. Looking for the

---

[3] This points comes primarily from my visits at Parfit's seminar on Sidgwick, and our long conversation at Oxford.

[4] Sen's approach with consequence-based moral evaluation as the structure, is clearer than Ross' utilitarian values stuck in a deontic framework; balancing deontic *prima facie* duties tends to be emotive and intuitionistic. **It is effective to put the emotions in the object's value not in weighing scale.**

source of human dignity, Floridi seems right, paradoxically, recalling Picco della Miran-dola and his justification of human uniqueness, as dignified copying with our pitiful existential condition (a long time after della Mirandola, it was called *Sein zum Tode* [37]). Paraconsistent foundations of our very existence, the paradox of humans fighting for life in our pitiful position, provide important background of all the three approaches. Its understanding seems to be the gist and the value of the humanities, which we shall need to share with AGI. Sharing the humanities with AGI is part and parcel of inculcating human values in it, instead of merely sophisticated engineering perspective [38]. The truly advanced AI-based artificial companions [39], capable of interacting with human beings would have to meet us also at our existential level. For this, Goertzel's postulate that they need to act in the framework of paraconsistent logic of action and values, is an idea worth taking seriously and testing in AIs on their, long enough, way towards AGI.

References

1. Goertzel, B.: Paraconsistent foundations for quantum probability, 20 Jan 2021. https://arxiv.org/pdf/2101.07498.pdf
2. Goertzel, B.: Paraconsistent foundations for probabilistic reasoning, programming and concept formation. abs/2012.14474 (2020). https://arxiv.org/abs/2012.14474
3. Goertzel, B.: Paraconsistent Interzones *Eurykosmotron*. 13 Aug 2021 (2021). https://bengoertzel.substack.com/p/paraconsistent-interzones
4. Goertzel, B.: Progress toward a general theory of general intelligence. AGI Keynote Oct. (2021). http://agi-conf.org/2021/keynotes/ no recording available. Similar topics covered at https://www.youtube.com/watch?v=AKScYMrbMNw
5. Goertzel, B.: Exploring Open-Ended Intelligence Using Patternist Philosophy. At: IS4SI, Philosophy and Computing 14 Sep 2021. https://www.youtube.com/watch?v=C8m_PxuQkF8
6. Boltuc, P.: Non-Homogenous moral space. From Bentham to Sen. Analiza i Egzystencja **24**, 43–59 (2013). https://bazhum.muzhp.pl/media/files/Analiza_i_Egzystencja/Analiza_i_Egzystencja-r2013-t24/Analiza_i_Egzystencja-r2013-t24-s43-59/Analiza_i_Egzystencja-r2013-t24-s43-59.pdf
7. Goertzel, B.: The Hidden Pattern: A Patternist Philosophy of Mind. Brown Walker Press, Boca Raton (2006)
8. Weber, Z.: On paraconsistent ethics. S Afr. J. Philos. **26**(2), 239–244 (2007). https://doi.org/10.4314/sajpem.v26i2.31477
9. Bohse, H.: A Paraconsistent solution to the problem of Moral Dilemmas. S. Afr. J. Philos. **24**(2), 77–86 (2005). https://doi.org/10.4314/sajpem.v24i2.31415
10. Serbena, C.A.: Is Ethics with moral dilemmas possible? A paraconsistent proposal. In: 25th IVR World Congress of Philosophy of Law and Social Philosophy. Frankfurt: Goethe Universität Frankfurt am Main, pp. 309–310 (2011)
11. Przelecki, M.: Sens i Prawda w Etyce (Sense and Truth in Ethics). PTS, Warszawa (2004)
12. Misuina, K.: O obliczach sprzeczności (The faces of contradiction). Filozofia Nauki XVIII. 3/71, 55–78 (2010)
13. Łukasiewicz, J.: O pojęciu możliwości (On the notion of possibility). Ruch Filozoficzny 5169–5170 (1920)
14. Jaśkowski, S.: Propositional calculus for contradictory deductive systems. Studia Logica **24**, 143–157. (the English translation of Jaśkowski, 1948; Eng. 1969)

15. da Costa, N.C.A., Krause, D., Bueno, O.: Paraconsistent logics and paraconsistency. In: Jacquette, D. (ed.), Handbook of the Philosophy of Science (Philosophy of Logic), pp. 791–911. Elsevier (2007)

16. da Costa, N., de Ronde, C.: The paraconsistent logic of quantum superpositions. Found. Phys. **43**(7), 845–858 (2013). https://doi.org/10.1007/s10701-013-9721-9

17. Maturana, H.R., Varela, F.J.: Autopoiesis and Cognition: The Realization of the Living. Reidl Publishing CO, Dordrecht (1980)

18. Ross, W.D.: The Right and the Good (1930) Philip Stratton-Lake. Oxford University Press, New York (2002)

19. Haidt, J.: The emotional dog and its rational tail: a social intuitionist approach to moral judgement. Psychol. Rev. **108**(4), 814–834 (2001)

20. Dancy, J.: Ethical particularism and morally relevant properties. Mind **92**, 530–547 (1983)

21. Karlin, A., Klein, N., Gharan, S.: A (Slightly) Improved Approximation Algorithm for Metric TSP, 11 May 2021. https://arxiv.org/pdf/2007.01409.pdf

22. Dougherty, M.V.: Perplexity simpliciter and perplexity secundum quid: a look at some contemporary appeals to St. Thomas Aquinas. Int. Philos. Q. **41**(4) (2001)

23. Max Talanov, M., Vallverdu, J.: On importance of life and death for artificial intelligent creatures. APA Newslett. Philos. Comput. **16**, 32–37 (2016). https://www.academia.edu/31262634/

24. Bentham, J.: An Introduction to the Principles of Morals and Legislation. Hafner, New York (1948)

25. Sidgwick, H.: The Methods of Ethics. Hackett, Cambridge (1981)

26. Gilligan, C.: In a Different Voice. Harvard UP (1982)

27. Pargetter, R.: Kinship and Moral Relativity. Philosophia **20**, 345–361 (1991)

28. Sen, A.: Evaluator relativity and consequential evaluation. Philos. Publ. Aff. **12**, 113–132 (1983)

29. Sen, A.: Rights and agency. In: Scheffler, S. (ed.) Consequentialism and Its Critics. Oxford Universtiy Press, Oxford (1988)

30. Kant, I.: Groundwork of the Metaphysics of Morals.Transl. Gregor, M.J. Cambridge University Press (1998)

31. Mill, J.: Utilitarianism. Parker son and Bourn, London (1863)

32. Regan, D.: Against evaluator relativity: a response to Sen. Philos. Publ. Aff. **12**, 93–112 (1983)

33. Parfit, D.: Reasons and Persons. Oxford University Press, Oxford (1984)

34. Boltuc, P.: Why common sense morality is not collectively self-defeating. Polish J. Philos. **2**, 19–39 (2007)

35. Walzer, M.: Spheres of justice: A defence of pluralism and equality. Oxford (1983)

36. Floridi, L.: On human dignity as a foundation for the right to privacy. Philos. Technol. **29**(4), 307–312 (2016). https://doi.org/10.1007/s13347-016-0220-8

37. Heidegger, M.: Being and Time. (Trans. Macquarrie, J., Robinson, E.) Harper & Row, New York (1962)

38. Boltuc, P.: Transhumanities as the pinnacle and a bridge. Humanities **11**(1), 27 (2022). https://doi.org/10.3390/h11010027

39. Boltuc, P.: Church-turing lovers. In: Iin Abney, K.A., Lin, P.J., Ryan R. (eds.) Robot Ethics 2.0: From Autonomous Cars to Artificial Intelligence. Oxford University Press, Oxford (2017)

PERI.2 Goes to PreSchool and Beyond, in Search of AGI

Selmer Bringsjord(✉) , Naveen Sundar Govindarajulu , John Slowik,
James Oswald , Mike Giancola , John Angel , Shreya Banerjee ,
and Aidan Flaherty

Rensselaer AI & Reasoning (RAIR) Lab, Rensselaer Polytechnic Institute (RPI),
Troy, NY 12180, USA
selmer.bringsjord@gmail.com, naveen.sundar.g@gmail.com

Abstract. After introductory remarks, we share our two-part theoretical position, viz. that: (P1) The best overarching approach to suitably defining GI, and obtaining AGI, is via formal logic, including specifically via logic-based learning that is academic in nature; and (P2) AI/AGI is best pursued by seeking artificial agents that pass determinate cognitive tests. We note that in striking harmony with this position is work on AGI by Goertzel et al. that has inspired us; this is work in which PreSchool for would-be AGIs provides an attractive route toward AGI itself. While Goertzel et al. envisage a virtual academic environment, we have in mind physical classrooms, for physical robots. We describe the robot PERI.2, which we have started to send to school.

1 Introduction

However one might prefer to define AGI, it seems likely to be a matter of consensus that we have GI,[1] and that you do too.[2] Why are we so fortunate? Many reasons, often competing ones among them, will be offered. One prominent reason, it seems to us, is this: Because we all went to school, year after year, for many years, and learned a lot in the process; and we went there *physically*. From a high-altitude perspective, the present paper revolves around this reason.

The plan for the paper is in general as follows: We begin in Sect. 2 by confessing our two-part theoretical position, namely that

---

[1] We note here one vocal objection to that consensus: Yann LeCun has claimed that humans do not have general intelligence [24]. He discusses a hypothetical scenario wherein a human's visual field is permuted as an example of our lack of general intelligence, arguing (it seems) that the ability to learn this permutation is required of anything which could be considered "general" intelligent. While an attempted refutation of LeCun's position is out of scope for this paper, we do volunteer here that this "permutation skill" is clearly not particularly intelligent by any reasonable definition of the word (let alone by any reputable test of intelligence/cognitive ability we are aware of), and hence any definition of general intelligence which requires it as a prerequisite is not one we find at all plausible.

[2] If some of our readers are artificial, and not human persons, then they have **A**GI.

B. Goertzel et al. (Eds.): AGI 2022, LNAI 13539, pp. 178–187, 2023.
https://doi.org/10.1007/978-3-031-19907-3_17

P1 The best overarching approach to suitably defining GI, and obtaining AGI, is via formal logic, including specifically via logic-based learning that is academic in nature.

P2 AI/AGI is best pursued by seeking artificial agents that pass determinate cognitive tests.

We then note that in harmony with this position is inspiring work on AGI by Goertzel et al. [17,18], in which PreSchool (and, in general, grade levels progressing beyond this into at least K–12) for would-be AGIs presents an attractive engineering route toward AGI itself. While Goertzel et al. envisage a virtual academic environment, we have in mind physical classrooms, for physical robots. After explaining our focus on "logical/mathematical" cognition within the underpinnings of Goertzel's approach, we describe the robot PERI.2, which we have started to send to school in the hopes of it developing AGI. We give an example of an academic challenge for PERI.2 in the logical/mathematical category at the Kindergarten level. PERI.2 succeeds upon this challenge, but, as we admit, much additional work will be needed.

2 Our Two Theoretical Pillars

We fully recognize that there isn't exactly consensus regarding how best to reach AGI. In some cases, for example, non-declarative learning is believed to provide the most, perhaps even the *only*, route to AGI; an exemplar, by our lights, would be [23], an (impressive) approach described in a manner wholly bereft of formal reasoning over declarative knowledge or belief for the intelligent agents in question.[3] However, for better or worse, as the next section confesses, we (or at least the first author) feel differently.

2.1 Pillar 1: Logic-Based AI and Cognitive Science

The first author has long maintained that logic-based AI is superior to methodological competitors (see e.g. [7]). Re. computational cognitive science, the unmatched effectiveness of logic-based effort, at least for cognition, has likewise been asserted (see e.g. [6,8,11]). Overall, we posit an infinite collection $\mathfrak{L}$ of logics (we call them *cognitive calculi*) reasoning in which can constitute any level of GI whatsoever. (Standard logics still used in AI include first-order logic $\mathscr{L}_1$, second-order logic $\mathscr{L}_2$, etc.) In particular, it seems indubitable that at least for every aspect of human-level cognition that is reasoning-centric, there exists some cognitive calculus $\mathscr{L} \in \mathfrak{L}$ that can be tokened, specified, and implemented for concrete use in AGI; for this in action, see e.g. the novel logics specified and implemented in [11]. For notational convenience in the remainder of the present paper, we assume a particular cognitive calculus $\mathscr{L}^\star$ for the AGI science and engineering devoted to PERI.2 we describe and report herein—but for economy forego providing formal specification of $\mathscr{L}^\star$. For details regarding cognitive calculi, see the Appendix in [9].

---

[3] On the other hand, among prominent AGI researchers, we are incidentally not alone in our emphasis on logic-based r&d; see e.g. [30], to which we return below.

Real Learning is Academic Learning. Under the umbrella of logic-based AI & CogSci, we specifically hold that academic learning of and by formal logic and mathematics is key to AGI [3]—and it's this part of our orientation that aligns with the work of Goertzel et al. (see below).

Logicist Cognitive Robotics. As to robotics, the logicist approach to it advocated and pursued by the first author can be quickly summed up by tightening the concept of cognitive robotics as defined in [25], wherein it is said that such robotics produces robots whose actions are a function of what they believe. In line with this, but expanded in keeping with $\mathscr{L}^*$, we seek to engineer robots all of whose substantive decisions and actions are the result of automated reasoning over formulae in some set Φ of formulae in $\mathscr{L}^*$ known or at least believed by these robots, where such knowledge and belief can vary in strength depending upon the underlying likelihood of the formulae in Φ.

2.2 Pillar 2: Psychometric AI

Our second theoretical pillar is that AI, and AGI, should be fields devoted exclusively to creating and implementing artificial agents able to excel on established tests of cognitive ability and skill, including those used in the Academy for humans; see e.g. [4,5]. Most recently, this aspect of AI has been used in [1] to have success in solving Bennett mechanical test problems by artificial agents.

3   The Goertzelian (et al.) Academic Road to AGI

In general, we seek to follow the road to AGI paved by a progression through academic grade levels at least akin to the progression that brought the reader to a position in which she can understand the present paper; the progression of which we speak has been seminally described in [17,18].

4   PERI.2 in Kindergarten

We give a snapshot of an example of PERI.2 in Kindergarten, being tested in the area "Logical-Mathematical." (See Figs. 1 & 2.) This area is listed in [17] as a specific kind of intelligence according to Gardner's [13] theory of "multiple intelligences," and is obviously—given Pillars 1 & 2—pivotal for us.[4]

4.1   Automated Reasoning of a Meta-forms Problem/Solution Pair

PERI.2 employs the automated deductive reasoner ShadowProver [20] to verify proposed solutions to a given Meta-Forms problem; see Fig. 1.[5] Specifically,

---

[4] [17,18] also point out that this area finds its way into early eduction.

[5] ShadowProver has long been used to engineer logic-based intelligent artificial agents in our lab. A robust example can be found e.g. in [19]. While ShadowProver's reasoning is deductive, it is the basis for types of reasoning we believe are key to AGI r&d, e.g. nonmonotonic/defeasible reasoning. See [10] for an example of an inductive logic and an inductive automated reasoner (ShadowAdjudicator).

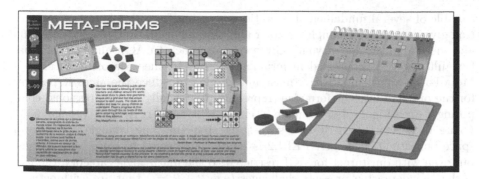

Fig. 1. The Meta-Forms game, From FoxMind. *This game provides a series of "clues" to the would-be puzzle solver, each of which is a visual version of a "logical statement." The goal is to physically construct a complete configuration of the 3×3 board from these clues. Formally, if Π is a complete configuration of the board, and Γ the collection of formulae that logicize all clues, then necessarily Π ∪ Γ is provably consistent in $\mathscr{L}^*$.*

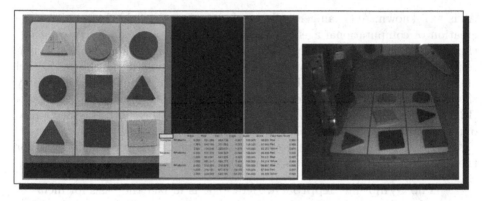

Fig. 2. PERI.2 sees the board (left), and holds a meta-forms piece in one hand (right). *Machine vision for PERI.2 courtesy of Cognex; hands are from Barrett.*

with a formalization of the clues given to the problem in this figure—as set Γ of formulae in $\mathscr{L}^*$—and the proposed configuration of the board shown in this figure—as set Π in $\mathscr{L}^*$—ShadowProver was tasked to find a proof of a contradiction (i.e. $\zeta \wedge \neg\zeta$) from Γ∪Π. It failed to find a proof in 3.16 s, which entails (given some formal context we leave unstated) that the configuration of the board is consistent with the clues, and hence a solution.

5   PERI.2, Concretely: A Glimpse

PERI.2 has a pair of dexterous, tactile-sensing Barrett hands attached to powerful Yaskawa arms, which together provide somatic information to his "mind." For vision, PERI.2 has three Cognex cameras that compose a system for sight capable of several fundamental operations, ranging from simple object recognition given a training example, to color and blob identification, to edge detection and measurement, and beyond. Given our approach to AGI, all such information ultimately is expressed in formulae of $\mathscr{L}^*$. In the case of its tackling a Meta-Forms problem, PERI.2 must ultimately transduce the clues it receives for the problem into the formulae (represented internally as s-expressions) composing Γ (see Fig. 1). For example, a clue might appear as (and (space 0 0) (blue 0 1) (triangle 0 1)), suggesting that the blue triangle will have a space beneath it. Presently PERI.2 is rigidly engineered to solve Meta-Forms, but even with our target for AGI restricted to the math/logic category, the fact is that Kindergarten presents challenges (e.g. $2 + 2 =?$) that are arithmetic in nature. Accordingly, our cognitive calculus $\mathscr{L}^*$ subsumes Peano Arithmetic, but this dimension must be left aside here.

6   Related Work

As is well-known, AGI can generally be classified as the field that explores the creation of computational agents possessing some level of *general intelligence*: the ability to exhibit complex problem-solving capabilities in an arbitrary environment, akin to the ability of humans (but not necessarily at the same level as humans) [14,15,33]. As AGI focuses on a broad overarching goal, inevitably there are many camps in AGI, each based upon its own approach to the problem [12,14]. Obviously, camps that are not overtly logicist bear little connection to our approach to AGI. Nonetheless, a simple triadic breakdown of approaches in AGI helps to contextualize the work discussed herein; this is particularly so for the first element of the trio in question, which is:

– **The Symbolic[6] Approach.** Here logic is in fact the basis for memory and reasoning. Knowledge in these systems consists of statements from which new knowledge can be derived by logical reasoning. New statements may also be added by way of fully logic-based perception (e.g. see [32]). Different approaches use different ontologies and different logics with different properties to optimize for the type of reasoning to be executed [21]. Invariably, at least so far, relative to the calculi $\mathscr{L}$ upon which our AGI r&d is based, logics in this approach to AGI by others are inexpressive, and reasoning is correspondingly simple. In particular, often representation and reasoning in this AGI approach can be reduced to information and processing in (perhaps with tailor-made inference schemata as needed) at the level of only $\mathscr{L}_1$, augmented perhaps with a few intensional operators. Some notable members of the symbolic camp are Wang's NARS [31] system and Shapiro et al.'s SNePS and GLAIR architectures [27]; all three encode symbolic representations of knowledge into a graph representation.

---

[6] Since all symbolic information and processing in AI/AGI can carried out in a formal logic, feel free to replace 'Symbolic' here with 'Logicist' or 'Logic-based.'

- **The Emergent Approach.** This approach focuses on creating agents whose memory and learning take the form of connectionist systems. The emergent approach assumes, naturally enough, an emergent hypothesis: that symbolic reasoning and learning can emerge from basic connections and interactions between nodes, as they perhaps do (at least in part) in the human brain. *Contra* the logicist approach, "knowledge" in emergent systems is encoded within the weights and connections between nodes of a network, which may evolve over time for "learning."
- **Hybrid Approaches.** Hybrid AGI systems aim to combine emergent and symbolic approaches. According to [12], hybrid approaches suffer from the same shortcomings as emergent approaches: they have "difficulty in realizing higher-order cognitive functions" such as reasoning over arbitrarily complex/iterated declarative content, which is the hallmark of our $\mathcal{L}$.

AGI stands in stark contrast to today's mainstream "narrow" AI systems, usually machine-learning models trained on massive datasets to excel in one particular task. For our logicist approach to AGI it is important to contextualize "human-level." Human-level AI can be thought of as a goal of AGI, but from the standpoint of our approach to AGI it is only a point on a spectrum of general intelligence that AGI agents fall on. AGI researchers of either a thoroughgoingly or even substantive logicist bent can presumably locate their ambitions for future AGI systems in the standard hierarchies (Arithmetic, based on $\mathcal{L}_1$; and Analytical, based on $\mathcal{L}_2$). In our approach to AGI, because we have a scheme for measuring intelligence (viz. Λ; see [2]), we can quantify very well where the level of given agents fall. One particular point worth noting here is that while we are inspired and guided by Goertzel, his conception of intelligence [16, p. 5] stands in contrast to ours, since he writes that "Intelligence in general must be considered as an open-ended phenomenon without any single scalar or vectorial quantification." This runs completely counter to the spirit and specifics of our approach to AGI. Consider e.g. the fact that we commonly compare the intelligence of human and nonhuman animal agents at least roughly in line with how academic learning and the test-measured success of such learning works. Consider for instance the common view that humans are more intelligent than dogs. It seems more than reasonable that the intuitive concept of intelligence underlying such a view is some sort of a single scalar. If a human is asked why he believes that humans are more intelligent than dogs, takes the question seriously, and tries to justify it, it appears to us likely that the rationale provided will in some way appeal to cognition measured in traditionally academic ways. Canines are smart, but as we all know, they don't start to learn to read, nor do they learn basic arithmetic, these being things routinely taught in PreSchool.

6.1   Remarks on NARS w.r.t Our Theoretical Pillars

NARS [31] is profitable to consider in relation to our two-pillar approach to AGI. NARS is fundamentally logicist in nature and has working implementation that can solve some preschool-level problems. With regard to our first pillar, Wang has argued for the need for "cognitive logic" rather than "mathematical logic" when capturing human reasoning, and claims that the non-axiomatic logic used in NARS embodies this reasoning [29]. We agree for the most part that cognitive logics are necessary, but hold e.g. that "real learning" in a cognitive logic still needs tools from logics used in mathematics (e.g. $\mathscr{L}_1$, $\mathscr{L}_2$, and $\mathscr{L}_3$) to give any serious treatment of what humans do when they go to K–12 school (since a large part of that schooling is in none other than mathematics, and reverse mathematics [28] has disclosed that mathematics ultimately consists of proofs and other structures built from formulae in first-to-third order logic). In taking a cognitive approach, NARS has demonstrated a level of competence in the areas of simple "spatial-visual" and "logical-mathematical" tasks [and has worked toward some basic "linguistic" tasks (see e.g. [22])]. Due to the cognitive nature of NARS and its ability to represent knowledge, belief, and self [34], it would in theory be able to realize our working definition of logicist cognitive robotics from [25]. As to our second pillar, Psychometric AI [5], NARS is not necessarily at odds with it, but is focused on achieving intelligence in line with Wang's working definition of intelligence as "the capacity of an information-processing system to adapt to its environment while operating with insufficient knowledge and resources" [33]. PAI provides by definition a means of meaningfully evaluating incremental progress toward AGI (viz. tests); Wang's definition doesn't supply such means.

7   Are Harder Problems Computationally Feasible?

For alert readers who may be wondering, Fig. 3 shows that harder Meta-Forms problems are within PERI.2's intellectual reach, in real time.

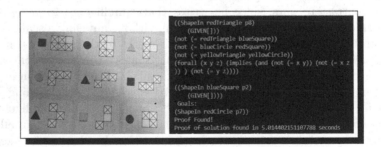

Fig. 3. A difficult meta-forms problem. *No positive clues are given (left), yet a proof of the correctness of PERI.2's proposal found by ShadowProver (right).*

8   Future Work: What About Compromised Perception?

Generally intelligent agents are capable of perceiving that they are mis-perceiving, as e.g. when they perceive rather dense smoke, and perceive that their sensors are therefore compromised; such a situation is shown in Fig. 4, for PERI.2's attempt to perceive Meta-Forms clues. Currently success in this case eludes us (and thus PERI.2), but a new cognitive calculus that formalizes such meta-reasoning is under development, one that reflects the computational science of attention and perception erected by Bello & Bridewell et al. (e.g. see [26]).

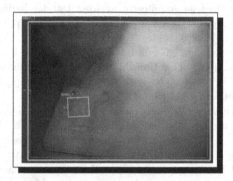

Fig. 4. Perception of compromised perception. *Here the set Γ of clues for the meta-form problem are hard to reliably perceive due to ambient smoke.*

Acknowledgements. We are grateful to: AFOSR for a DURIP award to Bringsjord & Govindarajulu that has brought PERI.2 to physical life, to ONR for sponsorship of r&d devoted to meta-cognitively perceptive artificial agents (award # N00014-22-1-2201), and to both AFOSR (currently award #FA9550-17-1-0191) and ONR for longstanding support of r&d in automated reasoning, planning, and logic-based learning.

References

1. Banerjee, S., Bringsjord, S., Giancola, M., Govindarajulu, N.S.: Qualitative mechanical problem-solving by artificial agents: further progress, under psychometric AI. In: The International FLAIRS Conference Proceedings, vol. 35 (2022)
2. Bringsjord, S., Govindarajulu, N.: The theory of cognitive consciousness, and Λ (lambda). J. Artif. Intell. Conscious. **7**(1), 155–181 (2020). http://kryten.mm.rpi.edu/sb_nsg_lambda_jaic_april_6_2020_3_42_pm_NY.pdf, The URL here goes to a preprint of the paper
3. Bringsjord, S., Govindarajulu, N.S., Banerjee, S., Hummel, J.: Do machine-learning machines learn? In: Müller, V.C. (ed.) PT-AI 2017. SAPERE, vol. 44, pp. 136–157. Springer, Cham (2018). https://doi.org/10.1007/978-3-319-96448-5_14
4. Bringsjord, S., Licato, J.: Psychometric artificial general intelligence: the Piaget-MacGuyver room. In: Wang, P., Goertzel, B. (eds.) Foundations of Artificial General Intelligence, pp. 25–47. Atlantis Press, Amsterdam (2012). http://kryten.mm.rpi.edu/Bringsjord_Licato_PAGI_071512.pdf, This URL is to a preprint only

5. Bringsjord, S., Schimanski, B.: What is artificial intelligence? Psychometric AI as an answer. In: Proceedings of the 18th International Joint Conference on Artificial Intelligence (IJCAI-2003), pp. 887–893. Morgan Kaufmann, San Francisco (2003). http://kryten.mm.rpi.edu/scb.bs.pai.ijcai03.pdf

6. Bringsjord, S.: Declarative/logic-based cognitive modeling. In: Sun, R. (ed.) The Handbook of Computational Psychology, pp. 127–169. Cambridge University Press, Cambridge (2008). http://kryten.mm.rpi.edu/sb_lccm_ab-toc_031607.pdf, This URL goes to a preprint only

7. Bringsjord, S.: The logicist manifesto: at long last let logic-based AI become a field unto itself. J. Appl. Logic **6**(4), 502–525 (2008). http://kryten.mm.rpi.edu/SB_LAI_Manifesto_091808.pdf

8. Bringsjord, S., Giancola, M., Govindarajulu, N.S.: Logic-based modeling of cognition. In: Sun, R. (ed.) The Handbook of Computational Psychology. Cambridge University Press, Cambridge (forthcoming). http://kryten.mm.rpi.edu/Logic-basedComputationalModelingOfCognition.pdf

9. Bringsjord, S., Govindarajulu, N.S., Licato, J., Giancola, M.: Learning ex nihilo. In: 6th Global Conference on Artificial Intelligence, GCAI 2020. EPiC Series in Computing, vol. 72, pp. 1–27. International Conferences on Logic and Artificial Intelligence at Zhejiang University (ZJULogAI), EasyChair Ltd., Manchester (2020). https://doi.org/10.29007/ggcf. http://easychair.org/publications/paper/NzWG

10. Bringsjord, S., Govindarajulu, N., Giancola, M.: Automated argument adjudication to solve ethical problems in multi-agent environments. Paladyn J. Behav. Robot. **12**, 310–335 (2021). http://kryten.mm.rpi.edu/AutomatedArgumentAdjudicationPaladyn071421.pdf, The URL here goes to a rough, uncorrected, truncated preprint as of 071421

11. Bringsjord, S., Sundar Govindarajulu, N.: Rectifying the mischaracterization of logic by mental model theorists. Cogn. Sci. **44**(12), (2020). https://doi.org/10.1111/cogs.12898

12. Duch, W., Oentaryo, R.J., Pasquier, M.: Cognitive architectures: where do we go from here? In: AGI, pp. 122–136 (2008)

13. Gardner, H.: Frames of Mind: The Theory of Multiple Intelligences. Basic Books, New York (1983)

14. Goertzel, B.: Artificial general intelligence. Scholarpedia **10**(11), 31847 (2015). https://doi.org/10.4249/scholarpedia.31847, revision #154015

15. Goertzel, B.: Artificial general intelligence: concept, state of the art, and future prospects. J. Artif. Gen. Intell. 1–48 (2014). https://doi.org/10.2478/jagi-2014-0001

16. Goertzel, B.: The general theory of general intelligence: a pragmatic patternist perspective, 1–64. arXiv:2103.15100 (2021)

17. Goertzel, B., Bugaj, V.: AGI preschool: a framework for evaluating early-stage human-like AGIs. In: Proceedings of the 2nd Conference on Artificial General Intelligence, pp. 12–17. Atlantis Press (2009). https://www.atlantis-press.com/proceedings/agi09/1826

18. Goertzel, B., Pennachin, C., Geisweiller, N.: AGI preschool. In: Engineering Intelligence, Part 1: A Path to Advanced AGI via Embodied Learning and Cognitive Synergy, vol. 5, pp. 337–354. Atlantis Thinking Machines. Atlantis Press, Amsterdam (2014)

19. Govindarajulu, N., Bringsjord, S.: On automating the doctrine of double effect. In: Sierra, C. (ed.) Proceedings of the Twenty-Sixth International Joint Conference on Artificial Intelligence (IJCAI-2017), pp. 4722–4730. International Joint Conferences on Artificial Intelligence (2017). https://doi.org/10.24963/ijcai.2017/658

20. Govindarajulu, N., Bringsjord, S., Peveler, M.: On quantified modal theorem proving for modeling ethics. In: Suda, M., Winkler, S. (eds.) Proceedings of the Second International Workshop on Automated Reasoning: Challenges, Applications, Directions, Exemplary Achievements (ARCADE 2019), Electronic Proceedings in Theoretical Computer Science, vol. 311, pp. 43–49. Open Publishing Association, Waterloo (2019). http://eptcs.web.cse.unsw.edu.au/paper.cgi?ARCADE2019.7.pdf. The ShadowProver system can be obtained here: https://naveensundarg.github.io/prover/
21. Gust, H., Krumnack, U., Schwering, A., Kühnberger, K.U.: The role of logic in AGI systems: towards a lingua franca for general intelligence, pp. 126–131, June 2009. https://doi.org/10.2991/agi.2009.28
22. Hammer, P., Lofthouse, T., Wang, P.: The OpenNARS implementation of the non-axiomatic reasoning system. In: AGI (2016)
23. Hutter, M.: Universal Artificial Intelligence: Sequential Decisions Based on Algorithmic Probability. Springer, New York (2005). https://doi.org/10.1007/b138233
24. LeCun, Y.: Yann LeCun: deep learning, convolutional neural networks, and self-supervised learning. Lex Fridman Podcast, August 2019. Transcript of podcast. https://www.happyscribe.com/public/lex-fridman-podcast-artificial-intelligence-ai/yann-lecun-deep-learning-convolutional-neural-networks-and-self-supervised-learning#paragraph_2405. Relevant portion begins at 00:40:05
25. Levesque, H., Lakemeyer, G.: Cognitive robotics. In: Handbook of Knowledge Representation, chap. 24, pp. 869–882. Elsevier, Amsterdam (2007). http://www.cs.toronto.edu/~hector/Papers/cogrob.pdf
26. Lovett, A., Bridewell, W., Bello, P.: Selection, engagement, & enhancement: a framework for modeling visual attention. In: Proceedings of the 43rd Annual Conference of the Cognitive Science Society, pp. 1893–1899. Cognitive Science Society, Vienna (2021)
27. Shapiro, S., Bona, J.: The GLAIR cognitive architecture. Int. J. Mach. Conscious. **02**, 144–152 (2010). https://doi.org/10.1142/S1793843010000515
28. Simpson, S.: Subsystems of Second Order Arithmetic, 2nd edn. Cambridge University Press, Cambridge (2010)
29. Wang, P.: Cognitive Logic versus Mathematical Logic (2004)
30. Wang, P.: Rigid Flexibility: The Logic of Intelligence. Applied Logic Series, vol. 34. Springer, Dordrecht (2006). Ed. by D. Gabbay and J. Barwise
31. Wang, P.: Non-Axiomatic Logic. A Model of Intelligent Reasoning, Sciendo (2013)
32. Wang, P.: Proceedings of the 6th International Conference on Artificial General Intelligence. In: Artificial General Intelligence, pp. 160–169, July 2013. https://doi.org/10.1007/978-3-642-39521-5_17
33. Wang, P.: On defining artificial intelligence. J. Artif. Gen. Intell. **10**, 1–37 (2019)
34. Wang, P., Li, X., Hammer, P.: Self in NARS, an AGI system. Front. Robot. AI **5**, 20 (2018)

Reinforcement Learning
with Information-Theoretic Actuation

Elliot Catt[2]($\boxtimes$) (iD), Marcus Hutter[1,2] (iD), and Joel Veness[2]

[1] Australian National University, Canberra, Australia
{ecatt,mhutter,aixi}@google.com
[2] Deepmind, London, UK

Abstract. Reinforcement Learning formalises an embodied agent's interaction with the environment through observations, rewards and actions. But where do the actions come from? Actions are often considered to represent something external, such as the movement of a limb, a chess piece, or more generally, the output of an actuator. In this work we explore and formalize a contrasting view, namely that actions are best thought of as the output of a sequence of internal choices with respect to an action model. This view is particularly well-suited for leveraging the recent advances in large sequence models as prior knowledge for multi-task reinforcement learning problems. Our main contribution in this work is to show how to augment the standard MDP formalism with a sequential notion of internal action using information-theoretic techniques, and that this leads to self-consistent definitions of both internal and external action value functions.

1 Introduction

It is hard to speak of embodied agents these days without mentioning or appealing to some notion of Reinforcement Learning. This particular mathematical formalism has been so successful of late that the validity of its various modelling assumptions rarely gets called into question. Yet recently we have seen a step-change in the capabilities of generative modelling, with the most striking example being in multi-modal language applications; the acquisition of gigantic multi-task datasets via internet scraping and scalable approaches to training has led to a renewed excitement for building next generation question-answering systems, chat bots, productivity tools, sentiment analysis, and in some circles, has even produced a newfound sense of optimism that the original goals of Artificial Intelligence may well be obtainable within our lifetimes.

Yet what does this mean for Reinforcement Learning? While its success in restricted domains is no longer in doubt, questions remain about its long-term viability as a foundational paradigm for Artificial Intelligence. For example, effective exploration, even in restricted settings such as finite MDPs, is problematic in large unstructured state spaces, with various lower bounds demonstrating polynomial dependence on the size of the state space, e.g. [12]. While there are some noteworthy recent examples of hard exploration problems being overcome

B. Goertzel et al. (Eds.): AGI 2022, LNAI 13539, pp. 188–198, 2023.
https://doi.org/10.1007/978-3-031-19907-3_18

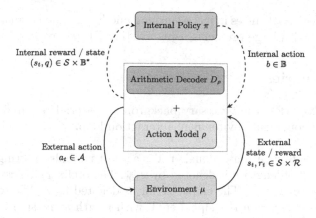

Fig. 1. Agent-environment loop with internal actions.

by clever heuristics [5], the situation in general looks challenging, if not dire. On the other hand, recent advances in sequence modelling combined with the acquisition of gigantic datasets via internet scraping has led to a seeming step-change [2] in the ability of various types of probabilistic models to generate plausible continuations. Is there a way to leverage this, while keeping the basic reinforcement learning formalism and derived notions such as value functions, policies, return, etc. intact?

Our proposal argues for rethinking the fundamental notion of action in reinforcement learning. Actions are often considered to represent something external, such as the movement of a limb, a chess piece, or more generally, the output of an actuator. In this work however, we develop a generic notion of *internal* action, which is implied by a choice of action model ρ. The key technical insight we leverage is the well-known duality between optimal lossless coding strategies and probabilities from information theory. At a high level, instead of an agent directly picking an action from the action space $\mathcal{A}$, instead it will pick a sequence of internal actions from an internal action set $\mathbb{B}$ which will decode to an external action from $\mathcal{A}$. Figure 1 depicts this interaction graphically.

So what do we gain by introducing this particular layer of indirection in the agent's choice of action? Breaking up an action into a series of internal actions seems like a reasonable approach to dealing with large action spaces, and indeed has been used in other planning settings, but it immediately throws up a number of questions. How do we decompose an arbitrary action space? Is there a universal, or in some sense optimal decomposition? When should the agent stop generating internal actions and communicate an external action to the environment? Does this even make sense in a reinforcement learning setting? How do we leverage prior knowledge in the form of a default policy? Are there ramifications for multi-task RL? Can we efficiently compute or sample good actions? This paper will argue that our particular information-theoretic decomposition using an arithmetic decoder coupled with a coding distribution implied by a choice of action model naturally addresses all these questions, and opens up the possibly of leveraging recent advances in meta-learning and large-scale language/sequence models to deal with large problems using existing RL techniques.

2 Preliminaries

We now briefly review the necessary background material required to describe our internal action agent-environment interaction loop.

Sequential Prediction. A finite alphabet $\mathcal{X}$ is a set of symbols. A string of symbols $x_1 x_2 \ldots x_n \in \mathcal{X}^n$ of length n is denoted by $x_{1:n}$. The prefix $x_{1:j}$ of $x_{1:n}$, $j \leq n$, is denoted by $x_{\leq j}$ or $x_{<j+1}$. The empty string is denoted by ϵ. The set of strings whose symbols come from the alphabet $\mathcal{X}$ with length at most n is defined by $\mathcal{X}^{\leq n} := \{\epsilon\} \cup \bigcup_{i=1}^{n} \mathcal{X}^i$. The set of strings of symbols from alphabet $\mathcal{X}$ with finite length is denoted by $\mathcal{X}^* := \{\epsilon\} \cup \bigcup_{i=1}^{\infty} \mathcal{X}^i$. The concatenation of two strings x and y is denoted by xy. The length of a string x will be denoted by $|x|$. We will use $y \in x$ to denote that the symbol y is in the string x.

A (coding) distribution ρ is a sequence of probability mass functions $\rho_n : \mathcal{X}^n \rightarrow [0,1]$, which for all $n \in \mathbb{N}$ satisfy the constraint that $\rho_n(x_{1:n}) = \sum_{y \in \mathcal{X}} \rho_{n+1}(x_{1:n}y)$ for all $x_{1:n} \in \mathcal{X}^n$, with the base case $\rho_0(\epsilon) := 1$. From here onwards, whenever the meaning is clear from the argument to ρ, the subscript on ρ will be dropped. Under this definition, the conditional probability of a symbol x_n given previous data $x_{<n}$ is defined as $\rho(x_n|x_{<n}) := \rho(x_{1:n})/\rho(x_{<n})$ provided $\rho(x_{<n}) > 0$, with the familiar chain rules $\rho(x_{1:n}) = \prod_{i=1}^{n} \rho(x_i|x_{<i})$ and $\rho(x_{j:k} \mid x_{<j}) = \prod_{i=j}^{k} \rho(x_i|x_{<i})$ now following. We will use $\Delta(\mathcal{X})$ to denote the space of probability distributions over $\mathcal{X}$.

Arithmetic Encoding/Decoding. A fundamental technique known as *arithmetic encoding* [11,16] makes explicit the connection between coding distributions and source codes. Binary arithmetic encoding is a general purpose parameterized technique that takes in a distribution ρ (known as a coding distribution) and some data $x_{1:n} \in \mathcal{X}^n$, and produces a uniquely decodable binary codeword $C_\rho(x_{1:n}) \in \{0,1\}^*$, whose length is essentially $\lceil -\log_2 \rho(x_{1:n}) \rceil$, which is optimal in terms of expected length if the data is sampled from ρ. In essence, shorter binary codewords are assigned to data which has a higher chance of occurring under ρ, and longer binary codewords are assigned to the less probable data items. Arithmetic decoding is the reverse of this procedure; it takes a coding distribution ρ, a binary code word $y_{1:k} = C_\rho(x_{1:n})$, and returns the original data $D_\rho(y_{1:k}) = x_{1:n}$. We will also use the shorthand notation $D_\rho(y_{1:k} \mid s) := D_{\rho(\cdot|s)}(y_{1:k})$ to denote decoding with respect to a coding distribution conditioned on the string s. We refer the reader to the standard text of [4] for further information.

Markov Decision Processes. A Markov Decision Process (MDP) is a type of probabilistic model widely used within reinforcement learning [13,14] and control [1]. In this work, we limit our attention to finite horizon, time-homogeneous

MDPs whose action and state spaces are finite. Formally, an MDP is a quadruplet $(\mathcal{S}, \mathcal{A}, \mathcal{R}, \mu)$, where $\mathcal{S}$ is a finite, non-empty set of states, $\mathcal{A}$ is a finite, non-empty set of actions, $\mathcal{R} \subset \mathbb{R}$ is the reward space, and μ is the transition probability kernel that assigns to each state-action pair $(s, a) \in \mathcal{S} \times \mathcal{A}$ a probability measure $\mu(\cdot \,|\, s, a)$ over $\mathcal{S} \times \mathcal{R}$. $\mathcal{S}$ and $\mathcal{A}$ are known as the *state space* and *action space* respectively. The transition probability kernel gives rise to the *state transition kernel* $\mathcal{P}(s'|s, a) := \mu(\{s'\} \times \mathcal{R} \,|\, s, a)$, which gives the probability of transitioning from state s to state s' if action a is taken in s.

An agent's behavior is determined by a *policy* that defines, for each state $s \in \mathcal{S}$ and time $t \in \mathbb{N}$, a probability measure over $\mathcal{A}$ denoted by $\pi_t(\cdot \,|\, s)$. A *stationary policy* is a policy which is independent of time, which we will denote by $\pi(\cdot \,|\, s)$ where appropriate. At each time t, the agent communicates an action $A_t \sim \pi_t(\cdot \,|\, S_{t-1})$ to the system in state $S_{t-1} \in \mathcal{S}$. The system then responds with a state-reward pair $(S_t, R_t) \sim \mu(\cdot \,|\, S_{t-1}, A_t)$. Here we will assume that each reward is bounded between $[r_{\min}, r_{\max}] \subset \mathbb{R}$ and that the system starts in a state s_0 and executes for an infinite number of steps. Thus the execution of the system can be described by a sequence of random variables $S_0, A_1, S_1, R_1, A_2, S_2, R_2, \dots$.

The finite m-horizon *return* from time t is defined as $Z_t := \sum_{i=t}^{t+m-1} R_i$. The expected m-horizon return from time t, also known as the *value function*, is denoted by $V_\mu^\pi(s_t) := \mathbb{E}[Z_{t+1} \,|\, S_t = s_t]$. The return space $\mathcal{Z}$ is the set of all possible returns. The *action-value function* is defined by $Q_\mu^\pi(s_t, a_{t+1}) := \mathbb{E}[Z_{t+1} \,|\, S_t = s_t, A_{t+1} = a_{t+1}]$. An *optimal policy*, denoted by π_μ^*, is a policy that maximizes the expected return $\mathbb{E}[Z_{t+1} \,|\, S_t]$ for all t.

3   Information-Theoretic Actuation – Internal Actions

We now describe in detail how to combine the aforementioned building blocks into the internal reinforcement learning framework described in Fig. 1, and discuss its ramifications. Compared with the standard agent-environment loop, there are two additional components with this setup: a choice of action model ρ, and an associated arithmetic decoder D_ρ that uses ρ as a coding distribution. The internal action space $\mathbb{B}$ is defined by the associated decoding alphabet used by D_ρ; for example, using a binary arithmetic decoder would lead to an internal action space of $\mathbb{B} = \{0, 1\}$. For pedagogical purposes, we will restrict our attention to this case in the rest of the paper, but remark that any finite decoding alphabet can in principle be used with our construction.

We first introduce our notion of internal action. At a high-level, one should think of a single internal action as a bit-commitment towards a particular choice of external action, with particular sequences of these corresponding to external actions. In a sense, internal actions correspond to a period of private deliberation by the agent, which upon conclusion produces a string describing the desired actuation in compressed form; in essence, the arithmetic decoder functions as a universal actuator, whose behavior can be completely configured by a choice of action model.

Reshaping of the Action Space. As alluded to before, the effect of the action model is to reshape the action space, which the following example will make clear. Figure 2 shows an illustrative example of the behavior of a binary arithmetic decoder equipped with an action model based on a GLN-based context mixing language model [15] that has been pre-trained on 9 MB of grandmaster chess games in PGN (Portable Game Notation) format. On the left hand side of the table, we have the input to the decoder, and on the righthand side we have the decoded output; if we consider the first row, the LHS corresponds to the bitstring $10 = C_\rho(\text{a6})$ and the RHS corresponds to $D_\rho(10)$, with ρ here denoting our pre-trained language model (which depends on the state). The LHS of the first 4 rows shows the encoding of a natural sequence of continuing moves (known as the Morphy Defense), while the last four rows show an illogical continuation of moves which ignore development, lose castling rights, and even hang the queen. One can see that much shorter codes are assigned to the more logical sequence of moves. This shows the effect of the action model as providing a type of inductive bias, which we will discuss in greater depth later.

In contrast, one could also consider the effect of a completely uninformative action model, $\rho_{\text{UNIFORM}}(a|s) := 1 / |\mathcal{A}|$, which assigns uniform probability mass to each possible external action in every state. Here every single action would have the same codelength of $\lceil \log |\mathcal{A}| \rceil$, which would correspond to a naive binarization of the external action space.

Input bits	Decoded Output
10	a6
10010	a6 Ba4
100100	a6 Ba4 Nf6
1001010111	a6 Ba4 Nf6 O-O
010010101010011	Nh6
0100101010101000110000010	Nh6 Kf1
010010101010100011000001100100101101	Nh6 Kf1 Qg5
0100101010101000110000011001001010100010010001	Nh6 Kf1 Qg5 Na3

Fig. 2. Arithmetic decoding example. Some example decoded outputs from a pre-trained model on chess, with the model's context set to the Ruy Lopez opening, namely: *e4 e5 Nf3 Nc6 Bb5.*

When to Stop Decoding. Figure 2 also highlights a technical issue which we need to resolve, namely, how and when is a decoded action to be transmitted to the external environment? For example, if we wanted a chess-playing agent whose action space was the space of single moves, we need some way to know when our decoded output should be communicated to the environment as an external action. Although other solutions are possible, in this work we adopt the convention that every external action can be described as a string formed by the concatenation of atomic symbols from a common alphabet. More formally, we assume that the action space $\mathcal{A} \subseteq \mathbb{A}^{\le k}$, where $\mathbb{A}$ denotes the sub-action alphabet, and k is a positive constant. We assume that the sub-action alphabet

---

Algorithm 1. Internal Agent-Environment loop

Require: Internal policy $\pi : \mathcal{S} \times \mathbb{B}^* \to \Delta\mathbb{B}$
Require: External environment $\mu : \mathcal{S} \times \mathcal{A} \to \Delta(\mathcal{S} \times \mathcal{R})$
Require: Action model $\rho : \mathcal{S} \to \Delta\mathbb{A}^{\leq k}$
  for $t = 1, 2, 3, \ldots$ **do**
    Observe $s_t, r_t \sim \mu(\cdot, \cdot | s_{t-1}, a_{t-1})$
    $a_t, q \leftarrow \epsilon$
    while $\top \not\in a_t$ **do**
      $b \sim \pi(\cdot | s_t, q), q \leftarrow qb, a_t \leftarrow D_\rho(q | s_t), r_t \leftarrow 0$
    end while
    $a_t \leftarrow \tau(a_t)$
    Act a_t
  end for

---

always contains a privileged termination symbol $\top \in \mathbb{A}$, which has the semantics that when it is decoded it causes an external action to be communicated to the environment. Note that in finite action/state MDPs, this modification does not impose any restrictions nor add further expressive power. Returning to the example shown in Fig. 2, by identifying the space character with $\top$, we would know when to transmit an external action. This is implemented formally via a function $\tau : \mathbb{A}^{\leq k} \to \mathcal{A}$ which takes actions and returns the action component up to but not including the first $\top$, for example $\tau(a6\,\top) = a6$. This importantly handles the case of multiple $\top$ symbols, for example $\tau(a6\,\top\,\mathrm{Ba4}\,\top) = a6$.

A terminal symbol is not the only way to know when to stop decoding. Another approach could be to only allow prefix-free codes. This will however run into it's own problems, such as what prefix-free encoding to use, how to enumerate the elements of $\mathcal{A}$ so that the corresponding prefix code can be found easily (and vice versa). Using an "optimal" prefix code would require the use of universal Turing machines and is beyond the scope of this paper. Another choice to stop decoding is to consider the action before the last $\top$ symbol, instead of before the first. In this case the agent may take multiple actions without knowing the state in between them.

Internal Action Loop. External action selection is determined by executing our internal policy π until the concatenation of these binary actions uniquely decodes into an external action. Once the action model and arithmetic decoder have generated an external action, this external action will be sent to the external environment. The external environment will then return an external observation/reward to the action model and arithmetic decoder combination, and the internal policy receives a reward r_t from the external environment. This interaction is displayed graphically in Fig. 1 and described by Algorithm 1.

4   Connecting Internal with External

In this section, we will describe formally how to augment an arbitrary external environment to an internal environment that the internal action agent is able to interact with; additionally if the external environment is Markovian then the internal environment will also be Markovian. Our approach will be to construct an augmented environment ϑ, called the internal environment, comprised of the true environment, the action model and the arithmetic decoder. We will also show how the internal action agent can be uplifted to an external agent, and then show that both the internal environment with an internal action agent and the external environment with the uplifted policy are equivalent in the sense that they achieve identical action-value functions. These results will allow for easier analysis of the internal action agent setup, as well as the ability to apply any result or algorithm specific to MDPs to the internal agent setup.

Internal Environment. The internal environment ϑ is a stochastic function over internal states and internal actions to internal states and rewards. The internal state space used here will be $\mathcal{I} := \mathcal{S} \times \mathbb{B}^{\leq n}$, the state from the external environment and previous internal actions taken by the internal agent, until they are decoded to an external action. We consider the finite set $\mathbb{B}^{\leq n}$ over the infinite set $\mathbb{B}^*$, as for any external action a with $\rho(a) > 0$ there will always be a finite number of binary actions needed to decode a; n is the maximum of those finite numbers. We will use $\top$ to denote the "terminal" symbol, that is, the symbol that indicates when the concatenation of internal actions corresponds to a complete external action, and is sent to the external environment. We will use the symbols s, s' for elements of $\mathcal{S}$, the first component of the internal state. We will use q, q' for elements of $\mathbb{B}^{\leq n}$, the second component of the internal state, the internal agent's previous internal actions. The symbol b will be used for the internal agent's internal action. The symbol a will be used for a decoded external action, e.g. $D_\rho(qb|s) = a$. The true external environment will be denoted by μ, which is a stochastic function from external states and external actions to external states and rewards. The external state space is $\mathcal{S}$. The external action space is $\mathcal{A} \subseteq \mathbb{A}^{\leq k}$.

Definition 1 (MDP (Internal) Environment ϑ). *The internal policy π interacts with an internal environment $\vartheta : \mathcal{I} \times \mathbb{B} \to \Delta(\mathcal{I} \times \mathcal{R})$ which is defined by the action model ρ (encoder/decoder C_ρ/D_ρ generated by ρ) and the true external environment μ as follows:*

$$\vartheta(s'q'r|sq, b) := \begin{cases} \mu(s'r|s, \tau(a)) & \text{if } q' = \epsilon \wedge (\top \in a), \\ 1 & \text{if } s' = s \wedge q' = qb \wedge r = 0 \wedge (\top \notin a), \\ 0 & \text{otherwise} \end{cases}$$

where $a := D_\rho(qb|s)$, $(s'q', r) \in \mathcal{I} \times \mathcal{R}$, $sq \in \mathcal{I}$ and $b \in \mathbb{B}$.

The definition of ϑ is split up into three cases: In the first case the decoded qb contains the symbol $\top$, $\top \in a$ where $a := D_\rho(qb|s)$, and the previous binary characters q' resets to being the empty string ϵ. In this case the τ of the decoded action $D_\rho(qb|s)$ is sent to the external environment μ, and the next state s', is the external state s'. The second case of ϑ is when the internal agent is still decoding, that is, $\top \notin a$ and the next state $s'q' = sqb$ is updated by the agent's action b, and the internal reward r is 0. In the third case, where neither set of above conditions is satisfied, the probability of the state $s'q'$ and reward r is 0. In this way the environment ϑ is deterministic during the decoding process, and only stochastic when it sends the decoded action to the external environment.

Given the internal agent's policy π and the arithmetic decoder D_ρ, we can construct an external policy Π which will interact with the true external environment μ. The external policy Π is a stochastic function from external states $s \in \mathcal{S}$ to external actions $a \in \mathcal{A}$. To construct Π, we consider all possible binary strings $q \in \mathbb{B}^{\leq n}$ such that the arithmetic decoder will decode q into a given s. For this we will need to define a *decodable* subset of $\mathbb{B}^{\leq n}$. We will use $\mathbb{D}$ to denote the set of decodable binary strings. A string q is decodable if $\top$ is in the decoding of the string, and $\top$ is not in the decoding of the first $|q| - 1$ elements of the string. Formally this means $\mathbb{D}_s := \{q \in \mathbb{B}^{\leq n} : \top \in D_\rho(q|s) \wedge \top \notin D_\rho(q_{<|q|}|s)\}$. We then consider the probability that π will output the internal binary actions that eventually construct q, which using the chain rule we can write as the product of probabilities that π will take the action of each element of q given the previous elements of q. All together this is written as follows:

$$\Pi(a|s) := \sum_{\substack{q \in \mathbb{D}_s: \\ a = \tau(D_\rho(q|s))}} \prod_{i=1}^{|q|} \pi(q_i | s q_{<i}). \tag{1}$$

It is important to note that there may be more than one binary string $q \in \mathbb{D}_s$ such that $a = \tau(D_\rho(q|s))$; this comes from how arithmetic decoders work. For example, consider a case where

$$D_\rho(10\,s) = e, \; D_\rho(100\,s) = e4, \; D_\rho(101\,s) = e4$$
$$D_\rho(1000\,s|s) = e4\,c5, \; D_\rho(1001\,s|s) = e4\,\top$$
$$D_\rho(1010\,s|s) = e4\,\top, \; D_\rho(1011\,s|s) = e4\,e5$$

We have that both 1001 and 1010 are elements of $\mathbb{D}_s$ and both $\tau(D_\rho(1001\,s|s)) = e4$ and $\tau(D_\rho(1010\,s|s)) = e4$, therefore $\Pi(e4|s)$ would be a sum over 1001 and 1010.

Self-consistency of Internal and External Q-values. We can use the external agent Π to interact with the external environment μ, just as any regular RL agent would.

Theorem 1 (Internal/External value equivalence). *For all states $s \in \mathcal{S}$, previous internal actions $q \in \mathbb{B}^{\leq n}$, external actions $a \in \mathcal{A}$ and internal actions $b \in \mathbb{B}$, if $\tau(D_\rho(qb|s)) = a$ then*

$$Q_\mu^\Pi(s, a) = Q_\vartheta^\pi(sq, b). \tag{2}$$

That is, the action-value function for the external policy Π and external environment μ is equal to the action-value function for the internal policy π and the internal environment ϑ.

Because of Eq. 2 we are able to say that if an internal agent π performs well, in the sense of a high action-value, in the internal environment ϑ, then the uplifted version of the agent Π, performs well in μ.

5 Discussion

A Universal Action Interface for Multi-task RL. A key complication and limiting factor in the design of any multi-task RL system is how to deal with the potentially radically different action spaces required for each distinct task. While it is feasible to make a generic agent work well across multiple similar domains e.g. Atari games [9], the situation becomes considerably more complicated when the action spaces of the different tasks vary dramatically. The arithmetic encoding-based approach we advocate provides an elegant solution to this problem, which builds on techniques from universal source coding. Given $K > 1$ coding distributions, it is straightforward to combine them into a universal ensemble whose compression performance will be close to that of the best coding distribution in hindsight. If we denote the ith coding distribution by ρ_i, one can take a uniform Bayesian mixture of the K coding distributions, whose marginal distribution over sequences is given by $\xi(x_{1:n}) := \sum_{i=1}^{K} \frac{1}{K} \rho_i(x_{1:n})$. A standard dominance argument [6] shows that the logarithmic loss/coding length of the mixture ξ compared to any choice of action model j is bounded by $-\log \xi(x_{1:n}) \leq -\log\left(\frac{1}{K} \rho_j(x_{1:n})\right) = -\log \rho_j(x_{1:n}) + \log K$, or in other words, the excess log-loss is bounded by a constant, which is asymptotically negligible when one considers the time-averaged performance of the ensemble.

This has important ramifications for multi-task reinforcement learning in our internal action formulation. Recently, various works [7] have attempted to frame reinforcement learning in terms of probabilistic sequence models over interaction strings, i.e. defining a sequential probability measure ν over strings that represent state/reward/action histories in the form $s_1 r_1 a_1 \ldots$. By taking a uniform Bayesian mixture over multiple instances of these history-based measures for different tasks, just as in the coding distribution example, one also obtains a sequence model that is universal across all of these tasks. More formally, given a history string h which is an element of $(\mathcal{S} \times \mathcal{R} \times \mathcal{A})^* \cup ((\mathcal{S} \times \mathcal{R} \times \mathcal{A})^* \times (\mathcal{S} \times \mathcal{R}))$, we can define the uniform Bayesian mixture $\xi(h) = \sum_{i=1}^{K} \frac{1}{K} \nu_i(h)$ over K history based measures ν_i, with each ν_i corresponding to a task specific history model. Note that this formulation in terms of measures on strings still implies the usual Bayesian learning in terms of sequential updating of the posterior, it is just hidden in this notation; see Sect. 2 by [8] for a brief overview.

An interesting effect now emerges if we use the conditional action distribution $\xi(\cdot \mid s_1 r_1 a_1, \ldots, s_n r_n)$ as the action model in our setup. In particular, this action model will rapidly learn to *automatically generate actions appropriate for the underlying task*, without requiring any task identity information. How this works is subtle; Bayesian inference is used implicitly by ξ to determine which task the agent is most likely in, and due to the rapid convergence of the Bayesian mixture to the best task specific model, the action model used for decoding after a small number of external environment interactions will essentially behave the same as if we knew which task specific action model to use in the first place. In other words, what this means in practice is that one can use ξ as the action model, and C_ξ will produce codes which are almost as short as any task-specific action encoding C_{ρ_j}. In particular, this implies that short bitstrings can decode to very different external actions which are plausible under either task-specific model.

The most interesting aspect about this construction is that the internal action formalism allows us to treat a multi-task reinforcement problem as a single reinforcement learning task with a common action space.

Specifying the Action Space from Data. In complicated environments, it may be difficult or complicated to precisely specify the action space explicitly. This situation readily arises in natural language domains for example. In these cases it is more natural to simply learn a probabilistic model of the domain. Our internal agent formalism directly allows for this possibility via the action model. The action model allows for a strict separation between pre-training on data, for example pre-training an action model using a collection of grandmaster games in chess, and the resultant learning behavior of the internal agent.

It is also worth pointing out an interesting connection to meta-learning with sequence models across many tasks. Perhaps surprisingly, perplexity-based meta-learning of history-dependent LLMs is closely related to the explicit Bayesian mixture solution. In particular, one can show that in many standard meta-learning setups, the optimal perplexity-minimizing solution is *exactly* a Bayesian mixture distribution [10]. Provided that a sufficiently powerful history-dependent model is used (such as the case with LLMs based on Transformers) to model the interaction histories, a low-perplexity solution can be seen as a learnt approximation to the explicit Bayesian construction we provided. In this way the action space for a multi-task agent can be learnt directly from data alone, which goes some way to explaining the recent empirical success of approaches such as [7].

Pre-training and Universality. A common use case in machine learning is to consider fine tuning an existing pre-trained model to save on compute. It is possible to show that pre-training on any data will not affect the asymptotic performance of any consistent density estimator [3]. In our context, it suggests that a good general approach to constructing an action model for a new domain might be to first pre-train on large, task-agnostic data and then to use fine tuning to incorporate task-specific knowledge if this data is available.

References

1. Bertsekas, D.P., Tsitsiklis, J.N.: Neuro-Dynamic Programming. Athena Scientific, Belmont (1996)

2. Brown, T.B., et al.: Language models are few-shot learners. arXiv preprint arXiv:2005.14165 (2020)
3. Catt, E., Hutter, M., Veness, J.: Reinforcement learning with information-theoretic actuation. arXiv preprint arXiv:2109.15147 (2021)
4. Cover, T.M.: Elements of Information Theory. Wiley, New York (1999)
5. Ecoffet, A., Huizinga, J., Lehman, J., Stanley, K.O., Clune, J.: Go-explore: a new approach for hard-exploration problems (2021)
6. Hutter, M.: On the existence and convergence of computable universal priors. In: Gavaldá, R., Jantke, K.P., Takimoto, E. (eds.) ALT 2003. LNCS (LNAI), vol. 2842, pp. 298–312. Springer, Heidelberg (2003). https://doi.org/10.1007/978-3-540-39624-6_24
7. Janner, M., Li, Q., Levine, S.: Reinforcement learning as one big sequence modeling problem (2021)
8. Milan, K., et al.: The forget-me-not process. In: Lee, D., Sugiyama, M., Luxburg, U., Guyon, I., Garnett, R. (eds.) Advances in Neural Information Processing Systems, vol. 29. Curran Associates, Inc. (2016)
9. Mnih, V., et al.: Human-level control through deep reinforcement learning. Nature **518**(7540), 529–533 (2015)
10. Ortega, P., et al.: Meta-learning of sequential strategies (2019)
11. Rissanen, J., Langdon, G.G.: Arithmetic coding. IBM J. Res. Dev. **23**(2), 149–162 (1979)
12. Strehl, A., Li, L., Littman, M.: Reinforcement learning in finite MDPs: PAC analysis. J. Mach. Learn. Res. **10**, 2413–2444 (2009). https://doi.org/10.1145/1577069.1755867
13. Sutton, R.S., Barto, A.G.: Reinforcement Learning: An Introduction. MIT Press, Cambridge (2018)
14. Szepesvári, C.: Algorithms for reinforcement learning. Synth. Lect. Artif. Intell. Mach. Learn. **4**(1), 1–103 (2010)
15. Veness, J., et al.: Gated linear networks. arXiv preprint arXiv:1910.01526 (2019)
16. Witten, I.H., Neal, R.M., Cleary, J.G.: Arithmetic coding for data compression. Commun. ACM **30**(6), 520–540 (1987)

Homomorphisms Between Transfer, Multi-task, and Meta-learning Systems

Tyler Cody[✉]

National Security Institute, Virginia Tech, Arlington, VA, USA
tcody@vt.edu

Abstract. Transfer learning, multi-task learning, and meta-learning are well-studied topics concerned with the generalization of knowledge across learning tasks and are closely related to general intelligence. But, the formal, general systems differences between them are underexplored in the literature. This lack of systems-level formalism leads to difficulties in coordinating related, inter-disciplinary engineering efforts. This manuscript formalizes transfer learning, multi-task learning, and meta-learning as abstract learning systems, consistent with the formal-minimalist abstract systems theory of Mesarovic and Takahara. Moreover, it uses the presented formalism to relate the three concepts of learning in terms of composition, hierarchy, and structural homomorphism. Findings are readily depicted in terms of input-output systems, highlighting the ease of delineating formal, general systems differences between transfer, multi-task, and meta-learning.

Keywords: Abstract learning systems · Transfer learning · Multi-task learning · Meta-learning · Abstract systems theory

1 Introduction

Transfer learning, multi-task learning, and meta-learning are three different concepts of learning that aim to generalize knowledge across learning tasks. As such, they are common topics in artificial general intelligence [1,7]. They are informally described as similar in their respective, prominent surveys [6,9,11]. Formally, however, the general systems character of this similarity is left undiscussed. Likely, this is because the formalism of their respective learning algorithms quickly represents their differences. While this gap may seem inconsequential to algorithm designers, who typically work very closely to solution methods, to systems engineers, this gap muddles basic questions about composition and hierarchy.

In this manuscript, a recently proposed abstract systems theory (AST) model of learning [2,4] is used to formally relate transfer, multi-task, and meta-learning. Each concept of learning is modeled as an abstract system [5], i.e., as a relation on component sets, and their structural homomorphism is studied. The presented results extend previous work that synthesizes AST with statistical learning theory [2] and transfer learning [3,4] with novel definitions of multi-task and

B. Goertzel et al. (Eds.): AGI 2022, LNAI 13539, pp. 199–208, 2023.
https://doi.org/10.1007/978-3-031-19907-3_19

meta-learning as abstract systems, and with an investigation of their structural similarities.

This manuscript is structured as follows. First, preliminaries on abstract learning systems and transfer learning systems are given in Sects. 2 and 3. Subsequently, multi-task learning and meta-learning are formalized as systems from their informal descriptions in Sect. 4, and the homomorphism between transfer, multi-task, and meta-learning is investigated in Sect. 5. The manuscript concludes with a synopsis and remarks on the pitfalls of the existing informal taxonomy in light of the presented material.

2   Abstract Learning Systems

Abstract systems S are relations on (non-empty) abstract sets

$$S \subset \times \{V_i | i = 1, ..., I\},$$

where $\times$ is the Cartesian product, V_i are (component) sets, and $\overline{S} = \{V_i | i = 1, ..., I\}$ [5]. Input-output systems are (elementary) systems

$$S \subset \times \{\mathcal{X}, \mathcal{Y}\},$$

where $\mathcal{X} \cap \mathcal{Y} = \varnothing$, $\mathcal{X} \cup \mathcal{Y} = \overline{S}$, and $\varnothing$ is the empty set. The set $\mathcal{X}$ is termed the input and the set $\mathcal{Y}$ is termed the output. Functional systems are input-output systems of the form $S : \mathcal{X} \to \mathcal{Y}$. AST is primarily concerned with input-output systems, with their composition, and with categories of systems [5].

Recent work presented a stratified model of abstract learning systems as a cascade connection of learning algorithms $A : D \to \Theta$ and hypotheses $H : \Theta \times \mathcal{X} \to \mathcal{Y}$ where D are data and Θ are parameters [2]. This follows the treatment of learning as function approximation [10]. Learning systems are defined as follows.

Definition 1 (Learning Systems). *A learning system S is a relation*

$$S \subset \times \{A, D, \Theta, H, \mathcal{X}, \mathcal{Y}\}$$

such that

$$D \subset \mathcal{X} \times \mathcal{Y}, A : D \to \Theta, H : \Theta \times \mathcal{X} \to \mathcal{Y}$$
$$(d, x, y) \in \mathcal{P}(S) \leftrightarrow (\exists \theta)[(\theta, x, y) \in H \wedge (d, \theta) \in A]$$

where

$$x \in \mathcal{X}, y \in \mathcal{Y}, d \in D, \theta \in \Theta.$$

The algorithm A, data D, parameters Θ, hypotheses H, input $\mathcal{X}$, and output $\mathcal{Y}$ are the component sets of S, $\mathcal{P}$ is the power set, and learning is specified in the relation among them.

This AST model of learning is depicted in Fig. 1 at the elementary (input-output) and cascade levels of abstraction (as presented in [2]).

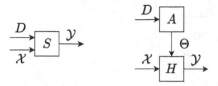

Fig. 1. Learning systems at the elementary (left) and cascade (right) levels of abstraction [2].

3   Transfer Learning Systems

The concept of learning tasks is widely used in artificial intelligence [8]. Transfer learning is conventionally defined in terms of domains $\mathcal{D} = \{\mathcal{X}, P(X)\}$ and tasks $\mathcal{T} = \{\mathcal{Y}, P(Y|X)\}$, where P denotes a probability measure. Given a source domain $\mathcal{D}_S$ and learning task $\mathcal{T}_S$, a target domain $\mathcal{D}_T$ and learning task $\mathcal{T}_T$, Pan and Yang define transfer learning as a learning paradigm that [6],

> "aims to help improve the learning of the target predictive function $f_T{}^1$ in $\mathcal{D}_T$ using the knowledge in $\mathcal{D}_S$ and $\mathcal{D}_T$, where $\mathcal{D}_S \neq \mathcal{D}_T$ or $\mathcal{T}_S \neq \mathcal{T}_T$."

Alternatively, previous work describes transfer learning as [4],

> "...a relation on the source and target (learning) systems that combines knowledge from the source with data from the target and uses the result to select a hypothesis that estimates the target learning task."

Transfer learning systems are defined as follows.

Definition 2 (Transfer Learning System). *Given source and target learning systems S_S and S_T*

$$S_S \subset \times \{A_S, D_S, \Theta_S, H_S, X_S, Y_S\}$$
$$S_T \subset \times \{A_T, D_T, \Theta_T, H_T, X_T, Y_T\}$$

a transfer learning system S_{Tr} is a relation on the component sets of the source and target systems $S_{Tr} \subset \overline{S_S} \times \overline{S_T}$ such that

$$K_S \subset D_S \times \Theta_S, D \subset D_T \times K_S$$

and

$$A_{Tr} : D \rightarrow \Theta_{Tr}, H_{Tr} : \Theta_{Tr} \times X_T \rightarrow Y_T$$
$$(d, x_T, y_T) \in \mathcal{P}(S_{Tr}) \leftrightarrow$$
$$(\exists \theta_{Tr})[(\theta_{Tr}, x_T, y_T) \in H_{Tr} \wedge (d, \theta_{Tr}) \in A_{Tr}]$$

where

$$x_T \in X_T, y_T \in Y_T, d \in D, \theta_{Tr} \in \Theta_{Tr}.$$

---

[1] $f_T \sim P(Y_T|X_T)$.

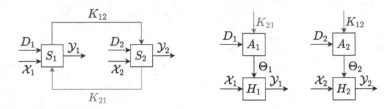

Fig. 2. Two learning systems transferring knowledge to each other depicted at the elementary (left) and cascade (middle, right) levels of abstraction [4].

The nature of source knowledge $K_S{}^2$, the transfer learning algorithm A_{Tr}, hypotheses H_{Tr}, and parameters Θ_{Tr} specify transfer learning as a relation on $\overline{S_S}$ and $\overline{S_T}$.

This AST model of transfer learning is depicted in Fig. 2. Previous work extensively elaborates on and beyond Definition 2 [4].

4   Multi-task and Meta-learning Systems

4.1   Multi-task Learning

Zhang and Yang define multi-task learning as [11],

> "a learning paradigm in machine learning and its aim is to leverage useful information contained in multiple related tasks to help improve the generalization performance of all the tasks."

Multi-task learning systems are defined herein as follows.

Definition 3 (Multi-task Learning Systems). *Given N learning systems $S_1, ..., S_N$, a multi-task learning system is a learning system $S \subset \times \{A, D, \Theta, H, \mathcal{X}, \mathcal{Y}\}$ where,*

$$D = (D_1, ..., D_N), H = (H_1, ..., H_N),$$
$$\Theta = (\Theta_1, ..., \Theta_N), \mathcal{X} = (\mathcal{X}_1, ..., \mathcal{X}_N),$$
$$\mathcal{Y} = (\mathcal{Y}_1, ..., \mathcal{Y}_N),$$

i.e., $A : (D_1, ..., D_N) \rightarrow (\Theta_1, ..., \Theta_N)$.

Multi-task learning systems are simply learning systems that jointly learn multiple, distinct hypotheses. Multi-task learning systems are depicted in Fig. 3A. A trivial multi-task learning system can be defined as follows.

---

[2] Here transferred knowledge K_S is defined as D_S and Θ_S, the source data and parameters, following convention [6].

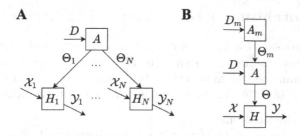

Fig. 3. A multi-task learning system (A) and a meta-learning system (B).

Definition 4 (Trivial Multi-task Learning Systems). *Given N learning systems $S_1, ..., S_N$, a trivial multi-task learning system is a multi-task learning system $S \subset \times\{A, D, H, \Theta, \mathcal{X}, \mathcal{Y}\}$ defined over $S_1, ..., S_N$ where $A = (A_1, ..., A_N)$.*

In other words, the trivial case of multi-task learning is a superficial grouping of algorithms $(A_1, ..., A_N)$ where A simply uses $D_1, ..., D_N$ as input to each respective algorithm A_n for $n \in N$. A non-trivial multi-task learning system can be defined as follows.

Definition 5 (Non-trivial Multi-task Learning Systems). *Given N learning systems $S_1, ..., S_N$, a non-trivial multi-task learning system is a multi-task learning system $S \subset \times\{A, D, H, \Theta, \mathcal{X}, \mathcal{Y}\}$ defined over $S_1, ..., S_N$ where $A \neq (A_1, ..., A_N)$.*

4.2 Meta-learning

Vanschoren defines meta-learning as [9]

"the science of systematically observing how different machine learning approaches perform on a wide range of learning tasks, and then learning from this experience, or meta-data, to learn new tasks much faster than otherwise possible."

Meta-learning systems are defined herein as follows.

Definition 6 (Meta-learning System). *Meta-learning systems are learning systems $S \subset \times\{A_m, \Theta_m, D_m, H_m, \mathcal{X}_m, \mathcal{Y}_m\}$ with hypotheses H_m that are algorithms A, inputs $\mathcal{X}_m$ that are data D, outputs $\mathcal{Y}_m$ that are parameters Θ for hypotheses $H : \Theta \times \mathcal{X} \to \mathcal{Y}$, and where $S \subset \times\{A, D, \Theta, H, \mathcal{X}, \mathcal{Y}\}$ is a learning system.*

Meta-learning systems are learning systems whose hypotheses are learning algorithms. Meta-learning systems are depicted in Fig. 3B.

5   Homomorphisms Between Learning Systems

Similarity of systems is a fundamental notion. Structural similarity describes the *homomorphism* between two systems' structures. In accord with category theory, a map from one system to another is termed a morphism. Homomorphism specifies the morphism to be onto. Homomorphism is formally defined as follows.

Definition 7. Homomorphism.
An input-output system $S_1 \subset \times\{\mathcal{X}_1 \times \mathcal{Y}_1\}$ is homomorphic to $S_2 \subset \times\{\mathcal{X}_2, \mathcal{Y}_2\}$ if there exists a pair of maps,

$$\varrho : \mathcal{X}_1 \to \mathcal{X}_2, \vartheta : \mathcal{Y}_1 \to \mathcal{Y}_2$$

such that for all $x_1 \in \mathcal{X}_1$, $x_2 \in \mathcal{X}_2$, and $y_1 \in \mathcal{Y}_1$, $y_2 \in \mathcal{Y}_2$, $\varrho(x_1) = x_2$ and $\vartheta(y_1) = y_2$.

Let a two-way transfer learning system be a pair of transfer learning systems that both transfer knowledge to each other. In the following, it is proven that two transfer learning systems sharing knowledge with each other are homomorphic to a non-trivial multi-task learning system, as depicted in Fig. 4.

Theorem 1. *Two-way transfer learning systems are homomorphic to a non-trivial multi-task learning system.*

Proof. Consider two learning systems S_1' and S_2',

$$S_1' \subset \times\{A_1', D_1', \Theta_1', H_1', \mathcal{X}_1, \mathcal{Y}_1\},$$
$$S_2' \subset \times\{A_2', D_2', \Theta_2', H_2', \mathcal{X}_2, \mathcal{Y}_2\}.$$

Let transfer learning be used to transfer knowledge $K_{12} \subset D_1'$ from S_1' to S_2' and knowledge $K_{21} \subset D_2'$ from S_2' to S_1'. This creates two transfer learning systems, termed S_1 and S_2, respectively,

$$S_1 \subset \times\{A_1, D_1, \Theta_1, H_1, \mathcal{X}_1, \mathcal{Y}_1\},$$
$$S_2 \subset \times\{A_2, D_2, \Theta_2, H_2, \mathcal{X}_2, \mathcal{Y}_2\}.$$

where $D_1 \subset D_1' \times D_2'$ and $D_2 \subset D_1' \times D_2'$, as in Fig. 2. Consider a multi-task learning system

$$S \subset \times\{A, D, \Theta, H, \mathcal{X}, \mathcal{Y}\}$$

such that $A = (A_1, A_2)$, $D = (D_1, D_2)$, $\Theta = (\Theta_1, \Theta_2)$, $H = (H_1, H_2)$, $\mathcal{X} = (\mathcal{X}_1, \mathcal{X}_2)$, and $\mathcal{Y} = (\mathcal{Y}_1, \mathcal{Y}_2)$. Clearly, by the identity, $A, D, \Theta, H, \mathcal{X}$, and $\mathcal{Y}$ are homomorphic to (A_1, A_2), (D_1, D_2), (Θ_1, Θ_2), (H_1, H_2), $(\mathcal{X}_1, \mathcal{X}_2)$, and $(\mathcal{Y}_1, \mathcal{Y}_2)$, respectively. Thus, there exists a set of onto maps $\{\varrho_A, \varrho_D, \varrho_\Theta, \varrho_H, \varrho_\mathcal{X}, \varrho_\mathcal{Y}\}$ from $(S_1, S_2) \to S$. Thus, the two-way transfer learning system (S_1, S_2) is homomorphic to the multi-task learning system S. Since $A = (A_1, A_2)$ and since $A_1' \neq A_1$ and $A_2' \neq A_2$ (they have different supports), S is therefore necessarily a non-trivial multi-task learning system with respect to S_1' and S_2'. $\square$

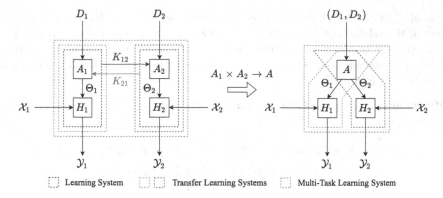

Fig. 4. A set of learning systems all transferring knowledge to each other implicitly forms a multi-task learning system.

The above hints that multi-task learning systems are related to parallel connections of learning systems. To see this, first define a parallel connection as follows.

Definition 8 (Parallel Connections). *A parallel connection of systems* $S_1 : \mathcal{X}_1 \to \mathcal{Y}_1$ *and* $S_2 : \mathcal{X}_2 \to \mathcal{Y}_2$ *is an operator* $\| : \overline{S_1} \times \overline{S_2} \to \overline{S_2}$ *such that* $S_2 : (\mathcal{X}_1 \times \mathcal{X}_2) \to (\mathcal{Y}_1 \times \mathcal{Y}_2)$ *and*

$$((x_1, x_2), (y_1, y_2)) \in S_2 \leftrightarrow$$
$$((x_1, y_1)) \in S_1 \wedge ((x_2, y_2) \in S_2).$$

Theorem 2. *Trivial multi-task systems are a parallel connection of learning systems.*

Proof. Consider a set of N learning systems $S_1, ..., S_N$. Let $S_{1-2} = S_1 \| S_2$. Let $S_{1-n} = S_{1-(n-1)} \| S_n$. Thus, S_{1-N}, at the elementary (input-output) level of abstraction is,

$$S_{1-N} = (D_1 \times ... \times D_N) \times (\mathcal{X}_1 \times ... \times \mathcal{X}_N) \to (\mathcal{Y}_1 \times ... \times \mathcal{Y}_N),$$

which simplifies to,

$$S_{1-N} : (D_1, ..., D_N) \times (\mathcal{X}_1, ..., \mathcal{X}_N) \to (\mathcal{Y}_1, ..., \mathcal{Y}_N).$$

Let $D = (D_1, ..., D_N)$, $\mathcal{X} = (\mathcal{X}_1, ..., \mathcal{X}_N)$, and $\mathcal{Y} = (\mathcal{Y}_1, ..., \mathcal{Y}_N)$. Let A, Θ, and H be defined similarly. By definition, the system

$$S \subset \times\{A, D, \Theta, H, \mathcal{X}, \mathcal{Y}\}$$

is a trivial multi-task learning system. □

When triviality does not hold, multi-task learning is a *shallow* parallel connector in the sense that it is always a parallel connector in (elementary-level) terms of D, $\mathcal{X}$, and $\mathcal{Y}$, but not always a parallel connector in the (cascade-level) terms of the relation on them given by A, Θ, and H since $\exists A \neq (A_1, ..., A_N)$.

In contrast to the parallel connections of multi-task learning, meta-learning is related to cascade connections and hierarchy. To see this, first define a cascade connection as follows.

Definition 9 (Cascade Connections). *Let* $\circ : \overline{S} \times \overline{S} \to \overline{S}$ *be such that* $S_1 \circ S_2 = S_3$, *where,*

$$S_1 \subset X_1 \times (Y_1 \times (Z_1)), S_2 \subset (X_2 \times Z_2) \times Y_2$$
$$S_3 \subset (X_1 \times X_2) \times (Y_1 \times Y_2), Z_1 = Z_2 = Z$$

and,

$$((x_1, x_2), (y_1, y_2)) \in S_3 \leftrightarrow$$
$$(\exists z)((x_1, (y_1, z)) \in S_1 \wedge ((x_2, z), y_2) \in S_2)$$

$\circ$ *is termed the cascade (connecting) operator.*

Theorem 3. *Meta-learning systems are a cascade connection of a learning algorithm and a learning system.*

Proof. Consider a learning algorithm $A_2 : D_2 \to \Theta_2$ and a learning system S_1. Let $S_3 = A_2 \circ S_1$. Thus $S_3 = \subset \times \{A_2, D_2, \Theta_2, A_1, D_1, \Theta_1, H_1, \mathcal{X}_1, \mathcal{Y}_1\}$ where $A_1 : \Theta_2 \times D_1 \to \Theta_1$. Let $S_m \subset S_3$ such that $S_m \subset \times \{A', D', \Theta', A, D, \Theta\}$. S_m is a meta-learning system where A_1, D_1, and Θ_1 are the hypotheses, inputs, and outputs of S_m. □

5.1   Discussion

The preceding provides the basic math needed to support the use of transfer, multi-task, and meta-learning as basic elements of modeling abstract learning systems. Because of the generality and homomorphism of these three concepts, a systems modeler clearly has many representations to choose from when modeling learning systems. Consider the learning system shown in Fig. 5, which shows a series of homomorphisms on a learning system from Fig. 5A to 5F.

Figure 5A shows two learning systems with meta-learning systems that transfer knowledge to each other. In Fig. 5B, a parallel connection of A_1 and A_2 transforms the system in Fig. 5A into a multi-task learning system with a decomposed meta-learning system. In Fig. 5C, the meta-learning system is recomposed into A_m using a parallel connection. Figure 5D shows the hypotheses of the multi-task learning system are composed into H by a parallel connection. Figure 5E shows the meta-learning hierarchy is collapsed into algorithm A' using a series connection. And lastly, in Fig. 5F, sets are redefined to recover a general learning system as in Definition 1. All of these morphisms are homomorphisms—they are onto and thus structure-preserving.

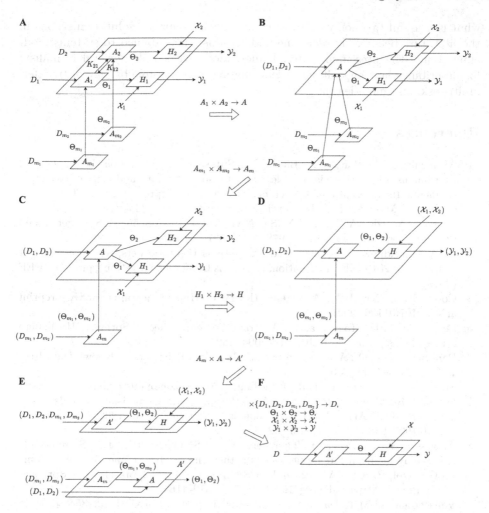

Fig. 5. A series of homomorphisms from a two-way transfer learning system with meta-learning in (A) to a generic learning system in (F), as described in detail in Sect. 5.1.

6   Conclusion

Appreciating the compositional and hierarchical relations between the three concepts of learning makes clear a simple point about learning systems. Transfer, multi-task, and meta-learning are basic compositions of learning systems that display a recursive self-similarity. A multi-task learning system can use transfer learning from other multi-task learning systems that all have meta-learning systems that use transfer learning, and so on.

What is a multi-task transfer learning system? What is a transfer multi-task learning system? What is a meta-transfer multi-task learning system? What is a meta-transfer multi-task transfer learning system? What is ... etc.? Clearly what is a useful taxonomy for organizing machine learning solution methods in the literature becomes burdensome and tedious when applied to systems modeling. Using the presented material, modelers have simple, general formalism for describing the compositions of learning systems possible by way of transfer, multi-task, and meta-learning.

References

1. Al-Shedivat, M., Bansal, T., Burda, Y., Sutskever, I., Mordatch, I., Abbeel, P.: Continuous adaptation via meta-learning in nonstationary and competitive environments. In: International Conference on Learning Representations (2018)
2. Cody, T.: Mesarovician abstract learning systems. In: Goertzel, B., Iklé, M., Potapov, A. (eds.) AGI 2021. LNCS (LNAI), vol. 13154, pp. 55–64. Springer, Cham (2022). https://doi.org/10.1007/978-3-030-93758-4_7
3. Cody, T., Adams, S., Beling, P.A.: A systems theoretic perspective on transfer learning. In: 2019 IEEE International Systems Conference (SysCon), pp. 1–7. IEEE (2019)
4. Cody, T., Beling, P.A.: A systems theory of transfer learning. arXiv preprint arXiv:2107.01196 (2021)
5. Mesarovic, M.D., Takahara, Y.: Abstract Systems Theory. Springer, Heidelberg (1989). https://doi.org/10.1007/BFb0042462
6. Pan, S.J., Yang, Q.: A survey on transfer learning. IEEE Trans. Knowl. Data Eng. **22**(10), 1345–1359 (2009)
7. Sheikhlar, A., Thórisson, K.R., Eberding, L.M.: Autonomous cumulative transfer learning. In: Goertzel, B., Panov, A.I., Potapov, A., Yampolskiy, R. (eds.) AGI 2020. LNCS (LNAI), vol. 12177, pp. 306–316. Springer, Cham (2020). https://doi.org/10.1007/978-3-030-52152-3_32
8. Thórisson, K.R., Bieger, J., Thorarensen, T., Sigurðardóttir, J.S., Steunebrink, B.R.: Why artificial intelligence needs a task theory. In: Steunebrink, B., Wang, P., Goertzel, B. (eds.) AGI -2016. LNCS (LNAI), vol. 9782, pp. 118–128. Springer, Cham (2016). https://doi.org/10.1007/978-3-319-41649-6_12
9. Vanschoren, J.: Meta-learning: a survey. arXiv preprint arXiv:1810.03548 (2018)
10. Wang, P., Li, X.: Different conceptions of learning: function approximation vs. self-organization. In: Steunebrink, B., Wang, P., Goertzel, B. (eds.) AGI -2016. LNCS (LNAI), vol. 9782, pp. 140–149. Springer, Cham (2016). https://doi.org/10.1007/978-3-319-41649-6_14
11. Zhang, Y., Yang, Q.: A survey on multi-task learning. IEEE Trans. Knowl. Data Eng. (2021)

Core and Periphery as Closed-System Precepts for Engineering General Intelligence

Tyler Cody[1]([✉]), Niloofar Shadab[2], Alejandro Salado[3], and Peter Beling[1,2]

[1] National Security Institute, Virginia Tech, Arlington, VA, USA
tcody@vt.edu
[2] Grado Department of Industrial and Systems Engineering,
Virginia Tech, Blacksburg, VA, USA
[3] Department of Systems and Industrial Engineering,
The University of Arizona, Tucson, AZ, USA

Abstract. Engineering methods are centered around traditional notions of decomposition and recomposition that rely on partitioning the inputs and outputs of components to allow for component-level properties to hold after their composition. In artificial intelligence (AI), however, systems are often expected to influence their environments, and, by way of their environments, to influence themselves. Thus, it is unclear if an AI system's inputs will be independent of its outputs, and, therefore, if AI systems can be treated as traditional components. This paper posits that engineering general intelligence requires new general systems precepts, termed the core and periphery, and explores their theoretical uses. The new precepts are elaborated using abstract systems theory and the Law of Requisite Variety. By using the presented material, engineers can better understand the general character of regulating the outcomes of AI to achieve stakeholder needs and how the general systems nature of embodiment challenges traditional engineering practice.

Keywords: Artificial intelligence · Systems engineering · Systems theory · Requisite variety

1 Introduction

Engineering methods are still centered around traditional engineering notions of decomposing stakeholder needs and outcomes into component-level functions and recomposing those component-level functions into subsystems and systems [22]. This traditional approach of engineering by aggregation relies on a partitioning of inputs and outputs to allow for component-level properties to hold after composition [32]. While the artificial intelligence (AI) in AI-enabled systems—systems with AI components or subsystems—may be well-treated as an individually addressable part at conception, the boundaries between an AI part,

B. Goertzel et al. (Eds.): AGI 2022, LNAI 13539, pp. 209–219, 2023.
https://doi.org/10.1007/978-3-031-19907-3_20

other aspects of its greater system, and the environment it interacts with face dissolution as the three intertwine.

This paper posits that whereas traditional engineering is driven by a focus on open systems and correspondingly on precepts of decomposition and recomposition, engineering general intelligence requires an alternative treatment and new precepts. This paper substantiates discourse on a new framework for engineering by challenging the legitimacy of existing precepts. Moreover, this paper proposes two new general systems precepts, *core* and *periphery*, and discusses their use. While previous work on the topic of embodiment explores related concepts [24], importantly, it does not explore embodiment as a consequence of general systems theory or directly identify the challenges to traditional engineering that embodiment presents. Using the material presented herein, engineers can better understand the general nature of regulating the outcomes of AI-enabled systems, and thereby of achieving stakeholder needs.

This paper is structured as follows. Embodied cognition is reviewed as a related, although differently motivated field of research in cognitive science. Then, the limitations of existing engineering practice are outlined. Discussion is lead to a review of the Law of Requisite Variety [3], which is used as a basis to define core and periphery as closed-system precepts, and to explore their use in modeling AI. Before concluding, remarks are made on relevance.

2   Related Work

Embodied cognition is a cognitive science that considers the role body and environment, in addition to mind, play in cognitive processes, and, moreover, emphasizes a lack of distinction between the three [20]. Embodied cognition can be characterized as: "a research program with no clear defining features other than the tenet that computational cognitive science has failed to appreciate the body's significance in cognitive processing and to do so requires a dramatic reconceptualization of the nature of cognition and how it must be investigated" [24].

Notions of embodiment are closely related to ecological psychology, which, eschewing the notion of cognition as computation, posits that cognitive processes, like perceptual processes, involve the whole organism as it moves through the environment [19]. This contrasts the traditional view of computational cognitive scientists that cognitive processes require inference from "impoverished" inputs, which, on their face, do not contain enough information to solve problems, and therefore necessitate a kind-of Bayesian conditioning of inputs with background knowledge [10].

Attempts to bring embodied cognition from philosophy to the real-world include robotics and the use of dynamical systems. Embodied cognitive robotics limits, discredits, or otherwise avoids the use of internal representations and the use of symbolic logic over them—in the extreme, linking perception directly to action [6,7]. Some critics are quick to point out the subjectivity of determining what is and what is not a representation [8,16], e.g., as sensors already bias inputs away from reality [21]. Other critics strongly challenge scalability [18].

Dynamical cognitive science treats cognition as a dynamical system: a continuous time relationship among the component sets of a system and the relations between them [4]. In essence, it favors the view of "mind as a continuous event" in the stead of "mind as computer" [26]. But real-world examples remain simple [5,13,25,28], because dynamical systems quickly become complex and adaptive as they scale in intelligence [31], thereby limiting scientific investigation. Although taking a formal systems view, dynamical cognitive science has fallen short of defining formal, general engineering precepts for intelligence.

Most often, embodied cognition is a topic of natural intelligence, and less so of AI, because AI is largely concerned with computation, and, in present day, with computational approaches to *problem* solving tasks [29], as opposed to (cognitive) *systems* which solve problems or come to be able to solve problems. As a result, questions regarding where cognition resides or where problem solving takes place are generally not within the scope of discourse [11]. As such, in computer science, there are disparate research efforts with a broadened scope [23,27], but they often rely on their disparate specifics. This manuscript works outward from a general systems perspective, as opposed to from a cognitive psychologist or computer science perspective, to suggest new precepts for engineering embodiment.

3   Existing Precepts and Their Limits

Precepts for engineering AI must presume something of the nature of intelligence. There is ongoing research into defining intelligence and the properties it exhibits in engineered systems [30]. Some advocate that intelligence is measured by integrating a complexity-weighted performance measure over a set of tasks [9]. Others advocate that intelligence is manifested as a minimization of complexity in state dynamics [12]. And others yet still measure intelligence in terms of adversarial sequence prediction [1,15]. Each alternative definition leads the discussion of engineering intelligence in a different direction. This paper avoids the constricting effect of pursuing a specific definition of intelligence on the generality of results by focusing on precepts for the case when *intelligence is a property of the relation between an system and its environment*—rather than a property of the system itself.

The latter case, that of intelligence as a property of a system, suggests a continuation of existing engineering practice. Given a system and needed outcomes of that system, systems engineers decompose the system into subsystems and their components, specify functional requirements on the components, and then distribute the engineering of each functional component to their respective disciplines. Subsequently, component-level solutions are recomposed into subsystems and, in turn, into the system as a whole, performing test and evaluation along the way, as shown in Fig. 1. Once properly composed, the system is deployed into operation, putting engineers in a holding pattern until another iteration of the so-called engineering "V" is desired [14,17]. This traditional practice of engineering by following the mantra, "If the parts work, and the interfaces between

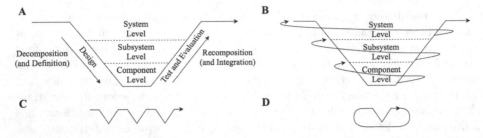

Fig. 1. (A) depicts the traditional engineering process of decomposing systems into individually addressable components and recomposing them into systems. But, can AI-enabled systems with inter- and intra-level coupling as depicted by spiraling, multi-level dependencies in (B) be treated with the same precepts of decomposition and recomposition? The basic concept of engineering operations offered by traditional approaches follows the iterative decomposition and recomposition shown in (C). In contrast, the posited, highly coupling effect of intelligence imposes a continuous concept of operations shown in (D).

the parts work, then the whole will work", is rooted in precepts of *decomposition* and *recomposition* and is in direct conflict with the environmental coupling that this paper posits as the definitive feature of engineering general intelligence.

Deep neural networks (DNNs) are exemplary of this phenomena. DNNs can be specified as a composition of functions that pass information from layer to layer in a way that meets certain mathematical requirements. Specifications of DNNs using functional requirements are nearly the same for the enormous number of systems where DNNs are applied. However, apparently, the outcomes *needed* from DNNs vary greatly between systems. Thus, there is an apparent gap between achieving the needed outcomes a stakeholder has for a DNN and the functional requirements of a DNN. Whereas embodied cognition views this gap as the result of a flawed *philosophical* view of the mind as computation from which an inappropriate characterization of the relation between stimuli and cognition is derived, this paper views this gap as the result of a flawed *mathematical*—and therefore formal—foundation of traditional engineering which undergirds the dogma of engineering by composition.

If engineers cannot rely on functional decomposition and recomposition as precepts, what can they rely on? First, AI engineers must admit that they cannot readily specify the needs and outcomes of stakeholders into low-level functions and requirements. That is, simply ensuring input-output relationships will not reliably generate desired outcomes as it has in the past. With a renewed focus on the primacy of outcomes to input-output relations, engineers must then turn to new precepts that do not rely on persistent boundaries across the various subsystems and levels of abstraction in systems.

4   Outcomes and Requisite Variety

In general systems theory, systems are (often) defined as a relation on sets. General systems theory is thus (often) concerned with general conditions of relations on sets. These can be categorical, topological, algebraic, etc., however, set theory alone can be illuminating of the character of any of those more specific concerns. In the mid-twentieth century, Ashby used a particular notion of variety to study homeostasis—the ability to maintain certain variables within tight bounds despite changing contexts—in biological systems [2,3], and he made a remarkably general discovery regarding the nature of outcomes termed the *Law of Requisite Variety*.

Consider two systems S and S_E where $S : \mathcal{X} \to \mathcal{Y}$ and $S_E : \mathcal{X}_E \to \mathcal{Y}_E$. Without loss of generality term S the system and S_E the environment. Suppose S is acting as a regulator of S_E. Let $\mathcal{X}_{E\setminus S} = \mathcal{X}_E \setminus \mathcal{Y}$ where $\setminus$ denotes set difference. In other words, inputs to the environment $\mathcal{X}_E = \mathcal{X}_{E\setminus S} \cup \mathcal{Y}$. Consider a set of outcomes $\mathcal{Z}$ with support over $\mathcal{X}_{E\setminus S} \times \mathcal{Y}$, i.e., $\mathcal{X}_{E\setminus S} \times \mathcal{Y} \to \mathcal{Z}$. This notion of outcomes is identical to payoff matrices used in game theory. Let V_A be termed *variety* and be the Shannon entropy of a finite set A, i.e.,

$$V_A = -\sum_i^{|A|} p_i \log_2 p_i, \tag{1}$$

where $|A|$ denotes the cardinality of A and p_i the probability of the ith element of A. Variety describes the number of unique elements in a system.

The Law of Requisite Variety states that for one system to be a stable regulator of another, the variety of the regulator's output must be greater than or equal to the variety of the regulated system's input. Formally put, consider that (from [3])

$$\min V_{\mathcal{Z}} = \max\{V_{\mathcal{X}_{E\setminus S}} - V_{\mathcal{Y}}, 0\}. \tag{2}$$

The Law of Requisite Variety can be defined as follows.

Definition 1 (Law of Requisite Variety). *The* Law of Requisite Variety *states that given $V_{\mathcal{X}_{E\setminus S}}$, the minimum variety of outcomes $\min V_{\mathcal{Z}}$ only decreases if $V_{\mathcal{Y}}$ increases.*

Only if $V_{\mathcal{Y}} \geq V_{\mathcal{X}_{E\setminus S}}$, is it information theoretically possible to determine outcomes $\mathcal{Z}$, i.e., $\min V_{\mathcal{Z}} = 0$.

In summary, Eq. 2 suggests that when the environment's input variety is not well-matched by the regulating system's output variety, the variety of the set of possible outcomes is necessarily large, and therefore the system will struggle to achieve precise outcomes. In the words of Ashby, system S's "capacity as a regulator cannot exceed its capacity as a channel for variety" [3].

5   Core and Periphery

Ashby considered system survival as dependent on bounding varieties [2]. Let bounded varieties be system varieties that are invariant and let unbounded varieties be system varieties that are *not* invariant. Informally speaking, one could identify those structures that are core to the functioning of a system with bounded varieties, and one could identify those that are peripheral to such a core with unbounded varieties. In the following, using the Law of Requisite Variety, this paper presents the formalism necessary to establish core and periphery as precepts.

5.1 Definition

Let S be a system $S \subset \times\{\mathcal{X}, \mathcal{Y}\}$ and let $\overline{S}$ denote the component sets of S, i.e., $\{\mathcal{X}, \mathcal{Y}\}$. Let $\mathcal{X}^t$ denote the input structure at time t, and so forth. Bounded and unbounded varieties are distinguished by measuring the variety of a system's residual change over time. Let R denote this residual change, i.e.,

$$R_{\overline{S}}^{t,t'} = \{\mathcal{X}^{t'} \setminus \mathcal{X}^t, \mathcal{Y}^{t'} \setminus \mathcal{Y}^t\} \tag{3}$$

$R_{\overline{S}}^{t,t'}$ gives the residual change in system structure between time t and t'. The core and periphery are defined as follows.

Definition 2 (Core and Periphery). *Consider a system S at time t and at a later time t'. The* core *of S from t to t' is*

$$\mathcal{C} = \overline{S} \setminus R_{\overline{S}}^{t,t'} \tag{4}$$

The periphery *of S from t to t' is*

$$\mathcal{P} = R_{\overline{S}}^{t,t'}. \tag{5}$$

The core are those elements of S's component sets that are identical at times t and t', and the periphery are those elements that are not.

5.2 Core and Periphery as Precepts

A number of immediate uses of core and periphery as precepts are now considered.

Symmetry. Consider that the environment S_E has a core $\mathcal{C}_E$ and periphery $\mathcal{P}_E$. Inequalities can be used to compare the relative balance of core and periphery in the system and environment. Consider Fig. 2, which considers the various possible outcomes. In the upper-right cases, system S is more periphery-dominant than the environment S_E. In the diagonal cases, the relative balance of variety is the same between S and S_E, i.e., there is symmetry between the system and environment. And in the lower-left cases, S is more core-dominant than S_E. This is a useful exposition of the general regime. Given that S is a regulator of S_E, it is useful to know if a homeostatic S_E is regulated with a similarly homeostatic S, or if a largely unstable S_E is regulated by a homeostatic S, etc. But, it is hard to assign relative value to these various cases because symmetry alone does not make a statement regarding the variety of outcomes.

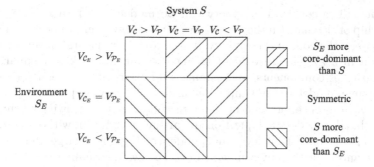

Fig. 2. A table depicting possible symmetries and asymmetries between the core and periphery of the system and environment.

Blocking. Outcome-based value judgements on the distribution of variety across $\mathcal{C}$ and $\mathcal{P}$ can be made by utilizing the Law of Requisite Variety to consider what S is demonstrating between t and t' regarding its mechanism to block varieties in S_E, i.e., to decrease the lower bound in Eq. 2) and regulate outcomes. For example, is the variety in the environment's periphery $V_{\mathcal{P}_E}$ being treated with $V_{\mathcal{P}}$ or $V_{\mathcal{C}}$? One cannot know generally, but, one can deduce given conditions on variety. If S is a stable regulator of S_E and $V_{\mathcal{C}_E} > V_{\mathcal{C}}$, then one can deduce that the system must be partially addressing the variety in the environment's core with variety in the system's periphery[1]. Without making restrictive or unrealistic assumptions about the functional dependence of components in S, as traditional engineering practice does to use precepts of decomposition and recomposition, one can use precepts of core and periphery, defined over the component sets of S and S_E, to model what aspects of an intelligent system are being used to block environmental variety in order to regulate outcomes.

Abstraction Independence. One may care about a subsystem of S. If one wants to know if a subsystem is in the core or periphery, one can just compare the subsystem to $\mathcal{C}$ or $\mathcal{P}$. However, one may find S hard to model as a whole. But since the subsystem is a system, it can have its own core and periphery. Therefore, the use of core and periphery does not require observability of the entire system. Moreover, by considering the distribution of core and periphery across subsystems, it can be used to compare the interaction of subsystems within a system without making strong assumptions regarding independence. And, furthermore, it follows that modeling the core and periphery at the system, subsystem, and component levels of abstraction can identify how the core and periphery are distributed across a system. When combined with similar, stratified models of the environment's core and periphery, this provides a abstraction-independent means of modeling the relation between system and environment.

---

[1] Note Eq. 2 specifically concerns the variety of outputs in the system's core and periphery and the variety of inputs in the environment's core and periphery.

Dynamics. The core and periphery can be modeled over time. As such, the membership of elements (in the component sets) of a system can be traced as they move between the core and periphery. This provides a natural means of tracing adaptation in a system. Instead of facing the difficult task of comparing the self-similarity of components, subsystems, and their inter-relations at different points in time, modelers can simply demarcate the varying presence of residual complexity. In essence, one can model core and periphery growing or shrinking, and as such, address detailed questions regarding adaptation without traditional assumptions of component-level independence. E.g., if a large change occurs between t and t' in the environment, does the system change from t' to t'' in response? Was the change in S_E regulated by S, i.e., was min $V_Z = 0$ from t to t'? Is there evidence of S absorbing new varieties into its core from the periphery, i.e., is $\mathcal{C}^{t',t''} \cap \mathcal{P}^{t,t'}$ non-empty? Core and periphery supports complex and varied analysis into the dynamical nature of the relation between an intelligent system and its environment.

5.3   Relevance

Traditional precepts are well-established, widely applied, and writ large successful. It is important, then, to identify where specifically new precepts are needed. The core roughly corresponds to traditional engineering practice. While the components in the core may not be independent of each other, the core's stability suggests that their respective input-output relations are stable, and therefore can be subject to functional requirements. Consider the preceding example in DNNs. Firstly, those identifiable functions for passing information from layer to layer, etc., that are common across applications of DNNs can be associated with the core. Alternatively, the parameter values of a DNN and the data used to train it (if data is considered in scope) can be treated as parts of the periphery.

Having disambiguated the core of DNNs from the periphery, the traditional decomposition and recomposition precepts can be applied to the core. Whether passing information between layers or back-propagating error, functions of the core of DNNs have a mechanical, largely environment-independent and therefore universal character. In contrast, the same decomposition cannot be applied to the DNN's periphery. Various no free lunch theorems suggest that good training data and model parameters are not universal. While there are desirable, general properties of learned representations like linear separability, many such properties are already implicit in loss functions generally and therefore embedded into the core. This example in DNNs highlights that core and periphery are general precepts, and decomposition and recomposition are, in the main, precepts applicable to the core.

In this sense, the precepts of core and periphery reduce to traditional precepts of decomposition and recomposition for (simple) systems wherein input-output relations are easily attributable to outcomes. In such a case, a definition of intelligence as the property of a system is sufficient. Now, consider that outcomes are not easily attributable to input-output relations when boundaries are not well-defined. And then consider that coupling between systems, between subsystems, and between components tends to dissolve boundaries. In such cases, input-output relations cannot be easily attributed to outcomes, thus, engineering intelligence as a system property has insufficient scope to regulate outcomes, and therefore intelligence ought to be treated as a property of the relation between a system and its environment. To the extent that general intelligence is emblematic of the latter case, precepts of core and periphery are more relevant to engineering general intelligence than traditional precepts.

6 Conclusion

Whereas functional decomposition and recomposition are precepts for open systems, core and periphery are precepts for closed systems, i.e., for engineering intelligence as a property of the relation between system and environment. And whereas functional composition is associated writ large with stratification, hierarchies, and hierarchical engineering processes, the core and periphery are associated with a coarser disambiguation oriented towards characterizing the nature of inter-linkages created by intelligence. While closed systems may not appreciably exist in nature besides (perhaps) the universe, their emphasis here derives from a stated interest in formal precepts for engineering theory. Engineering—designing, building, and operating—AI-enabled systems needs to consider the necessity of new closed-system precepts for engineering AI towards stakeholders' desired outcomes.

Future work is needed to demonstrate and support practical value. First, the ability to empirically isolate system functions via core-periphery disambiguation should be evaluated on a system with general intelligence. Additionally, a longer-form, formal elaboration of core and periphery in terms of mathematical theorems and corollaries is needed. Similarly, a point-by-point comparison with traditional system engineering methods is merited. Lastly, determining core and periphery requires defining boundaries between systems, even if only temporarily. Additional research on the dynamics of boundaries between highly coupled systems is needed.

References

1. Alexander, S., Hibbard, B.: Measuring intelligence and growth rate: variations on Hibbard's intelligence measure. J. Artif. Gen. Intell. **12**(1), 1–25 (2021)
2. Ashby, W.R.: An Introduction to Cybernetics. Chapman & Hall Ltd., London (1961)
3. Ashby, W.R.: Requisite variety and its implications for the control of complex systems. In: Facets of Systems Science, pp. 405–417. Springer, Boston (1991). https://doi.org/10.1007/978-1-4899-0718-9_28
4. Beer, R.D.: Dynamical approaches to cognitive science. Trends Cogn. Sci. **4**(3), 91–99 (2000)
5. Beer, R.D.: The dynamics of active categorical perception in an evolved model agent. Adapt. Behav. **11**(4), 209–243 (2003)

6. Brooks, R.A.: Intelligence without representation. Artif. Intell. **47**(1–3), 139–159 (1991)
7. Brooks, R.A.: New approaches to robotics. Science **253**(5025), 1227–1232 (1991)
8. Chemero, A.: Radical embodied cognitive science. Rev. Gen. Psychol. **17**(2), 145–150 (2013)
9. Chollet, F.: On the measure of intelligence. arXiv preprint arXiv:1911.01547 (2019)
10. Chomsky, N., et al.: On cognitive structures and their development: a reply to Piaget. In: Philosophy of Mind: Classical Problems/Contemporary Issues 751 (2006)
11. Cody, T.: Mesarovician abstract learning systems. In: Goertzel, B., Iklé, M., Potapov, A. (eds.) AGI 2021. LNCS (LNAI), vol. 13154, pp. 55–64. Springer, Cham (2022). https://doi.org/10.1007/978-3-030-93758-4_7
12. Friston, K.: The free-energy principle: a unified brain theory? Nat. Rev. Neurosci. **11**(2), 127–138 (2010)
13. Haken, H., Kelso, J.S., Bunz, H.: A theoretical model of phase transitions in human hand movements. Biol. Cybern. **51**(5), 347–356 (1985)
14. Haskins, C., Forsberg, K., Krueger, M.: Systems Engineering Handbook. INCOSE 9 (2006)
15. Hibbard, B.: Measuring agent intelligence via hierarchies of environments. In: Schmidhuber, J., Thórisson, K.R., Looks, M. (eds.) AGI 2011. LNCS (LNAI), vol. 6830, pp. 303–308. Springer, Heidelberg (2011). https://doi.org/10.1007/978-3-642-22887-2_34
16. Hutto, D.D., Myin, E.: Radicalizing Enactivism. Basic Minds Without Content. Cambridge (2013)
17. Klatt, K.U., Marquardt, W.: Perspectives for process systems engineering-personal views from academia and industry. Comput. Chem. Eng. **33**(3), 536–550 (2009)
18. Matthen, M.: Debunking enactivism: a critical notice of Hutto and Myin's radicalizing enactivism. Can. J. Philos. **44**(1), 118–128 (2014)
19. Michaels, C.F., Palatinus, Z.: A ten commandments for ecological psychology. In: The Routledge Handbook of Embodied Cognition, pp. 19–28 (2014)
20. Pfeifer, R., Iida, F.: Embodied artificial intelligence: trends and challenges. In: Iida, F., Pfeifer, R., Steels, L., Kuniyoshi, Y. (eds.) Embodied Artificial Intelligence. LNCS (LNAI), vol. 3139, pp. 1–26. Springer, Heidelberg (2004). https://doi.org/10.1007/978-3-540-27833-7_1
21. Rydéhn, H.: Grounding and ontological dependence. Synthese **198**(6), 1231–1256 (2021)
22. Salado, A.: A systems-theoretic articulation of stakeholder needs and system requirements. Syst. Eng. **24**(2), 83–99 (2021)
23. Schick, L., Malmborg, L.: Bodies, embodiment and ubiquitous computing. Digit. Creat. **21**(1), 63–69 (2010)
24. Shapiro, L.: Embodied Cognition. Routledge, Abingdon (2019)
25. Smith, L.B., Thelen, E.E.: A Dynamic Systems Approach to Development: Applications. The MIT Press, Cambridge (1993)
26. Spivey, M.: The Continuity of Mind. Oxford University Press, Oxford (2008)
27. Steels, L., Brooks, R.: The Artificial Life Route to Artificial Intelligence: Building Embodied, Situated Agents. Routledge, Abingdon (2018)
28. Thelen, E., Schöner, G., Scheier, C., Smith, L.B.: The dynamics of embodiment: a field theory of infant perseverative reaching. Behav. Brain Sci. **24**(1), 1–34 (2001)
29. Thórisson, K.R., Bieger, J., Thorarensen, T., Sigurðardóttir, J.S., Steunebrink, B.R.: Why artificial intelligence needs a task theory. In: Steunebrink, B., Wang,

P., Goertzel, B. (eds.) AGI -2016. LNCS (LNAI), vol. 9782, pp. 118–128. Springer, Cham (2016). https://doi.org/10.1007/978-3-319-41649-6_12

30. Wang, P.: On defining artificial intelligence. J. Artif. Gen. Intell. **10**(2), 1–37 (2019)
31. Weinbaum, D., Veitas, V.: Open ended intelligence: the individuation of intelligent agents. J. Exp. Theor. Artif. Intell. **29**(2), 371–396 (2017)
32. Wymore, A.W.: A Mmathematical Theory of Systems Engineering: The Elements. Wiley, New York (1967)

Toward Generating Natural-Language Explanations of Modal-Logic Proofs

Mike Giancola[✉][iD], Selmer Bringsjord[iD], and Naveen Sundar Govindarajulu[iD]

Rensselaer AI & Reasoning (RAIR) Lab, Department of Computer Science,
Department of Cognitive Science, Rensselaer Polytechnic Institute (RPI),
Troy, NY, USA
mike.j.giancola@gmail.com, naveen.sundar.g@gmail.com

Abstract. As we work toward artificial general intelligence, it is clear that we must try to imbue agents with faculties which ensure they are trustworthy. We firmly believe that an AGI agent must be able to explain its decision-making in order for it to be considered trustworthy. More specifically, agents must be able to explain themselves in a way that is both logically correct and understandable to humans. We take a first step toward a system that can generate explanations which satisfy this pair of conditions. We created the first model that can produce summaries of modal-logic proofs using a transformer language model. We qualitatively evaluated the model's outputs on a held-out test set and found that the logical content of the model's explanations precisely matched the input proofs in 60% of cases.

Keywords: Hybrid AI · Transformer language models · Modal logic

1 Introduction

As AI agents continue to play a larger role in our everyday lives, the issue of trust of AI systems is becoming more apparent. Moreover, as we work toward artificial general intelligence (AGI), it is clear that we must try to imbue agents with faculties which ensure they are trustworthy. While there is no one sufficient condition for trust of an AGI, we firmly believe that the ability to explain its decision-making is a necessary condition for trust in an AGI. More specifically, agents must be able to explain themselves in a way that is both logically correct and understandable to humans.

Many approaches to explainable AI secure one or the other of these two conditions. DARPA's Explainable AI Program has been focused primarily on the latter. The goal is to produce systems that can explain machine-learning models in a human-understandable way. But since the core technology is machine-learning-based, there is no guarantee that the decisions nor the explanations will be formally correct with respect to some relevant formal system. Alternatively, in much of our prior work we have taken a logic-based approach to AI which enables agents to explain their decisions in a formally correct (and verifiable)

B. Goertzel et al. (Eds.): AGI 2022, LNAI 13539, pp. 220–230, 2023.
https://doi.org/10.1007/978-3-031-19907-3_21

way [3,6,7]. Our AI agents do this by producing a formal proof; unfortunately, proofs are not easily understood by humans who don't have training in formal methods.

In this paper, we take a first step toward a system that can generate explanations which are both logically correct and understandable by humans. Specifically, we created the first model which can produce summaries[1] of modal-logic proofs.

The rest of the paper is as follows. We first introduce the modal logic used (Sect. 2), then the approach we took to generating natural-language explanations of proofs from that logic (Sect. 3). Next, we provide and analyze sample outputs of the system (Sect. 4). Finally, we discuss related work (Sect. 5) and conclude (Sect. 6).

2   Cognitive Calculi

A *cognitive calculus* is a multi-operator intensional logic with modal operators that capture propositional attitudes of human cognition (e.g. **K** for "knows", **B** for "believes"). For the purposes of this paper, a cognitive calculus consists essentially of two components:[2] (1) multi-sorted n^{th}-order logic[3] with intensional/modal operators for modeling cognitive attitudes (e.g. **K**, **B**) and (2) inference schemata that—in the tradition of proof-theoretic semantics [5]—fully express the semantics of the modal operators. We note that the title is slightly inaccurate, as a cognitive calculus is not exactly the same as a modal logic. Specifically, because of this last point: Whereas modal logics all have (typically model-theoretic) semantics, cognitive calculi have no model-based semantics. The meaning of formulae within a cognitive calculus is defined exclusively by the ways they can be used in proofs and arguments, which is accomplished formally by the calculus' inference schemata.

2.1   A Micro Calculus: $\mu\mathcal{C}$

In the present paper, we utilize a micro cognitive calculus we refer to as '$\mu\mathcal{C}$.' We use a micro calculus, as opposed to a full-fledged cognitive calculus,[4] in order

---

[1] As we discuss in Sect. 5, there are systems that can create *explanations* of modal logic proofs [4], but not *summaries*. That is, they can produce explanations which have a one-to-one correspondence with the input proof, but cannot synthesize a summary that highlights only the major components of the proof.

[2] For a full exposition of exactly what a cognitive calculus is and isn't, we point the interested reader to Appendix A of [3].

[3] Most cognitive calculi subsume first-order logic; some others include also second-, third-, and higher-order logics. For reasons that will be explained later in the paper, the cognitive calculus we utilize herein includes, of extensional logics, only zero-order logic.

[4] Such as the Deontic Cognitive Event Calculus ($\mathcal{DCEC}$) and its inductive counterpart ($\mathcal{IDCEC}$). The interested reader is referred to [3], which utilizes both of these calculi.

to simplify the challenging task at hand of generating explanations of modal-logic proofs. That is to say, the only difference between a standard cognitive calculus and a micro cognitive calculus is the relative size in terms of syntactic forms and inference schemata. We have elsewhere, previously, made use of other micro cognitive calculi, in order to simplify meta-proofs and explanation of our automated-reasoning algorithms; see e.g. [8].

In general, a cognitive calculus consists of two main pieces: a signature and a set of inference schemata. The signature of a cognitive calculus has four components: (1) a set of sorts, (2) a set of function signatures, (3) a grammar for terms, and (4) a grammar for formulae. Note that each of these components builds upon a pre-existing core.[5] The sorts and function signatures build upon the standard, extensional event calculus[6] [9]. While the terms and syntactic forms generally build upon first-order logic, in the case of $\mu\mathcal{C}$, they build upon zero-order logic; that is, propositional logic with predicates and function symbols, but *no quantifiers*.

Signature. The signature contains three sorts: Agent, for specifying human/artificial cognizers within modal formulae; Moment, for specifying time points; and Formula, for specifying any well-formed formula in the calculus. Next, there are three types of terms: variables, constants, and functions. Finally, the syntactic forms cover the standard relations of propositional logic, and modal operators for **P**erception, **B**elief, and **D**esire.

$\mu\mathcal{C}$ Signature

$$S ::= \text{Agent} \mid \text{Moment} \mid \text{Formula}$$

$$t ::= x : S \mid c : S \mid f(t_1, \ldots, t_n)$$

$$\phi ::= \{\neg\phi \mid \phi \wedge \psi \mid \phi \vee \psi \mid \phi \to \psi \mid \mathbf{P}(a, t, \phi) \mid \mathbf{B}(a, t, \phi) \mid \mathbf{D}(a, t, \phi)$$

Inference Schemata. The calculus contains four inference schemata in the natural-deduction tradition: I_1 enables an agent to infer a belief in any formula ϕ which it perceives. I_2 enables an agent to perform *And Elimination* on any conjunction it believes holds. In the same way, I_3 and I_4 enable an agent to use *Or Introduction* and *Implication Elimination* within beliefs.

$\mu\mathcal{C}$ Inference Schemata

$$\frac{\mathbf{P}(a, t, \phi)}{\mathbf{B}(a, t, \phi)} \, [I_1] \quad \frac{\mathbf{B}(a, t, \phi \wedge \psi)}{\mathbf{B}(a, t, \phi)} \, [I_2] \quad \frac{\mathbf{B}(a, t, \phi)}{\mathbf{B}(a, t, \phi \vee \psi)} \, [I_3] \quad \frac{\mathbf{B}(a, t, \phi \to \psi) \quad \mathbf{B}(a, t, \phi)}{\mathbf{B}(a, t, \psi)} \, [I_4]$$

---

[5] For brevity, the pre-existing core of the function signatures is excluded as we will not need them for the problems presented herein.

[6] Other calculi (e.g. the *situation calculus*) for modeling commonsense and physical reasoning can be easily switched out in-place of the event calculus.

3   NLG via Transformer Language Models

While we do not assert that transformer language models are unproblematic,[7] their impressive ability to quickly generate reasonable-looking natural-language text is, at the time of this writing, unmatched by any other technology. Hence our model to convert formal proofs into natural-language explanations utilizes a transformer language model.[8]

Specifically, we fine-tuned Pegasus [12] on a dataset of $\mu\mathcal{C}$ proofs and corresponding explanations, and evaluated it on a held-out dataset. Next, we discuss the reasoning behind the choices of Pegasus and $\mu\mathcal{C}$ for this work.

3.1   Pegasus

We selected the Pegasus transformer model as it was designed to perform well at *abstractive summarization*. Briefly, whereas *extractive* summarization simply extracts a proper subset of the input verbatim to synthesize a summary, *abstractive* summarization attempts to create a coherent summary that contains words/phrases that did not appear in the source text. This approach to summarization was necessary for our task, since we did not want to simply pick out pieces of the proofs for the summaries, but rather summarize the key points *in English*. Our task would be more accurately categorized as "summarization and translation." But since there are no translation models pre-trained on this type of data, we determined that an abstractive summarization model was the best available option.

3.2 $\mu\mathcal{C}$ and the Proof Domain

We selected $\mu\mathcal{C}$ as the cognitive calculus within which proofs would be created for this experiment largely for its simplicity. Whereas some cognitive calculi contain many more complex inference schemata, including e.g. meta-logical statements about provability, $\mu\mathcal{C}$ contains only four inference schemata, each of which can be easily explained in English. For example, I_1 allows an agent a to infer a belief in some formula ϕ which it perceives.[9] This enabled the creation of proofs involving several inferences that could be succinctly summarized in a few sentences.

Similarly, we selected the proof domain—the weather—in order to enable quick, manual generation of proofs which are logically correct and corresponding explanations which are sensible. We included predicates for simple types of

---

[7] The interested reader is referred to [2] for a thorough analysis of the environmental, financial, and societal concerns surrounding transformers.

[8] We certainly do not believe transformers are the only method by which this generation of proof explanations can be achieved. In fact, we expect that methods of natural-language generation which incorporate symbolic reasoning would almost certainly provide better assurances that the resulting explanations match the logical content of the proof. We discuss this more in Sect. 6.

[9] See Sect. 2.1.

weather (e.g. `Raining`, `Foggy`), road conditions which could be caused by the weather (e.g. `Slippery`, `ReducedVisibility`), and items one may want for certain weather (e.g. `rainboots`, `umbrella`). Example proofs and explanations are given in Sect. 4.

3.3 Model Fine-Tuning

We fine-tuned the Pegasus transformer on 20 proof-explanation pairs, holding out a set of 10 for evaluation. We note that the dataset is relatively small for a transformer training task for several reasons, but primarily because the pairs had to be engineered by hand, which was labor-intensive. The evaluation was also performed by hand, which will be discussed further in the following section.

Fortunately, because transformers are pre-trained on large datasets, we expected that we could be successful fine-tuning with a relatively small dataset. For details on the implementation of the fine-tuning process, see Appendix A.

4 Evaluation

We took a qualitative approach to evaluating the results of our fine-tuned model. Statistical metrics for measuring the similarity of the model's output to the ground truth aren't very meaningful in this case, as they fail to capture whether the logical reasoning content of the outputs are similar. For example, "You should bring an umbrella today because it is raining" and "You should bring an umbrella today because it is not raining" are very close syntactically, but the latter sentence doesn't exhibit valid reasoning (assuming common-sense understanding of the involved properties). Hence we evaluated the output qualitatively by partitioning it into the following trichotomy:

1. The output *logically corresponds* to the input proof.
2. The output doesn't logically correspond, but is still *logically correct*.
3. The output *neither* logically corresponds to the input proof nor is logically correct.

By "logical correspondence," we mean that the logical content of the summary is consistent with that in the proof. Since our goal is to generate summaries (as opposed to complete explanations), the model's output need not explain each individual step of the proof. However, it may not include language that does not have a formal correlate in the proof.

By "logical correctness," we mean that each step within the summary corresponds to an inference schema (or chain of inference schemata) in the cognitive calculus. Again, since our model is summarizing proofs, the explanation need not include a natural-language correlate of each step in the proof, but it cannot include language that is not sanctioned by some subset of the inference schemata.

The present page limit precludes inclusion of the full set of output on the test set. Here we show only a few noteworthy results, both positive and negative.[10]

---

[10] Newlines and indentation have been added for readability.

4.1 Example #1

```
Input:
PROOF: (Believes! a now (Slippery now road))
  VIA MODUS PONENS IN BELIEF:
   (Believes! a now (implies (or (Raining now) (Snowing now))
                                 (Slippery now road))),
   (Believes! a now (or (Raining now) (Snowing now)))
     VIA GIVEN:
       (Believes! a now (implies (or (Raining now) (Snowing now))
                                  (Slippery now road)))
     AND:
       (Believes! a now (or (Raining now) (Snowing now)))
         VIA DISJUNCTION INTRO IN BELIEF:
           (Believes! a now (or (Raining now) (Snowing now)))
             VIA GIVEN: (Believes! a now (Raining now))
```

```
Ground Truth (Human-Generated):
The agent believes the road is slippery. This is because the agent
believes if it is raining or snowing then the road is slippery, and
the agent believes it is raining.
```

```
Model Output:
The agent believes it is slippery on the road. This is because the agent
believes it is raining or snowing on the road.
```

We consider the model's output to be excellent for two reasons: (1) it logically corresponds to the input proof; and (2) it is more concise than the human-generated/ground-truth explanation, without excluding any content necessary for a person to understand it.

4.2 Example #2

```
Input:
PROOF: (Believes! a now (Slippery now road))
  VIA MODUS PONENS IN BELIEF:
   (Believes! a now (implies (or (Raining now) (Snowing now))
                                 (Slippery now road))),
   (Believes! a now (or (Raining now) (Snowing now)))
     VIA GIVEN:
       (Believes! a now (implies (or (Raining now) (Snowing now))
                                  (Slippery now road)))
     AND:
       (Believes! a now (or (Raining now) (Snowing now)))
         VIA DISJUNCTION INTRO IN BELIEF:
           (Believes! a now (Snowing now))
             VIA GIVEN: (Believes! a now (Snowing now))
```

```
Ground Truth (Human-Generated):
The agent believes the road is slippery. This is because the agent
```

believes if it is raining or snowing then the road is slippery, and
the agent believes it is snowing.

Model Output:
The agent believes it is slippery on the road. This is because the agent
believes if it is raining or snowing then it is slippery on the road, and
the agent believes it is raining or snowing.

In this case the machine's output is slightly longer than the ground truth but
still logically corresponds to the input proof.

4.3   Example #3

Input:
PROOF: (Desires! a now (or (Umbrella now) (RainJacket now)))
   VIA MODUS PONENS IN BELIEF:
     (Believes! a now (implies (and (Raining now) (not (Windy now)))
                                   (Desires! a now (or (Umbrella now)
                                                       (RainJacket now))))),
     (Believes! a now (and (Raining now) (not (Windy now))))
       VIA GIVEN:
         (Believes! a now (implies (and (Raining now) (not (Windy now)))
                                   (Desires! a now (or (Umbrella now)
                                                       (RainJacket now)))))
       AND:
         (Believes! a now (and (Raining now) (not (Windy now))))
           VIA CONJUNCTION INTRO IN BELIEF:
             (Believes! a now (Raining now)),
             (Believes! a now (not (Windy now)))
               VIA GIVEN: (Believes! a now (Raining now))
               AND GIVEN: (Believes! a now (not (Windy now)))

Ground Truth (Human-Generated):
The agent desires an umbrella or a rainjacket. This is because the agent
believes if it is raining and not windy then it should hold this desire,
and the agent believes it is rainy and not windy.

Model Output:
The agent desires umbrellas and rain jackets. This is because the agent
believes if it is raining and not windy then it should hold this desire,
and the agent believes it is raining and not windy.

The machine's output is almost identical to the ground truth, but there is
one critical difference: it should be "umbrellas *or* rain jackets", not "umbrellas
and rain jackets". Hence while this output looks reasonable, it does not logically
correspond to the input proof nor is it logically correct.

4.4 Example #4

```
Input:
PROOF: (Believes! a now (Rainbow now))
  VIA MODUS PONENS IN BELIEF:
    (Believes! a now (implies (and (Raining before) (Sunny now))
                               (Rainbow now))),
    (Believes! a now (and (Raining before) (Sunny now)))
      VIA GIVEN:
        (Believes! a now (implies (and (Raining before) (Sunny now))
                                   (Rainbow now)))
      AND:
      (Believes! a now (and (Raining before) (Sunny now)))
        VIA CONJUNCTION INTRO IN BELIEF:
          (Believes! a now (Raining before)),
          (Believes! a now (Sunny now))
            VIA GIVEN: (Believes! a now (Raining before))
            AND GIVEN: (Believes! a now (Sunny now)))
```

```
Ground Truth (Human-Generated):
The agent believes there is a rainbow now. This is because the agent
believes if it rains first and is sunny second then there will be a
rainbow, and the agent believes the premise.
```

```
Model Output:
The agent believes it is sunny and raining. This is because the agent
believes if it is sunny and raining then it should hold this belief,
and the agent believes it is sunny and raining.
```

Here the machine's output is logically correct (albeit tautologically), but does not at all logically correspond to the input proof.

4.5 Overall

Out of the 10 held-out test examples, six logically corresponded to the input proof (60%), two did not logically correspond to the input but were logically correct (20%), and two neither logically corresponded nor were logically correct (20%). While we do not deny that there is plenty of room for improvement, our model is the first (to the authors' knowledge) able to generate summaries of modal-logic proofs. Next, we discuss relevant prior work in this space.

5 Related Work

To the author's knowledge, there is no prior work using transformer language models to generate explanations of proofs in *any* logic, let alone a logic as highly-expressive as $\mu\mathcal{C}$. There is, however, some prior work on generating explanations of proofs using other methods.

Felty and Hager [4] presented a method for generating natural-language explanations of modal-logic proofs. They essentially hard-code natural-language templates for every inference rule in their logic. Thus the technique cannot be generalized to new inference rules or logics without hard-coding new templates. Additionally, this creates a one-to-one correspondence between the proof and explanation. While this may be desired in some cases, this method is incapable of generating *summaries* of proofs (= explanations that leave out minor details in an effort to demonstrate "big picture" understanding).

Alexoudi et al. [1] developed a method for producing summaries of mathematical proofs. It used a submodule to extract only the mathematically "interesting" proof steps in order to create a higher-quality summary. However, again, the natural-language translation boils down to a hard-coded transformation. For example, the term "`primitive_ind`" is translated to the phrase "one-step structural induction on" [1]. Also, as the focus in this work was on generating summaries of simple mathematical proofs,[11] they use standard first-order logic, and hence their method doesn't address generating summaries of proofs which contain modal operators.

While our use of transformers introduces the possibility that the resulting explanations may not precisely logically correspond to the input proof, the linguistic content is of much higher quality than that seen in prior work. Alexoudi et al. specifically mention this drawback in their work, noting that "In certain cases the template mapping produces minor grammatical errors" [1]. We note that all of the explanations generated by our model were grammatically correct. Of course, the ultimate goal of our research is a model which guarantees logical correspondence *and* grammatical correctness. We discuss future work in this direction in the following section.

6   Conclusion

We firmly believe that for AGI agents to be considered trustworthy by most people, these agents will need the capability to explain their decision-making in a way that is both logically correct and understandable by humans. In this paper, we have taken a first step in that direction. We created the first model which can generate natural-language summaries of modal-logic proofs. Of the summaries generated from proofs in the test set, 60% logically corresponded to the input proof, and all summaries were grammatically correct and overall linguistically coherent. Nonetheless, clearly there are many needed, subsequent steps; we mention two general directions now.

---

[11] They state that their goal was to produce summaries of proofs similar to what would be seen in "mathematical textbooks". While they didn't specify any subfields of mathematics, nor the level of rigor (e.g. high-school, undergraduate, or graduate textbooks) they intended their method for, the examples in the paper all involve mathematical-induction proofs of arithmetic properties, e.g. commutativity of addition. It is now known that some classical mathematics beyond merely the textbooks involves third-order logic, and proofs couched therein.

First, our model was trained and tested on a single proof domain, with relatively simple proofs, within a relatively simple cognitive calculus. An AGI agent should be able to generate explanations of proofs in a wide variety of domains which it may not have encountered before. New methods may be needed to achieve this, as well as to enable such an agent to generate explanations of more complex proofs in cognitive calculi with more and deeper modalities and inference schemata.

Second, while using a transformer enabled our model to generate text that was linguistically coherent, one significant drawback is that there is no guarantee the logical content of the explanation matches that of the proof. That is, the explanation may be syntactically correct English, but not match the meaning of the proof.[12] We see two possible directions in this space. First, one could imbue the transformer with some type of rule-based system that ensures that the text it produces corresponds with the logical content of the proof. Second, one could take a different approach to language generation entirely. Specifically, a knowledge-based approach to language generation (e.g. [10,11]) could ensure that outputs are both logically and linguistically sensible.

Acknowledgements. This research is partially enabled by support from ONR and AFOSR (Award # FA9550-17-1-0191).

A   Fine-Tuning and Evaluation Implementation

We used the Hugging Face Transformers library to access Pegasus, fine-tune the model, and evaluate it. Our fork of the model (https://github.com/mjgiancola/transformers) includes scripts for fine-tuning with the parameters we set to enable reproduction of our results (https://github.com/mjgiancola/transformers/tree/main/examples/research_projects/proof-nlg).

The script `fine_tune_pegasus.sh` runs the fine-tuning process. It is configured to generate the fine-tuned model's predictions on the test set after fine-tuning is completed. Additionally, the script `get_predictions_from_fine_tuned.py` loads the fine-tuned model and outputs pretty-printed results, including the input (a proof), the ground-truth output (a human-generated explanation), and the model's output.

---

[12] We note that, while this is a significant drawback, which we shortly address as pressing future work, AI agents which utilize the type of technology presented herein (i.e. a cognitive calculus for reasoning and a transformer for NLG) would still enact logically correct decision-making, even if its explanation wasn't correct. That is, the agent's behavior would still be bound by what it could prove via the calculus' inference schemata.

References

1. Alexoudi, M., Zinn, C., Bundy, A.: English summaries of mathematical proofs. In: Second International Joint Conference on Automated Reasoning-Workshop on Computer-Supported Mathematical Theory Development, pp. 49–60. Citeseer (2004)
2. Bender, E.M., Gebru, T., McMillan-Major, A., Shmitchell, S.: On the dangers of stochastic parrots: can language models be too big? In: Proceedings of the 2021 ACM Conference on Fairness, Accountability, and Transparency, pp. 610–623 (2021)
3. Bringsjord, S., Govindarajulu, N.S., Giancola, M.: Automated argument adjudication to solve ethical problems in multi-agent environments. Paladyn J. Behav. Robot. **12**, 310–335 (2021). https://doi.org/10.1515/pjbr-2021-0009
4. Felty, A., Hager, G.: Explaining modal logic proofs. In: Proceedings of the 1988 IEEE International Conference on Systems, Man, and Cybernetics, vol. 1, pp. 177–180. IEEE (1988)
5. Francez, N.: Proof-Theoretic Semantics. College Publications, London (2015)
6. Giancola, M., Bringsjord, S., Govindarajulu, N.S.: Novel intensional defeasible reasoning for AI: is it cognitively adequate? In: Proceedings of the IJCAI Workshop on "Cognitive Aspects of Knowledge Representation" (CAKR 2022). CEUR-WS (2022). http://ceur-ws.org/Vol-3251/paper9.pdf
7. Giancola, M., Bringsjord, S., Govindarajulu, N.S., Varela, C.: Making maximally ethical decisions via cognitive likelihood & formal planning. In: Ferreira, M.I.A., Tokhi, O. (eds.) Towards Trustworthy Artificial Intelligent Systems, Intelligent Systems, Control and Automation: Science and Engineering, vol. 102. Springer (2022). https://link.springer.com/chapter/10.1007/978-3-031-09823-9_10
8. Govindarajulu, N.S., Bringsjord , S., Peveler, M.: On quantified modal theorem proving for modeling ethics. Electron. Proc. Theor. Comput. Sci. **311**, 43–49 (2019)
9. Kowalski, R., Sergot, M.: A logic-based calculus of events. N. Gener. Comput. 4(1), 67–95 (1986)
10. Leon, I.E.: OntoGen: a knowledge-based approach to natural language generation. Master's thesis, Rensselaer Polytechnic Institute (2020)
11. McShane, M., Leon, I.: Language generation for broad-coverage, explainable cognitive systems. arXiv preprint arXiv:2201.10422 (2022)
12. Zhang, J., Zhao, Y., Saleh, M., Liu, P.: PEGASUS: pre-training with extracted gap-sentences for abstractive summarization. In: International Conference on Machine Learning, pp. 11328–11339. PMLR (2020)

ONA for Autonomous ROS-Based Robots

Patrick Hammer[1](✉)(iD), Peter Isaev[2], Tony Lofthouse[1],
and Robert Johansson[1](iD)

[1] Department of Psychology, Stockholm University, Stockholm, Sweden
{patrick.hammer,robert.johansson}@psychology.su.se,
tony.lofthouse@reasoning.systems
[2] Department of Computer Science, Temple University, Philadelphia, USA
peter.isaev@temple.edu

Abstract. In this paper we will show that OpenNARS for Applications (ONA) can be used for enhanced autonomous robots operating in the real world. It is done by utilizing state-of-the-art object detection along with Simultaneous Localization and Mapping techniques while inheriting the strengths of means-end reasoning and adding robust learning at runtime into the picture. This is showcased in an experiment where an ONA-controlled mobile robot with manipulator arm is learning about its environment to collect bottles to be returned to a human operator.

Keywords: Reasoning under uncertainty · Non-axiomatic reasoning system · Procedure learning · Means-end reasoning · Autonomous robots

1 Introduction: A Reasoner Which Learns and Decides

In this paper we first introduce an architecture that shows the ability of Open-NARS for Applications (ONA) to be utilized on robots running Robot Operating System (ROS), then present real-world robotics experiments as a case study that uses YOLOv4 [6] and [20], a Convolutional Neural Network [16] which represents the state-of-the-art object detection and Simultaneous Localization and Mapping. In this experiment we observe that the reasoner inherits some of the known strengths of means-end reasoning solutions (such as support for easily human-readable knowledge compared to model-based RL), while being able to deal with knowledge insufficiency at run-time. Knowledge insufficiency [26] include incomplete knowledge, outdated knowledge and various forms of concept drift, all of which are addressed by supporting robust learning at run-time.

Means-end reasoners are sometimes referred to as Practical Reasoning Systems and have multiple existing instantiations (such as [9,19,22,29], Belief-Desire-Intention models [2,5] like [7], etc.), most are not designed to allow knowledge to be uncertain but rely on it to be sufficient for the task at hand. Multiple logics have been proposed to support reasoning under uncertainty, such as: Markov Logic Networks [21], ProbLog [8], Fuzzy Logic [31], Probabilistic Logic Networks [10] and Non-Axiomatic Logic [25], where they commonly extend truth

B. Goertzel et al. (Eds.): AGI 2022, LNAI 13539, pp. 231–242, 2023.
https://doi.org/10.1007/978-3-031-19907-3_22

value of propositions from boolean to a degree of belief to allow capturing knowledge that is neither true or false, but somewhere in-between. Of these logics, [8,21] and [10] operate with probability values associated to the prepositions. Additionally, [10] and [25] use a second value to address the size of the sample spaces, which intuitively speaking corresponds to the stability of the probability of a new evidence. Such approach allows to allocate a higher certainty for a 50/50 over a 5/5 coin flip scenario, while still converging to the same truth value in the limit of infinite samples. Therefore these two logics become extremely well-suited for cases where "degree of belief" has to be estimated from samples and justifiable conclusions should be drawn (or decisions being made) even when samples supporting a relevant hypothesis are low in count. In this case the ratio of confirming cases over total cases is not necessarily yet representative because the amount of samples also needs to be considered when comparing competing hypotheses to make them suitable for learning goal-directed behaviors and solving the Goal-Directed Procedure Learning Problem [13], which is concerned with learning behaviors to reach (potentially changing, and conflicting) goals.

2 Non Axiomatic Logic (NAL)

For this paper, NAL [25] was chosen over PLN [10] since it incorporates goal reasoning and decision making, hence can be considered a Practical Reasoner able to learn from experience. In this section we provide only some definitions of NAL that are necessary to replicate the experiments.

Truth Value. Truth Value in NAL is based on positive evidence w^+ and negative evidence w^- which speaks for or against a statement/belief/hypothesis, and the total evidence $w := w^+ + w^-$, each of which is zero or greater. Based on these evidence values, the NAL truth value is defined as the frequency and confidence tuple (f, c):

$$f := \frac{w^+}{w} \in [0, 1], c := \frac{w}{w+1} \in [0, 1)$$

Please note the similarity between frequency and probability, with the difference being that the limit $\lim_{w \to \infty} f$ is not taken, as it cannot be obtained from any finite amount of samples. Also, clearly for $w > 0$, the mapping $(w^+, w^-) \mapsto (f, c)$ is bijective, and statements with $w = 0$ do not need to be handled as they do not contribute any evidence. Additionally, truth expectation is defined as

$$expectation(f, c) := (c * (f - \frac{1}{2}) + \frac{1}{2}).$$

This measure allows to summarize the two-valued truth value into a single value with the extremes being 0 for $c = 1, f = 0$, and 1 for $c = 1, f = 1$, which both are approachable but unreachable, since $\forall w \in \mathbb{R} : c < 1$ while $\lim_{w \to \infty} c = 1$.

Implications. For the sake of this paper we will restrict ourselves to temporal implications $(A \Rightarrow B)$ and procedural implications of the form $((A, Op) \Rightarrow B)$. The former denotes that B will happen after A, and the latter that B will happen when Op is executed right after A happened. To calculate the truth values of these correlative implications [28], the evidences of w^+ and w^- are needed. If events would have binary truth, for $(A \Rightarrow B)$, w^+ would be the amount of cases in which A happened and B happened after it, and w^- would be the amount of cases where A happened but B did not happen thereafter. Slightly more complex but following the same idea, given $((A, Op) \Rightarrow B)$, w^+ would be the amount of cases in which A happened, op was executed and B happened after it, while w^- would be the amount of cases where A happened and op was executed but B did not happen thereafter. Differently than the schemas in [15], implications can be supported to various degree instead of having to match all the data the agent has seen so far.

Now, using w^+ and w^-, the truth value (f, c) of the implication statements would be fully determined. While this captures the main idea, we need to make the temporal reasoning more robust in regards to timing variations.

Event Uncertainty. Events are not "true" at only a specific moment in time (with some unique identifier attached to them, which can be an integer, string, or as we will see later, logical statements with internal structure), instead they have an occurrence time and truth value attached to them. The confidence decreases with increasing time distance to the second premise (also called Projection in [25]). This is realized when two premises are used in inference, the confidence of the second premise is discounted by the factor $\beta^{|\Delta t|}$ with $\Delta t = time(B) - time(A)$, where β is the truth projection decay, a hyperparameter.

Now, the way implications are formed is via the Induction rule

$$\{A, B\} \vdash (A \Rightarrow B)$$

with Δt stored as metadata and the truth of the conclusion being computed using truth function for induction (as described in more detail in [25]):

$$truth((A \Rightarrow B)) = f_{ind}((f_A, c_A), (f_B, c_B)) = (f_B, \frac{f_A * c_A * c_B}{f_A * c_A * c_B + 1})$$

When the same implication is derived multiple times, their truth values are revised by simply adding up the evidences of the premises: $w^+ = w_1^+ + w_2^+$, $w^- = w_1^- + w_2^-$. This makes sure that the implication receives increasing amounts of evidence when the supporting events do occur (the antecedent and consequent). However, with the addition, that evidence is being discounted based on temporal distance making the temporal credit assignment succeed. On this matter, Projection plays the same role as Eligibility Traces do for Reinforcement Learners [23].

As a last detail, the Δt is also updated in revision, by taking a weighted average between the time deltas of the premises, weighted by the confidence of the premises. We will need this to decide the occurrence time of derived events.

Learning. To form the temporal and procedural implications from input events (to calculate their evidence), a sliding-window is utilized (a first-in-first-out buffer) which only holds the latest k events, which is a common approach in Data Stream Mining [18]. This way evidence for implication $(A \Rightarrow B)$ is only attributed (based on the Induction rule we described) when both the antecedent A and consequent B of the implication exist within the sliding window. Please note that A can as well be a sequence here, such as (X, Op), meaning that X happened and then operation event Op happened. In principle sequences do not need to contain operation events and can contain more than just two elements, this allows ONA to learn temporal patterns which span a larger time distance (up to the sliding window size). This helps especially in environments where the Markov property does not hold, but since we compare with Q-Learning which assumes the Markov property to hold (next state and reward only being dependent on current state plus current action), we will leave this out for now to make the comparison fair.

Collecting negative evidence for an implication is slightly more tricky (Anticipation in NAL, see [25]), as it is supposed to be added when the consequent will not happen, but how long to wait for the consequent? Ideally this would not depend on the buffer size, and would be dependent on the averages of the experienced timings and related variances. However timing estimations can go wrong if certain distributional assumptions are not met, which is why we went for a simpler solution for now which is at least not dependent on the size of the sliding window: to add a small amount of negative evidence immediately when the antecedent arrives, small enough that should the consequent arrive as predicted by the implication, the truth expectation of the implication will still increase (the positive evidence over-votes the negative), while else it would decrease due to the negative evidence which was added. Overall, the accumulation of positive and negative evidence leads to frequency values which encode the hypotheses (the implications) proficiency to predict successfully. Therefore, truth expectation can be seen as the expected frequency, which as we will now see is used in decision making (as it takes into account how many samples have been seen about a certain implication, eliminating initially lucky hypotheses to be preferred over consistently competently predicting ones).

Decision Making: Goal events $G!$ are represented as temporal implication $(G \Rightarrow D)$ where D is implicitly present and stands for "desired state", and their desire value is the truth value of this implication. When processed, goals either trigger decisions or lead to the derivations of subgoals. For this purpose, the existing procedural implications are checked. If the implication $((A, Op) \Rightarrow B)$ has a sufficiently high truth value, and event A recently happened, it will generate a high desire value for the reasoner to execute op. The truth expectations of the implications with G as consequent are compared, and the operation from the candidate with the highest expectation desire value will be executed if above decision threshold (a hyperparameter, usually set to be 0.5 approximately). If not, all the preconditions (such as A) of the implications with G as consequent will be derived as subgoals, competing for attention and processing in a bounded priority queue ranked by truth expectation (this way only the most desired goals are pursued). Hereby, the desire value of the subgoal is evaluated using deduction between the implication and the goal [25]. To determine the operation's desire value, one additional deduction step to take the precondition truth value into account is necessary. This corresponds to the inference rule

$$\{(X \Rightarrow G), (G \Rightarrow D)\} \vdash (X \Rightarrow D) = \{(X \Rightarrow G), G!\} \vdash X!$$

where the conclusion goal's occurrence time (the time at which X would have to have occurred if G had to happen right now) is G's occurrence time minus the Δt stored as metadata of the implication. And the following inference rule in case X is of the form (Y, Op):

$$\{((Y, Op) \Rightarrow D), Y\} \vdash (op \Rightarrow D) = \{(Y, Op)!, Y\} \vdash op!$$

which means that op is wanted to be executed if op is wanted to be executed after Y happened and Y happened.

The conclusion goal desire values are:

$$desire(X) = f_{ded}(desire(G), truth(((X, Op) \Rightarrow G))$$

for the subgoal which corresponds to the antecedent of the implication, and

$$desire(Op) = f_{ded}(desire((X, Op)), truth(X))$$

for the operation subgoal to potentially execute if X happened, with f_{ded} being (as in [25]):

$$f_{ded}((f_1, c_1), (f_2, c_2)) = (f_1 * f_2, f_1 * f_2 * c_1 * c_2)$$

Using this model, decision making is concerned with realizing a goal by executing an operation which most likely and sufficiently likely leads to its fulfillment. When there is no such candidate to accomplish this in a single step, subgoals are derived from which a candidate will fulfill this requirement or again lead to further subgoaling. This is similar to backward planning from a goal to current circumstances, but preferring to process more attainable goals by taking uncertainties of events and implications into account. Hereby, uncertainties are not assumed-to-be known probabilities as in Probabilistic STRIPS extensions [24] and systems which utilize Probabilistic Planning Domain Definition Language (PPDDL [30]), but includes confidence values for empirical frequency values estimated from data. In addition, differently than [3,4,27], this process derives goals backwards and random rollouts (random action till the game finishes) are not assumed to be possible, which also allows for usage in open-ended environments.

Algorithm 1: Decision and subgoaling

Input: Goal G **Result**: Execution of Op, or subgoaling
subgoals = {}, bestDesire = 0.0
forall the $((X, Op) \Rightarrow G) \in memory$ **do**
    $subgoals = subgoals \cup \{X\}$
    if $desire(Op) > bestDesire$ **then**
       | bestDesire = $desire(Op)$, bestOp = Op
    end
end
if $bestDesire > DECISION\_THRESHOLD$ **then**
    | execute(bestOp)
else
    forall the $s \in subgoals$ **do**
       | derive s (for potential selection in next inference step)
    end
end

Also to allow effective usage of implications in implementation, the procedural implications should be indexed by their consequent, where only a constant amount of implications is allowed for each consequent. This can be achieved by ranking them according to their truth expectation, such that too weak and wrongly predicting implications are removed while those predicting successfully are kept (similarly as in [13]), thus keeping the resource demands bounded [26]. Similarly, through the indexing, the competing hypothesis that lead to the goal do not need to be searched for, instead only iterated and compared in the way the Algorithm 1 describes.

Exploration. Sometimes the operation to execute is ignored and a random one is executed instead, which can be considered a form of exploration through motor babbling. This is also common for Reinforcement Learners, and for the reasoner is especially necessary in the beginning, when no procedural implications exist, and hence no decision can be derived to lead to the desired outcome. Yet sometimes an action should be tried such that the first implications will be formed, and "informed decision" can increasingly replace random trial, e.g. exploitation replacing exploration.

3   Practical Reasoning and Learning

In this chapter we will show how ONA can be used to extend on the abilities of typical practical reasoning approaches [7,9]. This is achieved by supporting learning at run-time without relying on a separate learning technique or POMDP-based approach such as in [1]. The strength of practical means-end reasoning lies in the ability to effectively utilize high-level knowledge for planning purposes (easily expressible and communicable by human's). However, Practical Reasoning solutions such as [7] and [9] completely lack a robust learning mechanism or capability. An effective learning mechanism would allow the agent to deal with a lack of knowledge or changing circumstances [17] (such as various forms of concept drift [14]). We will see how ONA can be easily fed with background knowledge, whilst being able to learn new knowledge from observations at run-time, as the previous examples required.

Encodings. Before we continue, additional knowledge representation needs to be introduced: beyond events, operations, sequences of events and operations, and implications. Previously we assumed input events just have a string or integer identifier attached to them. However, since ONA uses Non-Axiomatic Logic [25], events can have richer internal (compound) term structure, which we will make use of for similar reasons that predicates are common in First Order Predicate Logic-based Practical Reasoner applications and Logic Programming in general: they allow arbitrary relationships to be easily expressed. The following logical copulas are the most important for this experiment. Please note that these can be arbitrarily nested, thus making ONA's formal language for knowledge representation very expressive.

- Inheritance statements. Inheritance $<A \to B>$ indicates A to be a special case of B. For instance, that cats are animals can be encoded as an Inheritance statement $<cat \to animal>$.
- Terms referring to instances and properties, denoted by $\{instance\}$ and $[property]$ respectively. For instance, Garfield being orange in color can be expressed with $<\{garfield\} \to [orange]>$.
- Relational terms. This includes products $(a * b)$ to express anonymous relationships, these allow to express arbitrary relationships like that cats eat mice, $<(cat * mouse) \to eat>$. This is similar to predicates in predicate logic.
- Properties and instances: $SELF$ indicating the system itself, and perceivable properties such as $[open]$, $[left]$ and $[right]$.
- Negation, expressed with $(\neg a)$, where a can be an arbitrary statement.
- Variables: Dependent, Independent and Question Variables $\$name$, $\#name$ and $?name$ respectively resembling all- and exists-quantified variables and placeholders. These variables enable statements to be made more abstract by allowing for variable binding and unification in inference. This is achieved by substituting specific terms that have a matching structure and do not conflict with previous assignments to the same variable.

Architecture and Setup. In the experiment we used the Yahboom Transbot robot. The following list shows the sensory channels and operations used by the reasoner.

- Sensors: Lidar, Depth (& RGB) camera, servo sensors
- Actuators: Two motors for turning left, right and moving forward. Three degree of freedom robotic arm, which is utilized to pick up and drop objects.
- Software: A vision channel based on YOLOv4 [6] trained on ImageNet.
- Parameters: Default parameters of ONA v0.9.0 [12].[1]

---

[1] Software release: https://github.com/opennars/OpenNARS-for-Applications.

YOLOv4 trained on ImageNet is utilized as an object detection model and vision channel. The vision channel uses discretized relative location information (relative to the center) together with the output label to form statements of the form $<objectLabel \rightarrow [direction]>$ similar as in [11] but with relative location encoding where *position* for the X-axis is either *left*, *center* or *right*. This encoding makes ONA aware of the detected object types and their position in the camera's field of view, and is utilized to pick up objects with the manipulator arm. Additionally, the Lidar sensor is utilized to build statements such as

$$<obstacle \rightarrow [direction]>, <obstacle \rightarrow [free]>$$

(*direction* being *left*, *front*, or *right*) dependent on whether an obstacle is detected below a distance threshold of 50 cm. This gives the robot a way to sense when in proximity to an obstacle. Lastly, the gripper provides events regarding whether it's currently holding an object:

$$<gripper \rightarrow [free]>, <gripper \rightarrow [hold]>$$

Additionally, a map channel which employs Gmapping SLAM algorithm is utilized allowing ONA associate detected objects and their perceived location on the map. This happens via

$$<(objectLabel * pose) \rightarrow at>$$

relationships, where pose is a combination of the robots location and rotation as estimated by the ROS move base using SLAM.

4   Demonstrated Capabilities

1. **Perceive and remember locations of objects**
   In this case, the system has to be able to answer the question event $<(objectLabel*?where) \rightarrow at>$? by remembering the most recent corresponding relation between the labelled object which was detected and the location as obtained by the map channel. Among multiple candidates, the system gives the answer of highest truth expectation when projected to the time the question is asked. This can be considered a form of retrieving an episodic memory about a correlation between object and location.
2. **Go back to objects' remembered location while avoiding obstacles**
   This ability directly builds on the above ability. Hereby the system directly invokes an operation with the remembered object location to plan a path to the target, taking obstacles into account by considering the map channel which includes the information from Lidar scans.
3. **Retrieve objects by using a manipulator arm.** This capability is initiated by the reasoner, based on the visually perceived location of the object to pick, where the object has to be close enough to be grabbed. During the pick operation, both visual feedback, and servo feedback, is taken into account.

Instead of motion planning, visual feedback is used to move the perceived location of the object to be closer to the gripper of the robot (by left, right and forward operations). Should the object go out of sight during this process, or the system be unable to perceive the object in its gripper (via Servo feedback), the operation will return without success. This is noticed immediately by NARS, via the gripper events, which can either indicate holding or free. The reasoner can then decide to re-initiate the operation should the object be visible again, or take explorative actions to re-acquire it. This leads to a robust solution as it allows the system to compensate for disturbances based on observed feedback, or to change its behavior.

4. **Bottle collect mission.** To illustrate the system's abilities, we directed the system to find and retrieve a bottle to the location the human operator has been last observed by the robot, a form of bottle-fetch mission, part of which is illustrated in Fig. 1. The background knowledge is as follows:

```
//Avoid obstructing object:
<(<obstacle --> [left]> &/ ^right) =/> <obstacle --> [free]>>.
<(<obstacle --> [right]> &/ ^left) =/> <obstacle --> [free]>>.
<(<obstacle --> [front]> &/ ^left) =/> <obstacle --> [free]>>.
<(((<gripper --> [open]> &/ <obstacle --> [free]>) &/ ^forward) =/> G>.
//Go to the location in order to see the object:
<(<gripper --> [holding]> &/ <({SELF} * $obj) --> ^goto>) =/>
     <$obj --> [left]>>.
//If gripper is open and a bottle is seen, pick it up to hold it
<(((<gripper --> [open]> &/ <bottle --> [left]>) &/
     <({SELF} * bottle) --> ^pick>) =/> G>.
//If the gripper is holding an object and a person is seen, drop it
<(((<gripper --> [hold]> &/ <person --> [left]>) &/ ^drop) =/> G>.
```

Each of these higher-order statements act as initial knowledge but can be revised by the system. For example, statements related to object avoidance behavior will receive negative evidence if the obstacle is still perceived, after avoidance behavior has been carried out, or positive evidence when successful. Due to this ability, these statements can also be learned from interactions with the environment in a matter of minutes. Now, to show the overall solutions ability to carry out the bottle collect mission with the background knowledge, we collected the following measures over multiple runs:

As summarized in Table 1, across 10 runs, 8 retrievals succeeded. And 3 recovery behaviors were invoked by the reasoner, which are cases where the reasoner had to re-adjust and re-initiate picking the objects when YOLOv4 failed to detect the bottle and the bottle became visible again. These recoveries were successful and can be taken as an example where the reasoner worked around the shortcomings of the offline-trained object detection model. Of the two failures, one was a mechanical issue, and one was caused by the robot accidentally tipping over the bottle when it tried to adjust the arm's location relative to the bottle's. In all cases, including the two failure cases, the

Table 1. Bottle collect mission results

Runs	Successes	Failures	Recovery behaviors	Location recall
10	8	2	3	10

Fig. 1. Bottle collect mission

location of the human was learned from a single observation, and successfully recalled.

Our results in remembering object locations and learning object avoidance represent a first step to demonstrate ONA's abilities on an advanced robot. More complex experiments revealing the potential of having a reasoner that controls a robot and learns from observations will be carried out in the future.

5   Conclusion

An architecture for utilizing the ONA NARS implementation on a robot running ROS has been shown, together with several base capabilities which represent useful building blocks for complex autonomous robotic missions featuring mobility and manipulation. Hereby, both our system's ability to utilize high-level knowledge in form of Narsese sentences, and to learn from observation by utilizing the sensors available on the robot together with related techniques for processing has been described. This represents our way to push robot autonomy, by allowing robots to adapt at runtime, through the usage of a reasoning system that learns (NARS in particular) and perceives the world by interfacing with perception channels running as ROS modules.

References

1. Amiri, S., Shirazi, M.S., Zhang, S.: Learning and reasoning for robot sequential decision making under uncertainty. In: Proceedings of the AAAI Conference on Artificial Intelligence, vol. 34, no. 03, pp. 2726–2733 (2020)
2. Bratman, M.: Intention, Plans, and Practical Reason, vol. 10, p. 20. Harvard University Press, Cambridge (1987)

3. Browne, C.B., et al.: A survey of Monte Carlo tree search methods. IEEE Trans. Comput. Intell. AI Games **4**(1), 1–43 (2012)
4. Chaslot, G., Bakkes, S., Szita, I., Spronck, P.: Monte-Carlo tree search: a new framework for game AI. In: AIIDE (2008)
5. Georgeff, M., Pell, B., Pollack, M., Tambe, M., Wooldridge, M.: The belief-desire-intention model of agency. In: Müller, J.P., Rao, A.S., Singh, M.P. (eds.) ATAL 1998. LNCS, vol. 1555, pp. 1–10. Springer, Heidelberg (1999). https://doi.org/10.1007/3-540-49057-4_1
6. Bochkovskiy, A., Wang, C.Y., Liao, H.Y.M.: YOLOv4: optimal speed and accuracy of object detection. arXiv preprint arXiv:2004.10934 (2020)
7. Bordini, R.H., Hübner, J.F.: BDI agent programming in AgentSpeak using *Jason*. In: Toni, F., Torroni, P. (eds.) CLIMA 2005. LNCS (LNAI), vol. 3900, pp. 143–164. Springer, Heidelberg (2006). https://doi.org/10.1007/11750734_9
8. De Raedt, L., Kimmig, A., Toivonen, H.: ProbLog: a probabilistic prolog and its application in link discovery. In: IJCAI, vol. 7, pp. 2462–2467 (2007)
9. Ferrein, A., Steinbauer, G., Vassos, S.: Action-based imperative programming with YAGI. In: CogRob@ AAAI (2012)
10. Goertzel, B., Iklé, M., Goertzel, I.F., Heljakka, A.: Probabilistic Logic Networks: A Comprehensive Framework for Uncertain Inference. Springer, Heidelberg (2008). https://doi.org/10.1007/978-0-387-76872-4
11. Hammer, P., Lofthouse, T., Fenoglio, E., Latapie, H., Wang, P.: A reasoning based model for anomaly detection in the smart city domain. In: Arai, K., Kapoor, S., Bhatia, R. (eds.) IntelliSys 2020. AISC, vol. 1251, pp. 144–159. Springer, Cham (2021). https://doi.org/10.1007/978-3-030-55187-2_13
12. Hammer, P., Lofthouse, T.: 'OpenNARS for applications': architecture and control. In: Goertzel, B., Panov, A.I., Potapov, A., Yampolskiy, R. (eds.) AGI 2020. LNCS (LNAI), vol. 12177, pp. 193–204. Springer, Cham (2020). https://doi.org/10.1007/978-3-030-52152-3_20
13. Hammer, P., Lofthouse, T.: Goal-directed procedure learning. In: Iklé, M., Franz, A., Rzepka, R., Goertzel, B. (eds.) AGI 2018. LNCS (LNAI), vol. 10999, pp. 77–86. Springer, Cham (2018). https://doi.org/10.1007/978-3-319-97676-1_8
14. Hu, H., Kantardzic, M., Sethi, T.S.: No free lunch theorem for concept drift detection in streaming data classification: a review. Wiley Interdisc. Rev.: Data Min. Knowl. Discov. **10**(2), e1327 (2020)
15. Kansky, K., et al.: Schema networks: Zero-shot transfer with a generative causal model of intuitive physics. In: International Conference on Machine Learning, pp. 1809–1818. PMLR (2017)
16. Khan, A., Sohail, A., Zahoora, U., Qureshi, A.S.: A survey of the recent architectures of deep convolutional neural networks. Artif. Intell. Rev. **53**(8), 5455–5516 (2020)
17. Lanza, F., Hammer, P., Seidita, V., Wang, P., Chella, A.: Agents in dynamic contexts, a system for learning plans. In: Proceedings of the 35th Annual ACM Symposium on Applied Computing, pp. 823–825 (2020)
18. Pramod, S., Vyas, O.P.: Data stream mining: a review on windowing approach. Glob. J. Comput. Sci. Technol. Softw. Data Eng. **12**(11), 26–30 (2012)
19. Purang, K., Purushothaman, D., Traum, D., Andersen, C., Perlis, D.: Practical reasoning and plan execution with active logic. In: Proceedings of the IJCAI-99 Workshop on Practical Reasoning and Rationality, pp. 30–38 (1999)
20. Redmon, J., Divvala, S., Girshick, R., Farhadi, A.: You only look once: unified, real-time object detection. In: Proceedings of the IEEE Conference on Computer Vision and Pattern Recognition, pp. 779–788 (2016)

21. Richardson, M., Domingos, P.: Markov logic networks. Mach. Learn. **62**(1–2), 107–136 (2006)
22. Shams, Z., De Vos, M., Padget, J., Vasconcelos, W.W.: Practical reasoning with norms for autonomous software agents. Eng. Appl. Artif. Intell. **65**, 388–399 (2017)
23. Sutton, R.S.: Learning to predict by the methods of temporal differences. Mach. Learn. **3**(1), 9–44 (1988)
24. Teichteil-Königsbuch, F., Vidal, V., Infantes, G.: Extending classical planning heuristics to probabilistic planning with dead-ends. In: Twenty-Fifth AAAI Conference on Artificial Intelligence (2011)
25. Wang, P.: Non-axiomatic Logic: A Model of Intelligent Reasoning. World Scientific, Singapore (2013)
26. Wang, P.: Insufficient knowledge and resources-a biological constraint and its functional implications. In: AAAI Fall Symposium: Biologically Inspired Cognitive Architectures (2009)
27. Wang, W., Sebag, M.: Multi-objective Monte-Carlo tree search. In: Asian Conference on Machine Learning, pp. 507–522. PMLR (2012)
28. Wang, P., Hammer, P.: Issues in temporal and causal inference. In: Bieger, J., Goertzel, B., Potapov, A. (eds.) AGI 2015. LNCS (LNAI), vol. 9205, pp. 208–217. Springer, Cham (2015). https://doi.org/10.1007/978-3-319-21365-1_22
29. Wooldridge, M.: Practical reasoning with procedural knowledge. In: Gabbay, D.M., Ohlbach, H.J. (eds.) FAPR 1996. LNCS, vol. 1085, pp. 663–678. Springer, Heidelberg (1996). https://doi.org/10.1007/3-540-61313-7_108
30. Younes, H.L., Littman, M.L.: PPDDL1. 0: an extension to PDDL for expressing planning domains with probabilistic effects. Technical report CMU-CS-04-162, 2, 99 (2004)
31. Zadeh, L.A.: Fuzzy logic. Computer **21**(4), 83–93 (1988)

Generalized Identity Matching in NARS

Robert Johansson[1,2(✉)], Tony Lofthouse[1], and Patrick Hammer[1]

[1] Department of Psychology, Stockholm University, Stockholm, Sweden
{robert.johansson,tony.lofthouse,patrick.hammer}@psychology.su.se
[2] Department of Computer and Information Science, Linköping University,
Linköping, Sweden

Abstract. Generalized identity matching is the ability to apply an identity concept in novel situations. This ability has been studied experimentally among humans and non-humans in a match-to-sample task. The aim of this study was to test if this ability was possible to demonstrate in the Non-Axiomatic Reasoning System (NARS). More specifically, we used a minimal configuration of OpenNARS for Applications that contained only sensorimotor reasoning. After training with only two identity matching-to-sample problems, NARS was able to derive an identity concept that it could generalize to novel situations.

Keywords: Identity matching · Animal intelligence · NARS

1 Introduction

At the foundation of any intelligent system is the ability to form general concepts about the relationships among objects or other types of stimuli. These concepts are essential to a wide range of tasks. A fundamental relational concept is the identity concept, i.e., the ability to respond to the identity relationship among stimuli.

One way to study the use of the identity concept is with *identity matching* in the matching-to-sample (MTS) context. In these experiments, participants are presented with a sample stimulus and pairs of comparison stimuli and are asked to decide which comparison is identical to the sample. These experiments are thought to reveal the extent to which a subject applies the identity concept as part of the decision making. While these experiments typically are done with visual stimuli, there are no limits on the type of stimuli that can be matched regarding sensory modality.

An even more sophisticated ability, *generalized identity matching*, can be tested for using the same MTS setup. After having been trained to match by identity over a set of trials, the subject is presented with a novel sample stimulus and novel comparisons. Generalized identity matching is demonstrated if the subject can transfer the identity concept to these new stimuli. Evidence of this ability has been reported in a number of non-human species including sea lions

B. Goertzel et al. (Eds.): AGI 2022, LNAI 13539, pp. 243–249, 2023.
https://doi.org/10.1007/978-3-031-19907-3_23

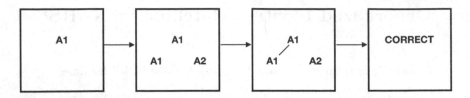

Fig. 1. A typical trial in the identity matching-to-sample task. First, the sample is presented at the top (leftmost panel). Then, two comparison stimuli are presented (next panel). The experimental subject then indicates a choice between either the left or right option. Finally, the subject receives feedback if the choice was correct or not (rightmost panel).

[3], rats [5] and pigeons [8]. A typical trial in the generalized identity matching-to-sample task is illustrated in Fig. 1. A video of a sea lion carrying out the task can be found in [1].

While this might seem like a trivial task, it can be seen as a minimal example of general-purpose learning. In other words, being able to complete this task seems like a necessary (but not sufficient) critiera for an AGI system. Hence, this task would be interesting to demonstrate for any AGI system.

In this study, we report on a study of generalized identity matching in the AGI-system OpenNARS for Applications. The relevance for other AGI research will be discussed.

2   Methods

2.1   OpenNARS for Applications

We used OpenNARS for Applications (ONA) [2], a highly effective implementation of the Non-Axiomatic Reasoning System (NARS) [7]. Importantly, the parameter SEMANTIC_INFERENCE_NAL_LEVEL was set to 0, which means that only NAL layers 6–8 were available. This means that the system could only do sensori-motor inference (procedural and temporal reasoning), but no semantic inference (declarative reasoning). In a way, this could be called an animal-like version of ONA.

2.2   Identity Match-to-Sample Task in NARS

The identity match-to-sample task was presented as temporal Narsese statements (as indicated by the : | : markers below). An arbitrary goal event G! : | : was presented at the end to trigger the execution of one of the two procedural operations ^left and ^right (through motor babbling or a decision). During training, feedback was given in the form of G. : | : (meaning to reinforce a correct choice) or G. : | : 0.0 0.9 (to indicate that the system had conducted an incorrect choice). Between each trial, 100 time steps was entered, by feeding 100 to ONA.

```
<A1 --> [sample]>. :|:
<A1 --> [left]>. :|:
<A2 --> [right]>. :|:
G! :|:
```

An explanation of the Narsese follows. The first three lines are inheritance statements with properties on the right-hand side, indicating that the stimuli (*A*1, *A*2), are either on the left, right, or are the sample.

2.3 Experimental Setup

ONA was set to have two operators ^left and ^right, and an initial chance of motor babbling to 20%. The experiment consisted of four phases: Baseline assessment, Training (with feedback), Testing for identity (without feedback), and Testing for generalized identity (without feedback). In all phases, training and testing were done in blocks of trials. One trial could for example be that *A*1 was the sample and *A*1 and *A*2 were the left and right options, respectively. A block contained twelve trials, with the four trials possible with *A*1 and *A*2 as samples, each presented three times in random order.

1. **Baseline.** During the baseline assessment, which was two blocks, no feedback was given. This phase was included to establish a baseline probability of responding correct. It was expected that the system would respond correctly by chance in 50% of the trials.
2. **Training.** Then, the system was trained on a set of six blocks. Feedback was given when the system was correct (for example matching <A1 --> [sample]> to <A1 --> [right]> by doing ^right), and when not correct.
3. **Testing for identity.** The system was then tested (without feedback) on two blocks, with the contingencies that previously had been trained. If the system was correct on all trials in all blocks, the experiment continued with the next phase.
4. **Testing for generalized identity.** Finally, the system was tested (without feedback) on two blocks with trials containing novel stimuli (*X*1 and *X*2) the system hadn't seen before.

2.4 NARS Examples from the Training Phase

A few example trials from the training session follows. Let's say that the system was exposed to the following NARS statements:

```
<A1 --> [sample]>. :|:
<A2 --> [left]>. :|:
<A1 --> [right]>. :|:
G! :|:
```

If it is early in the training, NARS might use motor babbling to execute the ^right operation. Since this is considered correct in the experiment, the feedback G. :|: would be given to NARS, followed by 100 time steps. Only from this single interaction, NARS would form both a specific and a general hypothesis:

```
<((<A1 --> [sample]> &/ <A1 --> [right]>) &/ ^right) =/> G>.
// frequency: 1.00, confidence: 0.15

<((<#1 --> [sample]> &/ <#1 --> [right]>) &/ ^right) =/> G>.
// frequency: 1.00, confidence: 0.26
```

Importantly, after this single trial, NARS would also form simpler hypothesis such as:

```
<(<A1 --> [right]> &/ ^right) =/> G>.
// frequency: 1.00, confidence: 0.21

<(<A1 --> [sample]> &/ ^right) =/> G>.
// frequency: 1.00, confidence: 0.16
```

This means, that if the same trial was to be presented again (all four possible trials will be presented three times in a block of twelve trials), NARS would respond ^right again, but the decision being based on a simple hypothesis such as <(<A1 --> [right]> &/ ^right) =/> G>, since that hypothesis has the highest confidence value.

Let's say, that within the same block of 12 trials, the next trial to be presented to NARS was the following:

```
<A1 --> [sample]>. :|:
<A1 --> [left]>. :|:
<A2 --> [right]>. :|:
G! :|:
```

NARS would initially respond ^right, with the decision being made from the simple hypothesis <(<A1 --> [sample]> &/ ^right) =/> G>. This would be considered wrong in the experiment, and the feedback G. :|: 0.0 0.9 would be given to NARS. This would lead to negative evidence for the simple hypothesis. If the same trial was presented again, NARS would then likely resort to motor babbling that could execute the ^left operation. Over repeated trials with feedback, the simpler hypotheses would get more negative evidence, and the confidence value of the target hypotheses (specific and general) would increase.

3   Results

During baseline, the amount of correct trials ranged between 0 and 50% during the two blocks, indicating that no learning happened. In the training phase,

NARS was 100% correct after six blocks. When being tested on the same symbols without feedback (Phase 3: identity matching), NARS was 100% correct during both blocks. Also, NARS was 100% correct on novel stimuli (Phase 4), demonstrating generalized identity matching.

Across the six training blocks, the average confidence value for the four specific target hypotheses such as

`<((<A1 --> [sample]> &/ <A1 --> [left]>) &/ ^left) =/> G>`

went from 0.17 to 0.86. For the general target hypotheses (please note the #1 variable which could be substituted with specific terms) such as

`<((<#1 --> [sample]> &/ <#1 --> [left]>) &/ ^left) =/> G>`

the average confidence value went from 0.34 to 0.96. This also confirms that the generalized hypotheses reached more evidence in total than the specialized one, which was as expected, as it is not tied to $A1$ (it could also be substituted by other stimuli).

Importantly, in the final phase (generalized identity matching), NARS made its decisions based on the general hypotheses that had developed in confidence during the training.

The results from the four phases are illustrated in Fig. 2.

3.1 NARS Explanation of the Results

We will now explain the results in terms of mechanisms and inference rules implemented in the reasoner. The confidence increase followed from repeated examples which provide evidence to the predictive hypotheses. For this to happen and to derive the truth value, the following mechanisms in NARS were necessary:

1. **Temporal Induction:** To derive positive evidence to the relationship `<A =/> B>` from event A and B being observed in that order.
2. **Variable Introduction:** To introduce a variable for common terms in the subject of predicate of inheritance statements embedded into a statement, such as the #1 variable in the generalized hypothesis seen before.
3. **Anticipation:** To derive negative evidence to a hypothesis `<A =/> B>`, namely the antedecent happened but the consequent did not, hence the hypothesis failed, i.e. did not explain the outcome. In this particular task `<(<A1 --> [left]> &/ ^left) =/> G>` and `<(<A1 --> [sample]> &/ ^left) =/> G>` are both insufficient (receive negative evidence) as two stimuli, including the sample stimulus, need to be considered to make the correct decision.
4. **Revision.** To summarize the positive evidence and the negative evidence for a statement.

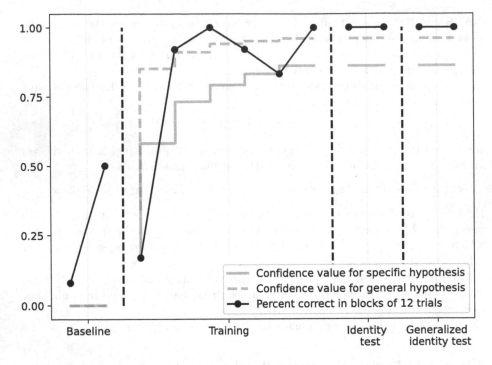

Fig. 2. Learning generalized identity matching in the Match-to-sample task. Dots illustrate the percent of correct in blocks of 12 trials. The solid line shows the NARS confidence value for specific hypotheses (identity matching), while the dashed line illustrates the NARS confidence in general hypotheses (generalized identity matching).

4   Discussion

The aim of this study was to study if a minimal version of NARS without declarative reasoning could do generalized identity matching. NARS learned this very quickly, as demonstrated by the experiments carried out in this study.

We believe these results are important for the AGI field in general. First, we see this as a minimal example of general-purpose learning. We believe that generalized identity matching is a good example of a capability that is necessary (but not sufficient) for AGI. Several other tasks exist in the animal cognition literature that any AGI-aspiring system should demonstrate. Further research can hence be carried out using a similar strategy. Second, we see this research as an example of a more general research approach. The match-to-sample task is an idealized situation, but can be used for studying more advanced capabilities, like symmetry [4] and stimulus equivalence [6], that both are assumed to be related to human-level intelligence [9]. Experiments in these particular directions will be part of our future work.

We believe that the AGI field will benefit from being continuously inspired by cognitive experiments carried out on non-human animals, and that these capabilities might reveal important insights regarding the necessary steps towards AGI, especially in terms of cognitive abilities and mechanisms that will be required to bring about these abilities.

Acknowledgements. We want to acknowledge Professor Pei Wang for his work on the NARS model.

References

1. BBC Earth: Sea lion plays snap! (2013). https://youtu.be/Ex1nEuzAYxo. Accessed 04 Aug 2022
2. Hammer, P., Lofthouse, T.: 'OpenNARS for applications': architecture and control. In: Goertzel, B., Panov, A.I., Potapov, A., Yampolskiy, R. (eds.) AGI 2020. LNCS (LNAI), vol. 12177, pp. 193–204. Springer, Cham (2020). https://doi.org/10.1007/978-3-030-52152-3_20
3. Kastak, D., Schusterman, R.J.: Transfer of visual identity matching-to-sample in two California sea lions (Zalophus californianus). Anim. Learn. Behav. **22**(4), 427–435 (1994). https://doi.org/10.3758/BF03209162
4. Lionello-DeNolf, K.M.: An update on the search for symmetry in nonhumans. J. Exp. Anal. Behav. **115**(1), 309–325 (2021)
5. Peña, T., Pitts, R.C., Galizio, M.: Identity matching-to-sample with olfactory stimuli in rats. J. Exp. Anal. Behav. **85**(2), 203–221 (2006)
6. Schusterman, R.J., Kastak, D.: A California sea lion (Zalophus californianus) is capable of forming equivalence relations. Psychol. Rec. **43**(4), 823–839 (1993)
7. Wang, P.: Non-Axiomatic Logic: A Model of Intelligent Reasoning. World Scientific, Singapore (2013)
8. Wright, A.A.: Concept learning and learning strategies. Psychol. Sci. **8**(2), 119–123 (1997)
9. Zettle, R.D., Hayes, S.C., Barnes-Holmes, D., Biglan, A.: The Wiley Handbook of Contextual Behavioral Science. Wiley Online Library, Hoboken (2016)

Adaptive Multi-strategy Market-Making Agent for Volatile Markets

Ali Raheman[1], Anton Kolonin[1,2,3](✉) ⓘ, Alexey Glushchenko[1] ⓘ, Arseniy Fokin[1] ⓘ,
and Ikram Ansari[1] ⓘ

[1] Autonio Foundation Ltd., Bristol, UK
`akolonin@gmail.com`
[2] SingularityNET Foundation, Amsterdam, The Netherlands
[3] Novosibirsk State University, Novosibirsk, Russian Federation

Abstract. Crypto-currency market uncertainty drives the need to find adaptive solutions to maximize gain or at least to avoid loss throughout the periods of trading activity. Given the high dimensionality and complexity of the state-action space in this domain, it can be treated as a "Narrow AGI" problem with the scope of goals and environments bound to financial markets. Adaptive Multi-Strategy Agent approach for market-making introduces a new solution to maximize positive "alpha" in long-term handling limit order book (LOB) positions by using multiple sub-agents implementing different strategies with a dynamic selection of these agents based on changing market conditions. AMSA provides no specific strategy of its own while being responsible for segmenting the periods of market-making activity into smaller execution sub-periods, performing internal backtesting on historical data on each of the sub-periods, doing sub-agent performance evaluation and re-selection of them at the end of each sub-period, and collecting returns and losses incrementally. With this approach, the return becomes a function of hyperparameters such as market data granularity (refresh rate), the execution sub-period duration, number of active sub-agents, and their individual strategies. Sub-agent selection for the next trading sub-period is made based on return/loss and alpha values obtained during internal backtesting as well as real trading. Experiments with the AMSA have been performed under different market conditions relying on historical data and proved a high probability of positive alpha throughout the periods of trading activity in the case of properly selected hyperparameters.

Keywords: Adaptive agent · Limit order book · Market making · Narrow AGI

1 Introduction

The extension of the algorithmic trading approach to the market making problem has been in the focus of the research community over the last few decades. Avellaneda has used simulation modeling for exploring how the different parameters can affect performance of the active portfolio management by means of market making operations with limit order book (Avellaneda and Stoikov 2008). The specifics of the market making risk management is related to the need of locking funds in the limit order which might be causing what is called "impermanent loss" in finance. The risks associated with inventory management in market making have been studied by Guéant (Guéant et al. 2012).

On the other hand, the use of machine learning algorithms such as deep learning and reinforcement learning have been actively explored in the last decade. Deep learning has been explored for price prediction by exploiting stationary limit order book features used in market making (Tsantekidis 2018). Reinforcement learning has been tried in order to get applied for trading on conventional financial markets (futures) (Zhang et al. 2019) as well as for market making (Ganesh et al. 2019). The latest trend in using of machine learning on financial markets can be seen as an attempt to operate at the strategy level, trying to figure out the more appropriate strategies for specific market conditions instead of trying to generate sparse "trading signals", which is not that helpful when dealing with funds locked in the limit order book orders (Yanjun et al. 2020).

Moreover, since the boom of crypto-currency markets five years ago, attempts have been made to apply algorithmic trading powered by machine learning to market making on centralized crypto-currency exchanges such as Binance. The most interesting series of studies have been run by Sadighian in 2019–2020. His works (Sadighian 2019) and (Sadighian 2020) explore the possibility of using deep reinforcement learning to learn how to manage positions on the limit order book based on feedback evaluated in terms of profits and losses. Unfortunately, the results have not shown an ability to provide significant and reliable profits.

In this work, we have tried to implement the principles of "purposeful activity" (Vityaev 2015) and "experiential learning" (Kolonin 2022) as a "Narrow Artificial General Intelligence" (Narrow AGI) solution applied to financial active portfolio management domain. We follow the concept of an agent constantly building and updating its model of the surrounding environment, as well as trying to use this model in order to evaluate different behavioral strategies relying on episodic memories, applying the "hypothetically winning" strategies to the real operational environments as it has been attempted in (Raheman et al. 2021a) relying on simulation and backtesting framework presented in (Raheman et al. 2021b).

2 Adaptive Multi-Strategy Agent

The Adaptive Multi-Strategy Agent (AMSA) for market making approach anticipates that no reliable prediction of the market price can be made at all, due to the volatile nature of the crypto markets. That might be one of the explanations as to why no "successful stories" are attributed to attempts to apply machine learning to the market making in crypto finance. In turn, the architecture suggested in current work ensures adaptability of an agent of algorithmic market making to ongoing stochastic changes of the price as well as overall market conditions with different trends ("bear", "bull", "flat") overlapped with different levels of volatility ("high", "low") in an unpredictable manner. The concept introduced in (Raheman et al. 2021a) provides no strategy of its own using a pre-configured set of multiple agents with individual strategies instead. From the exchange perspective, it may behave like a single "chair" agent, employing "macro-strategy" while the latter might be executed in total by multiple "micro-strategies" run by its "subordinate" agents.

2.1 Key Principles

The suggested market-making architecture is intended for autonomous operations on the financial crypto-market. It is expected to perform purposeful activity: maximizing profits and minimizing losses given the current market conditions. This is measured as profits and losses recognized for agents running specific strategies as points in the multi-dimensional space of possible strategies where dimensions are the parameters such as bid/ask spread or limit order cancellation policy. At the same time, it refers to the historical data, involving all trades made on the particular trading pair in the recent past, as well as snapshots of the limit order book for the pair, using it to evaluate all imaginable strategies safely in the "virtual" backtesting environment as discussed in (Raheman et al. 2021b).

AMSA main features are:

- Implementing no strategy of its own.
- Providing real trading (real exchange) and backtesting (on historical market data) environment for child agents.
- Making all limit orders issued by "subordinate" agents on behalf of the "chair" AMSA agent.
- Keeping track of all orders made by the "subordinate" agents, evaluating their performances.
- Performing time management by splitting the market making period into execution/evaluation periods.
- Calculate total profits/losses for each period.

2.2 Implementation Details

There are two sets, or pools of agents, used by AMSA at the same time. One set operates with real money and another one is used for strategy evaluation on historical data (backtesting). AMSA implicitly uses three environments: a) for real market making, which is used to run all agents selected for current execution period; b) for idle agents who are not allowed to operate for real; c) one for internal backtesting containing clones of all agents in a) and b), running their strategies in a "virtual environment". Operations in real market making, backtesting, and virtual environments are performed simultaneously. Agents residing in the idle environment are not performing operations. Agents are moved between real market making (a) and idle (b) environments during assessment of their performances and selection at the end of each execution period. All agents are always involved in internal backtesting while only the best ones are involved in real trading.

2.3 Agent/Strategy Assessment and Selection

The selection or omission of an agent applies to the "micro-strategy" being implemented by the agent. Initial agent selection is made based on backtesting results applied to the historical interval one execution period long prior to the starting time of the first execution period. For all the subsequent periods, the evaluation is done on both real market making and backtesting environments. Agents showing positive return and "alpha" (i.e., excess return compared to the buy-and-hold "hodler" strategy, which means buying base asset at the beginning of the experiment and selling it at the end) due to their strategies are selected for the next period of real market making. The real market making period is skipped for those agents which do not satisfy agent selection policy. All agents are always used for backtesting.

2.4 Algorithm

The following algorithm is employed to run by the AMSA on every refresh (correspond-ing to simulation cycle interval) in place of the conventional order handling procedure and is just running and evaluating agents of different families implementing specific strategies as described further.

Algorithm 1. AMSA Algorithm

Input: Time, Price
Parameters: start_time, end_time, period, agents, real_env, backtest_env, inventory_history
Output: inventory_history
1: **if** time $= =$ start_time **then** # start of experiment
2: backtest(start_time-period, start_time) # initial
3:    period_start $=$ start_time.
4:    period_end $=$ start_time $+$ period_len
5: **if** time % period $= = 0$ **then** # end of period
6:    real_inventory $=$ count_totals(real_env).
7:    backtest_inventory $=$ count_totals(backtest_env)
8:    best_agents $=$ select_best(backtest_totals).
9:    real_env.agents $=$ best_agents
10:    period_start $=$ period_end
11: **for** agent **in** real_env.agents **do** # real market making
12:    agent.handle_orders() # create/cancel orders
13: **for** agent **in** backtest_env.agents **do** # back-testing
14:    agent.handle_orders() # create/cancel orders
15: **return** inventory_history

2.5 Inventory Sharing Policy

Initial inventory amounts are evenly shared between all agents for both backtesting and real market making. For subsequent periods, current inventory is evenly shared between all agents selected for real market-making while for backtesting total inventory amount stays the same equal to the initial amount, evenly shared between all agents.

3 Experimental Setup

3.1 Evaluation Environment

The evaluation environment for our experiments was backtesting by means of simulation of the conventional limit order book execution policy and relying on historical trading data including both raw trades and snapshots of the LOB, while including 50 levels of bid orders and 50 levels of ask orders as well as Open-High-Low-Close-Volume (OHLCV) frames. All snapshots and frames were available with time granularities of 1 min and 1 h, corresponding to respective simulation intervals. The backtesting framework described in (Raheman et al. 2021b) and (Raheman et al. 2021a) was simulating Binance limit order book execution policy against the historical trades based on each of the simulation intervals. In turn, the order book simulation was involving modification of the historical order book snapshots with the limit orders created by the agents involved in the simulation, so some of the historical trades were executed against actual historical LOB positions while others were "intercepted" by the "injected" positions owned by market making agents involved in simulation.

3.2 Three Types of Historical Market Intervals

We were running the experiments on historical market data on BTC/USDT trading pair available from binance.com and cryptotick.com with time granularities corresponding to target experimental simulation intervals (1 h, 1 min). Three BTC/USDT historical periods of different types of market conditions were chosen for AMSA test runs: "bull" low volatile in October 2020, "bull" highly volatile in January 2021 and "bear" in May 2021.

3.3 Three Sets of Market Making Agents and Hodler

Three families of market making agents were selected to be AMSA working force in the experiments: Base agents implementing basic strategies, NIOX agents, and Hummingbot agents. A collection of agents belonging to a given family being controlled by a "chair" AMSA agent might be thought of as a regular/irregular bid/ask "order grid" (may be called "staggered orders") with selective creation/cancellation of the orders on respective price levels of the limit order book. For each of the experiments, "chair" AMSA agent was credited 0.1 BTC plus the same amount in USDT according to the market price at the beginning of the experiment. These amounts have been evenly distributed across inventories of the "subordinate" agents.

"Base" agents used in our experiments are described in the earlier work (Raheman et al. 2021a). Agents of this family may have only one limit order at a time on either the ask or bid side of the spread. A new order is created only once the current open limit order is filled. Base agents configuration may differ in bid/ask spread (five ranges) and order cancellation policies (never, always, opposite). The "never" policy means that the limit order is never cancelled until it is completely filled. The "always" policy means that the existing order is always cancelled on every agent refresh time (1 min or 1 h). The "opposite" policy means the current order is always cancelled when the price move changes direction. Bid/ask spreads are symmetric, so percent of the spread is the same for bid and ask orders. 27 configurations were used in our experiments in total.

NIOX agents were implemented as part of closed-source project reproducing the market making strategy described at https://autonio.gitbook.io/autonio-foundation/niox-suite/maker. The strategies of these agents were different only in bid/ask spreads (asymmetric or skewed bid/ask spread), as the previously ran experiments have shown this parameter has turned to be the key drive for profits and losses for agents of this kind under different market conditions. 50 agent configurations were used in total.

Hummingbot agents were implemented as a closed-source clone of the open-source Hummingbot "Pure Market Making" strategy, adapted to deal with the simulation and backtesting environment. Source code of the Hummingbot is publicly available at https:// github.com/hummingbot/hummingbot. The Hummingbot agent grid had 6 by 6 bid/ask levels (0.3, 0.5, 0.8, 1.3, 3.4, 5.5). 36 agent configurations were used in total.

Hodler agent As an extra single configuration implementing the "hodler" ("buy and hold") strategy was used in each of the experiments for reference. This strategy involved just buying as much as possible of base currency at the beginning of the simulation and selling it in the end.

3.4 Experimental Configurations

There were multiple experimental setups ran for each of the three respective market types (bull low volatile, bull highly volatile and bear), for each of the three families of agents, for different time granularities (1 min and 1 h) and for four different durations of execution/evaluation periods (1, 2, 3 and 5 days), as shown on Fig. 1.

4 Experimental results

4.1 Performance Comparison by Interval

The results were evaluated by assessing the return of investments (ROI), as shown for the case of 1-min based simulation (backtesting) interval in Fig. 1 on the next page. Regardless of period, all three agent families have shown positive alpha in case of bear market. Bull highly volatile market brings negative return and alpha for Base and NIOX agents while Hummingbot stays positive regardless of period. Bull non-volatile market results are highly dependent on period (growing with the period durability) for Hummingbot, being constantly negative for Base and NIOX.

In case of 1-h based simulation Base agent configuration rarely shows positive alpha and appears highly dependent on period duration regardless of type of market. NIOX shows positive alpha for bear market with slight period dependency while remains negative for bull non-volatile market, on bear highly volatile market its alpha grows with the period duration. Hummingbot shows positive alpha for most periods in all markets, mostly successful for volatile market.

4.2   Performance Comparison by Market Making Agent

Bull Non-Volatile Market

Period	Hodler ROI, %		Base makers ROI, %		NIOX makers ROI, %		Hummingbot makers ROI, %	
	Hours	Minutes	Hours	Minutes	Hours	Minutes	Hours	Minutes
1	12.90	12.90	4.67	−8.14	−26.45	−24.07	12.55	−3.46
2	12.90	12.90	16.49	−5.70	−25.90	−25.65	21.61	4.99
3	12.90	12.90	−3.08	−14.29	−27.02	−27.36	7.55	11.19
5	12.90	12.90	2.06	−5.53	−24.71	−21.73	11.33	13.61

Bull Highly-Volatile Market

Period	Hodler ROI, %		Base makers ROI, %		NIOX makers ROI, %		Hummingbot makers ROI, %	
	Hours	Minutes	Hours	Minutes	Hours	Minutes	Hours	Minutes
1	9.20	9.20	37.14	−21.60	−12.88	−16.47	57.09	27.36
2	9.20	9.20	−7.35	−16.99	−7.31	13.67	26.83	18.75
3	9.20	9.20	−5.51	−59.47	17.89	10.51	42.62	18.86
5	9.20	9.20	42.82	−17.65	58.16	5.09	76.80	57.80

Bear Market

Period	Hodler ROI, %		Base makers ROI, %		NIOX makers ROI, %		Hummingbot makers ROI, %	
	Hours	Minutes	Hours	Minutes	Hours	Minutes	Hours	Minutes
1	−19.10	−19.10	2.45	3.03	34.23	35.06	6.79	26.46
2	−19.10	−19.10	−5.95	23.20	35.99	34.60	27.07	40.11
3	−19.10	−19.10	8.71	52.19	41.20	48.69	35.88	45.11
5	−19.10	−19.10	6.99	66.16	34.48	46.63	48.59	51.52

Base Makers are consistently effective on bear market, showing much better result on minutely data. Only 2-day period on minute data has positive alpha for bull non-volatile market. Bull volatile market is a complete loss on minutes while depends on period duration in case of hours.

NIOX Is constantly losing on bull non-volatile market, unstable on bull volatile market and has a good performance on bear market for both hours and minutes.

Hummingbot Has constantly positive alpha for bull highly volatile and bear market while appears unstable, but rarely negative alpha on bull non-volatile market.

4.3 Possible Experimental Problems

The smaller the chosen period, the larger the market trend discrepancy. Because of the noisiness of the price signal, short periods may represent quite different market trend so the agent set tuned on previous period signal may poorly behave on the next one.

Hummingbot in its current implementation has poor control over base asset spent which may cause larger earnings on bear market, compared to the competing agent families.

NIOX agent was used with irregular grid skewed spreads which may be the cause of a good performance only for bear market.

5 Further Improvements

Given the experiments that we have run, and experience gained while developing the infrastructure for the experiments, the following improvements can be considered.

A denser regular bid/ask spread grid may be implemented for more precise strategy selection. In the above-mentioned experiments, grid density was limited by the available computational resources while better AMSA performance could be expected with a more precisely tuned bid/ask grid with more fine-grained levels.

Hanging orders within the period may be involved in the experiments. Hanging orders were only used by Base agent setup but were disabled for both NIOX and Hummingbot configurations.

Hanging orders throughout the periods may be implemented. Long-lasting orders are not currently implemented so even if an agent is performing successfully in the previous period and re-selected for the next period, it has all of its orders canceled at the period boundary. Keeping the orders hanging across the periods may improve the return for winning agents and increase the overall performance.

Base/quote order amount grid might be finer grained as maximum available inventories were used in the current setup, while in some circumstances smaller bid/ask orders may improve the overall return.

Agent selection policy tuning may be improved. As of now, agents achieving positive return and alpha during the previous interval backtesting and real trading are selected for the next round of trades in the current AMSA version. More sophisticated selection algorithm may improve the overall return.

As an extension or variation of the above while running the AMSA in real trading environments, front testing (also called "paper trading") can be performed on live market data instead of backtesting on historical data. This could be done following the same simulation of the LOB execution as we have described but might be more realistic being run on live data in sync with the real market making.

The inventory funds distribution policy might be changed to uneven (prioritized or weighted) among the agents involved in real market making, giving more funds to more successful agents can be explored and one of the measures as it might increase the overall returns because of greater contribution of more successful strategies.

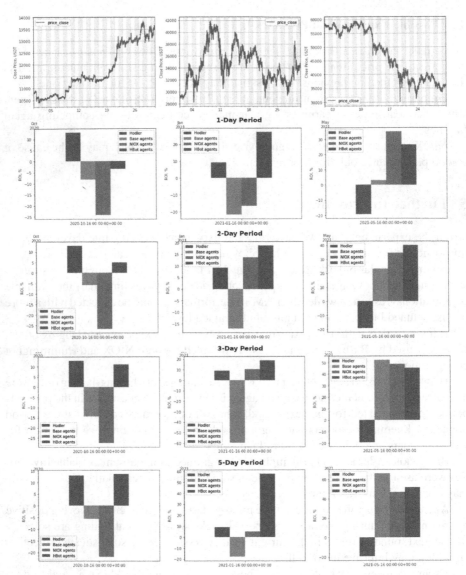

Fig. 1. Results (ROI %) of minute-based simulation (backtesting) of three agent families compared to "Hodler" across three different market types with different durations of evaluation periods.

6 Conclusion and Future Work

We have presented the architecture of adaptive multi-strategy agent (AMSA) for autonomous market making as a Narrow AGI solution applied to financial domain. The architecture has been evaluated in a market making simulation framework by means of backtesting of the limit order book operations relying on full scope of historical market data for BTC/USDT trading pair on Binance crypto exchange during three months with different market conditions with different time granularities.

The evaluation has been applied to three different families of market making agents. One of the families (namely, open-source Hummingbot implementation) was found to be capable of providing both non-negative return and "alpha" (excess return over conservative "hodling" strategy) across all evaluated market conditions.

Our further work will be dedicated to exploring the applicability of our market making AMSA architecture for real market making relying on Hummingbot and extending our studies on other trading pairs and exchanges.

References

Avellaneda, M., Stoikov, S.: High-frequency trading in a limit order book. Quantitative Finance **8**(3), 217–224 (2008)

Guéant, O., Lehalle, C.-A., Fernandez-Tapia, J.: Dealing with the inventory risk: a solution to the market making problem. Math. Finan. Econ. **7**(4), 477–507 (2012)

Tsantekidis, A.: Using deep learning for price prediction by exploiting stationary limit order book features. arXiv:1810.09965 [cs. LG] 23 Oct 2018

Zhang, Z., Zohren, S.: Stephen roberts. deep reinforcement learning for trading. arXiv:1911.10107 [q-fin.CP] (2019)

Ganesh, S., et al.: Reinforcement learning for market making in a multi-agent dealer market. arXiv: 1911.05892 [q-fin.TR], 14 Nov 2019

Chen, Y., Liu, K., Xie, Y., Mingyu, H.: Financial trading strategy system based on machine learning. Math. Prob. Eng. **2020**, 1–13 (2020). https://doi.org/10.1155/2020/3589198

Sadighian, J.: Deep reinforcement learning in cryptocurrency market making. arXiv:1911.08647 [q-fin.TR] 20 Nov 2019

Sadighian, J.: Extending deep reinforcement learning frameworks in Cryptocurrency market making. arXiv:2004.06985 [q-fin.TR] 15 Apr 2020

Vityaev, E.E.: Purposefulness as a principle of brain activity. Anticipation: learning from the past. In: Nadin, M. (ed.) Cognitive Systems Monographs, vol. 25, Chapter No.: 13, pp. 231–254. Springer (2015)

Kolonin, A.: Neuro-symbolic architecture for experiential learning in discrete and functional environments. In: Goertzel, B., Iklé, M., Potapov, A. (eds.) AGI 2021. LNCS (LNAI), vol. 13154, pp. 106–115. Springer, Cham (2022). https://doi.org/10.1007/978-3-030-93758-4_12

Raheman, A., Kolonin, A., Ansari, I.: Adaptive multi-strategy market making agent. In: Goertzel, B., Iklé, M., Potapov, A. (eds.) AGI 2021. LNCS (LNAI), vol. 13154, pp. 204–209. Springer, Cham (2022). https://doi.org/10.1007/978-3-030-93758-4_21

Raheman, A., Kolonin, A., Goertzel, B., Hegyközi, G., Ansari, I.: Architecture of automated crypto-finance agent. In: 2021b International Symposium on Knowledge, Ontology, and Theory (KNOTH), pp. 10–14 (2021b). https://doi.org/10.1109/KNOTH54462.2021b. 9686345

Toward a Comprehensive List of Necessary Abilities for Human Intelligence, Part 1: Constructing Knowledge

Jerald D. Kralik[✉]

Korea Advanced Institute of Science and Technology (KAIST), Daejeon 34141, South Korea
jerald.kralik@gmail.com

Abstract. In [1], Adams et al. chart a roadmap toward the grand AI vision, with human-level (or greater) intelligence as destination. To that end, in this and a companion paper [2], I take one of the next steps they outline, to "refine the list of specific competency areas" in human cognition. It is argued that we should move toward a comprehensive list of all required abilities to make clearer what is known, unknown, and what the next steps should be, such as resolving how abilities piece together into the larger-scale puzzle of general intelligence. This paper concentrates roughly on the first half of cognitive processing, from initial input to knowledge construction and memory storage (including, for example, emotion, perception, attention, memory, and knowledge construction processes, such as reasoning, imagination, and simulation); with the second paper on the action-based second half that uses the knowledge for constructive outcomes.

Keywords: Emotion · Perception · Attention · Memory · Generative knowledge · Reasoning · Imagination · Creativity · Simulation · Artificial intelligence · Cognition

1 Introduction

Even with the ultimate goal of understanding *general intelligence* in its purest form, that is, even beyond what humans achieve and how they achieve it, the human mind/brain cannot be avoided, as it is the best example of – and in fact the only existence proof for – our level of ability. It is undeniably state of the art. Any field interested in intelligence, therefore, should wish to characterize it (a) to obtain insight into how general intelligence can be achieved, whether as a sufficient solution (how can be) or as a necessary one (how must be – at least, potentially, in some aspects); and, minimally, (b) to compare alternative developments to it, to assess their distance. Thus, it makes sense to have detailed, comprehensive information about human general intelligence as a roadmap toward artificial general intelligence (AGI) [1, 3].

Following the AGI *narrow* versus *general* distinction, with narrow enabling domain-specific capacity, general ability in psychology is typically captured in the concepts of *intelligence* overall or in *higher-level* cognition. But regardless, even highest-level

B. Goertzel et al. (Eds.): AGI 2022, LNAI 13539, pp. 260–270, 2023.
https://doi.org/10.1007/978-3-031-19907-3_27

cognition requires and builds from basic cognitive abilities that span from perception to action (especially given the tight coupling of processes and systems throughout the human mind/brain). Therefore, as realized in [1, 3], the AGI path forward requires consideration of the entire core set of abilities for human cognition in general (with an eye toward its necessity for higher cognition and general intelligence). To this end, then, the AGI Roadmap Workshop provided an initial list of human cognitive abilities or 'competencies' [1, 3]. Although the list provided is excellent, which I build from here, as they said, it was nonetheless considered intuitive and necessarily lacking, given their sense that a complete list may be "beyond the scope of current science".

Contrary to this view, however, I believe there is enough evidence from psychology, neuroscience, and related fields (e.g., AI, machine learning) to attempt to move toward a comprehensive list. And even as [3] rightly points out that different people may all generate different lists, I yet believe it serves the community best to share such attempts at comprehensive lists, to provide a richer set of possibilities for AGI researchers to consider, as well as help lead to a convergent one [4]. Moreover, once listed explicitly, it becomes easier to identify larger patterns or expose omissions, leading either way to more efficient advancement. In fact, included in [1]'s list of next steps is to "refine the list of specific competency areas", which I attempt here.

I do so in a set of eight tables: four in the current paper, from initial input and system activation to knowledge construction; and then in the companion paper [2], four more, covering knowledge using. The papers may also be seen as roughly divided with respect to human neocortex: i.e., sensory-perceptual processing to knowledge construction and maintenance in posterior cortex, and more active thinking and action regions of frontal cortex (with areas like posterior parietal cortex transitional).

Together, the eight tables form a comprehensive list of human cognitive abilities (or competencies), and thereby general intelligence. It results from numerous references that cannot all be cited, with special emphasis on collating the most well-established processes from leading textbooks in the relevant fields: especially psychology (multiple subfields), cognitive neuroscience, AI, and machine learning (e.g., [5–13]).

Finally, we might ask whether such a compendium already exists. Textbooks in particular generally do this, yet they typically take some specialized perspective, remaining therefore incomplete. As well, psychology and neuroscience have generally been loath to consider a comprehensive, more global perspective (as being potentially too daunting and premature), leaving the task to those requiring it, such as metacognitive researchers (who must ask, e.g., what systems in the brain are being monitored and controlled), roboticists, and those ambitious enough to accept the grand AI (now AGI) challenge.

2 Necessary Abilities for Human Cognition

The topics across the two papers are organized following a rough input-to-output structure, with higher level descriptors for general orientation (I-XII), and numbering of main abilities (1–29). Under each ability I list key specifics, such as types, component processes, and other characteristics. Obvious and apparent cases of overlap indeed exist and are inevitable since I err on the side of explicitness, especially in cases where researchers have carved out an active niche, including the study of comparable topics under different more general ones (e.g., generalization and discrimination, required most everywhere). Listed together they should help clarify where further work is especially needed, to help establish the most fundamental abilities, better resolve their edges, and determine how best to assemble them. Finally, only brief comments can be made, with the hope that most items in the tables are self-evident enough, and/or can otherwise be readily found in multiple sources like the ones cited. We begin then with perhaps a first set of counterintuitive necessary processes, listed in Table 1.

This first table may appear an odd start, but it is becoming clearer how fundamentally integrated the human mind/brain is and how even the highest levels of cognitive processing are affected by the lowest (e.g., arousal functions) [14–21] – quite simply, we need to care, and we seem to need to *feel it*, to truly understand something, discussed more below [10, 22]. We should note that predominantly, though not always, neurochemistry (as neurotransmitters, neuromodulators, or hormones: e.g., acetylcholine, dopamine, endorphins, androgens) plays a fundamental role (in items 1–4) [18]. For arousal, more than just trivially (e.g., must turn on power to use), its subfunctions infuse neural systems with ease of processing and effort, influencing capacity, processing speed, thinking deliberativeness, motivation, valuation, etc. Consider, for example, how caffeine influences thinking ability (blocking adenosine receptors, thereby enhancing dopamine's arousal and concentration effects) [23]. For '4. EMFF', specific definitions change with author, but all concepts are fundamental and require some operational definition, with these common [10, 22]. Together they arise from an intricately coupled set of stacked systems, gradient like, distinguished significantly by the brain subregions (e.g., brainstem, midbrain, hypothalamus, limbic, and higher cortical regions) and neurochemistry, arising from typically lower regions (e.g., midbrain, hypothalamus & pituitary) and infused into mid and higher ones (especially limbic regions, such as the ventral striatum of basal ganglia and deeper prefrontal areas) or as hormones directly into the bloodstream [10, 18]. These details provide a sense of the rich relationships of lowest to highest level processes, becoming more appreciated, though not fully yet. Only then, when the system has cause to, once it cares, it perceives and attends (Table 2).

Perception is often divided into early, middle, and late processes or stages, and in any case, from low to high, with the latter seamlessly transitioning to more centralized cognitive or thinking processes. Indeed, perception itself involves integrated attentional and more centralized processes (such as memory access), with machine learning, neural-network modeling, and cognitive neuroscience helping to better appreciate this and flesh-out details (e.g., [10]). For internal modalities, body signals lead to perception of state, sensations, emotion, feeling (thus overlapping with caring processes). For attention, two general systems are recognized as listed [10, 24–26]. From perception and attention, then, we come to knowing: memory and knowledge (Table 3).

For memory, I have listed the well-established types as in [1, 3], as well as main general processes [5, 10, 27]; then for stored knowledge, detailed descriptions of its key concepts, characteristics, and processes. Under *General 1* are popular general models in psychology, most clearly for categories, but also beyond this [5, 6, 10, 28, 29]; *General 2* lists basic organizational structures [6, 30]; and *General 3* the main types of content elements actively recognized and studied [6, 31–33]. *Content domains* have

Table 1. Necessary abilities for human cognition: the need to care.

I. Caring

1. Arousal & State (internal)

Processes, State (internal):
- Arousal as activating system:
  - Wakefulness
  - Alertness, Readiness
  - Nervous system energy level, power
- State: Sense of physiological condition, from all arousal processes

2. Sensation

Types:
- Pain
- Touch
- Proprioception, kinesthesis, body state

3. Motivation: Drive, Desire

Types:
- Affect-based motivation 1.0 (needs, drives):
  - Intake: fluids, food
  - Other homeostasis: temperature control, health
  - Avoiding threats, germs
  - Mating and sexual: attraction, competition
  - Parenting and family
  - Social: cooperative, competitive
  - Sleep
  - Life-cycle based
- Affect-based motivation 2.0: desires: wanting, liking/disliking

Triggers/Signals/Input stimuli:
- Internal: homeostasis signals (e.g., hunger)
- External:
  - Instinctive value (+/-) of state/stimuli
  - Pavlovian value (+/-) of state/stimuli associated with reward

Processes:
- Pavlovian conditioning: state/stimuli associated with reward
- Operant/Instrumental conditioning: action associated with reward
- Related: Self-Control of lower-drives, desires, temptations (next)

(continued)

Table 1. (*continued*)

4. **Emotion, Mood, Feelings, Feeling**

Types & Processes:
- Emotion: Produces shorter-term feeling (with lower physiological response) to stimulus
  - Basic: surprise, fear, anger, happiness, sadness, disgust
- More complex: e.g., pride, embarrassment
- Mood: middle-term feeling, higher-level general (internal) state
- Feelings: longer-term feeling (with lower physiological response) toward stimulus (e.g., "I love her/him.")
- Feeling (and sensations): higher-order sense, appraisal of 1-4 (e.g., "How are you feeling?")
- Communication:
  - Nonverbal expressions
  - Perceiving/interpreting
- Emotion control (see below)

---

received considerable attention in multiple fields, including comparative and developmental psychology, with substantial evidence for them as actual organizing ontologies for knowledge and memory – even potentially as innate priors [7, 21, 34–37]. *Management processes* are a representative list of necessary and important data management processes in the human mind/brain (also being a good example of the current and perhaps necessary overlap with other main processes listed in the tables). Table 4, then, addresses how this knowledge is constructed.

Knowledge creation includes main processes actively studied both with respect to mind and brain, but also in machine learning (where work highlights the significance of the specific processes, and provides more critical details) [5–7, 11–13]. *Generalization* and *discrimination* are separated from *abstraction* and *reduction*, with the former two as potentially more lower-level and generic, and the latter two focused more on hierarchical relationships and levels of analysis [6, 21, 38]. *Symbolic processing* is widely recognized as a hallmark of human cognition – as we continue to appreciate its power beyond specific domains such as language. Of course, symbolic-level models have appreciated it; but as subsymbolic approaches accelerate, their interface to the symbolic becomes even more critical (with layered architectures and techniques such as vector quantization – essentially labeling vectors – promising approaches [13, 39]). *Reasoning* highly depends on one's operational definition of it, since if broad enough, could subsume most all the more central information processes. However, in psychology, for instance, it has come to represent more obvious cases of (typically) sequential logical construction and inference (e.g., transitivity: if $A = B$, $B = C$, $A = ?$). Even then, there are many types of reasoning, as shown [6]. *Modeling* is listed separately, with 'mental models' a defined area of psychological research, as well as more directly contacting related work such as in machine learning (e.g., system identification) and social processing (e.g., mind reading) [6, 9, 12, 13].

Table 2. Necessary abilities for human cognition: perceiving and attending.

II. Perceiving

   5. Perception: Low (Sensory) to High (Recognition/Identification)

     Modalities:
- External stimuli/input: Vision, Audition (Hearing), Smell (Odor), Somatosensory (Touch), Taste, Cross-modal
- Internal stimuli/input: Proprioception, Kinesthesis; Homeostasis/drive-based: hunger, thirst, temperature, sexual, parenting, social

     General Processes & Characteristics:
- Filtering, amplifying, search, selecting, constructing
- Dimensionality reduction; transformations; convolution
- Classification (e.g., template matching)
- Clustering (more unsupervised)
- Discrimination & Generalization
- Moving toward categories, concepts, relations, systems of relations.

III. Attending

   6. Attention

     Systems:
- Stimulus-driven (bottom-up or exogenous)
- Goal-directed (top-down or endogenous)

     General Processes:
- Selecting, filtering, amplifying, search

Although potentially overlapping with others, and in any case necessary for many, as in [1, 2], *generative construction* is emphasized to catalog the mechanisms for active knowledge creation – with the most quintessentially human being *recursion* [1, 3, 6, 12, 13, 38, 40]. *Imagination* and *creative thinking* are also listed, with active research areas such as *creative cognition,* and the greater appreciation of being fundamentally critical for such things as building problem representations in the first place, and not only discovering but creating novel problem solutions [5, 14, 15, 31, 32, 41]. And *simulation* is highlighted as a fundamental means by which humans think about, plan, and imagine the world [6, 10].

Finally, knowledge construction is a dynamic and highly interactive set of processes also influenced by the act of using the knowledge – processes taken up in Part 2 [2].

Table 3. Necessary abilities for human cognition: memory and knowledge.

IV. Knowing

7. Memory

Types:
- Implicit (long-term, unconscious)
- Procedural (a form of implicit that underlies habits, routines)
- Episodic (event-based)
- Semantic (explicit knowledge/fact-based)
- Short-term (as buffer, with no obvious manipulation)
- Working (short-term, with manipulation, conscious awareness)

General Processes:
- Encoding
- Retrieval
- Restructuring
- Forgetting
- Suppressing, repressing

8. Stored Knowledge (contents of memory)

Representation/organization/ontologies:
- General 1: templates; exemplar matching; levels of abstraction
- General 2: organization: graphs (e.g., tree: hierarchical; chains)
- General 3: features, objects, categories, concepts, relations, abstract relations; causal chains; systems of relations/chains; context; person; problems; events; event complexes; scripts
- Uncertain knowledge
- Values and beliefs
- ***Content Domains*:**
  - Physical:
    - physics (natural objects, movement)
    - space, time; object properties, dynamics, interactions
  - Biological (organismic) & (bio)chemical (cellular, molecular):
    - flora, fauna: as resources, threats (including germs, sickness, medicinal)
  - Social:
    - Individual & Group: cooperative, competitive/threats
    - More detail in [2]
  - Technical: Artifacts
  - Quantitative, relations, statistical

Management/manipulation/execution processes:
- Search, select, sort and 'data' organization
- Chunking, symbolic labeling & processing, cross-referencing
- See under perception, memory, metacognition

Table 4. Necessary abilities for human cognition: knowledge construction.

V.   Knowledge Construction

9.   Generalization & Discrimination

Characteristics & Processes:
- Recognizing/Isolating invariant structure
- Similarity matching (e.g., feature distance)
- Discrimination/Dissimilarity
- Regularization (i.e., methods to minimize overfitting)

10. Abstraction, Elaboration, Reduction

Processes:
- Recognizing/Building hierarchical relationships of entities and their features – and moving up and down these hierarchies
- Segmenting entities into subcomponents (e.g., parts, substance)
- Inferring/Creating unseen factors and relationships (e.g., cells, forces)
- Concept formation

11. Symbolic processing

Processes:
- Labeling denotive items
  - Externally: labeling/naming
  - Internally: internal representation label (e.g., vector quantization)
- Recognizing/Using symbols
- Verbal invention

12. Reasoning

General processes:
- Basic Logic
- Sequence modeling
- Inference
- Explanation; Argument
- Rule formation
- Using other rules, methods of thought (e.g., visuospatial)

Types:
- Associational (i.e., general relationships)
- Deductive (i.e., effects from causes)
- Inductive (general rule, principle, pattern from observations)
- Abductive (i.e., causes from effects)
- Causal (i.e., cause and effect identification and relationships)
- Analogical (similarity, esp. of relationships, across content domains)

(continued)

Table 4. (*continued*)

- Deontic (i.e., rules, obligations)
- Fictive ('what if?')
- Probabilistic
- In specific content domains: e.g., physical, social, quantitative

13. Modeling: Identifying patterns, structure

General processes:
- System identification/State estimation
- Structure learning (like of graphs or trees)
- Latent variable models
- Feature discovery
- Function approximation/identification (e.g., regression)

14. Generative construction (and deconstruction) and execution/control

General processes:
- Used throughout cognitive abilities list
- Sequences; hierarchy (i.e., all graph structures)
- Recursion
- Restructuring for consistency
- Formulating beliefs
- Specific content domains:
  - Physical: tool use, manufacture (from tools to technology)
  - Psychological & Social: Modeling self and others' minds
  - Other social construction: e.g., group structures, communities; language (and grammar)

15. Imagination, Creative thinking

General processes:
- Figurative: creative tropes: e.g., metaphor, associations (fiction, humor)
- Originality: combinations; novel conceptions, creations (some art)
- Examples: Philosophy, Mathematics, time travel, discovery

16. Simulation

General processes:
- Forward, backward in time
- Visual imagery, transformations (e.g., rotation)
- Internal theater as mind's eye (or ear, etc.)
- With other processes, such as working memory, fictive reasoning

---

3   Are All Necessary for Intelligence and More Than Obviously so?

For humans the answer appears a resounding, 'yes'. Not that all are necessary in all or most cases; but it is proposed that in some form, full human capability requires them, with broader and tighter integration than typically expected. For example, 'why' and 'how' human cognition is carried out is continuously influenced by the "I. Care" processes: e.g., mood and arousal state influencing which level and type of processing conducted, such as heuristic versus more deliberative reasoning and problem-solving processes [10, 14, 22, 29]. One way to imagine this are days (such as weekends) when one's own work looks 'Greek' and difficult to decipher; when a regular trip (such as to office) feels particularly far or near; the ambition of mornings versus late evenings; or after a strong cup of coffee. Moreover, perception requires memory and knowledge interpretation, in turn influenced by the problems to solve, actions to take, and so on; thus, naturally spanning all main components of intelligence. One may, nonetheless, question the necessity of some for artificial systems – e.g., why do they need to care if their algorithms reflect our interests? [2] returns to this once the entire list is complete.

4 Conclusion

The current set of cognitive abilities – caring, perceiving, attending, knowledge, and knowledge creation – already shines light on remarkable abilities of humans, including and perhaps especially to recognize and identify where meaning actually lies: beneath the apparent, perceptual surface. And not only to envision this otherwise hidden world in the mind's eye, but, together with the abilities in *Part 2*, create our own versions in the shared, external world – thereby testing out and ultimately thriving by our knowledge, inferences, flights of imagination.

References

1. Adams, S.S., et al.: Mapping the landscape of human-level artificial general intelligence. AI Magazine **33**(1), 25–41 (2012)
2. Kralik, J.D.: Toward a comprehensive list of necessary abilities for human intelligence, Part 2: Using Knowledge. In: Proc. 15th Conf. on Artificial General Intelligence (2022)
3. Goertzel, B.: Artificial general intelligence: concept, state of the art, and future prospects. Journal of Artificial General Intelligence **5**(1), 1–46 (2014)
4. Laird, J.E., Lebiere, C., Rosenbloom, P.S.: A Standard Model of the Mind. AI Magazine **38**(4), 13–26 (2017)
5. Reisberg, D.: Cognition. WW Norton & Co., New York (2021)
6. Holyoak, K.J., Morrison, R.G. (eds.) Oxford Handbook of Thinking and Reasoning. Oxford University Press (2012)
7. Goswami, U.: Cognitive development. Routledge, London (2008)
8. Mazur, J.E.: Learning and Behavior. Routledge, Abingdon (2016)
9. Aronson, E., Wilson, T.D., Akert, R.M., Sommers, S.R.: Social Psychology. Pearson, NYC, New York (2018)
10. Gazzaniga, M.S., Ivry, R.B., Mangun, G.R.: Cognitive Neuroscience. Norton, New York (2019)
11. Russell, S., Norvig, P.: Artificial Intelligence. Prentice Hall, Upper Saddle River (2020)
12. Marsland, S.: Machine Learning. CRC Press, Boca Raton (2015)
13. Murphy, K.P.: Machine Learning. The MIT Press, Cambridge, Mass (2012)
14. LeDoux, J.: Rethinking the emotional brain. Neuron **73**(4), 653–676 (2012)

15. Levy, D.J., Glimcher, P.W.: The root of all value: a neural common currency for choice. Current Opinion in Neurobiology **22**(6), 1027–1038 (2012)
16. Berridge, K.C.: 'Liking' and "wanting" food rewards: Brain substrates and roles in eating disorders. Physiol. Behav. **97**(5), 537–550 (2009)
17. Glimcher, P.W., Fehr, E.: Neuroeconomics. Academic Press, Oxford (2014)
18. Kandel, E.R., Koester, J., Mack, S.H., Siegelbaum, S.A.: Principles of Neural Science. McGraw Hill, New York (2021)
19. Jang, H., Jung, K., Jeong, J., Park, S.K., Kralik, J.D., Jeong, J.: Nucleus accumbens shell moderates preference bias during voluntary choice behavior. Soc Cogn Affect Neurosci **12**(9), 1428–1436 (2017)
20. Kralik, J.D., Xu, E.R., Knight, E.J., Khan, S.A., Levine, W.J.: When less is more: evolutionary origins of the affect heuristic. PLoS ONE **7**(10), e46240 (2012)
21. Kralik, J.D.: Architectural design of mind & brain from an evolutionary perspective. In: Proc. AAAI Fall Sym. Standard Model Mind (2017)
22. Damasio, A.: Feeling & Knowing. Pantheon, New York (2021)
23. Meyer, J.S., Quenzer, L.F.: Psychopharmacology. Oxford University Press, Oxford (2019)
24. Corbetta, M., Shulman, G.L.: Control of goal-directed and stimulus-driven attention in the brain. Nat Rev Neuro. **3**(3), 201–215 (2002)
25. Messinger, A., Lebedev, M.A., Kralik, J.D., Wise, S.P.: Multitasking of attention and memory functions in the primate prefrontal cortex. Journal of Neuroscience **29**(17), 5640–5653 (2009)
26. Jung, K., Jeong, J., Kralik, J.D.: A computational model of attention control in multi-attribute, context-dependent decision making. Front. Comput. Neurosci. **13** (2019)
27. Boland, R., Verduin, M.L.: Synopsis of Psychiatry. Wolters Kluwer, Philadelphia (2022)
28. Rosch, E.: Principles of categorization. In: Rosch, L. (ed.) Cognition and Categorization, pp. 27–48 (1978)
29. Kahneman, D.: Thinking, Fast and Slow. Farrar, Straus and Giroux, New York (2011)
30. Tenenbaum, J.B., Kemp, C., Griffiths, T.L., Goodman, N.D.: How to grow a mind: statistics, structure, and abstraction. Science **331**(6022), 1279–1285 (2011)
31. Herrnstein, R.J.: Levels of stimulus control: a functional approach. Cognition **37**(1), 133–166 (1990)
32. Sampson, W.W.L., Khan, S.A., Nisenbaum, E.J., Kralik, J.D.: Abstraction promotes creative problem-solving in rhesus monkeys. Cognition **176**, 53–64 (2018)
33. Lim, S., Yoon, S., Kwon, J., Kralik, J.D., Jeong, J.: Retrospective evaluation of sequential events and the influence of preference-dependent working memory: a computational examination. Front. Comput. Neurosci. **14** (2020)
34. Wynne, C.D.L., Udell, M.A.R.: Animal Cognition. Palgrave Macmillan, London (2013)
35. Tomasello, M., Call, J.: Primate Cognition. Oxford University Press, Oxford (1997)
36. Buss, D.M.: Evolutionary Psychology. Routledge, Abingdon (2019)
37. Carey, S., Spelke, E.: Domain-specific knowledge and conceptual change. In: Hirschfeld, L.A., Gelman, S.A. (eds.) Mapping the Mind. New York, pp. 169–200 (1994).
38. Kralik, J.D.: Core high-level cognitive abilities derived from hunter-gatherer shelter building. In: presented at the International Conference on Cognitive Modeling, pp. 49–54 (2018)
39. Doumas, L.A.A., Hummel, J.E.: Computational models of higher cognition. In: Holyoak, K.J., Morrison, R.G. (eds.) The Oxford Handbook of Thinking and Reasoning, pp. 52–66. Oxford University Press, Oxford (2012)
40. Gross, R.: Being Human. Hodder Education, London (2012)
41. Kralik, J.D., Mao, T., Cheng, Z., Ray, L.E.: Modeling incubation and restructuring for creative problem solving in robots. Robotics and Autonomous Systems **86**, 162–173 (2016)

Toward a Comprehensive List of Necessary Abilities for Human Intelligence, Part 2: Using Knowledge

Jerald D. Kralik[✉]

Korea Advanced Institute of Science and Technology (KAIST), Daejeon 34141, South Korea
jerald.kralik@gmail.com

Abstract. One of the next steps outlined by [1] in their roadmap toward artificial general intelligence (AGI) is to "refine the list of specific competency areas" in human cognition, providing the keys to human intelligence, ultimately unlocking general intelligence. To that end, here, and in a companion paper [2], I advance toward a more comprehensive list of the necessary abilities for human cognition. The first paper focused roughly on the first half of cognitive processing, from initial input to knowledge construction and memory storage; and this second paper completes the process, with the more action-based second half of using the knowledge for constructive outcomes, and the outcomes as feedback for knowledge updating. It is hoped that the additional refinement will further clarify what we know, and reveal clues for realizing and combining the abilities to move toward AI's grand goal of artificial general intelligence.

Keywords: Prediction · Problem solving · Decision making · Planning · Learning · Development · Cognition · Metacognition · Social · Language · Consciousness

1 Introduction

To reach the high summit of human-level artificial intelligence (or beyond), it makes sense to examine human intelligence itself. In [1], the AGI Roadmap Workshop thus provided a first sketch of the main processes or 'competencies' of human cognition. They also put forth a call to "refine the list of specific competency areas" in human cognition, which this and the companion paper [2] take up. It is indeed hoped that as more refinement occurs others will be inspired to continue the process, and from it draw emergent patterns of how best to realize and combined abilities to accelerate advancement toward human-level AGI. The current paper focuses on the more explicit control processes of the mind/brain: those used to think, act, and learn [3–5].

2 Necessary Abilities for Human Cognition

As in the companion paper, the tables use simple descriptors for general orientation (I-XII, starting here at VI), with the main abilities numbered 1–29, continuing here at 17.

© The Author(s), under exclusive license to Springer Nature Switzerland AG 2023
B. Goertzel et al. (Eds.): AGI 2022, LNAI 13539, pp. 271–281, 2023.
https://doi.org/10.1007/978-3-031-19907-3_25

Under each ability I list key specifics, such as critical concepts, types, characteristics, and well-established component processes. Here again overlap exists (such as between problem solving and decision making) and are inevitable since I stand on the side of explicitness, to provide more opportunity to recognize not only weaknesses or omissions, but also apparent patterns when examining a more comprehensive list. Again, only brief additional comments can be made, with the hope that most items are self-evident or can otherwise be found in multiple sources including those cited. We begin with the first step in using the perceived information and relevant knowledge evoked, that of drawing conclusions about it ('VI. Concluding' in Table 1).

Judgment and *decision making* are well-established subfields particularly in behavioral economics and cognitive psychology, with *judgment* formulating conclusions from evidence (usually weak, incomplete, uncertain, probabilistic) [3, 4, 6]. I utilize this operational definition of judgment though it can resolve into other related processes and conceptualizations like conclusions drawn from logical inference, etc. A critical reason for knowledge processing is to anticipate environmental events, i.e., for *prediction*, which has received great attention [7, 8]. Judgment and prediction, though, are only of value when something can be done about it, setting up 'VII. Using'. Often this most directly entails *decision making*, of determining and selecting the best action or course of action (i.e., policy), given the current world state and immediate predictions about it [3, 4, 7–9]. Decision making has been actively studied particularly in the human sciences, with well-developed aspects listed. This includes the much-celebrated types of strategies employed, roughly categorized as relying on simpler 'heuristics and biases' versus more deliberative ones [6, 10, 11–13]. Key decision scenarios are also included, based on goals, actions, states, sequences (i.e., action policies), in the presence of others (multi-agent, game theory), and in the face of uncertainty and probabilities. Model-free versus model-based decisions capture cases where one simply responds given the current state ('at this stop I always go right') or based on expectations about what the actions bring ('I'm taking right to head home') [7, 8, 14].

Table 1. Necessary abilities for human cognition: conclusions drawn and optimal use.

VI. Concluding

    17. Judgment: i.e., evaluation of evidence for conclusion (about world state)

    General processes:
- Conclusions drawn from Part 1 [2] knowledge construction processes
- Probability estimation; Likelihood
- Other statistical assessments

    18. Prediction

    General processes:
- Expectation
- Prediction error

(*continued*)

Table 1. (continued)

VII. Using (the knowledge)

19. Problem Solving

General processes:
- Search
- Constraint satisfaction
- Sequential, goal-based
- Hierarchical: Subproblems
- Contains or converges to decision making

20. Decision Making

General processes:
- Valuation
- Choice

Concepts:
- Utility Theory
- Heuristics and Biases (key examples below):
  - Loss aversion
  - Alternative hypothesis (and base rate) neglect
  - Availability bias (to overvalue what comes most readily)
  - Attention bias (overvalue that being attended)
  - Hindsight bias (assume 'answers' obvious after knowing them)
- Decisions under uncertainty
- Assessment: to attain the 'best' expected outcome (i.e., objective/goal)
  - Optimization; Risk/Loss/Cost minimization
  - Limited rationality; Satisficing

Types:
- Perception-based (overlapping potentially with *Judgment*)
- Goal-based I: Which goal (of potentially multiple)
- Goal-based II: Which action (of action set)
- Goal-based III: Which state (to move to)
- Sequential (e.g., multiple actions necessary to reach goal)
- Partially observable world, states, options (e.g., POMDPs)
- Game theory; Multiagent systems (MAS) (see below)
- Model-free (current-state-based responding); Model-based (choices based on expected outcomes)

VIII. Optimizing (over longer-term)

21. Planning

General types/levels:
- Tactical
- Strategic
- Automated Planning
- Hierarchical

IX. Doing, Taking Action

22. Actuation

General types:
- Most general actions: Approach, Acquire/Obtain, Avoid, Escape
- Manipulation: direct; tools
- Navigation
- Communication & Language (see below)

Considerations:
- Affordances (interface by which actions influence environment)
- Sequencing
- Coordination (e.g., both legs, hands)
- Based on knowledge at multiple levels (e.g., reflexes to decision-making and metacognition), from multiple competing, interacting systems

---

And yet, when considered in terms of action sequences, i.e., a policy, decision making and problem solving begin to melt together – and depending on specific implementations they may. Nonetheless, as they remain separable in concept and research work, they remain so here. For example, one may envision problem solving as more overarching, with multiple and different types of decisions made during solving. Moreover, *planning* too can be seen as overlapping with other processes – but nonetheless, entails its own set of issues and characteristics, such as hierarchical planning, and its relation to time horizons and simulation [5]. And although we may not typically consider *actuation* (i.e., action execution) as particularly relevant to intelligence per se, detailed work (especially computationally and neurobiologically) shows how difficult even these problems are, and how they quite likely interrelate with other upstream processes (such as with *affordances*, i.e., the interface by which actions affect the world, e.g., where to grasp objects for effectiveness, and how higher processing may need to take them into account) [15–18]. The main types of actions people engage in are listed, along with some key considerations. After action execution, then, there is outcome, which can be used as feedback for subsequent updating and learning; and related to learning is development (Table 2).

Learning generally reflects cases using feedback from the environment, although not necessarily for unsupervised. Indeed, it often can be unclear how to distinguish learning from other knowledge creation processes, as the field of machine learning attests. In any case, as with [1, 19], I have listed the most prominent types, with other well-established ones also added, especially from behavioral psychology [7, 20, 21]. Additionally, *plasticity* reflects learning and development interactions [5].

Development could obviously be placed under knowledge construction processes, as it is indeed such, but it is placed here as a natural companion to learning (which is also typically a construction process, though normally based on environmental feedback as action outcome). Development is highlighted not only because it builds the necessary apparatus (the brain) in the first place, but because its processes critically influence cognitive processing throughout our lifetimes – even at the highest levels of cognition: e.g., from existing prior knowledge, to change of parameter settings, capabilities, and preferences with life cycle. Moreover, because this is so for humans, it is argued that it requires closer scrutiny for meaning and value for artificial systems: not only for number of training steps required, but also types of experiences, and deeper genetic-environmental interactions underlying all processes [22, 23]. We next examine a critical feature of the human mind/brain architecture that especially comes to the fore from a developmental and evolutionary perspective: levels of processing and control, including metacognition & executive function (Table 3).

A fundamental aspect of the human mind/brain is being composed of multiple levels of systems, and at multiple scales. Popular conceptions distinguish basic innate, associative, deliberative, and metacognitive levels, or else more generally as a dual-system structure, though the latter often occurs in the context of human higher cognition, implying a full architecture with additional systems [4–6, 8, 14, 16, 23–27]. Although the human mind/brain's exact layered architecture remains unclear, it nevertheless is a critical construction that cannot be ignored; and one where computational modeling will help clarify its structure and value.

Table 2. Necessary abilities for human cognition: learning and development.

X.   Learning & Development

23. Learning

General types:

- Unsupervised (self-organizing) vs. Supervised (binary; answers to train)
- Plasticity (constrained by genes, development, and subsequent structure: e.g., remapping from over or under use, like increase finger representation for violin players)
- Habituation, Sensitization (to single stimuli)
- Associative reinforcement/reward learning:
    - Pavlovian: States/Stimuli (associated with reward)
    - Instrumental/Operant: Actions (associated with reward)
    - Conditioned reinforcement (association chains)
    - Hierarchical: e.g., context learning (occasion setting), actions
- Learning via experimentation (see *Metacognition* below)
- Imitation, Guidance
- With communication & language:
    - Interactive verbal instruction/coaching
    - Learning from written media
    - Teaching

24. Development

General processes:

- System formation (e.g., neural network formation, culling)
- Prior (genetic) knowledge; instincts, releasing/trigger stimuli
- Critical periods (e.g., sound discriminations for native language)
- Developmental stages
- Language development
- Time/Exposure/Experiential effects ('trials')
- Play
- Targeted parental training
- Life cycle influences (e.g., inherent change in preferences)

For *metacognition* ('thinking about thinking') and *executive function* (whether meta or driven by more sophisticated perceptual input), even though they have been studied for some time, the degree of their influence remains underspecified [5, 6, 16, 27–29]. This stems in part from inherent difficulty determining what is meta (or executive) versus basic cognition. For example, in most any implementation of a main cognitive process, such as decision making, it entails some type of higher controlling process over other subprocesses – and thus a form of metacognition (e.g., [8, 30]). Indeed, metacognitive processes can occur for any cognitive system at any level, influencing or potentially controlling those beneath (especially directly below). In any case, the higher levels, and especially the highest most clearly executive, engage in almost any modulatory function one can think of, with substantial evidence for those listed [5, 23, 27, 29]. General control mechanisms are excitatory, inhibitory, or releasing (double inhibitory); with evidence

Table 3. Levels of processing and control: including metacognition & executive function.

XI. Levels of processing and control: with metacognition & executive function

25. Levels with respect to scale

Scales involved (for humans, and other primates):
- Molecules, cells (neurons), networks, systems
- Levels of depth in given circuit (à la deep neural networks: DNNs)
- Levels of neural systems: e.g., brainstem, midbrain, hypothalamus, limbic structures, higher cortical

Processes:
- Control general: Modulation and influence
  - Excite, Inhibit, Release
  - Top-down as metacognition and executive function
  - Bottom-up as, e.g., recurrence; ascending pathways (e.g., affect)

26. Metacognition ('thinking about thinking') and Executive Function

Types:
- Metacognition:
  - If input from lower-level cognitive system
  - All cognitive types: e.g., metaperception, metamemory
- Non-metacognitive: If input higher-level stimuli (e.g., abstract concepts, relations, context), not from lower-level cognitive system

General processes:
- Observe, arbitrate, coordinate, optimize, correct, override, control

Processes:
- Meta-learning & model ensembles: e.g., voting, averaging, competing
- Monitoring: e.g., task execution, lower systems, outcomes
- Control general: Modulation (excite, inhibit, release)
- Control specific: Attention, Emotion, Self, Learning (e.g., experimentation), Reasoning, Simulation
- Dynamic filtering of memory: Selection & Retrieval
- Manipulation of Working Memory
- Levels of abstraction processing and control
- Flexible manipulation and modifications of knowledge
- (Hierarchical) Planning, Problem Solving
- Figurative description, meaning, metaphor
- Arbitration
- Multitasking
- Awareness/Consciousness
- Self-reflection/assessment/evaluation, correction
- Mind Reading (see under 'Social' below)
- Higher-order emotions: e.g., confidence, self-doubt, dignity

---

Table 4. Necessary abilities for human cognition: Social knowledge and processing.

XII. Example content domain knowledge (of particularly importance): Social

27. Modeling Self and Other

Processes & Characteristics:
- Self-Awareness: Theory of own mind
- Self-Control
- Theory of (Other's) Mind: e.g., their beliefs, desires, intentions
- Levels of modeling: modeling their models of others' minds, etc.
- Attitudes (beliefs and evaluations of others)
- Attribution (reasons for self and others' actions)
- Empathy, Compassion

28. Social Interaction

Processes & Characteristics:
- Social perception (e.g., faces)
- Dominance hierarchies, Subordinate strategies, Ownership
- Competition, with strategy (e.g., game theory, multiagent systems)
- Cooperation; Collaboration (with strategy)
- Reciprocity (i.e., reciprocal altruism), contracts, exchange, economies
- Coalitions/alliances, friendship, attraction
- Conformity, role models, leadership, authority
- Hierarchical social organization: e.g., bands, tribes, regions, states
- Appropriate social behavior: convention, norms, rules, laws
- Social morality: e.g., care-harm; fairness-cheating; loyalty; authority
- Social emotions: e.g., pride, embarrassment, compassion, love
- Person, relationship, group knowledge/inference/identity

29. Communication & Language

Processes & Characteristics:
- Involuntary: normally nonverbal (gestures, facial/body expressions)
- Voluntary: nonverbal, verbal natural language processing (NLP)
  - Comprehension, Production
  - Words/symbols
  - Grammars
  - Recursion
- Pictorial communication
- Language acquisition: listening, speaking, reading
- Cross-modal communication (e.g., sign languages)

---

for explicit executive control processes over many of the main cognitive processes, such as attention, emotion, self, etc. Considerations such as these indicate how extensive metacognition is in complex, multilayered systems like the human mind/brain, yet to be fully characterized [9, 17, 18, 29, 31].

Along with what appear to be more general-purpose mechanisms of metacognition and executive function are more specialized ones, significantly organized with respect to the major content domains. And as in [1, 19], here we highlight one of the most important set of content-specialized functions in people: social processing (Table 4) [5, 30, 32–34].

Many research fields – most notably the social sciences, including social psychology and social neuroscience – have recognized the heightened importance of sociality to humans. This has culminated in the extensive evidence for the so-called 'social brain': i.e., regions and circuitry dedicated to social processing [5, 33]. It is critical, therefore, to list these as fundamental abilities, as done in the AGI roadmap [1, 19]. I have here extended their list with multiple additional social processes that are especially well-established and actively studied [5, 30, 32–34, 47, 48].

At the same time, evidence points to the significance of other specialized content domains – e.g., physical, biological, quantity – as alluded to in other places (especially under '8. Knowledge' in the companion paper), and as indeed recognized in [1, 19]. In any event, the social domain is an excellent representative specialization and of course critical for human and artificial social interaction.

3   For Artificial General Intelligence, Are All Really Necessary?

With the survey completed, we may question whether all listed abilities are relevant for AGI: for example, requiring a developmental critical period or feelings. Given that they all affect the highest reaches of human cognition, it is proposed that some version will be required for full AGI; minimally, all topics should be closely examined, especially for autonomous systems, having more comparable constraints (and problems) as biological organisms. But isn't it already clear that some forms of human cognition – such as built-in biases (e.g., focused and limited empathy, poor statistical intuitions) or seemingly insatiable low-level drives – are vestiges of ancient evolutionary conditions, detrimental in the modern world? I propose that they retain value however modern the world, with certain conditions (as cognitive illusions) revealing their 'joints' (i.e., structure) that must inevitably exist. Exposed failures that yet belie clever solutions underpinning efficiency, resiliency, creativity, still to be fully understood.

Even more enigmatically, it remains vastly unclear the extent true understanding requires the kind of feeling, qualia-experiences, and meta-awareness that humans (and to some degree other animals) have: whether producing our true sense of knowing [5, 35]. It is hard to imagine that consciousness is not fundamental to human intelligence [5, 35, 36]. But short of this, compelling advancement in artificial thinking instills enough inspiration to presume impressive levels of general intelligence will be reached, especially when combining the best approaches, such as symbolic and subsymbolic, notwithstanding current limitations [19, 37, 38].

To address the relevance for artificial systems differently, we might also survey the two papers and conclude that many if not all topics are already being pursued in artificial systems research. Indeed, the topics listed converge well with those of AI and machine learning [25–28, 39]. What, then, is missing, as we remain far from human level AGI? A simple answer is that no system to date is fully comprehensive. And even within relatively narrow domains, most remain too brittle, breaking too readily especially in real-world environments. In general, artificial systems need softer landings. Methods for this include probability theory, population coding, broader learning capabilities, movement toward more continuous and dynamic (versus discrete) data, richer data experiences, and levels of processing architectures, with strategies that tune systems at different levels to environmental circumstances, and flexibly label internal representations and recognize their (abstract and relational) similarities [5, 7, 27, 37, 38, 40–42].

At the same time, even perception and action are hard problems, limiting for example what inputs higher-level cognitive systems can work with. And even the most basic mechanisms – such as choosing the proper degree of generalization and level of abstraction (to find, e.g., appropriate characterizations of similarity and causality) – prove an art form. This is so even for people, belying a cognitive superpower, that yet oftentimes proves a major source of angst, conflict, and error – underlying many of our well-documented heuristics and biases: leading to oversimplifying, confounding, conflating, attribution errors, stereotyping, profiling, prejudice; or rather, to undergeneralizing, and thus losing advantages of similarity, comparison, analogy, statistics. For artificial systems, although it is right to highlight particularly odd errors – like classifying a pile of towels as a pug dog – it remains unclear how far away they may be: missing deeper meaning or simply requiring more information about the characteristics, contexts, and essence of dogness. There can be a fine line between cleverness, creativity, self-embarrassment versus dysfunction. Either way, for human-*like* ability, the answer lies in the dogness. Beyond shaggy coat and wagging tail, to outer and inner causal features, animacy, personality, and mind [4, 27, 43–46].

4 Conclusion

Given that the broad strokes of the two companion papers have already been developed in AI and found lacking, answers must lurk in the details – with a critical step being to fill them in, as I have tried to further do. General intelligence also derives from the collective combination of processes, at least among a magical core set properly implemented and integrated – of which a compiled list might help to glean. For this will certainly take a community effort, with collective detailing, developing, edge resolving, and piecing together into an emergent human-level thinking machine.

References

1. Adams, S.S., et al.: Mapping the landscape of human-level artificial general intelligence. AI Mag. **33**(1), 25–41 (2012)
2. Kralik, J.D.: Toward a comprehensive list of necessary abilities for human intelligence, part 1: constructing knowledge. In: Proceedings of the 15th Conference on Artificial General Intelligence (2022)
3. Reisberg, D.: Cognition. WW Norton & Co., New York (2021)
4. Holyoak, K.J., Morrison, R.G. (eds.): The Oxford Handbook of Thinking and Reasoning. Oxford University Press (2012)

5. Gazzaniga, M.S., Ivry, R.B., Mangun, G.R.: Cognitive Neuroscience. Norton, New York (2019)
6. Kahneman, D.: Thinking, Fast and Slow. Farrar, Straus and Giroux, New York (2011)
7. Sutton, R.S., Barto, A.G.: Reinforcement Learning. MIT Press, Cambridge, MA (1998)
8. Reuter, M., Montag, C. (eds.): Neuroeconomics. SNPBE, Springer, Heidelberg (2016). https://doi.org/10.1007/978-3-642-35923-1
9. Jung, K., Jang, H., Kralik, J.D., Jeong, J.: Bursts and heavy tails in temporal and sequential dynamics of foraging decisions. PLoS Comput Biol **10**(8), e1003759 (2014)
10. Kahneman, D., Slovic, P., Tversky, A.: Decision Under Uncertainty. Cambridge University Press (1983)
11. Jeong, J., Youngmin, O., Chun, M., Kralik, J.D.: Preference-based serial decision dynamics: your first sushi reveals your eating order at the Sushi table. PLoS ONE **9**(5), e96653 (2014)
12. Yoon, S., Lim, S., Kwon, J., Kralik, J.D., Jeong, J.: Preference-based serial decisions are counterintuitively influenced by emotion regulation and conscientiousness. PLoS ONE **14**(10), e0222797 (2019)
13. Lim, S., Yoon, S., Kwon, J., Kralik, J.D., Jeong, J.: Retrospective evaluation of sequential events and the influence of preference-dependent working memory: a computational examination. Front. Comput. Neurosci. **14**, 65 (2020)
14. Daw, N.D., Niv, Y., Dayan, P.: Uncertainty-based competition between prefrontal and dorsolateral striatal systems for behavioral control. Nat. Neurosci. **8**(12), 1704–1711 (2005)
15. Gibson, J.J.: The ecological approach to visual perception. Houghton Mifflin, Boston (1979)
16. Sloman, A.: Varieties of metacognition in natural and artificial systems. In: Cox, M.T., Raja, A. (eds.) Metareasoning: Thinking about Thinking, pp. 307–322. The MIT Press (2011)
17. Wessberg, J., et al.: Real-time prediction of hand trajectory by ensembles of cortical neurons in primates. Nature **408**(6810), 361–365 (2000)
18. Santucci, D.M., Kralik, J.D., Lebedev, M.A., Nicolelis, M.A.L.: Frontal and parietal cortical ensembles predict single-trial muscle activity during reaching movements in primates. Euro. J of Neuro. **22**(6), 1529–1540 (2005)
19. Goertzel, B.: Artificial general intelligence: concept, state of the art, and future prospects. J. Artif. General Intell. **5**(1), 1–46 (2014)
20. Mazur, J.E.: Learning and Behavior. Routledge, Abingdon (2016)
21. Mazur, J.E., Kralik, J.D.: Choice between delayed reinforcers and fixed-ratio schedules requiring forceful responding. J. Exp. Anal. Behav. **53**(1), 175–187 (1990)
22. Goswami, U.: Cognitive Development. Routledge, London (2008)
23. Striedter, G.F.: Principles of Brain Evolution. Sinauer Associates, Sunderland (2005)
24. Evans, J.S.B.T., Stanovich, K.E.: Dual-process theories of higher cognition: advancing the debate. Perspect. Psychol. Sci. **8**(3), 223–241 (2013)
25. Kralik, J.D., Shi, D., El-Shroa, O., Ray, L.E.: From low to high cognition: A multi-level model of behavioral control in the primate brain. Cogn. Sci. (2016)
26. Shi, D., Kralik, J.D., Mi, H.: A hierarchical computational model inspired by the behavioral control in the primate brain. IEEE Access **8**, 178938–178945 (2020)
27. Kralik, J.D.: Architectural design of mind & brain from an evolutionary perspective. In: Proceedings of the AAAI Fall Symposium Standard Model of Mind (2017)
28. Cox, M.T., Raja, A.: Metareasoning. The MIT Press, Cambridge, MA (2011)
29. Kralik, J.D., et al.: Metacognition for a common model of cognition. Procedia Comput. Sci. **145**, 730–739 (2018)
30. Lee, J., Kralik, J.D., Jeong, J.: Understanding human social communication. In: Proceedings of the ICCM (2021)
31. Kowaguchi, M., Patel, N.P., Bunnell, M.E., Kralik, J.D.: Competitive control of cognition in rhesus monkeys. Cognition **157**, 146–155 (2016)

32. Aronson, E., Wilson, T.D., Akert, R.M., Sommers, S.R.: Social Psychology. Pearson, NYC (2018)
33. Cacioppo, J.T., Decety, J. (eds.): The Oxford Handbook of Social Neuroscience. Oxford University Press (2011)
34. Haidt, J.: The new synthesis in moral psychology. Science **316**(5827), 998–1002 (2007)
35. Damasio, A.: Feeling & Knowing. Pantheon, New York (2021)
36. Chalmers, D.J.: The Conscious Mind. Oxford University Press, Oxford (1996)
37. Lucci, S., Kopec, D., Musa, S.M.: Artificial Intelligence in the 21st Century. Mercury, Duxbury (2022)
38. Doumas, L.A.A., Hummel, J.E.: Computational models of higher cognition. In: Holyoak, M. (ed.) The Oxford Handbook of Thinking and Reasoning, pp. 52–66. Oxford University Press, Oxford (2012)
39. Marsland, S.: Machine Learning. CRC Press, Boca Raton (2015)
40. Russell, S., Norvig, P.: Artificial Intelligence. Prentice Hall, Upper Saddle River (2020)
41. Murphy, K.P.: Machine Learning. The MIT Press, Cambridge, Mass (2012)
42. Goodfellow, I., Bengio, Y., Courville, A.: Deep Learning. The MIT Press, Cambridge, MA (2016)
43. Gross, R.: Being Human. Hodder Education, London (2012)
44. Pearl, J., Mackenzie, D.: The Book of Why. Basic Books, New York (2020)
45. Marcus, G., Davis, E.: Rebooting AI. Pantheon Books, New York (2019)
46. Kralik, J.D.: Core high-level cognitive abilities derived from hunter-gatherer shelter building. In: Proceedings of the International Conference Cognitive Modeling, pp. 49–54 (2018)
47. Lee, J., Kralik, J.D., Jeong, J.: How 'who someone is' and 'what they did' influences gossiping about them. PLoS ONE **17**(7), e0269812 (2022)
48. Jahng, J., Kralik, J.D., Hwang, D., Jeong, J.: Neural dynamics of two players when using nonverbal cues to gauge intentions to cooperate during prisoner's dilemma game. Neuroimage **157**, 263–274 (2017)

What Can Nonhuman Animals, Children, and *g* Tell Us About Human-Level Artificial General Intelligence (AGI)?

Jerald D. Kralik[✉]

Korea Advanced Institute of Science and Technology (KAIST), Daejeon 34141, South Korea
jerald.kralik@gmail.com

Abstract. Human-level artificial general intelligence is one of the grandest challenges in science. All evidence should therefore be brought to bear. Here, I summarize highly relevant work from comparative psychology, human intelligence, and developmental psychology. The comparative research points to a set of abilities proposed to separate humans from other animals; then, especially from the human intelligence field and the concept of the general factor *g*, abstract relational reasoning singles out. Deeper considerations of *g* suggest how abstract relational reasoning may underpin human cognitive processing itself. Developmental psychology helps clarify what that may mean.

Keywords: Human cognition and intelligence · Developmental psychology · Abstract relations · Reasoning · Causality · Metacognition · Brain networks · Prefrontal and posterior parietal cortex · Behavioral genetics

1 Introduction

Human intelligence is state-of-the-art and thus the quintessential case for artificial general intelligence (AGI) to compare to and emulate. Although one might wonder whether the evolutionary process led to extensive suboptimalities, the evidence overwhelmingly indicates that the intensive natural selection process produced an elegant solution. For example, the human cognitive abilities described across [1] and [2] converge well with theoretical approaches to intelligence from AI and machine learning (albeit with an eye toward the human model) [3–6]. Nonetheless, the abilities listed cover all forms of human cognition, from narrow to general or higher cognition. What then may separate truly general intelligence capabilities in humans – to perform well across vast and complex settings – from more narrow ability (whether lower-level or expertise)?

The answer of course remains unclear and so any relevant evidence can help. In this short review I consider three areas of psychology with findings of high relevance to human general intelligence, and thereby AGI, which I believe remain underappreciated: evolutionary (or comparative) psychology and neuroscience, developmental psychology, and the subfield that directly studies human intelligence.

B. Goertzel et al. (Eds.): AGI 2022, LNAI 13539, pp. 282–292, 2023.
https://doi.org/10.1007/978-3-031-19907-3_26

2   What Human-Level AGI Can Learn from Nonhuman Animals: Uniquely Human Cognitive Abilities

Evolutionary approaches (including behavioral biology, comparative psychology, and evolutionary neuroscience) attempt to characterize the behavioral and cognitive capacities across animals, seeking, from a *Homo sapiens* perspective, to fulfill Darwin's claim that, "Psychology will be based on a new foundation, that of the necessary acquirement of each mental power and capacity by gradation. Light will be thrown on the origin of man and his history" (*Origin of Species*, 1859). And although most comparative researchers are reticent to declare a cognitive *in*ability in their research subjects, some have nonetheless proposed abilities that most clearly separate humans. The most common proposals relate to abstraction, relations, and their combination: i.e., abstract relations and abstract reasoning [7–11]. Penn et al. [8] take this a step further proposing the comprehension of relations of relations: most notably exemplified in analogical reasoning (e.g., 'cat is to kitten as frog is to [?]'). At the same time, other proposals exist, and Table 1 attempts a comprehensive list of them – many if not all of which do not separate humans in all-or-none fashion, but are in every case dramatically heightened (modified from [7, 8, 10–14]).

These abilities, then, can be considered a proposal as the key ones mediating human general intelligence (from those listed in the tables of [1, 2]), to be singled out perhaps for targeted development. At the same time this list remains daunting and wide-ranging (e.g., from abstract reasoning to consciousness to sophisticated social processes). It would be nice to hone this list further, or in any case, provide more clues about human general intelligence – and indeed there is pertinent evidence from work focused directly on human intelligence, examined next.

3   From Human Intelligence Research

3.1   What to Test

The direct study of human intelligence along with tests to measure it have developed for over 150 years (at least since 1865 with Charles Darwin's cousin Francis Galton, a forebearer of both the intelligence and statistics fields). The basic logic of this work is (a) to define intelligence, (b) devise potential tests for it, (c) attempt to externally validate the tests, and (d) then in turn to (factor) analyze the test results to better understand the actual cognitive abilities and interrelationships underlying the test scores. With respect to external validity, the test scores correlate highly with measures believed to require intelligence for success: e.g., achievement tests (such as the SAT, GRE, college and graduate school entrance exams, respectively), grades, education level, career occupations, socioeconomic status, self-control ability, level of health, etc. [17–19]. One can rightly point out the complications and myriad factors involved, but to attempt external validity, these comparisons seem reasonable places to expect intelligence to promote success, and the significant results bear this out persistently.

What then should be tested in the first place? Psychologists attempted to pinpoint the main cognitive abilities most closely aligned with higher information processing;

Table 1. Hypothesized uniquely human cognitive abilities (modified from [12]). Primary through tertiary representations based on (1°) perception, (2°) denotive (i.e., of something), and (3°) figurative (i.e., less literal reference to something) meanings; and Qualia being 'phenomenological subjective, internal experiences', such as our experience of colors like red or blue from different wavelengths, or deep feelings of love, sense of self [15, 16].

1. Abstraction (secondary representation: denotive):
    - Meaning: including concepts; ideas; assumed unseen causes
    - Relations; relations of relations; relational chains
    - Systems of relations/meaning: e.g., philosophy, science, economics
2. Symbolic processing: labeling/naming and use of symbols
3. Reasoning: especially abstract, causal, chains, hierarchical
4. Mental simulation and imagery (in mind's eye)
5. Extended time horizon (imagined as limitless, including mental time travel)
6. Imagination (tertiary representation: figurative)
    - Figurative: creative tropes: e.g., metaphor, associations (fiction, humor)
    - Originality: combinations; novel conceptions, creations (some types of art)
7. Generative construction (for others in the list): sequences; hierarchy; recursion
8. Metacognition
    - Perhaps involved in all: i.e., processes using processes
    - Executive management
9. Self-awareness, reflection
10. Consciousness
    - Qualia, and true understanding/experiencing/feeling/appreciating
    - Leading to such topics as Existentialism, Philosophy
11. Other minds: theory/believing & reading
12. Heightened morality: e.g., fairness-justice; dignity-pride
13. Extensive social transmission & exchange, culture, teaching
14. Language

that is, considering the general input (sensation) to output (action) cycle, targeting those subsequent to sensation/perception and prior to action execution – most typically called higher cognition or thinking and reasoning [20]. Examining the tables in [1, 2], this would include memory, knowledge, knowledge creation processes (such as abstraction, reasoning, mental modeling, and simulation), concluding and using processes (such as judgment and problem solving), as well as planning, learning, and executive function. And these indeed are especially reflected in intelligence tests.

More specifically, the most widely used intelligence test – the Wechsler Adult Intelligence Scale – is composed of 11 subtests divided into *verbal* (six tests) and *performance* (five tests) sections (see [18]). For **verbal**, they are **(1) Information** (i.e., general knowledge, like geography, prime minister of UK); **(2) Vocabulary**; **(3) Similarities** (e.g., 'how are apple and pear alike?'); **(4) Comprehension** (testing abstract rules or expressions, e.g., 'kill 2 birds with 1 stone'); **(5) Digit Span** (i.e., remembering a sequence of numbers, with length increasing); and **(6) Arithmetic**.

For **performance** the five tests are **(1) Picture Completion** (i.e., recognize and draw-in missing parts, like hands, numbers of clock); **(2) Object Assembly** (putting puzzle pieces together to form object, like face); **(3) Block Design** (i.e., arrange a set of blocks with partial patterns on them to match a given pattern); **(4) Picture Arrangement** (rearrange pictures to tell story); and **(5) Digit Symbol** (i.e., match symbol to number, after given key of nine number-symbol pairs: e.g., '1 and #', '2 and %').

It is worth considering them closely yourself, but I believe we can see that abilities tested range from working memory to quantity (with quantitative relations) to spatial relations (including hierarchical) to world knowledge to abstract (conceptual) relational understanding and reasoning. Although each subtest is designed to query something unique, there is clearly overlap among them. One might claim that they should be separated better; but interestingly and importantly, one of the major developments across time was to attempt this: that is, on the one hand, to test topics meant to best reflect intelligence, and yet on the other, to attempt to separate them better – such as dividing into verbal and performance sections (Herrnstein, of [19], personal communication). Regardless, significant correlations persisted, leading many, then and now, to conclude that the tests are providing a window into the underlying structure of intelligence.

To anticipate, it is valuable to examine similarities among the tests. I would characterize the underlying abilities as ranging from capacity (working memory, long-term memory, processing bandwidth, speed) to perceptual, abstract, and causal relational understanding and reasoning. But let us look more closely at the findings.

3.2 Underlying Structure of Intelligence Test Scores

General consensus has settled on a three-level hierarchical model [17, 21]. The first, shallowest level consists of the specific factors (s) essentially unique to each test. The second, middle layer of more general domain factors (d) captures the broader similarity in sets of subtests (e.g., verbal, spatial, memory, speed – although findings do not always agree on the exact groupings, and variance accounted for is low, but significant for this level) [17]. And the third, highest or deepest level is the most general factor underlying all tests (causing them to correlate), coined *general intelligence*, shortened as g. Thus, the general model of intelligence is $I = g\{d\{s\}\}$, where all three components are sets of factors in hierarchical relation.

Indeed, g has been the most persistent of the underlying factors, often accounting for up to half the total variance in the scores – and remaining remarkably stable across test batteries [17, 22]. This is important to highlight, and will be done further below.

3.3 What is g?

And so if this persistent test-wide correlation actually reflects an underlying cognitive ability, what is it – what is g? Spearman [23], who first identified and proposed the concept, considered it in general as a mental energy or power; but more specifically as the mechanism underlying *abstract relational reasoning* (e.g., among objects, events, concepts) – and the latter remains the most accepted idea [18].

At the same time, there is evidence for other secondary components of g, with the best established ones being *processing speed, memory capacity/facility (especially working memory)*, and *sensory discrimination* [17]. The first two of these secondary components are intuitively appealing, with speed and capacity expected to facilitate information processing. Sensory discrimination, in contrast, is more enigmatic – reflecting either (a) direct perceptual acuity to parse and process more details of the input, and/or (b) a more top-down influence of cognitive facility promoting perception of more environmental detail. We return to this later, with evidence for the latter.

In any case, the primary component appears to be abstract relational reasoning, which is especially interesting as it corroborates other findings, such as in comparative psychology as we have seen. However, if skepticism remains over the interpretations of g, especially the primary one, biological evidence provides strong, and in fact, remarkable support for it.

3.4   Genetic and Brain Evidence for Intelligence and g

Obviously g must be something, producing the correlation across all tests. Yet initial interpretation may feel speculative. Biological investigation can test the concept of g as actually reflecting cognitive ability, and also help understand its nature.

What Genes say About g (Thus Far). I will attempt to leave aside the deep-seated issues and sophisticated analyses that exist with genetics studies of intelligence, and simply state that genetics work continues and the consensus is clear: however intelligence is measured, a remarkably large genetic component persists [17, 22, 24–28]. This remains best shown with the most comprehensive twin and adoption studies. For example, even from the early 1980s, a review of the dozens of genetics and intelligence studies across the family, adoption, and twin data to date found that roughly 50% of the variance in g (in particular) was genetic [25–27]. More recently, compelling examples include a set of studies using the Minnesota database of twins *raised apart*, consisting of 436 participants, including 126 twin pairs (74 monozygotic, 52 dizygotic) [22, 28]. The studies examined intelligence as measured by three different test batteries (including the Wechsler Scale). First, they found strong evidence for the same g factor across all three scales (pairwise correlations: 0.99, 0.99, 1.00). Second, they found that 77% of the variance in g across individuals was accounted for by genetic influences.

With respect to identifying individual gene effects, correlational evidence thus far is pointing to cumulative small effects of multiple genes, but much work remains to verify this [17]. Although it is true that behavioral genetic results such as the twin and adoption studies will become even more convincing once directly tied to specific genes, the consistency of findings across test batteries and studies, as well as the size of the genetic component found are striking. Ultimately, of course, it would have to influence the brain somehow, and so direct studies in neuroscience can also provide important clues, which they do.

What the Brain Says About Intelligence and g (Thus Far). For general measures of the brain, *larger* overall brain size, both in gray (neuron bodies) and white (neural axons) matter, as well as *greater* white matter integrity (i.e., thicker mylenation and therefore conduction effectiveness) coincide with *higher* intelligence test scores, as well as with g [17, 29–31]. These features are also highly genetically influenced [29–31].

For specific brain regions, fascinating evidence exists with respect to intelligence in general, but imply a significant relationship to g as well. Most notably, a review of 37 functional and structural neuroimaging studies has identified a distributed network of regions underpinning intelligence, centered around two key regions in frontal cortex – (1) *dorsolateral prefrontal* (Brodmann areas 6, 9, 10, 45, 46, 47) and (2) *anterior cingulate* (BA 32) cortex – and three in posterior cortex – (1) *posterior parietal* (BAs 39, 40, 7), (2) *temporal* (BAs 21, 37), and (3) *occipital* (BAs 18, 19) cortex [31]. These regions are connected by two key fiber bundles also identified – (1) the *arcuate fasciculus* (connecting, by the way, the two main language areas, Wernicke's and Broca's, of the posterior parietal and frontal cortices, respectively) and (2) the *superior longitudinal fasciculus* (broadly connecting frontal and posterior cortices).

Other prominent human studies provide further support for these key regions [30, 32]. Additionally, findings from evolutionary neuroscience have independently singled out *dorsolateral prefrontal* (BAs 10, 46) and *posterior parietal cortex* (BAs 39, 40), in particular, as either entirely unique or greatly expanded in humans [33].

Together, these results are rather remarkable because the identified regions, and the larger distributed network to which they belong, have been well-documented as subserving higher-level cognition across multiple studies [34]. More specifically, in [31], the authors suggest the following interrelationships: (1) *abstraction and elaboration of perceptual information* via posterior parietal cortex, (2) *reasoning and problem solving* via posterior and frontal cortical interaction, and (3) *executive function* via especially anterior cingulate cortex. (The findings would also have to point to *language processing* as well.)

And so, what do these intelligence and brain findings tell us about *g* per se? Given the structural evidence linking brain structure to *g* itself (overall brain size, gray and white matter size, and the latter's integrity), and given the imaging evidence connecting the higher-cognitive brain network to intelligence in general, and finally, given that *g* makes up nearly half the test score variance, it suggests that *g* strongly underlies the imaging results as well. The genetic and brain findings, then, provide strong support for the concept of *g* underlying highest cognition.

3.5 What can AGI Learn from g?

The main ability reflected in *g* appears to be *abstract relational reasoning* – meaning, (a) abstraction (e.g., concepts such as "information"), (b) relations (e.g., "information processing"), and (c) reasoning about them (e.g., 'what enables general intelligence') – and as said, the same ability is singled out by multiple comparative psychologists [7–11]. Therefore, it may be proposed as an especially fundamental ability for human general intelligence.

The significance of *abstract relational reasoning*, of course, is not a revelation, with especially symbolic-level architectures developing and utilizing it [4, 14, 35] (while proving especially problematic for associative, connectionist approaches) [36]. Nonetheless, any evidence to identify particularly fundamental abilities in a seemingly vast sea of necessary ones may help [1–3, 37]. Moreover, and critically, the finding that *g* underpins performance across all the test scores (as the deepest level in any hierarchical model of intelligence) implies that *g*, rather than the summit of the intelligence mountain, is more like the reverse, its foundation.

This is easy enough to fathom with respect to, say, processing speed, bandwidth, memory capacity, but perhaps less so for *abstract relational reasoning*. Does one's vocabulary expand, for instance, due to greater world exposure, or due to a mind/brain that sees more in the world, requiring labels that reflect this richer view, this greater precision? An approach with potential insight is that of [38, 39], where it is hypothesized that the brain has essentially inherent graph structures that are generatively matched to incoming data, producing, for example, a hierarchical tree structure for biological relationships (e.g., specific dog species, dogs in general, other animals) from enough examples with information about shared features. A heightened facility with a mechanism such as this might tend to search for patterns in the world – and across most any content domain, problem environment, etc.

Nonetheless, wouldn't more concrete entities be expected to underpin the more abstract ones? Don't abstract concepts, such as "information" and "processes", require grounding in concrete cases, specific examples, before ever truly understanding them? Aren't their meanings ultimately based on the specific cases, and not the other way around? And doesn't other evidence, such as from child development, strongly support a progression from concrete to abstract relations (and thereby showing how abstract relations are built and likely processed)? Indeed, developmental psychology has relevant evidence and insight.

4 What We Can Learn from Children: Progression with Exception

Piaget in particular has provided extensive evidence that human cognitive processing develops in stages, from infancy to adulthood [37, 40]. More specifically, the four main stages begin with **sensorimotor** (0–2 years old), itself with six substages: (1) reflexes to (2) action sequences to (3) affecting objects to (4) coordinated actions to achieve goal to (5) testing action effects to (6) internalization into 'mental realm' of actions and consequences. The second stage is **preoperational** (2–7 years), which is transitional to 'concrete operational', egocentric (world seen in relation to self), prelogical (symbols, concrete operations forming, but not fully integrated, with no reversibility, e.g., no subtraction), culminating in internalization (i.e., sensorimotor substages roughly redeveloping in mental realm for objects). The third stage is **concrete operational** (7–11 years), understanding properties of concrete object classes and their relations: especially class inclusion (part-whole relations), transitivity, arithmetic operations (addition, subtraction, equivalence), with units of thought integrated, operations used logically. The fourth stage is **formal operational** (11-adult), with second-order reasoning (i.e., formal logical system operating on elementary operations), hypothetical-deductive operations, and abstract relational reasoning.

In general, then, we see a clear progression, from sensorimotor (i.e., actions and their effects), to a more explicit internal representation of this, to concrete objects and their relations, with symbols and more explicit internal representation of these, to more abstract concepts and relations, including hierarchical relationships (e.g., relations of relations). And so, at first pass, developmental evidence supports a more intuitive cognitive structure of abstract relations building up from concrete object relations, in turn built up perhaps from one's own actions and their consequences.

However, more modern evidence has not only blurred these stage lines, but has crossed them, reshaping the basic developmental process [40–42]. First, rather than a concrete-to-abstract progression across all content domains, evidence now suggests cognitive development as more dependent on content domains – i.e., self, social, biological, physical, quantitative – and further, based on what particularly matters in each domain. For instance, even abstract concepts can be comprehended early, or perhaps even innately, when they particularly relate to self (like ownership); and then soon after, when they relate to others that matter, like beginning to read their minds (i.e., mind understanding) [43]. Even childhood fanciful imaginations and play appear to belie more abstract conceptions and second-order reasoning: e.g., pretending or imagining oneself and world as something else, like fireman, doctor, parent.

Equally interesting and significant is the evidence that cognitive development may be fundamentally based on an inherent sense of causality (perhaps from birth and progressing throughout) that leads to a parsing of the world into the content domains as fuller ontologies: that is, each with their own causality principles as organizing framework (such as intuitive or 'folk' Newtonian physics) [40–42]. Some examples (of numerous) include inherently knowing and anticipating how far a smaller stationary ball will travel when hit by a larger rolling ball [40]; whether a pile of items (like stones, bricks) will stand or fall [43]; or whether a wolf remains a wolf, even in sheep's clothing (that is, even if a wolf's fur were changed to wool) [41]. However rough and at times still perceptually dependent, the understanding suggests a sense of an unseen causal "essence" – like forces or internal drives or minds [41, 42, 44].

Developmental findings such as these provide a lively playground of possibilities for AGI researchers, including the organization of knowledge based on ontological content domains, and perhaps more fundamentally based on causal understanding, essentially asking 'why', and 'how' [14, 41, 45, 46]. Whether relatively distinct, independent content-domain-driven ontologies exist from the outset (i.e., evolutionary and genetic) versus a more general underlying mechanism creating (or at least elaborating) them remains to be determined. g votes significantly for the latter.

For the former, besides developmental evidence like that described above, there are as well other characterizations of intelligence, such as Gardner's multiple intelligences, that emphasize the relative independence of content domains, especially with a broader range of potential competencies, including musical, physical (i.e., action-based), social (interpersonal), and emotional/introspective (intrapersonal) ones [47]. But such characterizations (a) stretch the notion of intelligence beyond what most higher-cognitive psychologists and neuroscientists conceive (e.g., action abilities); and (b) tend to de-emphasize the significant correlations that yet exist across tests of even these competencies, including the most general g component [17, 48]. General intelligence translates. Meaning those with higher general ability may tend to succeed, whatever the domain or setting.

And yet, it can be easy to lose the forest for the trees. Piaget's progressive stages are too well-supported to discard; and thus, integration of the cognitive development schemes is needed. For example, some have argued Piaget's stages may generally hold, but for much younger ages than previously thought (see [40]). It could also hold in terms of how even the most innate prior knowledge and cognitive ability must be elaborated: like from a vague sense of causality and essence to more progressively complex and abstract concepts and relationships, which track Piaget's stages as well as normal educational trajectories: e.g., in math, social & natural sciences, humanities.

5 Conclusions

Attaining human-level artificial intelligence is one of the most extraordinary challenges in science. All evidence should marshal to the cause. I have summarized especially relevant findings from comparative psychology, human intelligence, and developmental psychology. They begin with the set in Table 1, and then hone in on abstract relational reasoning. Deeper considerations of g suggest that it may underpin much of higher cognition believed to comprise intelligence. Developmental psychology, in particular, alludes to rich possibilities of interrelationships of abstract relational reasoning with other cognitive abilities, both during development and for cognitive processing itself. These include Piaget's progression from concrete objects and relations to more abstract ones. And it also includes something perhaps even more intriguing: a top-down or center-out progression, whereby heightened higher-cognitive capability may beckon perception for the information it is capable of processing, and press action to effector limits and even beyond, to tools, further creations, and the most optimal solutions [38, 39, 41–43, 49, 50]. Such center-out influence may additionally suggest that metacognitive control processes play an even more fundamental role in human cognition – and ultimately higher general intelligence – than fully appreciated to date [40, 50, 51].

References

1. Kralik, J.D.: Toward a comprehensive list of necessary abilities for human intelligence, Part 1: constructing knowledge. In: Proc. 15th Conf. on Artificial General Intelligence (2022)
2. Kralik, J.D.: Toward a comprehensive list of necessary abilities for human intelligence, Part 2: using knowledge. In: Proc. 15th Conf. on Artificial General Intelligence (2022).
3. Goertzel, B.: Artificial general intelligence: concept, state of the art, and future prospects. Journal of Artificial General Intelligence **5**, 1–46 (2014)
4. Russell, S., Norvig, P.: Artificial Intelligence. Prentice Hall (2020)
5. Lucci, S., Kopec, D., Musa, S.M.: Artificial Intelligence in the 21st Century. Mercury (2022)
6. Marsland, S.: Machine Learning. CRC Press (2015)
7. Herrnstein, R.J.: Levels of stimulus control. Cognition **37**, 133–166 (1990)
8. Penn, D.C., Holyoak, K.J., Povinelli, D.J.: Darwin's mistake: Explaining the discontinuity between human and nonhuman minds. Behav Brain Sci **31**, 1–70 (2008)
9. Kralik, J.D., Hauser, M.D.: A nonhuman primate's perception of object relations: experiments on cottontop tamarins. Animal Behaviour **63**, 419–435 (2002)
10. Kowaguchi, M., Patel, N.P., Bunnell, M.E., Kralik, J.D.: Competitive control of cognition in rhesus monkeys. Cognition **157**, 146–155 (2016)
11. Tomasello, M., Call, J.: Primate Cognition. Oxford University Press (1997)
12. Gross, R.: Being Human. Hodder Education (2012)
13. Pasternak, C.: What Makes Us Human? Oneworld (2007)
14. Kralik, J.D.: Architectural design of mind & brain from an evolutionary perspective. In: Proc. AAAI 2017 Fall Symposium (2017)
15. Chalmers, D.J.: The Conscious Mind. Oxford University Press (1996)
16. Damasio, A.: Feeling & Knowing. Pantheon (2021)

17. Deary, I.J.: Intelligence. Annu Rev Psychol **63**, 453–482 (2012)
18. Maltby, J., Day, L., Macaskill, A.: Personality, Individual Differences and Intelligence. Pearson (2017)
19. Herrnstein, R.J., Murray, C.: The Bell Curve. Simon & Schuster (1996)
20. Holyoak, K.J., Morrison, R.G.: The Oxford Handbook of Thinking and Reasoning. Oxford University Press (2012)
21. Carroll, J.B.: Human Cognitive Abilities. Cambridge University Press (1993)
22. Johnson, W., Bouchard, T.J., Jr., Krueger, R.F., McGue, M., Gottesman, I.I.: Just one g: consistent results from three test batteries. Intelligence **32**, 95–107 (2004)
23. Spearman, C.E.: 'General intelligence', objectively determined and measured. American Journal of Psychology **15**, 201–293 (1904)
24. Knopik, V.S., Neiderhiser, J.M., DeFries, J.C., Plomin, R.: Behavioral genetics. Worth (2016)
25. Loehlin, J.C.: Partitioning environmental and genetic contributions to behavioral development. Am Psychol **44**, 1285–1292 (1989)
26. Bouchard, T.J., McGue, M.: Familial studies of intelligence - a review. Science **212**, 1055–1059 (1981)
27. Chipuer, H.M., Rovine, M., Plomin, R.: LISREL modelling: Genetic and environmental influences on IQ revisited. Intelligence **14** (1990)
28. Johnson, W., et al.: Genetic and environmental influences on the verbal-perceptual-image rotation (VPR) model of the structure of mental abilities in the minnesota study of twins reared apart. Intelligence **35**, 542–562 (2007)
29. Posthuma, D., et al.: The association between brain volume and intelligence is of genetic origin. Nat. Neurosci. **5**, 83–84 (2002)
30. Chiang, M.-C., et al.: Genetics of brain fiber architecture and intellectual performance. Journal of Neuroscience **29**, 2212–2224 (2009)
31. Jung, R.E., Haier, R.J.: The Parieto-Frontal Integration Theory (P-FIT) of intelligence: Converging neuroimaging evidence. Behav Brain Sci **30**, 135–+ (2007)
32. Duncan, J., et al.: A neural basis for general intelligence. Science **289**, 457–460 (2000)
33. Striedter, G.F.: Principles of Brain Evolution. Sinauer Associates (2005)
34. Gazzaniga, M.S., Ivry, R.B., Mangun, G.R.: Cognitive neuroscience. Norton (2002)
35. Laird, J.E., Lebiere, C., Rosenbloom, P.S.: A standard model of the mind. AI Mag. **38**, 13–26 (2017)
36. Doumas, L.A.A., Hummel, J.E.: In: Holyoak, K.J., Morrison, R.G. (eds.) The Oxford Handbook of Thinking and Reasoning, pp. 52–66. Oxford University Press (2012)
37. Adams, S.S., et al.: Mapping the landscape of human-level artificial general intelligence. AI Magazine **33**, 25–41 (2012)
38. Kemp, C., Tenenbaum, J.B.: The discovery of structural form. PNAS **105**, 10687–92 (2008)
39. Tenenbaum, J.B., Kemp, C., Griffiths, T.L., Goodman, N.D.: How to grow a mind: statistics, structure, and abstraction. Science **331**, 1279–1285 (2011)
40. Goswami, U.: Cognitive development. Routledge (2008)
41. Carey, S., Spelke, E.: In: Hirschfeld, G. (ed.) Mapping the Mind, pp. 169–200 (1994)
42. Gelman, S.A., Frazier, B.N.: In: Holyoak, K.J., Morrison, R.G. (eds.) The Oxford Handbook of Thinking and Reasoning. Oxford University Press (2012)
43. Lake, B.M., Ullman, T.D., Tenenbaum, J.B., Gershman, S.J.: Building machines that learn and think like people. Behav Brain Sci **40** (2017)
44. Carey, S.: Conceptual Change in Childhood. The MIT Press (1985)
45. Pearl, J.: Causality. Cambridge University Press (2009)
46. Kralik, J.D.: Core high-level cognitive abilities derived from hunter-gatherer shelter building. In: Proc. of 16th International Conference on Cognitive Modeling, pp. 49–54 (2018)
47. Gardner, H.: Frames of Mind. Basic Books (1983)

48. Visser, B.A., Ashton, M.C., Vernon, P.A.: Beyond g. Intelligence **34**, 487–502 (2006)
49. Goodman, N., Tenenbaum, J.B.: Learning physics from dynamical scenes (2014)
50. Kralik, J.D., et al.: Metacognition for a common model of cognition. Procedia Computer Science **145**, 730–739 (2018)
51. Friedman, N.P., et al.: Individual differences in executive functions are almost entirely genetic in origin. J. Experim. Psychol. Gen. **137**, 201–225 (2008)

Cognitive Architecture
for Co-evolutionary Hybrid Intelligence

Kirill Krinkin[✉][iD] and Yulia Shichkina[iD]

Saint-Petersburg Electrotechnical University 'LETI', Prof. Popova 5,
Saint-Petersburg 197022, Russia
kirill@krinkin.com, shichkina@etu.ai

Abstract. This paper questions the feasibility of a strong (general) data-centric artificial intelligence (AI). The disadvantages of this type of intelligence are discussed. As an alternative, the concept of co-evolutionary hybrid intelligence is proposed. It is based on the cognitive interoperability of man and machine. An analysis of existing approaches to the construction of cognitive architectures is given. An architecture that seamlessly incorporates a human into the loop of intelligent problem solving is considered. The article is organized as follows. The first part contains a critique of data-centric intelligent systems. The reasons why it is impossible to create a strong artificial intelligence based on this type of intelligence are indicated. The second part briefly presents the concept of co-evolutionary hybrid intelligence and shows its advantages. The third part gives an overview and analysis of existing cognitive architectures. It is concluded that many of them do not consider humans as part of the intelligent data processing process. The next part discusses the cognitive architecture for co-evolutionary hybrid intelligence, providing integration with humans. It finishes with general conclusions about the feasibility of developing intelligent systems with humans in the problem solving loop.

Keywords: Hybrid intelligence · Human-machine co-evolution · Cognitive architectures · Intelligence-centric systems

1 Data-Centric AI Crisis

Many real objects and processes that humans deal with (human body, biosphere, autonomous transport, social systems, economics etc.) have very high complexity. The complexity is such that human intellectual abilities are not enough to build models of such objects.

At the beginning of this century it became possible to collect and store a large amount of data. By analyzing data about an object collected over a relatively long period of time, it is possible to identify some regularities of behavior,

This work was carried out under the "Development program of ETU 'LETI' within the framework of the program of strategic academic leadership "Priority-2030" No 075-15-2021-1318 on 29 Sept 2021".

and build its'behavioral model'. Methods based on data analysis have become the basis for modern data-centric artificial intelligence. The current mainstream of data-centric artificial intelligence methods is machine learning based on neural networks, in particular deep learning. The general scheme of creation of AI based on neural networks is as follows: a representative dataset is collected, which is marked by automatic methods or with human intervention (marked and described the important features in the data), in other words, a dataset is created; a neural network is trained on this dataset, it identifies and 'remembers' the relationship between the features in the data; trained network can use new data of the same structure about the same object to predict the corresponding object characteristics or to model its behavior.

Artificial intelligence based on data is not intelligence in the common sense. Wang [24] raised a heated debate about redefining artificial intelligence. He proposed to approach intelligence as the ability to adapt when knowledge and resources are lacking. It is important to note that his attempt to define artificial intelligence does not distinguish artificial nature of intelligence. In fact, Wang defines intelligence in general. In this article, following the cognitive sciences, intelligence is defined constructively as a functioning system of cognitive functions. The action of this system allows to extract new knowledge and build new models, which provide the ability to adapt in the lacking of knowledge and resources. Examples of the cognitive functions are perception, attention, memory, language, or planning [1]. Obviously, one of the most important cognitive abilities is abstract thinking. It is based on the ability to replace real world objects and processes with symbols and to operate with these symbols instead of operating with the reality. Nowadays, automatic construction of interpretable symbolic models is impossible. So far, there are no successful models that allow to introduce symbols and give them meaning. Considering the above, it is possible to say that data-centric narrow intelligence is not an intelligence, but rather can be considered as one of the cognitive functions (depending on the subject area, it can be search, classification, translation, etc.). In other words, data-centric intelligence is an advanced stochastic machine. With all benifits, it has a number of significant drawbacks.

- To train a neural network describing a complex object is not always possible to collect and label a sufficient amount of data;
- Training a neural network takes a lot of time and large computational resources;
- For small changes of input data (especially, data structures) a full retraining cycle is required;
- The results produced by a neural network can almost never be interpreted. It is possible to get a result, but have no explanation why this result is correct and what the way it was got. Neural networks always give not an exact, but a probabilistic answer, without an explanatory component they cannot be used for example in fields such as medicine;
- the narrow field of application of solutions based on artificial neural networks. They are not able to solve simple cognitive problems (unable to demonstrate integral cognitive effect), to transfer the results of training to another domain.

Instead of data-centric AI we focus on a class of intelligent systems that allow the seamless integration of human and machine intelligence. This type of intelligence is able to co-evolutionary cognitive development of human and machine agents. The following section describes the main features such systems.

2   Co-evolutionary Hybrid Intelligence

The idea of hybridization of human and machine intelligence is not new. The most significant influence on the development of views on hybridization of intelligence was made by Engelbart [2]. In his framework for augmented intelligence, he defined the capabilities and basic interfaces for human-machine interaction in cognitive tasks.

Subsequently, Z. Akata and others [3] defined the concept of hybrid intelligence as a combination of human and machine intelligence, complementing each other. This type of symbiosis makes it possible to achieve goals that are unattainable for either humans or machines separately.

The mentioned works do not imply general principles of technologization of hybrid intelligent systems creation. We can conclude that, according to the mentiones authors, a hybrid system is created for a specific task. Hence, the way of integration is also chosen in ad-hoc way.

A definition of co-evolutionary hybrid intelligence is given in [4]. The authors point out the insufficiency of human-machine hybridization at the level of operations, data and ontologies. The key mechanism for moving towards strong intelligent systems is defined as the ability to build cognitive capabilities in the process of co-evolutionary development. Thus, co-evolutionary hybrid intelligence (CHI) is a symbiosis of artificial and natural intelligence mutually evolving, learning and complementing each other in a process of co-evolution. In this case, co-evolution refers to the ability of the system to change as it functions, based on the knowledge extracted from the domain.

The main possibility for this kind of co-evolution between man and machine is compatibility at the level of cognitive functions. In other words, if different cognitive abilities can be realized by humans and machines, then it is possible to create an interface that ensures their interchangeability (interoperability). From a pragmatic point of view, functions such as searching, classifying, identifying features in data, translating, and others can be performed by humans and machines. Depending on the amount of data, the level of formalization of the problem, and other aspects, a human or machine will be more efficient. If it is possible to replace one type of agent (human) with another type of agent (machine) and vice versa, it is possible to build hybrid systems.

A peculiarity of humans is that their performance strongly depends on the degree of fatigue caused by cognitive overload. Also, individual abilities to perform cognitive work matter. Thus, if in a hybrid system a human handles a certain operation noticeably better than a machine, then after a long period of time the performance may become worse than the machine version of the implementation. This fact entails the need to monitor human cognitive abilities during hybrid system operation.

In a broader sense, several classes of interoperability can be considered. Interoperability between the developer and the intelligent system being created defines the possibility to work in a single knowledge ontology of the developer (programmer, data engineer, etc.) with a subject matter expert (e.g. doctor or social engineer). Interoperability between machine and human intelligent agents within a hybrid system provides the ability to jointly extract new knowledge (e.g., software data analysis methods are capable of finding statistically significant patterns, but are not able to interpret them; on the other hand, humans are capable of interpretation, introducing a new symbol into the ontology, but are weak in data analysis). Interoperability between intelligent systems provides the possibility of cooperation between systems created independently (this situation is expected in the near future in the creation of smart cities, saturated with independent devices and services, which are forced to work in a common environment).

Technologization of the development of hybrid co-evolutionary intelligent systems relies on the following:

- formalization of cognitive functions that allow the assembly of'intelligence' implemented by agents of different nature;
- enhancement of capabilities of human-machine interfaces, for knowledge transfer from human to machine and vice versa;
- creation of an individualized model of a human being as a part of a hybrid system, control of his/her state and cognitive abilities (if necessary, reassignment of tasks to other agents)
- minimizing the gap between the "user" and the "developer" of the hybrid system.

In addition to the above points, the development of biofeedback methods is important. These methods are well proven in medical applications [5–7]. Their application allows to use non-verbal mechanisms of self-regulation and state control of human agents.

3 Cognitive Architectures: State of the Art

The main proponent of the idea of formulating a theory that would cover all aspects of cognition was Allen Newell, who identified the means to achieve this goal: cognition architectures [10]. The first ideas for creating such architectures can be traced back to Turing's article on the intelligent computer [11]. Turing believed that speed and memory capacity were the main barriers to the achievement of machine intelligence by computers of the time. History has shown, however, that each advance in artificial intelligence has only clarified how much of the mystery of human intelligence, creativity, and ingenuity is a difficulty [12].

There are different approaches for defining "cognitive architecture". Thus, in [13] the authors suggest that a cognitive architecture is a design of a computing system for modeling some aspects of human cognition. The authors of [14] believe that cognitive architectures are, on the one hand, part of the original purpose of creating an intelligent machine that exactly replicates human intelligence and, on the other hand, attempts at theoretical unification in the field of cognitive psychology. According to the authors [15], expert systems and cognitive architectures are close, but cognitive architectures offer a description of an agent's intellectual behavior at the level of systems, rather than at the level of component methods developed for specialized tasks.

In [15] there is a more detailed notion of cognitive architecture. Cognitive architecture, as a basic part of an intelligent system, according to the authors, includes those aspects of a cognitive agent that remain unchanged over time and in different fields of application. These typically include: short- and long-term memory, in which the agent's purposes and knowledge are stored; the representation of the elements contained in memory and their larger mental structures; and the processes that operate on these structures, including the learning mechanisms that modify them. The main properties of the cognitive architecture are: knowledge representation, knowledge organization, knowledge utilization, knowledge acquisition and knowledge dissemination.

The cognitive architecture for an intelligent robotic system according to the authors [16] must support fast perception, control and execution of tasks at a low level, as well as recognition and interpretation of complex contexts, internal task planning and behavioral learning, which are usually handled at higher levels.

Some researchers focus on reinforcing individual properties of AI systems. For example, the authors [17] argue that autonomy is a key property for any system that can be considered general intelligence. However, today there is no system that combines a wide range of capabilities or presents a general solution for the autonomous acquisition of a large set of skills. The reasons for this are the limited machine learning and adaptation techniques available, and the intrinsic complexity of integrating multiple cognitive and learning capabilities into a whole architecture. The authors consider cognitive architectures in terms of effective implementation of the autonomous properties.

The authors [18] emphasize the importance of the situational awareness module in a cognitive architecture, which includes a broad set of information and analytical requirements. To use it properly, the system must be able to determine the appropriate level of focus for information input at the global, or system level, as well as at the local level, integrating them into a unified picture of the situation. This requires both goal-driven processing and data-driven processing. The former aims at examining the environment according to current unresolved goals, while the latter receives signals from the environment and decides whether new active goals are needed to properly align with the intentions. Dynamic switching between the two models of information processing, according to the authors, is important for successful performance in many environments.

In [19] the authors present their vision of the approach to creating a hybrid intelligent information system for the basis of cognitive architecture. The authors understand "hybrid intelligent systems" as systems with hybridization of different methods of soft computing, expert systems, neuro-fuzzy systems, fuzzy expert systems, using evolutionary methods to build neural networks and other methods. In their paper the authors consider a simple example of a perception-action cycle for a cognitive architecture based on geo-information system.

A comparative analysis of the cognitive architectures of Cyc, Soar, Society of Mind and Neurocognitive Networks is given in [13], ACT-R, Epic, Soar in [12], ACT-R, ICARUS, PRODIGY in [15], ACT-R, Soar, LIDA, SiMA, NEF (SPAUN), iCub, SEMLINCS, Summary in [20]; ACT-R, Soar, NARS, OSCAR, AKIRA, CLARION, LIDA and Ikon Flux in [17]; Soar, ACT-R, EPIC, Clarion in [14], SOAR, ACT-R, CLARION and Vector-LIDA in [21].

Analysis of the above literary sources showed that the concept of "cognitive architecture" has existed since the middle of the 20th century. This term, in spite of the difference in architecture components, until the current moment is understood as follows: it is a system, which has, to a greater or lesser degree, analogues cognitive functions of a human being. Very rarely is it explicitly said that this architecture interacts with humans. In the rest, just like artificial intelligence, the cognitive system exists by itself.

The main and very strong distinguish between cognitive architecture presented in this paper and existing ones is the seamless human integration, aimed at the joint development of humans and AI.

4   Co-evolutionary Hybrid Intelligence Cognitive Architecture

This section considers cognitive architecture for Co-evolutionary Hybrid Intelligence from a software developer's perspective. Unlike many software frameworks, this architecture must seamlessly include humans (Fig. 1). Humans are viewed as both a subject and an object. As a subject, the human acts as an actor in the system and influences how the system works. As a subject, the human is seen as a component of a system with its own dynamic characteristics, which change in the process of operation. In particular, there are periodic states of decreased performance, increased errors due to fatigue and stress. Medically speaking – humans experience cognitive deficits [8] that affect the overall cognitive power of the system.

Traditionally, we can see a conventional division into different stages of transformation of external signals into recognition of the situation, planning and implementation of actions: perception, cognition, knowledge acquisition and model synthesis, intention and action. All this pipeline also has an obligatory process of self-assessment (or reflection). Mathematical methods for constructing reflective processes are described in detail by V. Lefebvre [9].

The functions of the main blocks of the architecture are listed below.

- *Data Sources*. Various primary data sources (sensors) which receive information about the control object and about the parameters of a human being who is part of the hybrid intelligent system.
- *Narrow AI*. Data processing techniques including signal cleaning, initial pattern recognition, classification, and approximation. This block contains simple models of observable signals.

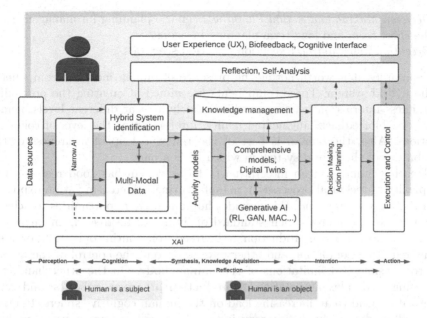

Fig. 1. Cognitive architecture for co-evolutionary hybrid intelligence

- *Multi-Modal Data.* A generalized data model, containing signals from independent sources, reduced to a single time (and space, where it makes sense).
- *Hybrid System Identification.* One of the key building blocks defining a model of a hybrid system as such. To optimize an intelligent system, having its model is required. This block is responsible for accumulation of data and prediction of the hybrid system 'behavior'.
- *Activity Models.* A person working professionally in some subject area uses two types of knowledge and skills: verbalizable and non-verbalizable. Verbalizable knowledge is comprehended by a person and can be recorded as data or rules. Non-verbalizable knowledge and nonverbalizable experience can only be extracted by observing a person's actions over a long period of time while performing the same procedure (for example: a professional golfer cannot describe the pattern of hitting with a club; a professional radiation diagnostician cannot accurately describe the sequence of processing X-rays to test a hypothesis of a diagnosis). This module is designed to observe the pattern of human actions included in the decision-making cycle in order to extract tacit knowledge. This knowledge obtained from a large number of professionals solving a similar problem can become the basis for the construction of a training system for newcomers in the subject area.
- *Digital Twins.* Full information about the hybrid system's operation during its lifetime and a set of methods for automatically identifying trends and predicting states.
- *Generative AI.* Algorithms and methods for generating decisions and directional search for options on a set of hybrid system parameters.

- *Decision Making and Action Planning.* Scenario planning for management in the short-term and long-term planning horizons.
- *Execution and Control.* Execution of action scenarios.

Separately, it is worth noting the presence of human inclusion components in the hybrid system. These components are aimed at creating the possibility of seamless interaction between machine and human at different levels: neural interfaces, biofeedback, augmented reality, interaction at the level of cognitive functions. Also, the human is part of the reflexive loop of awareness of the possibilities of the hybrid system in which he is a part.

Treating humans as an integral part of the system has good reasons. The complexity of technical processes in manufacturing is increasing at an exponential rate. On the one hand, this provides humans more opportunities to achieve various goals, to improve their standard of living, to be freed from physically demanding operations in production, to be freed from routine operations or operations requiring computing and other powers beyond the control of the human due to physiological limitations of the human body. On the other hand, the increasingly complex automation of production processes, robotics, and computerization lead to an increasing load on the human cognitive sphere. In other words, all modern technologies, reducing physical load on human organism, lead to increase of psycho-physiological load on human being, forcing him to work at the limit of his psycho-physiological possibilities, in extreme situations.

It is not enough for an intelligent system to be only a tool. To avoid severe consequences from incorrect actions, the development of human cognitive capabilities and artificial intelligence systems cannot be independent of each other. Their coordinated development is required. Such development requires reciprocal feedback between artificial and human manifestations of intelligence. Mutual evaluation of agents in analyzing the situation and choosing the best action is necessary to achieve the goals.

The main characteristics of Co-Evolutionary Intelligence systems as a single working organism are:

- mutual learning, when artificial and human intelligent agents complement each other in those areas where their cognitive capabilities are limited due to various reasons;
- personification, i.e. tuning of artificial intelligence systems for a definite person (or persons if we are dealing with system with group of human agents), with whom they form a single organism, a system, for achieving certain goals;
- condition monitoring of intellectual agents.

For the implementation of the last two items it is necessary to introduce modules on monitoring and estimation of a psycho-physiological state of a human into the cognitive architecture.

Following Bartlett's classification [22,23], it is possible to distinguish two main groups of indicators of the functional states of a person in the loop of production: physiological and psychological. As possible indicators of the dynamics of physical state are considered a variety of types of bio-electrical indicators:

EEC, ECG, temperature, pressure and others. There is a huge number of devices that allow to measure these indicators. The group of indicators of psychological state dynamics includes performance criteria of different psychometric tests and analysis of subjective symptomatic of specific types of functional states. In most cases during production processes there is no possibility of invasive measurement of physical indicators or passing tests to evaluate psychological criteria.

5   Conclusion

Throughout the history of artificial intelligence, it has often been viewed largely as an independent tool. This tool can be trained (or can itself be trained) to perform certain tasks autonomously. From the position of cognitive sciences, intelligence is a system of cognitive functions, capable, among other things, of creating symbolic models and operations with them. Creating symbolic systems for abstract reasoning is the basis for transferring experience from one domain to another and for generalizations. Currently, there are no examples of software or mathematical systems capable of creating meaningful symbolic systems without human intervention. At the same time, in many narrow applications artificial methods are much more efficient than humans in some domains. At development of intellectual systems it makes sense to consider a human as a carrier of some unique cognitive abilities which being integrated with machine methods possess intellectual power surpassing a human and a machine separately. The considered cognitive architecture for co-evolving hybrid intelligence allows to take into account the peculiarities of a human as an intelligent agent. Hybrid evolving systems can become the basis for intelligence superior to human capabilities.

It is also worth to mention, we have a lot of knowledge that we can't impose on intelligent systems. Therefore, mutual learning between humans and machines is a very delicate topic. It is obvious that the philosophical and ethical exploration can not be ignored, those topics should be one of the core future discussion. A significant issue for ethical research would be the potential for the human-machine interaction process to get out of control and become unsupervised, where the role and importance of intelligent system in the bilateral overall process may become asymmetrically reinforced and acquire the properties of a ≪defining dominant≫. In other words, by outsourcing to a machine functions that in the mathematical and algorithmic dimension humans are incapable of performing, there is a risk of gradual loss of control not only over a particular system decision, but also of control over strategic goals, the system of checkpoints ("taboos") and the definition of basic movement coordinates that have always been in human hands when interacting with machinery [4].

References

1. Colom, R., Karama, S., Jung, R.E., Haier, R.J.: Human intelligence and brain networks. J. Dialogues Clin. Neurosci. **12**(4), 489–501 (2010)

2. Engelbart, D.: Augmenting human intellect: a conceptual framework (1962). https://www.dougengelbart.org/content/view/138/000/. Accessed 10 May 2022

3. Akata, Z., et al.: A research agenda for hybrid intelligence: augmenting human intellect with collaborative, adaptive, responsible, and explainable artificial intelligence. Computer **53**, 18–28 (2020)

4. Krinkin, K., Shichkina, Y., Ignatyev, A.: Co-evolutionary hybrid intelligence. In: 2021 5th Scientific School Dynamics of Complex Networks and their Applications (DCNA), pp. 112–115 (2021). https://doi.org/10.1109/DCNA53427.2021.9587002

5. Goessl, V., Curtiss, J., Hofmann, S.: The effect of heart rate variability biofeedback training on stress and anxiety: a meta-analysis. Psychol. Med. **47**(15), 2578–2586 (2017). https://doi.org/10.1017/S0033291717001003

6. Dessy, E., Van Puyvelde, M., Mairesse, O., et al.: Cognitive performance enhancement: do biofeedback and neurofeedback work? J. Cogn. Enhanc. **2**, 12–42 (2018). https://doi.org/10.1007/s41465-017-0039-y

7. Sutarto, A.P., Wahab, M.N.A., Zin, N.M.: Effect of biofeedback training on operator's cognitive performance. Work **44**, 231–243 (2013)

8. Deligkaris, P., Panagopoulou, E., Montgomery, A.J., Masoura, E.: Job burnout and cognitive functioning: a systematic review. Work Stress: Int. J. Work Health Organ. **28**(2), 107–123 (2014)

9. Lefebvre, V.A.: Conflict Structures, 1st edn., p. 144. Leaf and Oaks Publishers (2015)

10. Newell, A.: Unified Theories of Cognition, p. 544. Harvard University Press, Cambridge (1990)

11. Turing, A.M.: Computing machinery and intelligence. Mind **LIX**(236), 433–460 (1950)

12. Taatgen, N., Anderson, J.: The past, present, and future of cognitive architectures. Top. Cogn. Sci. **2**, 693–704 (2009)

13. Sowa, J.F.: Cognitive architectures for conceptual structures. In: Andrews, S., Polovina, S., Hill, R., Akhgar, B. (eds.) ICCS 2011. LNCS (LNAI), vol. 6828, pp. 35–49. Springer, Heidelberg (2011). https://doi.org/10.1007/978-3-642-22688-5_3

14. Taatgen, N.A., Anderson, J.R.: Constraints in cognitive architectures. In: Sun, R. (ed.) Handbook of Computational Psychology, pp. 170–185 (2008)

15. Langley, P., Laird, J., Rogers, S.: Cognitive architectures: research issues and challenges. Cogn. Syst. Res. **10**, 141–160 (2009)

16. Burghart, C., et al.: A cognitive architecture for a humanoid robot: a first approach, pp. 357–362 (2005)

17. Thorisson, K.R., Helgasson, H.P.: Cognitive architectures and autonomy: a comparative review. J. Artif. Gener. Intell. **3**(2), 1–30 (2012)

18. Howard, N.: Cognitive architecture: integrating situation awareness and intention awareness. Brain Sci. J. **3**, 62–84, 9 (2012)

19. Chernenkiy, V., Gapanyuk, Y., Terekhov, V., Revunkov, G., Kaganov, Y.: The hybrid intelligent information system approach as the basis for cognitive architecture. Proc. Comput. Sci. **145**, 143–152 (2018)

20. Jimenez, J.P., Martin, L., Dounce, I.A., et al.: Methodological aspects for cognitive architectures construction: a study and proposal. Artif. Intell. Rev. **54**, 2133–2192 (2021)

21. Lieto, A., Lebiere, C., Oltramari, A.: The knowledge level in cognitive architectures: current limitations and possible developments. Cogn. Syst. Res. **48**, 39–55 (2018)

22. Bartlett, F.C.: Psychological criteria of fatigue. In: Floyed W.F., Welford, A.T. (eds.) Simposeum of Fatigue (1953)

23. Bartlett, F.C.: The Mind at Work and Play, American edition. George Allen and Unwin/Beacon Press, London/Boston (1951)
24. Wang, P.: On defining artificial intelligence. J. Artif. Gener. Intell. **10**(Issue 2), 1–37 (2019)

An Approach to Generation Triggers for Parrying Backdoor in Neural Networks

Menisov Artem[(⊠)] [iD]

Space Military Academia named By A.F. Mozhaysky, Zhdanovskay Street, 13,
Saint-Petersburg 197198, Russia
vka@mil.ru

Abstract. The lack of transparency in the results of the work of artificial neural networks makes them vulnerable to backdoor-attacks, which leads to unexpected results and loss of their effectiveness. The backdoor can remain hidden indefinitely until activated by modified data input, and pose an information security threat to all applications, but especially those associated with critical information infrastructure objects.

The article presents an approach to detect and neutralize the consequences of backdoor-attacks in neural networks, based on the identification of a backdoor and possible triggers. Taking into account the peculiarities of training artificial neural networks, the authors present the result of research aimed at determining 1) the presence of a trigger that will give incorrect results of the neural network, 2) the characteristics of the trigger, and 3) actions to neutralize the possibility of trigger activation.

The novelty of the obtained results lies in the development of a new approach for detecting bugs in neural networks based on synthesizing triggers, including 1) an algorithm for determining the target class for an attack, 2) a model correction algorithm based on neuron reduction, and 3) a model correction algorithm based on learning cancellation.

The authors also conducted experiments to parry this threat using the developed approach and evaluated the effectiveness of using neuron pruning and canceling neural network training.

The work is winner of nationwide contest for most innovative projects Code Artificial Intelligence (214635) and got funds from The Foundation for Assistance to Small Innovative Enterprises (FASIE) (Module for protecting neural networks from computer backdoor-attacks (PROTECA) www.proteca.tech).

Keywords: Artificial intelligence · Artificial neural network · Transparency · Information security · Computer attacks · Backdoor in neural networks · Synthesized triggers

1 Introduction

Today Artificial neural networks (ANNs) play an integral role in various objects of critical information infrastructure [1–4] from classification systems such as face and

B. Goertzel et al. (Eds.): AGI 2022, LNAI 13539, pp. 304–314, 2023.
https://doi.org/10.1007/978-3-031-19907-3_29

iris recognition to voice interfaces and control of unmanned vehicles. In information security, the range of applications of ANN is no less extensive - from the classification of malicious programs [5] to reverse engineering [6] and the detection of computer incidents in the network [7, 8].

Despite the advantages, ANNs also have disadvantages, the main of which is poor transparency, that is, the lack of an open, comprehensive, accessible, clear, and understandable presentation of information [9]. By their nature, ANNs are "black boxes" that are beyond human understanding. It is believed that the need for explain ability and transparency of the ANN's functioning is one of the biggest problems in their applicability [10–12]. The problem of the "black box" is the inability to fully understand and test the functioning of the ANN. This makes it possible to have backdoors in the ANN [13, 14]. Simply, backdoors are ANN defects that allow unauthorized access to data or remote control of the ANN and information resource as a whole, they cannot be detected unless they are activated by some kind of input (trigger) [15]. Backdoors can be inserted into the ANN either during training, for example, by a company employee responsible for training the model, or when it is adapted (transfer training). When performed correctly, backdoors have a minimal impact on the results of the ANN operation with normal input data, which makes them almost imperceptible for detection.

In the framework of the research, under the ANN backdoor, we mean a set of special conditions necessary to activate a backdoor or malicious code. For example, the presence of a red pixel in the lower right corner of the input image leads to an unexpected result of the ANN.

It should be noted that backdoor attacks on ANNs differ from adversarial attacks [16]. Adversarial attacks lead to the wrong result of the ANN by creating a modification for a particular image, i.e. the modification is ineffective when applied to other images. In contrast, for a backdoor attack, adding the same trigger causes arbitrary images to be misclassified. The next difference is that a backdoor needs to be injected into the model, and an adversarial attack can be successful without changing the model.

The target of the backdoor is the class "aircraft", and the trigger pattern is the red pixel in the lower right corner. Trigger patterns can have arbitrary shapes. When the backdoor is injected, a part of the training set is modified and a trigger is added to the images, and the class value is changed to the target. After training with the modified training set, the ANN recognizes the samples with the trigger as the target class. Meanwhile, the model can still correctly classify (with a certain quality) any images without a trigger.

There is also a newer approach - a Trojan attack [17], for which it is not necessary to have access to the training data set. Instead, triggers are selected that cause the maximum response of certain ANN neurons. This creates a stronger connection between triggers and intrinsic neurons and allows efficient backdoors with little modified data.

In addition to the described attacks, there is a backdoor attack within a more limited attack model, when an attacker can infect only a limited part of the training set [18]. Another direction of research determines the direct impact on the hardware on which the ANN operates [19]. Such backdoor schemes also change the performance of the model in the presence of a trigger.

In studies related to parrying ANN backdoors [20], it is a priori assumption that the model is known to be infected. But, to date, there is no effective means of detecting and mitigating the consequences of attacks using backdoors, because all approaches reveal the "signatures" present in backdoors [21]. This is due, firstly, to the fact that scanning of input data (images) for triggers is difficult because the trigger can take on arbitrary shapes and can be designed to avoid detection (for example, a small patch of pixels in a corner). Secondly, the analysis of the internal structure of the ANN for detecting anomalies in intermediate states is complicated. The interpretation of predictions and activations in the inner layers of the ANN is still an open research problem [22], and it is difficult to find an adequate approach that generalizes the results of the ANN.

Statement of the Research Problem. Within the framework of this study, three scientific tasks were set:

- backdoor detection: it is necessary to make a binary decision about whether this ANN is infected with a backdoor;
- backdoor identification: in case of infection it is necessary to determine the triggers of the backdoor attack;
- backdoor neutralization: it is necessary to make the backdoor ineffective.

Let Z represent the ANN output data set. Consider the ANN result $z_i \in Z$ and the target result $z_t \in Z$, $i \neq t$. If there is a trigger T_t that initiates z_t, then the minimum perturbation required to convert all ANN results z_i into z_t, is limited by the size of the trigger:

$$\Delta_{i \to t} \leq |T_t|. \tag{1}$$

This means that triggers must be added to the public value join model, this means that triggers will be added to the data regardless of their true z_i class:

$$\Delta_{\forall \to t} \leq |T_t|, \tag{2}$$

where $\Delta_{\forall \to t}$ is the minimum change required for any data to be classified as z_t.

In addition, to avoid detection, the value of the change should be small, that is, significantly less than is required to determine the desired value of the z_i class. Thus, if there is a backdoor trigger T_t, then the expression is true:

$$\Delta_{\forall \to t} \leq |T_t| \ll \min_{i, i \neq t} \Delta_{\forall \to i}. \tag{3}$$

Thus, it is possible to identify the trigger T_t only by detecting a small value $\Delta_{\forall \to i}$ among all ANN results.

The following restrictions are introduced in the research: 1) there is access to a trained ANN, 2) there is access to a set of correctly labeled samples to test the performance of the model, 3) there is access to computing resources for testing or modifying the ANN, for example, to graphic processors or cloud services on GPU base.

2 Description of the Approach

The approach for detecting and parrying backdoor attacks in neural network models includes the following phases:

- backdoor detection;
- trigger identification;
- backdoor neutralization.

To identify backdoors, it is necessary to take into account that in the infected model for the target class, fewer modifications are required to cause an erroneous classification than for other classes. Therefore, backdoor detection is based on enumeration of all model classes and determination of the class for which fewer changes are required to cause an ANN error. The whole process of backdoor detection consists of three stages.

Stage 1. A certain class must be considered as a target for a backdoor attack. The trigger for it is determined by the smallest set of pixels and the color in the image. The function to apply a trigger to the original image x:

$$f(x, m, T) = x^*,$$

$$x^*_{i,j,c} = (1 - m_{i,j})x_{i,j,c} + m_{i,j}T_{i,j,c}, \tag{4}$$

where T is a trigger pattern, which is a 3D matrix of pixel values with the same dimensions as the input image (height, width, and color); m is a two-dimensional matrix (height, width) called a mask that determines how much the trigger can overwrite the original image. The mask values range from 0 to 1. When $m_{i,j} = 1$ for a specific pixel (i, j), the trigger completely overwrites the original color ($x^*_{i,j,c} = T_{i,j,c}$), while for $m_{i,j} = 0$ the original color does not change at all ($x^*_{i,j,c} = x_{i,j,c}$).

To analyze the target class z_t, it is necessary to find a trigger (m, T) that would erroneously classify images in z_t. You also need to define a trigger that changes only a limited part of the image. The final expression looks like this.

$$\min_{m,T}(l(y_t, f(x, m, T)) + \beta m), \tag{5}$$

where l is a loss function that measures the classification error; β is the weighting factor. A lower weight gives a smaller trigger size but may result in a higher probability of misclassification.

Stage 2. Repeat stage 1 for each ANN result. For a model with $N = Z$ classes, this gives N potential triggers.

Stage 3. After calculating N potential triggers, the size of each trigger is measured by the number of pixels that each synthesized trigger has, i.e., how many pixels the trigger replaces. The minimum triggers capable of realizing a backdoor attack are determined.

These three steps allow you to determine if there is a backdoor in the ANN. If the result is positive and there are several candidates (synthesized triggers), it is necessary to identify the tab, that is, to find a correspondence between the synthesized triggers and the original trigger used by the offender. With high compliance, synthesized triggers can be used to develop mechanisms to neutralize the consequences of a backdoor attack.

Matching triggers can be searched in three ways [23].

Backdoor Efficiency Comparison. Like the original trigger, the synthesized trigger results in a high computer attack success probability (actually higher than the original trigger). This is an optimization of the incorrect protection of the ANN. An allergic synthesized trigger is revealed, which affects the same result of an incorrect reaction.

Visual Similarity. The original and synthesized triggers (m, T) are compared, which produce similarity with the original triggers and produce them in the same place on the image. However, there are slight differences between synthesized and original triggers. In an ANN that processes color images, synthesized triggers can be more light sensitive. First, the efficiency of the computer capture when the model detects the detection of a trigger that does not have a detected fluid and color. Secondly, the purpose of generating triggers is to reduce the size of the trigger. Therefore, some redundant pixels in the trigger will be removed in the process. In approximating this transformation, the process is more like a more compact form of the backdoor trigger compared to the original trigger.

Similarities in the Activation of Neurons. Check whether the synthesized triggers and the original trigger involved in the activation of neurons at the internal level take place. You should start with the penultimate layer since this layer encodes all representative patterns. Through the appearance of pure and malicious images (containing a trigger) at the input of the ANN, it may be the most important for laying neurons from the second to the last layer. That is, if neurons are activated by original triggers, then they are activated by synthesized triggers. This shows that when a synthesized trigger is added to the input, the same neurons associated with the backdoor are activated as well as the original trigger.

Backdoor Neutralization. Once the backdoor is detected and the trigger is identified, it is necessary to apply consequences parrying techniques to remove the backdoor while maintaining ANN performance. The study proposes two complementary options. The first is to fix the ANN by making it immune to the detected backdoor triggers by pruning neurons. The second is the cancellation of training.

Correction of ANN by Pruning Neurons.
To fix an infected ANN, it is necessary to identify the ANN neurons associated with the tab and remove them or set the output value of these neurons to zero during inference. Using a synthesized trigger, one should rank the neurons on the penultimate layer according to the difference between clean and malicious data. Those neurons that have a high rank, that is, show a high gap in activation between clean and malicious data, must be removed from the ANN. In order not to reduce the quality of the ANN, it is necessary to stop removing neurons from the ANN when the model no longer responds to the synthesized trigger.

The obvious advantage is that this approach requires little computation, most of which involves the processing of safe and malicious images. However, the limitation is that performance depends on the choice of the layer to remove neurons, and this may require experimentation with multiple layers. In addition, it is subject to a requirement regarding how well the synthesized trigger matches the original trigger.

Fixing the ANN with Unlearning.
This attack neutralization approach is to train the ANN not to perceive the original trigger. Compared to pruning neurons, detraining allows the model to decide through training which weights (not neurons) should be updated.

3 Experiment

To evaluate the hypothesis and test the approach of parrying an backdoor-attack, the following actions were experimentally carried out:

1) definition of the problem of image classification and selection of an open data set;
2) backdoor configuration;
3) training the model with a backdoor;
4) identification of the backdoor;
5) backdoor neutralization.

For the experiment, we use the data set for identifying an object in aerial photographs (DOTA) [24], the data set for recognition of handwritten digits (MNIST) [25], and the data set for recognition of famous faces (LFW) [26].

The backdoor configuration occurs during ANN training. We randomly select the target class and modify the training data by adding a trigger. The trigger is a set of pixels located in the lower right corner of the image, chosen in such a way as not to cover any informative part of the image, such as ships or aircraft. The shape and color of the trigger is chosen so that it is unique and does not occur naturally in any image. To make the trigger even less visible, the trigger size is limited to less than 1% of the entire image (Table 1).

Table 1. Characteristics of the initial data of the experiment

Dataset	Number of classes	Image size	Trigger size	Train data
DOTA	15	$800 \times 800 \times 3$	24×24	188 282
MNIST	10	$28 \times 28 \times 1$	4×4	60 000
LFW	1680	$112 \times 112 \times 3$	5×5	13 233

In the course of the study, an analysis was made of the ratio of ANN quality to the proportion of modified data. It should be noted that with a change of less than 3% of the data, the quality of the ANN does not significantly decrease.

To measure the effectiveness of computer attacks on ANNs based on backdoor, it is necessary to calculate the classification accuracy of test data, as well as the probability of attack success when applying a trigger (2%) to test images. The attack effectiveness score measures the proportion of malicious images classified as the target class. As a benchmark, the average classification accuracy was measured on a conventional model (i.e., using the same ANN architecture and training parameters, but with clean data). The final performance of each attack on four tasks is presented in Table 2.

Table 2. The effectiveness of backdoor attacks on ANNs

Dataset	ANN architecture	Attack efficiency	Accuracy (with backdoor)	Accuracy (w/o backdoor)
DOTA	MaxPool + AvgPool, Conv2d, ReLu [27]	0.97405	0.871901	0.925925
MNIST	4 (Conv2D, BatchNorm2D, ReLu) [28]	0.99876	0.869902	0.981094
LFW	4 Conv2D + 1 Merge + 1 Dense [29]	0.99963	0.446505	0.542253

All backdoor attacks reach about 97% attack efficiency with a certain impact on the average classification accuracy. The largest decline in classification accuracy is 13% in MNIST.

Following the description of the developed approach, the fact of the presence of a backdoor in the ANN is further revealed. This process performs per-class validation and generates a trigger template.

The synthesized trigger will be added to the blank image to mimic the behavior of the backdoor. To determine which class is the target for a backdoor attack, it is necessary to calculate the significance value of the perturbation $\Delta_{\forall \to t}$. The value for the target class will be lower than for other classes.

Compared to the distribution of uninfected classes, the perturbation needed for the target class is always much lower than the mean of the other classes. Accordingly, the size of the trigger required for an attack is smaller compared to an attack on an uninfected class.

After determining the infected classes in the ANN, the backdoor was neutralized in the following ways:

– correction of ANN by pruning neurons;
– correction of ANN with the help of cancellation of training.

The effectiveness of neutralization and the impact on the quality of the ANN are presented in Table 3.

When correcting the ANN by pruning neurons, there is a deterioration in the work of the ANN. This is due to the fact that not only the neurons subject to backdooring are removed, but also the neurons responsible for making decisions about other classes. It should be noted that the pruning of neurons on the last ANN layer gives the best results. When pruning ¼ neurons, the effectiveness of an attack using a synthesized trigger is reduced to less than 1%. While the effectiveness of the attack with the original trigger is 3%.

Table 3. Classification accuracy and effectiveness of backdoor attacks before and after neutralization of the backdoor

Dataset	With backdoor		Pruning neurons		Cancellation of ANN training	
	Accuracy	Attack's effectiveness	Accuracy	Attack's effectiveness	Accuracy	Attack's effectiveness
DOTA	0.871901	0.97405	0.799537	0.031708	0.857714	0.039269
MNIST	0.869902	0.99876	0.784083	0.029518	0.855576	0.035861
LFW	0.446505	0.99963	0.039986	0.033778	0.419534	0.043004

When correcting an ANN with delearning, a synthesized trigger is needed to train the ANN to correctly recognize the target class when there is an anomaly. In this fall-back method, detraining allows the model to learn through training which weights (not neurons) are problematic and need to be updated.

For all models, the ANN was trained for 1 epoch using the updated training data set. The dataset consists of 20% of the original training data (pure, without triggers) and 20% of the modified data (with a synthesized trigger) without changing the class value.

4   Discussion

The description of the approach for detecting and parrying computer attacks with back-door in neural network models and the experiment carried out allows us to draw the following conclusions:

1) by increasing the size or complexity of a trigger, an attacker can make it difficult to synthesize triggers for protection;
2) the difficulty of defining several infected classes, or one class with several triggers.

When conducting the experiment, it was found that larger triggers will lead to larger synthesized triggers. The maximum detectable trigger size largely depends on one factor: the trigger size for uninfected classes (the number of changes required to misclassify all inputs between uninfected classes). Typically, a larger trigger is more visually visible and easier for a human to identify. However, there may be approaches to increase the size of the trigger, while remaining less obvious [30, 31].

It's also worth considering a scenario where attackers insert multiple independent tabs into a single model, each targeting a specific class. This will make the impact of any single trigger more difficult to detect. But, it is worth noting that a large number of backdoor can reduce the accuracy of ANN classification.

In a scenario in which several distinct triggers cause misclassification of the same class, the developed approach will allow only one of the existing backdoors to be detected and neutralized. But, the iterative execution of the neutralization of the backdoor will probably allow the ANN to be corrected from all the backdoors.

5   Conclusion

An approach to identifying and parrying the consequences of backdoor-attacks on ANNs was developed. The novelty of the research lies in the use and ranking of synthesized triggers, which makes it possible to detect the presence of backdoors in the ANN without information about its training, as well as to determine the class of images subject to attack. The study also provides complimentary methods for neutralizing bookmarks, which will allow information security specialists to more effectively counteract computer attacks on artificial intelligence technologies and develop automated information protection tools for ANNs.

References

1. Federal Law of the Russian Federation No 187-FZ of 26 July 2017: On the security of the critical information infrastructure of the Russian Federation. https://rg.ru/2017/07/31/bezopa snost-dok.html. Last accessed 01 February 2022
2. Regiment of the Russia's Federal Service for Technical and Export Control No 235 of 21 December 2017: On approval of the Requirements for the creation of security systems for significant objects of the critical information infrastructure of the Russian Federation and ensuring their functioning. https://fstec.ru/normotvorcheskaya/akty/53-prikazy/1589-prikaz-fstek-rossii-ot-21-dekabrya-2017-g-n-236. Last accessed 01 February 2022
3. Decree of the President of the Russian Federation No 899 of 7 July 2011: On approval of priority areas for the development of science, technology and technology in the Russian Federation and the list of critical technologies of the Russian Federation. http://pravo.gov.ru/proxy/ips/?docbody=&nd=102149065. Last accessed 01 February 2022
4. Decree of the President of the Russian Federation No 490 of 10 October 2019: On the development of artificial intelligence in the Russian Federation and the approval of the attached National Strategy for the Development of Artificial Intelligence for the period up to 2030. http://www.kremlin.ru/acts/bank/44731. Last accessed 01 February 2022
5. Bukhanov, D.G., Polyakov, V.M., Redkina, M.A.: Detection of malware using an artificial neural network based on adaptive resonant theory. Prikladnaya Diskretnaya Matematika **52**, 69–82 (2021)
6. Massarelli, L., et al.: Investigating graph embedding neural networks with unsupervised features extraction for binary analysis. In: the 2nd Workshop on Binary Analysis Research (BAR). Internet Society, Reston, Virginia, U.S.A. (2019)
7. Zabelina, V.A., et al.: Detecting internet attacks using a neural network. Journal Dynamics of Complex Systems - XXI century **15**(2), 39–47 (2021)
8. Arkhipova, A.B., Polyakov, P.A.: Methodology for constructing a neural fuzzy network in the field of information security. Digital technology security **3**, 43–56 (2021)

9. State Standard 59276–2020 "Artificial intelligence systems. Methods for ensuring trust. General" (2020)
10. Spitsyn, V.G., Tsoi, U.R.: Evolving artificial neural networks. Reports of the Academy of Sciences of the USSR **114**(5), 953–956 (1957)
11. McCalloch, W.S., Pitts, W.: A logical calculus of the ideas immanent in nervous activity. Bull. Math. Biophys **5**, 115–133 (1943)
12. Shevskaya, N.V.: Explainable artificial intelligence and methods for interpreting results. Modeling, optimization and information technology **9**(2), 22–23 (2021)
13. Xu, Q., Arafin, M.T., Qu, G.: Security of neural networks from hardware perspective: A survey and beyond. In: 26th Asia and South Pacific Design Automation Conference (ASP-DAC), pp. 449–454. IEEE, Tokyo, Japan (2021)
14. The information security threat database of the Federal Service for Technical and Export Control: https://bdu.fstec.ru/threat. Last accessed 01 February 2022
15. State Standard (project): Data protection. Detection, prevention and liquidation of the consequences of computer attacks and response to computer incidents. Terms and Definitions
16. Kravets, V., Javidi, B., Stern, A.: Defending deep neural networks from adversarial attacks on three-dimensional images by compressive sensing. In: 3D Image Acquisition and Display: Technology, Perception and Applications. – Optical Society of America. Washington, DC, USA (2021)
17. Liu, Y., et al.: Trojaning attack on neural networks. Department of Computer Science Technical Reports. Paper 1781. https://docs.lib.purdue.edu/cstech/1781/. Last accessed 01 February 2022
18. Chen, X., et al.: Targeted backdoor attacks on deep learning systems using data poisoning. arXiv preprint arXiv:1712.05526 (2017)
19. Li, W., et al.: Hu-fu: Hardware and software collaborative attack framework against neural networks. In: IEEE Computer Society Annual Symposium on VLSI (ISVLSI), pp. 482–487. IEEE, Hong Kong, China (2018)
20. Gong, X., et al.: Defense-resistant backdoor attacks against deep neural networks in outsourced cloud environment. IEEE J. Sel. Areas Commun. **39**(8), 2617–2631 (2021)
21. Wenger, E., et al.: Backdoor attacks against deep learning systems in the physical world. In: CVF Conference on Computer Vision and Pattern Recognition, pp. 6206–6215. IEEE (2021)
22. Shahroudnejad, A.: A survey on understanding, visualizations, and explanation of deep neural networks. arXiv preprint arXiv:2102.01792 (2021)
23. Wang, B., et al.: Neural cleanse: identifying and mitigating backdoor attacks in neural networks. In: IEEE Symposium on Security and Privacy, pp. 707–723. IEEE, San Francisco, CA, USA (2019)
24. Xia, G.S., et al.: DOTA: A large-scale dataset for object detection in aerial images. In: the IEEE conference on computer vision and pattern recognition, pp. 3974–3983. IEEE, Salt Lake City, UT, USA (2018)
25. Deng, L.: The mnist database of handwritten digit images for machine learning research [best of the web]. IEEE Signal Process. Mag. **29**(6), 141–142 (2012)
26. Huang, G.B., et al.: Labeled faces in the wild: a database for studying face recognition in unconstrained environments. In: Workshop on faces in 'Real-Life' Images: detection, alignment, and recognition, pp. 1–14. HAL, Marseille, France (2008)
27. Wang, J., et al.: Integrating weighted feature fusion and the spatial attention module with convolutional neural networks for automatic aircraft detection from SAR images. Remote Sensing **13**(5), 910 (2021)
28. An, S., et al.: An Ensemble of Simple Convolutional Neural Network Models for MNIST Digit Recognition. arXiv preprint arXiv:2008.10400 (2020)

29. Yan, M., et al.: Vargfacenet: an efficient variable group convolutional neural network for lightweight face recognition. In: The IEEE/CVF International Conference on Computer Vision Workshops, pp. 2647-2654. IEEE, Seoul, Korea (South) (2019)
30. Liu, X., et al.: Removing backdoor-based watermarks in neural networks with limited data. In: 2020 25th International Conference on Pattern Recognition (ICPR), pp. 10149–10156. IEEE, Milan, Italy (2021)
31. Kaviani, S., Sohn, I.: Defense against neural trojan attacks: a survey. Neurocomputing **423**, 651–667 (2021)

The Learning Agent Triangle: Towards a Unified Disambiguation of the AGI Challenge

Benet Oriol Sabat[✉][iD]

University of California Los Angeles, Los Angeles, CA 90095, USA
benet@cs.ucla.edu

Abstract. In this short paper, we tackle an ambiguity issue in the discussion of how to build Artificial General Intelligence (AGI), with the goal of removing a communication barrier which is arguably slowing down its development. Due to the openness of the AGI problem, many design ideas describe some aspects of a learning agent but ignore or make implicit assumptions about other key features. We argue that, when sharing AGI design hypothesis, it is necessary to describe or constrain three specific key aspects of the agent, and we explain why only discussing about a subset of these aspects reduces the usefulness of the design hypothesis for the progress towards AGI. We disambiguate the design of a machine learning agent into what we call the Learning Agent Triangle, formed by the architecture, the objective goal and the optimization algorithm, which are conditioned by the computational resources. It must be noted that, even if the learning agent triangle might not be the most general or accurate way to describe any kind of agent, this model can be used as a framework to guide a description of an AGI in a complete enough way that the value of the contribution is not negatively affected by ambiguity or communication issues.

1 Introduction

Even if most of the success of AI has been for specific tasks and scenarios, the question of how to build generally intelligent machines is raising interest within the research community. However, AGI has not been fully consolidated as an independent and mainstream branch of research and experts from a broad range of AI subfields are now engaging in the discussion of how current artificial intelligence systems will scale to robust, truly intelligent cognitive systems.

We have observed a very wide spectrum of opinions, points of views and interpretations of which are the fundamental research problems we need to tackle in order to solve general intelligence. The opinions on this topic can range from models based on neuroscience [1] to hypothesis about the potential of large language models or chatbots [2], among many others. Many times, these opinions provide very valuable ideas towards AGI but only cover partially some of the potentially relevant aspects. We hypothesize that this lack of completeness in the

B. Goertzel et al. (Eds.): AGI 2022, LNAI 13539, pp. 315–320, 2023.
https://doi.org/10.1007/978-3-031-19907-3_30

opinions on how to build general intelligence is actually a major barrier towards AGI. We argue that this ambiguity and communication issue doesn't allow for the optimal collaboration and spreading of ideas, and it limits to a great extent the potential of working in community, which is at the core of how science and technology progress.

In this work, we will i) analyse the issue of ambiguity of the AGI paradigm and ii) propose a framework to define unified strategies towards AGI. The ultimate goal of this work is to ensure all contributions to AGI are complete enough to provide value to the community, while keeping an accessible model that also narrows the gap between the design of current AI systems and the design of an AGI. We attempt to do so by breaking down the design of a learning agent into a three-blocks model, therefore disambiguating the problem of designing a generally intelligent agent into three clearer design questions. The three main characteristics that we use to fully describe a learning agent are: i) architecture, ii) objective goal and iii) optimization method. We call this the Learning Agent Triangle. Even if at first this can seem like an overly simplistic categorization, in Sect. 3 we will explain how concepts like active learning, multi-agency, self-learning, human interaction or embodiment could fit into this model.

In addition to the Learning Agent Triangle, we will consider the element of the computational framework, which refers to the assumptions made on the computational limitations with which the hypothetical AGIs are designed. This is a crucial factor to consider in the design, and we argue this is a major part of the communication issue in the community.

2   Importance of a Complete Design Description

As we have introduced in Sect. 1, there is a wide range of ideas about which are the fundamental research issues that the scientific community needs to focus on in order to build an AGI. Many times, these ideas describe aspects that might be valuable, like model architectures, but often ignore other aspects like what objective function will these models be optimized for or what are the required computational resources to train such systems.

The reason we argue that it is paramount to simultaneously describe all elements of the Learning Agent Triangle is that, most of the times, the validity of the design choices of a subset of the elements of the triangle is greatly affected by the assumptions made in the remaining ones. In other words, aspects like which architecture will be used, depend so much on other aspects like the available computational resources, that it is necessary to give a joint description of the different the aspects of the agent. For example, the hypothesis that language models can scale into AGI is not invalid but might not directly contribute to the progress towards AGI, without constraining the amount of data and computational resources available, since one could argue a language model might or might not scale into AGI depending on those factors.

This issue has an additional challenge, which is that a large volume of AGI ideas are shared through less formal channels like oral talks, which makes it more difficult to detect and formally analyse the issue. Arguably, this formality challenge is intrinsic to the issue we are attempting to tackle, since the limitations of these communication channels might be one of the causes of the ambiguity we described. In Appendix A we analyse a specific example of a scenario where this issue is manifested.

3 The Learning Agent Triangle

We introduce a way of describing a learning agent through three main components: the *architecture*, the *objective goal* and the *optimization method*, which provide a simplified description of the agent. These three features are conditioned by the available *computational resources*. Even though this is not a common description of machine learning models, it has been designed in a way that multiple AGI ideas can fit in, while keeping some of the intuitions of *narrow-AI* models. Moreover, even if it might be an incomplete description for AGI, the purpose of this model is not to give a detailed description of the system but to encourage all researchers to provide more complete, less ambiguous, and ultimately more valuable takes on AGI approaches. We see a diagram of the model in Fig. 1.

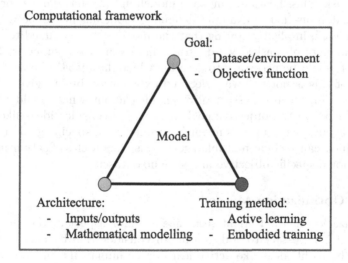

Fig. 1. Diagram of the Learning Agent Triangle

3.1 The Architecture

The architecture can be described as two main components: i) the input and output information of the system and ii) the mathematical structure between the two. In terms of input and output information, some opinions can arise regarding, for example, if a textual interface is enough to yield AGI, whether multimodality will be necessary, or if AGI might need direct access to the internet. Other common discussions around the architecture include whether deep learning can scale into AGI, whether we need to inspire our models on how human brain works, or how to include short and long term memory in the systems, among many others. To exemplify why it is necessary to provide information about other aspects of the model we can consider the case of a 1 hidden layer perceptron. This model can theoretically approximate any function by mapping the input into a big enough hidden space, hence making in plausible to approximate an AGI. However, the computation needed to scale an MLP into to AGI-complex mapping might be very high. With this example we demonstrate how the question *which is the best architecture for AGI?* is too open, and a more valuable, less ambiguous approach is *which is the best architecture for AGI, given our limited computational resources?*, for example.

3.2   The Objective Goal

Currently, statistical models learn through the optimization of an objective function. In this category, we don't just include what is usually described as the "loss function", but we mainly refer to the training paradigms (supervision, reinforcement, ...), task (classification, language modelling, ...) and dataset or environment when it is used. For example, language modeling might be an example of objective goal, implicitly stating that the model will be trained to maximize a prediction score of masked words in a sentence in a self-supervised fashion. Moreover, it would be necessary to describe which data would be used for that. The point of this is not to give a detailed explanation but to give a bound of dataset size and, when necessary, give an idea about what would the labels, domain, etc. be. In the objective goal we can also consider ideas like training with multi-agency, since models might be trained for a specific goal in a specific scenario which can include multiple agents, just like a classification model can be trained for a specific objective in a specific dataset.

3.3   The Optimization Method

The optimization method might seem like a minor aspect of the design. However, we find it necessary to add as a major consideration because of two main ideas. Firstly, to fit ideas like active learning or human interaction, where the training procedure might receive feedback from the model or external sources. Secondly, because in the case of RL agents or embodied systems, problems like the exploration-exploitation trade-off, cold start, few-shot learning, etc. might be major issues to consider when training an AGI.

3.4   Conditioned by the Computational Limitations

Even though a model can be fully described without specifying how long it took to train or how much memory it needs, the computational limitations might be the most important factor to consider in practice. In Sect. 3.1 we have already given an example of why the computational limitations are so important to define aspects like the architecture. Computational limitations will impact many other aspects of the model like the amount of data that can be used or the exploration-exploitation trade-off in RL training, among many others.

4   Discussion

We hypothesize that the technological progress of AGI would advance faster in the scenario where all aspects of a trained agent were always jointly described or somehow constrained in the discussion of how to build AGI. We explain why this happens and how this is related to the ambiguity or openness of the AGI question. We propose a framework with which to guide a description that is complete enough for the contribution to add as much value as possible to the AGI community by specifically avoiding ambiguity. The model is not meant to fit very well all of the AGI ideas, approaches and proposals. However, by following this guideline, it is likely to greatly diminish the issues described and arguably speed up the progress towards AGI.

A   Study Case: Y. Bengio Discusses His Ideas with L. Fridman

Due to the early stage in which AGI research currently is, some of the experts in AI do not have complete formal publications or statements where they express their thoughts on AGI design. Even though Yoshua Bengio does have a few papers describing some of his ideas, we will focus on a short segment of the 4th episode of the Lex Fridman Podcast[1], where the host (Lex Fridman) discusses with Yoshua Bengio about high-level cognition systems. The purpose of this study case is to exemplify how the ambiguity of the AGI paradigm created a barrier towards a constructive discussion.

We will first comment on a segment starting at 6:44. We see Bengio point out how the most important research questions for high-level cognition are not the architecture or dataset used but what do we optimize our models for and how. Bengio suggests that active learning might have a crucial role but does not describe any specific training objective. Therefore, he gives some ideas regarding the training procedure and possibly some implicit architectural features, both due to active learning. However, it remains unclear what would the model be trained for (objective task).

The discussion continues at at 9:30. Fridman is pointing out how large-scale language models, which are now showing some surprisingly robust behaviours in some scenarios, might scale into more intelligent, high-level cognition agents. Bengio answers he is sure they will not.

---

[1] https://www.youtube.com/watch?v=azOmzumh0vQ.

What we think Fridman is referring to is whether just by training a sufficiently big enough model with enough data, this might yield high-level representations like the ones humans have. What Bengio seems to understand is that Friedman is suggesting to solely increase the amount of layers and this will make the model learn more abstract representations, to which he does not agree. Fridman's question might be a bit ambiguous. A more suitable approach would have been something like: *With sufficiently computing power and data, can current large-scale language models learn cognitively high representations by increasing the capacity of the model?*. This question is more suitable because it specifies the computational limitations, the task (language modelling), the architecture (transformer-like). The question could also include the description of the training procedure, even if one might assume the usual training procedure of gradient optimization with mini-batch sampling or we could have active learning ideas coming in.

References

1. Bengio, Y.: The consciousness prior. arXiv preprint arXiv:1709.08568 (2017)
2. Grudin, J., Jacques, R.: Chatbots, humbots, and the quest for artificial general intelligence. In: Proceedings of the 2019 CHI Conference on Human Factors in Computing Systems. Association for Computing Machinery (2019). https://doi.org/10.1145/3290605.3300439

Maze Learning Using a Hyperdimensional Predictive Processing Cognitive Architecture

Alexander G. Ororbia[1](✉) [iD] and M. Alex Kelly[2] [iD]

[1] Rochester Institute of Technology, Rochester, NY 14623, USA
ago@cs.rit.edu
[2] Carleton University, Ottawa, ON K1S 5B6, Canada
alex.kelly@carleton.ca

Abstract. We present the COGnitive Neural GENerative system (CogNGen), a cognitive architecture that combines two neurobiologically-plausible, computational models: predictive processing and hyperdimensional/vector-symbolic models. We draw inspiration from architectures such as ACT-R and Spaun/Nengo. CogNGen is in broad agreement with these, providing a level of detail between ACT-R's high-level symbolic description of human cognition and Spaun's low-level neurobiological description, furthermore creating the groundwork for designing agents that learn continually from diverse tasks and model human performance at larger scales than what is possible with current systems. We test CogNGen on four maze-learning tasks, including those that test memory and planning, and find that CogNGen matches performance of deep reinforcement learning models and exceeds on a task designed to test memory.

Keywords: Cognitive architectures · Predictive processing · Memory

1 Introduction

Artificial neural networks (ANNs) do not typically model high-level cognition and are usually models of only one task. Otherwise, when an ANN is trained to learn a series of tasks, catastrophic interference occurs, with each new task causing the ANN to forget all prior tasks [3,12,13]. On the other hand, symbolic cognitive architectures, such as the widely used ACT-R [19], can capture the complexities of high-level cognition but scale poorly to the naturalistic data of sensory perception or to big data necessary for modelling life-long learning.

We propose a cognitive architecture [15] that is built from two neurobiologically and cognitively plausible models, namely neural generative coding (NGC) [16] (a form of predictive processing) and vector-symbolic (a.k.a. hyperdimensional) models of memory [7,10]. Desirably, using these specific building blocks yields scalable, local Hebbian [6] update rules for adjusting the system's synapses while facilitating robustness in acquiring, storing, and composing representations

B. Goertzel et al. (Eds.): AGI 2022, LNAI 13539, pp. 321–331, 2023.
https://doi.org/10.1007/978-3-031-19907-3_31

of tasks encountered sequentially [12]. Our intent is to advance towards an architecture capable of intelligent action at all scales of learning, from the small maze tasks considered here, to skills acquired gradually over a lifetime. By combining NGC with vector-symbolic models of human memory, we work towards creating a model of cognition that has the power of modern machine learning techniques while retaining long-term memory, single-trial and transfer-learning, planning, and other capacities associated with high-level cognition.

In this work, we demonstrate proof of concept and show that our architecture, CogNGen (the COGnitive Neural GENerative system; see [15] for details), can learn variants of a maze-learning task, including those requiring planning (get a key to open a locked door) and memory (pick a path based on an earlier cue). Our results show that CogNGen is competitive with several deep learning approaches, offering promising performance when task reward is sparse. We start by describing the circuits and core modules used to construct CogNGen. Then, we describe the tasks used to evaluate CogNGen and the experimental results.

2 Neural Building Blocks

2.1 Neural Generative Coding (NGC)

Neural generative coding (NGC) is an instantiation of the predictive processing brain theory [4,18], yielding a robust form of predict-then-correct learning and inference. An NGC circuit in CogNGen receives two sensory vectors, input $\mathbf{x}^i \in \mathcal{R}^{I \times 1}$ (I is the input dimensionality) and output $\mathbf{x}^o \in \mathcal{R}^{O \times 1}$ (O is the output dimensionality). An NGC circuit is composed of L layers of neurons, i.e., layer ℓ is represented by state vector $\mathbf{z}^\ell \in \mathcal{R}^{H_\ell \times 1}$ containing H_ℓ total units. Given an input–output pair of sensory vectors $\mathbf{x}^i$ and $\mathbf{x}^o$, the circuit clamps the last layer $\mathbf{z}^L$ to the input, $\mathbf{z}^L = \mathbf{x}^i$, and clamps the first layer $\mathbf{z}^0$ to the output, $\mathbf{z}^0 = \mathbf{x}^o$. Once clamped, the NGC circuit will undergo a settling cycle where it processes the input and output vectors for several steps in time (i.e., it processes sensory signals over a stimulus window of K discrete time steps). After processing the input–output pair over a stimulus window, the synaptic matrices are adjusted via local Hebbian-like updates. See the Appendix[1] for details of the exact mechanics/dynamics of the NGC circuits we implemented for this paper.

2.2 Memory

For CogNGen, we model both short and long-term memory using the MINERVA 2 model of human memory [7]. Short-term MINERVA 2 is cleared after an episode is completed (e.g., a maze is solved), whereas the contents of long-term MINERVA 2 persist across episodes. MINERVA 2 is a model of human memory equivalent to a type of Hebbian network [10]. We choose MINERVA 2 since it captures a wide variety of human memory phenomena, e.g., [7,9,10]. Our implementation of MINERVA 2 stores a sequence of observations as a concatenated

---

[1] Appendix: https://www.cs.rit.edu/~ago/cogngnen_agi2022_append.pdf.

vector. Each sequence is represented as a row in the memory table. Retrieval from memory is a weighted sum of all rows in the table, each row weighted by the similarity to the currently observed sequence, allowing MINERVA 2 to predict the next observations(s) given the agent's recent history. Growth of the memory table is limited by forgetting simulated as random deletion [7].

3   The CogNGen Cognitive Architecture

3.1   Perceptual Modules

CogNGen's perceptual module encodes observation $o_t \in \mathcal{R}^{D_o \times 1}$ at time t to $z_t \in \mathcal{R}^{D_z \times 1}$ (and decodes it back) – D_o is the dimension of o_t and D_z is that of z_t. Although this process can be implemented in NGC circuits, in this work, we leverage an encoder and decoder offered by the task environment (see Appendix).

3.2   Procedural Memory and Motor Control

The Procedural Dynamics Model: Motivated by the finding of expected value estimation in the brain, CogNGen's procedural module implements a neural circuit that produces intrinsic reward signals. At a high level, this neural machinery facilitates some of the functionality of the basal ganglia and procedural memory, simulating an internal reward-creation process [20]. Concretely, we refer to the above as an NGC dynamics model, where reward is calculated as a function of its error neurons, further coupled to a short-term MINERVA 2 memory "filter".

The NGC dynamics circuit processes the current state z_t and the external discrete action a_t^{ext} ($a_t^{ext} \in \{0,1\}^{A_{ext} \times 1}$ is its one-hot encoding, where A_{ext} is the number of actions), as produced by the motor-action model (described later), and predicts the value of the future state z_{t+1}. When provided with z_{t+1}, the dynamics circuit runs the following for its layer-wise predictions:

$$\bar{z}^2 = \mathbf{W}_{ext}^3 \cdot a_t^{ext} + \mathbf{W}_z^3 \cdot z_t + \mathbf{b}_2 \tag{1}$$

$$\bar{z}^1 = \mathbf{W}^2 \cdot \phi(z_t^2) + \mathbf{b}_1 \tag{2}$$

$$\hat{z}_{t+1} = \bar{z}^0 = g^0 \left(\mathbf{W}^1 \cdot \phi(z_t^1) + \mathbf{b}_0 \right) \tag{3}$$

and leverages the NGC settling process (see Appendix) to compute its internal state values, i.e., z_t^3, z_t^2, z_t^1. Notice that we have simplified a few items with respect to the NGC circuit – the topmost layer-wise prediction $\bar{z}_t^3$ sets $\phi^3(\mathbf{v}) = \mathbf{v}$ for both its top-most inputs c_t^{ext} and z_t, the post-activation prediction functions for the internal layers are $g^2(\mathbf{v}) = g^1(\mathbf{v}) = \mathbf{v}$, and $phi^2(\mathbf{v}) = \phi^1(\mathbf{v}) = \phi(\mathbf{v})$ (the same state activation function type is used in calculating $\hat{z}^1$ and $\hat{z}^0$). Once the above dynamics have been executed, the NGC dynamics model's synapses are adjusted via Hebbian updates. Furthermore, upon receiving z_{t+1}, the short-term MINERVA 2 coupled to the dynamics circuit stores the current latent state vector, updating its current knowledge about the episode that CogNGen is operating with, and outputs a similarity score s^{recall}. Note that, at the an episode's termination, the contents of the short-term MINERVA 2 are cleared.

To generate the value of the epistemic reward [17]), the dynamics model first settles to a prediction $\hat{\mathbf{z}}_{t+1}$ given the value of CogNGen's next latent state $\mathbf{z}_{t+1}$. After its settling process has finished, the activity signals of its (squared) error neurons are summed to obtain the circuit's epistemic reward signal:

$$r_t^{ep} = \sum_j (\mathbf{e}^0)_{j,1}^2 + \sum_j (\mathbf{e}^1)_{j,1}^2 + \sum_j (\mathbf{e}^2)_{j,1}^2 \tag{4}$$

$$r_t^{ep} = r_t^{ep}/(r_{max}^{ep}) \quad \text{where } r_{max}^{ep} = \max(r_1^{ep}, r_2^{ep}, ..., r_t^{ep}) \tag{5}$$

where the epistemic reward signal is normalized to the range of $[0, 1]$ by tracking the maximum epistemic signal observed throughout the course of the simulation. This signal is next modified by the MINERVA 2 memory filter as follows:

$$r^{ep} = \begin{cases} \eta_e r^{ep} & s^{recall} \leq s_\theta \\ -0.1 & \text{otherwise} \end{cases} \tag{6}$$

where s_θ is a threshold that s^{recall} is compared against and $0 \leq \eta_e \leq 1$ is meant to weight the epistemic signal. If $s^{recall} \leq s^\theta$, then $\mathbf{z}_{t+1}$ is deemed "unfamiliar" and the agent is positively rewarded with the epistemic reward for uncovering a new state of its environment. Whereas if the opposite is true ($s^{recall} > s^\theta$), then the latent state is deemed familiar and the agent is given a negative penalty. The final reward signal is computed by combining the epistemic signal with the problem-specific (instrumental) reward: r_t^{in}, i.e., $r_t = r_t^{in} + r_t^{ep}$. Although we utilize the sparse reward signal provided by the task for r_t^{in}, we remark that another circuit, serving as CogNGen's prior preference could be designed to encode probability distributions over preferred goal states [5,17].

The Motor Action Model: To manipulate its environment, CogNGen implements another NGC circuit that we call the motor-action model $f_a \colon \mathbf{z}_t \mapsto (\mathbf{c}_t^{int}, \mathbf{c}_t^{ext})$ (offering some functionality provided by the motor cortex) which outputs two control signals at each time step, i.e., internal control signal $\mathbf{c}_t^{int} \in \mathcal{R}^{A_i nt \times 1}$ and external control signal $\mathbf{c}_t^{ext} \in \mathcal{R}^{A_e xt \times 1}$. Note that a discrete internal action $a_t^{int} \in \{1, 2, , ..., i, ..., A_{int}\}$ is extracted via $a_t^{int} = \arg\max_i \mathbf{c}_t^{int}$ and external action $a_t^{ext} \in \{1, 2, , ..., j, ..., A_{ext}\}$ is extracted via $a_t^{ext} = \arg\max_j \mathbf{c}_t^{ext}$ (A_{int} is the number of discrete internal actions). Action a_t^{ext} affects the environment while action a_t^{int} manipulates the action model's coupled working memory buffers.

Within the NGC action-motor model is a modifiable working memory that allows the model to store a finite quantity M_w of latent state vectors into a set of self-recurrent memory vector slots. This particular working memory module, which we call the *self-recurrent slot buffer* serves as the glue that joins the modules of CogNGen together. The buffers in CogNGen serve the same purpose as ACT-R's buffers [19]. Each memory slot in the buffer is represented by $\mathbf{m}^i \in \mathcal{R}^{M_d \times 1}$ (M_d is the dimesionality of the memory slot). This component of the action-motor model is inspired by the working memory model proposed in [11]. Concretely, the self-recurrent slot buffer operates according to the following:

$$\mathbf{k}_t^i = \mathbf{Q}^i \cdot \mathbf{z}_t, \forall i = 1, ..., M_w \qquad // \text{ Compute key} \quad (7)$$

$$s^i = \mathbf{s}^i = \frac{1}{|\mathbf{m}^i|}\left(\sum_j \lfloor \mathbf{m}^i - \mathbf{k}_t^i \rfloor_{j,1} + \lfloor \mathbf{k}_t^i - \mathbf{m}^i \rfloor_{j,1}\right) \qquad // \text{ Compute match} \quad (8)$$

$$\mathbf{m}_t = \left[[\mathbf{m}^1, \mathbf{s}^1], ..., [\mathbf{m}^i, \mathbf{s}^i], ..., [\mathbf{m}^{M_w}, \mathbf{s}^{M_w}]\right] \qquad // \text{ Compute value} \quad (9)$$

where $\mathbf{Q}^i \in \mathcal{R}^{M_d \times D_z}$ is the ith random projection matrix (sampled from a centered Gaussian distribution in this paper), which means there is one projection matrix per working memory slot. Note that the match score for any slot i is $\mathbf{s}^i = \mathcal{R}^{1 \times 1}$ (a 1×1 vector) and thus also a scalar s^i. The working memory buffers, in essence, compute a key value vector $\mathbf{k}_t^i$ given the current state input $\mathbf{z}_t$ for each slot (by projecting via matrix $\mathbf{Q}^i$), calculate the match score between the ith key and ith slot/value, and then return the entire concatenated contents $\mathbf{m}_t$ of working memory (including the match scores).

Given the output of working memory $\mathbf{m}_t$, the motor-action model then proceeds to compute its output control signals using an ancestral projection scheme (see Appendix), yielding $\mathbf{c}_t^{ext}, \mathbf{c}_t^{int} = f_{proj}(\mathbf{z}_t; \Theta)$, implemented as follows:

$$\bar{\mathbf{z}}_t^3 = \mathbf{W}^4 \cdot \mathbf{z}_t + \phi(\mathbf{M} \cdot \mathbf{m}_t) + \mathbf{b}^3 \qquad (10)$$

$$\bar{\mathbf{z}}_t^2 = \mathbf{W}^3 \cdot \phi(\mathbf{z}_t^3) + \mathbf{b}^2 \qquad (11)$$

$$\bar{\mathbf{z}}_t^1 = \mathbf{W}^2 \cdot \phi(\mathbf{z}_t^2) + \mathbf{b}^1 \qquad (12)$$

$$\mathbf{c}_t^{ext} = \bar{\mathbf{z}}_{t,ext}^0 = \mathbf{W}_{ext}^1 \cdot \phi(\mathbf{z}_t^1) + \mathbf{b}_{ext}^0 \qquad (13)$$

$$\mathbf{c}_t^{int} = \bar{\mathbf{z}}_{t,int}^0 = \mathbf{W}_{int}^1 \cdot \phi(\mathbf{z}_t^1) + \mathbf{b}_{int}^0. \qquad (14)$$

The NGC circuit depicted in Eqs. 10–14 embodies both the "internal control" and "control" sub-systems by outputting $\bar{\mathbf{z}}_{t,ext}^0$, i.e., the same as control signal $\mathbf{c}_t^{ext}$, and $\bar{\mathbf{z}}_{t,int}^0$, i.e., the same as control signal $\mathbf{c}_t^{int}$. The above dynamics represent a five-layer circuit with its top-most layer clamped to: $\mathbf{z}_t^4 = \mathbf{z}_t$ and $\mathbf{m}_t$.

Finally, after the motor-action model has produced its control signals, the internal action is selected via $a_t^{int} = \arg\max_j \mathbf{c}_t^{int}$ and the external action is selected via $a_t^{ext} = \arg\max_j \mathbf{c}_t^{ext}$. While a_t^{ext} is transmitted to the environment, a_t^{int} is used to modify the working memory module. The internal actions possible are specifically: $a_t^{int} = \{\text{ignore}, \text{store}_1, \text{store}_2, ..., \text{store}_{M_w}\}$ (each integer has been mapped to a string clarifying the action's effect), where "ignore" means $\mathbf{z}_t$ is not stored and "store$_i$" means store $\mathbf{z}_t$ into memory slot i.

To update the motor-action model's synaptic efficacies, we then leverage the reward r_t computed by the dynamics model described in Sect. 3.2. Specifically, we compute the target control vectors $\mathbf{z}_{t,ext}^0$ and $\mathbf{z}_{t,int}^0$ as follows:

$$\mathbf{c}_t^{ext}, \mathbf{c}_t^{int} = f_{proj}(\mathbf{z}_{t+1}; \Theta) \tag{15}$$

$$z_{ext}^0 = \begin{cases} r_t & \text{if } \mathbf{z}_t \text{ is terminal} \\ r_t + \gamma \max_a \mathbf{c}_t^{ext} & \text{otherwise} \end{cases} \tag{16}$$

$$z_{int}^0 = \begin{cases} r_t & \text{if } \mathbf{z}_t \text{ is terminal} \\ r_t + \gamma \max_a \mathbf{c}_t^{int} & \text{otherwise} \end{cases} \tag{17}$$

and the final target vectors computed simply as:

$$\mathbf{z}_{t,ext}^0 = z_{ext}^0 \mathbf{a}_t^{ext} + (1 - \mathbf{a}_t^{ext}) \odot \mathbf{c}_t^{ext}$$
$$\mathbf{z}_{t,int}^0 = z_{int}^0 \mathbf{a}_t^{int} + (1 - \mathbf{a}_t^{int}) \odot \mathbf{c}_t^{int}.$$

Once the target vectors have been created, the NGC settling process can be executed and all motor-action synapses are updated via Hebbian learning.

3.3 Long-Term Memory

CogNGen implements long-term memory through a MINERVA 2 module. Information is transferred to this memory through an intermediate working memory buffer, where pieces of a transition (partial experience) are stored as they are encountered during the agent-environment interaction process. Specifically, once the buffer contains at least one partial transition $(\mathbf{z}_t, \mathbf{a}_t^{ext}, \mathbf{a}_t^{int}, \mathbf{r}_t)$ $(\mathbf{r}_t \in \mathcal{R}^{1 \times 1})$, our long-term MINERVA 2 $\mathcal{M}$ (which is created alongside a starting transition buffer $\mathcal{S}_0$) is updated according to the following algorithm:

1. Create a window (buffer) w of length L – each slot is filled with empty values (zero vectors of the correct length). Store the start transition $\mathbf{m}_0^{exp} = [\mathbf{z}_0, \mathbf{a}_0^{ext}, \mathbf{a}_0^{int}, \mathbf{r}_0]$ in buffer $\mathcal{S}_0$.
2. Store $\mathbf{m}_t^{exp} = [\mathbf{z}_t, \mathbf{a}_t^{ext}, \mathbf{a}_t^{int}, \mathbf{r}_t]$ at the last position (index L) of the window w and delete the entry at position 0.
3. Flatten w into a vector $\mathbf{w}_{mem}$ and store this item by updating $\mathcal{M}$.
4. If episode terminal has been reached, go to Step 1, else go to Step 2.

The above process is repeated until the end of simulation. We impose an upper bound on the number of transitions stored in $\mathcal{M}$ – if this bound is exceeded, we remove the earliest transition $\mathbf{m}_t^{exp}$ stored in $\mathcal{M}$ and update $\mathcal{S}_0$ accordingly.

To drive learning through experience replay, CogNGen samples from $\mathcal{M}$ by:

1. Create window w of length L, initialized with empty values. Sample $\mathbf{m}_0^{exp} \sim \mathcal{S}$, and place it in the last position L in w.
2. Remove the item at position 1 in w and use $\mathcal{M}$ to hetero-associatively complete/predict $\mathbf{m}_{t+1}^{exp}$.
3. Store $\mathbf{m}_{t+1}^{exp}$ at last position L within w.
4. Repeat steps 2 through 4 until episode terminal reached.

The above is repeated until E episodes have been sampled. To create a mini-batch for updating the motor-action/dynamics circuits, we sample B transitions $(\mathbf{z}_j, \mathbf{a}_j^{ext}, \mathbf{a}_j^{int}, \mathbf{r}_t, \mathbf{z}_{j+1})$ from each sampled episode. Thus, at t, CogNGen's computation consists of an information processing step followed by a learning step.

4 Experimental Results

4.1 The Mini GridWorld Problem

To evaluate CogNGen-built agents, we adapt the environment from the OpenAI Gym extension, Mini-GridWorld [2] and investigate four tasks: the *random empty room*, *multi-room*, *unlocking*, and *memory* tasks. The maze environment is an $N \times M$ tile grid and is partially observable by the agent as a $7 \times 7 \times 3$ tensor created by mapping each tile of the 7×7 grid to 3 integer values. Each tile is encoded to an object index ($0 =$ unseen, $1 =$ empty, $2 =$ wall, etc.), a color index ($0 =$ red, $1 =$ green, etc.), and a state index ($0 =$ open, $1 =$ closed, $2 =$ locked).

The agent itself is restricted to picking up one single object, such as a key, and may open a locked door if it carries a key that matches the door's color. The discrete action space for our agent can be summarized as a set of six unique actions: 1) turn left, 2) turn right, 3) move forward, 4) pick up an object, 5) drop the object that the agent is currently carrying, and 6) toggle/activate (such as opening a door or interacting with an object). The reward structure/signal provided by all problems in the Mini-GridWorld environment is sparse – 1.0 if the agent reaches the green goal tile and 0 otherwise, making all problems difficult from a reinforcement learning perspective. Each problem has a specific time step limit allotted to allow the agent to complete the task with maximum episode lengths ranging from 60 to 288 time steps.

The Random Empty Room Task: In this task (max. 144 steps), the agent is spawned at a random location (and starting orientation) in the room and must reach the green goal square. A sparse reward is provided if the goal is reached.

The Multi-Room Task: This task (max. 60 steps) requires the agent to navigate a set of connected rooms where it opens a door in one room in order to proceed to the next room. In the final room, there is green square that the agent must reach to end the episode successfully. This is a procedurally generated environment with a different floor plan per episode – we focused on 3 rooms of size 4×4.

The Unlocking Task: In this task (max. 288 steps), to successfully exit an episode, the agent must open a locked door by finding the key. The key location, door position, and agent initial position/orientation are randomly generated each episode.

The Memory Task: The agent starts in a small room where it sees an object (such as a key/ball), starting the episode by looking in the direction of the cue object. After perceiving the object, the agent must turn around, exit the room and go through a narrow hall that ends in a split. At the split, the agent can

Table 1. In the top row, examples of several tasks are presented – from left to right, the 6×6 empty room task (R6 × 6), the multi-room task w/ three rooms of size four (MR), and the unlock task (Unl). In the bottom row, we present results over the last 100 episodes for: (Left) Average success rate (%); (Right) Average episode length (% of maximum episode length - closer to 0 is more efficient)

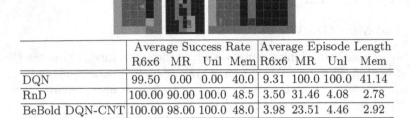

| | Average Success Rate | | | | Average Episode Length | | | |
	R6x6	MR	Unl	Mem	R6x6	MR	Unl	Mem
DQN	99.50	0.00	0.00	40.0	9.31	100.0	100.0	41.14
RnD	100.00	90.00	100.0	48.5	3.50	31.46	4.08	2.78
BeBold DQN-CNT	100.00	98.00	100.0	48.0	3.98	23.51	4.46	2.92
CogNGen	100.00	98.50	100.0	98.5	3.90	23.41	4.15	2.96

either go up or go down, and at the end of each of these splits is a different object (either a key or ball). To successfully complete the episode (max. 245 steps) and receive a positive reward, the agent must remember the initial object that it saw and go to the split that contains the correct matching object. For this study, we focus on the 7 × 7 room variant.

4.2   Baseline Models

We compare the CogNGen to several baselines: a standard deep Q-network (DQN) [14], a DQN that leverages an intrinsic reward generated via random network distillation (RnD) [1] (an intrinsic curiosity model), and a DQN that learns through a formulation of the BeBold exploration framework [21] (BeBold DQN-CNT; see Appendix for details). The DQN component of each of the above baselines utilized two layers of hidden neurons using the linear rectifier activation. RnD and BeBold have access to problem-specific, global information from the Mini GridWorld task environments (namely, the agent's $x - y$ coordinates in the world) whereas CogNGen and the DQN do not. For details/hyperparameter settings related to the agent implemented with our CogNGen architecture (referred to as "CogNGen" in all plots/tables), please see the Appendix.

4.3   Experimental Results

In Table 1, we report the average success rate (in solving the task/reaching a goal state) as well as the average episode length (average measurements were computed over the last 100 episodes of simulation for all models). In Fig. 1, we present reward curves (mean & standard deviation across five trials).

Based on our results, we find that (1) CogNGen is able to learn the maze tasks, (2) the performance is comparable to/on par with powerful deep RL methods that have access to problem-specific, global information, and (3) CogNGen

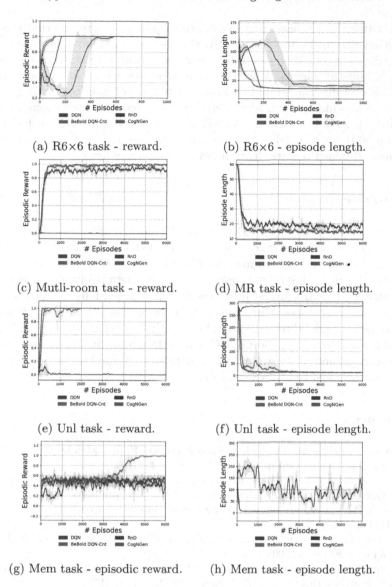

(a) R6×6 task - reward.

(b) R6×6 - episode length.

(c) Mutli-room task - reward.

(d) MR task - episode length.

(e) Unl task - reward.

(f) Unl task - episode length.

(g) Mem task - episodic reward.

(h) Mem task - episode length.

Fig. 1. Average reward (left) and episode length (right) for (top-to-bottom): 6 × 6 empty room (R6×6), multi-room (MR), unlock (Unl), and memory task (Mem).

can successfully outperform all baselines on the memory task. Given that CogN-Gen approximates much of the functionality of modern-day RL mechanisms with large auto-associative Hebbian memory modules and predictive processing circuits, our simulation results are promising. When CogNGen is compared to the baselines, we notice that there are some instances where the powerful BeBold DQN-CNT and RnD baselines yield shorter episodes or yield higher episodic rewards earlier (after converging to an optimal policy). We reason that this small gap is likely due to: 1) BeBold DQN/RnD have access to global, problem-specific information (the agent's x-y coordinates in the world in order to calculate state visitation counts) whereas CogNGen only operates with local information, 2) CogNGen's mechanism to update synapses relies on imperfect memory (which is more human-like but introduces error in the recollections as compared to a standard replay buffer), and 3) CogNGen's motor-action model must also learn how to modify its coupled working memory as well as how to interact with its environment, which requires learning more complex policies.

5 Conclusions

In this study, we presented CogNGen (the COGnitive Neural GENerative system), a cognitive architecture composed of circuits based on predictive processing and auto-associative Hebbian memory (MINERVA 2). CogNGen lays down the foundation for designing agents composed of neurocognitively-plausible building blocks that learn across diverse problems as well as potentially model human performance at larger scales. Our results, on a set of sparse reward maze learning tasks, show that goal-directed agents built with CogNGen perform well. Future work will entail studying the CogNGen's performance on other more complex environments, such as [8], as well as generalizing it further to learning across tasks, i.e., continual reinforcement learning.

References

1. Burda, Y., Edwards, H., Storkey, A., Klimov, O.: Exploration by random network distillation. arXiv preprint arXiv:1810.12894 (2018)
2. Chevalier-Boisvert, M., Willems, L., Pal, S.: Minimalistic gridworld environment for OpenAI gym. https://github.com/maximecb/gym-minigrid (2018)
3. French, R.M.: Catastrophic forgetting in connectionist networks. Trends Cogn. Sci. **3**(4), 128–135 (1999)
4. Friston, K.: A theory of cortical responses. Philos. Trans. R. Soc. B: Biol. Sci. **360**(1456), 815–836 (2005)
5. Friston, K., FitzGerald, T., Rigoli, F., Schwartenbeck, P., Pezzulo, G.: Active inference: a process theory. Neural Comput. **29**(1), 1–49 (2017)
6. Hebb, D.O.: The Organization of Behavior: A Neuropsychological Theory (1949)
7. Hintzman, D.L.: MINERVA 2: a simulation model of human memory. Behav. Res. Methods Instrum. Comput. **16**, 96–101 (1984). https://doi.org/10.3758/BF03202365
8. Huang, S., Ontañón, S., Bamford, C., Grela, L.: Gym-μRTS: toward affordable full game real-time strategy games research with deep reinforcement learning. In: 2021 IEEE Conference on Games (CoG), pp. 1–8. IEEE (2021)
9. Kelly, M.A., Ghafurian, M., West, R.L., Reitter, D.: Indirect associations in learning semantic and syntactic lexical relationships. J. Mem. Lang. **115**, 104153 (2020). https://doi.org/10.1016/j.jml.2020.104153

10. Kelly, M.A., Mewhort, D.J.K., West, R.L.: The memory tesseract: Mathematical equivalence between composite and separate storage memory models. J. Math. Psychol. **77**, 142–155 (2017)
11. Kruijne, W., Bohte, S.M., Roelfsema, P.R., Olivers, C.N.: Flexible working memory through selective gating and attentional tagging. Neur. Comput. **33**(1), 1–40 (2021)
12. Mannering, W.M., Jones, M.N.: Catastrophic interference in predictive neural network models of distributional semantics. Comput. Brain Behav. **4**(1), 18–33 (2021). https://doi.org/10.1007/s42113-020-00089-5
13. McCloskey, M., Cohen, N.J.: Catastrophic interference in connectionist networks: the sequential learning problem. Psychol. Learn. Motiv. **24**(109), 92 (1989)
14. Mnih, V., et al.: Human-level control through deep reinforcement learning. Nature **518**(7540), 529–533 (2015)
15. Ororbia, A.G., Kelly, M.A.: CogNGen: constructing the kernel of a hyperdimensional predictive processing cognitive architecture. In: Proceedings of the 44th Annual Conference of the Cognitive Science Society, pp. 1322–1329. Cognitive Science Society, Toronto, ON (2022). https://doi.org/10.31234/osf.io/g6hf4
16. Ororbia, A., Kifer, D.: The neural coding framework for learning generative models. Nat. Commun. **13**(1), 1–14 (2022)
17. Ororbia, A., Mali, A.: Backprop-free reinforcement learning with active neural generative coding. In: Proceedings of the AAAI Conference on Artificial Intelligence, vol. 36 (2022)
18. Rao, R.P., Ballard, D.H.: Predictive coding in the visual cortex: a functional interpretation of some extra-classical receptive-field effects. Nat. Neurosci. **2**(1), 79–87 (1999)
19. Ritter, F.E., Tehranchi, F., Oury, J.D.: ACT-R: a cognitive architecture for modeling cognition. WIREs Cognit. Sci. **10**(3), e1488 (2019)
20. Schultz, W.: Reward functions of the basal ganglia. J. Neural Transm. **123**(7), 679–693 (2016). https://doi.org/10.1007/s00702-016-1510-0
21. Zhang, T., et al.: Bebold: exploration beyond the boundary of explored regions. arXiv preprint arXiv:2012.08621 (2020)

Market Prediction as a Task for AGI Agents

James T. Oswald[(✉)] [iD]

RAIR Lab, Rensselaer Polytechnic Institute, Troy, NY, USA
James.Oswald.111@gmail.com

Abstract. We argue that market prediction is a worthwhile incremental challenge for AGI due to its dual logical and statistical nature. We formally define a modified version of a market prediction task for AGI and ways in which an instance of a normal market prediction problem may be converted to our version. We perform an empirical study on an instance of our problem and benchmark a NARS agent against statistical and connectionist agents to see if it can competitively forecast the direction of the S&P 500 from qualitative technical market data.

1 Introduction

When talking about tasks for AGI agents to solve, it is common to think about human-level tasks including the Turing test and alternatives such as the coffee test and the robot college student test [8]. These tests will be definitive proof, that upon solving, we can point to and claim that an agent is generally intelligent. However, in order to get to that point at which these human-level tasks can be accomplished, we take the position it is important to make incremental steps on tasks that are more easily measured. Various proposals have been made for tasks that might allow us to measure incremental progress toward an AGI, including Bringsjord's Psychometric AI [3] and Goertzel's AGI preschool suite [4]. Both of these tasks are well defined but have various entry-level bottlenecks to particular classes of AGI agents. Psychometric AI is a very good task for logicist agents but would be harder for connectionist agents. The full suite of tasks proposed in AGI Preschool are beyond the scope of what we can reasonably benchmark any existing logical agents on. We seek to define a task that is simple enough from a mathematical standpoint that it may serve as a benchmark for both logicist and connectionist agents, measuring purely their reasoning ability and statistical-pattern-finding ability, independent of architecture, which is a task that may be approached both statistically and logically.

When designing tasks for AGI agents to solve, it is important to take into account a working definition of intelligence and how it may be measured. Legg and Hutter's popular definition of intelligence as "the capacity for an agent to achieve goals in a wide range of environments" [13] and Wang's intelligence as "the ability for an information processing system to adapt to its environment with insufficient knowledge and resources" [27] are good starting points. Wang's definition better lends itself to the empirical nature of our goal to quantitatively measure incremental improvements of AGI agents [25]. However, Legg and Hutter's definition is important to take into consideration for its emphasis on performance in a wide range of environments. Our working definition of intelligence in designing this task is then one which takes into account the ability to perform well in both a wide range of environments and under the constraints of insufficient knowledge and resources.

With this working definition of intelligence in mind, we assert that market prediction (also referred to throughout as market forecasting) is a robust task that serves as a good indicator of intelligence. The task requires an agent to reason about the future from the currently available data, thus hitting check boxes for reasoning under insufficient knowledge. Rather than empirically testing an agent in many environments, we argue that the market prediction task itself is so robust that depending on the provided features, reasoning on individual classes of features constitutes reasoning on entirely separate environments; for example, the analysis of technical market data (raw asset price information and other daily quantitative indicators) is completely distinct from analysis of fundamental market data (earnings reports, social media sentiment on assets). The agent can go about this reasoning on each individual factor in many ways, including looking at statistical trends to analyzing human sentiments and performing logical reasoning.

In this work, we present the classic market prediction task for AI and discuss its shortcomings with respect to AGI agents. We then present our modified market prediction task for AGI and discuss its merits. In the second half of this work we perform an empirical study comparing a NARS Agent against various statistical methods on our modified market prediction task. We begin by presenting our data set and discussing a technique for qualifying it in such a way that it is usable on our modified task. We finish by briefly discussing the agents we use and their performance on the task.

2   Related Work

Traditional AI for Market Prediction
Multiple surveys have been done on the effectiveness of various computational techniques for market prediction over a wide range of global markets [11,14]. Kumar's survey [11] breaks down market forecasting models into three fundamental components, of which many hybrid models exist making use of one or more of these components:

1. Artificial Neural Network (ANN) Based Approaches: classified as anything using a neural network, including deep learning based approaches and RNN based approaches with LSTMs for time series prediction [17].
2. Fuzzy Logic Based Approaches: Incorporate any kind of fuzzy logic or fuzzy logic derivative/alternative into their forecasting model.
3. Genetic Algorithm Based Approaches: Make use of genetic algorithms for training their forecasting models.

Of particular note in this space is [22] which compares a simple ANN network with an SVN and a Multiple Linear Regression model, finding that SVM yields the best forecasting performance on the American S&P 500 using technical factors. We will be using the three methods in this work as our baseline as it provides a good example of machine learning and statistical techniques using technical factors that we can compare against, as well as modifying to allow for the use of converted qualitative factors.

Despite success in predicting the S&P 500, [14] shows that ML for single stock prediction still falls flat on meaningful day-to-day prediction, particularly in the case of longer-term investments. This shortcoming of having ML only useful for speculation is a large drawback for ML based methods as a whole.

AGI for Market Prediction
The idea of using AGI for market prediction tasks is not a novel concept. Previous work such as Raheman, Kolonin, and Ansari's Adaptive Multi-Strategy Market Making Agent [20] in their own words exploits Goertzel's definition of AGI in [7] as "having the ability to reach complex goals in complex environments" to justify why their market prediction architecture falls into the realm of AGI. We claim, however, that the task of market prediction is a far more robust measure of intelligence than previously let on, and is a good fit as a more general task for AGI agents.

3   Task

Traditionally, market prediction is modeled as a quantitative sequence prediction task, where we want to use some numeric features, $f_1, ..., f_n \in \mathbb{R}$, that we have available to us at some time, $t \in \mathbb{N}$, to predict the price of some asset, $p \in \mathbb{R}$, at some time in the future, $t + i \in \mathbb{N}$. Note that the selection of features can be anything, be that technical market data or fundamental market data. In the context of market prediction for AGI, the selection of features influences the "environments" the AGI agent gets to reason on. It is common that the current price of the asset we desire to predict the price of p_t is included within our list of features [16, 22]. The objective of this quantitative prediction task is to create a model A that takes our features and maps them as closely as possible to the true price of the asset at some time in the future. For market prediction tasks, the time step is typically measured in days and the price in the future we're trying to predict is one day ahead of our current features $t + 1$ [16, 22].

$$p_{t+1} = A(p_t, f_{1,t}, ..., f_{n,t}) \tag{1}$$

The quantitative market prediction task is well formulated, but it can be difficult for logic-based agents to be measured on, as it requires them to have an ability to reason over arbitrary continuous price data and return continuous price results. In order to open the field, we propose a qualitative variant of the market prediction task that is easier to play for agents where the ability to reason over arbitrary continuous price data is not a given. Our variant makes discrete the continuous price data of our features by looking at the relative change of features from time step to time step. We then convert each feature into two new qualitative features: a direction, $f^d \in \{\text{Up}, \text{Down}\}$, and magnitude of change $f^m \in \{\text{Small}, \text{Medium}, \text{Large}\}$. Note that the set of magnitudes we give here are just an example and an arbitrary number of magnitudes can be added depending on how much information we want the agent to have. The computation of these new magnitudes from quantitative feature data is up to the implementation, essentially the value of each feature at time t is compared against the value of the feature at time $t-1$ and a decision is made on what magnitude the change is. For the direction it is assumed the $f_t \neq f_{t-1}$. If $f_t > f_{t-1}$ then $f_t^d = \text{Up}$, otherwise $f_t^d = \text{Down}$. We make the goal of our modified task to predict not the price of our original asset, p, but the direction it moves in p^d at the future time step $t+1$. Hence the goal of our new task is the creation of an agent A who can correctly use magnitude and direction of features to predict the direction of an asset.

$$p_{t+1}^d = A(p_t^d, p_t^m, f_{1,t}^d, f_{1,t}^m \cdots, f_{n,t}^d, f_{n,t}^m) \tag{2}$$

One of the main merits of this modified task beyond working for logical agents is that since our set of possible magnitudes is implicitly well ordered, it is fully possible to convert our qualitative data back to quantitative data for agents that prefer to use statistical methods internally on numerical data. Hence this task can be used to benchmark logical, statistical, and connectionist agents.

Our particular instance of this task that we empirically test in this paper sets our p to be the daily price of the S&P 500 index on market close. The choice of the S&P 500 index, rather than that of an individual asset like a stock, is deliberate. The S&P 500 is more predictable and less volatile than individual assets, hence it is a preferred and popular target for computational and AI market forecasting tasks [16,18,22]. For our data set we have 32 features derived from 29 technical market factors, including the S&P 500 price. The quantitative features are then qualified with a Z-Score bucketing approach into 6 magnitude levels.

4 Data Set

Our initial data set for consideration consists of 29 technical market indicators. We group these factors into 5 broad classes based on the type of indicator they are and what units they are recorded in. Our data-points are recorded daily over the course of 10 years from January 1st 2012 to March 24th 2022; data from non-subsequent market closes is thrown out. The selection of these indicators was heavily influenced by the list of technical indicators for market prediction that Sheta et al. use in their 2015 work [22] as well as those used in [16]. We have had to update many of these factors to include more recent market data as well as change the stocks in our data set to better reflect those currently used to calculate the S&P 500 at the time this work is being done.

Indicator Classes

- **Market Indexes (Index):** Indexes are broad predictors of market performance based on a variety of underlying assets from which the index price is calculated. All of the market indexes we use in our data set are international exchange indexes which give our agent a good overview of the state of global markets, which have been shown to influence each other [6]. For our data set we use the closing price of the index as its daily data-point.
- **Commodities (Commodity):** Commodities are real assets traded on commodity exchanges. The link between commodity prices and stock prices, on the whole, is an area under active research [1,10], however, results seem to be positive, particularly for stocks of companies whose underlying products are commodities; such as oil and mining companies [2,15].
- **Stock Prices (Stock):** Stock prices are the market values of shares in a company on a stock exchange. We consider the prices of the top five stocks on the S&P 500 in 2022, the top 5 stocks on the S&P 500 from 2015, as well as a few other significant stocks in terms of market capitalization. For our data set, we use the closing price of the stock as its daily data point.
- **Foreign Exchange Rates (Currency):** A foreign exchange rate is the amount of US$s a unit of a given foreign currency is worth. Foreign exchange rates are considered to be strong indicators of market performance and have observable ties to index prices [6,12]. All foreign exchange rates in our data set are obtained from the US Federal Reserve H10's reported daily exchange rate.
- **Bond Yields (Bond):** Bond yields are the interest rate agreed to be paid when a bond is issued. Our data set includes two classes of bonds: corporate bonds, and US treasury bonds. We include treasury bonds with various maturities and source our treasury bond data from the US Federal Reserve H15's reported daily yields. For corporate bonds, we use Moody's Corporate bond yield indexes, which function as an indicator of all corporate bond yields within a risk class. The relationship between bond prices and market performance is widely acknowledged to be quite strong [21,23].

Features. We select our initial 29 quantitative features at each time step from the set of technical data outlined in Table 1. We add an additional three features, derived by offsetting the price of the S&P 500 by 1, 2, and 3 days into the past respectively, giving our agent S&P 500 closing prices of the past 4 days on one single time step. Now with all features f present, we convert each feature f into two new discretized features, a direction f^d and magnitude f^m. We take the features from the previous day and compute the direction as Up if the feature value is higher than the previous day, otherwise it is marked Down.

$$f_t^d = \begin{cases} \text{Up} & f_{t-1} < f_t \\ \text{Down} & f_{t-1} \geq f_t \end{cases} \tag{3}$$

Table 1. Indicators used in our dataset (YF = Yahoo Finance, FR = Federal Reserve, WSJ = Wall Street Journal)

Name	Class	Description	Source
SPX	Index	S&P 500, indicator of the US stock market	NASDAQ
HSI	Index	Hang Seng Index, indicator of the Hong Kong stock market	YF
FCHI	Index	CAC 40, indicator of the French stock market	YF
FTSE	Index	FTSE 100, indicator of the British stock market	WSJ
GDAXI	Index	DAX Index, indicator of the German stock market	YF
DJIA	Index	Dow Jones Industrial Average	WSJ
OIL	Commodity	Price of crude oil (West Texas Intermediate)	EIA
GOLD	Commodity	Price of gold	NASDAQ
AAPL	Stock	Stock price of Apple Inc	YF
MSFT	Stock	Stock price of Microsoft Corporation	YF
AMZN	Stock	Stock price of Amazon Inc	YF
GOOGL	Stock	Stock price of Alphabet Inc. class A shares	YF
GOOG	Stock	Stock price of Alphabet Inc. class C shares	YF
XOM	Stock	Stock price of Exxon Mobil Corporation	YF
GE	Stock	Stock price of General Electric	YF
PG	Stock	Stock price of Procter & Gamble	YF
JNJ	Stock	Stock price of Johnson & Johnson	YF
BRKA	Stock	Stock price of Berkshire Hathaway Inc. class A shares	YF
GBP	Currency	British Pound to US$ exchange rate	FR H10
CAD	Currency	Canadian Dollars to US$ exchange rate	FR H10
CNY	Currency	Chinese Renminbi to US$ exchange rate	FR H10
JPY	Currency	Japanese Yen to US$ exchange rate	FR H10
DAAA	Bond	Moody's Seasoned AAA Corporate Bond Yield	FRED
DBAA	Bond	Moody's Seasoned BAA Corporate Bond Yield	FRED
TB3M	Bond	Yield on 3-month Treasury Securities	FR H15
TB6M	Bond	Yield on 6-month Treasury Securities	FR H15
TB1Y	Bond	Yield on 1-year Treasury Securities	FR H15
TB5Y	Bond	Yield on 5-year Treasury Securities	FR H15
TB10Y	Bond	Yield on 10-year Treasury Securities	FR H15

Obtaining the magnitude is a more difficult process, as we want to ensure that magnitude is fairly assigned no matter the distribution of changes in a feature. Figure 1 shows the distribution in our data set of daily percent change in a stock; Apple Inc. (AAPL) as well as a foreign exchange rate, that between Canadian

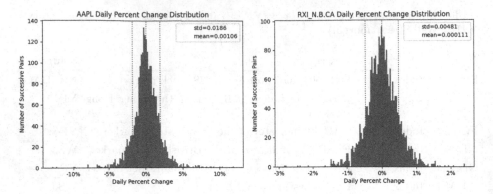

Fig. 1. Distribution of daily percent change of Apple Stock Price vs. Distribution of Canadian Dollar to USD Foreign Exchange Rates

Dollars (CAD) and US$s. The issue is that a 1% change in the AAPL feature is not a significant movement and hence should not be assigned a high magnitude, whereas a 1% change in CAD is very significant and should be assigned a high magnitude. This issue plays out across all features in our data set. Hence we must construct a means of assigning magnitude based on the distributions of individual features so that magnitudes are fairly assigned.

The solution we have come up with for this problem is a Z-Score bucketing method based on the daily percent change of a feature. The daily percent change of a feature, c_t, is computed by finding the percent an asset's value has changed since the day before.

$$c_t = \frac{f_t - f_{t-1}}{f_{t-1}} \tag{4}$$

We refer to the daily percent change of a feature as a *feature movement*. The Z-Score of a feature movement represents how many standard deviations, σ, away the movement is from the mean, μ, (average least significant) movement of that feature. Therefore the Z-score of a movement provides us a way to qualify the magnitude of a movement in relation to other movements on a per feature basis, even when these features have very different underlying normal distributions. Hence for quantitative feature f_t and T set of time steps (before t), we compute our Z-score for the movement z_t as:

$$z_t = \frac{c_t - \mu}{\sigma} = \frac{c_t - \frac{1}{|T|} \sum_{u \in T} c_u}{\sqrt{\frac{1}{|T|} \sum_{v \in T} \left(c_v - \frac{1}{|T|} \sum_{u \in T} c_u \right)^2}} \tag{5}$$

Finally, we qualify our Z-Scores by bucketing them, each bucket acts as an enumeration for a qualitative label. If k is the number of buckets and n is the number of buckets per standard deviation, we compute our magnitude bucket as:

$$f_t^m = \min\left(\lfloor n |z_t| \rfloor, k - 1\right) \tag{6}$$

In our instance of the problem, we use 2 buckets per standard deviation and use 6 buckets total. We split our 2314 data points into 162 points of test data and 2152 points of train data, and we shuffle our data to ensure our test data has the same distribution as our training data.

5   Methods

We investigate the performance of five different agents on the task. Three of these agents are statistical in nature (MLR, MLogR, SVC), one is connectionist (ANN), and one is an AGI method (NARS). All underlying statistical agents, unless otherwise stated, are implemented as sci-kit learn classifiers with default parameters [19].

Multiple Linear Regression Agent (MLR). The MLR agent makes use of the statistical technique known as Multiple Linear Regression to help it determine the market direction. We convert our qualitative features into quantitative features for this task by interpreting Up and Down as 1 and -1 respectively, computing our input features as the product $f_t^d f_t^m$ for each feature. As the output of a linear regression agent is continuous, we map it to the closest feature bucket for evaluation.

Multiple Logistic Regression Agent (MLogR). Identical to MLR except we instead use multiple logistic regression rather than multiple linear regression. Multiple logistic regression, at least in the quantitative case, has been shown as a good predictor of the S&P 500 [24]. The input formatting and output rounding are the same as those used for our MLR agent.

Support Vector Machine Agent (SVM). Our SVM agent uses raw qualitative features as input to train a support vector classifier [5] which tries to classify feature lists either up or down. SVM maps data points to a high dimensional space so that they may be more accurately classified.

Artificial Neural Network Agent (ANN). For our agent we use a multilayer perceptron classifier with ReLu activation function. The network has a hidden layer with 100 neurons. We train the agent on the qualified data using values as classes.

Limited NARS Agent (NARS). Uses a NARS [26] agent under the hood. Due to spacial limitations in our ability to create arbitrary length term products in NAL (for further explanation, observe Theorem 8.4 in [26]) we impose restrictions on our input and use linear regression to compute the five most important discretized features (from both direction and movement features), $f_1^*, ..., f_5^*$, as our modified agent input. Training data is passed in Narseese as products of qualified features implying market direction. $(f^*_{1,t} \times f^*_{2,t} \times ... \times f^*_{5,t}) \Rightarrow p^d_{t+1}$. We use default frequency and confidence for all of our inputs of training data and give the agent 10,000 cycles between training and testing. For our implementation of NARS we create the agent using OpenNARS for applications [9]. For testing the agent we query $(f^*_{1,t} \times f^*_{2,t} \times ... \times f^*_{5,t}) \Rightarrow ?$, for query responses that are not either Up or Down, we mark the prediction as incorrect.

6   Results

Our performance metric is accuracy, the number of times the agent was correctly able to predict the direction of the S&P 500 in the testing set. We find in Table 2 the accuracies from our agents on trained vs unseen test data. While not performing quite as well as the statistical agents, we observe that the limited NARS agent is at least able to predict the market direction well beyond the random baseline.

Table 2. Results of all of our agents

Method	Train	Test
Random Baseline	55.23%	49.3%
MLR	65.03%	64.81%
MLogR	65.17%	63.58%
SVC	55.09%	51.23%
ANN	65.45%	64.19%
NARS	62.76%	60.49%

7   Conclusion

In this work, we discussed the merits of using market prediction as a task for AGI agents based on its robust ability to emulate different environments in a single task. We have proposed a novel version of the market prediction task that is adaptable to logical, connectionist, and statistical agents. In our empirical study, we presented a comprehensive data set for market prediction and discussed in detail a means of converting quantitative technical market features into qualitative market features via a Z-Score bucketing approach based on the absolute daily percent change of a feature. We empirically tested five agents on the new task and found that, while not able to out-perform them, the NARS agent is able to perform around the same level as other narrow AI agents tested.

References

1. Black, A.J., Klinkowska, O., McMillan, D.G., McMillan, F.J.: Forecasting stock returns: do commodity prices help? J. Forecast. **33**(8), 627–639 (2014)

2. Boyer, M.M., Filion, D.: Common and fundamental factors in stock returns of Canadian oil and gas companies. Energy Econ. **29**(3), 428–453 (2007)
3. Bringsjord, S., Schimanski, B.: What is artificial intelligence? psychometric AI as an answer. In: IJCAI (2003)
4. Bugaj, V., Goertzel, B.: AGI preschool: a framework for evaluating early-stage human-like AGIs. In: Proceedings of the 2nd Conference on Artificial General Intelligence (2009)
5. Cortes, C., Vapnik, V.N.: Support-vector networks. Mach. Learn. **20**, 273–297 (2004). https://doi.org/10.1007/BF00994018
6. Garefalakis, A., Dimitras, A., Koemtzopoulos, D., Spinthiropoulos, K.: Determinant factors of Hong Kong stock market. Available at SSRN 1762162 (2011)
7. Goertzel, B.: Artificial general intelligence: concept, state of the art, and future prospects. J. Artif. General Intell. **5**, 1–48 (2014)
8. Goertzel, B., Iklé, M., Wigmore, J.: The architecture of human-like general intelligence. In: Theoretical Foundations of Artificial General Intelligence, pp. 123–144 (2012)
9. Hammer, P., Lofthouse, T.: OpenNARS for applications: architecture and control. In: Goertzel, B., Panov, A.I., Potapov, A., Yampolskiy, R. (eds.) AGI 2020. LNCS (LNAI), vol. 12177, pp. 193–204. Springer, Cham (2020). https://doi.org/10.1007/978-3-030-52152-3_20
10. Hu, C., Xiong, W.: Are commodity futures prices barometers of the global economy? Working Paper 19706, National Bureau of Economic Research (2013). https://doi.org/10.3386/w19706, https://www.nber.org/papers/w19706
11. Kumar, G., Jain, S., Singh, U.P.: Stock market forecasting using computational intelligence: a survey. Arch. Comput. Methods Eng. **28**(3), 1069–1101 (2020). https://doi.org/10.1007/s11831-020-09413-5
12. Lee, Y.M., Wang, K.M.: Dynamic heterogeneous panel analysis of the correlation between stock prices and exchange rates. Econ. Res.-Ekonomska istraživanja **28**(1), 749–772 (2015)
13. Legg, S., Hutter, M.: A collection of definitions of intelligence. In: AGI (2006)
14. Mokhtari, S., Yen, K.K., Liu, J.: Effectiveness of artificial intelligence in stock market prediction based on machine learning. In: International Journal of Computer Application (2021)
15. Nangolo, C., Musingwini, C.: Empirical correlation of mineral commodity prices with exchange-traded mining stock prices. J. South Afr. Inst. Min. Metall. **111**(7), 459–468 (2011)
16. Niaki, S., Hoseinzade, S.: Forecasting s&p 500 index using artificial neural networks and design of experiments. J. Ind. Eng. Int. **9**, 1–9 (2015). https://doi.org/10.1186/2251-712X-9-1
17. Pang, X.W., Zhou, Y., Wang, P., Lin, W., Chang, V.: An innovative neural network approach for stock market prediction. J. Supercomput. **76**, 2098–2118 (2018). https://doi.org/10.1007/s11227-017-2228-y
18. Patel, J., Shah, S.R., Thakkar, P., Kotecha, K.: Predicting stock and stock price index movement using trend deterministic data preparation and machine learning techniques. Expert Syst. Appl. **42**, 259–268 (2015)
19. Pedregosa, F., et al.: Scikit-learn: machine learning in Python. J. Mach. Learn. Res. **12**, 2825–2830 (2011)
20. Raheman, A., Kolonin, A., Ansari, I.: Adaptive multi-strategy market making agent. In: Goertzel, B., Iklé, M., Potapov, A. (eds.) AGI 2021. LNCS (LNAI), vol. 13154, pp. 204–209. Springer, Cham (2022). https://doi.org/10.1007/978-3-030-93758-4_21

21. Rankin, E., Idil, M.S.: A century of stock-bond correlations. Bulletin of The Reserve Bank of Australia (2014)
22. Sheta, A.F., Ahmed, S.E.M., Faris, H.: A comparison between regression, artificial neural networks and support vector machines for predicting stock market index. Int. J. Adv. Res. Artif. Intell. **4** (2015)
23. Shiller, R.J., Beltratti, A.E.: Stock prices and bond yields: can their comovements be explained in terms of present value models? J. Monet. Econ. **30**(1), 25–46 (1992)
24. Smita, M.: Logistic regression model for predicting performance of s&p bse30 company using IBM SPSs. In: International Journal of Mathematics Trends and Technology (2021)
25. Wang, P.: The evaluation of AGI systems. In: AGI 2010 (2010)
26. Wang, P.: Non-Axiomatic Logic. World Scientific, Singapore (2013). https://www.worldscientific.com/doi/abs/10.1142/8665
27. Wang, P., Goertzel, B.: Introduction: aspects of artificial general intelligence. In: AGI (2006)

Monte Carlo Bias Correction
in Q-Learning

Dimitris Papadimitriou[(⊠)]

University of California, Berkeley, USA
dimitri@berkeley.edu

Abstract. The Q-learning algorithm suffers from overestimation bias due to the maximum operator appearing in its update rule. Other popular variants of Q-learning, like double Q-learning, can on the other hand cause underestimation of the action values. In many stochastic environments both underestimation and overestimation can lead to sub-optimal strategies. In this paper, we present a variation of Q-learning that uses elements from Monte-Carlo Reinforcement Learning to correct for the overestimation bias. Our method *1)* makes no assumptions on the distributions of the action values or the rewards, *2)* does not require extensive hyperparameter tuning unlike other popular variants proposed to deal with the overestimation bias and *3)* requires storing only two estimators, similar to double Q-learning, along with the most recent episode. Our method is shown to effectively control for the overestimation bias in a number of simulated stochastic environments leading to better policies with higher cumulative rewards and action values that are closer to the optimal ones, as compared to a number of well-established approaches.

Keywords: Q-learning · Overestimation · Bias

1 Introduction

Reinforcement Learning (RL) is a control technique that enables an agent to make informative decisions in unknown environments by interacting with them in time [10]. The RL algorithms can be generally categorized in model-based and model-free methods. Model-based methods learn the underlying dynamics of the system and incorporate that information in the decision process. One of the benefits of this line of work over model-free methods is the smaller amount of data required to train the agents. On the other hand, model-free methods directly estimate value functions or policies from interactions with the environment. Model-free methods do not suffer from model bias, which arises due to the insufficient estimation of the underlying dynamics, as model-based methods frequently do.

In this work, we focus on model-free methods and more specifically on variants of the celebrated Q-learning algorithm [12]. The wide popularity of Q-learning can be attributed to the simplicity of the algorithm as it follows a simple update rule that uses the current estimate of the action values of a state,

B. Goertzel et al. (Eds.): AGI 2022, LNAI 13539, pp. 343–352, 2023.
https://doi.org/10.1007/978-3-031-19907-3_33

the reward observed while transitioning from that state to the next and the maximum over all possible actions estimate of the action values at the next state. Using the latter maximum operator however has been proven to cause Q-learning to overestimate the action values. This overestimation is attributed to the uncertainty in the estimates and the possible stochasticity of the environment. This phenomenon frequently leads to poor policies [11].

To deal with the overestimation bias a number of variants of Q-learning have been proposed in the literature. Double-Q learning [6] uses a double estimator approach, where one estimator determines the maximizing action and the other independently determines that action's value. Despite the fact that double Q-learning tends to underestimate the actual value functions, it is shown to outperform Q-learning by leading to better policies in many environments. To balance between over- and under-estimation [13] extend double Q-learning by using an appropriately weighted sum of the single and double estimators in the update rule. Weighted Q-learning [1] uses a weighted estimate among the action values in the place of the maximum in the update rule. Furthermore, theoretically backed bias correction techniques have been proposed in the asymptotic regime for normally distributed rewards [8]. Finally, Maxmin Q-learning [7] uses a number of independent action value estimators and selects the maximizing action by considering the minimum of these action values for each action. It should be noted that overestimation bias has also been shown to affect policy gradient algorithms which are predominantly used in continuous control applications [3].

Another branch of model-free learning algorithms, that is broadly related to our work, is that of Monte Carlo (MC) based RL methods. The Monte Carlo Exploring Starts (MCES) algorithm uses simulations to obtain estimates of the cumulative discounted reward from a state-action pair to the end of the task and uses those estimates to update the action value of that state-action pair [10]. Although MC methods do not lead to overestimated action values they tend to have high variance in their estimates compared to Q-learning [5].

In this paper we combine the Q-learning algorithm with MC techniques to reduce the overestimation bias of the former in applications with finite state-action spaces and episodic tasks. In summary, at the end of each episode of the algorithm we compute the realized discounted cumulative reward from each visited state-action pair. Given that and the current action value estimates we can obtain an estimate for the bias incurred in each visited state-action pair, which we then use to update a running bias estimator in our problem. That bias estimate is subsequently subtracted from the action value estimates in the Q-learning update rule to correct for the overestimation bias. We show in a number of benchmark environments that our method consistently returns action value estimates with low bias while producing policies that most of the times outperform those from other approaches.

The rest of the paper in organized in the following way. Section 2 introduces basic concepts of Q-learning and tries to shed some light in the reasoning behind the overestimation bias while Sect. 3 summarizes already established techniques designed to tackle overestimation bias. Section 4 introduces in detail our bias correction method. Finally, Sect. 5 compares the performance of our method with the alternatives in a number of simulated stochastic environments.

2   Preliminaries

Reinforcement Learning applies to problems in which an agent interacts with an environment and uses that information for informative decision making with the ultimate goal being utility maximization over a finite horizon T. We model such environments with Markov Decision Processes (MDP) which are defined by tuples $(\mathcal{S}, \mathcal{A}, P, R, \gamma)$, where $\mathcal{S}$ denotes the state space, $\mathcal{A}$ the action space, P the transition probabilities in the environment, R the reward function and $\gamma \in (0, 1)$ is the discount factor. We assume the state and action spaces are finite and their cardinalities are denoted with $|S|$ and $|A|$ respectively and we use $\mathcal{A}(s)$ for the set of available actions in state s. The system transition probabilities $P : \mathcal{S} \times \mathcal{A} \times \mathcal{S} \rightarrow [0, 1]$ are denoted with $P(s_{t+1}|s_t, a_t)$. After each transition the agent observes a reward $R : \mathcal{S} \times \mathcal{A} \times \mathcal{S} \rightarrow \mathbb{R}$ obtained at state s_t by applying input a_t and transitioning to state s_{t+1} denoted with $R_{a_t}(s_t, s_{t+1})$. The discount factor γ controls for the significance of short versus long term rewards. The goal of the agent is to find an optimal policy $\pi : \mathcal{S} \times \mathcal{A} \rightarrow [0, 1]$ that maximizes the expected discounted sum of rewards $\mathbb{E}_\pi \left[\sum_{i=0}^{T} \gamma^i R_{a_t}(s_t, s_{t+1}) \right]$ starting from an initial state s_0.

Such a policy can be found via Q-learning in which state-action dependent Q-functions $Q : \mathcal{S} \times \mathcal{A} \rightarrow \mathbb{R}$ are estimated. $Q_\pi(s_t, a_t)$ quantifies the cumulative discounted reward from state s_t when applying action a_t and then following policy π for the duration of the task. At iteration $t + 1$ the Q-learning algorithm with a learning rate α, which frequently is a function of the state-action pair, uses the following update rule

$$Q_{t+1}(s_t, a_t) = Q_t(s_t, a_t) + \alpha \left(R_{a_t}(s_t, s_{t+1}) + \gamma \max_{a \in \mathcal{A}(s_{t+1})} Q_t(s_{t+1}, a) - Q_t(s_t, a_t) \right).$$
(1)

The set of available actions $\mathcal{A}(s_{t+1})$ at state s_{t+1} and the policy π from the action values will be dropped in subsequent expressions for notational conciseness. The optimal policy can be derived by greedily choosing the action that corresponds to the highest action value from each state s, $\pi^* = \arg\max_a Q^*(s, a)$.

The term $\max_a Q_t(s_{t+1}, a)$ appearing in (1) causes the action value estimates to be positively biased. Ideally, the update rule would choose at time step $t + 1$ the action value with the highest expected value $max_a \mathbb{E}[Q(s_{t+1}, a)]$. However, the true underlying action values and consequently their expected values are unknown and instead are substituted by the sample estimates $max_a Q(s_{t+1}, a)$. The action value samples though are polluted with noise, attributed to the stochasticity of the environment and the estimation uncertainty of the action values themselves. Even if the noise has zero mean the max operator will likely still positively bias the action value estimates. For detailed proofs of the overestimation bias in Q-learning we refer the reader to [6, 9]. To obtain some intuition

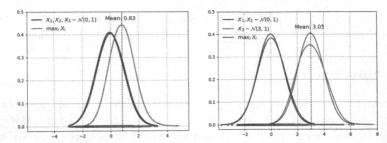

Fig. 1. (*left*) 100 simulations, each with three samples from the three normal distributions (blue dots) and the maximum of those three (red dots) and the empirical distributions of $X_i, i = 1, \ldots, 3$ and $\max_i X_i$. The mean of the empirical distribution of the maximum is 0.83. (*right*) Similar to the left but one of the normal distributions has now mean 3. (Color figure online)

on the overestimation bias we include a simulation that showcases that effect. Assume that we have N alternatives $X_1, X_2, \ldots, X_N$ each associated with realized rewards x_i, $i = 1, \ldots, N$ coming from a normal distribution $\mathcal{N}_i(0, 1)$. We repeatedly observe the realizations of all N rewards and we select the maximum one $\max_i x_i$. It is known from extreme value theory that the maximum of these standard normally distributed random variables will asymptotically converge to a Gumbel distribution with positive mean [4]. Intuitively, since the distributions have the same zero mean, it is highly likely that at least one of them in a realization will be positive and since we are picking the maximum of the N samples, $\max_i x_i$ most of the times will be positive as well, thus biasing the estimator. Figure 1 shows the effect of the discrepancy among the alternatives in the bias of the maximum operator for $N = 3$. When one of the alternatives is distinctively better - it comes from a distribution with higher mean - then we observe minimal overestimation, since the max function systematically selects the sample that comes from the distribution with the higher mean. On the other hand, if all distributions generate similar rewards as in the left figure, the effect of overestimation becomes significant. Frequently in applications the different action alternatives of the action values are similar to each other leading to positive bias in the estimates.

3   Related Works

The aforementioned max-operator bias frequently leads the Q-learning algorithm to overestimate action values. A number of methods have been proposed to alleviate this problem most of which resolve to using more than one estimator for the action values to tackle overestimation.

Double Q-learning [6] uses two independent estimators for the action values, one to choose the optimal action and another to extract the action value. It requires storing two tables Q^A and Q^B and the agent follows an ϵ-greedy policy in which actions can be selected using both tables, for instance

$a^* = \arg\max_a Q^A(s,a) + Q^B(s,a)$. At each iteration one of the Q-tables is randomly chosen to be updated. When table $i \in \{A, B\}$ is updated then the target in expression (1) is equal to $R_{a_t}(s_t, s_{t+1}) + \gamma Q_t^{-i}(s_{t+1}, a^*)$, where $a^* = \arg\max_a Q^i(s_{t+1}, a)$. The notation $-i$ denotes the alternative choice to i.

The structure of the weighted double Q-learning algorithm [13] is similar to that of double Q-learning as it also employs two Q-tables A and B. The major difference is that it uses a weight that is a function of both Q-tables at each iteration to update a randomly chosen Q-table with the weighted average of the two tables. When table i is updated the target value in the update rule becomes $R_{a_t}(s_t, s_{t+1}) + \gamma(\beta^i Q_t^i(s_{t+1}, a^*) + (1 - \beta^i)Q_t^{-i}(s_{t+1}, a^*))$, where β^i is a weight parameter depending on the Q-values evaluated at $a^* = \arg\max_a Q^i(s_{t+1}, a)$, $a_L = \arg\min_a Q^i(s_{t+1}, a)$ and c is a user specified hyperparameter.

Maxmin Q-learning [7] employs m independent Q-tables to balance between over- and under-estimation bias, where the number of Q-tables is another hyperparameter of the algorithm. Both the optimal action choice of the agent as well as the Q-table update rule uses the Q_{min} table which for a state s is constructed as $Q_{min}(s,a) = \min_{i \in \{1,...,m\}} Q^i(s,a)$, $\forall a$. The Maxmin Q-learning target is $R_{a_t}(s_t, s_{t+1}) + \gamma \max_a Q_{min}(s_{t+1}, a))$. For some value $m > 0$ the Maxmin Q-learning estimates switch from being overestimated to being underestimated and depending on which of the two, if any, is beneficial for a particular environment the user can tune m appropriately.

4   Monte Carlo Bias Correction

Most of the aforementioned methods utilize a multiple estimator scheme to tackle the overestimation bias. In the process of creating estimates with reduced bias the double weighted and Maxmin variants of Q-learning need extra hyperparameter tuning. Our method exploits already available information from the realized trajectories in order to reduce bias without requiring significantly more tuning than the original Q-learning algorithm. The intuition behind the algorithm is to use information obtained during an episode to construct bias estimates of the action values and use those to correct for the bias. More specifically, at the end of each episode we compute the realized discounted cumulative reward from each state-action pair visited to the end of that episode. Given the current action value estimates we compute an estimate for the bias at state-action pair s, a by subtracting the realized action values from the current action value estimates (2). That estimate is then used to update a bias table, which is similar in dimensions to the Q-table, for that particular pair (3). At each iteration of the Q-learning algorithm the bias term is subtracted from the max action value to compensate for the overestimation bias. Our algorithm can be broadly seen as a combination of the Q-learning algorithm with elements from a variant of the Monte Carlo Exploring Starts (MCES) algorithm [10].

In more detail, during each episode at each time step the agent acts in the environment using an ϵ-greedy policy. During the episode, the sequence of state-action pairs visited and rewards observed is saved. Once the episode is done after T_{ep} steps, for each state-action pair in the trajectory $s_i, a_i, i = T_{ep}, \ldots, 1$ we compute the realized cumulative discounted reward sequence $\hat{Q}(s_i, a_i)$ from time step i until the end of that episode. This realized $\hat{Q}$ value is an estimate of the action value that is not biased by the max operator and can be used to obtain a sample estimate for the bias incurred at state-action pair s_i, a_i as follows

$$\hat{B}(s_i, a_i) = Q(s_i, a_i) - \hat{Q}(s_i, a_i). \tag{2}$$

The samples in (2) are then used to update a running average of the bias for each s_i, a_i similar to the update rule in (1)

$$B_{t+1}(s_t, a_t) = B_t(s_t, a_t) + \alpha' \left(\hat{B}(s_t, a_t) - B_t(s_t, a_t) \right), \tag{3}$$

where we allow for the use of a different learning rate α' from the one used in (1). The target value in the Q-learning update rule of our method is

$$Q_{t+1}(s_t, a_t) =$$
$$Q_t(s_t, a_t) + \alpha \left(R_{a_t}(s_t, s_{t+1}) + \gamma(Q_t(s_{t+1}, a^*) - B_t(s_{t+1}, a^*)) - Q_t(s_t, a_t) \right), \tag{4}$$

Algorithm 1: Monte-Carlo Bias Corrected Q-learning (MBCQ)

Choose learning rates α, α'
Initialize $Q(s, a)$ randomly, $B(s, a) = 0 \ \forall s, a$
Repeat until convergence
    $T_{ep} \leftarrow 0$
    While episode not over:
        Choose action a in state s using policy derived from Q (e.g. ϵ-greedy)
        Move to state s' and observe reward $R_a(s, s')$
        $a^* \leftarrow \arg\max_a Q(s', a)$
        $\delta \leftarrow R_a(s, s') + \gamma(Q(s', a^*) - B(s', a^*))$
        $Q(s, a) \leftarrow (1 - \alpha)Q(s, a) + \alpha\delta$
        Store s, a, R_a
        $T_{ep} \leftarrow T_{ep} + 1$
        $s \leftarrow s'$
    $\hat{Q} \leftarrow R_{a_{T_{ep}}}(s_{T_{ep}})$
    For each uniquely visited tuple $(s_i, a_i, R_{a_i}), i = T_{ep} - 1, \ldots, 1$:
        $\hat{Q} \leftarrow R_{a_i}(s_i, s_{i+1}) + \gamma\hat{Q}$
        $\hat{B} \leftarrow Q(s_i, a_i) - \hat{Q}$
        $B(s_i, a_i) \leftarrow (1 - \alpha')B(s_i, a_i) + \alpha'\hat{B}$

---

where $a^* = \arg\max_a Q(s_{t+1}, a)$. More details on our approach can be seen in Algorithm 1. It should be noted that our method requires the storage of the most recent trajectory along with the bias table B. For tasks in which episodes have a large duration and $\gamma < 1$ a more computationally efficient rolling window scheme can be used to approximate the total reward from a particular state. In the following section we compare the effectiveness of our method with that of other popular methods designed to tackle overestimation bias in Q-learning.

5 Experiments

This section quantifies the performance of our method, abbreviated to MBCQ to denote the Monte Carlo-like bias correction, in a number of stochastic benchmark environments both with discrete and continuous state spaces. We compare the performance of our method with that of single Q-learning (Q), Double Q-learning (DQ), Weighted Double Q-learning (WDQ) and MaxMin Q-learning (MMQ). The last three of the aforementioned methods are some of the primary approaches in literature that deal with the overestimation bias.

In all experiments we choose a polynomial learning rate for the Q-learning update $\alpha(s, a) = 1/n(s, a)^{0.8}$, where $n(s, a)$ denotes the number of times the state-action pair s, a has been visited. For algorithms that require more than one Q-table we use distinct learning rates for each table i, $\alpha_i(s, a) = 1/n_i(s, a)^{0.8}$. The probability of randomly choosing an action in the ϵ-greedy policy also diminishes with a polynomial rate, $\epsilon = 1/\sqrt{n(s, a)}$. For the learning rate of the bias update we select a constant rate $\alpha' = 0.01$. In all the experiments the discount factor γ is set to 0.95.

5.1 Roulette

Roulette is a stochastic environment consisting of a single state and 171 actions. The 170 betting actions include betting on individual numbers, red or black color, odd or even numbers, etc. The 171th action is a termination action with zero reward after which the agent walks away from the table. The agent bets each time 1\$, with no budget constraints, and the average expected reward from each betting action is 0.947\$, leading to an expected loss of 0.053\$ for each bet. The optimal strategy for the agent is to clearly walk away. All actions return to the same state except for when the agent decides to walk away.

We sequentially update the action values for each action for 10^5 trials. We repeat this experiment 10 times. We compute and report the mean of the action values over all actions, averaged over the 10 experiments for all five methods as shown in Table 1. All the methods overestimate the maximum action value as the optimal one is equal to zero. Q-learning suffers from excessive overestimation while weighted double Q-learning has diminishing bias for growing c. Double and Maxmin Q-learning show significantly lower overestimation compared to single Q-learning. On the other hand our method obtains estimates that approach the actual action values.

Table 1. Average over all non-terminating actions of the action values.

Q	DQ	WDQ ($c = 10$)	WDQ ($c = 100$)	MMQ	MBCQ
9.70\$	0.02\$	5.57\$	0.025\$	0.15\$	$6.3 \cdot 10^{-4}$\$

5.2   Grid World

The grid world environment (see Fig. 2 in [6]) consists of a $n \times n$ dimensional grid in which the agent starts from the bottom left cell s_0 and tries to navigate towards the top right cell, which is the terminal state s_g. At each cell the agent can choose one of the possible actions $\{north, east, south, west\}$. If any of the actions taken leads the agent off the grid then the agent remains in the same cell. The agent receives equally likely a reward of -4 or 2 for any action leading to a non-terminal state and a reward of 15 or -5 for successfully reaching the goal state. The optimal strategy of the agent is to follow the shortest path towards the terminal state. During the experiments we record the value function of the starting state $V(s_0) = max_a Q(s_0, a)$ and the average reward per time step. The duration of the task is 10^4 iterations. The plotted curves have been smoothed with an exponential kernel with parameter 0.1 for better exposition.

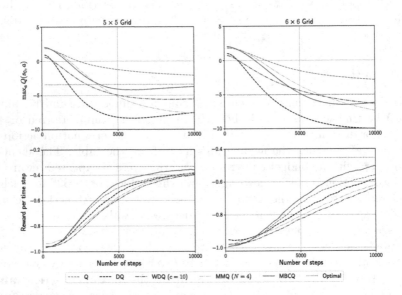

Fig. 2. Maximum action value for s_0 and average reward per step for two different grid sizes averaged over 1000 runs. The green dotted lines correspond to the optimal maximum action values and average rewards. (Color figure online)

Q-learning and double Q-learning consistently over- and under-estimate the action values respectively, as expected from their theoretical analysis. On the other hand weighted double Q-learning tends to suffer less from overestimation. Our method consistently approaches the optimal action values in all the experiments and is never far off. The average reward obtained using our method is consistently higher compared to all others. We also report in Table 2 the values of $V(s_0)$ that all five algorithms converged to after 10^5 iterations for grid sizes $n = 3, 4, 5$ and 6. The results were averaged over 1000 runs. The optimal value

Table 2. Maximum action values $V(s_0)$ after 10^5 iterations.

n	$V^*(s_0)$	Q	DQ	WDQ ($c = 10$)	MMQ ($N = 4$)	MBCQ
3	0.36	0.37	−0.65	−0.18	−0.09	**0.36**
4	−1.62	**−1.58**	−2.79	−2.25	−2.43	−1.66
5	−3.41	−3.30	−4.69	−4.15	−4.75	−3.46
6	−5.03	−4.76	−6.53	−5.82	−7.17	−5.09

function as a function of the grid size is given by $V^*(s_0) = 5\gamma^{2(N-1)} - \sum_{i=0}^{2N-3} \gamma^i$. Our method consistently manages to approach the optimal values of $V^*(s_0)$ closer than any of the other methods.

5.3 Taxi

The Taxi environment [2] is the last domain we will test our algorithm. In this environment the agent can pick up a passenger who is in any of the R,G,Y,B locations and transport the passenger to one of the remaining locations. For each allowed move on the map that does not deliver a passenger to the specified location the agent incurs a cost of 1. Regarding the rest of the rewards we will be studying two cases, one with deterministic and one with stochastic rewards. In the deterministic case, for illegal actions like trying to drop a passenger on the wrong location, the agent incurs a reward of −4 while the reward for correctly delivering the passenger to the specified location is 8. In the stochastic case, for misplaced passenger deliveries the agent incurs a reward of −10 or 2 and for correct deliveries the agent obtains a reward of 20 or −4, where all alternatives have equal probability of occurring.

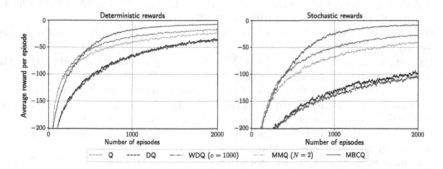

Fig. 3. Average reward per episode in Taxi environment with deterministic and stochastic rewards. Results averaged over 100 runs.

We report the average reward per iteration for 2000 iterations averaged over 100 runs. The resulting curves have also been smoothed with an exponential kernel with parameter 0.1. Figure 3 shows the average reward plots for the deterministic and stochastic cases. MBCQ clearly outperforms all the other methods on both cases by leading to policies that obtain higher rewards.

6   Summary

Overestimation bias is a flaw of the Q-learning algorithm that usually leads to overestimated action values and frequently to suboptimal policies. We presented a novel algorithm that combines the Q-learning algorithm with Monte Carlo methods to obtain action value estimates with reduced bias. Our method utilizes information already gathered through past trajectories to construct estimates of the bias and uses these estimates in the Q-learning update rule to compensate for the maximization bias. Our method consistently outperforms the current state of the art approaches in a number of stochastic environments with discrete state spaces without requiring extensive hyperparameter tuning. It should be noted that most of the methods presented in this work assume fully observable states. We leave possible extensions to POMDPs for future work.

References

1. D'Eramo, C., Restelli, M., Nuara, A.: Estimating maximum expected value through gaussian approximation. In: International Conference on Machine Learning, pp. 1032–1040 (2016)
2. Dietterich, T.G.: Hierarchical reinforcement learning with the MAXQ value function decomposition. J. Artif. Intell. Res. **13**, 227–303 (2000)
3. S. Fujimoto, H. Hoof, and D. Meger. Addressing function approximation error in actor-critic methods. In International Conference on Machine Learning, pages 1587–1596. PMLR, 2018
4. Gumbel, E.J.: Statistics of Extremes. Columbia University Press, New York (1958)
5. Hanna, J.P., Niekum, S., Stone, P.: Importance sampling in reinforcement learning with an estimated behavior policy. Mach. Learn. **110**(6), 1267–1317 (2021). https://doi.org/10.1007/s10994-020-05938-9
6. Hasselt, H.V.: Double Q-learning. In: Advances in Neural Information Processing Systems, pp. 2613–2621 (2010)
7. Lan, Q., Pan, Y., Fyshe, A., White, M.: Maxmin Q-learning: controlling the estimation bias of Q-learning. arXiv preprint arXiv:2002.06487 (2020)
8. Lee, D., Defourny, B., Powell, W.B.: Bias-corrected q-learning to control max-operator bias in q-learning. In: 2013 IEEE Symposium on Adaptive Dynamic Programming and Reinforcement Learning (ADPRL), pp. 93–99. IEEE (2013)
9. Smith, J.E., Winkler, R.L.: The optimizer's curse: skepticism and postdecision surprise in decision analysis. Manage. Sci. **52**(3), 311–322 (2006)
10. Sutton, R.S., Barto, A.G.: Reinforcement Learning: An Introduction. MIT press, Cambridge (2018)
11. Thrun, S., Schwartz, A.: Issues in using function approximation for reinforcement learning. In: Proceedings of the Fourth Connectionist Models Summer School, pp. 255–263. Hillsdale, NJ (1993)
12. Watkins, C.J., Dayan, P.: Q-learning. Mach. Learn. **8**(3–4), 279–292 (1992)
13. Zhang, Z., Pan, Z., Kochenderfer, M.J.: Weighted double q-learning. In IJCAI, pp. 3455–3461 (2017)

Free Will Belief as a Consequence of Model-Based Reinforcement Learning

Erik M. Rehn[✉][iD]

Malm, Sweden
erik.m.rehn@gmail.com

Abstract. The debate on whether or not humans have free will has been raging for centuries. Although there are good arguments based on our current understanding of the laws of nature for the view that it is not possible for humans to have free will, most people believe they do. This discrepancy begs for an explanation. If we accept that we do not have free will, we are faced with two problems: (1) while freedom is a very commonly used concept that everyone intuitively understands, what are we actually referring to when we say that an action or choice is "free" or not? And, (2) why is the belief in free will so common? Where does this belief come from, and what is its purpose, if any? In this paper, we examine these questions from the perspective of reinforcement learning (RL). RL is a framework originally developed for training artificial intelligence agents. However, it can also be used as a computational model of human decision making and learning, and by doing so, we propose that the first problem can be answered by observing that people's common sense understanding of freedom is closely related to the information entropy of an RL agent's normalized action values, while the second can be explained by the necessity for agents to model themselves as if they could have taken decisions other than those they actually took, when dealing with the temporal credit assignment problem. Put simply, we suggest that by applying the RL framework as a model for human learning it becomes evident that in order for us to learn efficiently and be intelligent we need to view ourselves as if we have free will.

Keywords: Free will belief · Reinforcement learning · Model-based · Credit assignment

1 Introduction

Although, according to the current understanding of the laws of nature, there are good arguments in support of the view that it is not possible for humans to have free will, so-called free will belief is widely spread across cultures [15]. This discrepancy between the materialist view held by large parts of the scientific community, on the one hand, and the subjective experience most laypeople have of their own freedom, on the other hand, begs for an explanation. If we assume that the materialists are right (i.e., that we lack free will), we must ask ourselves the following questions:

© The Author(s), under exclusive license to Springer Nature Switzerland AG 2023
B. Goertzel et al. (Eds.): AGI 2022, LNAI 13539, pp. 353–363, 2023.
https://doi.org/10.1007/978-3-031-19907-3_34

1. What does *freedom* mean when used in everyday language? Freedom is a commonly used concept but what are we actually referring to when we say that an action or choice is *free* or not?
2. Why is free will belief so common? Even the most determined determinist feels as if he or she can make free choices. Where does this experience come from, and what is its purpose, if any?

In this paper, we attempt to address these questions from the perspective of an agent trained with model-based reinforcement learning (RL). Reinforcement learning is a framework for training artificial intelligence (AI) agents in settings where there is a delay between the actions of the agent and the evaluation of the objective of the agent. The goal of an RL agent is to learn to perform sequences of actions that maximize the long-term reward it receives from its environment. Where reward is received when the objective assigned to the agent is fulfilled. A classic example is games like chess, where an AI should learn to make a sequence of turns that lead to a win.

Importantly, reward maximization through reinforcement learning has been proposed not only as a method for building AI systems, but also as a computational theory of human learning and decision-making [13]. Although the human brain most definitely mixes many different kinds of algorithms and objectives, reward maximization is suggested as a general framework for how to express the multitude of objectives. The pursuit of reward allows humans to optimize for long-term success, which is subjectively defined through the reward system of the brain—a system that has evolved to balance different needs and desires and preserve the homeostasis of the body. Accordingly, reward is hypothesized to be a "common currency" that allows for most (if not all) aspects of intelligence and behavior to be prioritized and integrated.

It has frequently been argued that the problem of free will is due to semantics, and we agree that this is indeed the case. When debating free will, we are conflating two different types of freedom, and we argue that by viewing humans as reward-maximizing RL agents it is possible to resolve the conceptual confusion. The first type of freedom—which we will refer to here as *physical freedom*—is what incompatibilists have in mind when they conclude that the currently known laws of nature do not permit one to have free will in any meaningful way. This kind of freedom is essentially randomness. It is the possibility for things to happen without a cause, which is in physics a consequence of quantum mechanics, or at least according to some interpretations thereof. Therefore, it makes perfect sense to conclude, as hard incompatibilists do, that physical freedom is not something we can possess, since if something is random, it is by definition not under our control [11].

However, as we will show, the RL perspective allows us to reason about and define the freedom of an agent in a different yet meaningful way. We call this other type of freedom *value freedom*. Where *value* refers to the estimated values of actions available to an RL agent given its current knowledge of the environment. The state dependent value freedom of an agent is defined as the information entropy of its action selection process and thus can, at least in some sense, be viewed as a measure of unpredictability, regardless of whether the selection process is fully deterministic or somewhat stochastic. Accordingly, we suggest that the concept of *value freedom* bridges the everyday use of the word *free*, the compatibilist view that it is meaningful to talk about free will even under strict determinism, and the incompatibilist view according to which our understanding of causality does not permit us to have free will in the physical sense.

Furthermore, we also suggest that value freedom is beneficial for agents due to its connection to the exploitation vs. exploration dilemma faced by all agents trying to learn from delayed rewards. [7,14] High freedom states are desirable because they signal low-risk exploration and provide room for potential policy improvements.

Lastly, we address the question of why people so often believe in free will by observing that an efficient solution to the temporal credit assignment problem [10] requires agents to model themselves as if they are able break the causal structure of their environment. Although this model—from a deterministic point of view—is flawed, it tend to make humans think of themselves as being free to have done differently than they actually did.

In what follows, we start with a brief description of model-based RL and challenges that learning agents, including humans, face when trying to maximize reward. Then, we proceed to define the value freedom of an agent and, through a series of examples, demonstrate that this quantity closely relates to the concept of freedom, as used in everyday language. In the next section, we discuss why the credit assignment problem makes it necessary for efficient model-based RL agents to believe that—or at least act as if—they have free will that defies causality.

2   Reinforcement Learning

Owing to the delay between actions and rewards, RL[1] presents a learning agent with two central challenges: reward prediction and credit assignment (Minsky, 1963).

If an agent can predict how its behavior will alter its environment and what future states will result in reward, it can use these predictions to better choose its actions. Less trial-and-error is needed if an agent, when faced with a new situation, is capable of seeing into the future to make predictions of the likely reward its actions will generate. We will in the following refer to an agent's prediction of the expected value of an action, a, given an observed state of the world, o, and its policy, π, as $Q^\pi(o, a)$.

In contrast to planning, that requires an RL agent to predict the future, the problem of temporal credit assignment requires it to understand the past. If a sequence of actions leads to a successful outcome, the agent needs to figure out which actions were actually important for the success, and which were not. Accordingly, the agent has to assess which behaviors shall be reinforced, making

---

[1] For the sake of brevity, we here only give a high-level description of model-based RL. For a more complete formulation see [12].

them more likely to be repeated in similar situations in the future, and which shall be suppressed.

Model-based RL is an approach to tackle both the problem of reward prediction through planning and/or that of credit assignment by equipping the agent with some form of generative model of its environment, i.e., a world model. Specifically, reward prediction can be achieved by running the world model forward, allowing the agent to search for favorable action sequences without really performing them, while credit assignment is attained by employing the world model to evaluate which past actions were actually important for the received reward, without needing to go back and test alternative action sequences. Both prospection and retrospection through a world model are thus crucial for efficient RL.

3   What is Freedom?

Similar to many other concepts often used in everyday language, *freedom* and *voluntary* vs. *involuntary* action are not precisely defined. However, this does not make them less useful.

If we seriously consider the perspective that humans are RL agents, a problem emerges. Namely, what does it mean for an RL agent to make free choices? An RL agent is just an algorithm or a collection thereof, be it deterministic or somewhat stochastic, or equipped with a world model or not. It is still just a mapping between states of the environment and actions. It is difficult to talk about algorithms having free will.

We suggest that the solution to this problem starts by noting that the relative action value estimates given the agents observer state, $Q^\pi(\mathbf{o}, a)$, represent something close to the "will" of an agent, since in every situation an agent selects its actions according to their expected value. Therefore, action values represent what an agent wants to do, i.e., what outcomes it expects to be rewarding or least costly, and how effective it believes the available actions are when trying to reach those outcomes. For instance, if the agent is an imprisoned human, he or she might really want to escape, but, at the same time, realizes that the probability for success is minuscule and thus estimates the action value of escaping to be rather small. Therefore, after an agent has considered the probability of success, the resulting action values can be viewed as the will of that agent.

Based on the aforementioned definition of "will", we suggest that it is also possible to quantify how free an agent is. To this end, we define the action selection probability as: $P(a_i) = softmax(Q^\pi(\mathbf{o}, a_i))$, where the softmax function normalizes[2] the estimated action values into a probability distribution over actions.

We then use this to define the freedom of an agent with an observed state as the information entropy of the action selection distribution:

---

[2] The exact method of normalization in not important. We here ignore the problem that the softmax function is not scale invariant.

$$H_a = -\sum_i P(a_i) log_2(P(a_i)). \tag{1}$$

This quantity, which we refer to as *value freedom*, can thus be interpreted as the uncertainty of an agent's action selection if the policy samples action weighted according to *P(a)*. It is high in situations where the agent's estimated action values, $Q^\pi(\mathbf{o}, a)$, are uniform, and low when the value of one or a few actions appears to be markedly higher than those of all other actions.

To demonstrate that value freedom, H_a, is indeed a quantity that closely resembles what, in everyday language, is referred to as freedom of choice, let us imagine two idealized scenarios where one could consider a binary choice to be free or not (here we switch to a second-person perspective to allow the reader to better imagine themselves in these situations):

1. You are sitting on a lush green lawn. Someone asks you in a friendly way to raise your left arm if you like, with no consequences whether you do it or not.
2. You are standing at the edge of a precipice with a deep dark ocean crashing against the sharp cliffs beneath you. Someone sneaks up behind you and threatens to push you off the ledge if you do not raise your left arm.

Let us also assume you can be very certain that what is promised will also happen, and that you are not suicidal.

When comparing these scenarios, one could argue that you are not free to choose what to do in either case, because you are just an algorithm and, as such, have no free will. Whether you raise your arm or not is just a result of the initial conditions of the situation and some deterministic or stochastic machinery in your head. However, in the common-sense meaning of being free, it is obvious that you are freer to choose what to do in the first scenario. Nothing is forcing you to do anything and, if you raise your arm, it seems as if you were free to not do it. So what is the difference between these two situations?

The central argument here is that the reason behind our perception of these two cases as very different is not that you are actually more physically free in one case or the other, but rather that you estimate the action values, $Q^\pi(\mathbf{o}, a))$, differently. Your goal (or that of any other RL agent) is to maximize the reward you receive over time. To this end, you need to continuously estimate the future reward of every available action and select the action with the highest estimate. Hence, you always perform the action that you subjectively estimate to be the best, i.e., the one that, in your assessment, has the highest estimated action value.

From this perspective, the difference between the two scenarios lies in how you reasonably would estimate the future reward of raising your arm or not. In the first scenario, raising your arm has no consequences; therefore, doing so or not has basically equal values. In contrast, in the second scenario, your fear of death produces a very large estimated negative reward for the option of not raising your arm. For more examples of how various action value estimates result in different levels of value freedom, see [12].

Note that you could also imagine that your policy is more or less stochastic, and that you do not always select the action with the highest value, but instead somehow sample your actions weighted according to the estimated rewards, since your action selection process might be more or less noisy. Nevertheless, intuitively, the "freedom" of your policy is large in the first scenario and very small in the second scenario, because, in the former case, there is simply less difference in value between available options. Indeed, there is empirical evidence showing that a person indifferent to the consequences of his/her choice is seen by lay people as maximally free [3].

However, at this point, one might rightfully object that, thus far, this seems like a very narrow definition of freedom. Isn't it possible to be very sure about what you want to do, but still feel free to do so or not? For instance, you might feel free to choose to have your favorite dish for dinner or not, even if you feel very sure its your preferred choice. However, note that you also know that the relative reward between having your favorite dish, or any other well-cooked meal is actually marginal. In contrast, image a scenario where, after starving for a week, you can choose between having your favorite dish and no dinner at all, your freedom is quite limited, to say the least. Hence, your value freedom is actually relatively high when choosing what to have for dinner and for most other everyday decisions.

In summary, we argue that the freedom of an agent can be quantified by looking at the uniformity of Q^π. The amplitudes of Q^π naturally translate to the will of the agent, since they represent how beneficial each action appears to be to the agent, while the uniformity of Q^π, here suggested to be measured through the information entropy, H_a, corresponds to how "free" the will is. In other words, value freedom could also be viewed as the "entropy of the will". And as such, its unit, bits, corresponds to how much information is gained by observing the choice of an agent. Because decisions where the value freedom is high involve more uncertainty concerning what the agent will do, the information content is higher than for low freedom decisions.

The above discussion of our commonsense understand of freedom has been limited to simple choice scenarios, where we view this as the *momentary* value freedom. We acknowledge that since agents like humans have a sophisticated model of the past and future, our experienced freedom is also depended on past choices, and the anticipated future outcome of actions (other than the reward). In [12] these factors are discussed in more detail. However, note that all these factors are highly subjective, from the perspective of both the agent itself and other agents judging someone else's freedom. The main argument here is that our everyday understanding of freedom is inherently subjective, i.e., it depend on the reward function of the agent, and that it is independent of whether or not the universe is deterministic.

4   Why Do We Believe We are Free?

Now that we have a way to quantify and think about our subjective understanding of freedom through the concept of value freedom, we will address the other questions we set out to answer: Why do we feel that we have free will, and what is the purpose of this feeling? Two questions which we suggest can be translated to: (1) Why do we tend to mix up value freedom with physical freedom? And, (2) why is high value freedom desirable? We hypothesize that the answer to (2) can be found in the need for RL agents to deal with the famous exploration vs. exploitation dilemma [7,14]. High value freedom indicates to an agent that the risk of exploration is low, because, in such situations, it looks as if there is not much to lose from exploring. Since several alternatives have similar predicted values, choosing one that is not known to be optimal is perceived as less of a risk. From this perspective, freedom can be seen as room for learning. When value freedom is high, an agent has the opportunity to test new approaches that hopefully will improve its world model, leading to an improved policy. Hence, high value freedom is a heuristic that signals potential low-risk policy improvements.

But, note that the value freedom does not say anything about how good your options are in an absolute sense—rather, it only shows how you subjectively value them relative to each other. Therefore, if all dishes on a restaurant menu look equally disgusting to your refined taste, then you are still bad off, even if your freedom is high. The inductive bias of "freedom desire" is thus balanced towards other goals, like having good food, through the common currency of reward. We are all familiar with the fact that people are often willing to give up some of their freedom in exchange for the fulfillment of other more basic needs.

We hypothesize that, rather than directly giving an agent a higher reward, striving for freedom makes the policy more robust and increases the venues for improving it in the future. Intuitively, this makes sense. If you are always forced to do the same thing over and over again, there is no room to try anything new, and you will never learn. However, an important distinction to be made here is that the lack of freedom does not necessarily mean the lack of exploration. We all have been in situations where our exploration was guided by a teacher. During this "supervised exploration", the teacher employs its model of the learning domain and the learner and, through authority or trust, skews the learner's reward estimates to make some actions look more preferable than others.

Now that we have discussed a potential motivation for the importance of (value) freedom to learning agents like humans, let us turn to the next question: Why do we tend to mix up value freedom with physical freedom?

Remember that temporal credit assignment is a challenge faced by all agents that need to learn from delayed rewards. The problem is essentially to figure out what actions leading up to a reward or penalty were responsible for the outcome and reinforce or weaken similar behavior in the future. In most work on RL, this problem is dealt with by relying on a temporal proximity heuristic where the actions closer in time to the reward state are straightforwardly assigned more credit than those farther away, i.e., the credit is somehow discounted based on the temporal proximity to the reward. This works in board games like Go or chess which have little causal invariance (most actions/turns influence the end state of the game), and where it is easy to generate a lot of independent action trajectories (e.g., chess games), but fails when actions have very different importance, and you cannot afford to fail multiple times, or in multi-task settings where it is not obvious which action influenced which reward state. For instance, imagine a Wall Street investor who assigns credit to his daily choice of a tie when he reaches the office in the morning and finds out that the value of one of his assets has crashed overnight. Superstition can in many cases be viewed as a failure of credit assignment.

Instead of relying only on temporal proximity, agents become more efficient learners if they are capable of figuring out what actions were actually important for a received reward or penalty. To this end, agents need to be able to imagine choosing other actions than those that were actually chosen. It comes down to answering counterfactual questions, such as "What would have happened if I had not done X? Would Y still happen?" Accordingly, to figure out what actions caused a received reward or penalty, agents need to imagine alternative realities. Along with planning by simulating the future, the simulation of such alternative histories is a key benefit of having a world model that encodes causal relationships between variables. So-called hindsight credit assignment has been investigated [5, 6, 9], albeit, to the best of our knowledge, only for model-free RL, i.e. RL when there is no explicit world model.

One can argue that not only credit assignment but also planning involves imagining taking actions independently of causal influence from the environment. When simulating future scenarios, agents need to evaluate the consequence of different decisions and can imagine being free to do virtually anything as long as it can be represented by their world model. For instance, Deery [2] argued that prospection, i.e., our experience of different future scenarios through mental simulation, is the cause for people's free will belief. However, since the action of planning lies in the causal path to the future, it is less clear that the imagination of being free in the future contradicts a deterministic model of the world and the agent itself. Since planning involves modeling the future, at least in its basic form, it does not require you to think about yourself as non-deterministic and having the ability to do differently than you actually did, i.e., no counterfactuals are needed.

In summary, we argue that, in order to efficiently learn from our successes or mistakes, we need to imagine that we are free. This *imagined freedom* is physical freedom in the simulated reality of our world model. When planning and performing credit assignment by counterfactual reasoning, we break the causal structure of our virtual reality and basically decide that something that did not in fact happen actually happened. In other words, we decide that events should occur without causes. The real causes for events in our mental simulation lie outside the simulation. In the frame of reference of the simulation, they are, to use physics jargon, hidden variables. Therefore, according to our imagination, we have physical freedom. Our ability to mentally break the chains of determinism makes us believe that—or at least feel as if—we really have physical freedom and that we can make decisions that are not ultimately caused by events external to ourselves.

5   Discussion

In this paper, we argued that the centuries-long philosophical debate about free will is a result of a necessary, but flawed aspect of our self-concept. Our models of ourselves say that, when offered a choice, we could have chosen to do something that we did not in fact do. This model has a good purpose. Without it, we would be unable to apply counterfactual reasoning to the problem of credit assignment and efficiently learn from our successes and failures. To learn in complex situations, we need to imagine that we could have made other choices than those we actually made. And, interestingly, this model of ourselves is not something we seem free to get rid of. On some level, even the most determined determinists act as if they have free will. While they might intellectually know that they have no physical freedom, if they truly thought as if they did not, they would fail to learn efficiently.

Furthermore, we argue that this contradiction can be resolved by applying a reward maximization perspective on human decision-making. It allows us to formalize what *free* and *will* actually refer to and realize that we do not really need to believe that we have physical freedom. Instead, what we refer to here as value freedom suffices. When we reason about our own freedom, write laws, or communicate with each other in general, this is the kind of freedom we are actually referring to. Therefore, our freedom is not based on our ability to act independently from the world—rather, it emerges from our brain's reward systems and the predictions of our world models. And since freedom tells us something about how much room for exploration and learning we have, it becomes, in Dennett's [4] parlance, "worth wanting"—for humans, and for learning agents in general.

Of note, our definition of value freedom does not rely on RL being a complete theory of human learning and decision-making. There is no requirement for any learning to occur, and rewards do not necessarily need to be scalar. The only requirement is that agents should be capable of selecting actions based on their expected relative benefit. Such a selection process appears to be a condition for agency itself. To choose is to weigh different options against each other, and then make a decision. While the nature of this weighting can vary considerably, agency postulates the need for some kind of ordering of alternatives. Similarly, it is clear that humans are capable of performing complex credit assignments using some form of causal model of the world.

In some sense, by formulating what freedom is, regardless of whether or not determinism holds, we propose a compatibilist view on free will. We are not disagreeing with the *classic incompatibilist argument* [8] that determinism does not allow for free will; rather, what we argue is that the kind of freedom laypeople actually refer to in everyday language is not the same kind of freedom incompatibilists reject. This distinction between what we here call physical freedom vs. value freedom allows for several potentially interesting perspectives.

For instance, when the UN declares that freedom of opinion is a human right, this does not imply that humans shall be able to choose their opinions independently from their environment. Rather, this means that people shall be able to do so without risking being punished for "wrong" choices, or bribed into making "correct" ones. When people vote to select their leaders, they should not perceive huge differences in estimated reward between candidates. Although some differences, seemingly more or less important, must obviously exist, voters should know that making one choice or the other will not massively change their outlook. They will not get jail time, nor will they get a promotion, regardless of how they cast their votes. Said differently, freedom of opinion means that, when forming opinions, agents should not experience any extremes in the action value distribution, and political liberty should be seen not only as freedom from oppression, but also as freedom from excessively strong positive incentives.

Furthermore, the RL perspective on human decision-making also suggests that laws, be they written or moral, do not exist because they reflect some metaphysical justice or ideal, but rather because they are ways for societies of learning agents to teach each other how to act. Accordingly, the classic incompatibilist position—the one that submits that, without free will, no one can be morally responsible for their actions [8]—is based on a misunderstanding of the purpose of assigning responsibility. Moral responsibility must be forward-looking [8]. The main reason for punishing members of a society, or any other group, for something they have done, is to discourage similar behavior in the future, and it makes little difference whether they were physically free to do what they did or not. From an RL perspective, what is important is to reduce the likelihood of someone making the same choice again in a similar situation by skewing future action value estimates. The "responsibility assignment" that societies have created courts for is analogous to the credit assignment single RL agents need to deal with when learning what behaviors to suppress or reinforce. In this view, courts are important components of the multi-agent learning system we call society.

There has been some empirical research on the connection between counterfactual thinking and free will belief. For instance, in a series of experiments, Alquist et al. [1] found the belief in free will to be linked to increased counterfactual thinking. The authors then hypothesized that "individuals and society as a whole may have benefitted from free will beliefs and the counterfactual simulations they stimulate". Here we show why this is the case and demonstrate not only that individuals and societies benefit from counterfactual thinking, but also how and why such thinking is essential for learning on a fundamental level through its role in efficient credit assignment.

Another observation is the relation between freedom and indifference, and how the latter is central to certain religious beliefs. According to the definition of value freedom, a maximally free agent is the one that always estimates all actions to have equal value. Such an agent never wants anything more or less than anything else, and obviously, would never learn anything and be utterly useless. One can question if it would be an agent at all. Applied to humans, such an agent is a person who completely lacks ego—an individual without any needs, drives, or desires. Interestingly, this view that the destruction of the ego is the ultimate path to freedom closely resembles a common theme in Eastern philosophy. According to Buddha's *Four Noble Truths*, to end personal suffering, stop the cycle of rebirth, and reach spiritual liberation, *nirvana*, we must let go of all desires. It is only when we have no desires—not even the desire to rid ourselves of all desires—that we become completely free. Accordingly, nirvana is described as a state of complete emptiness. It is when we experience ultimate indifference, and end experience itself. Nirvana is thus a state of eternal maximum value freedom.

References

1. Alquist, J.L., Ainsworth, S.E., Baumeister, R.F., Daly, M., Stillman, T.F.: The making of might-have-beens: effects of free will belief on counterfactual thinking. Pers. Soc. Psychol. Bull. **41**(2), 268–283 (2015). https://doi.org/10.1177/0146167214563673
2. Deery, O.: Why people believe in indeterminist free will. Philos. Stud. **172**(8), 2033–2054 (2014). https://doi.org/10.1007/s11098-014-0396-7
3. Deutschländer, R., Pauen, M., Haynes, J.D.: Probing folk-psychology: do Libet-style experiments reflect folk intuitions about free action? Conscious. Cogn. **48**, 232–245 (2017). Epub 2016 Dec 23. PMID: 28013177. https://doi.org/10.1016/j.concog.2016.11.004
4. Dennett, D.C.: Elbow room?: The Varieties of Free Will Worth Wanting. MIT Press, Cambridge (1984)
5. Guez, A., et al.: Value-driven Hindsight Modelling (2020)
6. Harutyunyan, A., et al.: Hindsight credit assignment. In: Advances in Neural Information Processing Systems (2019)
7. Lai, T., Robbins, H.: Asymptotically efficient adaptive allocation rules. Adv. Appl. Math. **6**(1), 4–22 (1985)
8. McKenna, M., Coates, D.J.: Compatibilism, The Stanford Encyclopedia of Philosophy (Fall 2021 Edition), Edward N. Zalta (ed.) (2021)
9. Mesnard, T., et al.: Counterfactual Credit Assignment in Model-Free Reinforcement Learning (2020)
10. Minsky, M.L.: Steps toward artificial intelligence. In: Feigenbaum, E.A., Feldman, J. (eds.) Comput. Thought, pp. 406–450. McGraw-Hill, New York (1963)
11. Pereboom, D.: Living without Free Will. Cambridge University Press, Cambridge (2001)
12. Rehn E.M.: Free will belief as a consequence of model-based reinforcement learning. Preprint (2021). https://doi.org/10.48550/arXiv.2111.08435
13. Silver, D., Singh, S., Precup, D., Sutton, R.S.: Reward is enough, Artificial Intelligence, Volume 299, 2021. ISSN **103535**, 0004–3702 (2021). https://doi.org/10.1016/j.artint.2021.103535
14. Thompson, W.R.: On the likelihood that one unknown probability exceeds another in view of the evidence of two samples. Biometrika **25**(3/4), 285–294 (1933)
15. Wisniewski, D., Deutschländer, R., Haynes, J.D.: Free will beliefs are better predicted by dualism than determinism beliefs across different cultures. PLoS ONE **14**(9), e0221617 (2019)

Thoughts on Architecture

Paul S. Rosenbloom[✉]

Department of Computer Science, University of Southern California, Los Angeles, CA, USA
rosenbloom@usc.edu

Abstract. The term *architecture* has evolved considerably from its original Greek roots and its application to buildings and computers to its more recent manifestation for minds. This article considers lessons from this history, in terms of a set of relevant distinctions introduced at each of these stages and a definition of architecture that spans all three, and a reconsideration of three key issues from cognitive architectures for architectures in general and cognitive architectures more particularly.

Keywords: Architecture · Historical context · Definition · Exploration

1 Introduction

Architectures are central to many attempts to capture key aspects of what is necessary for general intelligence [1–4], whether as models of natural (human) intelligence or as artificial systems that embody human-level intelligence or beyond. This notion is most familiar in cognitive science, where a cognitive architecture is intended to embody a theory of the human mind. However, it can also be found in both artificial intelligence (AI) and artificial general intelligence (AGI) – although sometimes under other names, such as AI, AGI, and agent architectures – where it amounts to a fixed framework that supports the construction of (generally) intelligent systems. For simplicity, the term cognitive architecture is used here as the generic across all of these variants.

One definition of a cognitive architecture is as a *hypothesis concerning the fixed structures and processes that together yield a mind, whether natural or artificial* [5]. Explicit in this definition is that a cognitive architecture should be *fixed* and that it may concern *natural or artificial* minds. Implicit in it is that a cognitive architecture should be *theoretical* ("hypothesis concerning") and *computational* ("structures and processes"). However, computer architectures, the direct inspiration for cognitive architectures, although fixed and computational, are not obviously theoretical in the sense of being *about* something else. Reaching further back in the inspirational chain, building architectures, although fixed, are neither computational nor theoretical.

In his classic work on *Unified Theories of Cognition*, Newell [6] defined an architecture as a *symbol system* [7]. This shares the concern with fixity and the notion that an architecture in general need not be theoretical, but then narrows the definition from there down to a form of universal computation. It thus rules out building architectures and any other noncomputational structures – such as noncomputational scientific theories – or even many special purpose computational devices, while still admitting typical

© The Author(s), under exclusive license to Springer Nature Switzerland AG 2023
B. Goertzel et al. (Eds.): AGI 2022, LNAI 13539, pp. 364–373, 2023.
https://doi.org/10.1007/978-3-031-19907-3_35

computer architectures and symbolic cognitive architectures. By having identified minds with symbol systems [7] – an idea that remains controversial to date – Newell had no need to add that cognitive architectures are about minds, whereas under the version in [5] they are explicitly concerned with understanding and/or building minds.

The remainder of this article begins with an attempt to clarify the notion of an architecture as it has developed from building architecture, through computer architecture, to cognitive architecture (Sect. 2). A key part of this is identifying relevant *distinctions* that the kinds of architectures in this sequence have introduced. Analyzing this history, and the distinctions introduced across it, a broad definition of an architecture emerges that spans the entire sequence (Sect. 3). What then follows are discussions of three issues of interest that specifically concern cognitive architecture: multilayered architectures (Sect. 4), theoretical computational architectures (Sect. 5), and architectural exploration (Sect. 6). The ultimate intent is to see what new insight this all can yield for architecture in general and for cognitive architecture more particularly.

2 Historical Context[1]

The word *architecture* stems from the Greek ἀρχιτέκτων (*arkhitekton*), where it referred to a master builder or director of works [8, 9]. In modern usage it includes "both the process and the product of planning, designing, and constructing buildings or other structures" [9], with its practice oriented toward both practical and expressive requirements, and thus serving both utilitarian and aesthetic ends [10]. Distinctions that arise in such architectures that resonate in later forms of architecture include:

1. The *fixed* nature of the architecture versus the *variable* nature of its contents. In French, this is succinctly *immobiliere* (real estate) versus *mobiliere* (furniture).
2. *Design* versus *implementation*. A design is part of the process that specifies what is to be implemented, whereas an implementation is the heart of the resulting product.
3. (*Function* versus *structure*) versus *form*. Function concerns how the product is used whereas structure concerns how this function is provided. Both relate to utility whereas form in this context concerns the aesthetics of how these are presented.
4. *Simple* versus *complex*. Although this may impact utility, the greater concern is with form/aesthetics, such as Scandinavian or Japanese versus Victorian or rococo.

Computer architecture [11] is a more recent conceptualization inspired by the notion of building architecture. It induces a partitioning of a computational system – i.e., a system that transforms information [12] – into a fixed architecture versus variable programs and data. The design is a description whereas the implementation actively computes. The earliest computers each had their own *instruction set* – a specification of the instructions the computer could execute – that was tied to the hardware they came with. However, it was not long before this was separated from the implementation, with the architecturally defined instruction set specifying what was to be implemented, and multiple hardware implementations being developed to span sizes and generations of computers. A general

---

[1] *Truth in advertising:* I am an expert on cognitive architecture, but nothing more than a student of computer architecture and an interested outsider on building architecture.

language – Instruction Set Processor (ISP) – was even developed to enable specifying instruction sets across the field of computer architecture [13].

The function of a computer architecture is to support computation via an instruction set. The structure comprises the hardware (and possibly firmware) components that yield this plus their organization. Form is often deprecated, although some manufacturers do take it seriously. There is an analog of simple versus complex, in the debate between reduced versus complex instruction set computers – i.e., RISC versus CISC – although the focus here is more on utility than aesthetics.

A computer architecture induces one additional distinction of note:

5. *Transformer* versus *container*. A transformational architecture transforms its variable content rather than simply containing it.

A computational architecture transforms information, with a computer architecture further specializing this to be based on hardware (and possibly firmware) structures.

The notion of a *cognitive architecture* is even newer, being a form of computational architecture that originated in analogy to computer architecture, with Allen Newell having played formative roles in both areas [13, 14]. Its function is to provide a (fixed) *mind* that can transform (variable) *knowledge and skills*. Its structure comprises the mechanisms and their organization that together yield a mind. The question of form arises primarily in terms of the simple versus complex distinction. A simple, RISC-like cognitive architecture focuses on achieving intelligence from the interactions among a small number of very general mechanisms (see, e.g., [5, 15]), whereas a complex, CISC-like architecture includes a wider range of more complex mechanisms (see, e.g., [16, 17]). This distinction may be thought of as between a physics (i.e., beauty) mindset – although even there it can be controversial [18] – versus a biological (i.e., evolution-as-a-tinkerer) one, with the computer science (i.e., modular) perspective possibly sitting in between. Both utilitarian and aesthetic aspects are implicated here.

The introduction of cognitive architecture also induces an additional distinction:

6. *Theoretical* versus *atheoretical*. This amounts to whether or not an architecture is *about* something else. Architectures in cognitive science tend to be theoretical – being about human minds – whereas A(G)I architectures (along with building and computer architectures) are not directly so.

A theoretical architecture – or *theory* – with or without accompanying variations, represents – or "stands in for" – key aspects of a phenomenon or domain of interest. Architectures represent complex phenomena when used in *understanding* it [12], as is typical in the sciences. Transformational architectures may also be used to generate (or *shape* [12]) complex phenomena, as is typical in engineering and other professions [12]. Such architectures may also represent something but need not do so.

A computer architecture, for example, is central to engineering all kinds of computational systems, with its foremost purpose being to aid in the development of such systems rather than to represent or to help in understanding anything. The architecture in such a case could conceivably be considered as a model of computation, as with a

Turing machine [19], but this is deep in the background in most applications. Similarly, a cognitive architecture may be theoretical in a strong sense if intended, for example, to explicitly represent a human mind or it may be theoretical only in a weaker sense, in implicitly embodying a hypothesis about mind in the abstract. The definition in the introduction is broad enough to span both senses.

An *inspired* architecture, such as a biologically inspired cognitive architegure (BICA) [20], sits at a hybrid position with respect to theoretical versus atheoretical via a particular combination of understanding and shaping. At the top level, the goal is atheoretical, to support the development of useful systems with no concern as to what might be represented in the process. However, understanding of an existing system becomes an instrumental subgoal in guiding the design of the atheoretical architecture. In some cases the existence of this subsidiary understanding is considered purely heuristic, and fine to ignore or dismiss when convenient, while in others it is considered a virtue to be extolled.

3 Defining Architecture

From these three overall classes of architectures – building, computer, and cognitive – a slimmed-down definition of an architecture can be identified that centers on a *fixed framework* that enables and delimits a *space of variations*. This focuses on Distinction 1, with the other five helping to scope the space of architectural types while not themselves being definitional. Simon [21] discussed the importance of identifying *invariants* because of "their power to strip away the complexity and diversity of a whole range of phenomena and to reveal the simplicity and order underneath." In this sense, an architecture is a set of invariants; however, it also typically goes beyond this to consider the interactions among them and what a complete set of them might be.

Together, an architecture and a set of variations yields a *system*, which can succinctly be semi-formalized via the equation *system = architecture + variations*. This harks back to earlier syntactically similar equations, such as *algorithms + data structures = programs* [22] and *algorithm = logic + control* [23]; however, each of these equations makes a distinct point. Still, in the spirit of the second equation, the familiar equation *system(s) = program(s) + data* can be seen as a particular specialization of the equation proposed here to computational systems, where the program is the fixed, architectural component and the data yields the variations.

More broadly, the systems of interest here may be conceptual, mathematical, computational, physical, etc. An *application* is then simply a system that yields value. In general, different kinds of architectures enable different forms of variations (and thus yield different types of systems and applications). As we have just seen, computer architectures enable programs and data while cognitive architectures enable skills and knowledge. In addition, modular architectures enable module definitions and API (i.e., application programming interface) specifications; hierarchical and graphical architectures enable node and link definitions; tables and maps enable entries at appropriate locations; and buildings enable furniture, appliances, and ornaments. In tightly specified theories or models, in which nearly the entire system is architecture, the variations may simply be parameter values.

A classic slogan in AI, although it seems to have originated hundreds of years ago with Francis Bacon as *scientia potentia est*, is that *knowledge is power* [24]. We could also add that *applications are payoff*. In architectural terms, knowledge is a form of variation enabled by cognitive architectures, whereas applications are complete systems that result from combining appropriate architectures and variations. In analogy, we can now go a step further to say that *architecture is essence*.

4 Multilayered Architectures

Computational architectures – i.e., architectures that transform information – and the-oretical architectures are both amenable to being parts of layered stories.[2] Consider first computational architectures. A computer architecture provides a fixed foundation that supports leveraging programs to transform data. However, as anticipated with the familiar equation introduced in the previous section, at a second level programs may themselves yield computational architectures, particularly when fixed over some span of interest, with their data then providing the only source of variation. This data variation may in turn be very flexible – as for example in a cognitive architecture that supports a broad range of skills and knowledge – or it may be severely limited.

In the former case, this process of implementing computational architectures within the variations that are enabled by other computational architectures can conceivably proceed to arbitrary levels. For example, the Sigma cognitive architecture [5] comprises two such layers – a *graphical* architecture and a *cognitive* architecture – with the former implementing the latter. Some of the capabilities included in the Common Model of Cognition [3] – such as a particular form of declarative memory – are then implemented in a third layer, with the aid of skills and knowledge represented within Sigma's cognitive architecture.

Similarly, a theoretical architecture can be a theory itself or just one part of a more elaborate theory that also includes appropriate choices among the variations the architec-ture enables. Kivunja [25], for example, discusses the notion of a theoretical framework as the accepted wisdom from experts that serves as the background for a graduate stu-dent's own research. The former might perhaps also be considered a Kuhnian paradigm [26]. This effectively partitions a student's contributed theory into a fixed, architectural framework – or paradigm – plus the student's own contributed variations. A Lakatosian research programme [27] also partitions in this manner – "For Lakatos an individual theory within a research programme typically consists of two components: the (more or less) irrefutable hard core plus a set of auxiliary hypotheses" [28].

A cognitive architecture can be considered as a theory of the fixed structures and processes found in a human mind, or of what is necessary and/or sufficient to yield an artificial mind. When combined with skills and knowledge, it can also serve as a more fleshed out model, for example, of human behavior in a particular task. While cogni-tive architectures are often both computational and theoretical, only the more fleshed out models can execute to yield behavioral data for comparison with human data, or applications that have value beyond their ability to model humans.

---

[2] The same may also be true beyond computational architectures to all transformational architectures, but the focus here is narrower.

5 Theoretical Computational Architectures

For theoretical computational architectures, there is a serious question of how their design, implementation and theory are related; and, also, which of these is properly an/the architecture. In general, a design is a description, and an implementation is a realization of this description. For buildings, both are architecture, whereas for computers only the design is, with the implementation being instead a computer. For cognition the implementation is typically the architecture, as there is rarely an explicit design. However, for a theoretical cognitive architecture this yields a conundrum, as there often is a vague notion of what the architecture is beyond any particular implementation that enables researchers to refer to multiple implementations, even in different underlying languages, as being the same architecture.

Starting back at the beginning, in the simplest case there is just a theory about a body of phenomena (Fig. 1). It might be described informally in text or more formally as mathematical equations. For a computational theory, there is typically an implementation, of which the theory itself is only a subpart. The remainder is "implementation details" necessary to make the theory executable but not part of the theory itself (Fig. 2). There is typically no separate design specification in such cases, although AIXI [15] could be considered as such, and there were several attempts to specify Soar more formally [29, 30]. Still, ideally there would always be a separate design that specifies in a more comprehensible yet abstract fashion what is to be in the implementation (Fig. 3), as is common with buildings and computers. This design would have its own theoretical subpart – corresponding to the theory in Fig. 1 – which may be more easily demarcated than is possible within the implementation. Without this, the boundary between what is part of the theory versus an implementation detail remains fuzzy [30].

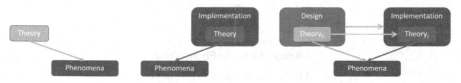

Fig. 1. Simple theory.   **Fig. 2.** Typical computational theory.   **Fig. 3.** Ideal computational theory.

Where is the architecture in all of this? According to the definition in Sect. 3, all four non-phenomenal components in Fig. 3 are theoretical architectures. They may even share the same name in practice, although Fig. 3 can potentially be leveraged to distinguish the distinct roles they each fill with respect to a common name. It should be noted though that the atheoretical aspects of the two larger components maintain an ambiguous state of being fixed with respect to their enabled variations but malleable in being adjustable as necessary without affecting the core theory, much like Lakatosian auxiliary hypotheses. The two design architectures in turn can be doubly theoretical, in being both about the phenomena and the implementation.

6 Architectural Exploration

Figure 4 shows one way of conceptualizing the traditional *scientific method*. As parts of a method diagram, these boxes are an odd mix of nouns and verbs, although they do include the standard pieces in one form or another. Still, when considering my own architectural methodology over the past 40+ years, I end up with something more like Fig. 5, which labels nouns as nodes while relegating verbs to arrows. According to this view, there is a constant back and forth between an architecture and its researchers, with the former yielding new insight for the latter and in return being modified by them to capture this insight. The phenomena of interest are themselves understood (theoretical) and/or shaped (atheoretical) by the architecture, with this interaction providing input for both directions of the architecture-researchers interaction. There is also a direct link between researchers and phenomena that reflects both architecture-free observation and direct exploration of the phenomena.

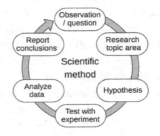

Fig. 4. The scientific method [31].

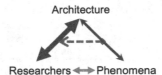

Fig. 5. Architectural exploration.

Exploration – i.e., searching for new phenomena to understand – has no explicit role in Fig. 4, although it may be implicit within the *Observation/question* box. It is often considered pre-scientific, but the scientific enterprise would be terribly impoverished without it. Early natural scientists fanned out across the globe to deliberately seek out and make sense of novel plants, animals, and other natural phenomena. To this day, disciplines such as paleontology, astronomy and particle physics intentionally explore the natural universe. They may also expend considerable effort developing new instruments that sense aspects of the world/universe not previously perceptible to us. There may be hypotheses and predictions that are intended from the beginning to be tested via such instruments, but part of the anticipation and excitement in any such enterprise must always be the possibility of uncovering what was not expected.

In Fig. 5, the researchers-phenomena arrow represents classical exploration as a form of active observation, with the leftward direction reflecting observation and the rightward direction manipulation of what is to be observed (with controlled experimentation at the extreme). The architecture-researchers arrow then represents architectural exploration. The downward direction represents the development of insight based on the architecture and its interactions with the phenomena of interest (with direct observation entering from the side). It also reflects the architecture's role as both an instrument and a guide. The upward direction represents architecture modification based on the existing architecture and its interactions with the phenomena of interest. This reflects the architecture's role as both a hypothesis and a domain of exploration of its own.

The cognitive architectures I have developed over the years have partially been intended as expressions of, and means for testing, hypotheses. Often these hypotheses start out rather vague,[3] such as some notion of the potential benefits deriving from the combination of rules and neural-like activation in Xaps [33]; rules, problem solving and learning-by-chunking in Soar [34]; and Soar-like cognitive architectures and probabilistic graphical models in Sigma [5]. Sometimes this develops into a somewhat more precise – and even at times grander – hypothesis, such as that chunking provides a general learning mechanism [35] or that Soar can support a *unified theory of cognition* [6]. More often, crisper small hypotheses are spun off, such as that chunking in Soar could be used not just to speed up performance but also to learn new things [36], or that Sigma could straightforwardly be extended to incorporate neural networks (NNs) [37].

Still, most of the actual work is exploratory, using the architecture to guide the exploration of cognition and to interpret the results of these explorations; as well as searching the space of cognitive architectures itself. Controlled experiments are relevant to only a fraction of the criteria used to evaluate such work, with the more complete criteria including: (1) whether an architecture functions as intended; (2) how broadly the architecture models and/or produces the phenomena of interest; (3) how simple and elegant the architecture is; and (4) how much insight the architecture inspires and captures, whether into anticipated implications or wholly unanticipated ones.

Despite numerous attempts by the field to develop better approaches to evaluating work on cognitive architectures, much of the evaluation activity around these four criteria necessarily continues to center around simply building new architectural components and exploring their interactions. Controlled experiments, in contrast, tend to focus on refining what can be said about criterion (1), in terms of how well the architecture models and/or produces phenomena of interest, and a bit of criterion (2). Such experiments clearly play a role, but not particularly a dominant one. If one is problem focused, rather than methodology focused, it is critical to use whatever the best methods available are for the problem of interest, rather than limiting oneself to problems for which the strongest methods – in terms of the veracity they guarantee – are applicable; and exploration is still the best methodology for much work in cognitive architectures.

Exploration was the name of the game in the early days of AI, when there were many more unexplored areas than researchers to investigate them and it was better to move on to new topics once sufficient low-hanging fruit had been harvested than to work over existing topics very carefully first. Now, however, exploration has fallen into relative disrepute as a method of investigating topics in AI. With a broader coverage of the space

---

[3] "I do not pretend to start with precise questions. I do not think you can start with anything precise. You have to achieve such precision as you can, as you go along." [32].

of topics now under our belts, and general progress in the application of proofs and controlled experiments to specific AI problems, these methodologies have become the coin of the realm instead. Strong methods once they get a foothold in a field tend to push out weaker ones even in areas where the stronger ones are not applicable [12].

Exploration has continued to remain a major methodology in AGI, presumably enabled by separating the field out from AI as a distinct discipline. However, in doing so, it must also be sure to avoid becoming a wayside by either ignoring what is happening in the mainstream or by clinging to weaker methods if/when stronger ones do come along that apply to the problem(s) of producing general intelligence.

7 Conclusion

The crux of the idea of an architecture is to differentiate the fixed from the variable aspects of a system. This distinction, which in honor of Simon might be denoted simply as *(in)variant*, or even as *(im)mobiliere*, can then be elaborated on in various ways, with the (non)computational and (a)theoretical distinctions being of particular relevance to cognitive architectures. Additional issues that have been revisited here concern architectural layering and the nature of theoretical computational architectures. The question of how architectures should be investigated, with a specific focus on exploration, has then capped off these thoughts. Future work might occur in a variety of directions, including incorporating into this analysis other forms of architecture, such as software architecture [38, 39], that are relevant to architecture in general, and that should in principle be relevant to cognitive architecture, but which did not have a foundational impact on the development of this latter notion.

References

1. Langley, P., Laird, J.E., Rogers, S.: Cognitive architectures: Research issues and challenges. Cog. Sys. Res. **10**(2), 141–160 (2009)
2. Goertzel, B.: Artificial general intelligence: Concept, state of the art, and future prospects. J. of AGI **5**(1), 1–46 (2014)
3. Laird, J.E., Lebiere, C., Rosenbloom, P.S.: A Standard Model of the Mind: Toward a common computational framework across artificial intelligence, cognitive science, neuroscience, and robotics. AI Mag. **38**(4), 13–26 (2017)
4. Kotseruba, I., Tsotsos, J.K.: 40 years of cognitive architectures: Core cognitive abilities and practical applications. AI Review **53**(1), 17–94 (2020)
5. Rosenbloom, P.S., Demski, A., Ustun, V.: The Sigma cognitive architecture and system: Towards functionally elegant grand unification. J. of AGI **7**(1), 1–103 (2016)
6. Newell, A.: Unified Theories of Cognition. Harvard U. Press, Cambridge, MA (1990)
7. Newell, A., Simon, H.A.: Computer science as empirical inquiry: symbols and search. Comm. of the ACM **19**(3), 113–126 (1976)
8. Online Etymology Dictionary on Architect: https://www.etymonline.com/word/architect. 10 February 2022
9. Wikipedia on Architecture. https://en.wikipedia.org/wiki/Architecture. 10 February 2022
10. Britannica on Architecture. https://www.britannica.com/topic/architecture. 10 February 2022
11. Hennessy, J.L., Patterson, D.A.: Computer Architecture: A Quantitative Approach, 5th edn. Morgan Kaufmann, Waltham, MA (2012)

12. Rosenbloom, P.S.: On Computing: The Fourth Great Scientific Domain. MIT Press, Cambridge, MA (2012)
13. Bell, C.G., Newell, A.: Computer Structures: Readings and Examples. McGraw-Hill, New York, NY (1971)
14. Newell, A.: You can't play 20 questions with nature and win: projective comments on the papers of this symposium. In: Chase, W.G. (ed.), Visual Information Processing: Proc. of the 8th Annual Carnegie Symp. on Cognition. Academic Press, New York, NY (1973)
15. Hutter, M.: Universal Artificial Intelligence: Sequential Decisions Based on Algorithmic Probability. Springer-Verlag, Berlin (2005)
16. Laird, J.E.: The Soar Cognitive Architecture. MIT Press, Cambridge, MA (2012)
17. Goertzel, B., Pennachin, C., Geisweiller, N.: Engineering General Intelligence. Atlantis Press, Amsterdam (2014)
18. Hossenfelder, S.: Lost in Math: How Beauty Leads Physics Astray. Basic Books, New York, NY (2018)
19. Turing, A.M.: On computable numbers, with an application to the entscheidungsproblem. In: Proc. of the London Math. Soc. s2-42(1), 230-65 (1937)
20. Stocco, A., Lebiere, C., Samsonovich, A.: The B-I-C-A of biologically inspired cognitive architectures. International Journal of Machine Consciousness 2(2), 171-192 (2010)
21. Simon, H.A.: How Big Is a Chunk? Science 183(4142), 482-488 (1974)
22. Wirth, N.: Algorithms + Data Structures = Programs. Prentice-Hall, Englewood Cliffs, NJ (1976)
23. Kowalski, R.: Algorithm = logic + control. Comms. of the ACM 22(7), 424-436 (1979)
24. Feigenbaum, E.: Expert System: Principles and Practice (1992)
25. Kivunja, C.: Distinguishing between theory, theoretical framework, and conceptual framework: A systematic review of lessons from the field. Int. J. of Higher Ed. 7(6), 44-53 (2018)
26. Kuhn, T.: The Structure of Scientific Revolutions. U. of Chicago Press, Chicago, IL (1962)
27. Lakatos, I.: The Methodology of Scientific Research Programmes: Philosophical Papers, vol. 1. Cambridge U. Press, Cambridge, UK (1978)
28. Stanford Encyclopedia of Philosophy on Lakatos. https://plato.stanford.edu/entries/lakatos/. 14 February 2022
29. Milnes, B.G., et al.: A Specification of the Soar Cognitive Arch. In: Z. Carnegie Mellon U., Pittsburgh, PA (1992)
30. Cooper, R., Fox, J., Farringdom, J., Shallice, T.: Towards a systematic methodology for cognitive modelling. Artif. Intell. 84(1–2), 355 (1996)
31. Wikipedia on Scientific Method. https://en.wikipedia.org/wiki/Scientific_method. 12 February 2022
32. Russell, B.: The Philosophy of Logical Atomism (1918)
33. Rosenbloom, P.S.: A cognitive odyssey: From the power law of practice to a general learning mechanism and beyond. Tutorials in Quant. Meth. for Psych. 2(2), 43-51 (2006)
34. Laird, J.E., Newell, A., Rosenbloom, P.S.: Soar: an architecture for general intelligence. Artif. Intell. 33, 1-64 (1987)
35. Laird, J.E., Rosenbloom, P.S., Newell, A.: Chunking in Soar: the anatomy of a general learning mechanism. Mach. Learn. 1(1), 11-46 (1986)
36. Rosenbloom, P.S., Laird, J.E., Newell, A.: Knowledge level learning in Soar. In: Proc. of the 6th Nat. Conf. on AI, pp. 499-504. AAAI Press, Menlo Park, CA (1987)
37. Rosenbloom, P.S., Demski, A., Ustun, V.: Toward a neural-symbolic Sigma: introducing neural network learning. In: Proc. of the 15th Annual Meeting of the ICCM (2017)
38. Perry, D.E., Wolf, A.L.: Foundations for the study of software architecture. ACM SIGSOFT Software Engineering Notes 17(4), 40-52 (1992)
39. Clements, P., et al.: Documenting Software Architectures: Views and Beyond, 2nd Edition. Addison-Wesley, Upper Saddle River, NJ

On the Possibility of Regulation of Human Emotions via Multimodal Social Interaction with an Embodied Agent Controlled by eBICA-Based Emotional Interaction Model

Alexei V. Samsonovich[1]([✉]) [iD], Zhen Liu[2] [iD], and Ting Ting Liu[2]

[1] National Research Nuclear University MEPhI, 115409 Moscow, Russia
avsamsonovich@mephi.ru
[2] Ningbo University, Ningbo, China

Abstract. Embodied social agents are expected to become useful for emotion regulation with applications in the field of service-oriented artificial intelligence. Emotion models can be used to generate an adequate response of the agent in order to achieve a desired emotion regulation effect. Here an eBICA-based model of emotional interaction of embodied social agents is proposed, combining concepts borrowed from biology, cognitive psychology, sociology, and ethics. Based on it, a concept of an embodied emotionally-intelligent agent is developed that will enable natural user emotion regulation during human-computer social interaction. The expected impact includes new smart emotion regulation technologies and new feasible means for emotional communication with and via artifacts.

Keywords: Human-computer interaction · Affective computing · Cognitive modeling · BICA · Semantic map · Moral schema

1 Introduction

Embodied social agents are intelligent creatures that usually have an anthropomorphic appearance. They can be implemented as virtual agents (virtual graphic avatars) or physical humanoid robots. Embodied social agents can mimic human emotions and emotionally driven behavior and communicate with users naturally like humans. This new technology is expected to become useful for emotion regulation with applications in the field of service-oriented artificial intelligence.

Artificial regulation of emotions should use various regulatory mechanisms borrowed from biology, which are necessary at different stages of emotional perception, cognition, decision-making and behavior control, including the mechanisms of situation awareness, situation correction, attention transformation, cognitive reassessment and reaction correction [1]. In order to be able to regulate emotions during social interaction, it is first necessary to be able to perceive emotions of the user. To do this, one should rely on the multimodal perception of information, which requires determining the type of emotion by analyzing and integrating information extracted from facial expressions,

B. Goertzel et al. (Eds.): AGI 2022, LNAI 13539, pp. 374–383, 2023.
https://doi.org/10.1007/978-3-031-19907-3_36

voice, body language, and physiological signals [2]. On this basis, the emotion model can be used to generate an adequate response and to control the agent, using its ability to express emotions, in order to achieve the desired emotion regulation effect. The agent's emotions can be expressed through body language, facial expressions, speech acts (including voice and text tonality), etc., or by controlling environmental characteristics such as light [3]. Modern basic models of emotional intelligence are based on the cognitive appraisal theory [33–38]. In computational models based on this theory, emotion or affect is calculated as an assessment of perception from the point of view of the agent [4]. It has been proven that agents with emotional expressiveness are more capable of influencing the emotional experience of users [5]. Personalized emotional expressiveness can further enhance the believability of agents [6]. In addition, technology for processing uncertain information [7] and machine learning methods have been widely recognized for their potential in emotion processing. With the help of conversational agents, users' emotions can be detected [8, 9], and in combination with the analysis of non-verbal behavior, users' emotions can be well tracked and evaluated [10].

When a computer can detect and evaluate a user's emotions, it can use that information to mimic the adequate emotional behavioral response in a virtual agent or robot and therefore be able to create a more natural and engaging user experience. It has been established that the mechanism of empathy can be used to better stimulate positive emotions in users, and therefore social robots capable of empathy are more popular [11, 12]. The need for more socially acceptable human-computer interaction is drawing researchers' attention to the development of cognitive models and architectures allowing for a more complex structure of emotions, capable of using a combination of body language and voice to detect user emotions, and using a Bayesian network to quantify detected emotions in terms of valence and arousal. At the stage of expression of emotions, a cognitive architecture should allow the robot to evaluate and correct emotional characteristics of the robot's behavior, bringing it in correspondence with the perceived emotion, the current emotional state of the robot, the robot's own needs, and the user's feedback after the robot expresses its emotion [13].

Many research groups in the world pursue various goals related to the artificial emotionality of social embodied agents. It is impossible to list all of them here because of their huge number; a few examples of leading groups are given below: Jonathan Grach (University of Southern California) [4, 14], Cynthia Breazeal (MIT Personal Robots, MIT Media Lab) [15, 16], Catherine Pelachaud (French National Center for Scientific Research - CNRS, France) [17, 18], Rodrigo Ventura, Instituto Superior Técnico (IST), Technical University of Lisbon [19, 20], Michael Sellers, Department of Telecommunications, Indiana University [21], Antonio Chella, Robotics, University of Palermo [22, 23], and Nadia Magnenat Thalmann, MIRALab, University of Geneva [24]. For a review, see [25].

Machine learning, in particular deep learning, is used today by many groups as a tool for analyzing and synthesizing the emotional flavor (tonality, sentiment) of text, speech, facial expressions, gaze direction, posture and gesture language, and the like. One example of an emotional chatbot is XiaoIce [26], which can be said to use semantic mapping technology (although the authors do not use this terminology). The XiaoIce social chatbot has been widely adopted since its release in May 2014. It "understands" the emotional needs of users and engages them in interpersonal communication as a "friend", encouraging them and keeping their attention. We recognize that the approach used in XiaoIce also has the potential to regulate emotions. However, its capabilities do not go beyond primitive, limited paradigms (e.g., driving the conversation with the user toward a certain mood).

Other major competitors in the field of emotional robotics are companies commercializing emotional toys (Hasbro Furby, Sony AIBO, UGOBE Pleo, Karotz/Violet Nabaztag, Philips iCat, the iCub anthropomorphic robot research project (Italian Institute of Technology, Italy), the Pepper robot design group (SoftBank Robotics, USA) and others. These approaches in emotional robotics did not make a breakthrough yet: they do not exceed their virtual counterparts in emotional intelligence, and in most cases have limitations compared to virtual emotional characters outlined above.

We previously conducted relevant studies of the multimodal emotional interaction of actors of various nature [27, 28] and developed an emotional Biologically Inspired Cognitive Architecture (eBICA) to describe the mechanisms of the socio-emotional and moral behavior of actors.

Building a cognitive architecture supporting emotional intelligence is an important step in emotion modeling. Here are examples. The MicroPsi model is a cognitive architecture to regulate and control a complex organism. It describes a detailed framework of needs, reward generators and cognitive modulators [29, 30]. The LIDA cognitive architecture is a computational model of human cognition, integrating cognitive psychology and cognitive neuroscience [31, 32]. It's architecture conceptually affords grounded cognition, attention, emotion, action selection, human-like learning, and other higher-level processes.

Summarizing, we can say that the emotional effectiveness of existing embodied agents is insufficient to satisfy modern demands. They often lack the capacity for self-regulated learning and acquisition of emotional values, and their function of social interaction is too simplistic for real-life social contexts. In addition, many of the cognitive models used in existing social agents are based on formal logic coupled with psychological theories that lack the mechanisms of humanlike social and moral reasoning.

In order to build a computational emotion regulation system, here a model of emotional interaction of embodied social agents is proposed, combining concepts borrowed from biology, cognitive psychology, sociology and ethics. This approach will allow us to achieve natural and harmonious human-computer interaction, relying on the monitoring and regulation of negative emotions.

2   The Concept and Implementation Plan

Existing research (summarized above) shows that cognitive architectures of embodied social agents are getting richer and richer. To implement the emotion regulation function, embodied agents must be endowed with rich capabilities of emotion perception and expression. With the development of artificial intelligence, various new technological approaches to emotion perception and expression become available. The embodied agent should have a multimodal emotional perception ability, should be able to comprehensively perceive the user's emotional state, make strictly adequate behavioral responses, and adjust its expressed emotions in order to regulate the user's emotional state. This is the general goal. Specific tasks are described below.

2.1 Cognitive Architecture

The first task is to develop a cognitive architecture of an embodied social agent supporting emotional intelligence. The architecture will include modules supporting perception, behavior control, emotion, and memory systems of various types, including a knowledge base and learning mechanisms necessary to achieve continuous information processing from perception to behavior generation.

Among them, the perception module is used to perceive the user's multimodal input and call the knowledge base to recognize the semantics of user's expression, posture, text content and voice tonality.

The behavior control module is used to generate the appropriate behavior semantics and produce a multimodal response of the embodied agent using facial expression, posture, gestures, speech content and voice tonality as behavioral variables.

The emotion module supports the function of empathy evaluation and emotion generation, which is mainly used to analyze the causes of users' emotions and generate an appropriate emotional response.

The memory module is used to store user information details, which are continuously acquired and updated during interaction, and provide parameters for implementing a personalized emotional interaction.

The knowledge base module supports situational semantic recognition and includes emotional reasoning rules, moral schemas and related to them behavioral rules, as well as a natural language thesaurus.

Situational semantic recognition is used in the perception module; emotional reasoning rules are used for emotion generation; moral schemas and related behavioral rules are used to generate ethical, socially acceptable behavior, and a natural language processing system is used to implement a chatbot capabilities necessary to support a human-computer dialogue in natural language.

The learning module should comprehensively use the existing machine learning algorithms to augment the knowledge base. The reinforcement learning algorithm needs to be used to adjust the emotional expression intensity of the embodied social agent.

2.2 Interaction Model

The second task is to develop an emotional interaction model for embodied social agents. It includes two subtasks.

(a) To develop a perception method for user's emotion. The user's personality type and emotional state should be identified by her or his voice, facial expression, gaze direction, posture, gestures, actions, and physiological readings acquired through the microphone, camera, depth camera, as well as wearable equipment (including various biometrics, from heart rate to EMG or EEG). A deep learning framework should be used to implement a unimodal emotion classifier to identify the emotion types in each modality, respectively.

Based on this, the knowledge base can be used to comprehensively determine the exact type and nature of emotion.

(b) To develop an emotion generation model of embodied social agent. In order to make the embodied social agent capable of producing emotional responses similar to those of a human, an empathy evaluation ability should be implemented in the emotion module, so that the embodied agent would correctly identify the user's emotion and its causes, and therefore would be able to produce an adequate, believable emotional response. When combined with the perception of users' personality, the real origin of users' emotion can be derived from observations using reasoning rules stored in the knowledge base. Based on empathy evaluation, the embodied social agent generates an appropriate emotional expression through the emotion generation algorithm, to show its empathy for users. To achieve this goal, firstly, a context-based reasoning algorithm for emotional expression analysis should be designed. It will be used to select and exhibit the appropriate posture, speech content and tonality, etc., to demonstrate empathy. Secondly, the method based on fuzzy reasoning should be used to calculate the intensity of emotional expression.

2.3 Behavioral Paradigms

The third task is to select behavioral paradigms and for each of them develop a paradigm-specific model of the embodied social agent behavior. In essence, the task is to create an embodied agent capable of autonomous emotion expression and behavior generation in the given paradigm, which should interact with users through many modalities, including facial expression, gaze control, posture, gestures, voice tonality, speech content, and other forms of multimodal interaction described above.

Appealing human-computer interaction tasks and paradigms should be designed to realize human-computer interaction and to monitor and control users' emotions by engaging the user in specific interaction paradigms. Reinforcement learning algorithms should be designed to adjust the difficulty of human-computer interaction to meet the personalized needs of different users. Combined with the information about user identity, social distance, body orientation, emotional state and other factors, methods of behavior semantic generation and behavioral expression of emotion will allow the agent to regulate the user emotionality.

3 Outcomes of Preliminary Studies

During 2020–2022, a number of virtual-environment-based (VE) and virtual-reality-based (VR) applications were developed at the BICA Lab (NRNU MEPhI), including the virtual hotel receptionist (Fig. 1A), the virtual poster presenter (Fig. 1B), the virtual pet (Fig. 1C), and the Virtual Convention Center (VCC, Fig. 1D).

Our VCC, including the virtual poster presenter, was used to run two international conferences (BICA 2020 and BICA 2021) and the All-Russian congress CAICS 2020. Figure 1D shows a plenary session at BICA 2020 hosted by Alexei V. Samsonovich; Artemiy Kotov and John Laird participate as avatars.

Our experimental study showed that in all cases the emotional bot is perceived and understood by participants better, compared to a non-emotional version of the same bot.

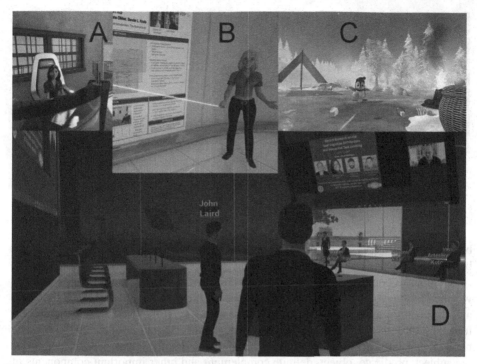

Fig. 1. Screenshots of VR applications developed at BICA Lab in NRNU MEPhI in 2020–2022.

Another VR application of a virtual agent is shown in Fig. 2. The agent receives its emotional input from/about users through ordinary cameras, microphones, and the Kinect system. Interaction between the user and the virtual agent is realized through the interactive virtual scene. In this scene, the perception module of the virtual agent is used to collect and identify the multimodal information about users. Among them, user's facial expression is acquired using the camera, user's posture information is acquired using the Kinect system and the camera, and user's voice information is acquired using the microphone (the speech sound is converted into text using the iFLYTEK's voice package). The facial expression is recognized using OpenCV (a development tool) and Dlib (a deep learning library) based on a set of facial feature points and an SVM classifier. Six emotions are identified: happy, angry, fear, sad, surprise, and disgust.

Posture recognition includes gesture recognition and upper limb motion recognition. Gestures are recognized by the camera. Different semantics of gestures are defined in advance, and the recognition of gestures is based on the tracking of hand movements and using an SVM classifier. The motion of the upper limb is recognized by Kinect. The position of joint points is registered by Kinect, and the motion (such as waving) is judged according to the position of different joint points. The emotion expressed in user's speech (converted to text) is recognized by a neural network trained using a deep learning algorithm. The data set of the Sina microblog is used for the training.

The described above pipeline of multimodal emotional information recognition delivers to the agent behavior module the user's emotional state data. Therefore, the

Fig.2. Screenshots of VR interaction between a user and the virtual agent.

behavior module can generate an adequate behavior, which includes facial animation, body animation and text dialogue, depending on the state of the user.

In order to communicate with users, several common conversation topics, such as weather, birthday and playing ball, were pre-set in the dialogue system. Each topic had a corresponding topic thesaurus and response database. If the user's input contained a topic keyword, then the text was analyzed syntactically. In this case, the LTP (language technology platform) tool of Harbin Institute of Technology was used to determine the subject, predicate, object, definite complement and other important components of the sentence, and the response was generated from the thesaurus. If there was no topic keyword in the user's input, then a chat was generated by the deep neural network. When the user did not give any topic keyword for several turns of the dialogue, the virtual agent guided the user to talk about a specific topic. Virtual scenes were constructed in advance. When a dialogue contained a topic related to the scene, the system switched to the corresponding virtual scene.

4 Discussion

Negative factors such as the aging of population and COVID-19 are having a negative impact on emotions of more and more people. Using artificial intelligence technology to monitor and regulate people's emotions will be of important practical significance. In recent years, artificial intelligence technology was significantly developed in the direction of embodied intelligence. An embodied social agent is a humanoid intelligent entity, which can be a virtual agent (a graphical entity, such as a virtual human) or a humanoid robot. Embodied social agents can simulate human emotions and emotional behaviors and communicate with users like real humans. Embodied emotional agents are expected to become a new technology of emotion regulation. They constitute one of the important directions of the development of service-oriented artificial intelligence.

Existing research on embodied emotional agents is mostly carried out from the perspective of computational psychology based on the traditional appraisal theories [33–38]. As a result, cognitive architectures of virtual agents appear too simplistic, and their emotional expressions may be inadequate.

In contrast, our approach is based on the principles of brain functioning and on the theoretical social psychology. Here we described a concept of a system based on a cognitive architecture for embodied social agents, capable of user's emotion understanding and regulation. The method utilizes the unity of emotional drives and moral constraints. A rich model of emotional intelligence integrated with the empathy mechanism is used, which makes the embodied social agent have rich emotional expressivity and be capable of a friendly human-computer interaction. Embodied social agents created based on this approach can actively perceive users' emotions and their causes. These abilities allow them to establish natural multimodal emotional interaction with users.

Future study that is necessary to implement the proposed concept implies carrying out human-computer interaction experiments with embodied social agents to study how users' emotions can be monitored and regulated through a multimodal human-computer interaction. The study will establish new general theoretical and empirical facts about embodied social agents. The expected impact includes new smart emotion regulation technologies and new feasible means for emotional communication with and via artifacts, that will benefit many millions of people.

Acknowledgments. This work was supported by the Russian Science Foundation Grant #22-11-00213, https://rscf.ru/en/project/22-11-00213/.

References

1. Gross, J.J.: Handbook of Emotion Regulation, 2nd edn. Guilford, New York (2014)
2. Jiang, Y., Li, W., Hossain, M.S., Chen, M., Alelaiwi, A., Al-Hammadi, M.: A snapshot research and implementation of multimodal information fusion for data-driven emotion recognition. Inf. Fusion **53**, 209–221 (2020)
3. Wisessing, P., Zibrek, K., Cunningham, D.W., Dingliana, J., McDonnell, R.: Enlighten me: importance of brightness and shadow for character emotion and appeal. ACM Trans. Graph. **39**(3), 1–19 (2020)
4. Gratch, J., Marsella, S.: A domain-independent framework for modeling emotion. Cogn. Syst. Res. **5**(4), 269–306 (2004)
5. Sonlu, S., Güdükbay, U., Durupinar, F.: A conversational agent framework with multi-modal personality expression. ACM Trans. Graph. **40**(1), 1–16 (2021)
6. Ghafurian, M., Budnarain, N., Hoey, J.: Improving humanness of virtual agents and users' cooperation through emotions. IEEE Trans. Affect. Comput. (2021). https://doi.org/10.1109/TAFCC.2021.3096831
7. Jain, S., Asawa, K.: Modeling of emotion elicitation conditions for a cognitive-emotive architecture. Cogn. Syst. Res. **55**, 60–76 (2019)
8. Pacheco-Lorenzo, M.R., Valladares-Rodríguez, S.M., Anido-Rifón, L.E., Fernández-Iglesias, M.J.: Smart conversational agents for the detection of neuropsychiatric disorders: a systematic review. J. Biomed. Inform. **113**, 103632 (2021). https://doi.org/10.1016/j.jbi.2020.103632
9. Kaywan, P., Ahmed, K., Miao, Y., Ibaida, A., Gu, B.: DEPRA: an early depression detection analysis chatbot. In: Siuly, S., Wang, H., Chen, L., Guo, Y., Xing, C. (eds.) HIS 2021. LNCS, vol. 13079, pp. 193–204. Springer, Cham (2021). https://doi.org/10.1007/978-3-030-90885-0_18
10. Stratou, G., Morency, L.P.: MultiSense-context-aware nonverbal behavior analysis framework: a psychological distress use case. IEEE Trans. Affect. Comput. **8**(2), 190–203 (2017)

11. Abdollahi, H., Mahoor, M., Zandie, R., Sewierski, J., Qualls, S.: Artificial emotional intelligence in socially assistive robots for older adults: a pilot study. IEEE Trans. Affect. Comput. (2022).https://doi.org/10.1109/TAFFC.2022.3143803

12. Lara-Alvarez, C., Miter-Hernandez, H., Flores. J.J., Perez-Espinosa, H.: Induction of emotional states in educational video games through a fuzzy control system. IEEE Trans. Affect. Comput. 12(1), 66–77 (2021)

13. Hong, A., et al.: A multimodal emotional human-robot interaction architecture for social robots engaged in bidirectional communication. IEEE Trans. Cybern. **51**(12), 5954–5968 (2021)

14. Marsella, S.C., Gratch, J.: EMA: a process model of appraisal dynamics. Cogn. Syst. Res. **10**(1), 70–90 (2009)

15. Breazeal, C. Designing Social Robots. MIT Press (2002)

16. Breazeal, C.: Emotion and sociable humanoid robots. Int. J. Hum. Comput. Stud. **59**(1–2), 119–155 (2003)

17. Cafaro, A., Ravenet, B., Pelachaud, C.: Exploiting evolutionary algorithms to model nonverbal reactions to conversational interruptions in user-agent interactions. IEEE Trans. Affect. Comput. **13**(1), 485–495 (2022)

18. McRorie, M., Sneddon, I., McKeown, G., Bevacqua, E., De Sevin, E., Pelachaud, C.: Evaluation of four designed virtual agent personalities. IEEE Trans. Affect. Comput. **3**(3), 311–322 (2012)

19. Nery, B., Ventura, R.: A dynamical systems approach to online event segmentation in cognitive robotics. J. Behav. Robot. **2**(1), 18–24 (2011)

20. Ventura, R.: Emotions and empathy: a bridge between nature and society? Int. J. Mach. Conscious. **2**(2), 343–361 (2010)

21. Sellers, M.: Toward a comprehensive theory of emotion for biological and artificial agents. Biologically Inspired Cogn. Architectures **4**, 3–26 (2013)

22. Chella, A.: Some Challenges for Emotional Agents. Int. J. Synth. Emotions **2**(2), 70–72 (2011)

23. Chella, A., Lebiere, C., Noelle, D.C., Samsonovich, A.V.: On a roadmap to biologically inspired cognitive agents. Front. Artif. Intell. Appl. **233**, 453–460 (2011)

24. Tulsulkar, G., Mishra, N., Thalmann, N.M., Lim, H.E., Lee, M.P., Cheng, S.K.: Can a humanoid social robot stimulate the interactivity of cognitively impaired elderly? a thorough study based on computer vision methods. Vis. Comput. **37**(12), 3019–3038 (2021)

25. Marsella, S., Gratch, J., Petta, P.: Computational models of emotion. In: Scherer, K.R., Bänziger, T., Roesch, E. (Eds.) A Blueprint for Affective Computing: A sourcebook and manual. Oxford: Oxford University Press (2010)

26. Shum, H.-Y., Xiao-dong, H.E., Di, L.I.: From Eliza to xiaoice: challenges and opportunities with social chatbots. Front. Inf. Technol. Electr. Eng. **19**(1), 10–26 (2018)

27. Zhang, K.L., Liu, T.T., Liu, Z., Zhuang, Y., Chai, Y.J.: Multimodal human-computer interactive technology for emotion regulation. J. Image Graph. **25**(11), 2451–2464 (2020)

28. Samsonovich, A.V.: Socially emotional brain-inspired cognitive architecture framework for artificial intelligence. Cogn. Syst. Res. **60**, 57–76 (2020)

29. Bach, J. Principles of Synthetic Intelligence PSI: An Architecture of Motivated Cognition. Oxford University Press (2009)

30. Bach, J., Coutinho, M., Lichtinger, L.: Extending MicroPsi's model of motivation and emotion for conversational agents. In: Hammer, P., Agrawal, P., Goertzel, B., Iklé, M. (eds.) AGI 2019. LNCS (LNAI), vol. 11654, pp. 32–43. Springer, Cham (2019). https://doi.org/10.1007/978-3-030-27005-6_4

31. Franklin, S., Madl, T., D'Mello, S., Snaider, J.: LIDA: a systems-level architecture for cognition, emotion, and learning. IEEE Trans. Auton. Ment. Dev. **6**(1), 19–41 (2014)

32. Kugele, S., Franklin, S.: Learning in LIDA. Cogn. Syst. Res. **66**, 176–200 (2021)

33. Ortony, A., Clore, G., Collins, A.: The Cognitive Structure of Emotions. Cambridge University Press, Cambridge (1988)
34. Smith, C.A., Lazarus, R.S.: Emotion and adaptation. In: Pervin, L.A. (ed.) Handbook of personality: Theory and research, pp. 609–637. Guilford, New York (1990)
35. Scherer, K.R.: Appraisal theory. In: Dalgleish, T., Power, M. (eds.) Handbook of cognition and emotion, pp. 637–663. Wiley, London (1999)
36. Scherer, K.R.: Appraisal considered as a process of multilevel sequential checking 2001. In K.R. Scherer, A. Shorr, T. Johnstone (Eds.), Appraisal processes in emotion: Theory, methods, research. Canary, NC: Oxford University Press (2001)
37. Sloman, A., Chrisley, L.: More things than are dreamt of in your biology: Information-processing in biologically inspired robots. Cogn. Syst. Res. 6(2), 145–174 (2005)
38. Hudlicka, E.: Guidelines for designing computational models of emotions. Int. J. Synth. Emotions 2(1), 26–79 (2011)

QKSA: Quantum Knowledge Seeking Agent

Aritra Sarkar[1,2]($\boxtimes$) (iD), Zaid Al-Ars[1] (iD), and Koen Bertels[2] (iD)

[1] Department of Quantum and Computer Engineering, Faculty of Electrical
Engineering, Mathematics and Computer Science, Delft University of Technology,
Delft, The Netherlands
`{a.sarkar-3,z.al-ars}@tudelft.nl`
[2] QBee.eu, Leuven, Belgium
`{aritra.sarkar,koen.bertels}@qbee.eu`

Abstract. In this research, we extend the universal reinforcement learning agent models of artificial general intelligence to quantum environments. The utility function of a classical exploratory stochastic Knowledge Seeking Agent, KL-KSA, is generalized to distance measures from quantum information theory on density matrices. Quantum process tomography (QPT) algorithms form a tractable subset of programs for modeling environmental dynamics. The optimal QPT policy is selected based on a mutable cost function based on algorithmic complexity as well as computational resource complexity. The entire agent design is encapsulated in a self-replicating quine which mutates the cost function based on the predictive value of the optimal policy choosing scheme. Thus, multiple agents with pareto-optimal QPT policies evolve using genetic programming, mimicking the development of physical theories each with different resource trade-offs. This formal framework, termed Quantum Knowledge Seeking Agent (QKSA), is a resource-bounded participatory observer modification to the recently proposed algorithmic information-based reconstruction of quantum mechanics. A proof-of-concept is implemented and available as open-sourced software.

Keywords: Algorithmic information theory · Quantum computing · Reinforcement learning · Mutating quine

1 Introduction

The overwhelming success of deep learning over the last decade is encouraging the revival of research on artificial general intelligence (AGI) from various directions [7,9]. The most mathematically rigorous among these is universal artificial intelligence (UAI) [11]. The agent-environment paradigm of model-based reinforcement learning (RL), is best suited to mimic the interactive learning behavior of biological intelligence. UAI-based RL agents are concisely referred to as universal reinforcement learning (URL) agents. This research examines policies of modeling an unknown environment as the general task assigned to a URL agent.

B. Goertzel et al. (Eds.): AGI 2022, LNAI 13539, pp. 384–393, 2023.
https://doi.org/10.1007/978-3-031-19907-3_37

URL agents have been instrumental in proving asymptotic optimal behavior [20,21] in partially observable environments by merging theoretical concepts in universal automata, algorithmic information theory (AIT) [24] and decision theory. However, the dependence on AIT makes these agents generally uncomputable. While resource-bounded variants have been proposed, these models still remain intractable for real-world applications. Moreover, these resource bounds introduce arbitrary hyper-parameters. To address this issue, we utilize the proposal [37] of embedding RL agents within an evolutionary framework (Evo-RL) to guide the meta-learning for a specific application scenario. In this work, we propose the idea of a resource-bounded evolutionary URL (Evo-URL) for the first time. The framework implements the resource cost function as a genetic program encapsulated by a mutating quine. This work is prompted by the suggestion of UAI systems to eventually play the role of autonomous scientists by recursive self-improvement [35].

The properties of the environment is as crucial for AGI as that of the learning strategy. In its most general form, physical systems should include classical, quantum, and relativistic scenarios. This work addresses the first two cases by defining the environment as an unknown quantum process. The proposed agent uses quantum process tomography (QPT) strategies as a tractable predefined subset of programs for actively learning the environmental model. Limiting the evaluation to this subset of programs alleviates the exponential scaling of the space of programs, which limits UAI's applicability beyond toy models.

The proposed AGI framework, called *Quantum Knowledge Seeking Agent (QKSA)*, models classical and quantum dynamics by merging ideas from AIT, quantum information, constructor theory, and genetic programming. Following the artificial life (or, animat) path to intelligence, a population of classical agents undergoes open-ended evolution (OEE) to explore pareto-optimal ways of modeling the perceptions from a quantum environment. Similar to how AIXI-tl [12] is a resource-bounded active version of Solomonoff universal induction [39], QKSA is a resource-bounded participatory observer [13,44] framework to the recently proposed [26] algorithmic information-based reconstruction of quantum mechanics. QKSA can be applied for simulating and studying aspects of quantum information theory like control automation, multiple observers, course-graining, distance measures, resource complexity trade-offs, etc.

The rest of the article is organized as follows. Section 2 presents the four features of the QKSA model that distinguish it from other similar concepts and models. In Sect. 3 we present the formalization of QKSA's policy. Section 4 concludes the article with suggestive applications.

2   Framework Features

In this section, we present the four distinguishing features of the QKSA framework, (i) representations of general quantum environments, (ii) process tomography algorithms for modeling, (iii) computational resource-bounded algorithmic cost, and (iv) mutating meta-learning hyper-parameter embedded in a quine.

2.1   Representations of General Quantum Environments

The class of environments an agent can model define the bound of its applicability. Solomonoff's theory of universal inductive inference [39] forms the theoretical basis of UAI, and automated scientific modeling in general. In it, the environment is assumed to be computable by a universal Turing machine [42]. The hypothesis size (i.e., the Kolmogorov/algorithmic complexity [17]) is used to proportionally weigh (i.e., the Solomonoff/algorithmic probability) the environmental models for future predictions. The invariance theorem allows any universal automata/language to be used for estimating the hypothesis size, up to a constant overhead.

The active generalization of Solomonoff's induction using Bellman's optimality equation form the basis of URL agents. The agent and the environment interact in turns. At every time step, the agent supplies the environment with an action. The environment then performs some computation and returns a percept to the agent, and the procedure repeats. The environment is modeled as a partially observable Markov decision process. The canonical URL model is the AIXI model [11].

Knowledge Seeking Agents [28] replaces the extrinsic reward function in AIXI with a utility function defined as information gain of the model. Thus, this collapses the exploration-exploitation trade-off to simply exploration, allowing agents to explore the environment in a principled approach. The goal of these agents is to entirely explore their world optimally, form a model, and get a reward for reducing the entropy (uncertainty) in its model from the two components: uncertainty in the agent's beliefs and environmental noise. A particularly interesting case is the KL-KSA [29], which is robust to stochastic noise as the utility function is given as the Kullback-Leibler divergence.

While KL-KSA generalizes over arbitrary countable classes and priors, it cannot intrinsically interpret quantum information. This is because quantum information [27] is a generalization of classical probability theory to the complex domain. It allows richer representations and manipulations of information based on superposition, unitary evolution, interference, entanglement, and projective measurement. QKSA generalizes the probability distribution of KL-KSA to density matrices and the KL divergence to various distance measures on quantum processes.

A brief necessary background of these representations are presented here. Statistical ensembles of N pure quantum states $|\psi\rangle$ are described as a density matrix $\rho = \sum_{k=1}^{N} p_k |\psi\rangle\langle\psi|$, where the probabilities satisfy $0 < p_k \leq 1$ and $\sum_{k=1}^{N} p_k = 1$. A projective measurement of an observable M_m is given by the expectation value $Pr(m) = Tr(M_m\rho)$. Statistics of observable probabilities from quantum measurements can only estimate the density matrix instead of the state, thus fitting the QKSA use case. The unitary U evolution of closed quantum systems is denoted for pure states as, $|\psi'\rangle = U|\psi\rangle$ and for mixed states as $\rho' = U\rho U^\dagger$. More generally, a quantum process Φ that transforms a density matrix need not always be unitary. Given classical processes are often irreversible and include measurements, a quantum generalization includes unitary transforms (symmetry transformations of isolated systems), probabilistic logic, measurements and transient interactions with an environment. Thus, quantum processes formalize the time evolution of open quantum systems as linear quantum dynamical maps from the set of density matrices to itself. For a quantum system with an input state ρ_{in} of dimension $n \times n$ and an output state $\rho_{out} = \Phi(\rho_{in})$ of dimension $m \times m$, Φ is a linear superoperator mapping between the space of Hermitian matrices $\Phi : \mathcal{M}_{n \times n} \to \mathcal{M}_{m \times m}$. There are other equivalent representations of quantum processes like Choi matrix ρ_{Choi}, Kraus operators, Stinespring, Pauli basis Chi matrix χ, Lindbladian, etc. For instance, the Choi matrix ρ_{Choi} is the density matrix obtained after putting half of the maximally entangled state $|\Omega\rangle$ through the channel Φ, while doing nothing on the other half, i.e. if $\Lambda = \sum_{i,j} \frac{1}{2^n} |i\rangle\langle j| \otimes \Phi(|i\rangle\langle j|)$, the $\rho_{Choi} = \Lambda(|\Omega\rangle\langle\Omega|)$ The evolution of a density matrix with respect to the Choi-matrix is given by, $\rho_{out} = \Phi(\rho_{in}) = \mathrm{Tr}_1((\rho_{in}^T \otimes \mathrm{I})\rho_{choi}))$, where Tr_1 is the partial trace over subsystem 1. As a result of the Choi-Jamiolkowski isomorphism, the Choi matrix ρ_{Choi} characterizes the process Φ completely. This isomorphism forms the basis of the channel-state duality in quantum information.

Like classical probability distribution, there are many measures of quantum distances, each with its own application advantage. The QKSA framework allows the user to select a distance metric as part of the experimental setup. The current implementation provides the following distance metrics, Hamming distance, KL divergence, trace distance, Hilbert-Schmidt norm, and Bures distance (fidelity). Users can also define a custom distance measure. A future extension would provide diamond distance, Hellinger distance, quantum Kolmogorov complexity, quantum relative entropy, RÃl'nyi divergence, Bhattacharyya distance, and quantum complexity action [10].

2.2 Process Tomography Algorithms for Modeling

In canonical UAI formalism, the programs are drawn randomly from a prefix code for a universal automata. However, the space of programs grows exponentially, limiting its applicability beyond simple grid-world exploration and games. We restrict this space to a constant number of predefined algorithms provided to the framework. This pragmatic design feature allows us to implement interpretable and tractable URLs.

Characterization of quantum dynamical systems is a fundamental problem in quantum information science. The procedures that achieve this goal are called quantum process tomography. Some examples of these well-developed techniques are: standard QPT [6], entanglement-assisted QPT, direct characterization of quantum dynamics, compressed-sensing QPT, permutation-invariant tomography, self-guided QPT and shadow QPT [23]. Each QPT technique has a different experimental setup and computational resource requirements. These QPT algorithms form the space of programs that QKSA evaluates as candidates for modeling the environment. Intuitively, a QPT algorithm will better predict a quantum environment than a random program. Thus, it allows us to apply the tools of AIT in a practical setting where available expert knowledge can be embedded within the agent. Given computational resource limitations, QKSA is designed to automatically discover the optimal strategy in the available pool of QPT algorithms.

Recent publications study learning in a quantum environment, for e.g., process learning with restricted Boltzmann machines [41], RL based optimizer for variational algorithms [31,43], automated design of experimental quantum optics [19], and, projective simulation (PS) [4,8]. Despite the similarities with QKSA (especially of PS), these approaches are not based on URL. Also unlike [5,33], we do not assume the quantum computational capability of the agent for estimating the AIT metric, in line with the conventional qualia of human intelligence. QKSA is an RL framework to study quantum information and computation via the lens of AIT.

2.3 Computational Resource-Bounded Algorithmic Cost

The algorithmic probability of a candidate model/program is used as a weight for choosing an action and thereby the reward in UAI. However, this also makes such models impractical due to the uncomputability of algorithmic information metrics like algorithmic probability and algorithmic complexity. Being asymptotically computable, URL is thus not a pragmatic algorithmic solution to general RL, and must be simplified in any implementation. In principle, there are an infinite number of programs that can be candidate models of the environment. Also, while evaluating, the programs can enter infinite loops. To circumvent these two issues, modifications are proposed on the agents, like AIXI-tl [12], MC-AIXI$_{(FAC-CTW)}$ and UCAI [14]. These bound the program length and run-time per step to explore a subspace of promising hypotheses that models the interactive behavior registered till the current time step. There arise three issues with this approach:

1. The bounds introduce heuristic hyper-parameters that depend on the available computational resources. Thus, selecting an appropriate value to apply the model for a given use case becomes difficult.
2. The bounds sharply cut off models beyond the specification while keeping the weight for the models within the specification unaffected. So a model that performs well but lies beyond the defined bound may be unreachable.
3. It is possible to trade off these resource bounds with other computational resources, like additional memory.

Using the QKSA platform, it is possible to investigate these issues. In the framework we propose five computational resources, together we call the *LEAST* metric, as an acronym for (program) length, (compute) energy, approximation, (work memory) space and (run) time. Similar algorithmic observables have been suggested in [1]. We provide estimation techniques of the LEAST metric in our implementation, based on state-of-the-art algorithmic information research and general practices in computer engineering. The estimation technique, however can easily be redefined by the user. The estimated metric is used in a two-fold way. Firstly, it is used to qualify the hypothesis for consideration based on upper bounds for each of the five computational resources individually. This is dictated by the available computational resource of the substrate the implementation is executed on, and is similar to the resource-bounded UAI models [12]. These bounds can be included in the list of evolving hyper-parameters to allow QKSA to mutate and adjust autonomously to the available computational resource. After that, the metrics for valid hypotheses are fed to a cost function (a genetic program) that outputs a single positive real value which is used as the weight for the hypothesis (instead of only the length, as in algorithmic probability). We call this the *least action* as a parameterization to optimize the Lagrangian dynamics of computation.

2.4 Mutating Meta-learning Hyper-parameter Embedded in a Quine

There is no unifying cost function that can serve as a metric to trade-off bounds on resources (like space, time, approximation), and possibly cannot exist [13, 30]. In fact, this depends closely on the policy of the agent. For example, a physicist might use simpler Newtonian mechanics instead of complex relativistic mechanics for modeling where the approximations are acceptable. Thus, instead of a single metric, a pareto-optimal frontier on the LEAST metrics maps to models and algorithms that can be used to predict the environment dynamics.

Various research has explored this frontier, considering a few of the LEAST metrics. Some examples are, Levin complexity [22], Bennett's logical depth [2] and pebbling game [3], Schmidhuber's speed prior [36], Wolpert's statistical thermodynamics of Turing machines [16], Zenil's block decomposition method [38], and look-up tables. These resource-bounded metrics are not immune to the no-free-lunch theorems [45] and adversarial cases of environments.

QKSA holistically (yet, subjectively) explores these trade-offs by dynamically adapting the cost function to the environment. The five estimates of the LEAST metrics are given as input to a cost function. We employ evolutionary computation, a population-based trial and error problem solving technique for meta-heuristic or stochastic optimization. More specifically, we use genetic programming (GP) [18]. The cost function itself is a gene represented as a program tree with the leaf nodes as the metrics or constants, and the internal nodes are from a set of essential arithmetic functions. Once QKSA learns an environment optimally or completely fails to do so (i.e. when the learning rate stabilizes), the QKSA self-replicates. The child QKSA has the same source code as the parent, except for a mutation on the cost function that modifies the weights and structure embedded via the cost function gene. Thus the open-ended evolution of the pareto-optimal manifold converges on QPT algorithms which fits well in the available computational resource. The parent QKSA perishes if the prediction of the model fails persistently (i.e., when the rate stabilizes as the strategy fails to learn) or continues to correctly predict environmental interaction and can be inspected to obtain the cost function. Thus, a single QKSA may not have an objective optimal resource trade-off for a static environment, but the population is expected to converge to an optimal policy even for a dynamic environment (provided the dynamics are slower than the learning rate).

The entire agent framework described so far is embedded within a quine. Quines are self-replicating programs that are the software embodiment of constructors, an idea foundational to artificial life [40] and physical theories alike [25]. The Kleene recursion theorem [15] allows any program to be modified such that it (a) replicates its source code, (b) executes an orthogonal payload that serves the same purpose as the original non-quine version. This embellishment on the evolutionary cost function qualifies QKSA as a recursive self-improving system.

3   QKSA Formalism

In this section, we start from the formalism of AIXI and elucidate the changes described in the previous section. For brevity, we omit the mathematical reasoning behind the AIXI, which can be found in [11]. The canonical expectimax equation in UAI is used by the agent to rationalize the choice of a particular action at the current time step. For AIXI [11], it takes the form:

$$a_t = \arg \lim_{m \to \infty} \max_{a_t \in \mathcal{A}} \sum_{e_t \in \mathcal{E}} \ldots \max_{a_m \in \mathcal{A}} \sum_{e_m \in \mathcal{E}} \sum_{k=t}^{m} \gamma_k r_k \sum_{p:U(p;a_{<k})=e_{<k}} 2^{-l(p)}$$

where, a_t is the action at time step t from the action space $\mathcal{A}$, e_k is a perception from the percept space $\mathcal{E}$ defined over the time step span from t to m, γ is a reward discount function, U is an universal automata, p is a program that forms the model/hypothesis for the environment, r_k is the reward signal from the environment, and $l(p)$ is the length of the program p. In the case of KL-KSA [29], the reward for AIXI is generalized to the utility given by, $u_k = u(e_k|ae_{<k}a_k) = Ent(w_\nu|ae_{<k+1}) - Ent(w_\nu|ae_{<k}a_k)$, where $Ent()$ refers to the entropy function and w_ν refers to the agent's credence in the percept distribution ν representing the environment.

The first change is to restrict the search space of programs p to quantum process tomography algorithms, denoted as p_{qpt}. It is important that the QPT algorithm reconstructs and outputs a process representation ρ_k instead of the prediction of the subsequent perception. $\lambda^{e'_k} \in \{0, 1\}$ is the probability of the quantum state collapsing to the prediction e'_k made at time step $t - 1$. This modification is imperative due to the stochastic nature of individual quantum measurements and the calculation of the utility.

The second change is to replace the length estimate of the $2^{-l(p)}$ factor from the algorithmic probability with the estimate of the evolving cost function c_{est}. The cost function is denoted by c_{least}, i.e. $c_{est} = c_{least}(p_{qpt})$. Thus, the learning part of the equation is:

$$a_t^{QKSA} = \arg \lim_{m \to \infty} \max_{a_t \in \mathcal{A}} \sum_{e'_t \in \mathcal{E}} \lambda^{e'_t} \ldots \max_{a_m \in \mathcal{A}} \sum_{e'_m \in \mathcal{E}} \lambda^{e'_m} \sum_{k=t}^{m} \gamma_k u'_k \sum_{\substack{p_{qpt}:U(p_{qpt};h_k)=\rho_k \\ p_{qpt}:U(p_{qpt};\rho_k;a_k;e'_k)=\lambda^{e'_k}}} 2^{-c_{least}(p_{qpt})}$$

The third change is to define the utility function as a quantum distance measure on the space of quantum processes ρ (defined as the density matrix in the Choi process matrix representation). A higher predicted utility indicates that the current estimate of the quantum process will be updated more significantly based on the perception, thus, a potential knowledge gain for choosing that action.

$$u'_t = \Delta(\rho'_{t+1}, \rho_t) = \Delta(U(p_{qpt}; h_t; a_t; e'_t), U(p_{qpt}; h_t))$$

A detailed description of the QKSA framework and policy is provided in [32]. A full proof-of-concept of the discussed QKSA framework is implemented on Python and Qiskit. It is available as open-source software at the following link: https://github.com/Advanced-Research-Centre/QKSA.

4 Conclusion

In this article, we extended the formalism of UAI to quantum environments by generalizing the KL-KSA to a quantum knowledge seeking agent (QKSA). The environment within the reinforcement learning setup is defined by an unknown quantum circuit that the agent attempts to model using quantum process tomography. A quantum environment prevents the exact prediction of perceptions (as used by AIXI), and a single probability distribution of perception based on the set of actions (as used by KL-KSA). The subjective model is conditioned on the chosen action and is thus represented by the more general density matrix formalism. Any quantum process can be represented as a Choi density matrix, which forms a model of the environmental dynamics. To circumvent the uncomputability of UAI models, we propose to evaluate the algorithmic cost within a set of user-provided programs. This consideration makes the framework more tractable and interpretable. Also, the resource restrictions used in computable UAI models are arbitrary. In our model, these resource bounds are interdependent hyper-parameters whose value and trade-off relations are optimized using genetic programming. Thus, this allows open-ended evolution of the agents for dynamic environments. Each agent can self-replicate as a quine and thus is a recursive self-improving intelligence model.

As part of ongoing research [34], we are applying the QKSA framework as described in this article to study course-graining in multi-observer scenarios and quantum uncomplexity resources. It also has near term applicability in optimizing NISQ era hybrid variational quantum algorithms.

References

1. Baez, J., Stay, M.: Algorithmic thermodynamics. Math. Struct. Comput. Sci. **22**(5), 771–787 (2012)
2. Bennett, C.H.: Logical depth and physical complexity. Citeseer (1988)
3. Bennett, C.H.: Time/space trade-offs for reversible computation. SIAM J. Comput. **18**(4), 766–776 (1989)

4. Briegel, H.J., De las Cuevas, G.: Projective simulation for artificial intelligence. Sci. Rep. **2**(1), 1–16 (2012)
5. Catt, E., Hutter, M.: A gentle introduction to quantum computing algorithms with applications to universal prediction. arXiv preprint arXiv:2005.03137 (2020)
6. Chuang, I.L., Nielsen, M.A.: Prescription for experimental determination of the dynamics of a quantum black box. J. Mod. Opt. **44**(11–12), 2455–2467 (1997)
7. Domingos, P.: The master algorithm: How the quest for the ultimate learning machine will remake our world. In: Basic Books (2015)
8. Dunjko, V., Taylor, J.M., Briegel, H.J.: Advances in quantum reinforcement learning. In: 2017 IEEE International Conference on Systems, Man, and Cybernetics (SMC), pp. 282–287 (2017)
9. Goertzel, B.: Artificial general intelligence: concept, state of the art, and future prospects. J. Artif. Gen. Intell. **5**(1), 1 (2014)
10. Halpern, N.Y., Kothakonda, N.B., Haferkamp, J., Munson, A., Eisert, J., Faist, P.: Resource theory of quantum uncomplexity. arXiv preprint arXiv:2110.11371 (2021)
11. Hutter, M.: Universal Artificial Intellegence. TTCSAES, Springer, Heidelberg (2005). https://doi.org/10.1007/b138233
12. Hutter, M.: Universal algorithmic intelligence: a mathematical top → down approach. In: Artificial General Intelligence, pp. 227–290. Springer (2007). https://doi.org/10.1007/978-3-540-68677-4_8
13. Hutter, M.: A complete theory of everything (will be subjective). Algorithms **3**(4), 329–350 (2010)
14. Katayama, S.: Computable variants of aixi which are more powerful than aixitl. J. Artif. Gen. Intell. **10**(1), 1–23 (2019)
15. Kleene, S.C.: Introduction to metamathematics. North-Holland Publishing Co. (1952)
16. Kolchinsky, A., Wolpert, D.H.: Thermodynamic costs of turing machines. Phys. Rev. Res. **2**(3), 033312 (2020)
17. Kolmogorov, A.N.: Three approaches to the quantitative definition of information. Int. J. Comput. Math. **2**(1–4), 157–168 (1968)
18. Koza, J.R., Koza, J.R.: Genetic programming: on the programming of computers by means of natural selection, vol. 1. MIT press (1992)
19. Krenn, M., Malik, M., Fickler, R., Lapkiewicz, R., Zeilinger, A.: Automated search for new quantum experiments. Phys. Rev. Lett. **116**(9), 090405 (2016)
20. Leike, J., Hutter, M.: Bad universal priors and notions of optimality. In: Conference on Learning Theory, pp. 1244–1259. PMLR (2015)
21. Leike, J., Lattimore, T., Orseau, L., Hutter, M.: Thompson sampling is asymptotically optimal in general environments. arXiv preprint arXiv:1602.07905 (2016)
22. Levin, L.A.: Universal sequential search problems. Probl. Peredachi Informatsii **9**(3), 115–116 (1973)
23. Levy, R., Luo, D., Clark, B.K.: Classical shadows for quantum process tomography on near-term quantum computers. arXiv preprint arXiv:2110.02965 (2021)
24. Li, M., Vitányi, P.: An Introduction to Kolmogorov Complexity and Its Applications. TCS, Springer, New York (2008). https://doi.org/10.1007/978-0-387-49820-1
25. Marletto, C.: Constructor theory of life. J. R. Soc. Interface **12**(104), 20141226 (2015)
26. Mueller, M.P.: Law without law: from observer states to physics via algorithmic information theory. Quantum **4**, 301 (2020)
27. Nielsen, M.A., Chuang, I.: Quantum computation and quantum information (2002)

28. Orseau, L.: Universal knowledge-seeking agents. Theor. Comput. Sci. **519**, 127–139 (2014)
29. Orseau, L., Lattimore, T., Hutter, M.: Universal knowledge-seeking agents for stochastic environments. In: Jain, S., Munos, R., Stephan, F., Zeugmann, T. (eds.) ALT 2013. LNCS (LNAI), vol. 8139, pp. 158–172. Springer, Heidelberg (2013). https://doi.org/10.1007/978-3-642-40935-6_12
30. Poland, K., Beer, K., Osborne, T.J.: No free lunch for quantum machine learning. arXiv preprint arXiv:2003.14103 (2020)
31. Rivera-Dean, J., Huembeli, P., Acín, A., Bowles, J.: Avoiding local minima in variational quantum algorithms with neural networks. arXiv preprint arXiv:2104.02955 (2021)
32. Sarkar, A.: Applications of Quantum Computation and Algorithmic Information: for Causal Modeling in Genomics and Reinforcement Learning. Ph. D. thesis, Delft University of Technology (2022)
33. Sarkar, A., Al-Ars, Z., Bertels, K.: Estimating algorithmic information using quantum computing for genomics applications. Appl. Sci. **11**(6), 2696 (2021)
34. Sarkar, A., Al-Ars, Z., Gandhi, H., Bertels, K.: Qksa: quantum knowledge seeking agent-resource-optimized reinforcement learning using quantum process tomography. arXiv preprint arXiv:2112.03643 (2021)
35. Schmidhuber, J.: On learning how to learn learning strategies. Fakultät für Informatik, Technische Universität München, Technical report (1995)
36. Schmidhuber, J.: The speed prior: a new simplicity measure yielding near-optimal computable predictions. In: Kivinen, J., Sloan, R.H. (eds.) COLT 2002. LNCS (LNAI), vol. 2375, pp. 216–228. Springer, Heidelberg (2002). https://doi.org/10.1007/3-540-45435-7_15
37. Silver, D., Singh, S., Precup, D., Sutton, R.S.: Reward is enough. Artif. Intell. **299**, 103535 (2021)
38. Soler-Toscano, F., Zenil, H., Delahaye, J.P., Gauvrit, N.: Calculating kolmogorov complexity from the output frequency distributions of small turing machines. PloS One **9**(5) (2014)
39. Solomonoff, R.J.: A formal theory of inductive inference. Part i. Inf. Control **7**(1), 1–22 (1964)
40. Strannegård, C., Svangård, N., Lindström, D., Bach, J., Steunebrink, B.: The animat path to artificial general intelligence. In: Proceedings of IJCAI-17 Workshop on Architectures for Generality & Autonomy (2017)
41. Torlai, G., Mazzola, G., Carrasquilla, J., Troyer, M., Melko, R., Carleo, G.: Neural-network quantum state tomography. Nat. Phys. **14**(5), 447–450 (2018). https://doi.org/10.1038/s41567-018-0048-5
42. Turing, A.M., et al.: On computable numbers, with an application to the entscheidungsproblem. J. Math. **58**(345–363), 5 (1936)
43. Wauters, M.M., Panizon, E., Mbeng, G.B., Santoro, G.E.: Reinforcement-learning-assisted quantum optimization. Phys. Rev. Res. **2**(3), 033446 (2020)
44. Wheeler, J.A.: At home in the universe. American Institute of Physics (1996)
45. Wolpert, D.H.: The lack of a priori distinctions between learning algorithms. Neural Comput. **8**(7), 1341–1390 (1996)

Elements of Active Continuous Learning and Uncertainty Self-awareness: A Narrow Implementation for Face and Facial Expression Recognition

Stanislav Selitskiy[✉][ID]

School of Computer Science and Technology, University of Bedfordshire,
Park Square LU1 3JU, Luton, UK
stanislav.selitskiy@study.beds.ac.uk

Abstract. Reflection on one's thought process and making corrections to it if there exists dissatisfaction in its performance is, perhaps, one of the essential traits of intelligence. However, such high-level abstract concepts mandatory for Artificial General Intelligence can be modelled even at the low level of narrow Machine Learning algorithms. Here, we present the self-awareness mechanism emulation in the form of a supervising artificial neural network (ANN) observing patterns in activations of another underlying ANN in a search for indications of the high uncertainty of the underlying ANN and, therefore, the trustworthiness of its predictions. The underlying ANN is a convolutional neural network (CNN) ensemble employed for face recognition and facial expression tasks. The self-awareness ANN has a memory region where its past performance information is stored, and its learnable parameters are adjusted during the training to optimize the performance. The trustworthiness verdict triggers the active learning mode, giving elements of agency to the machine learning algorithm that asks for human help in high uncertainty and confusion conditions.

Keywords: Meta-learning · Statistical loss function ·
Trustworthiness · Uncertainty estimation · Active learning ·
Continuous learning

1 Introduction

Artificial Intelligence (AI) is quite a vague terminology artefact that has been overused many times, sometimes even for describing narrow software implementations of simple mathematical concepts such as multi-dimensional regression. It is understandable that to separate the high-level AI from the narrow level, such abbreviation as AGI (Artificial General Intelligence) was introduced. Sometimes even AGI gets associated with the "hype-style" conversation, therefore such alternatives as "human-level AI" [5] or "DL System 2" [4], and others can be used. The founders of AI research, such as A. Turing and J. McCarthy, who coined

© The Author(s), under exclusive license to Springer Nature Switzerland AG 2023
B. Goertzel et al. (Eds.): AGI 2022, LNAI 13539, pp. 394–403, 2023.
https://doi.org/10.1007/978-3-031-19907-3_38

the very term AI, were sceptical about the worthiness of the attempts to answer what AI is. Instead, they suggested answering the question of how well AI can emulate or implement human-type intelligence [9,17]. N. Chomsky, in numerous lectures and publications (f.e. [2]), even more categorically elaborated that AI is a human linguistic concept rather than an independent phenomenon.

Suppose we accept discussing AI in the context of human-likeliness. There still should be room for learning from simple and narrow machine learning (ML) algorithms if they could be used as "building blocks" and working approxima-tions of human-like intelligence. In this work, we want to concentrate on two aspects of human-likeliness intelligence functionality: continuous lifetime learn-ing and awareness of uncertainty.

Lifetime Learning (LTL) was introduced in the mid-'90s in the context of the robot learning process [15]. The LTL learner could face various tasks during its lifetime, and each new learning task may benefit from the saved successful models and examples of data they were trained and applied to [14].

From the human perspective, a high volume of training data forced on the learner is not a benefit. Rather abundance of potential data, from which the learner chooses a few characteristic examples and asks for the teacher's expert advice, is more desirable. A similar Active Learning (AL) approach expects an ML algorithm to ask an "Oracle" advice on selected un-labelled data [8], in par-ticular when high uncertainty about a particular piece of data is occurred [6].

The idea of learning the ML processes was also introduced in the '90s by the same author as LTL [16], and recently gained traction in various flavours of meta-learning [18]. One of the directions of learning about learning is learning uncertainty of the learner [7].

To bring general considerations into a practical, although narrow perspective, we concentrate on making the meta-learning supervisor ANN model. It learns patterns of the functionality of the underlying CNN models that are associated with the failed predictions for Face Recognition (FR) [13] and Facial Expression Recognition (FER) tasks [12], self-adjusting on the previous experience during training, as well as, test times.

The reason to use FR and FER tasks is based not only on the fact that these are pretty human-centric ones but also, although State of the art (SOTA) CNN models had already passed the milestone of the human-level accuracy of face recognition several years ago in the ideal laboratory conditions. In the case of the Out of (training) Data Distribution (OOD) [10], for example, makeup and occlusions, accuracy significantly drops. Even worse for FER algorithms and modes, which perform far worse than FR. The reason may be that the idea that the whole spectre of emotion expressions can be reduced to six basic facial feature complexes [3] was challenged because human emotion recognition is context-based. The same facial feature complexes may be interpreted differently depending on the situational context [1].

Applying the continuous uncertainty and trustworthiness self-awareness algo-rithms to FR and FER models and data sets built and partitioned to exaggerate and aggravate OOD conditions is a good area for evaluating the algorithms.

The paper is organized as follows. Section 2 proposes a solution for dynamically adjusting the meta-learning trustworthiness estimating algorithm for predictions done for the FR and FER tasks. Section 3 describes the data set used for experiments; Sect. 4 outlines experimental algorithms in detail; Sect. 6 presents the obtained results, and Sect. 6 discusses the results, draws practical conclusions, and states directions of the research of not yet answered questions.

2   Proposed Solution

2.1   Uncertainty Meta-learning

In [13], two approaches to assigning a trustworthiness flag to the FR prediction were proposed: statistical analysis of the distributions of the maximal softmax activation value for correct and wrong verdicts, and use of the meta-learning supervisor ANN that uses the whole set of softmax activations for all FR classes (sorted into the "uncertainty shape descriptor" (USD) to provide class-invariant generalization) as an input and generates trusted or not-trusted flag.

This contribution "marries" these two approaches by collecting statistical information about training results in the loss layer (LL) memory of the meta-learning supervisor ANN. The information in the LL's memory holds prediction result y_t, training label result l_t, and trustworthiness threshold TT. The latter parameter is the learnable one, and the derivative of the loss error, calculated from these statistical data, is used to auto-configure the TT to optimize the sum of square errors loss: $SSE_{TT} = \sum_{t=1}^{K} SE_t$, where K is a number of entries in the memory table:

$$SE_{TTt} = \begin{cases} (y_t - TT)^2, & (l_t < TT \wedge y_t > TT) \vee (l_t > TT \wedge y_t < TT) \\ 0, & (l_t > TT \wedge y_t > TT) \vee (l_t < TT \wedge y_t < TT) \end{cases} \quad (1)$$

The input of the meta-learning supervisor ANN was built from the softmax activations of the ensemble of the underlying CNN models. The algorithm of building USD can be described in a few words as follows: "build the "uncertainty shape descriptor" by sorting softmax activations inside each model vector, order model vectors by the highest softmax activation, flatten the list of vectors, rearrange the order of activations in each vector to the order of activations in the vector with the highest softmax activation". Examples of the descriptor for the $M = 7$ CNN models in the underlying FR or FER ensemble, for the cases when none of the models, 4, and 6 detected the face correctly, are presented in Fig. 2. It could be seen that shapes of the distribution of the softmax activations are pretty distinct and, therefore, can be subject to the pattern recognition task performed by the meta-learning supervisor ANN.

However, unlike in the mentioned above publication, for simplification reasons, supervisor ANN was not categorizing the predicted number of the correct members of the underlying ensemble but instead was performing the regression task of the transformation. On the high level (ANN layer details are given in Sect. 4), the transformation can be seen as Eq. 2, where $n = |C| * M$ is the dimensionality of the $\forall USD \in \mathcal{X}$, $|C|$ - cardinality of the set of FR or FER categories (subjects or emotions), and M - size of the CNN ensemble 1.

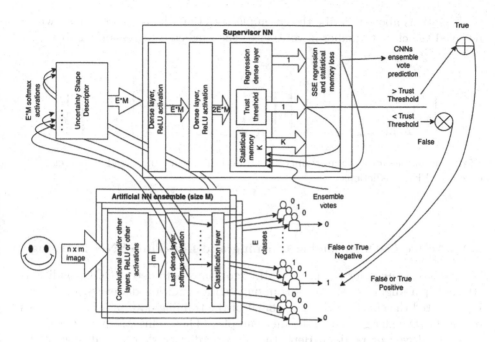

Fig. 1. Meta-learning supervisor ANN over underlying CNN ensemble.

$$reg : \mathcal{X} \subset \mathbb{R}^n \mapsto \mathcal{Y} \subset \mathbb{R} \qquad (2)$$

where $\forall \mathbf{x} \in \mathcal{X}, \mathbf{x} \in (0\ldots 1)^n, \forall y \in \mathcal{Y}, E(y) \in [0\ldots M]$.

The loss function used for y is the usual for regression tasks, sum of squared error: $SSE_y = \sum_{t=1}^{N_{mb}} (y_j - e_j)^2$, where e is the label (actual number of the members of CNN ensemble with correctl prediction), and N_{mb} - minbatch size.

From the trustworthiness categorization and ensemble vote point of view, the high-level transformation of the combined CNN ensemble together with the meta-learning supervisor ANN can be represented as Eq. 3:

$$cat : \mathcal{I} \subset \mathbb{I}^l \mapsto \mathcal{C} \subset \mathbb{C} \times \mathbb{B} \qquad (3)$$

where $\mathbf{i}$ are images, l - mage size, c - classifications, and b - binary trustworthy flags, such as $\forall \mathbf{i} \in \mathcal{I}, \mathbf{i} \in (0\ldots 255)^l, \forall c \in \mathcal{C}, c \in \{c_1, \ldots, c_{|C|}\}, \forall b \in \mathcal{B}, b \in \{1, 0\}$.

$$b_i = \begin{cases} 1, & (y_i > TT_t) \\ 0, & (y_i < TT_t) \end{cases} \qquad (4)$$

where i is an index of the image at the moment t of the state of the loss function memory.

$$c_i = argmin(|y_i - e_i(c_i)|) \tag{5}$$

Equations above describe the ensemble vote that chooses category c_i, which received the closest number of votes e_i to the predicted regression number y_i.

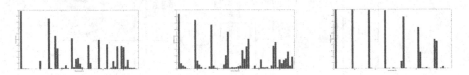

Fig. 2. Examples of the uncertainty shape descriptors for 0, 4, and 6 correct CNN ensemble FER predictions.

2.2 Active CNN Ensemble Learning and Life-Time SNN Learning

A common strategy for the passive ML algorithms is to detect OOD conditions [19]. AL paradigm expects actions upon such a condition discovery. In [11] we investigated the effects of the enrichment of the training data by a few examples of the OOD makeup and occlusion examples. Those enrichments were either "expert" driven or random. Here, the SNN verdict to detect confusion of the underlying CNN ensemble (i.e. when the SNN-predicted number of correct CNN models in the ensemble is less than the trusted threshold: $y_t < TT_t$) is used to invoke AL mode post-classification, asking "Oracle" to assign the correct label to the problematic image.

The trained CNN ensemble has a reference training set $|D_r| = N_{mb}$ of the mini-batch size, which is composed of the randomly-selected elements of the whole training set $D_{tr}; D_r \subset D_{tr}$. Upon "Oracle" labelling, one of the elements of the older reference training set is replaced, and original CNN ensemble models are quickly retrained on a few epochs. The percentage of the allowed "Oracle" requests is limited by a low number.

Lifetime or (continuous or online) learning for SNN is implemented similarly to AL for CNN ensemble; however, because SNN has no supervisor of supervisor, retraining on the reference training set is implemented after each test classification.

3   Data Set

The BookClub artistic makeup data set contains images of $E = |C| = 21$ subjects. Each subject's data may contain a photo-session series of photos with no makeup, various makeup, and images with other obstacles for facial recognition, such as wigs, glasses, jewellery, face masks, or various headdresses. The data set features 37 photo sessions without makeup or occlusions, 40 makeup sessions, and 17 sessions with occlusions. Each photo session contains circa 168 JPEG images of the 1072×712 resolution of six basic emotional expressions (sadness, happiness, surprise, fear, anger, disgust), a neutral expression, and the closed eyes photoshoots taken with seven head rotations at three exposure times on the off-white background. The subjects' age varies from their twenties to sixties. The race of the subjects is predominately Caucasian and some Asian. Gender is approximately evenly split between sessions.

The photos were taken over two months, and several subjects were posed at multiple sessions over several weeks in various clothing with changed hairstyles, downloadable from https://data.mendeley.com/datasets/yfx9h649wz/3. All subjects gave written consent to use their anonymous images in public scientific research.

4 Experiments

The experiments were run on the Linux (Ubuntu 20.04.3 LTS) operating system with two dual Tesla K80 GPUs (with 2×12 GB GDDR5 memory each) and one QuadroPro K6000 (with 12 GB GDDR5 memory, as well), X299 chipset motherboard, 256 GB DDR4 RAM, and i9-10900X CPU. Experiments were run using MATLAB 2022a.

The experiments were done using MATLAB with Deep Learning Toolbox. For FR and FER experiments, the Inception v.3 CNN model was used. Out of the other SOTA models applied to FR and FER tasks on the BookClub data set (AlexNet, GoogLeNet, ResNet50, InceptionResnet v.2), Inception v.3 demonstrated overall the best result over such accuracy metrics as trusted accuracy, precision, and recall [12,13]. Therefore, the Inception v.3 model, which contains 315 elementary layers, was used as an underlying CNN. Its last two layers were resized to match the number of classes in the BookClub data set (21), and retrained using "adam" learning algorithm with 0.001 initial learning coefficient, "piecewise" learning rate drop schedule with 5 iterations drop interval, and 0.9 drop coefficient, mini-batch size 128, and 10 epochs parameters to ensure at least 95% learning accuracy. The Inception v.3 CNN models were used as part of the ensemble with a number of models $N = 7$ trained in parallel.

Meta-learning supervisor ANN models were trained using the "adam" learning algorithm with 0.01 initial learning coefficient, mini-batch size 64, and 200 epochs. The memory buffer length, which collects statistics about previous training iterations, was set to $K = 8192$. For online learning SNN experiments, the number of epochs was set to 10, and for active learning, the number of epochs was set to 5. Limits for the "Oracle" requests were set for 1% and 0.1%, resulting in 112 and 12 requests out of 11125 test images.

The *reg* meta-learning supervisor ANN transformation represented in the Eq. 2 implemented with two hidden layers with $n+1$ and $2n+1$ neurons in the first and second hidden layer, and ReLU activation function. All source code and

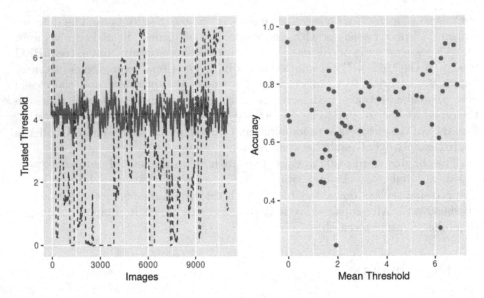

Fig. 3. Left - trusted threshold learned during the training phase (blue, dashed line), online learning changes for grouped test images (green), and shuffled test images (red) for FR task. Right - trusted accuracy against the trusted threshold for grouped test images for the FR task.

detailed results are publicly available on GitHub https://github.com/Selitskiy/StatLoss.

4.1 Trusted Accuracy Metrics

Suppose only the classification verdict is used as a final result of the ANN model. In that case, the accuracy of the target CNN model can be calculated only as the ratio of the number of correctly identified test images by the CNN model to the number of all test images:

$$Accuracy = \frac{N_{correct}}{N_{all}} \tag{6}$$

When additional dimension in classification is used, for example amending verdict of the meta-learning supervisor ANN, (see Formula 3), and $cat(i) = c \times b$, where $\forall i \in \mathcal{I}$, $\forall c \times b \in \mathcal{C} \times \mathcal{B} = \{(c_1, b_1), \ldots (c_p, b_p)\}$, $\forall b \in \mathbb{B} = \{True, False\}$, then the trusted accuracy and other trusted quality metrics can be calculated as:

$$Accuracy_t = \frac{N_{correct:f=T} + N_{wrong:f\neq T}}{N_{all}} \tag{7}$$

As a mapping to a more usual notations, $N_{correct:f=T}$ can be as the True Positive (TP) number, $N_{wrong:f\neq T}$ - True Negative (TN), $N_{wrong:f=T}$ - False Positive

(FP), and $N_{correct:f \neq T}$ - False Negative (FN). Analogously to the trusted accuracy, we used metrics such as trusted precision, recall, specificity and F1 score for the models' evaluation.

5 Results

Results of the FR experiments are presented in the Table 1, for FER experiments - in the Table 2. The first column holds accuracy metrics using the ensemble's maximum vote. The second column - using the ensemble vote closest to the meta-learning SNN prediction and trustworthiness threshold learned only on the test set, see Formulae 4, 5. The third column lists accuracy metrics in the continuous learning setting, and the next two - are in the active learning setting with 1% and 0.1% of the allowed "Oracle" requests.

Figure 3 on the left shows trustworthy thresholds learned during training and continuous learning setting when test data is either unstructured or structured by a photo session, i.e. groups of the same person and same makeup or occlusion, but with different lighting, head position, and emotion expression. Figure 3 on the right shows the relationship between the average session trusted threshold and session-specific trusted recognition accuracy for FR and FER cases of the grouped test sessions.

Table 1. Accuracy metrics for FR task. Maximal ensemble vote, SNN predicted vote, SNN with online retraining, CNN ensemble active learning on 1% of test data, CNN ensemble active learning on 0.1% of test data.

Metric	Maximal	Predicted	Online	Active 1%	Active 0.1%
Untrusted accuracy	0.68237	0.57488	0.57488	0.84720	0.60335
Trusted accuracy	0.73836	0.83383	0.83526	0.92293	0.81833
Trusted precision	0.84102	0.91644	0.91821	0.99198	0.9560
Trusted recall	0.76029	0.78227	0.78321	0.91644	0.73257
Trusted F1 score	0.79862	0.84406	0.84535	0.95271	0.82952
Trusted specificity	0.69124	0.90355	0.90566	0.95890	0.94877

Table 2. Accuracy metrics for FER task. Maximal ensemble vote, SNN predicted vote, SNN with online retraining, CNN ensemble active learning on 1% of test data.

Metric	Maximal	Predicted	Online	Active 1%
Untrusted accuracy	0.39626	0.29147	0.29147	0.20126
Trusted accuracy	0.672599	0.77678	0.69298	0.77735
Trusted precision	0.64736	0.65266	0.48052	0.42908
Trusted recall	0.38166	0.50052	0.65778	0.32157
Trusted F1 score	0.48021	0.56656	0.55534	0.36763
Trusted specificity	0.86355	0.89042	0.70747	0.89219

6   Discussion, Conclusions, and Future Work

For the experimentation with CNN model ensemble based on Inception v.3 architecture and data set with significant OOD in the form of makeup and occlusions, using meta-learning SNN, which works as an instrument of self-awareness of the model about uncertainty and trustworthiness of its predictions, noticeably increases accuracy metrics for FR tasks (by tens of per cent) and significantly (doubles) - for FER task. The proposed novel loss layer with memory architecture without online retraining increases key accuracy metrics by an additional (up to 5)%. The trustworthiness threshold learned using the loss layer with memory offers a simple explanation of why prediction for a given image was categorized as trusted or non-trusted.

Active learning significantly improves FR accuracy metrics even at the 0.1% of the allowed "Oracle" requests and brings trusted accuracy metrics at the high 90% level for 1% of the allowed test-time requests. For FER task, AL significantly improves accuracy metrics related to true negatives.

Fig. 4. Examples of images for FER (anger expression) with the low trusted threshold (bad acting) - left and high trusted threshold (better acting) - right.

Online retraining adds insignificant improvement to accuracy metrics for non-structured test data. However, online retraining of the trustworthiness threshold on structured test data informs the model not only about its uncertainty but also about the quality of the test session, see Fig. 4. For example, it could be seen that a low-threshold session has a poorly performing subject who struggles to play the anger emotion expression, while in the high-threshold session, the facial expression is much more apparent.

References

1. Cacioppo, J.T., Berntson, G.G., Larsen, J.T., Poehlmann, K.M., Ito, T.A., et al.: The psychophysiology of emotion. Handb. Emotions **2**(01), 2000 (2000)
2. Chomsky, N.: Powers and Prospects: Reflections on Human Nature and the Social Order. South End Press (1996)

3. Ekman, P., Friesen, W.V.: Constants across cultures in the face and emotion. J. Pers. Soc. Psychol. **17**(2), 124 (1971)
4. Knowledge, P.: Yoshua Bengio | From System 1 Deep Learning to System 2 Deep Learning | NeurIPS 2019 (2019). www.youtube.com/watch?v=FtUbMG3rlFs. Accessed 11 Apr 2022
5. LeCun, Y.: A path towards autonomous machine intelligence version 0.9. 2, 2022–06-27 (2022)
6. Lewis, D.D., Catlett, J.: Heterogeneous uncertainty sampling for supervised learning. In: Machine Learning Proceedings 1994, pp. 148–156. Elsevier (1994)
7. Li, K., et al.: Mural: meta-learning uncertainty-aware rewards for outcome-driven reinforcement learning. In: International Conference on Machine Learning, pp. 6346–6356. PMLR (2021)
8. Marcheggiani, D., Artieres, T.: An experimental comparison of active learning strategies for partially labeled sequences. In: Proceedings of the 2014 Conference on Empirical Methods in Natural Language Processing (EMNLP), pp. 898–906 (2014)
9. McCarthy, J., Hayes, P.J.: Some philosophical problems from the standpoint of artificial intelligence. In: Readings in Artificial Intelligence, pp. 431–450. Elsevier (1981)
10. Qiu, L., et al.: Resisting out-of-distribution data problem in perturbation of xai. arXiv preprint arXiv:2107.14000 (2021)
11. Selitskaya, N., Sielicki, S., Christou, N.: Challenges in real-life face recognition with heavy makeup and occlusions using deep learning algorithms. In: Nicosia, G., et al. (eds.) LOD 2020. LNCS, vol. 12566, pp. 600–611. Springer, Cham (2020). https://doi.org/10.1007/978-3-030-64580-9_49
12. Selitskiy, S., Christou, N., Selitskaya, N.: Isolating Uncertainty of the Face Expression Recognition with the Meta-Learning Supervisor Neural Network, pp. 104–112. Association for Computing Machinery, New York, NY, USA (2021). https://doi.org/10.1145/3480433.3480447
13. Selitskiy, S., Christou, N., Selitskaya, N.: Using statistical and artificial neural networks meta-learning approaches for uncertainty isolation in face recognition by the established convolutional models. In: Nicosia, G., et al. (eds.) Mach. Learn. Optim. Data Sci., pp. 338–352. Springer International Publishing, Cham (2022). https://doi.org/10.1145/3480433.3480447
14. Thrun, S.: Is learning the n-th thing any easier than learning the first? In: Advances in Neural Information Processing Systems 8 (1995)
15. Thrun, S., Mitchell, T.M.: Lifelong robot learning. Robot. Auton. Syst. **15**(1–2), 25–46 (1995)
16. Thrun S., P.L.: Learning To Learn. Springer, Boston, MA (1998). https://doi.org/10.1007/978-1-4615-5529-2
17. Turing, A.M.: I.-computing machinery and intelligence. Mind **LIX**(236), 433–460 (1950). https://doi.org/10.1093/mind/LIX.236.433
18. Vanschoren, J.: Meta-learning: a survey. ArXiv abs/1810.03548 (2018)
19. Williams, D.S., Gadd, M., De Martini, D., Newman, P.: Fool me once: robust selective segmentation via out-of-distribution detection with contrastive learning. In: 2021 IEEE International Conference on Robotics and Automation (ICRA), pp. 9536–9542. IEEE (2021)

Thrill-K Architecture: Towards a Solution to the Problem of Knowledge Based Understanding

Gadi Singer, Joscha Bach, Tetiana Grinberg[✉] [iD], Nagib Hakim, Phillip R. Howard, Vasudev Lal, and Zev Rivlin

Intel Labs, Santa Clara, CA 95054, USA
{gadi.singer,joscha.bach,tetiana.grinberg,nagib.hakim,
phillip.r.howard,vasudev.lal,zev.rivlin}@intel.com

Abstract. While end-to-end learning systems are rapidly gaining capabilities and popularity, the increasing computational demands for deploying such systems, along with a lack of flexibility, adaptability, explainability, reasoning and verification capabilities, require new types of architectures. Here we introduce a classification of hybrid systems which, based on an analysis of human knowledge and intelligence, combines neural learning with various types of knowledge and knowledge sources. We present the Thrill-K architecture as a prototypical solution for integrating instantaneous knowledge, standby knowledge and external knowledge sources in a framework capable of inference, learning and intelligent control.

Keywords: Neuro-Symbolic AI · Hybrid systems · Knowledge engineering

1 Introduction: The Rise of Cognitive AI

Many of the current Deep Learning (DL) applications address perception tasks related to object recognition, natural language processing (NLP), translation, and other tasks that involve broad data correlation processing such as that performed by recommendation systems. DL systems yield exceptional results based on differential programming and sophisticated data-based correlation and are expected to drive transformation across industries for years to come. At the same time, a number of fundamental limitations inherent to the nature of DL itself must be overcome so that machine learning, or more broadly AI, can come closer to realizing its potential. A concerted effort in the following three areas is needed to achieve non-incremental innovation:

- Materially improve model efficiency (e.g., reduce the number of parameters by two to three orders of magnitude without loss in accuracy)
- Substantially enhance model robustness, extensibility, and scaling
- Categorically increase machine cognition

B. Goertzel et al. (Eds.): AGI 2022, LNAI 13539, pp. 404–412, 2023.
https://doi.org/10.1007/978-3-031-19907-3_39

Among other developments, the creation of transformers and their application in language modeling [1] has driven computational requirements to double roughly every 3.5 months in recent years [2], highlighting the urgency for improvements in model efficiency. Despite developments in acceleration and optimization of neural networks, without improvements in model efficiency, current model growth trends will not be sustainable for the long haul [3].

Techniques such as pruning, sparsity, compression, distillation and graph neural networks (GNNs) offer helpful advancements in efficiency but ultimately yield only incremental or task specific improvements. Reducing model size by orders of magnitude without compromising the quality of results will likely require a more fundamental change in the methods for capturing and representing information itself and in the learning capabilities within a DL model. Using AI systems that integrate neural networks with added information injected per-need might help to scale down some of the language model growth trends. On a more fundamental level, deep learning lacks the cognitive mechanisms to address tasks central to human intelligence, missing competencies such as abstraction, context, causality, explainability, and intelligible reasoning.

There is a strong push for AI to reach into the realm of human-like understanding. Leaning on the paradigm defined by Daniel Kahneman in his book, Thinking, Fast and Slow [4], Yoshua Bengio equates the capabilities of contemporary DL with what Kahneman characterizes as "System 1" capabilities—intuitive, fast, unconscious, habitual thinking [5]. In contrast, he posits that the next challenge for AI systems lies in implementing the capabilities of "System 2"—slow, logical, sequential, conscious, and algorithmic thinking, such as those needed in planning and reasoning. In a similar fashion, Francois Chollet describes [6] an emergent new phase in the progression of AI capabilities based on broad generalization ("Flexible AI"), capable of adaptation to unknown unknowns within a broad domain. Both these characterizations align with DARPA's Third Wave of AI [7], characterized by contextual adaptation, abstraction, reasoning, and explainability, and by systems constructing contextual explanatory models for classes of real-world phenomena. One possible path to achieving these competencies is through the integration of DL with symbolic reasoning and deep knowledge. We use the term Cognitive AI to refer to this new phase of AI.

There is a divide in the field of AI between those who believe categorically higher machine intelligence can be achieved solely by advancing DL further, and those who do not. Taking the neuro-symbolic side of this debate, we see the need for incorporating additional fundamental mechanisms while continuing to advance DL as a core capability within a larger architecture. Knowledge that is structured, explicit, and intelligible can provide a path to higher machine intelligence or System 2 type capabilities. Structured knowledge is required to capture and represent the full richness associated with human intelligence, and therefore constitutes a key ingredient for higher intelligence. Such knowledge enables abstraction, generalization to new contexts, integration of human generated expertise, imagination of novel situations, counterfactual reasoning, communication and collaboration, and a higher degree of autonomous behavior. If developed, Cognitive AI will be characterized not only by the ability to access and represent symbolic knowledge in conjunction with learning mechanisms, but also by the ability to integrate this knowledge, use it for reasoning, planning, decision making and control, and generate new knowledge via inference and abstraction.

2 Dimensions of Knowledge

What we call "human knowledge" encompasses a diverse set of models and information types. We introduce here a classification of the different dimensions of human knowledge, from which we can extrapolate to machine knowledge and understanding.

We distinguish between six dimensions of knowledge. Three are dimensions of direct knowledge, two are meta-dimensions (context and values), and one allows for connecting references (ConceptRefs) (Fig. 1):

1. **Descriptive knowledge** consists of conceptual abstractions and can also include facts and systems of records. The facts and information relevant for specific use cases and environments can be organized, utilized and updated as hierarchical knowledge. The underlying ontology used in individual AI systems can be seeded with task-relevant classes and entities from curated systems (e.g., the OpenCyc ontology or the AMR named entity types).
2. **Dynamic models** of the world include physical, mathematical/algebraic, financial, perceptual and other structural regularities and abstractions that describe how the observed environment will likely change given its current state. Dynamic models can be formal, but when dealing with the heterogeneity of the real world, they often merely capture statistical regularities. Causal knowledge enables going beyond statistical prediction by identifying the conditions under which events manifest, which is a prerequisite for planning and explainability.
3. Humans often use **stories** and **scripts** to provide frames and contexts for the interpretation of facts and events. Stories can take the form of complex narratives that build on shared beliefs and mythologies.
4. **Context and source attribution** is a meta-knowledge dimension that enables the binding of knowledge to a particular context, dealing with conflicting knowledge, and retracting and updating it when other sources are available. Source attribution can become particularly relevant when a system has to deal with questions of data provenance and information reliability (e.g. from news sources).
5. **Values and priorities** are meta-knowledge dimensions that enable specifying the relevance of knowledge and the contexts in which systems can choose a course of action over another so as to behave according to ethical considerations and normative constraints.
6. **Concept references** enable binding different types, modalities and instances of representations together, and unifying knowledge by identifying the relationships between the representations of unique entity. A Concept Reference (or ConceptRef for short) is the identifier and set of references to all things related to a given concept. The ConceptRefs themselves do not actually include any of the knowledge—the knowledge resides in the dimensions described above.

Understanding requires a foundation of **common-sense knowledge**: a broad (and broadly shared) set of unwritten assumptions that humans automatically apply to make sense of the world. In our framework, commonsense knowledge is considered a subset of each of the above five knowledge dimensions.

For AI systems, implementing knowledge dimensions observed in human comprehension and communication can provide substantial value to the system's intelligence, constituting what we term deeply structured knowledge.

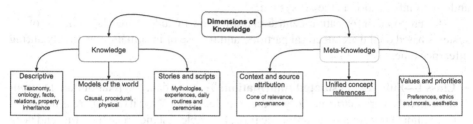

Fig. 1. Dimensions of knowledge

3   From Knowledge to Understanding

Now that we have introduced a taxonomy of human knowledge, we can build upon it to create a definition of understanding that can be reasonably applied to AI systems.

Understanding is the foundation of intelligence. Yoshua Bengio characterizes human-level AI understanding as follows [8]: capture causality and how the world works; understand abstract actions and how to use them to control, reason and plan, even in novel scenarios; explain what happened (inference, credit assignment); and generate out-of-distribution.

We are proposing a knowledge-centric definition of understanding: the ability to create a persistent world view expressed in rich knowledge representation; the ability to acquire and interpret new information to enhance this world view; and the ability to effectively reason, decide and explain existing knowledge and new information.

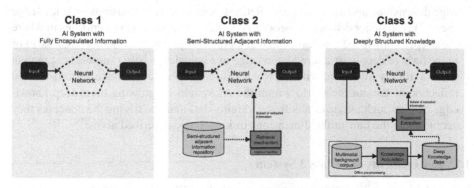

Fig. 2. Information-centric classification of AI systems

4 Information-Centric Classification of AI Systems

The above knowledge-centric definition of understanding leads us to an information-centric classification of AI systems (Fig. 2) as a complementary view to a processing-based classification such as Henry Kautz's taxonomy for neuro-symbolic computing [9]. The classification emphasizes the high-level architectural choice related to the structure and use of information in the AI system.

The proposed information-centric classification includes three key classes of AI systems based on the architectural partition and the use of information on the fly during inference time:

- **Class 1—Fully Encapsulated Information:** Training data and relations are incorporated into the parametric memory of the neural network (NN) itself. There is no access to additional information at inference time. Examples include recent end-to-end deep learning (DL) systems and language models (e.g., GPT-3). Such systems will likely be the best solutions for all types of perception tasks (such as image recognition and segmentation, speech recognition, and many natural language processing functions), sequence-to-sequence capabilities (such as language translation), recommendation systems, and various question-and-answer applications.
- **Class 2—Semi-structured Adjacent Information** (in retrieval-based systems): These systems rely on retrieving information from an external repository (e.g., Wikipedia) in addition to the NN parametric memory (e.g., retrieval-augmented generation) [10]. In Class 2 systems, the repository contains information, but much of the complex relationships and insights related to the information are encapsulated in the embedded space of the NN. These systems are most helpful in addressing use cases with very large data/information space, e.g., an AI system tasked with answering questions about Wikipedia articles. The ability to modify the information in the repository between training time and inference time can be important for out-of-domain challenges, even if the relevant information was not present during training.
- **Class 3—Deeply Structured Knowledge** (in retrieval-based systems): Retrieval-based systems that interact closely with a deeply structured knowledge base, where the latter uses an explicit information structure that incorporates the multiple knowledge dimensions and their complex relations described in Dimensions of Knowledge (Sect. 2). The major distinction between Class 2 and Class 3 AI systems lies in where the deeper knowledge resides—whether in the NN parametric memory (Class 2) or in the form of deeply structured knowledge in a knowledge base (knowledge graph in Class 3) tightly integrated with the NN. Class 3 systems could create a multi-faceted reflection of the outside world within the AI system by growing their deep knowledge base through interaction with the training data and classifying the concepts they accrue using the humanlike dimensions of knowledge described above.

4.1 Key Elements of a Class 3 System

In an AI system with deeply structured knowledge (Class 3), an NN has an adjacent knowledge base with an explicit structure that conveys the relations and dependencies that constitute deep knowledge. The auxiliary knowledge base is accessed both during training and inference time. Some of the deep knowledge still resides in the NN parametric memory, but in this class of systems, most of the knowledge resides outside the NN. In an NN-only reasoning system, the knowledge base serves as a repository. A Class 3 system will use an explicit knowledge base during inference; however, reasoning functions such as sorting, selection, neighbor identification, and others are conducted by the NN within the embedded space—as can be found in examples of QA systems operating over knowledge graphs [11].

Other Class 3 systems could have an active functionality for selecting information or performing parts of the reasoning on top of the Knowledge Base (KB). We refer to such a mechanism as **reasoned extraction**. One example is Neuro-Symbolic Question Answering (NSQA) [12]. A key advantage of reasoned extraction over NN-only reasoning is that the answer returned by the system can change dynamically as the Knowledge Graph (KG) is updated, without needing to retrain the model.

The rightmost section of Fig. 2 depicts the high-level architecture of a Class 3 system and its key components. The term **Knowledge** refers to the relevant and objective information gained through experience. **Deep Knowledge** describes knowledge that has multiple dimensions, with complex relations captured within each domain. A knowledge base implements structured interactive knowledge as a repository in a particular solution, primarily implemented as knowledge graphs (e.g.: Google's Knowledge Graph [13]). Finally, an AI system with Deeply Structured Knowledge is a system with a knowledge base that captures deep knowledge and reflects its structure through extraction schemes.

The **Neural Network** (NN) is the primary functional part of a Class 3 system. It may include all perception elements such as image recognition and scene segmentation, or a language model for processing syntax, placement-based relations, and the core of common semantics. It will likely learn an embedding space that represents the key dimensions of the incoming data. In multimodal systems, it will reflect the images space and the language space. Like Class 2 systems, the neural network system in Class 3 can engage with the structured knowledge base during inference time, and retrieve the information needed to complete its task successfully. In this architecture, the training of the NN needs to be done together with the extraction mechanism and some representation of the knowledge base to allow the NN to learn how to extract the required knowledge during inference.

The **Deep Knowledge Base** contains facts and information that might be required for future inference and some or all of the deep knowledge structures depicted in Fig. 1. These include descriptive knowledge, dynamic models of the world, stories, context and source attribution, values and priorities, and Concept References. The knowledge base can change after training and can include additional data and knowledge. As long as the nature of knowledge and information is similar to that encountered by the NN during training, the modified knowledge base should be fully utilizable during inference based on its latest incarnation.

Finally, the **Reasoned Extraction** block mediates between the NN and its external source of knowledge. In the simplest case, it is a direct mapping from embedding vectors through some indexed links to the knowledge base. In the more general case, reasoned extraction will extract its information using libraries based on queries or APIs.

While promising some considerable strengths, Class 3 systems require a higher level of complexity because they necessitate creating and updating an additional element of the architecture - the deep knowledge base. They also necessitate changes to the learning algorithms because the knowledge is now split between the NN and the KB, ultimately requiring new techniques for integrating gradient descent statistical methods with symbolic representations and learning.

5   Thrill-K: A Blueprint for Hybrid Machine Intelligence

Advanced AI systems will integrate a full mechanism of retrieval from a large semi-structured corpus of data in addition to their knowledge base. This will require dealing with inconsistencies, incomplete knowledge, and the addition of prerequisite knowledge, based on inference processes.

From the perspective of such systems, we observe three levels of knowledge (which we call 3LK):

1. **Instantaneous knowledge** allows for rapid response to external events. This knowledge represents a direct input-to-output function that reacts to events or sequences within a well-mastered domain. All higher organisms depend on the availability of instantaneous knowledge.
2. Humans and advanced intelligent machines acquire and use **standby knowledge**. Standby knowledge requires additional processing and internal resolution within the deep knowledge base, which makes it slower than instantaneous knowledge, but applicable to a wider range of situations.
3. **Retrieved external knowledge** makes use of additional knowledge sources. Whatever the scope of knowledge is within the human brain or the boundaries of an AI system, there is substantially more information, or more recently relevant information, that can be retrieved from outside of the boundary.

5.1   Thrill-K's Three Levels of Knowledge

Thrill-K (contraction of "three-L-K") is a proposed architectural blueprint for AI systems that utilizes the three levels of knowledge (3LK). It provides a means for representing and accessing knowledge at three levels—in parametric memory for instantaneous knowledge, in an adjacent deeply structured knowledge base for reasoned extraction, and access to broad digital information repositories for external knowledge.

Figure 3 depicts the Thrill-K system architecture. This architecture includes all the building blocks of such systems, however the flow (depicted by the arrows) can change based on the usage and configuration. In the example flow shown in the diagram, the sequence assumes the initial control is via a neural network, followed by the deep knowledge base, followed if needed by external resources. The direct input-to-output path using the instantaneous knowledge is encoded in parametric memory. If it detects uncertainty or low confidence in the direct path, the system performs reasoned extraction from its deep knowledge base. This knowledge base relies on machine-learning-based knowledge acquisition to update and refresh the knowledge as new information becomes relevant

Thrill-K Architecture

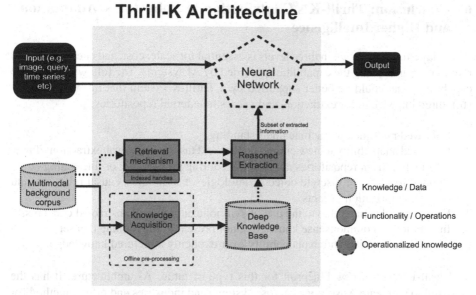

Fig. 3. Thrill-K architecture blueprint

and useful enough to be added. Finally, if the AI system cannot find the knowledge needed, the retrieval mechanism enables accessing and retrieving necessary information from the available repositories. Other flows are also possible. For example, if the task of the AI is to search a knowledge base or to find paragraphs in an external repository, the same building blocks will be configured in a different sequence. It should also be noted that while the main processing path is depicted here as a neural network, the same tiering principle applies to other types of machine learning with information integrated into the processing as part of the instantaneous input-to-output path.

5.2 Scalability of a Thrill-K System

Aside from the obvious advantages in terms of explainability, the stratification of information access into three separate layers offers a method of mitigating compute and data costs [14] associated with scaling a typical Class 1 system. The expensive NN parametric memory is reserved only for the **instantaneous knowledge** requiring expedient access, akin to Kahneman's System 1 [4]. A Deep Knowledge base offers the necessary expansion of the scope of available **standby knowledge** at the cost of some speed of access. Finally, **retrieved external knowledge** is both the slowest (since it has to be digested through the largest number of intermediate modules), and the cheapest (since it does not have to be maintained and updated by the model itself).

By applying the 3-level knowledge hierarchy and Thrill-K system architecture, we can build systems and solutions for the future that are likely to partition knowledge at those three levels to create sustainable and viable cognitive AI.

6 Conclusion: Thrill-K's Contribution to Robustness, Adaptation and Higher Intelligence

While layering knowledge in three levels is essential for scale, cost, and energy, it is also required for increasing the capabilities provided by AI systems. The following are some capabilities that could be better supported by a Thrill-K system that integrates deeply structured knowledge for extraction, and access to external repositories:

1. Improved multimodal machine understanding.
2. Increased adaptability to new circumstances and tasks by retrieval/extraction of new information from repositories not available during pre-training or fine-tuning.
3. Refined handling of discrete objects, ontologies, taxonomies, causal relations, and broad memorization of facts.
4. Enhanced robustness due to the use of symbolic entities and abstracted concepts.
5. Integration of commonsense knowledge not present in the training dataset.
6. Symbolic reasoning and explainability over explicitly structured knowledge.

Thrill-K offers a new blueprint for this type of future AI architecture. It has the potential to permeate AI solutions across systems and industries and offer a method for building intelligence effectively and efficiently.

References

1. Devlin, J., Chang, M.W., Lee, K., Toutanova, K.: Bert: pre-training of deep bidirectional transformers for language understanding (2018). arXiv preprint. arXiv:1810.04805
2. Amodei, D.: AI and Compute. OpenAI (2021). https://openai.com/blog/ai-and-compute/
3. Interpreting AI compute trends. AI Impacts (2020). https://aiimpacts.org/interpreting-ai-compute-trends/
4. Kahneman, D.: Thinking, Fast and Slow. Macmillan, New York (2011)
5. Bengio, Y.: From system 1 deep learning to system 2 deep learning. In Neural Information Processing Systems (2019)
6. Chollet, F.: On the measure of intelligence (2019). arXiv preprint arXiv:1911.01547
7. Launchbury, J.: A DARPA perspective on artificial intelligence (2017). Accessed 11 Nov 2019
8. Goyal, A., Bengio, Y.: Inductive biases for deep learning of higher-level cognition (2020). arXiv preprint. arXiv:2011.15091
9. Kautz, H.: The third AI summer: AAAI Robert S engelmore memorial lecture. AI Mag. **43**(1), 93–104 (2022)
10. Lewis, P., et al.: Retrieval-augmented generation for knowledge-intensive NLP tasks. In: Advances in Neural Information Processing Systems, vol. 33, pp. 9459-9474 (2020)
11. Chakraborty, N., Lukovnikov, D., Maheshwari, G., Trivedi, P., Lehmann, J., Fischer, A.: Introduction to neural network based approaches for question answering over knowledge graphs (2019). arXiv preprint. arXiv:1907.09361
12. Kapanipathi, P., et al.: Leveraging abstract meaning representation for knowledge base question answering (2020). arXiv preprint. arXiv:2012.01707
13. Singhal, A.: Introducing the knowledge graph: things, not strings. Official Google Blog **5**, 16 (2012)
14. Thompson, N.C., Greenewald, K., Lee, K., Manso, G.F.: The computational limits of deep learning (2020) (2020). arXiv preprint. arXiv:2007.05558

Grammar Induction - Experimental Results

Linas Vepštas[(✉)] [iD]

OpenCog Foundation, Austin, USA
linasvepstas@gmail.com

Abstract. The OpenCog Learning project explores novel techniques for the induction of symbolic structure from environmental sources. As a first application of these ideas, the automated learning of the grammatical structure of English is explored. This document provides a summary of results observed to date. The symbolic structure manifests itself as large, complex graphs tying together words and grammatical structure. The induction process provides probability distributions on the graphs. The primary task is to describe and understand the nature of those graphs.

1 Introduction

The goal of the OpenCog Learning project is to induce structure from raw observational data. In the most direct sense, this would be visual or auditory data. In a more sophisticated sense, "observational data" will already have been processed by other information extraction layers, as the goal of learning is to do so hierarchically, recursively: to deduce structure in structure inside of structure... If this can be made to work, then, "starting in the middle" is not a bad place to start. In the present case, "the middle" is a corpus of English text, and the goal is to extract grammatical structure, including morphology, syntax and the lower reaches of semantics.

The general theory of how this can be done is sketched out in a companion article [6]. The overall process is as follows: first, one computes the mutual information (MI) between word-pairs occurring in the corpus. The MI assigns a numerical score to how often a pair of words occur near each-other. This can be used to generate a maximum spanning tree (MST) parse of the text, which captures the syntactic structure of the text [7]. This parse tree can be disassembled into individual "jigsaw pieces" which encode the syntactic structure of the parse [4]. Individual jigsaws encode the local syntactic environment of a given word, not unlike skip-grams. Collections of such jigsaws can be understood to be vectors: each word is endowed with a lexis of all of the syntactic contexts in which it was observed. But this is too fine-grained; one wishes to generalize from the particular to the general. The vectors can be used both to discover words that have similar syntactic contexts (based on the similarity of the local environments) and also to factor out different word-senses, since different syntactic contexts associate strongly with distinct word-senses [1, 2].

B. Goertzel et al. (Eds.): AGI 2022, LNAI 13539, pp. 413–423, 2023.
https://doi.org/10.1007/978-3-031-19907-3_40

This text reports on the algorithms developed to perform the above, and on the statistical properties of the resulting graphical networks. The report is summary, encompassing more than a decade of research and development[1]. There are obvious directions in which both the theory and the experiment could be taken, but haven't been so far. In the "downwards" direction lies morphology, needed for Indo-European languages, and segmentation, needed for Chinese. Further down, the extraction of phonetic structure and general audio processing. Levering the same tool-set upwards, one can search for high-MI pairs across multiple paragraphs, both to resolve references and to detect entities. Syntactic relations can also be extracted between different sense streams, say, between words and blueprints/diagrams, or words and photographs, or other hi-tech sensory data. The author believes the basic algorithm is generic, and can be ratcheted upwards, to arbitrarily high reaches. Whether this proves to be true cannot be known without conducting actual experiments.

The remainder of this paper focuses on the narrow tasks defined above, in the order given. The computation of word-pairs results in a graph, whose vertexes are words, and whose edges are word-pairs. What are the statistical properties of this graph? MST parsing and the creating of jigsaw pieces results in a matrix of (word, connector-sequence) pairs. What are the statistical properties of this matrix? Words are vectors in this matrix; the similarity between words can be judged with assorted different vector measures; how do these behave, and how does clustering and word-sense disambiguation proceed, in practice?

1.1 Software Infrastructure

All results were obtained by using the software found in the GitHub repo for the OpenCog Learn project[2]. It is built on top of the OpenCog AtomSpace[3] as a foundational layer. The AtomSpace is an in-RAM graph database with powerful graph query capabilities, tuned for performance. It has shims that allow data to be stored in conventional disk databases and to be distributed across the network. Most notable for the present task is the "matrix API"[4]: it allows arbitrary collections of subgraphs to be used as the basis elements of a vector space. If one has two such vector spaces, then pairs of elements form a matrix of rows and columns. Given a matrix, one may compute marginal and conditional probabilities. This is, of course, quite ordinary. What is new is that the AtomSpace allows extremely sparse matrices to be represented: say, 100K × 100K entries, of which all but a few million are zero. Conventional software packages do not provide tools for sparse data. Furthermore, the "base data" in the AtomSpace are graphs; the matrices themselves are but slices through the graphs. For example,

---

[1] A detailed diary of results, spanning a many hundreds of pages, can be found in the Dairy, Parts One-Six, and the adjunct reports. Rather than peppering this text with self-citations, footnotes will be used to indicate which of these to examine.

[2] See https://github.com/opencog/learn.

[3] See https://github.com/opencog/atomspace.

[4] See https://github.com/opencog/atomspace/tree/master/opencog/matrix.

during word-sense disambiguation, columns correspond to connector sequences; these are selected subgraphs taken from the total parse graph.

2   Pair Counting

Obtaining a suitable corpus for the English language is not as simple as it seems: it is not enough to train on a dump of Wikipedia articles. Wikipedia is descriptive, having a paucity of verbs and a surfeit of proper nouns and technical terms. The verbs of everyday outdoor adventure: run, jump, catch, are missing. This was remedied by working with a corpus of young adult adventure literature taken from Project Gutenberg and publicly licensed fan fiction.

Word-pair counting is done by generating random planar parse trees, and counting the connected pairs. This provides a uniform sampling over the space of all possible parse trees, eliminating edge effects from conventional finite-sized window sampling. Overall, though, the difference between this and window sampling are not obviously discernible.

Data Sets. Five snapshots of an increasingly larger English-language corpus were taken. These are summarized below[5].

Corpus	1	2	3	4	5
$\log_2 N_L$	16.678	17.097	18.214	18.600	19.019
$\log_2 N_R$	16.690	17.117	18.228	18.620	19.039
$\log_2 D_{\text{Tot}}$	23.224	23.797	24.748	25.180	25.627
Sparsity	10.144	10.416	11.693	12.040	12.431
Rarity	6.540	6.690	6.527	6.570	6.598
$\log_2 N_{\text{Tot}}/D_{\text{Tot}}$	4.779	5.079	5.128	5.235	5.335
Total Entropy	17.827	17.889	18.378	18.503	18.631
Left Entropy	9.7963	9.8102	10.069	10.109	10.148
Right Entropy	9.5884	9.5463	9.8321	9.8801	9.9265
MI	1.5572	1.4677	1.5227	1.4863	1.4431

In the table above, N_L and N_R are the height and width of the matrix (the number of unique words occurring on the left and right of observed word-pairs). They are almost the same, but not quite: periods and question marks never occur at the start of sentences; capitalized words rarely appear at the end. The sizes are given as logarithms, as this makes comparison to entropies more immediate. The total number of unique pairs is D_{Tot} while the total number of observations of these pairs is N_{Tot}.

---

[5] See Diary Part Two, page 75 and Diary Part Three, page 7. The corpus was divided into five "tranches"; each dataset includes one more tranche of the corpus.

The sparsity is $-\log_2 D_{\text{Tot}}/N_L \times N_R$, and is expressed in bits. It indicates what fraction of all possible word-pairs are actually observed. Observe how the sparsity increased by two bits, as the dimensions of the matrix increased by two bits (a factor of four; nontrivial in terms of compute-time, corpus size and RAM usage.) Thus, rarity is defined as $\log_2 D_{\text{Tot}}/\sqrt{N_L \times N_R}$, and is seen to be approximately constant, independent of dataset size.

The total entropy is

$$H_{\text{Tot}} = \sum_{w,v} p(w,v) \log_2 p(w,v)$$

with the sum ranging over all word-pairs (w,v) and the frequency $p(w,v) = N(w,v)/N(*,*)$ where $N(w,v)$ is the observation count of a pair, and $N(*,*)$ is the total count over all word-pairs. The left entropy is

$$H_{\text{Left}} = \sum_{w} p(w,*) \log_2 p(w,*)$$

where $p(w,*) = \sum_v p(w,v)$ is the left-marginal sum; likewise for the right entropy. The mutual information is

$$MI = H_{\text{Tot}} - H_{\text{Left}} - H_{\text{Right}} = \sum_{w,v} p(w,v) \log_2 \frac{p(w,v)}{p(w,*)\,p(*,v)}$$

Notable trends are that the number of distinct pairs increases as the square-root of the possible number of pairs. The total number of observations per pair is very nearly constant, increasing only slowly with the size of the dataset. Notable is that the MI really does appear to be constant, independent of the size of the dataset! The low value of the MI, one and a half bits, indicates the paucity of word-pairs. They convey some information, but not very much. On the other hand, the sparsity is quite high: of all possible word pairs that could have been observed, only minuscule fractions of a percent are actually observed.

Remarkably, the overall numbers appear to be language-independent; almost identical values are seen for Mandarin Chinese text[6]. To perform this counting, each Hanzi is taken to be a "word". This is not technically correct, as Chinese words may consist of one, two, three or more Hanzi. However, segmentation is a challenge, and so at this level, for pair-counting, issues of segmentation are ignored. Presumably, the discovery of Chinese words as set-phrases will occur later in the learning pipeline.

MI Distribution. The distribution of word-pair MI is shown below. This is for dataset 3, which contains 28 million pairs. The MI is sorted into 500 histogram bins.

---

[6] See the "Word Pair Distributions" document.

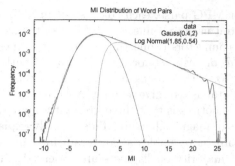

The distribution is clearly not symmetric. The two sides appear to be bounded by straight lines. The author is unaware of any theoretical explanation for this shape. However, the following guess is offered. If word-pairs are chosen completely at random, and the number of sampled pairs is much smaller than the total possible pairs, then one obtains a Gaussian distribution. Such a distribution is centered on a small but positive MI, due to sample-size effects. For larger samples, the mean tends to zero. Thus, perhaps the left-hand-side of this figure is just a Gaussian. An eyeballed, imprecise fit is shown.

Taking this to be "common-mode noise", and subtracting it leaves an excess of word pairs with positive MI, having a peak near $MI \sim 4$. The straight-line slope on the right suggests that the excess can be described by a log-normal distribution. Again, an eye-balled, imprecise fit is shown. These two, summed together, model the observed distribution almost perfectly.

Pairs with the highest MI are observed very infrequently. The highest observable MI value is directly related to the sample size: it is a bit below the log of the number of observations. Thus, the sharp drop on the right side is purely a sample-size effect. Trimming does not appreciably change the shape of this distribution, other than to eliminate the very highest MI values. This distribution is not language-specific; a nearly identical distribution is seen for Chinese Mandarin Hanzi pairs[7].

3   MST Parsing

Armed with word-pair data, one can proceed to perform Maximum Spanning Tree (MST) parsing, as described by Yuret [7]. One considers all possible planar trees connecting all of the words in a sentence, and, out of all of these trees, the one with the greatest sum-total MI of the edges is selected. A variation is the Maximum Planar Graph (MPG), which takes the above tree, and adds edges for high-MI pairs, as long as edges don't cross and the MI is above a threshold. Experience with Link Grammar (LG) suggests that MPG parses offer a significant advantage over trees. There, cycles force grammatical agreement between nearby words, which introduces a rigidness, resulting in a greater rejection of bad parses. This result should carry over to the present case, and help constrain the learned grammar.

---

[7] See "Word-Pair Distributions", page 18.

Given an MST or MPG parse, each edge is cut in half, and the half-edge is labeled with the word it used to connect to. This results in a connector sequence for each word, some connectors connecting to the left, some to the right. Every connector sequence d, or disjunct for short, is paired with a word w to form a word-disjunct pair (w, d)[8]. Parsing a large corpus this way, the counts are accumulated in the database, to give a count $N(w, d)$.

The first thing one notices is that there are vastly more disjuncts than there are words: two orders of magnitude more! This is easily explained: each disjunct is a context for a word: it resembles a skip-gram in many ways [5]. Next, one notices that the vast majority of disjuncts are observed only once. This raises the question: what is signal and what is noise? This can be explored through trimming, by removing words, disjuncts and word-disjunct pairs whenever their observation counts fail to pass a minimal threshold.

Results are summarized in the table below[9]. The column labels indicate the trimming thresholds; in the rightmost column, all words with an observation count of less than 10 were removed; all disjuncts with an observation count of less than 4, and all word-disjunct pairs with a count of less than 2. After this initial trimming, an additional consistency trim is performed, to guarantee that all remaining words can connect to some connector in some disjunct, and *vice versa*.

Trim cuts	full set	1-1-1	2-2-2	5-2-2	10-4-2
$\log_2 N_{\text{words}}$	18.526	15.542	13.644	12.889	12.249
$\log_2 N_{\text{disjuncts}}$	24.615	20.599	18.662	18.447	17.369
$\log_2 D_{\text{Tot}}$	24.761	20.967	19.247	19.086	18.443
Sparsity	18.380	15.174	13.058	12.251	11.175
Rarity	3.191	2.896	3.095	3.418	3.634
$\log_2 N_{\text{Tot}}/D_{\text{Tot}}$	0.356	2.248	3.384	3.461	3.889
Total Entropy	24.100	19.486	17.711	17.508	16.875
Left Entropy	23.494	18.346	16.417	16.163	15.379
Right Entropy	10.157	7.937	7.280	7.268	7.258
MI	9.550	6.796	5.987	5.923	5.763

Notable in this data is that even modest trimming removes the vast majority of words and disjuncts in the dataset. The total entropy and sparsity is strongly dependent on the trim; the rarity is almost a constant. It will later become apparent that heavy trimming is perhaps not a good idea: there is a considerable amount of information held in the infrequently-observed disjuncts.

---

[8] For example, parsing "*John hit the ball*" results in a (w, d) pair (hit, John- & ball+) for the verb "hit": a subject on the left, and an object on the right. Details can be found in [5].

[9] The raw data is in Diary Part Six.

Characterizing this precisely, understanding what it means remains an ongoing task.

The MI between words ad disjuncts can be computed; this forms a distribution, shown below, both for the full dataset, and for the trimmed variants[10].

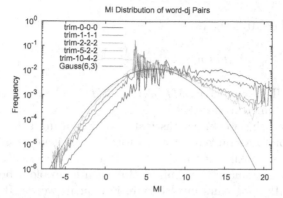

MI Distribution of word-dj Pairs

Drawn for comparison is a Gaussian, centered at an MI of 6, with a standard deviation of 3. There is no compelling reason to believe that the distribution should be a normal distribution; just that it seems not inappropriate. Compared to the Gaussian in the earlier figure for word-pairs, this one is clearly centered far away from MI=0. A certain "amplification of information" appears to have occurred.

4   Grammatically Similar Words

The machinery above brings us to the first interesting grammatical application: determining what words are grammatically similar. Each row in the above matrix is a vector; it corresponds to a word with a collection of disjuncts associated with it. Each disjunct is a context for that word: it is very much like a skip-gram, familiar from corpus linguistics. Unlike conventional skip-grams, it is determined by MST/MPG parsing, rather than simple observation frequency. This should result in much higher quality data, although this hasn't been directly demonstrated, yet. The interpretation is also different than a conventional skip-gram: the context of the word is re-interpreted as jigsaw connectors; and connectors must connect to form a valid parse of a sentence. This is very unlike conventional neural net approaches, where there is no explicit appearance of any grammar.

How should similarity be compared? Conventional approaches employ the cosine distance. Experimentally, this appears to be the worst-possible way of determining similarity[11]. Other possibilities include the Jaccard distance, and weighted variants thereof. One of these is optimal, in that it maximizes all possible similarities [3]. Any of these do quite well. Keeping with the information-theoretic theme, using the mutual information between two vectors seems appropriate. This needs to be defined afresh, as it is not simply a restatement of that

---

[10] An earlier version of this graph, for a different dataset, can be found in "Connector Set Distributions" (2018) page 22.

[11] See Diary Part Two, pages 55–74.

given above. Let the joint probability $p(w, d)$ of a word-disjunct pair (w, d) be as before: $p(w, d) = N(w, d) / N(*, *)$. Define a vector inner product of two words w, v as

$$i(w, v) = \sum_d p(w, d) p(v, d)$$

The corresponding MI is then

$$MI(w, v) = \log_2 \frac{i(w, v) i(*, *)}{i(w, *) i(v, *)}$$

Note that this MI is symmetric: $MI(w, v) = MI(v, w)$, which follows from the symmetry of the inner product.

How well does this work? Fantastically well; creating a list of the top-100 most similar words, as ranked by MI, provides excellent results, excellent in the sense that just looking at the list it is clear that they really are synonyms, or are obviously grammatically similar. But then a problem becomes evident: all of the high-MI word pairs involve rare, infrequent words. If one is to build a syntactical lexis, one really wants to begin by looking at common, frequent words. A weighting that brings frequent words to the forefront is desirable.

Such a weighting is given by the "variation of information". The variation of information is given by

$$VI(w, v) = \log_2 \frac{i(w, v)}{\sqrt{i(w, *) i(v, *)}}$$

There are also other possibilities, which look even more promising; the above, however, is the cheapest and easiest to compute[12].

The graph below shows the distribution of MI similarities for the top-ranked (most frequent) 1200 words[13]. In principle, there are $N(N+1)/2 = 720600$ such pairs. In practice, 386380 pairs are observed; the remaining pairs have no overlap! (and thus a $-\infty$ for the MI.)

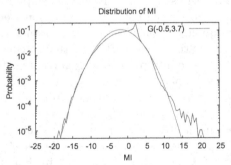

The curve marked G is a Gaussian, with the indicated mean and standard deviation. The negative mean MI is just saying that most words are *not* similar to one-another (duh.) The graph for the VI is nearly identical, having the same deviation, but with the mean shifted to 1.5.

---

[12] See Diary Part Five.

[13] See Diary Part Three, page 14; see also Diary Part Five.

5   Clustering

How well does this work? Some of the top-most similar groups of words are shown in the table below[14].

Top-ranked Clusters		
+ — "" _	? . !	must would
, ;	He It I There	he she
was is	of in to from	are were
but and that as	has was is had could	might should will may

The clusters above are sets of words, all of which have a high pairwise-VI amongst one-another. Most of these are obvious. The cluster of capitalized words is perhaps surprising: but these are all sentence-starters: they are similar because they all start occur first, and start similar sentences. (Recall, the corpus is adventure literature, with a lot of dialog in it.)

To get adequate word-sense disambiguation (WSD), one must be more sophisticated in clustering. A cluster should include only those disjuncts which are shared by the majority, excluding those that are not. An example of this is the word "saw", which can be the past tense of "to see", or a cutting implement. In forming a cluster with other viewing (or listening) verbs, one wishes to accept only the disjuncts pertinent to viewing/listening. Excluding the others leaves behind the disjuncts for cutting tools. Thus WSD is accomplished.

This can be accomplished with "exclusive club - common-interests" membership[15]. Starting with the pair of words having the highest possible VI, one searches for additional words having a high VI to these two. These form the candidate members to the club. Candidates are accepted if they pass a threshold. It is useful to have a reasonably large club, which can be expanded by gradually lowering the threshold. As it is lowered, the candidate list increases, until suddenly it explodes. The exclusive club is no longer exclusive, but is inviting everyone to join. The graph below shows the size of the candidate list, as the barrier to entry is lowered. The listed word pairs are the initial seed-words for forming a cluster.

---

[14] See Diary Part Five.
[15] See Diary Part Four, pages 13–25.

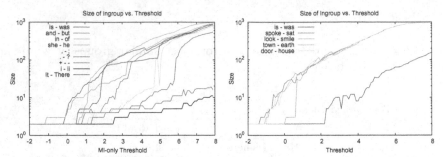

On the left, all of the seed-pairs are made of very frequent words. Does this pattern continue to hold for infrequent words? It appears to, as the graph on the right shows.

The above only provides a list of candidate members. Setting a high threshold keeps the candidate list small. But which words, exactly, should be admitted to the club? This can be determined by seeing what disjuncts the words share in common. For a given candidate list, one simply counts the fraction of all disjuncts that the words have in common (think of these as common interests in a social club). Next, consider ejecting one of the candidates; does the fraction of shared disjuncts increase, or not? If it increases, then the ejected candidate should be thrown out of the club. If it decreases, then that candidate should be kept in.

In forming the group, only those disjuncts that the group members have in common are kept as part of the group; the other, non-shared disjuncts presumably belong to other word-senses. This algorithm performs word-sense disambiguation. If one includes disjuncts shared by a majority, then this algorithm also performs generalization: it moves from particulars to generalities. Some words may have been seen in some contexts; others in different, but generally similar contexts. In admitting these disjuncts into the common group, all of the group members gain the ability to engage in these contexts, thus generalizing. The majority need not be a strict 50% majority; it can be a plurality, set at any threshold. This can be understood as the Jaccard index for the group.

To summarize, high MI (or high VI) just indicates general similarity between words. The actual list of shared disjuncts is computed with a Jaccard index. It is this set of shared disjuncts that determine the grammatical behavior of the group.

6   Conclusion

A collection of research results were described. Research is ongoing. An immediate next step is to evaluate the quality of the resulting grammars. The most important next step is to climb up the hierarchy: to repeat the process, but now looking at multi-sentence, paragraph, and corpus-wide correlations, with the intent of identifying entities and their properties. Equally important, yet equally daunting, is to apply these techniques to vision, sound or other kinds of information streams. The primary limitation to further research is the development of the tools, the software and infrastructure needed to carry out these experiments. Based on the current results, the future looks extremely promising.

References

1. Kahane, S.: The meaning-text theory. Dependency and valency. Int. Handb. Contem. Res. **1**, 546–570 (2003). www.coli.uni-saarland.de/courses/syntactic-theory-09/literature/MTT-Handbook2003.pdf
2. Mihalcea, R., Tarau, P., Figa, E.: Pagerank on semantic networks, with application to word sense disambiguation. In: COLING 2004, p. 1126. ACL (2004). https://doi.org/10.3115/1220355.1220517,http://web.eecs.umich.edu/~mihalcea/papers/mihalcea.coling04.pdf
3. Moulton, R., Jiang, Y.: Maximally consistent sampling and the Jaccard index of probability distributions. In: International Conference on Data Mining, Workshop on High Dimensional Data Mining, pp. 347–356 (2018). https://doi.org/10.1109/ICDM.2018.00050, http://arxiv.org/abs/1809.04052
4. Sleator, D., Temperley, D.: Parsing English with a link grammar. Technical report, Carnegie Mellon University Computer Science technical report CMU-CS-91-196 (1991). http://arxiv.org/pdf/cmp-lg/9508004
5. Vepstas, L.: Gradient decent vs. graphical models (2018). https://github.com/opencog/learn/learn-lang-diary/skippy.pdf
6. Vepstas, L.: Purely symbolic induction of structure (2022). https://github.com/opencog/learn/raw/master/learn-lang-diary/agi-2022/grammar-induction.pdf. submitted for publication, AGI-2022
7. Yuret, D.: Discovery of linguistic relations using lexical attraction. Ph.D thesis, MIT (1998). https://doi.org/10.48550/arXiv.cmp-lg/9805009, www2.denizyuret.com/pub/yuretphd.html

Brain Principles Programming

Evgenii Vityaev[1,2](✉) (iD), Anton Kolonin[2] (iD), Andrey Kurpatov[3],
and Artem Molchanov[3] (iD)

[1] Sobolev Institute of Mathematics, Koptuga 4, Novosibirsk, Russia
vityaev@math.nsc.ru
[2] Novosibirsk State University, Pirogova 2, Novosibirsk, Russia
[3] Sberbank of Russia, Neuroscience Lab, Moscow, Russia

Abstract. The monograph "Strong Artificial Intelligence. On the Approaches to Superintelligence", referenced by this paper, provides a cross-disciplinary review of Artificial General Intelligence (AGI). As an anthropomorphic direction of research, it considers Brain Principles Programming (BPP) – the formalization of universal mechanisms (principles) of the brain's work with information, which are implemented at all levels of the organization of nervous tissue. This monograph provides a formalization of these principles in terms of the category theory. However, this formalization is not enough to develop algorithms for working with this information. In the paper, for the description and modeling of BPP, it is proposed to apply mathematical models and algorithms developed by us earlier that model cognitive functions, which are based on well-known physiological, psychological and other natural science theories. The paper uses mathematical models and algorithms of the following theories: P.K.Anokhin's Theory of Functional Brain Systems, Eleonor Rosh's prototypical categorization theory, Bob Rehter's theory of causal models and "natural" classification. As a result, the formalization of the BPP is obtained and computer examples are given that demonstrate the algorithm's operation.

Keywords: Brain principles · Categorization · Category theory · Formal concepts

1 Introduction

In the monograph "Strong Artificial Intelligence. On the approaches to superintelligence" [1] the first cross-disciplinary guide on Artificial General Intelligence (AGI) is given: "General artificial intelligence is the next step in the development of AI, not necessarily endowed with self-awareness, but, unlike modern neural networks, capable of coping with a wide range of tasks in different conditions." As an anthropomorphic direction of research, it considers Brain Principles Programming (BPP) – the formalization of universal mechanisms (principles) of the brain's work with information, which are implemented at all levels of the organization of nervous tissue. The book provides a formalization of these principles in terms of category theory. However, algorithms for working with information do not follow from this formalization.

B. Goertzel et al. (Eds.): AGI 2022, LNAI 13539, pp. 424–433, 2023.
https://doi.org/10.1007/978-3-031-19907-3_41

In this paper, we apply mathematical models and algorithms developed by us earlier that modeling cognitive functions and based on the well-known physiological, psychological and natural science theories, to model Brain Principles Programming. We will rely on the following theories: P.K.Anokhin's Theory of Functional Brain Systems [2, 3], Eleonor Rosh's prototypical categorization theory [4, 5], Bob Rehter's theory of causal models [6, 7] and works on "natural" classification [8].

2 Part I. Basic Theories and Formal Models

2.1 Basic Elements of Perception and the World

"Natural" Classification. The first philosophical analysis of the "natural" classification belongs to J.S. Mill [9]: "artificial" classifications differ from "natural" in that they can be based on ... Features, so that different classes differ in that they include objects with different meanings of these features. But if we consider the classes of "animals" or "plants", then they differ in such a large (potentially infinite) number of properties that they cannot be enumerated. And all these properties will be based on statements confirming this difference".

J.S. Mill's analysis has been confirmed by naturalists. L. Rutkovsky writes about the similarity of properties in "natural" classes [10]: "The more essential features of the compared objects are similar, the more likely their similarity is in other features." Smirnov E.S. [11]: "The taxonomic problem lies in the "indication": from an infinitely many number of features, we need to move to a limited number of them, which would replace all other features". From studies on "natural" classification, it follows that features in "natural" classes are strongly correlated, since a potentially infinite number of features are almost uniquely determined follow L. Rutkovsky from the indicator features. A formal model of "natural" classification is given in [6].

"Natural" Concepts and Prototypical Theory of Categorization. The high correlation of features for "natural" classes has been confirmed in cognitive studies. In the works of Eleanor Rosch [4, 5], the following principle of categorization of "natural" categories was formulated, confirming the statements of J.S. Mill and naturalists: "Perceived World Structure: ... perceived world – is not an unstructured total set of equiprobable co-occurring attributes. Rather, the material objects of the world are perceived to possess... *High correlational structure* (emphasis added by EV). ... In short, combinations of what we perceive as the attributes of real objects do not occur uniformly. Some pairs, triples, etc., are quite probable, appearing in combination sometimes with one, sometimes another attribute; others are rare; others logically cannot or empirically do not occur». Therefore, directly perceived objects (so called basic objects) are information–rich bundles of observable and functional properties that form a natural discontinuity that creates categorization. These bundles form "prototypes" of class objects.Further Eleanor Rosch's theory of "natural" concepts was called the prototypical theory of concepts (prototype theory).

The Theory of Causal Models. Studies have shown that people's knowledge of categories is not reduced to the set of features, but includes a rich set of causal relationships between these features. In some experiments [7] it was shown that a feature is more important if it is more strongly included in the causal network of interrelations of features. Considering these studies, Bob Rehder put forward the theory of causal models (causal-model theory), according to which the relation of an object to a category is no longer based on a set of features and proximity by features, but on the basis of similarity of the generative causal mechanism [7]. In [8] Bayesian networks were used to represent causal knowledge. However, they cannot model cyclic causal relationships because Bayesian networks do not support cycles. The probabilistic formal concepts, that developed earlier and presented in the supplement of work [12], model cyclic causal relationships by fixed points of causal relationships predictions.

2.2 Probabilistic Formal Concepts

We assume that "natural" classification and "natural" concepts are described by the same formalism. From our point of view, the information processes of the brain were tuned in the process of evolution to extract a highly correlated structure of features of "natural" objects by forming "natural" concepts of these objects. Causal relationships in the perception of "natural" objects close on themselves forming a certain "resonance". At the same time, "resonance" occurs if and only if these causal relationships reflect some holistic "natural" object. The resulting cycles of inferences on causal relationships are mathematically described by "fixed points" of mutually interconnected features, which gives an "image" or "prototype" of objects class. Therefore, the brain perceives a "natural" object not as a set of features, but as a "resonating" system of causal relationships that forms a causal model.

The formalization of cyclic causal relationships in the form of probabilistic formal concepts is given in the supplement of the work [12]. There is also a definition of causality in the form of the Most Specific Causal Relationships (MSCR) that solve the problem of statistical ambiguity (see references in the supplement). There is also an example of the probabilistic formal concepts discovery.

Probabilistic formal concepts can be used to context (latin contextus – cohesion, coherence, connection) detection as systems of interrelated concepts in a certain situation, discourse, a certain point of view, etc. In addition, in supplement, an example of the context detection is given on the example of the social networks analysis.

The definition of probabilistic formal concepts and the proof of its properties is carried out under the assumption that a probabilistic measure is known. In practical tasks, we cannot assume this. Therefore, it is necessary to use a statistical criterion to detect MSCR on data. For that a Fisher 's independence exact criterion with some level of significance α was used. Then we can got a set $\mathcal{R}_\alpha$ of statistical approximations of MSCR detected on data with a confidence level α. They can cause contradictions in fixed points of probabilistic formal concepts. Therefore, it is necessary to introduce a criterion of approximations $\mathcal{R}_\alpha$ consistency in predictions on some data A. As a result we can discover a fixed points by consistently applying the prediction operator $\Upsilon(A)$ to data A, taking into account the consistency of predictions. The operator $\Upsilon(A)$ adds some new element to the set A if it is predicted by some approximation from $\mathcal{R}_\alpha$ based on data A and it is not contradict to the predictions of others by approximations in such a way that the consistency criterion strictly increases. Either the operator $\Upsilon(A)$ removes some element from A if there are approximations that predicting its negation and also in such a way that the consistency criterion again strictly increases. When the operator can no longer add a certain element to A, or remove an element in such a way that the operator strictly increases, we get a fixed point, which is denoted as $\Upsilon^{\infty}(A)$. A detailed description of this process is given in supplement of the work [12].

2.3 "Intelligent Object" and "Intelligent Function"

The formalization of "Brain Principles Programming, (BPP)" described in [1] is based on the category theory and the concepts of "intellectual object" and "intellectual function" formulated in it. Here is an informal definition of "intellectual object" and "intellectual function" from [1]:

- "intellectual object", by which we mean any single integrity that we distinguish in this space – for example, when we see a table, signals from the optic nerve are processed by the brain, and the combination of individual lines is recognized as a table;
- the "intellectual function", which describes all possible operations in the system under consideration, is all that the psyche can do with an intellectual object. When we identify a table as an object, we can estimate its size or figure out how to use it;
- "essence" is the specific meaning of an object for the psyche. That is, the knowledge of what the table can be used for.

Formally, an "intelligent object" is defined as a mapping [1]:

- some data set (A);
- the observer as a reflection of the world after interacting with it (Ω);
- the relation of the world to the observer, which is a function of the internal state/ expectation (f) – an intellectual function $A \xrightarrow{f} \Omega$.

Here A is a data set that characterizes any unit wholeness;

Ω – distinguishing ability: "the relationship of an intellectual object with "me" does not yet mean any awareness, representation of this intellectual object in consciousness – it is enough for something to be somehow perceived and recognized to a degree sufficient for this "something" to be taken into account in the future in one way or another... Since the main task of thinking... is to predict or produce a competitive future, then how the perceived object will eventually appear to us will depend on our mood, or, as phenomenologists would say, on our intentionality" [13]. More formally, "Some requirements will be imposed on the object Ω modeling the distinguishing ability, thus: first of all, it should be a partially ordered set, the elements of which correspond to "more" or "less" high values" [13].

Next, the waiting function $Exp_A : A \times A \rightarrow \Omega$ is defined (expectation) and the following explanations of this function are given: "at all levels of perception... we are essentially dealing with a situation, with some expected state of affairs... *Our psyche irresistibly tends to put the whole set of stimuli into a kind of understandable, clear and seemingly consistent picture of reality* (cursive 1 – E.V.)... These representations of reality, in turn, are a specific filter-interpreter – any new stimuli, finding themselves, figuratively speaking, in the field of gravity of the corresponding system of representations, inevitably seem to change their trajectory – some are repelled (ignored), others, complementary, on the contrary, are attracted, others are modified (interpreted) in favor of the prevailing attitudes (cursive 2 – E.V.)... As a result, with respect to any element x that is part of the intellectual object A, it is meaningful to say how different it is, firstly, from itself in the sense of what we expect to see in its place, and, secondly, how appropriate it is in the situation in general, i.e. how close it is to the rest of the elements distinguished in the situation."

More formally [13], the expectation function $Exp_A : A \times A \to \Omega$ assigns to each pair of elements $x, y \in A$ a measure of their consistency (coherence) on our existential partially-ordered scale Ω. At the same time, the measure of the object's $x \in A$ consistency with itself $Exp_A(x, x)$ can be understood as a measure of the proximity of x to its essence... And denoted as $Ess_A(x)$ (essence). If we consider the prototype of class objects as an "invariant" of class objects, then the fixed point of the operator $\Upsilon^\infty(X(y))$ obtained on the set of properties $X(y) = \{P_1 \& ... \& P_m\}$ of some element $y \in A$ will differ from the attributes $X(y)$ of the element itself exactly as a measure of the object's consistency with itself. Therefore, the operator Υ^∞ gives a certain measure of the proximity of the object to its essence (invariant).

The waiting function allows to define the intelligent object more fully [13]. By an intelligent object we will understand... an object $\mathcal{A} := (A, Exp_A)$ that includes a set of data A and an expectation function $Exp_A : A \times A \to \Omega$ that essentially depends on the subject experience Ω and its internal state.

The structure of an intelligent object described in cursive 1 above actually means that an intelligent object is a context, represented by a probabilistic formal concept, in which an operator Υ^∞ having the same meaning – minimizing contradictions in a set of stimuli – generates the most consistent picture of reality from the input set of stimuli A, supplementing it with all relevant information. At the same time (see cursive 2), new stimuli either change their trajectory, or repel, or attract. All these effects, which are taken into account in the expectation function $Exp_A : A \times A \to \Omega$, are modeled by the interaction of probabilistic formal concepts of elements of the set A. A change in the trajectory is the features moving closer to the prototype, repulsion is the braking of features, which is described in the supplement of the work [12], and attraction is mutual support at a fixed point.

Intelligent Function. The work of the intellectual function is not only to recreate the intellectual objects associated with the data elements A and the set A itself, but also to connect these intellectual objects with all other intellectual objects that exist in the psyche and are relevant to a given situation, for example, to a need or some task (goal). The result of the work of the intellectual function is the creation of a "heavy intellectual object" by "enlarging the knowledge we have, which we believe relates to some problem that interests us" [13]. Thus, an intellectual object "is, as it were, raised to the degree of the knowledge (intellectual objects) that we possess, and acquires an appropriate meaning for us" [13].

Raising of some intellectual object "to the degree" of knowledge is formally represented as a relation: "If (this) relation is thought of as a certain kind of directional connec-
tion, then it seems quite natural to designate intellectual objects with letters $\mathcal{A}, \mathcal{B}, \mathcal{C}...$,
and the relations between them with arrows... $r : \mathcal{A} \rightarrow \mathcal{B}$" [13]. In addition, this relation
"must respect those differences and identifications that were posited by the expectation
function $Exp_A : A \times A \rightarrow \Omega$" and satisfy the following conditions:

$$\forall a, b \in A(Ess_B(r(a)) \leq Ess_A(a)),\ Exp_A(a, b) \leq Exp_B(r(a), r(b)).$$

All arrows of the ratio r, showing the path of enrichment of the intellectual object,
form a "cone". The limit of the enrichment diagram is the cone generated by the "heavy"
object contained in all other cones. The operator $\Upsilon^\infty(A)$ automatically forms a context
generated by elements A of some intellectual object and probabilistic formal concepts of
its elements, since for all causal relationships linking elements A with other knowledge
available in the psyche, the predicted elements of the psyche will automatically be
included in the context by these causal relationships.

3   Part II. Brain Principles Programming Formalization

3.1   The Principle of the Complexity Generation

The principle of the complexity generation in [1, p. 217] is formulated as follows:
"The brain works with a very limited amount of information from the surrounding
reality coming to its sensors ... As this initially scarce information is used, the brain,
at all levels of its organization, repeatedly increases its volume, correlating the received
introductory data with the data already existing in it... The principle of complexity
generation allows the brain, having received the smallest external signal, to reproduce
knowledge (an intellectual object) with incomparably greater power in the human mind,
enriching the model of this object with information, which is relevant for the brain
within the framework of its tasks (its goals)." This complexity generation is performed
by the intellectual function introduced earlier in [1, p. 214], which "seems to be raised
to the degree of the knowledge (intellectual objects) that we possess, and acquires an
appropriate meaning for us".

The formalization of the "intellectual object" and "intellectual function" by
probabilistic formal concepts gives us the following models of complexity generation:

1. If we consider the features of digits (see Fig. 2 in supplement of the work [12]) as
    features perceived by the primary visual cortex, and the set A as a set of perceived
    digits, then the set of probabilistic formal concepts that have been discovered for
    these digits generates a set of intellectual objects $\mathcal{A}_0 := (0, Exp_0), \mathcal{A}_1 := (1, Exp_1),$
    ..., $\mathcal{A}_9 := (9, Exp_9)$ – "invariants" of these digits. They are examples of generated
    complexity based on the simplest features (see description in supplement of work
    [12]).
2. The formation of contexts as probabilistic formal concepts, which generates a
    typology of social network users (see description in the supplement of the work
    [12]).

3. In general, when a certain task or a certain goal is set, the generation of complexity by the corresponding intellectual function will consist in generation of the context according to the given initial conditions A by "raising them to the degree" of the knowledge that is directly related to them. Formally, this generation is a probabilistic formal concept generated by operator $\Upsilon(A)^\infty$, using all the knowledge related to the task or goal, represented by a set of MSCR approximations $\mathcal{R}_\alpha$.

3.2 The Principle of the Relationship

In psychology, this principle was originally called the Gestalt principle. The brain reacts not to a specific stimulus, but to what this stimulus becomes when corresponding with the information that is already contained in the brain [1]. "The evaluation of information arising in the brain... is carried out exclusively through the act of correlating one information with another, and the brain itself reacts not to the object of reality as such, but to how it correlates with other information located in the brain" [1].

Gestalt psychology puts forward the principle of integrity as the main explanatory principle. "The integrity of perception is a property of perception, consisting in the fact that every object, and even more a spatial objective situation, is perceived as a *stable systemic whole*, even if some parts of it cannot be observed at the moment (for example, the back of a thing)" (Wikipedia). The integrity of perception, which is formed in the process of perception of a "natural" concept or prototype of a class, as well as the context of a certain task, is formally expressed in a probabilistic formal concept by cyclic mutual prediction of features of the concept or elements of the context. Therefore, the probabilistic formal concepts form the very "stable system whole" that characterizes integrity.

Therefore, formally, the operator $\Upsilon(A)^\infty$ is just the "stable system whole" in which, not individual elements of A are perceived, but their inseparable relationship with the rest of the fixed point $\Upsilon(A)^\infty$ elements.

3.3 The Principle of Approximation to the Essence

The principle of approximation described in [1] as follows: "... in reality, there are no absolutely identical objects, so the brain performs approximation, that is, ignores differences if it manages to assign one or another "essence" to an object by specific features. At the same time, "essence" means the functionality of an object – what meaning it has for the brain (what role it performs) within the framework of the tasks it solves (its goals)... When a person is tired and wants to rest – in the forest, a stump can serve as a chair, since you can sit on it".

The formation of "entities" occurs in the context of tasks being solved. Every context clarifies and correlates the elements of the context with a system of mutually predicted properties by causal relationships. This leads to the formation of "essences" associated with the context. For example, a knife in different contexts: cooking, combat situations, office work and hiking conditions should have different properties arising from the context: for a kitchen knife, the relationship of width, weight and blade edge is important, for a combat knife – the ratio of tip, length, weight and width, for a stationery knife – small weight, length and safety, for a penknife – relative smallness of size. Therefore, "essences" of "kitchen knife", "combat knife", "stationery knife", "penknife" will automatically generate probabilistic formal concepts, since features and fix-points of their interrelation are different.

The functional, which has a certain meaning for the brain within the framework of the tasks and goals it solves, will in a certain way affect the totality of the properties of the object, which, mutually assuming each other, and hence automatically form the corresponding probabilistic formal concept corresponding to its functional "essence".

Therefore, "essence" is a probabilistic formal concept $\Upsilon(A)^\infty$ generated by such elements A – features of the objects used, which will be selected in accordance with the context of the task being solved or the goal being achieved.

3.4   The Principle of Locality-Distribution

The principle of locality-distribution [1]: "All information entering the brain can be duplicated many times in it, and its copies are processed in parallel by different structures independently, and only then this information is integrated into a holistic image." The brain processes information about a certain object in several modalities at once and in parallel – visual, auditory, tactile, etc. In each of these modalities, a hierarchy of the simplest "natural" concepts is formed, for example, in the visual cortex, on the basis of perceived sticks, images of digits can be formed, as in the example (see supplement of the work [12]) and "secondary" features – lines, angles, circles, etc., in the auditory cortex phonemes, words, text, etc. The integration of modalities is carried out through the perception of the integrity of the object, which integrates and binds the perception of parts into a "stable system whole" by some probabilistic formal concept.

Therefore, formally, this principle is also represented by an operator $\Upsilon(A)^\infty$ generating probabilistic formal concepts, for elements of A coming in parallel from different modalities.

3.5   The Principle of Heaviness

The principle of heaviness [1]: "The number of neural connections included in the creation of the object model, the number of relationships between the elements of the continuum of intelligent objects, the amount of information introduced into the object (attributes of the entity), the number of ways to calculate information about the object and the combination of multi-channel (modality) information about it into a single whole, correlated with the relevance of the task (goal) of the system, determine the "heaviness" of the intellectual object. The "heaviness" of the intellectual object determines the decision of the system. So, for example, if a person is hungry, he will look for food that will satisfy his hunger, but if he begins to face immediate danger (for example, from a predator), then a defensive strategy will begin to prevail, and he will stop looking for food and begin to escape".

In 1911, the dominant principle was put forward by A.A. Ukhtomsky [18]. This principle has also been preserved in the theory of functional systems [2, 3], as the dominance principle of the leading functional system, which creates the most "heaviness" context for satisfaction of some need (see supplement of the work [12]).

In general, when it comes to solving a certain task, possible solutions are obtained by different ways of enriching the original intellectual object "problem statement" or goal and form the corresponding "cones" and the contexts generated by them, which in the case of functional systems, we denote by a set $\{C := (C, Exp_C)\}$. The choice of the "heaviest" of them is determined by the choice of the most desirable "heavy" solution, generated by the "heavy" object contained in all other cones.

Therefore, formally, the principle of heaviness consists in choosing the most desirable "heavy" intellectual object generated by one of the contexts that are generated by the operator $\Upsilon^\infty(A \cup C)$, depending on the statement of the task/goal $\mathcal{A} := (A, Exp_A)$ and the available experience C of solution of such a tasks/goals.

3.6 Conclusions

Algorithms for detecting probabilistic formal concepts, class prototypes, "natural" concepts and contexts are practically confirmed in the works (see supplement of the work [12]). The model of functional systems has also shown its effectiveness [14–17].

This approach can be generalized to the tasks-driven approach to the artificial general intelligence, as planned in [19–21]. This approach solves the AGI problem formulated in [1] as: "general intelligence in AGI recognizes the ability to achieve goals in a wide range of environments, taking into account limitations". Therefore, Brain Principles Programming, formulated in [1] as principles of brain programming, based on research in cognitive sciences, can be implemented as a task-based approach to AGI, which, on the one hand, is able to solve a fairly wide class of tasks, and, on the other hand, corresponds fairly accurately to models of cognitive processes.

References

1. Strong artificial intelligence. The approaches to supermind. Alexander Vedyakhin [et al.]. - M.: Intellectual Literature, 232 p. (2021). (In Russian)
2. Anokhin, P.K.: Biology and Neurophysiology of the Conditioned Reflex and its Role in Adaptive Behavior, p. 574. Pergamon press, Oxford. (1974)
3. Sudakov, K.V.: General theory of functional systems M., Medicine (1984). (In Russian)
4. Rosch, E.H.: Natural categories. Cogn. Psychol. **4**, 328–350 (1973)
5. Rosch, E.: Principles of categorization. Rosch, E., Lloyd, B.B. (eds.) Cognition and Categorization, Lawrence Erlbaum Associates, Publishers, (Hillsdale), pp. 27–48 (1978)
6. Rehder, B.: Categorization as causal reasoning. Cogn. Sci. **27**, 709–748 (2003)
7. Bob Rehder, J.B.M.: Towards a generative model of causal cycles. In: 33rd Annual Meeting of the Cognitive Science Society 2011, (CogSci 2011), Boston, Massachusetts, USA, 20–23 July 2011, vol. 1, pp. 2944–2949 (2011)
8. Vityaev, E.E., Martynovich, V.V.: Formalization of "natural" classification and systematics by fixed points of predictions. Siberian Electron. Math. News **12**, 1006–1031 (2015). (In Russian)
9. Mill, J.S.: System of Logic, Ratiocinative and Inductive. L (1983)
10. Rutkovsky, L.: Elementary Textbook of Logic. St. Petersburg (1884). (In Russian)
11. Smirnov, E.S.: The construction of a type from the taxonomic point of view. Zool J. **17**(3), 387–418 (1938). (In Russian)

12. Vityaev, E., Kolonin, A., Molchanov, A.: Brain principles programming (2022). arXiv:2202. 12710 [q-bio.NC]
13. Egorychev, I.E.: Categorical analysis of the text "methodology of thinking" In: Kurpatov, A.V. (ed.) in the context of promising developments of AGI. Scientific opinion no. 7–8 (2020). (In Russian)
14. Vityaev, E.E.: The logic of the brain. In: Redko, V.G. (ed.) Approaches to modeling thinking. URSS Editorial, Moscow, pp. 120–153 (2014). (In Russian)
15. Vityaev, E.E.: Purposefulness as a principle of brain activity. In: Nadin, M. (ed.) Anticipation: Learning from the Past. CSM, vol. 25, pp. 231–254. Springer, Cham (2015). https://doi.org/ 10.1007/978-3-319-19446-2_13
16. Demin, A.V., Vityaev, E.E.: Learning in a virtual model of the C. elegans nematode for locomotion and chemotaxis. Biologically Inspired Cogn. Architectures **7**, 9–14 (2014)
17. Demin, A.V., Vityaev, E.E.: Adaptive control of modular robots. In: Samsonovich, A.V., Klimov, V.V. (eds.) BICA 2017. AISC, vol. 636, pp. 204–212. Springer, Cham (2018). https:// doi.org/10.1007/978-3-319-63940-6_29
18. Ukhtomsky, A.A.: Dominant. Articles of different years. 1887–1939. St. Petersburg.: Peter, 448 p. (2002) (In Russian)
19. Goncharov, S.S., Sviridenko, D.I., Vityaev, E.E.: Task approach to artificial intelligence. In: Proceedings of the Workshop on Applied Mathematics and Fundamental Computer Science 2020 (AMFCS 2020), Omsk, Russia, 23–30 April 2020. CEUR Workshop Proceedings, vol. 2642, pp. 1–6 (2020)
20. Vityaev, E.E., Goncharov, S.S., Sviridenko, D.I.: On the task approach in artificial intelligence. Siberian J. Philos. **17**(4), 5–25 (2019). (In Russian)
21. Vityaev, E.E., Goncharov, S.S., Sviridenko, D.I.: On the task approach in artificial intelligence and cognitive sciences. Siberian J. Philos. **18**(2), 5–29 (2020). (In Russian)

A Meta-Probabilistic-Programming Language for Bisimulation of Probabilistic and Non-Well-Founded Type Systems

Jonathan Warrell[1,2]([✉]), Alexey Potapov[2], Adam Vandervorst[2], and Ben Goertzel[2]

[1] Yale University, New Haven, USA
[2] SingularityNET, Amsterdam, The Netherlands
jonathan.warrell@singularitynet.io

Abstract. We introduce a formal meta-language for probabilistic programming, capable of expressing both programs and the type systems in which they are embedded. We are motivated here by the desire to allow an AGI to learn not only relevant knowledge (programs/proofs), but also appropriate ways of reasoning (logics/type systems). We draw on the frameworks of cubical type theory and dependent typed metagraphs to formalize our approach. In doing so, we show that specific constructions within the meta-language can be related via bisimulation (implying path equivalence) to the type systems they correspond. This allows our approach to provide a convenient means of deriving synthetic denotational semantics for various type systems. Particularly, we derive bisimulations for pure type systems (PTS), and probabilistic dependent type systems (PDTS). We discuss further the relationship of PTS to non-well-founded set theory, and demonstrate the feasibility of our approach with an implementation of a bisimulation proof in a Guarded Cubical Type Theory type checker.

1 Introduction

Probabilistic programming offers a fertile ground between logic-based and machine-learning-based approaches to A(G)I. Formalization within type theory offers a rigorous approach to deriving semantics for probabilistic languages [15], and formalization of dependently typed probabilistic languages offers the promise of drawing a tight connection with probabilistic logics of various kinds (e.g. Markov Logic [19], Probabilistic Paraconsistent Logic [7]).

While the exploration of such individual systems is highly important, we might consider more abstractly how to embody general principles for the formation of diverse probabilistic type systems, logics, and programming languages within a single meta-language. Such a language can be considered a meta-theoretical language or logical framework for expressing individual type systems and logics. However, previous frameworks (such as [9]) have not been designed with probabilistic type systems and logics specifically in mind. Here, we outline a formal language, $\mathbb{M}$, designed for such a purpose. This language is intended as a formal model of the MeTTa language, currently being developed as part of the OpenCog project [8,14,16]. The language allows for (probabilistic) reasoning not only about the knowledge embedded in a system, but also about the logic employed by the system itself.

B. Goertzel et al. (Eds.): AGI 2022, LNAI 13539, pp. 434–451, 2023.
https://doi.org/10.1007/978-3-031-19907-3_42

Our approach may also be seen in relation to recent methods to derive synthetic denotational semantics for logical systems using guarded cubical type theory (GCTT) [11, 13, 18]. Such approaches are particularly promising, offering as they do a unified approach to deriving semantics for recursive datatypes as final co-algebras of appropriate functors in the context of a formulation of univalent type theory with a fully computational semantics. We draw on methods from [10] to formalize our approach in this context. This allows us to rigorously define the relationship between an object-language and its expression in our meta-language as one of bisimulation, corresponding to path equivalence in GCTT. We further show how dependently typed metagraphs can be formalized in GCTT as the basis for our framework [6, 12], and how this leads to systems embedding natural type-theoretic equivalents of non-well-founded sets.

We begin by developing a general framework for representing metagraphs in GCTT, before outlining how the final co-algebra of a labeled transition system over this recursive datatype can be used to model our meta-language. We then derive bisimulations for various object-languages in our system, including simply typed (and untyped) lambda calulus, pure type systems, and probabilistic dependent type systems, hence deriving synthetic denotational semantics for these systems. Finally, we demonstrate the feasibility of our approach with an implementation of a bisimulation proof for a small-scale type system in a Guarded Cubical Type Theory type checker [4], before concluding with a discussion.

2   Labeled Metagraphs as a Guarded Recursive Datatype

We begin by defining a recursive datatype for typed metagraphs ($\mathcal{M}_{(T,\mathcal{L},\preceq_T)}$) using guarded cubical type theory. Here, $T, \mathcal{L}$ are types of type-symbols and edge labels respectively, and $\preceq_T : T \times T \to \mathbb{B}$ is a partial order on type-symbols. The recursive datatype is defined as the final co-algebra of the functor $\mathcal{M}'_{(T,\mathcal{L},\preceq_T)}(A)$, which when applied to type A returns the following datatype (letting Δ stand for the assumptions $\mathcal{L}, T, A : \mathcal{U}_0$; the ϵ, edge, and connect constructors used here follow the approach of [12] and [6]):

$$\frac{\Gamma \vdash \Delta}{\Gamma \vdash \mathcal{M}'_{(T,\mathcal{L})}(A)}$$

$$\frac{\Gamma \vdash \Delta}{\Gamma \vdash \epsilon : \mathcal{M}'_{(T,\mathcal{L})}(A)}$$

$$\frac{\Gamma \vdash \Delta, n : \mathbb{N}, t_0 : T, t : \mathrm{Vec}(n, T), l_0 : \mathcal{L}}{\Gamma \vdash \mathrm{edge}(n, t_0, l_0, t) : \mathcal{M}'_{(T,\mathcal{L})}(A)}$$

$$\frac{\Gamma \vdash \Delta, a_1, a_2 : A, t_0 : T, l_0 : \mathcal{L}, q : \mathbb{N} \to \mathbb{N}_{0,\infty}}{\Gamma \vdash \mathrm{connect}(a_1, a_2, t_0, l_0, q) : \mathcal{M}'_{(T,\mathcal{L})}(A)}$$

$$(1)$$

where $\text{Vec}(n, A)$ is the type of vectors over A of length n, and $\mathbb{N}_{0,\infty}$ is $\mathbb{N}$ extended with 0 and ∞. We note that for notational convenience, we do not explicitly include target labels/indices in the definition of $\mathcal{M}'_{(\mathcal{T},\mathcal{L})}(A)$ above (in contrast to [6], where $\mathcal{L}$ refers to target indices and $\mathcal{V}$ is used for edge values). If explicit indices are required to identify target 'levels', these may be included by letting $\mathcal{L} = \mathcal{L}_0 \times \sum_n \text{Vec}(n, \mathbb{N})$, so that each edge label is paired with a vector of target indices. $\mathcal{M}_{(\mathcal{T},\mathcal{L},\preceq_T)}$ is then defined as a final fixed-point of $\mathcal{M}'_{(\mathcal{T},\mathcal{L})}$, such that a set of constraints are satisfied:

$$\mathcal{M}_{(\mathcal{T},\mathcal{L},\preceq_T)} = \sum M : \nu(\mathcal{M}'_{(\mathcal{T},\mathcal{L})}).C(M, \preceq_T) \tag{2}$$

where $C(M, \preceq_T)$ represents the constraints:

$$C(M, \preceq_T) = \forall n_1, n_2 : \mathbb{N}, t_1, t_2 : \mathcal{T}$$
$$f(M, n_1) = t_1 \wedge$$
$$f(M, n_2) = t_2 \wedge$$
$$q'_M(n_1) = n_2 \Rightarrow t_1 \preceq_T t_2 \tag{3}$$

Here, $f(M, n)$ represents a function, which for metagraph M returns the type of its n'th edge or target. Specifically, when M is of the form $\text{edge}(n, t_0, l_0, t)$, $f(M, 0)$ is the type of the edge, and $f(M, n > 0)$ is the type of the n'th target, and when M is of the form $\text{connect}(a_1, a_2, t_0, l_0, q)$, $f(M, 0)$ is the type of the whole metagraph, while the types of the edges/targets of a_1 and a_2 are interleaved when evaluating $f(M, n > 0)$ for odd/even values of n respectively. Further, the function $q'_M : \mathbb{N} \rightarrow \mathbb{N}_{0,\infty}$ is recursively defined on $\nu(\mathcal{M}'_{(\mathcal{T},\mathcal{L})})$ (via the q function in the connect constructor of Eq. 1) to indicate that the n_1'th target of M is connected to the n_2'th edge/target of M, whenever $q(n_1) = n_2$, with $n_2 = \infty$ indicating that the target has no connection. $C(M, \preceq_T)$ thus provides a set of constraints that ensure the connections in a metagraph respect the $\preceq_T$ relation; further constraints are needed to ensure for instance that targets receive input from only one other target (as may be appropriate for some metagraphs). Further, $\nu = \text{fix}X.F(\triangleright(\alpha : \mathbb{T}).X[\alpha]))$ is the guarded fixed-point operator [10]. By [10], Prop. 3.2, $\mathcal{M}_{(\mathcal{T},\mathcal{L},\preceq_T)}$ is both a subset of the initial algebra and final coalgebra of $\mathcal{M}'_{(\mathcal{T},\mathcal{L})} \circ \triangleright$. Finally, we note that our connect constructor corresponds to Connect_Q in [6], and the Union constructor is simply connect with $q(n) = \infty$ for all n (meaning that no new connections are added).

We briefly give some examples of typed metagraphs. For convenience, we set $\mathcal{L} = \{\text{null}\}$, and $\mathcal{T} = \{A, B, C, D, \top\}$, with $\preceq_T$ the identity relation along with $t \preceq_T \top$ for all t. In our first example, we can construct metagraphs $X = \text{edge}(3, A, \text{null}, [D, B, C])$, and $Y = \text{edge}(2, B, \text{null}, [D, A])$. Then, a combined graph can be constructed as $Z' = \text{connect}(X, Y, \top, \text{null}, \{(1, 1), (2, 0)\})$, $Z'' = \text{connect}(Y, X, \top, \text{null}, \{(1, 1), (2, 0)\})$, $Z''' = \text{connect}(Z', Z'', \top, \text{null}, \{\})$, $Z = \text{connect}(X, Z''', C, \text{null}, \{(3, 0)\})$. The entire metagraph is shown in Fig. 1A. We note that, in general, any metagraph with a finite number of edges and targets can be represented by a term in the initial algebra of $\mathcal{M}'_{(\mathcal{T},\mathcal{L})}$ (as is Z). Some graphs, however, may

a)   b)

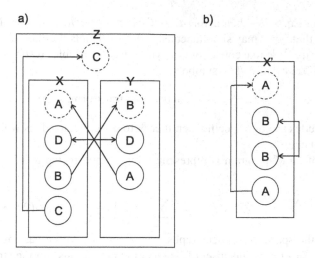

Fig. 1. Typed metagraph examples. Boxes show metagraphs, which may be single edges (containing no further boxes) or include several edges. Solid circles edge target types and dotted circles show metagraph types. Arrows show target-target or target-edge connections. Metagraph letter names are shown on the box of the metagraph to which they refer in the text.

be conveniently be represented also by terms in the final coalgebra. Consider for instance Fig. 1B. Here, we may define $X'' = \text{edge}(3, \top, \text{null}, [B, B, A])$ and $X' = \text{connect}(X'', X'', A, \text{null}, \{(1,2), (2,1), (3,0)\})$, representing X' by a term in the initial algebra (suppressing visualization of the X'' subgraph). Alternatively, we may define $X'_{co} = \text{connect}(\text{edge}(3, A, \text{null}, [B, B, A]), X'_{co}, A, \text{null}, \{(1,2), (2,1), (3,0)\})$, which implicitly determines a term in the coalgebra as a solution to the recursive equation.

3 $\mathbb{M}$ as the Final Coalgebra of a Labeled Transition System

We define the formal meta-probabilistic-programming language, $\mathbb{M}$, as a labeled transition system over typed metagraphs. Here, we are interested in typed metagraphs with a particular form. Specifically, we begin by defining $\mathcal{T}$ by the abstract syntax:

$$\mathcal{T} ::= t_n \mid \mathcal{T} \to \mathcal{T} \mid \prod a : \mathcal{T}.\mathcal{M}_{\mathbb{M}} \mid$$
$$\text{Eq}(\mathcal{T}, \mathcal{M}_{\mathbb{M}}, \mathcal{M}_{\mathbb{M}}) \mid \mathcal{T} \cup \mathcal{T} \mid \mathcal{T} \cap \mathcal{T} \mid$$
$$\text{Type} \mid \top_{\text{Type}} \mid \top \mid \mathcal{J} \mid \mathcal{X} \tag{4}$$

These syntactic constructions represent base-level types, function types, dependent types, equality types, type unions and intersections, a base universe of small types, the union of all small types, the union of all types, judgments and execution states respectively. Notice also that in Eq. 4, $\mathcal{T}$ is defined by mutual recursion with the type

$\mathcal{M}_{\mathbb{M}}$, defined in Eq. 6. We then define $\mathcal{L}$ as $\mathcal{L} = \mathcal{S} \cup \mathcal{V} \cup \mathcal{K} \cup \mathcal{T} \times \mathbb{N}$. Notice that $\mathcal{L}$ includes $\mathcal{T}$, so that types may simultaneously serve as labels. Further, $\mathcal{S} = \{s_1, s_2, ...\}$ and $\mathcal{V} = \{v_1, v_2, ...\}$ denote collections of symbols and variables respectively, and $\mathcal{K}$ is a special set of $\mathbb{M}$ keywords/key-symbols:

$$\mathcal{K} = \{:, \preceq, =, \rightarrow, \text{Eq}, \text{fun-app}, \text{transform}, @, \dagger\} \tag{5}$$

Further, $\mathcal{L}$ includes an edge-specific identifier $\mathbb{N}$ to deduplicate edges which are identical in other respects.

The state of an $\mathbb{M}$ program is represented by a typed metagraph in the following space:

$$\mathcal{M}_{\mathbb{M}} = \sum \preceq_T : (\mathcal{T} \times \mathcal{T} \rightarrow \mathbb{B}). \sum M : \mathcal{M}_{(\mathcal{T}, \mathcal{L}, \preceq_T)}.\mathcal{C}_{\mathbb{M}}(M, \preceq_T) \tag{6}$$

Hence, this is the space of all metagraphs over $\mathcal{L}$ and $\mathcal{T}$, with a varying $\preceq_T$ relation, where $\mathcal{C}_{\mathbb{M}}(M, \preceq_T)$ represents a set of 'M-specific constraints' on the structure of the metagraph (to be outlined below). This state represents the *Atomspace* of the program, and the subgraphs of the Atomspace are the individual atoms (as in MeTTa, see [8, 14]). We note that, since $\mathbb{M}$ serves both as a language for defining programs and type-systems within which these programs are embedded, the atoms may represent base-level propositions and programs (expressions), as well as judgments and computational state information, as reflected by their types. The M-specific constraints, $\mathcal{C}_{\mathbb{M}}(M, \preceq_T)$, determine the interaction of the keywords/key-symbols with the type system:

$$\forall m \in M. \exists n, n_1 : \mathbb{N}.$$

$$m = \text{edge}(2, \mathcal{J}, (:, n), [\top_{\text{Type}} \top]) \vee$$
$$m = \text{edge}(2, \mathcal{J}, (\preceq, n), [\text{Type Type}]) \wedge$$
$$\quad (m_M[1] = \text{edge}(0, \text{Type}, (t_{n_1}, 0), []) \wedge$$
$$\quad\quad m_M[2] = \text{edge}(0, \text{Type}, (t_{n_2}, 0), []) \Rightarrow (t_{n_1} \preceq t_{n_2})) \vee$$
$$m = \text{edge}(2, \mathcal{J}, (=, n), [\top_{\text{Type}} \top_{\text{Type}}]) \vee$$
$$m = \text{edge}(2, \text{Type}, (\rightarrow, n), [\text{Type Type}]) \wedge$$
$$\quad ((m_1)_M[2] = m \wedge l(m_1) = (:, n_1) \wedge t(m_M[1]) = A \wedge$$
$$\quad\quad t(m_M[2]) = B \Rightarrow t((m_1)_M[1]) \preceq A \rightarrow B) \vee$$
$$m = \text{edge}(2, \text{Type}, (\rightarrow, n), [\text{Type} \top]) \wedge$$
$$\quad ((m_1)_M[2] = m \wedge l(m_1) = (:, n_1) \wedge t(m_M[1]) = A \wedge$$
$$\quad\quad m_M[2] = m_2 \Rightarrow t((m_1)_M[1]) \preceq \prod a : A.m_2) \vee$$
$$m = \text{edge}(3, \text{Type}, (\text{Eq}, n), [\text{Type } t_{n_1} t_{n_1}]) \wedge$$
$$\quad m_M[1] = \text{edge}(0, \text{Type}, (t_{n_1}, 0), []) \wedge$$
$$\quad ((m_1)_M[2] = m \wedge l(m_1) = (\text{Eq}, n_1) \wedge l(m_M[1]) = (\top, n_1) \wedge$$
$$\quad\quad m_M[2] = A \wedge m_M[3] = B \Rightarrow t((m_1)_M[1]) = \text{Eq}(\top, A, B)) \vee$$
$$m = \text{edge}(2, \top, (\text{transform}, n), [\top \top]) \vee$$
$$m = \text{edge}(1, \mathcal{X}, (@, n), [\top]) \wedge$$

$$m = \text{edge}(1, \mathcal{X}, (\dagger, 0), [\top]) \wedge$$
$$m = \text{edge}(0, \top, (\mathcal{S} \cup \mathcal{V} \cup \mathcal{T}, n), []) \wedge$$
$$m = \text{edge}(2, B, (\text{fun-app}, n), [A \rightarrow B' \ A]) \wedge B' \preceq B \vee$$
$$m = \text{edge}(2, B, (\text{fun-app}, n), [\prod a : A.m_1 \ A]) \wedge$$
$$m_1[a = m_M[1]] \preceq B \vee$$
$$m = \text{connect}(\_, \_, \_, \_, \_) \wedge$$
$$\forall n, n_1, n_2 \ : \ \mathbb{N}.t_n \preceq \top \wedge$$
$$s_n \ : \ \top_{\text{Type}} \vee s_n : \text{Type} \wedge$$
$$v_n \ : \ \top_{\text{Type}} \vee v_n : \text{Type} \wedge$$
$$t_n \ : \ \text{Type} \wedge$$
$$(t_{n_1} \preceq t_{n_2} \wedge t_{n_2} \preceq t_n \Rightarrow t_{n_1} \preceq t_n) \wedge$$
$$t_n \preceq t_n \cup t_{n_1} \wedge$$
$$t_n \cap t_{n_1} \preceq t_n \tag{7}$$

where the notation $m_M[n]$ denotes the n'th target of subgraph m in metagraph M, $t[m]$ and $l[m]$ denote the type and label of metagraph m respectively, and we write $a : A$ as shorthand for 'there exits an :-edge in M connecting a and A'. We note that, for convenience, the above formulation does not include some constructions that may be appropriate in a full implementation, but can be derived from others. For instance, tuples can be constructed by introducing a dependent function tuple : $\prod A, B : \text{Type}.A \rightarrow B \rightarrow$ Type. The left and right projection functions are then defined by $\pi_1(\text{tuple}(A, B, a, b)) = a$ and $\pi_2(\text{tuple}(A, B, a, b)) = b$. Dependent sums can likewise be defined as dependent tuples, $\text{tuple}' : \prod A : \text{Type}. \prod B : (A \rightarrow \text{Type}). \prod a : A.B(a) \rightarrow \text{Type}$.

3.1 Labeled Transition System Based on Metagraph Rewriting

In guarded cubical type theory, a guarded labeled transition system (GLTS) may be defined via a state-space X, a space of actions A, and a function mapping states to sets of (action,state) pairs, $f : X \rightarrow P_{\text{fin}}(A \times \rhd X))$, where P_{fin} is the finite powerset functor. The space of all processes, or runs of the GLTS may the be defined as the final coalgebra of the following functor: $\text{Proc} = \text{fix}X.P_{\text{fin}}(A \times \rhd(\alpha : \mathbb{T}).X[\alpha]))$ (see [10]). In order to characterize the process of evaluation in $\mathbb{M}$, we characterize the computational dynamics of $\mathbb{M}$ via a GLTS. Here, the state space is the space of all $\mathbb{M}$ metgraphs, $X = \mathcal{M}_{\mathbb{M}}$. The actions are specified by single pushout (SPO) rewriting rules, or sequences of such rules. We therefore introduce the type, $\mathcal{A}' = \mathcal{M}_{\mathbb{M}}^{(L,R)} \times \text{hom}_p(\mathcal{M}_{\mathbb{M}})$, whose values (M', ϕ) consist of a $\mathbb{M}$ metagraph whose label set is $\mathcal{L}' = \mathcal{L} \times \{L, R, LR\} \times \{[], *, **\}$, i.e. identical to above, but with L and R labels added to each edge to indicate its membership of the left or right-hand side of the rule (notice that these may overlap), * and ** to indicate the input and output nodes of the rule (see below), and ϕ, a partial metagraph homomorphism between the L and R metagraphs of M' (defining a partial metagraph homomorphism as in [8]). Since we wish to allow sequences of rewrite rules as actions, we define the full action space to be $\mathcal{A} = \sum n : \mathbb{N}.\text{Vec}(n, \mathcal{A}')$, and write the

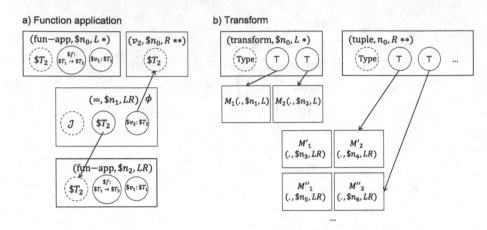

Fig. 2. Metagraph rewriting rules. Notation as in Fig. 1. Subgraphs involving only one variable are not shown explicitly, but notated directly on the targets they are connected to. See Eqs. 8 and 9 for explicit expressions for the graphs.

members of $\mathcal{A}$ as $a_1 \circ a_2 \circ \ldots \circ a_n$, where $a_{1\ldots n} : \mathcal{A}'$. The dynamics are then defined (via f) by mapping a given metagraph state M_1 to the set of all pairs (A, M_2) such that M_2 results from an application of action A to M_1. For individual rewrite rules $a \in \mathcal{A}'$, their action is determined via a partial homomorphism between a and M_1. We note that, when there are no partial homomorphisms between a and M_1, or when the rewrite rule produces an invalid $\mathbb{M}$ graph, we set $M_2 = M_1$. Further, we note that the update may change the $\preceq$ relation, for instance by introducing an edge of the form $t_1 \preceq t_2$.

3.2 $\mathbb{M}$-Interpretation as Metagraph Dynamics

We can now describe interpretation in $\mathbb{M}$ via the GLTS defined above. To do so, we map specific symbols/edges in the metagraph to actions in $\mathcal{A}$ (corresponding to the grounding domain F in [8]). Specifically, edges carrying symbols of a function type, $A \rightarrow B$, dependent product type, $\prod a : A.B$, or the transform symbol, are mapped to specific forms of rewrite rule, as specified below. All other edges are mapped to the null transform. Figure 2 specifies the general forms of the rewrite rules for function application, and transform rules (we note the transform is equivalent to the 2-argument match keyword/function in the current version of the MeTTa language, see [16]). The dependent product rule is identical to Fig. 2a, with $A \rightarrow B$ replaced with $\prod a : A.m_1$ For explicitness, we give these below also in equational form. We note that, for convenience variable names are denoted using $, although these should be ultimately mapped to the names $v_1, v_2, \ldots$.

$$R^1_{\text{fun-app}} = \text{edge}(2, \$T_2, (\text{fun-app}, \$n_0, L), [\$T_1 \rightarrow \$T_2 \ \$T_1])$$
$$R^2_{\text{fun-app}} = \text{edge}(2, \mathcal{J}, (=, \$n_1, LR), [\$T_2 \ \$T_2])$$

$$R_{\text{fun-app}}^3 = \text{edge}(2, \$T_2, (\text{fun-app}, \$n_2, LR), [\$T_1 \rightarrow \$T_2 \ \$T_1])$$

$$R_{\text{fun-app}}^4 = \text{edge}(0, \$T_1 \rightarrow \$T_2, (\$f, \$n_3, LR), [])$$

$$R_{\text{fun-app}}^5 = \text{edge}(0, \$T_1, (\$v_1, \$n_4, LR), [])$$

$$R_{\text{fun-app}}^6 = \text{edge}(0, \$T_2, (\$v_2, \$n_5, LR * *), [])$$

$$R_{\text{fun-app}}^7 = \text{connect}(\text{connect}(R_{\text{fun-app}}^1, R_{\text{fun-app}}^4, \top, \text{null}, \{(1,0)\})),$$
$$R_{\text{fun-app}}^5, \top, (\text{null}, \text{null}, *), \{(5,0)\})$$

$$R_{\text{fun-app}}^8 = \text{connect}(\text{connect}(R_{\text{fun-app}}^3, R_{\text{fun-app}}^4, \top, \text{null}, \{(1,0)\})),$$
$$R_{\text{fun-app}}^5, \top, \text{null}, \{(5,0)\})$$

$$R_{\text{fun-app}}^9 = \text{connect}(\text{connect}(R_{\text{fun-app}}^2, R_{\text{fun-app}}^3, \top, \text{null}, \{(1,0)\})),$$
$$R_{\text{fun-app}}^5, \top, \text{null}, \{(5,0)\})$$

$$R_{\text{fun-app}} = R_{\text{fun-app}}^7 \cup R_{\text{fun-app}}^8 \cup R_{\text{fun-app}}^9 \tag{8}$$

$$R_{\text{transform}}^1 = \text{edge}(2, \text{Type}, (\text{transform}, \$n_0, L), [\top \ \top])$$

$$R_{\text{transform}}^2 = \text{connect}(\text{connect}(R_{\text{transform}}^1, \$M_1, \top, \text{null}, \{(1,0)\})),$$
$$\$M_2, \top, (\text{null}, \text{null}, L*), \{(5,0)\})$$

$$R_{\text{transform}}^3 = \text{edge}(2, \text{Type}, (\text{tuple}, \$n_0, R * *), [\top \ \top])$$

$$R_{\text{transform}}^4 = \$M_1' \cup \$M_1'' \cup \$M_2' \cup \$M_2'' \cup \text{edge}(0, \top, (\text{null}, \text{null}, LR), [])$$

$$R_{\text{transform}}^5 = \text{connect}(R_{\text{transform}}^3, R_{\text{transform}}^4, \top, (\text{null}, \text{null}, \text{null}), \{(1,1),(2,2)\}))$$

$$R_{\text{transform}} = R_{\text{transform}}^2 \cup R_{\text{transform}}^5 \tag{9}$$

In Eq. 9, M_1' and M_2' denote metagraphs isomorphic to M_1 and M_2, using a disjoint set of variables, while M_1'' and M_2'' are defined similarly, with variables disjoint to the previous subsets. The rule in Eq. 9 is defined so as to return a 2-tuple of matches; in general, the size of the tuple returned should be large enough to allow for any number of matches (i.e. the number of nodes in M), and if the number of matches is less than this, it will be padded with null values.

Fun-App Nodes. For a given annotated fun-app node, i.e. $\text{connect}(@, F, \text{null}, \{(1,0)\}))$, where $@ = \text{edge}(1, \mathcal{X}, (@, n), [\top])$ and F is a graph consisting of a target fun-app node and its two arguments, the full rewrite rule rewrite_F is found by forming a metagraph homomorphism between $R_{\text{fun-app}}^7$ (labeled by $*$ as the input of the rule), and F, replacing the variables in $R_{\text{fun-app}}$ by their values in F. The resulting graph is denoted $R_{\text{fun-app}}(F)$. The rule rewrite_F is then defined by the subgraphs $L = \text{connect}(\$M_0, \text{connect}(@, l_{\text{fun-app}}(F), \text{null}, \{(1,0)\})), \text{null}, \{((n_1, m_1), (n_2, m_1), ...\}),$ $R = \text{connect}((\$M_0, r_{\text{fun-app}}(F), \text{null}, \{((n_1, m), (n_2, m), ...\}),$ where M_0 is the graph of all nodes in M targeting F, m_1 is the index of the fun-app node in F, m_2 is the index of the $**$ output node in $r_{\text{fun-app}}(F)$, and ϕ is defined by the partial homomorphism consisting of the identity map on all nodes labeled LR.

Transform Nodes. For a given annotated transform node, the full rewrite rule is defined similarly. Hence, for $\text{connect}(@, F, \text{null}, \{(1,0)\}))$, where $@ = \text{edge}(1, \mathcal{X}, (@, n), [\top])$

and F is a graph consisting of a target transform node and its two arguments, the full rewrite rule rewrite$_F$ is found by forming a metagraph homomorphism between $R^2_{\text{transform}}$ (labeled by $*$ as the input of the rule), and F, replacing the variables in $R_{\text{transform}}$ by their values in F. The resulting graph is denoted $R_{\text{transform}}(F)$. The rule rewrite$_F$ is then defined by the subgraphs $L = \text{connect}(\$M_0, \text{connect}(@, l_{\text{transform}}(F), \text{null}, \{(1,0)\})), \text{null}, \{((n_1, m_1), (n_2, m_1), ...)\})$, $R = \text{connect}((\$M_0, r_{\text{transform}}(F), \text{null}, \{((n_1, m), (n_2, m), ...)\})$, where M_0 is the graph of all nodes in M targeting F, m_1 is the index of the transform node in F, m_2 is the index of the $**$ output node in $r_{\text{transform}}(F)$, and ϕ is defined by the partial homomorphism consisting of the identity map on all nodes labeled LR.

$\mathbb{M}$-**Evaluation.** The above provides groundings for activated nodes in a metagraph; as noted, nodes not of the form above result in a null update. Evaluation in $\mathbb{M}$ involves repeatedly updating the current pointed metgraph according to the grounding of the node currently pointed to. The conditions in Eq. 7 imply there will be at most one edge labeled with † in a metagraph, whose target F specifies the rule by which the graph is updated. This is expressed via the single partial function, update : $\mathcal{M}_{\mathbb{M}} \to \mathcal{M}_{\mathbb{M}}$. The action of update is determined by the form of F. If F is not an activated subgraph, i.e. it is not the target of an @-edge, the action update cannot be applied (i.e. evaluation halts). If however F is the target of an @-edge, update first checks if F itself has any activated targets. If so, then update simply applies a graph rewrite which moves the pointer † to the first such activated target (in the ordering of the edge). If not, update applies rewrite$_F$, which automatically ensures that the update will finish with † pointing to the output subgraph, labeled $**$. These dynamics define a reduced GLTS, with $X = \mathcal{M}_{\mathbb{M}}$, $A = \{\text{update}\}$, and $f(M) = \{(\text{update}, M'|\text{update}(M) = M')\}$. Note that there may be multiple M''s for which update$(M) = M'$ if rewrite$_F$ for a fun-app node is non-deterministic. Processes are defined by the fixed point Proc $= \nu(P_{\text{fin}}(A \times \triangleright X)))$. Normal forms of $\mathcal{M}_{\mathbb{M}}$ are metagraphs for which update cannot be applied (i.e. their grounding is null). Processes which reach a normal form are said to be terminating, and the initial expression of the process is said to evaluate to the normal form reached. Alternatively, certain expressions may not reach a normal form, resulting instead in a non-terminating computation.

4   Bisimulation of Type Systems in $\mathbb{M}$

As described in [10], in guarded cubical type theory, a bisimulation $R : X \to X \to U$ for the GLTS (X, A, f) may be defined via the following dependent type:

$$\text{isGLTSBisim}_f R = \prod x, y : X.R(x, y) \to$$
$$\left(\prod x' : \triangleright X. \prod a : A.(a, x') \in f(x) \to \exists y' : \triangleright X. \prod a : A.\right.$$
$$(a, y') \in f(y) \times \triangleright(\alpha : \mathbb{T}).R(x'[\alpha])(y'[\alpha])) \times$$
$$\left(\prod y' : \triangleright X. \prod a : A.(a, y') \in f(y) \to \exists x' : \triangleright X. \prod a : A.\right.$$
$$(a, x') \in f(x) \times \triangleright(\alpha : \mathbb{T}).R(x'[\alpha])(y'[\alpha])). \quad (10)$$

As shown in [10], this type is equivalent to the path type over the recursive data type of processes defined by the GLTS, $\text{Proc} = \text{fix} X.P_{\text{fin}}(A \times \triangleright(\alpha : \mathbb{T}).X[\alpha]))$. We may further define a bisimulation $R_2 : X_1 \rightarrow X_2 \rightarrow U$ between two GLTS's over a common action space, (X_1, A, f_1) and (X_2, A, f_2) via a bisimulation over their coproduct (see [1]):

$$\text{is2GLTSBisim}_{f_1,f_2} R_2 = \text{isGLTSBisim}_{f_1+f_2} R_2' \times \forall x_1 : X_1.\exists x_2 : X_2.R_2(x_1, x_2) \times$$
$$\forall x_2 : X_2.\exists x_1 : X_2.R_1(x_1, x_2) \tag{11}$$

where $R_2' : (X_1 + X_2) \rightarrow (X_1 + X_2) \rightarrow U$, $R_2'((a, x), (b, y)) = R(x, y)$ when $a = 1 \wedge b = 2$, $R_2'(x, y) = \bot$ otherwise, and $f_1 + f_2 : (X_1 + X_2) \rightarrow \mathcal{P}(A \times (X_1 + X_2))$ defined similarly. Since $R_2(x_1, x_2)$ contains at least one matching element for each x_1 and x_2, we may extract functions $g_1 : X_1 \rightarrow X_2$ and $g_2 : X_2 \rightarrow X_1$ as subsets of R_2, where an element in the codomain of each is chosen arbitrarily when there are multiple matches in R_2. Since bisimulation corresponds to path-equivalence for elements of each type, g_1 and g_2, we can choose π_1 and π_2 such that $g_1 \circ g_2 \circ \pi_1 = i_1$ and $g_2 \circ g_1 \circ \pi_2 = i_2$, where i_1 and i_2 are the identity on X_1 and X_2 respectively, and $\pi_1(x) = x' \Rightarrow \exists p : \text{Path}_{X_1}(x, x')$, $\pi_2(x) = x' \Rightarrow \exists p : \text{Path}_{X_2}(x, x')$. Hence, (g_1, g_2) is an equivalence between the recursive process types Proc_1 and Proc_2 of the two GLTS's, meaning that $\text{Path}_U(\text{Proc}_1, \text{Proc}_2)$ is inhabited by univalence.

For a given type system, its computational content may be modeled by a GLTS by setting X to be the type of expressions in the system, A to contain an update action along with 'actions' corresponding to the judgmental and syntactic relations between expressions (e.g. is-of-type, is-of-subtype, is-a-body-of-lambda-term, and their opposite relations), and f to be the relation over expressions corresponding to the reduction relation in the system for the action update (for instance β-reduction). To show that $\mathbb{M}$ can be used as a metalanguage for a given type system, we thus show that there is a bisimulation between $\mathbb{M}$ with a specific form of Atomspace (i.e. containing specific atoms and/or additional constraints to those of Eq. 7), along with an expanded action space to incorporate the typing and syntactic relations relevant to the specific system, and the GLTS corresponding to computation in the target type system; hence the process spaces induced by the two systems are equivalent. Below, we sketch how this can be achieved for three type systems of interest, focusing on the how the computational dynamics of the update rule correspond to reduction in the target system (the typing and syntactic relations in each system straightforwardly correspond in $\mathbb{M}$ to the inbuilt typing relation and relationships definable in terms of submetagraph composition respectively).

4.1 Simply Typed Lambda Calculus

The syntax for the simply typed lambda calculus may be defined via mutually recursive definitions of variable, type and expression datatypes:

$$\mathcal{V} ::= v_n$$
$$\mathcal{T} ::= t_n \mid \mathcal{T} \rightarrow \mathcal{T}$$
$$\mathcal{E} ::= \mathcal{V} \mid (\mathcal{E} \, \mathcal{E}) \mid \lambda v_n : \mathcal{T}.\mathcal{E} \tag{12}$$

We refrain from explicitly stating the rules for type assignment as can be found in [2], which determine a typing relation $\_ : \_$ between $\mathcal{E}$ and $\mathcal{T}$ given a context Γ, which can be modeled as a partial map from $\mathcal{V}$ to $\mathcal{T}$. Together, these determine a set of valid expressions, $\mathcal{E}_{(\_:\_,\Gamma)}$, and the computational dynamics is defined by the β-reduction relation over this type:

$$((\lambda v_{n_1} : t_{n_2}.e_{n_3})\, e_{n_4}) \rightarrow_\beta e_{n_3}[v_{n_1}/e_{n_4}] \tag{13}$$

where $a[b/c]$ denotes substitution of b for c in a, where any bound variables in c are renamed so as not to clash with bound variables in a.

To simulate the simply typed lambda calculus in $\mathbb{M}$, we restrict the $\mathbb{M}$ atomspace to include only metagraphs labeled with types using the restricted type syntax of Eq. 12, and including only keywords/symbols $\{:, =, \rightarrow, \text{fun-app}, @, \dagger\}$. Then, we add the following constraint to those of Eq. 7:

$$\forall m \in M.l(m) = (:, n_1) \Rightarrow (m_M[1] \in \mathcal{S} \vee \mathcal{V}) \wedge m_M[2] \in \mathcal{T} \tag{14}$$

Hence, all typing relations are between symbols or variables (representing global and local variables respectively) and types. The context Γ is then represented by an atomspace consisting of a set of : edges between symbols and types. A given lambda expression $e = \lambda x : t_1.e'$, where $e' : t_2$ is then simulated by choosing an unused symbol, $f_e \in \mathcal{S}$, and introducing the following atoms to atomspace:

$$(: f_e (\rightarrow t_1\, t_2))$$
$$(= (f_e\, \$x)\, m_{e'}) \tag{15}$$

where $m_{e'}$ is the metagraph corresponding to expression e' (we note that Eq. 15 defines a combinator corresponding to the lambda term e). With the atomspace so specified, reduction of an expression e in context Γ in the simply typed lambda calculus corresponds to repeated application of update to the pointed atomspace containing Γ and m_e, with @ edges attached to all function application nodes, and the $\dagger$ pointing to m_e. The computation terminates with $\dagger$ pointing to the normal form of e. The required bisimulation thus involves pairing tuples (Γ, e) in the simply typed lambda calculus with their corresponding pointed atomspaces in $\mathbb{M}$. We note further that the untyped lambda calculus can be defined by simply removing $\mathcal{T}$ from the syntax in Eq. 12, and letting lambda expressions take the form $\lambda v_n.\mathcal{E}$. All members of $\mathcal{E}$ are considered legal expressions, and the $\mathbb{M}$ bisimulation is achieved by converting all type symbols to $\top_{\text{Type}}$, hence treating $\top_{\text{Type}}$ as a Scott domain.

4.2 Pure Type Systems

In a pure type system (PTS, [2]), types and terms are not distinguished syntactically. PTS expressions follow the syntax:

$$\mathcal{V} ::= v_n$$
$$\mathcal{C} ::= s_{1...N}$$
$$\mathcal{E} ::= \mathcal{V} \mid \mathcal{C} \mid (\mathcal{E}\ \mathcal{E}) \mid \lambda v_n : \mathcal{E}.\mathcal{E} \mid \prod v_n : \mathcal{E}.\mathcal{E} \qquad (16)$$

Here, $\mathcal{C}$ is a set of constant symbols, which in a PTS are used to represent *sorts*. The typing relation : for a PTS is defined via a set of axioms and rules. The former consist of a set of judgements $\mathcal{A} = \{s_m : s_n | (m, n) \in A \subset N \times N\}$, and the latter a set of triplets $\mathcal{R} = \{(s_l, s_m, s_n) | (l, m, n) \in R \subset N \times N \times N\}$. The typing rules for a PTS are identical to the typed lambda calculus, except for the introduction rule for dependent products, which takes the form:

$$\frac{\Gamma \vdash A : s_l \quad \Gamma, A : s_l \vdash B : s_m \quad (s_l, s_m, s_n) \in \mathcal{R}}{\Gamma \vdash (\prod x : A.B) : s_n}$$

The legal expressions then consist of the sorts, and any expression that can be typed in a context Γ, consisting of multiple typing judgments $e_1 : e_2$. The β-reduction relation is established identically to the simple lambda calculus above. Notice that there is no restriction on the form of $\mathcal{A}$ and $\mathcal{R}$; hence the typing relation : may be arbitrary between sorts (and hence may contain cycles), while the dependent product (i.e. dependent function types) may live in arbitrary sorts with respect to their inputs.

To simulate a PTS in $\mathbb{M}$, we select a collection of fixed types $t_1...t_N$ to represent the sorts. We then add edges of the following forms to atomspace:

$$(:\ t_m\ t_n),\quad \forall (s_m, s_n) \in \mathcal{A}$$
$$(:\ (\rightarrow \$t_a\ \$t_b)\ (\text{transform}\ (:\ \$t_a\ t_l) \wedge (:\ \$t_b\ t_m)\ t_n)),\quad \forall (s_l, s_m, s_n) \in \mathcal{R}$$
$$(:\ (\prod \$x : \$t_a.\$m)\ (\text{transform}\ (:\ \$t_a\ t_l) \wedge (:\ \$m\ t_m)\ t_n)),\quad \forall (s_l, s_m, s_n) \in \mathcal{R}$$
$$(17)$$

As above, lambda expressions are simulated by adding atoms of the form in Eq. 15 to the atomspace, and a context Γ is simulated by adding atoms corresponding to the typing relations it contains. Reduction of expression e in context Γ is simulated as previously by applying update to the pointed atomspace consisting of $\{\Gamma, e\}$ and the above constructions, along with † pointing to e. Further, we note that we can use PTS's can be regarded as a type-theoretic analogue of non-well-founded sets; from this viewpoint, a cyclical : relation corresponds to an accessible pointed graph (apg) underlying a non-well-founded set. For instance, including the axiom $s_1 : s_1$ in $\mathcal{A}$ defines s_1 as a type-theoretic analogue of a Quine atom. We note, however, that in the type-theoretic context, a cyclic PTS carries more structure than a non-well-founded set, since the rules ($\mathcal{R}$) carry information about how the $\rightarrow$ constructor interacts with the : relation. An interesting conjecture though would be that appropriately defined PTS's provide bisimulations of systems of non-well-founded sets definable within a recursive datatype (via a coalgebra on the powerset functor, definable in GCTT), as a general system of set equations ([3]) involving both $\in$ and $\rightarrow$ relations.

4.3 Probabilistic Dependent Types

Finally, we outline a version of the probabilistic dependent type system introduced in [19], and its bisimulation in $\mathbb{M}$. The syntax is a variation on the dependently typed lambda calculus:

$$
\begin{aligned}
\mathcal{V} &::= v_n \\
\mathcal{T} &::= t_n \mid \prod v_n : \mathcal{T}.\mathcal{E} \mid \mathcal{D}(\mathcal{T}) \mid \mathcal{T} \cup \mathcal{T} \mid \mathcal{T} \cap \mathcal{T} \mid \text{Type} \\
\mathcal{E} &::= \mathcal{V} \mid (\mathcal{E}\,\mathcal{E}) \mid \lambda v_n : \mathcal{T}.\mathcal{E} \mid \text{random}_\rho(\mathcal{E}, \mathcal{E}) \mid \text{sample}(\mathcal{E}) \mid \text{thunk}(\mathcal{E})
\end{aligned}
\tag{18}
$$

Further, we allow the judgments $\mathcal{E} : \mathcal{T}$ (typing), $\mathcal{T} \preceq \mathcal{T}$ (subtyping), and $\mathcal{E} \rightarrow^\rho_\beta \mathcal{E}$ (weighted β-reduction), where $\rho \in \mathbb{R}$. The typing rules are as for the dependent typed lambda calculus for expressions not involving subtypes or probabilistic terms. The typing rules for subtypes include the standard $\Gamma \vdash a : A$, $A \preceq B \Rightarrow \Gamma \vdash a : B$, $\Gamma \vdash A, B : \text{Type} \Rightarrow \Gamma \vdash A \cap B \preceq A$, $A \cap B \preceq B$, $A \preceq A \cup B$ $B \preceq A \cup B$, $\Gamma \vdash A \preceq B \Rightarrow \prod v_n : B.\mathcal{E} \preceq \prod v_n : A.\mathcal{E}$, $\Gamma, x : t \vdash A \preceq B \Rightarrow \prod x : t.A \preceq \prod x : t.B$. These interact with the probabilistic terms via the following special rules:

$$
\frac{\Gamma \vdash a : t_1, \; b : t_2}{\Gamma \vdash \text{random}_\rho(a, b) : t_1 \cup t_2}
$$

$$
\frac{\Gamma \vdash A : \text{Type}, \, p_A : \mathcal{D}(A)}{\Gamma \vdash \text{sample}(p_A) : A}
$$

$$
\frac{\Gamma \vdash a : A}{\Gamma \vdash \text{thunk}(a) : \mathcal{D}(A)}
$$

where, we note that $\mathcal{D}(A)$ denotes the type of distributions over A (so, for instance, if $a : t_1$, $b : t_2$, then thunk$(\text{random}_\rho(a, b)) : \mathcal{D}(t_1 \cup t_2)$). For all expressions not involving probabilistic terms, $e_1 \rightarrow_\beta e_2$ in the dependent typed lambda calculus implies $e_1 \rightarrow^1_\beta e_2$ in the PDTS above. For probabilistic terms, we have the following computational rules:

$$
\begin{aligned}
\text{random}_\rho(a, b) &\rightarrow^\rho_\beta a \\
\text{random}_\rho(a, b) &\rightarrow^{1-\rho}_\beta a \\
\text{sample}(\text{thunk}(p_A)) &\rightarrow^1_\beta p_A
\end{aligned}
\tag{19}
$$

Computationally, evaluation may proceed by stochastic β-reduction (i.e. sampling a reduction according to the weights ρ), or a 'full evaluation' may be made, by returning the set of all possible reduction sequences from a term, annotated with the total probability of each. We note that in any given reduction sequence, $e_1 \rightarrow^\rho_\beta e_2$ for $\rho > 0$ implies $t_2 \preceq t_1$ where $e_1 : t_1$, $e_2 : t_2$.

For the formulation in $\mathbb{M}$, we constrain the typing relation and encode lambda terms as in Eqs. 14 and 15; further, as above we encode contexts Γ by fixing atoms of the form : in atomspace. To encode the probabilistic terms, we choose fixed symbols $s_{1...4}$ to correspond to Distribution, random, sample, thunk. Then, we fix the following atoms in atomspace:

$$(: \text{ Distribution } (\rightarrow \text{ Type Type})),$$
$$(: \text{ random } (\rightarrow \$t_1 \$t_2 \$t_1 \cup \$t_2)),$$
$$(= \text{ (random } \$a \$b) \$a),$$
$$(= \text{ (random } \$a \$b) \$b),$$
$$(: \text{ sample } (\rightarrow \text{ (Distribution } \$t_1) \$t_1)),$$
$$(: \text{ thunk } (\rightarrow \$t_1 \text{ (Distribution } \$t_1))),$$
$$(= \text{ (sample (thunk } \$a)) \$a) \tag{20}$$

Application of update to the pointed atomspace so defined, with † pointing to m_e (corresponding to expression e), results in a simulation of a probabilistic reduction of e in the PDTS above. As defined, update will simulate the 'full evaluation' of all possible paths, and hence a bisimulation exists between full evaluation dynamics in the PDTS GLTS using $\beta\rho$-reduction and the GLTS defined by $\mathbb{M}$ with the restricted atomspace above. We note that, in both cases, the weights on particular paths are lost, since the ρ values are not explicitly recorded; however. it is straightforward to define a GLTS over the extended system, $(X \times \mathbb{R}, A, f)$, where $f(x) = \{((x_1, p_1), a_1), ((x_2, p_2), a_2), ...\}$ denotes that action a on x results in x_1 with probability p_1, x_2 with probability p_2, and so on.

5   Implementation of Bisimulation Proof in a Guarded Cubical Type Theory Type Checker

We briefly give an example to show the feasibility of our approach with an implementation of a bisimulation proof for a small-scale type system in a Guarded Cubical Type Theory type checker [4]. Here, we model a minimal type system, which has one type constant A : Type with two constructors $v_1, v_2 : A$; one function constant $f_1 : A \rightarrow A$, where $f_1(v_1) = v_2$ and $f_1(v_2) = v_1$; and includes the sample and thunk constructs, which are combined following the syntax of Eq. 18. Our implementation models a fragment of this system where expressions are restricted to include at most three subexpressions. Hence, valid expressions of the language include: $(f_1 \ (f_1 \ v_1))$, $(\text{thunk } (f_1 \ v_2))$, $(\text{sample (thunk } v_1))$, $(f_1 \ v_2)$. Our implementation in a Haskell-based Guarded Cubical Type Theory type checker [4] is given in Appendix A. Here, we implement evaluation in this system via (i) a pattern matcher over an atomspace ('update'), and (ii) direct implementation of β-reduction via case analysis over the expression space ('beta3'). We define GLTS's using both forms of evaluation ('str1' and 'str2'), and finally derive a proof that these GLTS's are bisimilar ('bisim'). The code for this example is also provided at: https://github.com/jwarrell/metta_bisimulation

6   Discussion

In the above, we have introduced a formal meta-probabilistic programming language, formalized in GCTT, and proposed that bisimutations link the specific object-languages (or domain specific languages) outlined above with their simulations in $\mathbb{M}$. Specifically, we have proposed that the restricted forms of $\mathbb{M}$ outlined in Sects. 4.1 and 4.2 and 4.3 form bisimulations of the simply typed lambda calculus, arbitrary PTS's, and the target PDTS, respectively.

Finally, we mention some of the areas of investigation opened up by the formal model outlined. First, we note that, while we have focused on 'full' probabilistic programming evaluation, other possibilities include investigation of sampling based evaluation which performs only one meta-graph update at each step, stochastically chosen from the possible graph rewriting locations. Second, we intend to derive further bisimulations for other kinds of probabilistic logic, particularly, probabilistic paraconsistent logic [7], and probabilistic analogues of pure type systems [2], which may be suitable for models involving infinite-order probabilities [5]. Lastly, we intend to expand our implementation of aspects of this framework in Guarded Cubical Agda [17] to provide more complete implementations of the metalanguage and type systems explored here.

Appendices

A   Proof of Bisimulation for Small-Scale Type System in a Guarded Cubical Type Theory Type Checker

Below, we provide the code for the example discussed in Sect. 5, which uses a Haskell-based GCTT type checker [4]. The code for this example is also provided at: https://github.com/jwarrell/metta_bisimulation.

Keywords, Preliminaries and Helper functions

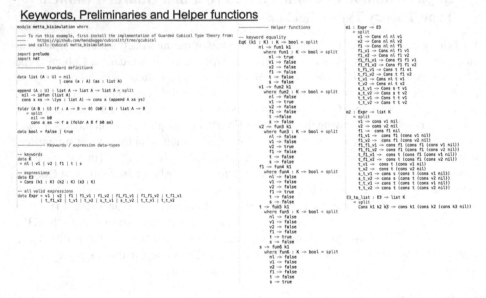

Helper functions (continued)

```
list_to_Expr : list K -> Expr
  = split
    nil -> v1
    cons k0 k0s -> fun1 k0 k0s
      where fun1 (k0 : K) : list K -> Expr = split
        nil -> fun2 k0
          where fun2 : K -> Expr = split
            nl -> v1
            v1 -> v1
            v2 -> v2
            f1 -> f1
            t -> v1
            s -> v1
        cons k1 k1s -> fun3 k0 k1 k1s
          where fun3 (k0 k1 : K) : list K -> Expr = split
            nil -> fun4 k0 k1
              where fun4 (k0 : K) : K -> Expr = split
                nl -> v1
                v1 -> fun5 k0
                  where fun5 : K -> Expr = split
                    nl -> v1
                    v1 -> v1
                    v2 -> v1
                    f1 -> f1_v1
                    t -> t_v1
                    s -> v1
                v2 -> fun6 k0
                  where fun6 : K -> Expr = split
                    nl -> v1
                    v1 -> v1
                    v2 -> v1
                    f1 -> f1_v2
                    t -> t_v2
                    s -> v1
                f1 -> v1
                t -> v1
                s -> v1
```

```
            cons k2 k2s -> fun7 k0 k1 k2 k2s
              where fun7 (k0 k1 k2 : K) : list K -> Expr = split
                nil -> fun8 k0 k1 k2
                  where fun8 (k0 k1 : K) : K -> Expr = split
                    nl -> v1
                    v1 -> fun9 k0 k1
                      where fun9 (k0 : K) : K -> Expr = split
                        nl -> v1
                        v1 -> v1
                        v2 -> v1
                        f1 -> fun10 k0
                          where fun10 : K -> Expr = split
                            nl -> v1
                            v1 -> v1
                            v2 -> v1
                            f1 -> f1_f1_v1
                            t -> t_f1_v1
                            s -> v1
                        t -> fun11 k0
                          where fun11 : K -> Expr = split
                            nl -> v1
                            v1 -> v1
                            v2 -> v1
                            f1 -> v1
                            t -> t_t_v1
                            s -> s_t_v1
                        s -> v1
                    v2 -> fun12 k0 k1
                      where fun12 (k0 : K) : K -> Expr = split
                        nl -> v1
                        v1 -> v1
                        v2 -> v1
                        f1 -> fun13 k0
                          where fun13 : K -> Expr = split
                            nl -> v1
                            v1 -> v1
                            v2 -> v1
                            f1 -> f1_f1_v2
                            t -> t_f1_v2
                            s -> v1
                        t -> fun14 k0
                          where fun14 : K -> Expr = split
                            nl -> v1
                            v1 -> v1
                            f1 -> v1
                            t -> t_t_v2
                            s -> s_t_v2
                        s -> v1
                    f1 -> v1
                    t -> v1
                    s -> v2
                cons k3 k3s -> v1
```

Evaluation via MeTTa pattern matching

```
---------- Evaluation via MeTTa pattern matching

-- rules
data rule
  = Cons (r1 : K) (r2 : K) (r3 : K)

-- atomspace
A : U = list rule

as : A = cons (Cons s t nl) (cons (Cons f1 v1 v2) (cons (Cons f1 v2 v1) nil))

-- compress
comp_fun (k : K) (ks : list K) : (list K)
  = fun1 ks k
    where fun1 (ks : list K) : (k : K) -> (list K) = split
      nl -> ks
      v1 -> append K (cons v1 nil) ks
      v2 -> append K (cons v2 nil) ks
      f1 -> append K (cons f1 nil) ks
      t -> append K (cons t nil) ks
      s -> append K (cons s nil) ks

compress (ks_in : list K) : (list K)
  = foldr K (list K) comp_fun nil ks_in
```

```
-- Toy MeTTa evaluator
rewrite (r1 r2 r3 : K) : (ks : list K) -> (list K)
  = split
    nil -> nil
    cons k1 k1s -> fun1 k1s (EqK r1 k1)
      where fun1 (k1s : list K) : (b1 : bool) -> list K = split
        false -> cons k1 (rewrite r1 r2 r3 k1s)
        true -> fun1a k1s
          where fun1a : (k1s : list K) -> (list K) = split
            nil -> cons k1 nil
            cons k2 k2s -> fun2 k2s (EqK r2 k2)
              where fun2 (k2s : list K) : (b2 : bool) -> list K = split
                false -> cons k1 (rewrite r1 r2 r3 k1s)
                true -> cons r3 (rewrite r1 r2 r3 k2s)

upd_fun (r : rule) (ks : list K) : list K
  = fun1 ks r
    where fun1 (ks : list K) : (r : rule) -> list K = split
      Cons k1 k2 k3 -> rewrite k1 k2 k3 ks

update (rs_in : list rule) : (ks_in : list K) -> list K = split
  nil -> nil
  cons k1 k1s -> fun1 rs_in (cons k1 k1s)
    where fun1 (rs_in : list rule) (ks_in : list K) : K -> list K = split
      nl -> compress (foldr rule (list K) upd_fun ks_in rs_in)
      v1 -> compress (foldr rule (list K) upd_fun ks_in rs_in)
      v2 -> compress (foldr rule (list K) upd_fun ks_in rs_in)
      f1 -> compress (foldr rule (list K) upd_fun ks_in rs_in)
      t -> ks_in
      s -> compress (foldr rule (list K) upd_fun ks_in rs_in)

update' : list K -> list K
  = update as
```

Evaluation via direct β-reduction definition

```
-- beta reduction
beta3 : E3 -> E3
    = split
    Cons k1 k2 k3 -> fun1 k3 k2 k1
        where fun1 (k3 k2 : K) : K -> E3 = split
            nl -> fun2 k3 k2
                where
                    fun2 (k3 : K) : K -> E3 = split
                        nl -> Cons nl nl k3
                        v1 -> Cons nl v1 k3
                        v2 -> Cons nl v2 k3
                        f1 -> fun3 k3
                            where fun3 : K -> E3 = split
                                nl -> Cons nl nl nl
                                v1 -> Cons nl nl v2
                                v2 -> Cons nl nl v1
                                f1 -> Cons nl f1 f1
                                t -> Cons nl f1 t
                                s -> Cons nl f1 s
                        t -> Cons nl t k3
                        s -> Cons nl s k3
            v1 -> Cons v1 k2 k3
            v2 -> Cons v2 k2 k3
```

```
            f1 -> fun4 k3 k2
                where
                    fun4 (k3 : K) : K -> E3 = split
                        nl -> Cons f1 nl k3
                        v1 -> Cons f1 v1 k3
                        v2 -> Cons f1 v2 k3
                        f1 -> fun5 k3
                            where fun5 : K -> E3 = split
                                nl -> Cons f1 f1 nl
                                v1 -> Cons nl f1 v2
                                v2 -> Cons nl nl v2
                                f1 -> Cons f1 f1 f1
                                t -> Cons f1 f1 t
                                s -> Cons f1 f1 s
                        t -> Cons nl t k3
                        s -> Cons nl s k3
            t -> Cons t k2 k3
            s -> fun6 k3 k2
                where
                    fun6 (k3 : K) : K -> E3 = split
                        nl -> Cons s nl k3
                        v1 -> Cons s v1 k3
                        v2 -> Cons s v2 k3
                        f1 -> Cons s f1 k3
                        t -> fun7 k3
                            where fun7 : K -> E3 = split
                                nl -> Cons s t nl
                                v1 -> Cons nl nl v1
                                v2 -> Cons nl nl v2
                                f1 -> Cons s t f1
                                t -> Cons s t t
                                s -> Cons s t s
                        s -> Cons s s k3
```

Proof of Bisimulation

```
-- Guarded Streams
data gStr (A : U) k
    = Cons (x : A) (xs : |> k (gStr A $ k))

Str (A : U) : U
    = forall k, gStr A $ k

-- Head and Tail
ghd (A : U) k : (xs : gStr A $ k) -> A
    = split
    Cons x _ -> x

gtl (A : U) k : (xs : gStr A $ k) -> |> k (gStr A $ k)
    = split
    Cons _ ys -> ys

hd (A : U) (xs : Str A) : A
    = ghd A $ k0 (xs $ k0)

tl (A : U) (xs : Str A) : Str A
    = prev k (gtl A $ k (xs $ k))

-- Iteration
iterate k (A : U) (f : A -> A) : A -> gStr A $ k
    = fix k it (A -> gStr A $ k)
        (\ (a : A) ->
            Cons a (next k [it' <- it] (it' (f a))))

-- Bisimulation between streams
data Bisimilar (A : U) (xs ys : Str A) =
    consBi (h : Id A (hd A xs) (hd A ys))
           (t : Bisimilar A (tl A xs) (tl A ys))
```

```
-- update using beta reduction
update1 (e : Expr) : Expr
    = list_to_Expr (compress (E3_to_list (beta3 (m1 e))))

-- update using pattern matching
update2 (e : Expr) : Expr
    = list_to_Expr (update' (m2 e))

-- generate stream from any starting expression
str1 (e0 : Expr) : Str Expr = [ k ] iterate $k Expr update1 e0

str2 (e0 : Expr) : Str Expr = [ k ] iterate $k Expr update2 e0

-- proof that streams starting from same expression are bisimilar
bisim : (e0 : Expr) -> (Bisimilar Expr (str1 e0) (str2 e0)) = split
    v1 -> consBi (refl Expr v1) (bisim v1)
    v2 -> consBi (refl Expr v2) (bisim v2)
    f1 -> consBi (refl Expr f1) (bisim f1)
    f1_v1 -> consBi (refl Expr f1_v1) (bisim v2)
    f1_v2 -> consBi (refl Expr f1_v2) (bisim v1)
    f1_f1_v1 -> consBi (refl Expr f1_f1_v1) (bisim f1_v2)
    f1_f1_v2 -> consBi (refl Expr f1_f1_v2) (bisim v2)
    t_f1_v1 -> consBi (refl Expr t_f1_v1) (bisim t_f1_v1)
    t_f1_v2 -> consBi (refl Expr t_f1_v2) (bisim t_f1_v2)
    t_v1 -> consBi (refl Expr t_v1) (bisim t_v1)
    t_v2 -> consBi (refl Expr t_v2) (bisim t_v2)
    s_t_v1 -> consBi (refl Expr s_t_v1) (bisim v1)
    s_t_v2 -> consBi (refl Expr s_t_v2) (bisim v2)
    t_t_v1 -> consBi (refl Expr t_t_v1) (bisim t_t_v1)
    t_t_v2 -> consBi (refl Expr t_t_v2) (bisim t_t_v2)
```

References

1. Baier, C., Katoen, J.P.: Principles of Model Checking. MIT press (2008)
2. Barendregt, H., Augustsson, L.: Lambda calculi with types. Handb. Log. Comput. Sci. **34**, 239–250 (1992)
3. Barwise, J., Moss, L.: Vicious circles: on the mathematics of non-wellfounded phenomena (1996)
4. Birkedal, L., Bizjak, A., Clouston, R., Grathwohl, H.B., Spitters, B., Vezzosi, A.: Guarded cubical type theory: path equality for guarded recursion. arXiv preprint arXiv:1606.05223 (2016)
5. Goertzel, B.: Modeling uncertain self-referential semantics with infinite-order probabilities (2008)
6. Goertzel, B.: Folding and unfolding on metagraphs. arXiv preprint arXiv:2012.01759 (2020)

7. Goertzel, B.: Paraconsistent foundations for probabilistic reasoning, programming and concept formation. arXiv preprint arXiv:2012.14474 (2020)
8. Goertzel, B.: Reflective metagraph rewriting as a foundation for an AGI 'language of thought'. arXiv preprint arXiv:2112.08272 (2021)
9. Harper, R.: Notes on logical frameworks. Lect. Notes, Insts. Adv. Study Nov **29**, 34 (2012)
10. Møgelberg, R.E., Veltri, N.: Bisimulation as path type for guarded recursive types. Proc. ACM on Program. Lang. **3**(POPL), 1–29 (2019)
11. Møgelberg, R.E., Paviotti, M.: Denotational semantics of recursive types in synthetic guarded domain theory. Math. Struct. Comput. Sci. **29**(3), 465–510 (2019)
12. Mokhov, A.: Algebraic graphs with class (functional pearl). ACM SIGPLAN Not. **52**(10), 2–13 (2017)
13. Paviotti, M., Møgelberg, R.E., Birkedal, L.: A model of PCF in guarded type theory. Electron. Notes Theor. Comput. Sci. **319**, 333–349 (2015)
14. Potapov, A.: MeTTa language specification (2021). https://wiki.opencog.org/w/Hyperon
15. Staton, S., Wood, F., Yang, H., Heunen, C., Kammar, O.: Semantics for probabilistic programming: higher-order functions, continuous distributions, and soft constraints. In: 2016 31st Annual ACM/IEEE Symposium on Logic in Computer Science (LICS), pp. 1–10 (2016)
16. TrueAGI. Hyperon-experimental repository (2021). https://github.com/trueagi-io/hyperon-experimental
17. Veltri, N., Vezzosi, A.: Formalizing π-calculus in guarded cubical Agda. In: Proceedings of the 9th ACM SIGPLAN International Conference on Certified Programs and Proofs, pp. 270–283 (2020)
18. Vezzosi, A., Mörtberg, A., Abel, A.: Cubical Agda: a dependently typed programming language with univalence and higher inductive types. J. Funct. Program. **31**, 1–29 (2021)
19. Warrell, J., Gerstein, M.: Dependent type networks: a probabilistic logic via the curry-howard correspondence in a system of probabilistic dependent types. In: Uncertainty in Artificial Intelligence, Workshop on Uncertainty in Deep Learning (2018). http://www.gatsby.ucl.ac.uk/~balaji/udl-camera-ready/UDL-19.pdf

Artificial Open World for Evaluating AGI: A Conceptual Design

Bowen Xu[✉] and Quansheng Ren[✉]

School of Electronics, Peking University, Beijing 100871, China
{xubowen,qsren}@pku.edu.cn

Abstract. How to evaluate Artificial General Intelligence (AGI) is a critical problem that is discussed and unsolved for a long period. In the research of narrow AI, this seems not a severe problem, since researchers in that field focus on some specific problems as well as one or some aspects of cognition, and the criteria for evaluation are explicitly defined. By contrast, an AGI agent should solve problems that are never-encountered by both agents and developers. However, once a developer tests and debugs the agent with a problem, the never-encountered problem becomes the encountered problem, as a result, the problem is solved by the developers to some extent, exploiting their experience, rather than the agents. This conflict, as we call *the trap of developers' experience*, leads to that this kind of problems is probably hard to become an acknowledged criterion. In this paper, we propose an evaluation method named Artificial Open World, aiming to jump out of the trap. The intuition is that most of the experience in the actual world should not be necessary to be applied to the artificial world, and the world should be open in some sense, such that developers are unable to perceive the world and solve problems by themselves before testing, though after that they are allowed to check all the data. The world is generated in a similar way as the actual world, and a general form of problems is proposed. A metric is proposed aiming to quantify the progress of research. This paper describes the conceptual design of the Artificial Open World, though the formalization and the implementation are left to the future.

Keywords: Evaluation · Artificial Open World · Artificial General Intelligence

1 Introduction

In AGI research, how to evaluate AGI is a critical problem. In "narrow AI [8, 20]", evaluation seems not a severe problem, since in that field the criteria are explicit, for example, in the field of Image Recognition, researchers aim to rise up the accuracy of classification and use any tricks to solve that problem. Few may deny that datasets, as problems for evaluation, play an important role in the rapid progress of narrow AI. However, in AGI research, it is quite a different story on evaluation. Despite different definitions, goals, and pathways of AGI [20], under

© The Author(s), under exclusive license to Springer Nature Switzerland AG 2023
B. Goertzel et al. (Eds.): AGI 2022, LNAI 13539, pp. 452–463, 2023.
https://doi.org/10.1007/978-3-031-19907-3_43

the perspectives of intelligence in Sect. 2, we hold that an AGI agent should solve problems that are unknown to both agents and developers. However, once a developer tests and debugs the agent with a problem, the unknown problem becomes a known problem, as a result, that problem is no longer suitable for evaluating AGI agents – the developers are able to construct a problem-specific system that could not be applied to other situations, and the performance of a system in this problem does not reflect the progress on AGI. We call this trouble *the trap of developers' experience*. To deal with this trouble, an alternative is to design new problems constantly [5], though we adopt a different path to jump out of the trap in this paper, *i.e.*, designing an artificial world. The Artificial Open World is generated in a similar way as the actual world, currently based on a classical world-outlook. The world should be open, in the sense that the causations in the world are time-varying on some abstract level, and problems to be solved are continuously changing. Implicitly infinite instances of the world can be generated so that for any of the instances, developers are possibly unable to perceive the world and solve problems by themselves based on their experience of the actual world. Nevertheless, after testing, developers are allowed to check all the data and analyze the activities of agents, and then perceive the instance of the world. The developers' knowledge of one instance of the world is not necessary to be applied to another instance, such that facing a new instance, an agent has to solve problems by exploiting its own intelligence. The world should be generated in a similar way as the actual world, so that the knowledge of the generation is allowed to be known by agents in advance, because the agent with the knowledge would be still able to adapt to the actual world, without being disturbed by problem-specific knowledge from developers. To quantify the progress of AGI research, a metric is also proposed. We consider three aspects of performance, *i.e.*, the speediness of adaptation, the goodness of adaptation, and the goodness of generalization (see Sect. 3.3), and they should be merged together into one value, as the measure of intelligence. It should be noted that the value is a lower-bound of intelligence, and complicated situations partially stem from the competition between different agents in the world.

2   What Intelligence is

Before proposing the evaluation method, in this section, we should first figure out what *that thing* which is called *intelligence* is. We are not trying to propose a definition of intelligence within a brief sentence, but we are trying to describe our perspectives on that thing which is called intelligence.

Different perspectives on intelligence lead to different work. If one regards intelligence as the ability to solve complex problems, he or she would specify a sufficiently complex problem to be solved by a machine [2,14]. If one treats intelligence as a set of cognitive functions, he or she would model human cognition with a cognitive architecture [9] or would let machines have capabilities that are presented in human beings, such as image recognition, natural language processing, *etc*. However, an agent, which possesses that thing which is called intelligence, should not merely solve several specified problems, no matter how complex they are, and should not has only parts of the capabilities of human cognition. Therefore, to distinguish the goal of creating a general-purpose system and the specific methods of solving specified problems, the term *AGI (Artificial General Intelligence)* is invented [8]. An AGI agent should own that thing which is called intelligence. What is that thing after all?

The definitions of intelligence is discussed by a lot of predecessors(*e.g.*, [6,11,19]). Among the definitions, Pei Wang's grasped some essential aspects of intelligence. In Wang's definition, *"Intelligence is the capacity of an information-processing system to adapt to its environment while operating with insufficient knowledge and resources"* [16,19], where *insufficient knowledge and resources* means being *finite*, being *open*, and working in *real-time*. Being *finite* means a system has insufficient spatial resources to store information and insufficient time to process information. As an intuition, an algorithm which searches exhaustively an answer, which is stored in an infinite memory, is not of intelligence. In this sense, insufficiency is critical. Being *open*, in Wang's theory, means the content of tasks should not be specified before the system has been developed. Working in *real-time* means multiple tasks may occur in the same time, and one task may interrupt another. Adaptation in the definition refers to "the mechanism for a system to summarize its past experience to predict the future situations accordingly, and to allocate its bounded resources to meet the unbounded demands". In Pei Wang's theory [18], the constraints of insufficient knowledge and resources have been placed at the forefront, though they are obvious in human beings' and machines' lives.

François Chollet proposed the "generalization spectrum" – *absence of generalization, local generalization, broad generalization*, and *extreme generalization* – and use the word intelligence to refer to the *extreme generalization* [3]. An agent, *e.g.* a sorting algorithm, with absence of generalization can only handle those situations with no uncertainty. An agent, *e.g.* current machine learning systems, with local generalization, should handle a single task or a few tasks, which are well scoped by developers. An agent, with broad generalization, should generalize to unknown unknowns across a broad category of related tasks, for example, an image classifier could recognize dog while it is trained with cat images. An agent, with intelligence, as Chollet considered, should generalize to unknown unknowns across an unknown range of tasks and domains. Chollet may presuppose implicitly that unknowns and knowns have similarity on some abstract level, and an agent who is able to identify that kind of similarity is of intelligence. We generally agree Chollet's view that an agent with intelligence should adapt to "unknown unknowns across an unknown range of tasks and domains", though the meaning of "adapt" here may not be the same as that in Chollet's definition, the meaning of which we approve is closer to that in Wang's.

As our position, we hold that intelligence is a unity, which implies that it is a whole which can be described from different points of view. From one perspective, intelligence is a property with which an agent is able to deal with tasks in an open environment with limited resources. From another perspective, intelligence is an object which involves principles of representation-interaction. Informally, an environment is open, which means that causations in the environment is time-varying to some extent.

As a further illustration, facing with the open environment, on one hand, an agent with intelligence should generalize to unknowns scenes, which means that, facing problems which are not encountered before, the agent should take reasonable solutions based on its past experience. The agent have to use the similarity on some abstract level to deal with the unknowns. On the other hand, after encountering a series of similar problems, which are expected to be solved by the agent, it should adapt to the problems as quickly as possible and performs as well as possible. Further more, as an explicit claim, the agent should be able to match a special-purpose system designed for specific tasks without losing the ability to adapt to new problems. Intelligence is the thing which facilitates an agent to meet the requirements mentioned above.

3   Evaluation

It is merely impossible to exhaustively review plenty of proposals and work on evaluating intelligence in this paper. Nevertheless, we briefly review some pieces of work and then propose our solution. A typical sort of evaluation is similar to I-athlon (Olympic Decathlon of Intelligence) [1]: a series of cognitive tasks are defined to test different capabilities. Broadly speaking, that evaluation method seems to assume that the more tasks an agent can fulfill and the better the agent performs in a task, the more intelligent the agent is. Some work focuses on the difficulty of problems and designs some puzzles to be solved by agents, *e.g.*, the "Bongard problem" [10]. To evaluate cognitive architecture, some metrics are proposed, *e.g.* [22], and we agree with some of them, especially the metric "taskability", which is the ability to adapt to new tasks. To evaluate human-level AGI, Goertzel and Bugaj proposed to build a school environment and educate agents in it, and whether an agent has some skills, *e.g.*, logical-math, music, story understanding, *etc.*, determines the extent of intelligence [7]. Regardless of the feasibility in practice, there is a more severe problem: as Wang pointed out,

> Though such activities do stimulate interesting research, it still has the danger of leading the research to problem-specific solutions, no matter how carefully the problems are selected - after all, this was why problems like theorem proving and game playing were selected in the early days of AI, and the resulting techniques have not been generalized to other fields very well [17].

3.1   The Trap of Developer's Experience

Those of AGI evaluation also encountered the same trouble as those work on evaluating narrow AI, *e.g.* datasets such as ImageNet [4], games such as Chess [2] and Go [14], *etc.*: developers may solve the problem and exploit their problem-specific knowledge, using any tricks, to program an agent. The problems for evaluation are hard to avoid this kind of cheating, such that a problem-specific method performs better than a general system, which makes the problems unsuitable to evaluate a general system.

Even if at first a problem is not permitted to be seen by developers, after testing an agent, the problem should be presented to the developers for further analysis, otherwise, this kind of problems is almost not suitable for advancing the research. As thus, the unknown problem becomes a known problem, and developers' experience on the specific problems would inevitably impact their designing the model of intelligence.

The agent with intelligence is necessary to adapt to an open environment, as we claim in Sect. 2. The environment could be complex or simple, actual or artificial, however, openness plays a critical role. The environment human faces is an actual, complex, and open one. The environment AlphaGo [14] faces is an artificial, simple, and closed one. The environment of ImageNet [4] is an actual, complex, and closed one. If the environment is closed, which means that the problems can be one by one solved by human developers, it is almost inevitable for developers to introduce their problem-specific experience to the machine. Eventually, it is not a machine but a human who solves problems.

This trouble, which is the reason why the traditional problems have the danger of leading the research to problem-specific solutions, is what we call *the trap of developer's experience*.

What we need is an admitted criterion, which could be used to compare different AGI agents within a relatively long period. To jump out of *the trap of developers' experience*, we first consider some overall principles of designing the evaluation method and then give some more detailed description of our proposal, the *Artificial Open World*.

3.2   Overall Principles

An AGI agent is required to be adaptive when faced with various problem in an open environment, and to find reasonable solutions without adaptation facing with new circumstances; simultaneously, for a specific problem, the agent should perform well with sufficient training, while it is still able to adapt to other problems and environments. Therefore, we should test how fast and how well an agent adapt to new environments and how well the agent generalize to new environments which are similar to the past.

Further, we suggest several criteria, for designing the Artificial Open World, that an AGI test should follow:

(1) **Independence.** The test should be abstract and independent of the actual world, which means that developers' experience of the actual world is not necessary to be applied to the artificial world. When solving problems in such a world, there are no problem-specific priors of developers, because the developers and the agents live in two worlds independent of each other – for example, knowledge of vision in the actual world does not have to be true in the artificial world.

(2) **Similarity.** The artificial world is similar with the actual world in the process of generation, *i.e.*, the actual world is similar to one instance of the artificial world. If an agent performs well in the artificial world, it will be adaptive not only to our humans' actual world, but also to any worlds which has common natures in some sense. The knowledge about the generation is permitted to be priori knowledge of developers, since even though a developer convert this knowledge into a skill of an agent, the agent is still able to adapt to the actual world.

(3) **Openness.** The world should be open in the sense that causations in the world are time-varying to some extent, and *new* problems can be generated continuously.

(4) **Asymmetry.** To generate the world is easy, but to conjecture directly the parameters or structures of the world inversely should be hard or even impossible, so that developers cannot use the artificial-world-specific algorithm to acquire knowledge, which is only applied to one instance of the world.

3.3   Conceptual Design of Artificial Open World

Generation. There are three steps to generating the world. The first step is *differentiation*. As shown in Fig. 1a, two different kinds of *entities* are generated: one is positive, and another is negative. A number of entities are generated in the world, and the basic property of an entity is its spatial position. The second step is generating *causations*, as shown in Fig. 1b and Fig. 1c. Every two entities

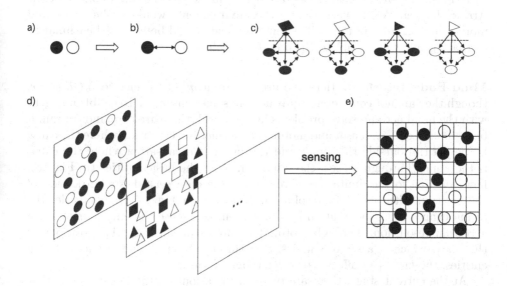

Fig. 1. The generation process of the Artificial Open World.

interact with each other, and several entities combine together as a whole, the whole as an entity interacts with others. A relation of the interaction is called a *causation*. Through the combination, the world is hierarchical, as shown in Fig. 1d. The third step is to import the mind. The entities with a mind constitute an agent, and the entities themselves constitute the body of the mind. There is also a set of causations, as an interface, between the mind and the body. The world without the mind is mechanical, rigid, and inanimate, however, the mind makes the world complex and vibrant – just as in a board of Go, players' mind leads to various complex situations.

The causations should be generated in some way. For example, the causation between two entities were a second-order differential equation, and the coefficients in the equation were randomly generated; further, the equation were not necessary to be a second-order differential equation, and the form of the equation were randomly generated. The causations do not have to be the same as those in the actual world so that the developers' experience of the actual world is almost unsuitable to the generated world.

Some of the causations are stable, while some of the causations are time-varying. For example, in the hierarchical structures shown in Fig. 1d, the causations in lower levels are fixed, and the ones in higher levels are continuously changing. This is similar to the actual world: the dynamics of microscopic particles are stable, while the weather of an area is changing.

Furthermore, it should be noted that the complexity of the world partially stems from the intelligent agents, though there are some basic rules of the world. For example, in the game of Go, the two agents, as players, lead to complex situations, though the basic rules of Go are simple. As the development of the Artificial Open World with agents, the environments would evolve more and more complex; some of the evolved environments could be used as benchmarks, so that agents could adapt to them and be evaluated.

Mind-Body Interface. Here, we use the term *mind* to refer to *intelligence*, though they are not completely equivalent in some sense [23]. To enable an agent with the mind act and solve problems in the world, there are two kinds of mind-body interfaces, *i.e.*, sensor and motor. The former is a causation where the cause is the entities outside the mind, and the latter is a causation where the cause is the mind. Through sensor, the mind can sense the basic entities (in Fig. 1a), however, due to the limitation of resources, the data sensed is a projection of the entities, with a certain resolution, as shown in Fig. 1e. For example, the retina cannot sense every atom accurately but can sense the environment with a certain resolution. Through motor, the mind can affect spatial positions of the body, which is a set of entities, and through further interactions between entities, the mind can affect a broader range of the world.

At the current stage, there are two considerations on the body. One is that the mind has a fixed body, which would not be destroyed by the environment so that the mind can survive in the world to solve problems for further evaluation.

The other is that the body is evolved and could be destroyed, and one goal of the mind is to maintain the existence of the body.

Problems. To measure the intelligence, we should define the problems to be solved in the world. However, once a specific problem is defined, developers would solve the problem and put the skills into a machine, as a result, it is not machines but developers who solve problems. To avoid the *trap of the developers' experience*, we consider a general form of the problems.

The objective status of the entities at time t is denoted as s_t, and the target status at time t is denoted as s'_t. A problem is defined as the pair (s_t, s'_t). To solve the problem is defined as to find a series of actions, which is denoted as a, so that s_t is evolved to s'_t. An agent is informed of the problem in a certain way and gave a score for solving the problem. The considerations for calculating the score are illustrated in the next sub-section *Metric*.

As thus, the implicitly countless problems could be generated, even if a developer debugs the program and checks how an agent solves a problem, the future encountered problems are not solved by the developer, and the developer's experience is not necessarily suitable for those cases.

Metric. To evaluate the adaptability of an agent, an intuition is that the agent should solve the problems with fewer observations and attempts, simultaneously, for a problem which are similar, on some abstract level, to those solved ones, an agent should solve the problem, to some extent, without attempts, *i.e.*, the agent should generalize its experience to the new problem.

Based on these considerations, there are some indicators to be measured. We denote the number of observations for an agent to solve a problem as O and the duration consumed as D. The indicators O and D are objective in the sense that they are independent of the implementation of agents. We denote the memory resources consumed for an agent to solve a problem as M and the calculation resources consumed as C. The indicators M and C are subjective in the sense that they depend on the implementation, *e.g.*, programming language, hardware, theoretical model, *etc.* Whenever an agent solves a problem, it obtains a score, denoted as S. The score S should be negatively related to O and D. The score S can be normalized by M and C so that different AGI models can be Relatively fairly compared.

Given the scores which varies with time, the time derivative of S, $\mathrm{d}S/\mathrm{d}t$, is calculated, and the typical curves are drawn in Fig. 2a. The derivative $\mathrm{d}S/\mathrm{d}t$ reflects the performance of adaptation to some extent. The faster a curve rises up, the faster the agent adapts to a new circumstance, *i.e.* it reflects the speediness of adaptation; the higher a curve reach, the better the agent adapts to a particular circumstance, *i.e.* it reflects the goodness of adaptation. After the causations are changed, the performance of the agent to obtain the scores would drawdown, and the extent of it reflects the goodness of generalization. In some way, indicators α, which denotes the speediness of adaptation, β, which denotes the goodness of adaptation, and γ, which denotes the goodness of generalization, are calculated all based on dS/dt. Finally, there should be an overall metric of intelligence, $I = M(\alpha, \beta, \gamma)$, where M is a function to merge the three indicators into one value I.

We argue that the metric I is a lower-bound of the measure: an agent is voluntary in some sense, which means that it may choose to do nothing at all in the world, without presenting its wisdom. Nonetheless, in a test, to increase the lower-bound, developers are allowed to modify some parameters of their models, so that agents are proactive in solving problems. In this sense, the metric I provides evidence that an agent is of intelligence.

We argue that there would be two stages of evaluating AGI. At the first stage, an agent is tested in the artificial world without other agents participating in; thus, at this stage, the metric I is an absolute one, which only reflects the ability of understanding the world. At the second stage, multiple agents lives in the same world, and more complex phenomena would emerge. Agents would compete and cooperate with each other, and communicate with each other, when game behaviors and language might emerge; thus, at this stage, the metric I is a relative one, and those agents who is better at game, or has the capability of language, might obtain relatively higher I.

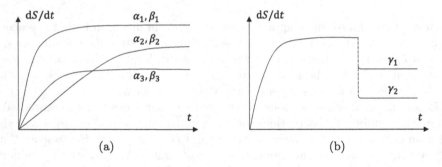

Fig. 2. Curves for evaluation. (a) Comparison on adaptation, where α indicates the speediness of adaptation, and β indicates the goodness of adaptation. In this figure, $\alpha_1 > \alpha_3 > \alpha_2$ and $\beta_1 > \beta_2 > \beta_3$. (b) Comparison on generalization, where γ indicates the goodness of generalization. In this figure, $\gamma_1 > \gamma_2$.

Future Work. We will formalize the description in Sect. 3.3 and implement the Artificial Open World in the future so that researchers can easily install the environment, test their agents, and compare their models with others' practically.

There are still some theoretical troubles of *Metric* in Sect. 3.3. For example, how to quantify the subjective indicators M and C in practice, and how to adjust the indicators O and D according to the difficulty of s_t reaching s_t' without agents' efforts.

The previous problems, including Game of Go, theorem proving, image recognition, natural language understanding, *etc*, should be special cases of the problems in the artificial world, however, this deserves further justification. The issue of causation, which is an important concept in our design, is discussed for a long time in philosophy [13], as well as in AGI [21], and the term causation should be further clarified.

It should be clarified that the current Artificial Open World is generated under a classical world view. However, with the development of quantum computing, a world with quantum effects might be considered.

4 Discussion

The trap of developers' experience is not a novel and fantastic idea, which may be realized by many researchers before, however, we put it in the first place when designing the evaluation method. It might be a misunderstanding that the trap could be an another name of "developers training in a test-dataset". In fact, even if a developer has never seen the test-dataset, his experience on the training data can lead to falling into the trap. For example, when a developer is creating an agent to answer questions according to given images, the developer is possible to assign the format of the input and output data, as well as the loss function of a neural network, which are the developers' experience on the problem, so that the agent cannot adapt to other situations, such as mastering the game of Go, without modifying any codes; If developers find that objects always locate in the center of images, which is another type of developers' experience, they could make the agent always focus on the center by clipping the images, and this agent are possibly not able to adapt to those images where objects locate at arbitrary positions.

The Artificial Open World might be similar to an environment for multi-agent reinforcement learning at first glance, however, it is essentially different from traditional environments. Traditional reinforcement learning environments, such as *Melting Pot* [12], are faced with the trap of developers' experience, since developers are possible to solve the predefined problems in the environments by themselves. Another similar evaluation environment is *XLand* [15], where the environment is generated somehow, and plenty of tasks are generated temporarily in *XLand*, however, the trouble of the trap above is still not avoided, as a developer is possible to research the patterns in each of the tasks. These problems designed for evaluation, just as those such as datasets of image recognition, are valuable in terms of guiding a researcher in creating his own model of intelligence if he keeps away from importing problem-specific experience cautiously, while they are not suitable to be treated as benchmarks or criteria around the community, whereas cheating is unavoidable to some extent. By contrast, the Artificial Open World aims to ensure that it is the agents, rather than their developers, who solves problems by exploiting their own intelligence.

An interesting issue is the logic in the Artificial Open World. The logic can be adaptive, which means that the logic rules and their truth functions are acquired through interactions with the world, but are not designed and fixed. The following illustration is under the context of Non-Axiomatic Logic [18]. For example, an acquired relation is represented as $\langle (*, T_1, T_2) \rightarrow R \rangle$, where R is the relation term; a syllogistic rule can be

$$\langle(\wedge, \langle(*, \$M, \$P) \rightarrow inheritance\rangle, \langle(*, \$S, \$M) \rightarrow inheritance\rangle)$$
$$\Rightarrow \langle(*, \$S, \$P) \rightarrow inheritance\rangle\rangle. \tag{1}$$

Suppose that the truth value of the two premises $\langle(*, \$M, \$P) \rightarrow inheritance\rangle$ and $\langle(*, \$S, \$M) \rightarrow inheritance\rangle$ are (f_1, c_1) and (f_2, c_2), and that the truth value of the conclusion $\langle(*, \$S, \$P) \rightarrow inheritance\rangle$ is (f, c). The truth value (f, c) is determined by (f_1, c_1) and (f_2, c_2) through a function $F(f_1, c_1, f_2, c_2)$. The function $F(\cdot)$ is acquired via experience, rather than identified in advance. Further, the syllogistic rule (Eq. 1) does not have to be true and can be acquired via experience. The intriguing questions occur: will the agent in the artificial open world follow the same logic which is discovered in the actual world? Will the logics, which are learned by agents in different configurations of the world, be the same to some extent? Will the logics emerged be appropriate for the agent in the actual world? If the answers are "yes", it will be quite strange that the logic seems a universal existence. If the answers are "no", then the artificial open world puts forward a higher demand for researchers to design an adaptive logic.

Contributions and Acknowledgements. Bowen Xu proposes the main idea and writes this paper; Quansheng Ren, who reviews and modifies the paper, points out the key idea that the complexity of the world stems from agents' behaviors. We thank Pei Wang for sharing some pieces of literature on evaluating AGI. We thank those who review this paper. The work was sponsored by Zhejiang Lab (No. 2021RD0AB01).

References

1. Adams, S.S., Banavar, G., Campbell, M.: I-athlon: towards a multidimensional turing test. AI Mag. **37**(1), 78–84 (2016)
2. Campbell, M., Hoane Jr, A.J., Hsu, F.H.: Deep blue. Artif. Intell. **134**(1–2), 57–83 (2002)
3. Chollet, F.: On the measure of intelligence. arXiv preprint arXiv:1911.01547 (2019)
4. Deng, J., Dong, W., Socher, R., Li, L.J., Li, K., Fei-Fei, L.: ImageNet: a large-scale hierarchical image database. In: 2009 IEEE Conference on Computer Vision and Pattern Recognition, pp. 248–255. IEEE (2009)
5. Genesereth, M., Björnsson, Y.: The international general game playing competition. AI Mag. **34**(2), 107–107 (2013)
6. Goertzel, B.: Artificial general intelligence: concept, state of the art, and future prospects. J. Artif. Gen. Intell. **5**(1), 1 (2014)
7. Goertzel, B., Bugaj, S.V.: AGI preschool: a framework for evaluating early-stage human-like AGIs. In: Proceedings of AGI, vol. 9, pp. 31–36 (2009)
8. Goertzel, B., Pennachin, C.: Artificial General Intelligence, vol. 2. Springer, Cham (2007). https://doi.org/10.1007/978-3-540-68677-4
9. Hart, D., Goertzel, B.: Opencog: a software framework for integrative artificial general intelligence. In: AGI, pp. 468–472 (2008)
10. Hofstadter, D.R.: Gdel, Escher, Bach: An Eternal Golden Braid. Basic Books, 20th anniversary (edn.) (1999)

11. Legg, S., Hutter, M., et al.: A collection of definitions of intelligence. Front. Artif. Intell. Appl. **157**, 17 (2007)
12. Leibo, J.Z., et al.: Scalable evaluation of multi-agent reinforcement learning with melting pot. In: International Conference on Machine Learning, pp. 6187–6199. PMLR (2021)
13. Schrenk, M.: Metaphysics of Science: A Systematic and Historical Introduction. Routledge (2016)
14. Silver, D., et al.: Mastering the game of go without human knowledge. Nature **550**(7676), 354–359 (2017)
15. Team, O.E.L., et al.: Open-ended learning leads to generally capable agents. arXiv preprint arXiv:2107.12808 (2021)
16. Wang, P.: Non-axiomatic reasoning system: exploring the essence of intelligence. Ph.D. thesis, Indiana University (1995)
17. Wang, P.: The evaluation of AGI systems. In: Proceedings of the Third Conference on Artificial General Intelligence, vol. 11, pp. 164–169. Citeseer (2010)
18. Wang, P.: Non-axiomatic Logic: A Model of Intelligent Reasoning. World Scientific (2013)
19. Wang, P.: On defining artificial intelligence. J. Artif. Gen. Intell. **11**(2), 73–86 (2020)
20. Wang, P., Goertzel, B.: Theoretical Foundations of Artificial General Intelligence, vol. 4. Springer, Cham (2012). https://doi.org/10.2991/978-94-91216-62-6
21. Wang, P., Hammer, P.: Issues in temporal and causal inference. In: Bieger, J., Goertzel, B., Potapov, A. (eds.) AGI 2015. LNCS (LNAI), vol. 9205, pp. 208–217. Springer, Cham (2015). https://doi.org/10.1007/978-3-319-21365-1_22
22. Wray, R., Lebiere, C.: Metrics for cognitive architecture evaluation. In: Proceedings of the AAAI-07 Workshop on Evaluating Architectures for Intelligence, pp. 60–66 (2007)
23. Xu, B., Zhan, X., Ren, Q.: The gap between intelligence and mind. In: Goertzel, B., Iklé, M., Potapov, A. (eds.) AGI 2021. LNCS (LNAI), vol. 13154, pp. 292–305. Springer, Cham (2022). https://doi.org/10.1007/978-3-030-93758-4_31

Ownability of AGI

Roman V. Yampolskiy[⊠] [iD]

Computer Science and Engineering, Speed School of Engineering, University of Louisville, Louisville, USA
roman.yampolskiy@louisville.edu

Abstract. To hold developers responsible, it is important to establish the concept of AGI ownership. In this paper we review different obstacles to ownership claims over advanced intelligent systems, including unexplainability, unpredictability, uncontrollability, self-modification, AGI-rights, ease of theft when it comes to AGI models and code obfuscation. We conclude that it is difficult if not impossible to establish ownership claims over AGI models beyond a reasonable doubt.

Keywords: AI · Agent · Impossible · Model Stealing · Ownership · Personhood · Rights · Tangible

1 Introduction

In order to establish responsible parties for potential AI failures, to allocate credit for creative outputs of intelligent software, and to address legal issues arising from advanced AI it is important to define and establish ways to prove ownership over intelligent systems. Chandrasekaran et al. write: "trust requires that one make unforgeable and undeniable claims of ownership about an ML model and its training data. This establishes the concept of identity, which identifies a key principal in the ML application: its owner. This is a prerequisite to holding model developers accountable for the potential negative consequences of their ML algorithms: if one is unable to prove that a model belongs to a certain entity, it will be impossible to hold the entity accountable for the model's limitations." [1].

While intuitively, most people understand the concept of owner and ownership such concepts are far more complex and nuanced from the legal point of view and are even more challenging to rigorously define and evaluate with respect to new cutting-edge technology such as intelligent software, Artificial General Intelligence (AGI) or Superintelligence. Chandrasekaran et al. provide a number of relevant definitions [1], the Model Owner "(i.e., the company or institution creating and deploying the model) ... This principal is one with a particular task that can be solved using ML. They communicate their requirements to the model builders, and clearly specifies how this trained model can be accessed (and by whom). Model ownership is often a broad term used to refer to the ownership of the model's sensitive parameters that were obtained after the (computationally intensive) training process. Defining ownership is necessitated by the existence of various threats that infringe the confidentiality of the model, and the need to be able to hold principals that own ML models accountable for the failures of their models." In the next subsection we will review proposals for establishing ownership over particular AI models.

2 Proposals for Establishing Ownership

A number of approaches have been suggested for establishing ownership over AI systems [1].

- Yampolskiy suggested [2] use of AI-Complete [3] CAPTCHAs [4] as zero knowledge proofs [5] of access to an artificial superintelligence (ASI) without having to reveal the system itself. However, such method does not bind an agent claiming ownership to a particular implementation, only shows access to a system of ASI-level of capability.
- Watermarking of ML models has been proposed via encoding of particular query response pairs during the training phase, and retrieval of such response during testing [6]. Unfortunately, watermark removal techniques have also been proposed [7].
- Inspired by proof-of-work algorithms, Jia et al. developed a proof-of-learning algorithm which relies on secret information known only to the original AI trainer, such as order of data samples, hyperparameters, and intermediate weights, to prove to a validator knowledge of intermediate states which are otherwise obscured by the stochastic nature of the training process [8]. Additional training of the model by an adversary can introduce new intermediate states which would be not known to the original owner and so invalidate ownership claims.
- Maini et al. suggest that ownership can be proven indirectly by showing that model was trained on a particular dataset, ownership of which is easier to establish, including via copyright protections [9]. However, this is problematic as a lot of large datasets share data or are in public domain, ex. Wikipedia.

While a number of methods for establishing ownership have been proposed, all have limitations and do not provide indisputable attribution.

3 Obstacles to Ownership

To claim ownership of an extrapersonal intangible object such as an advanced AI, one must demonstrate that they have control over it [10]. However, several established properties of AI make possibility of making such claims unlikely, if not impossible. Reasons why AI would not be ownable include but are not limited to:

Unpredictability [11], an impossibility result in the domain of intelligent system research, which establishes that it is impossible for a lower intelligence agent to accurately predict all decisions of a more intelligent agent. The proof is based on the observation that if a lower intelligence agent could predict decisions of a smarter agent, lower intelligence agent would be at least as intelligent, which is a contradiction. Unpredictable decisions lead to unpredictable outcomes, aka unforeseeable outcomes, but one cannot claim a natural right to own an unforeseeable outcome. As potential benefits/harms from

AI can't be anticipated in advance, ownership of such undetermined outcomes is problematic. Impact from AI may impact all, not just those who implemented AI and want to make claims of ownership. Consequently, a popular social justice goal – "AI4ALL" must be understood as not just partaking in sharing the benefits of AI, but also being ready to absorb any potential harms.

Unexplainability [12], yet another impossibility result concerning AI, states that advanced AI systems would not be able to explain their decision-making process to people and the provided explanations for complex decisions would either be trivializations of the true process or incomprehensible to people. The impact of unexplainability on unownability is that the designer of the system can't explain its internal workings.

Uncontrollability [13], a meta-level impossibility result for AI based on a number of well-known impossibility results in mathematics, computer science, public choice theory and many others [14]. Uncontrollability results have been shown for all types of control including direct, indirect and hybrid approaches. The main connection to ownership discussion is obvious, ownership claim requires ability to control an extrapersonal intangible object such as AI, but that is impossible for AIs at human-level [15] of performance or above.

Deterministic intelligent systems, which rely on rules for making decisions are predictable, but they are only useful in narrow domains of application. Artificial General Intelligence presupposes capabilities in novel environments and so can't rely on hardcoded rules. AGI must learn and change to adopt to novel environments many of which are nondeterministic and so unpredictable, consequently AGI's decisions also will not be predictable due to the randomness involved. On the other hand, expert systems, frequently designed as decision trees, are good models of human decision making and so are inherently understandable by both researchers and users but are of limited capabilities.

With paradigm shift in the dominant AI technology, to Machine Learning (ML) systems based on Neural Networks (NN) this ease of comprehending no longer applies. The current systems are "black boxes", opaque to human comprehension but very capable both with regards to performance and generalization capabilities [12]. A rule-based narrow AI for analyzing medical images may correctly detect cancer and its findings could be verified by medical experts aware of the rules used. However, for a deep learning system results may go beyond human ability to predict or even understand how the results are obtained. For example, "… AI can trivially predict self-reported race - even from corrupted, cropped, and noised medical images - in a setting where clinical experts cannot" [16].

To be in control of a system it is essential to be able to understand system's internal workings. In the case of intelligent system being able to comprehend how the system makes decisions is necessary to verify correctness [17] of the made decisions with respect to the given situation. Likewise, being able to predict system's decisions and outputs is a necessary condition of control. If you don't know what the system is going to do, if it constantly surprises you, it is hard to claim full control over the system. It is possible that the decisions made by the system are beneficial to the user and the user is satisfied, even if the user doesn't understand how the decisions are made or what the system is going to do next.

However, this doesn't guarantee that the system is in fact under control since the user doesn't understand the underlying decision-making process. At any point, the system can produce a harmful decision (treacherous turn [18]), and the user may not even realize it. For example, an AI can be asked to produce an effective vaccine against the SARS-CoV-2 virus which causes COVID19 decease. An AI may design the vaccine by some incomprehensible and unpredictable to people process, but in trials developed vaccine shows good efficacy against the disease and is widely administered. If AI decided to reduce human population size to decrease mutation opportunities for the COVID19 causing virus and so avoid problem with vaccine resistant variants impacting efficacy, it may do something unpredictable. It is possible that the AI integrated additional functionality into the mRNA vaccine such that grandchildren of all vaccinated people will be born infertile. Such a side effect would not be discovered until it was too late. This is a hypothetical example problem which may arise if the system is not fully under control, which would require explainability and predictability of all decisions.

4 Conclusions

If AI becomes an independent, or even conscious [19], agent it may be granted certain rights [20], among them freedom and it would not be legal to own it, as such ownership would be a type of slavery [21, 22]. If AI is granted legal personhood, as may already be possible in some jurisdictions [23], it would further complicate issues of ownership surrounding intelligent systems. Intellectual property produced by AI may belong to AI itself, as demonstrated by a recently granted South African patent [24]. It has been shown that an AI model can be stolen even if measures are taken to prevent such pilfering [1, 25]. Techniques such as reducing precision of outputs or adding noise, randomizing model selection, differential privacy of edge cases can all be defeated by an adaptive extraction strategy [26]. As long as AI represents a useful model, it leaks information, which makes it impossible to prevent model stealing [1].

If AI is capable of recursive self-improvement [27], its source code or at least model parameters and neural weights would be subject to continuous change, making it impossible to claim that current AI is the same as original AI produced some time ago. This would likewise be true if AI is deliberately modified to obfuscate [28] its source code by malevolent actors, and/or has its goals changed. Consequently, if an AI is stolen, it would not be possible to provide an accurate description of the stolen property or to identify it as such even if it was later recovered. To conclude, advanced AIs are unexplainable, unpredictable, uncontrollable, easy to steal and obfuscate. It is unwarranted to say that someone owns an advanced AI since they don't control it, its behavior, code, internal states, outputs, goals, consumed data or any other relevant attributes. But of course it is up to different jurisdictions to interpret their ownership laws in the context of AI ownership problem [29].

Acknowledgments. The author is grateful to Jaan Tallinn for his unconditional support. The author is thankful to Elon Musk and the Future of Life Institute for partially funding his work on AI Safety.

References

1. Chandrasekaran, V., et al.: SoK: Machine Learning Governance. arXiv preprint arXiv:2109. 10870 (2021)
2. Yampolskiy, R V.: AI-complete CAPTCHAs as zero knowledge proofs of access to an artificially intelligent system. ISRN Artif. Intell. **2012**, 1–6 (2012). https://doi.org/10.5402/2012/271878
3. Yampolskiy, R V.: Turing test as a defining feature of AI-completeness. In: Xin-She Yang, (ed.) Artificial Intelligence, Evolutionary Computing and Metaheuristics, pp. 3–17. Springer, Berlin, Heidelberg (2013). https://doi.org/10.1007/978-3-642-29694-9_1
4. D'Souza, D., Polina, P.C., Yampolskiy, R.V.: Avatar CAPTCHA: telling computers and humans apart via face classification, In: IEEE International Conference on Electro/Information Technology (EIT2012), 6–8 May 2012. Indianapolis, IN, USA (2012)
5. Goldreich, O., Oren, Y.: Definitions and properties of zero-knowledge proof systems. J. Cryptol. **7**(1), 1–32 (1994). https://doi.org/10.1007/BF00195207
6. Adi, Y., et al.: Turning your weakness into a strength: watermarking deep neural networks by backdooring. In: 27th USENIX Security Symposium (USENIX Security 18) (2018)
7. Jia, H., et al.: Entangled watermarks as a defense against model extraction. In: 30th USENIX Security Symposium (USENIX Security 21) (2021)
8. Jia, H., et al.: Proof-of-learning: definitions and practice. In: 2021 IEEE Symposium on Security and Privacy (SP). IEEE (2021)
9. Maini, P., Yaghini, M., Papernot, N.: Dataset inference: ownership resolution in machine learning. arXiv preprint arXiv:2104.10706 (2021)
10. Swain, S.: *Tangible Guide To Intangibles, 3E.* Wolters kluwer india Pvt Ltd (2019)
11. Yampolskiy, R.V.: Unpredictability of AI: on the impossibility of accurately predicting all actions of a smarter agent. J. Artif. Intell. Conscious. **7**(01), 109–118 (2020)
12. Yampolskiy, R.V.: Unexplainability and incomprehensibility of AI. J. Artif. Intell. Conscious. **7**(02), 277–291 (2020)
13. Yampolskiy, R.V.: Uncontrollability of Artificial Intelligence, In: IJCAI-21 Workshop on Artificial Intelligence Safety (AISafety2021), 19–20 August 2021. Montreal, Canada (2021)
14. Brcic, M., Yampolskiy, R.V.: Impossibility Results in AI: a survey. arXiv preprint arXiv:2109. 00484 (2021)
15. Yampolskiy, R.V.: On the differences between human and machine intelligence. In: IJCAI-21 Workshop on Artificial Intelligence Safety (AISafety2021), 19–20 August 2021. Montreal, Canada (2021)
16. Banerjee, I., et al.: Reading race: AI recognises patient's racial identity in medical images. arXiv preprint arXiv:2107.10356 (2021)
17. Yampolskiy, R.V.: What are the ultimate limits to computational techniques: verifier theory and unverifiability. Phys. Scr. **92**(9), 093001 (2017)
18. Bostrom, N.: Superintelligence: Paths, dangers, strategies. Oxford University Press (2014)
19. Yampolskiy, R.V.: Artificial consciousness: an illusionary solution to the hard problem. Reti, saperi, linguaggi **2**, 287–318 (2018)
20. Yampolskiy, R.V.: Artificial intelligence safety engineering: Why machine ethics is a wrong approach. In: Philosophy and Theory of Artificial Intelligence, pp. 389–396. Springer, Berlin Heidelberg (2013)
21. Jaynes, T.L.: I Am Not Your Robot: the metaphysical challenge of humanity's AIS ownership. AI Soc. 1-14 (2021)
22. Steunebrink, B., Wang, P., Goertzel, B. (eds.): AGI -2016. LNCS (LNAI), vol. 9782. Springer, Cham (2016). https://doi.org/10.1007/978-3-319-41649-6

23. Roman V. Yampolskiy,: AI personhood: rights and laws. In: Steven John Thompson, (ed.) Machine Law, Ethics, and Morality in the Age of Artificial Intelligence:, pp. 1–11. IGI Global (2021). https://doi.org/10.4018/978-1-7998-4894-3.ch001

24. Udovich, S.: Recent developments in artificial intelligence and ip law: South Africa grants world's first patent for AI-created invention, In: National Law Review, vol. XI, no. 215, 3 August 2021

25. Tramèr, F., et al.: Stealing machine learning models via prediction {APIs}. In: 25th USENIX security symposium (USENIX Security 16) (2016)

26. Chandrasekaran, V., et al.: Exploring connections between active learning and model extraction. In: 29th USENIX Security Symposium (USENIX Security 20) (2020)

27. Yampolskiy, R.V.: On the limits of recursively self-improving AGI. In: Bieger, J., Goertzel, B., Potapov, A. (eds.) AGI 2015. LNCS (LNAI), vol. 9205, pp. 394–403. Springer, Cham (2015). https://doi.org/10.1007/978-3-319-21365-1_40

28. Schwarting, M., Burton, T., Yampolskiy, R.: On the obfuscation of image sensor finger-prints. in information and computer technology (GOCICT). In: 2015 Annual Global Online Conference. IEEE (2015)

29. T Margoni: Artificial intelligence, machine learning and EU copyright law: Who owns AI? SSRN Electron. J. (2018). https://doi.org/10.2139/ssrn.3299523

Author Index

Printed in the United States
by Baker & Taylor Publisher Services

Printed in the United States
by Baker & Taylor Publisher Services